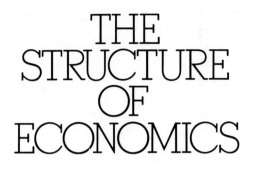

THE
STRUCTURE
OF
ECONOMICS

THE STRUCTURE OF ECONOMICS

A MATHEMATICAL ANALYSIS

EUGENE SILBERBERG

Associate Professor of Economics
University of Washington

McGraw-Hill Book Company

New York St. Louis San Francisco Auckland Bogotá Düsseldorf Johannesburg London Madrid
Mexico Montreal New Delhi Panama Paris São Paulo Singapore Sydney Tokyo Toronto

THE STRUCTURE OF ECONOMICS: A MATHEMATICAL ANALYSIS

4567890 FGRFGR 8321

This book was set in Times Roman. The editors were J. S. Dietrich and Shelly Levine Langman; the cover was designed by Albert M. Cetta; the production supervisor was Dominick Petrellese. The drawings were done by ECL Art Associates, Inc.
Fairfield Graphics was printer and binder.

Library of Congress Cataloging in Publication Data

Silberberg, Eugene.
    The structure of economics.

    Includes index.
    1. Economics, Mathematical.   I.   Title.
HB135.S54   330'.01'51   77-24429
ISBN 0-07-057453-7

To
Rachel
Marc
Aron
and Jane

CONTENTS

Preface   **xiii**

CHAPTER 1
COMPARATIVE STATICS AND THE PARADIGM
OF ECONOMICS   1

1.1 Introduction   1
1.2 The Marginalist Paradigm   2
1.3 Theories and Refutable Propositions   6
1.4 Theories versus Models; Comparative Statics   11
1.5 Examples of Comparative Statics   12

CHAPTER 2
REVIEW OF CALCULUS (ONE VARIABLE)   21

2.1 Functions, Limits, Continuity   21
2.2 Derivatives   26
2.3 Differentials   29
2.4 The Chain Rule   31
2.5 The Product and Quotient Rules   33
2.6 Implicit Functions   34
2.7 Elasticity   35
2.8 Maxima and Minima   36
2.9 Two Important Functions: $y = e^x$, $y = \log_e x$ 41
2.10 The Mean-Value Theorem   48
2.11 Taylor's Series   48
2.12 Integration   53
2.13 Differential Equations   60

CHAPTER 3
FUNCTIONS OF SEVERAL VARIABLES   62

3.1 Functions of Several Variables   62
3.2 Level Curves: I   63
3.3 Partial Derivatives   64
3.4 The Total Differential of a Function of Several Variables   70
3.5 The Chain Rule   72
3.6 Level Curves: II   79
3.7 Homogeneous Functions and Euler's Theorem   84
     Appendix to Chapter 3   94

CHAPTER 4
UNCONSTRAINED MAXIMA AND MINIMA:
TWO INDEPENDENT VARIABLES   100

4.1 First-Order Necessary Conditions   100
4.2 Sufficient Conditions for Maxima and Minima   102
4.3 An Extended Footnote   106
4.4 An Application of Maximizing Behavior:
     The Profit-Maximizing Firm   107
4.5 The Long Run and the Short Run: An Example of the
     Le Chatelier Principle   114
4.6 Analysis of Finite Changes: A Digression   117
     Appendix to Chapter 4   118

CHAPTER 5
MATRICES AND DETERMINANTS   122

5.1 Matrices   122
5.2 Determinants, Cramer's Rule   124
5.3 Application of Determinants to Comparative Statics   131
5.4 The Implicit-Function Theorem   134
     Appendix to Chapter 5   140

CHAPTER 6
CONSTRAINED AND UNCONSTRAINED MAXIMA AND
MINIMA OF FUNCTIONS OF SEVERAL VARIABLES   147

6.1 Unconstrained Maxima and Minima   147
6.2 The Theory of Constrained Maxima and Minima:
     First-Order Necessary Conditions   154
6.3 Constrained Maximization with More than One Constraint:
     A Digression   158

6.4 Second-Order Conditions 159
6.5 General Methodology 164
6.6 The Envelope Theorem **168**

CHAPTER 7
THE DERIVATION OF COST FUNCTIONS 173

7.1 The Cost Function 173
7.2 Marginal Cost 176
7.3 Average Cost 178
7.4 A General Relationship between Average and Marginal Costs 178
7.5 The Cost-Minimization Problem 179
7.6 The Factor-Demand Curves 185
7.7 Comparative Statics Relations 190
7.8 Elasticities; Further Properties of the Factor-Demand Curves 202
7.9 The Average-Cost Curve 208
7.10 Analysis of Firms in Long-Run Competitive Equilibrium 209

CHAPTER 8
THE DERIVATION OF CONSUMERS' DEMAND FUNCTIONS 214

8.1 Introductory Remarks: The Behavioral Postulates 214
8.2 Utility-Maximization 223
8.3 The Relationship between the Maximum-Utility Model and the
Cost-Minimization Model 233
8.4 The Slutsky Equation: The Comparative Statics of the
Utility-Maximization Model 239
8.5 Elasticity Formulas for Money-Income-Held-Constant and
Real-Income-Held-Constant Demand Curves 250
8.6 Concluding Remarks; Special Cases 253

CHAPTER 9
THE COMPARATIVE STATICS OF MAXIMIZATION MODELS 263

9.1 Profit-Maximization 263
9.2 Cost-Minimization 275
9.3 The Comparative Statics of Maximization Systems 284

CHAPTER 10
COST AND PRODUCTION FUNCTIONS: SPECIAL TOPICS 300

10.1 Homogeneous and Homothetic Production Functions 300
10.2 The Cost Function: Further Properties 303

10.3   The Duality of Cost and Production Functions   309
10.4   Elasticity of Substitution; the Constant-Elasticity-of-Substitution
       (CES) Production Function   313

CHAPTER 11
SPECIAL TOPICS IN CONSUMER THEORY   324

11.1   Revealed Preference and Exchange   324
11.2   The Strong Axiom of Revealed Preference and Integrability   332
11.3   The Composite-Commodity Theorem   342
11.4   Consumer's Surplus   350

CHAPTER 12
MAXIMIZATION WITH INEQUALITY AND
NONNEGATIVITY CONSTRAINTS   366

12.1   Nonnegativity   366
12.2   Inequality Constraints   374
12.3   The Saddlepoint Theorem   379
12.4   Nonlinear Programming   383
12.5   An "Adding-up" Theorem   386
       Appendix to Chapter 12   389

CHAPTER 13
GENERAL EQUILIBRIUM I: LINEAR MODELS   393

13.1   Introduction: Fixed-Coefficient Technology   393
13.2   The Linear Activity-Analysis Model: A Specific Example   401
13.3   The Rybczynski Theorem   408
13.4   The Stolper-Samuelson Theorem   410
13.5   The Dual Problem   412
13.6   The Simplex Algorithm   420

CHAPTER 14
GENERAL EQUILIBRIUM II: NONLINEAR MODELS   431

14.1   Tangency Conditions   431
14.2   General Comparative-Statics Results   439
14.3   The Factor-Price Equalization and Related Theorems   444
14.4   Summary and Conclusions   462

CHAPTER 15
WELFARE ECONOMICS   467

15.1 Social Welfare Functions   467
15.2 The Pareto Conditions   471
15.3 The Classical "Theorems" of Welfare Economics   480
15.4 A "Nontheorem" about Taxation   483
15.5 The Theory of the Second Best   484
15.6 Public Goods   486
15.7 Consumer's Surplus as a Measure of Welfare Gains and Losses   489
15.8 The Coase Theorem with an Application to the
      Theory of Sharecropping   494

CHAPTER 16
EQUILIBRIUM, DISEQUILIBRIUM, AND THE STABILITY
OF MARKETS   504

16.1 Three Sources of Refutable Hypotheses   504
16.2 Equilibrium and Stability   508
16.3 Multimarket Equilibrium and Stability   516
16.4 Stability with Lagged Adjustment   522
16.5 Overview and Conclusions   526

Hints and Answers   531

Index   539

PREFACE

The subject of this book, technically speaking, is metaeconomics, rather than economics itself. That is, we shall be concerned with the methodology of economics, with how meaningful theorems are derived in economics. In particular, we shall explore the mathematical structures which allow for the statement of hypotheses which are at least in principle refutable.

A word or two is in order regarding the level of mathematics used in this book. The only mathematical prerequisite for the bulk of the book is one quarter of calculus. Chapter 2 is included for those students or classes where the calculus of functions of one variable is not generally known. It is not intended as a perfect substitute for a full course in calculus, but it may suffice for many individuals. A student who knows how to differentiate and integrate elementary functions of one variable, such as polynomials, logarithms, exponents, and the like, and who is familiar with the chain rule for differentiating composite functions can probably skip or at least skim Chapter 2. Students need less be concerned with their ability to rederive all the theorems and concepts contained in a first-semester or quarter course in calculus than with their ability to use the results of those theorems. More advanced mathematics is presented as the need arises.

Although the mathematics we shall use is elementary, it is extremely useful to us. The late G. H. Hardy wrote, in his delightful essay *A Mathematician's Apology* (Cambridge University Press, 1973) that

> It is the dull and elementary parts of applied mathematics, as it is the dull and elementary parts of pure mathematics, that work for good or ill. Time may change all this. No one foresaw the applications of matrices and groups and other purely mathematical theories to modern physics, and it may be that some of the "highbrow" applied mathematics will become "useful" in as unexpected a way; but the evidence so far points to the conclusion that, in one subject as in the other, it is what is commonplace and dull that counts for practical life.

Moreover,

> The general conclusion, surely, stands out plainly enough. If useful knowledge is, as we agreed provisionally to say, knowledge which is likely, now or in the comparatively near future, to contribute to the material comfort of mankind, so that mere intellectual satisfaction is irrelevant, then the great bulk of mathematics is useless.

But this is precisely what an economist would expect. Hardy was observing the law of diminishing returns in the application of mathematical tools to science. A large gain in clarity and economy of exposition can be had from the incorporation of elementary algebra and calculus into scientific analysis. The gain from adding mathematical analysis and topology to one's kit of tools, however, is apt to be less than the previous gain. And perhaps, when such fields of mathematics as number theory and abstract algebra are brought to bear on a problem, their marginal product will be found to be approximately 0, fitting Hardy's definition of "useless."

In this book we shall explore the insights that elementary mathematics affords the study of economics. We shall not explore these issues to their fullest mathematical generality. While generality is a desirable entity, i.e., it is an economic "good," its production entails increasing costs due to the above-mentioned law of diminishing returns. Likewise, mathematical rigor, while desirable, is also costly. Hence, we shall often be satisfied with intuitive, heuristic proofs of many mathematical propositions. The student is referred to mathematics texts for rigorous discussion of certain issues and concepts.

It is hoped that the mathematics in this book will have been expounded to that unobservable margin where, for most students, the marginal gains from increased rigor just equal the marginal cost of such rigor. It is hoped that the more mathematically trained students (and professors) will not find this margin offensive.

All students of neoclassical mathematical economics owe an intellectual debt to certain earlier writers. In particular, the theme stressed by Paul Samuelson throughout *Foundations of Economic Analysis*, that the meaningful propositions in economics are the statements about how decision or choice variables change when the parameters of a system change, rather than the mere laying out of "equilibrium conditions" (which are empirically empty), is the guiding principle of this book as well.

I have benefitted from the stimulating company of past and present colleagues. Steven Cheung's comments and guidance on the matters discussed in Chapter 1 have been enormously valuable. Thomas Borcherding's early and persistent encouragement, and Terry Johnson's diligent note-taking, helped get the book off the ground. William Schworm and Eliezer Appelbaum provided assistance on the chapters on general equilibrium, as did Carl Pearson on Chapter 3. In addition to the above, Yoram Barzel, Robert Cahn, John Floyd, Donald Gordon, Allan Hynes, Levis Kochin, Ferdinand LaMenthe, and James Quirk have been important intellectual influences.

J. Stephen Dietrich's advice on the content and scope of the book was excellent. John Drabicki and Scott Saunders provided superb comments and corrections on earlier versions of the manuscript. Matt Thompson's diligent proofreading was very valuable.

Lastly, Georgiana Schuder's intelligent typing and editorial remarks, plus some last minute assistance from Patricia Kellerman, greatly eased the burdensome task of transforming thoughts to a finished book.

Eugene Silberberg

CHAPTER ONE

COMPARATIVE STATICS AND THE PARADIGM OF ECONOMICS

1.1 INTRODUCTION

Students who have come this far in economics will undoubtedly have encountered the standard textbook definition of economics which goes something like, "Economics is the science which studies human behavior as a relationship between ends and scarce means which have alternative uses."† This is indeed the substantive content of economics in terms of the class of phenomena generally studied. To many economists (including the author), however, the most striking aspect of economics is not the subject matter itself, but rather the conceptual framework within which the above-mentioned phenomena are analyzed. After all, sociologists and political scientists are also interested in how scarce resources are allocated and how the decisions of individuals are related to that process. What economists have in common with each other is a methodology, or paradigm, in which *all* problems are analyzed. In fact, what most economists would classify as *noneconomic* problems are precisely those problems which are incapable of being analyzed with what has come to be called the *neoclassical* or *marginalist* paradigm.

The history of science includes many paradigms or schools of thought. The ptolemaic explanation for planetary motion, in which the earth was placed at the center of the coordinate system (perhaps for theological reasons), was replaced by the copernican paradigm which moved the origin to the sun. When this was done,

---

† Taken from Lionel Robbins' classic monograph, "An Essay on the Nature and Significance of Economic Science," p. 15, MacMillan & Co., Ltd., London, 1932.

1

the equations of planetary motion were so vastly simplified that the older school was soon replaced (though the ptolemaic paradigm is essentially maintained in problems of navigation). The newtonian paradigm of classical mechanics served admirably well in physics, and still does, in fact, in most everyday problems. For study of fundamental processes of nature, however, it has been found to be inadequate and has been replaced by the einsteinian paradigm of relativity theory.

In economics, the classical school of Smith, Ricardo, and Marx provided explanations of the growth of productive capacity, the gains from specialization and trade (comparative advantage), and the like. One outstanding puzzle persisted: the diamond-water paradox. The classical paradigm, dependent largely on a theory of value based on inputs, was incapable of explaining why water, which is essential to life, is generally available at modest cost, while diamonds, an obvious frivolity, are expensive, even if dug up accidentally in one's backyard (considering the opportunity cost of withholding one from sale).† With the advent of marginal analysis, beginning in the 1870s and continuing in later decades by Jevons, Walras, Marshall, Pareto, and others, the older paradigm was supplanted. Economic problems came to be analyzed more explicitly in terms of individual choice. Values were perceived to be determined by consumers' tastes as well as production costs, and the value placed on goods by consumers was not considered to be "intrinsic," but rather depended on the quantities of that good and other goods available.

The structure of this new paradigm was explored further by Hicks, Allen, Samuelson, and others. As this was done, the usefulness and limitations of the new paradigm became more apparent. It is with these properties that this book is concerned.

1.2 THE MARGINALIST PARADIGM

Let us consider the definition of economics in more depth. Economics, first and foremost, is an *empirical science*. *Positive* economics is concerned with questions of *fact*, which are in principle either true or false. What *ought* to be, as opposed to what *is*, is a normative study, based on the observer's value judgments. In this text we shall be concerned only with positive economics, the determination of what *is*. (For expositional ease the term *positive* will generally be dropped.) Two economists, one favoring, say, more transfers of income to the poor, and the other favoring less, should still come to the same conclusions regarding the effects of such transfers. Positive economics consists of propositions which are to be tested against facts, and either confirmed or refuted.

But what *is* economics, and what distinguishes it from other aspects of social science? For that matter, what is social science? *Social science is the study of human behavior*. One particular paradigm of social science, i.e., the conceptual

---

† Of course, being different commodities with different "quantity" measurements, it is not possible to say that diamonds are *more* expensive than water.

framework under which human behavior is studied, is known as the *theory of choice*. This is the framework which will be adopted throughout this book. Its basic postulate is that individual behavior is fundamentally characterized by individual choices, or decisions.†

This fundamental attribute distinguishes social science from the physical sciences. The atoms and molecular structures of physics, chemistry, biology, etc., are not perceived to possess conscious thought. They are, rather, passive adherents to the laws of nature. The choices humans make may be pleasant (e.g., whether to buy a Porsche or a Jaguar) or dismal (e.g., whether to eat navy beans or potatoes for subsistence), but the aspect of choice is asserted to be pervasive.

Decisions, i.e., choices, are a consequence of the scarcity of goods and services. Without scarcity, whatever social science might exist would be vastly different than the present variety. That goods and services are scarce is a second, though not independent postulate of the theory of choice. Scarcity is an "idea" in our minds. It is not in itself observable. However, we *assert* scarcity because to say that certain goods or services are *not* scarce is to say that we can all—you, me, everybody—have as much as we want of that good at any time, at zero sacrifice to us all. It is hard to imagine such goods. Even air, if it is taken to mean *fresh* air, is not free in this sense; society must in fact sacrifice consumption of other goods, through increased production costs, if the air is to be less polluted.

Scarcity, in turn, depends upon postulates about individual preferences, in particular that people prefer more goods to less. If such were not the case, then goods, though *limited* in supply, would not necessarily be *scarce*.

The fact that goods are scarce means that choices will have to be made somehow regarding both the goods to be produced in the first place and the system for rationing these final goods to consumers, each of whom would in general prefer to have more of those goods rather than less. This problem, which is often taken as the definition of economics, has many aspects. How are consumers' tastes formed, and are those tastes dependent on ("endogenous to") or independent of ("exogenous to") the allocative process? How are decisions made with regard to whether goods shall be allocated via a market process or through the political system? What system of *rules*, i.e., *property rights*, is to be used in constraining individual choices? The issues generated by the scarcity of goods involve all the social sciences. All are concerned with different aspects of the problem of choice.

We now come to the fundamental conceptualization of the determinants of choice upon which the neoclassical, or marginalist, paradigm is based. We shall assert that for a wide range of problems individual choice can be conceived to be determined by the interaction of two distinct classifications of phenomena:

1. tastes, or preferences
2. opportunities, or constraints

---

† A complicating feature, not relevant to the present discussion but also peculiar to the social sciences, is that the participants often have a vested interest in the results of the analysis.

Under heading 1, tastes, are all the subjective things one would like to do. All the hypothetical exchanges one would be willing to make at various terms of trade constitute an individual's preferences. Some people would gladly exchange 2 pounds of coffee for 1 of tea; others, the reverse. These hypothetical offers are based on our subjective evaluations of the relative desirability of goods. They are our *tastes*.

Because of scarcity, our tastes are not given free reign. We cannot all have as much as we would like of all goods. Thus, the other determinants of choice are the opportunities faced by individuals for acting on their preferences. For given tastes, the opportunities or constraints are the determinants of choice.

What sorts of things enter the classification of *opportunities?* Strictly speaking, the answer is: all factors, which can be directly measured, which affect behavior. Certainly, the money prices of goods and the money incomes of individuals play a major part. In most everyday decisions to exchange goods and services, prices and income are the major constraints. More fundamentally, however, the constraints on behavior are the system of laws and the property rights in a given society. Without these rights, prices and money income would be largely irrelevant. Ordinary exchange is difficult or impossible if the traders have not previously agreed as to who owns what in the first place, and whether contracts entered into are enforceable. Laws also determine various restrictions on trading. During the winter of 1973–1974, gasoline was quoted at a certain price, but in many parts of the country it was unavailable for exchange. The *price* of the good loses meaning if the good is unavailable at that price. The same situation existed during World War II when goods were price-controlled. Then, the property rights individuals enjoyed over their goods no longer included the right to sell the good at a mutually satisfactory price with the buyer. Hence, the system of laws and the property rights endowed to the participants in a given society are a fundamental part of their opportunity set.

In addition to the above, technology and the law of diminishing returns constitute the other important constraints in economic analysis. Together with the system of laws and the property rights, technology determines the production possibilities of a society, i.e., the limits on total consumption.

One thing of which we can be quite certain is that tastes and opportunities vary widely, from individual to individual and from place to place. That tastes differ can be evidenced by the observation that even when the opportunities facing two individuals are largely the same, i.e., they have equal incomes, shop at the same stores, and are equal under the law, they often purchase widely different bundles of goods and services. Some people live in small houses and drive big cars; others, in similar circumstances, buy large houses and drive small cars. On the other hand, census figures attest to large differences in incomes among individuals in the United States; the same seems to be true in most other societies. How can any sensible analysis of choice be made under these horrendously complicated conditions? The answer to this important question is given by the paradigm of choice peculiar to the subspeciality of social science known as economics.

Of the two classifications of phenomena affecting choice, *opportunities* are in principle observable and measurable, whereas tastes are not. Prices are generally posted, or otherwise available; incomes are usually known to people; laws and property rights can be complicated but are at least on the books, and their enforceability can be determined. In contrast, tastes are not in general observable. It is in fact precisely for this reason that we make *assertions*, or *postulates*, about individual tastes. If tastes were observable, assertions about their nature would not be needed.

Observations of a person's consumption habits, i.e., the baskets of goods purchased, do not constitute observations of tastes. Actual consumption depends on opportunities as well as tastes. The generally nonobservable nature of the preferences of individuals requires that they be postulated, or asserted.

To answer all questions of choice, even about a well-defined situation, both tastes and opportunities must be included. Unfortunately, this situation cannot be realized in actual practice. However, it is still often possible to analyze problems of choice in a narrower, but still fruitful manner. Suppose we assume that whatever people's tastes are, they do not change very much, if at all, during the course of investigation of some problem in social science. Certain decisions will be made by individuals, given those tastes and the opportunities they face. If, now, the *opportunities* faced by those individuals *change, in an observable fashion*, then we can expect the decisions of individuals to somehow *change*, and those *changes in decisions, or choices, can be attributed to the changes in opportunities.* That is, while it may not be possible to predict the original choices made by individuals, it may still be possible to predict how those choices *change* when opportunities change. This is the paradigm of economics, a paradigm which distinguishes economics from the other facets of social science.

In terms of the methodology outlined above, then, economics is that discipline within social science (the general theory of choice) which seeks explanations of human events on the basis of the *changes* in opportunities faced by individuals. Economists do *not* thereby assert that tastes or preferences of individuals do not matter. Quite the contrary. Preferences are *asserted* to affect individual choices, as mentioned above. What the paradigm of economics recognizes is that it is possible to obtain answers regarding *marginal* quantities, i.e., how total quantities *change*, without a specific investigation of individual preferences.

How can we be sure that tastes do not in fact change? The truth is, we can't. Tastes may in fact change. Attitudes on many issues, e.g., divorce, sex outside of marriage, etc., appear to have undergone substantial changes over the years. The paradigm of economics does not rule out changes in tastes; it merely seeks explanations in terms of changes in opportunities. Tastes are *assumed* to be constant. If the events, i.e., the facts over which the theory is tested, confirm the theory; i.e., if they are consistent with the predictions of the theory, then the theory, including the assumption of constant tastes, may be useful, especially if it is frequently successful. If the price of bread, for example, is lowered, the standard economic theory predicts that the quantity of bread purchased will increase. The economist will assume that the increase was due to the change in price, but it might have been due to a sudden craving for bread on the part of consumers. With one such observation, it will be impossible to tell whether it was tastes or opportunities that caused the change in consumption of bread. Confidence in the explanation based on changing opportunities will be built up only if the propositions so derived have wide application and are successful in predicting events in numerous trials. Moreover, economists (this author included) believe that these explanations based on changes in opportunities are sufficiently robust to merit serious study.

1.3 THEORIES AND REFUTABLE PROPOSITIONS

In the past several pages we have used the terms *theory*, *propositions*, and *confirm* as well as other phrases that warrant a closer look. In particular, what is a theory, and what is the role of theories in scientific explanations?

It is sometimes suggested that the way to attack any given problem is to "let the facts speak for themselves." Suppose one wanted to discover why motorists were suddenly waiting in line for gasoline, often for several hours, during the winter of 1973–1974, the so-called energy crisis. The first thing to do, perhaps, is to get some facts. Where will they be found? Perhaps the government documents section of the local university library will be useful. A problem arises. Once there, one suddenly finds oneself up to the ears in facts. The data collected by the United States federal government and other governments fill many rooms. Where should one start? Consider, perhaps, the following list of "facts."

1. Many oil-producing nations embargoed oil to the United States in the fall of 1973.
2. The gross national product of the United States rose, in money terms, by 11.5 percent from 1972 to 1973.
3. Gasoline and heating oil are petroleum distillates.
4. Wage and price controls were in effect on the oil industry during that time.
5. The average miles per gallon achieved by cars in the United States has decreased due to the growing use of antipollution devices.
6. The price of food rose dramatically in this period.
7. Rents rose during this time, but not as fast as food prices.
8. The price of tomatoes in Lincoln, Nebraska was 39 cents per pound on September 14, 1968.
9. Most of the pollution in the New York metropolitan area is due to fixed, rather than moving, sources.

The list goes on indefinitely. There are an infinite number of facts. Most readers will have already decided that, e.g., fact 8 is irrelevant; and most of the infinite number of facts that might have been listed are irrelevant. But why? How was this conclusion reached? Can fact 8 be rejected solely on the basis that *most* of us would agree to reject it? What about facts 4 and 5? There may be less than perfect agreement on the relevance of some of these facts.

Facts, by themselves, do not explain events. Without some set of axioms, propositions, etc., about the nature of the phenomena we are seeking to explain, there is simply no way in which to sort out the relevant from the irrelevant facts. The reader who summarily dismissed fact 8 as irrelevant to the events occurring during the energy crisis must have had some behavioral relations in mind which suggested that the tomato market in 1968 was not a determining factor. Such a notion, however rudimentary, is the start of a *theory*.

The Structure of Theories

A theory, in an empirical science, is a set of explanations or predictions about various objects in the real world. Theories consist of three parts:

1. A set of *assertions*, or postulates, denoted $A = \{A_1, \ldots, A_n\}$, concerning the behavior of various *theoretical constructs*, i.e., idealized (perhaps mathematical) concepts, which are ultimately to be related to real world objects. These postulates are generally universal-type statements, i.e., propositions of the form: all x have the property p. Examples of such propositions in economics are the statements that "firms maximize wealth (or profits)," "consumers maximize utility," and the like. At this point, terms such as *firms, consumers, prices, quantities*, etc., mentioned in these behavioral assertions, or postulates, are ideas yet to be identified. They are thus referred to as theoretical constructs.
2. If behavioral assertions about theoretical constructs are to be useful in empirical science, these postulates must be related to real objects. The second part of a theory is therefore a set of *assumptions*, or *test conditions*, denoted $C = \{C_1, \ldots, C_n\}$, under which the behavioral postulates are to be tested. These assumptions include statements to the effect that "such-and-such variable p, called the *price of bread* in the theoretical assertions, in fact corresponds to the price of bread posted at xyz supermarket on such-and-such date."

   Note that we are distinguishing the terms assertions and assumptions. There has been a protracted debate in economics over the need for realism of assumptions. The confusion can be largely eliminated by clearly distinguishing the behavioral postulates of a theory (the assertions) from the specific test conditions (the assumptions) under which the theory is tested.

   If the theory is to be at all useful, the assumptions, or test conditions, must be *observable*. It is impossible to tell whether a theory is performing well or badly if it is not possible to tell whether the theory is even relevant to the objects in question. The postulates A are universal statements about the behavior of abstract objects. They are not observable; therefore, debate as to their realism is irrelevant. Assumptions, on the other hand, are the link between the theoretical constructs and real objects. Assumptions *must* be *realistic*, i.e., if the theory is to be validly tested against a given set of data, the data must conform in essential ways to the theoretical constructs.

   Suppose, for example, we wish to test whether a rise in the price of gasoline reduces the quantity of gasoline demanded. It will be observed that the money price of gasoline has been rising generally since World War II and that gasoline consumption has also been rising. Does this refute the behavioral proposition that higher prices lead to less quantity demanded? Perhaps the data, specifically the assumptions about prices, are not realistic. Does the reported series of prices really reflect the intended characteristics of the theoretical construct: price of gasoline? A careful statement of the law of demand involves changes in *relative* prices, not absolute money prices, and other things, e.g., incomes and other prices, are supposed to be held fixed. When compensated by price-level changes, the *real* price of gasoline, i.e., the price of gasoline relative to other goods, has indeed been falling, thus tending to *confirm* the law of demand. But in order to test the law of demand with this datum, the assumptions about income, prices of closely related goods, etc., must also be realistic, i.e., conform to the essential aspects of the theoretical constructs.

We say *essential aspects* of the theoretical constructs because it is impossible to describe, in a finite amount of time and space, every attribute of a given real object. The importance of *realism* of assumptions is to make sure that the attributes not specified do not significantly affect the test of the theory. In the foregoing example, money prices were an *unrealistic* measure of gasoline prices; i.e., they did not contain the attributes intended by the theory. The assumptions, or test conditions, of a theory *must*, therefore, be realistic; the assertions, or behavioral postulates are never realistic because they are unobservable.

3. The third part of a theory comprises the events $E = \{E_1, \ldots, E_n\}$ that are predicted by the theory. The theory says that the behavioral assertions A imply that if the test conditions C are valid (realistic), then certain events E will occur. For example, the usual postulates of consumer behavior (utility maximization with diminishing marginal rates of substitution between commodities), which we shall denote A, imply that if the test conditions C hold, where C includes decreasing relative price of gasoline with real incomes and other prices to be held fixed—that is, these assumptions are in fact *observed* to be true—then the event E, *higher gasoline consumption*, will be observed. Note that *both* the assumptions, or test conditions C and the events E must be observable. Otherwise, we can't tell whether the theory is applicable.

The logical structure of theories is thus that the assertions A imply that if C is true, then E will be true. In symbols, this is written

$$A \to (C \to E)$$

where the symbol $\to$ means *implies*. By simple logic, the symbolic statement can also be written

$$(A \cdot C) \to E$$

That is, the postulates A *and* assumptions C together imply that the events E will be observed.

Refutable Propositions

We have spoken casually of *testing theories*. What is it that is being tested, and how does one go about it? In the first place, there is no way to test the postulates *A* directly. Suppose, to take a classic example, one wished to test whether a given firm maximized profits. How would you do it? Suppose the accountants supplied income statements for this year and past years together with the corporate balance sheets. Suppose you found that the firm made $1 million this year. Could you infer from this that the firm made *maximum* profits? Perhaps it could have made $2 million, or $10 million. How would you know?

Maybe we should ask an easier question. Is the firm *minimizing* profits? Certainly not, you say. After all, it made a million dollars. Well, maybe it was in such a good business that there was simply no way to make less than a million dollars. No, you insist, if the owners of this firm were out to minimize profits, we should expect to see them giving away their goods free, hiring workers at astronomical salaries, throwing sand into the machinery, and indulging in a host of other bizarre behaviors. Precisely. The way one would *infer* that profits were being minimized would be to predict that if such behavior were present, then the given firm would engage in certain predicted events, specified in advance, such as the actions named. Since the object in question is undoubtedly a firm, i.e., the test conditions or assumptions *C* are realistic, and the events predicted by profit-minimization do not occur, the behavioral assertion *A*, that the firm minimizes profits, is refuted. *But the postulates are refutable only through making logically valid predictions about real, observable events based on those postulates, under assumed test conditions, and then discovering that the predictions are false.* The postulates are not testable in a vacuum. They can only be tested against real facts (events) under assumed, observable test conditions.

We have not, however, shown that firms maximize profits. But, we do know something. It will not be possible to determine whether firms maximize profits on the basis of whether we think that that is a sensible or achievable goal. The way to test the postulate of profit-maximization is to derive from that postulate certain behavior that should be observed under certain assumptions. Then, if the events predicted do indeed occur, we shall have evidence as to the validity of the postulate. The theory will be confirmed. But will it be *proved*? Alas, no. The nature of logic forbids us to conclude that the postulates *A* are true, even if *C* and *E* are known to be true. This is such a classic error it has a name: It is called the fallacy of *affirming the consequent*. If *A* implies *B*, then if *B* is true, one cannot conclude that *A* is true. For example, "If two triangles are congruent, then they are similar," is a valid proposition. However, if two triangles are known to be similar, one cannot conclude that they are also congruent, as counterexamples are easily demonstrated.

A striking example of why theories cannot be proved is presented in Fig. 1-1. The theory that the earth is round is to be tested by having an observer on the seashore note that when ships come in from afar, first the smoke from the smokestacks is visible, then the stacks, and so on, from the top of the ship on down.

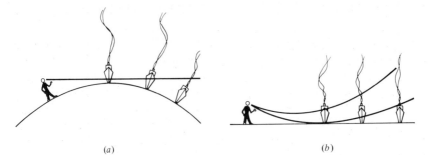

(a)

(b)

Figure 1-1 *Two Theories of the Shape of the Earth.* In Fig. 1-1*a*, a round earth is postulated. Under the assumption that light waves travel in straight lines, ships coming in from afar become visible from the top down, as they approach the shore. This is confirmed by actual observation. However, this does not *prove* that the earth is round. In Fig. 1-1*b*, a flat earth is postulated. However, under the assumption that light waves travel in curves convex to the surface of the earth, the same events are predicted. Therefore, on the basis of this experiment alone, no conclusion can be reached concerning the shape of the earth!

Panel *a* shows why this is to be expected. It does, in fact, occur every time. However, panel *b* shows that an alternative theory leads to the same events. Here, the earth is flat, but light waves travel in curves convex to the surface of the earth. The same events are predicted. There is no way, on the basis of this experiment, to determine which theory is correct. It is always possible that a new theory will be developed which will explain a given set of events. Hence, theories are in principle, as a matter of logic, unprovable. They can only be confirmed, i.e., found to be consistent with the facts. The more times a theory is confirmed, the more strongly we shall believe in its postulates, but we can never be *sure* that it is true.†

What types of theories are useful in empirical science, then? The only theories that are useful are those which might be wrong, i.e., might be refuted, but are not refuted. A theory which says that it will either rain or not rain tomorrow is no theory at all. It is incapable of being falsified, since the predicted "event" is logically true. A theory which says that if the price of gasoline rises, consumption will either rise or fall is similarly useless and uninteresting, for the same reason. The only theories which are useful are those from which *refutable hypotheses* can be inferred. The theory must assert that some event E will occur and, moreover, it must be possible that E will *not* occur. Such a proposition is, at least in principle, refutable. The facts may refute the theory; for if E is false, then as a matter of logic $(A \cdot C)$ is false. (If nonoccurrence of the event E is always attributed to false or unrealistic test conditions or assumptions C then the theory is likewise nonrefutable.)

The paradigm of economics, therefore, in order to be useful, must consist of refutable propositions. Any other kind of statement is useless. In the various chapters of this book, we shall demonstrate how such refutable hypotheses are derived from behavioral postulates in economics.

† See Irving M. Copi, "Introduction to Logic," 4th ed., Macmillan, New York, 1972.

1.4 THEORIES VERSUS MODELS; COMPARATIVE STATICS

The testing of a theory usually involves two fairly distinct processes. First, the purely logical aspects of the theory are drawn out. That is, it is shown that the behavioral postulates imply certain behavior for the variables of the theory. Then, at a later stage, the theoretical constructs are applied to real data, and the theory is tested empirically. The first stage of this analysis is what we shall be concerned with in this book. To distinguish the two phases of theorizing, we shall employ a distinction introduced by A. Papandreou† and amplified by M. Bronfenbrenner.‡ The purely logical aspect of theories will be called a *model*. A model becomes a theory when assumptions relating the theoretical constructs to real objects are added. Models are thus logical systems. They cannot be true or false empirically; rather, they are either logically valid or invalid. A theory can be false either because the underlying model is logically unsound or because the empirical facts refute the theory (or both occur).

The notion of a refutable proposition is preserved, however, even in models. A refutable proposition in a logical system means that when certain *conceptual* test conditions occur, the theoretical variables will have restricted values. Suppose that in a certain model, if a variable denoted p, ultimately to mean the price of some good, increases, then another variable x ultimately to mean the quantity of that good demanded, can validly be inferred to, say, decrease, as a matter of the logic of the model, then a refutable proposition is said to be asserted. The critical thing is that the variable x is to respond in a given manner, and it must be possible for x not to respond in that manner.

The logical simulation, usually with mathematics, of the testing of theories in economics is called the *theory of comparative statics*. The word *statics* is an unfortunate misnomer. Nothing really static is implied in the testing of theories. Recall that, in economics, theories are tested on the basis of *changes* in variables, when certain test conditions or assumptions change. The use of the term comparative statics refers to the absence of a prediction about the *rate* of change of variables over time, as opposed to the *direction* of change.

The testing of theories is simulated by dividing the variables into two classes:

1. Decision, or choice, variables.
2. Parameters, or variables exogenous to the model, i.e., not determined by the actions of the decision maker. The parameters represent the *test conditions* of the theory.

Let us denote the decision or choice variable (or variables) as x, and the

---

† Andreas Papandreou, "Economics as a Science," J. B. Lippincott Company, Philadelphia, 1958.
‡ Martin Bronfenbrenner, A Middlebrow Introduction to Economic Methodology, in S. Krupp (ed.), "The Structure of Economic Science," Prentice-Hall, Inc., Englewood Cliffs, N.J., 1966.

parameters of the model as α. To be useful, the theory must postulate a certain set of choices x as a function of the test conditions α

$$x = f(\alpha) \tag{1-1}$$

That is, given the behavioral postulates A, then if certain test conditions C, represented in the model by α, hold, then certain choices x will be made. Hence, x is functionally dependent on α, as denoted in equation (1-1), above.

As an empirical matter, economists will rarely, if ever, be able to test relations of the form (1-1) directly; i.e., formulate hypotheses about the actual amount of x chosen for given α. As mentioned earlier, to do this would require full knowledge of tastes as well as opportunities. The neoclassical economic paradigm is therefore based on observations of *marginal* quantities only. These marginal quantities are the responses of x to *changes* in α.

Mathematically, for "well-behaved" (differentiable) choice functions, it is the properties of the derivative of x with respect to α, or

$$\frac{dx}{d\alpha} = f'(\alpha) \tag{1-2}$$

that represents the potentially refutable hypotheses in economics. Most frequently, all that is asserted is a sign for this derivative. For example, in demand theory, prices p are exogenous, i.e., parameters, while quantities demanded x are choice variables. The law of demand asserts (under the usual qualifications) that $dx/dp < 0$. Since it is possible that $dx/dp > 0$, and since this would contradict the assertions of the model, the statement $dx/dp < 0$ is a potentially refutable hypothesis. *Comparative statics is that mathematical technique by which an economic model is investigated to determine if refutable hypotheses are forthcoming.* If not, then actual empirical testing is a waste of time, since no data could ever refute the theory.

1.5 EXAMPLES OF COMPARATIVE STATICS†

To illustrate the above principles, let us consider three alternative hypotheses about the behavior of firms. Specifically, suppose we were to postulate that:

1. Firms maximize profits π, where π equals total revenue minus cost.
2. Firms maximize some utility function of profits $U(\pi)$, where $U'(\pi) > 0$, so that higher profits mean higher utility. Thus, profits are desired not for their own sake, but rather for the utility they provide the firm owner.
3. Firms maximize total sales, i.e., total revenue only.

---

† The material in this section requires some knowledge of elementary calculus techniques. The student should review parts of Chap. 2 first if these tools are unfamiliar.

By what means shall these three theories be tested and compared? It is not possible to test theories by introspection. Contemplating whether these postulates sound to us like "reasonable" behavior is not an empirically reliable test. Also, asking firm owners if they behave in these particular ways is similarly unreliable. The only way to test such postulates is to derive from them potentially refutable hypotheses and ultimately to see if actual firms conform to the predictions of the theory.

What sorts of refutable hypotheses emerge from these behavioral assertions? Among the logical implications of profit-maximization is the refutable hypothesis that if a per-unit tax is applied to a firm's output, the amount of goods offered for sale will decrease. This hypothesis is refutable because the reverse can be true. We therefore begin our first example by *asserting* that firms maximize profits, in order to derive this implication.

Example 1 Let $R(x) =$ total revenue function (depending on output x)

$\quad\quad C(x) =$ total cost function

$\quad\quad tx =$ total tax revenue collected, where the per-unit tax rate t is a parameter determined by forces beyond the firm's control

If the firm sells its output in a perfectly competitive market, i.e., it is a *price taker*, then

$$R(x) = px$$

where p is the parametrically determined market price of x. If the firm is not a perfect competitor, then p is determined, along with x, via the demand curve, and revenue is simply some function of output, $R(x)$.

In the general case, the tax rate t represents the only parameter, or test condition, of the model. The first model thus becomes

maximize $\quad\quad\quad\quad \pi(x) = R(x) - C(x) - tx \quad\quad\quad\quad\quad$ (1-3)

By simple calculus, the first-order conditions for a maximum are

$$R'(x) - C'(x) - t = 0 \quad\quad\quad\quad\quad (1\text{-}4)$$

the prime denoting first derivative.

For a maximum, sufficient second-order conditions are:

$$R'' - C'' < 0 \quad\quad\quad\quad\quad (1\text{-}5)$$

Condition (1-4) is the choice function for this firm in implicit form. It states that the firm will choose that level of output such that marginal revenue (MR) equals marginal cost (MC) plus the tax (t). If the firm is a perfect competitor, then $R'(x) = p$, and $R''(x) = 0$. Equations (1-4) and (1-5) then become, respectively,

$$p - C'(x) - t = 0 \qquad (1\text{-}4')$$

$$-C''(x) < 0 \qquad (1\text{-}5')$$

We shall pursue the model from the standpoint of a firm with an unspecified revenue function $R(x)$. Application of the model to the perfectly competitive case will be left as a problem for the student.

Equation (1-4) is a well-known application of "marginal" reasoning. Equation (1-4) states that a firm will produce at a level such that the incremental (marginal) gain in revenues is exactly offset by the incremental cost (including, of course, the tax). This condition, however, does not guarantee a maximum of profits. It is also perfectly consistent with minimizing profits with the same cost and revenue functions, since the same first-order conditions are implied. What we mean to express is that as long as marginal receipts exceed marginal cost, the firm will produce at a higher rate, and if marginal receipts are less than marginal costs, the output will be reduced. This idea is given a precise statement by equation (1-5), which says that receipts are increasing at a slower rate than costs. Or, in terms of the marginal-revenue and marginal-cost curves, equation (1-5) says that the marginal-cost curve cuts the marginal-revenue curve from below.

Notice that we do not assert that the "optimum" output for a firm is where marginal revenue equals marginal cost; this is a value judgment, not a statement about behavior. Likewise, equation (1-4) does not represent what this firm does *in equilibrium.* Equation (1-4) is a *necessary* event, logically deduced from the assertion of maximization of profits. If equation (1-4) is not observed, it constitutes a refutation of the model, not *disequilibrium* or *nonoptimal* behavior. Thus, we *assert* that firms act as if they are obeying equations (1-4) and (1-5), and on that account we make predictions about their behavior.

To simply assert $MR = MC + t$, however, is not likely to be useful. One is not likely to observe these marginal relationships. Just as tastes are difficult to observe, the total revenue and total cost functions and, hence, their derivatives, will likely not be known. However, a prediction about the response of the firm to a change in the economic environment, i.e., some test condition—in this case, a change in the tax rate—*is*, nonetheless, possible. Even if profit-maximization, marginal revenue, and marginal cost are not directly observable, tax rates and quantities sold *are* potentially observable. And profit-maximization contains implications about these observable quantities.

How can equations (1-4) and (1-5) be used to obtain predictions about marginal responses? Upon closer observation we notice that equation (1-4) is an implicit relationship between x and t. Under certain mathematical conditions this implicit relationship between the variable x and the parameter t can be solved for the explicit choice function:

$$x = x^*(t) \qquad (1\text{-}6)$$

That is, if we knew the equations of the MR and MC curves, *then as long as the firm can be counted on to always obey the appropriate marginal relations,* no matter what tax rate prevails, we can, in principle, solve for the explicit relationship which states how much output will be produced at each tax rate. Again, although it would be desirable to know the exact form of equation (1-6), the economist will not typically have this much information. Hence, predictions about *total* quantities will not generally be forthcoming. However, we can, nonetheless, make predictions about *marginal* quantities.

If equation (1-6) is substituted into equation (1-4), the *identity*

$$R'(x^*(t)) - C'(x^*(t)) - t \equiv 0 \tag{1-7}$$

results. This is an identity because the left-hand side is 0 for all values of t. It is 0 for all values of t precisely because $x^*(t)$ is that level of output that the firm chooses in order to *make* the left-hand side of (1-7) always equal 0. That is, the firm, by always equating MR to MC plus the tax, for any tax rate, transforms the equation (1-4) into the identity (1-7). Since we are interested in what happens to x as t *changes*, the indicated mathematical operation is the differentiation of identity (1-7) with respect to t, keeping equation (1-6) in mind. The student must observe that this differentiation makes sense *only if x is a function of t*. Otherwise, the symbol dx/dt has no meaning. It is premature to simply differentiate *equation* (1-4) with respect to t until such functional dependence is formally implied. It is the assertion that the firm will *always* equate at the margin, i.e., obey equation (1-4) *for any tax rate,* that allows the specification of equation (1-6): the functional dependence of x upon t. The resulting identity, (1-7), *can* be validly differentiated on both sides; equation (1-4) cannot be. This step is often left out, yet it is critical from the standpoint of clearly understanding the implied economic relationships as well as mathematical validity.†

Performing the indicated differentiation of identity (1-7),

$$R''(x)\frac{dx^*}{dt} - C''(x)\frac{dx^*}{dt} - 1 \equiv 0 \tag{1-8}$$

Equivalently, assuming $(R'' - C'') \neq 0$,

$$\frac{dx^*}{dt} \equiv \frac{1}{R'' - C''} \tag{1-9}$$

Since $R'' - C'' < 0$ by the sufficient second-order conditions for profit-maximization, this implies

$$\frac{dx^*}{dt} < 0$$

---

† As an example of the latter, differentiation of both sides of the identity $(x + 1)^2 \equiv x^2 + 2x + 1$ is valid; differentiation of both sides of the equation $x^2 + 3x - 4 = 0$ yields nonsense. The difference is that the former holds for *all* x, whereas the latter holds only for $x = -4$ and $x = +1$.

The student will do well to consider what has been accomplished here. The postulate of profit-maximization (not observable), as specified in equation (1-3), has led to the refutable proposition that output will decline as the tax rate the firm faces increases. In addition, nothing has been assumed as to the specific functional form of the demand or cost curves, and hence the result holds for all specifications of those functions. A prediction about *changes* in the choice variable, that is, marginal adjustment of output when the parameter facing the decision maker changes, has been rather easily derived, i.e., shown to be implied by a single behavioral assertion. This is the goal of comparative statics; the limitations and abilities of the methodology to accomplish that goal are the subject of this book.

Example 2 Consider now the second above-mentioned behavioral postulate. Let us suppose that profits are desired not for their own sake, but, rather, for the utility derived from them. Thus, let us now assert that the firm owner maximizes $U(\pi)$, where $U'(\pi) > 0$, so that increased profits mean increased utility. The function $U(\pi)$ is some unspecified ordinal measure of the "satisfaction" that this firm owner gains from earning profits. It might seem that since we have replaced a potentially observable quantity, profits, with an unobservable variable, utility, that this theory will be devoid of refutable implications. Let us see.

The objective function is now

maximize $\qquad U(R(x) - C(x) - tx) = U(\pi)$ $\qquad\qquad$ (1-10)

The firm's choice function, as before, is found by setting the derivative of $U(\pi)$ with respect to x equal to 0. Using the chain rule

$$\frac{dU}{d\pi}\frac{d\pi}{dx} = 0$$

or $\qquad U'(\pi)[R'(x) - C'(x) - t] = 0$ $\qquad\qquad$ (1-11)

Since $U'(\pi) > 0$, the choice function (1-11) is equivalent to the previous one for simple profit-maximization:

$$R'(x) - C'(x) - t = 0 \qquad\qquad (1\text{-}4)$$

Since the implicit functions (1-4) and (1-11) are equivalent, their solutions

$$x = x^*(t) \qquad\qquad (1\text{-}12)$$

are identical. Thus, these firms will act identically; they have the same explicit choice functions (1-6) and (1-12) governing the response of output to tax rates. One technicality must not be overlooked, however. We must check that the point of maximum profits is also *maximum*, rather than minimum, utility; i.e., we have to check the second-order conditions for this problem. Otherwise we might be discussing two entirely different points, and the derivatives dx/dt at those points would in general differ. The second-order conditions for the two problems are, however, identical: we have, for the first-order condition

$$\frac{dU(\pi)}{dx} = U'(\pi)[\pi'(x)] = 0$$

Thus, using the product rule

$$\frac{d^2U(\pi)}{dx^2} = U'(\pi)[\pi''(x)] + [\pi'(x)]\{[U''(\pi)][\pi'(x)]\}$$

Since $d\pi/dx = 0$ by the first-order conditions

$$\frac{d^2U(\pi)}{dx^2} = U'(\pi)\pi''(x) \tag{1-13}$$

Since $U'(\pi) > 0$, $d^2U(\pi)/dx^2 < 0$ if and only if $d^2\pi/dx^2 < 0$, that is, the second-order conditions for the two models are identical.

These two theories of behavior are equivalent in the sense that they yield the same refutable hypotheses. Even if more parameters are introduced into $\pi(x)$, the first- and second-order equations will be identical. Thus, no set of data could ever distinguish whether a firm was maximizing profits, or some arbitrary increasing function of profits, $U(\pi)$. We shall never know if the firm is really maximizing log π, or e^π, or π^3 (*not* π^2; why?), or whatever. These behavioral postulates all yield the same refutable hypotheses. One is as good as the other.

Example 3 Consider now the last of the three hypotheses about firm behavior, the maximization of total sales. If such a firm were taxed at rate t, the objective function would be

maximize $\qquad\qquad \phi(x) = R(x) - tx \tag{1-14}$

The implicit choice function of this firm is the first-order condition for a maximum

$$\phi'(x) = R'(x) - t = 0 \tag{1-15}$$

The second-order conditions for maximizing $\phi(x)$ are

$$\phi''(x) = R''(x) < 0 \tag{1-16}$$

The *explicit* choice function of this firm is the solution of (1-15) for output as a function of the tax rate, or

$$x = x^{**}(t) \tag{1-17}$$

This choice function will in general indicate a different level of output for any given tax rate than the choice function (1-6) or (1-12). If the revenue function $R(x)$ were actually known, then this theory (sales-maximization) would be operationally distinguishable from the prior two theories, since different choices are implied. However, if it turns out that $R(x)$ is not directly observable (indeed, this is the empirically likely situation), then the only refutable proposition will concern the sign of dx^{**}/dt. This model, like the previous ones, implies a negative sign for this derivative. Substituting (1-17) into (1-15) and differentiating with respect to t

$$R''(x)\frac{dx^{**}}{dt} \equiv 1$$

or

$$\frac{dx^{**}}{dt} \equiv \frac{1}{R''(x)} < 0 \tag{1-18}$$

using the sufficient second-order conditions (1-16). Hence, *unless the revenue and cost functions are somehow known, the sales-maximization and profit-maximization postulates are equivalent, in the sense that no observation of* **changes** *in tax rates and* **changes** *in quantities sold will ever distinguish these two theories.* If $R(x)$ and $C(x)$ are unobservable, and $dx^*/dt < 0$ is implied for *any* $R(x)$ and $C(x)$ which satisfy the second-order conditions, then the same observations are implied for $C(x) \equiv 0$, i.e., sales-maximization. The reader is cautioned against assuming that there is *no* test which could separate these hypotheses. There may be, for example, reasons why the long-term survivability might differ for firms which maximized profits as opposed to sales.

Example 4 There is nothing in the previous examples which restricts the analysis to noncompetitive firms. For competitive firms, output price p is taken as given. The firm is a price taker; it cannot influence output price by its own choices regarding output levels. The revenue function, $R(x)$, for a competitive firm is simply px, price times quantity. Since this is a special case of $R(x)$, the previous analysis applies to competitive firms as well: a tax on output will lead to decreases in total output produced.

In this model, however, a new parameter p appears. Does the postulate of profit-maximization imply a refutable hypothesis regarding changes in p? The objective function is

maximize $$\pi(x) = px - C(x) \tag{1-19}$$

The first-order condition for maximization yields the implicit choice function

$$p - C'(x) = 0 \tag{1-20}$$

Here, marginal revenue = price p. Hence, this relation says that the firm will set marginal cost equal to price. However, unless we know the cost function, this information will not be very useful.

The sufficient second-order condition for maximizing π is

$$\frac{d^2\pi}{dx^2} = -C''(x) = -MC'(x) < 0 \tag{1-21}$$

That is, the marginal cost function of the firm must be upward-sloping.

The explicit choice function is found by solving (in principle) equation (1-20) for the choice variable x in terms of the parameter p

$$x = x^*(p) \tag{1-22}$$

This function is the firm's supply function. It tells how much x will be offered for sale at any given price p. Strictly speaking, the marginal cost function is *not* the supply function of the firm. In the MC function, output x is the *independent* variable, marginal cost (which equals price at the chosen point) is the *dependent* variable. For the supply function, output is the dependent variable, dependent upon price. Thus, the supply function is really the *inverse* of the MC function. How will x *change* when p *changes*? Substituting (1-22) back into (1-20), the identity

$$p - C'(x^*(p)) \equiv 0 \tag{1-23}$$

results. The left-hand side is *always* zero, because we are now postulating that the firm will *always* set price equal to marginal cost *for any price*. Hence, this is an identity—the left-hand side vanishes completely. Since the derivative dx^*/dp is desired, differentiate identity (1-23) with respect to p, using the chain rule for $C'(x^*(p))$

$$\frac{dp}{dp} - \frac{dC'(x)}{dx}\frac{dx^*}{dp} \equiv 0$$

or

$$-C''(x)\frac{dx^*}{dp} \equiv -1$$

and thus, since $C'' \neq 0$

$$\frac{dx^*}{dp} \equiv \frac{1}{C''(x)} > 0 \tag{1-24}$$

since $C''(x) > 0$ by the sufficient second-order conditions for a maximum (1-21). Thus, the behavioral postulate of profit maximization yields the refutable hypothesis that if the output price to competitive firms is somehow raised, output levels will increase. The supply function is upward-sloping. Given this mathematical property of the model, the theory can be tested using real data on the assumption that the firms in question correspond to the theoretical construct of the firm used in the model. But empirical testing is worthwhile only because the model yields refutable implications.

PROBLEMS

1 Consider the following alleged exception to the law of demand: "As the price of diamonds fall, the quantity of diamonds demanded will also fall since the prestige of owning diamonds will similarly fall." Why is this not an exception to the law of demand? What test condition is being violated? How would one test the law of demand for diamonds? (*Hint*: Do jewelry stores ever lower prices on diamonds? What results?)

2 What is the difference between an assertion and an assumption? Which is observable, which is not? Which must be "realistic"?

3 It is often argued that Americans have a "love affair" with big cars. This explanation of why Americans drive, on average, larger cars than other people, is based on *tastes*. Is there any evidence which suggests that these choices are based on differing *opportunities*?

4 Why do economists limit their analyses to marginal rather than total quantities? Do economists believe that marginal quantities are more useful than the corresponding total quantities?

5 What is the difference between a theory and a model?

6 Is there a trade-off between the realism of the assumptions of a theory and the *tractability*, i.e., the empirical usefulness, of the theory?

7 In regard to problem 6, is it necessary to have the latest theory of molecular action to make penicillin and other "wonder drugs"? How detailed a theory of the firm is necessary to predict the effects of tariffs on a given industry?

8 Consider a monopolist whose total cost function is $C = kx^2$ and who faces the demand curve $x = a - bp$.

(*a*) What restrictions on the values of the parameters a, b, and k would you be inclined to assert, a priori?

(*b*) Find the explicit function $x = x^*(t)$. Confirm that for the restricted values of a, b, and k placed in part (*a*) that $x^{*\prime}(t) < 0$, i.e., output decreases as the tax increases.

(*c*) What restrictions does the hypothesis of profit maximization place on the parameters a, b, and k? Are these weaker or stronger than your a priori restrictions?

(*d*) Substitute your $x^*(t)$ function into the first-order relation for maximization and confirm that an identity in t results.

(*e*) Confirm that, for this specification of the model, profit-maximization alone implies $x^{*\prime}(t) < 0$.

9 Show that an increase of a per-unit tax on a perfect competitor will lower that firm's output.

10 Show why a monopolist has no supply function. (*Hint:* In example 1 in this chapter, how would $x = x^*(p)$ be defined?)

11 Consider a firm which has as its behavioral postulate the minimization of total costs, irrespective of revenues. How will this theory of the firm differ from those discussed in examples 1 through 3 in this chapter?

BIBLIOGRAPHY

Alchian, Armen A.: Uncertainty, Evolution and Economic Theory, *Journal of Political Economy*, **58:** 211–221 (1950).

Bronfenbrenner, Martin: A Middle-brow Introduction to Economic Methodology, in S. Krupp (ed.), "The Structure of Economic Science," Prentice Hall, Inc., Englewood Cliffs, N.J., 1966.

Friedman, Milton: The Methodology of Positive Economics, from "Essays in Positive Economics," The University of Chicago Press, Chicago, 1953, pp. 3–43. The provocative essay that started the current debates on methodology.

Gordon, Donald: Operational Propositions in Economic Theory, *Journal of Political Economy*, **63:** 150–161 (1955).

Hempel, Carl: "The Philosophy of Natural Science," Prentice Hall, Inc., Englewood Cliffs, N.J., 1966. An extremely lucid discussion of theories and theoretical testing.

Kuhn, Thomas S.: "The Structure of Scientific Revolutions," The University of Chicago Press, Chicago, 1962.

Nagel, Ernst: Assumptions in Economic Theory, *American Economic Review*, May 1963, pp. 211–219. Clarifies the meaning of "assumptions" used ambiguously by Friedman.

Papandreou, Andreas: "Economics as a Science," J. B. Lippincott Company, Philadelphia, 1958.

Robbins, Lionel: "An Essay on the Nature and Significance of Economic Science," MacMillan & Co., Ltd., London, 1932.

Samuelson, Paul A.: "Foundations of Economic Analysis," Harvard University Press, Cambridge, Mass., 1947.

CHAPTER TWO

REVIEW OF CALCULUS (ONE VARIABLE)

2.1 FUNCTIONS, LIMITS, CONTINUITY

Consider a *variable x*. By the term *variable*, we mean that x is a number which can take on a whole range of values. In economics, two common variables are price and quantity of a good. Most often, these variables are restricted to nonnegative values, though, occasionally, inputs in a production process are referred to as "negative outputs." Occasionally, in economics the variable x is a *complex number* of the form $a + bi$, where $i = \sqrt{-1}$. We shall not deal with complex numbers in this chapter. In general, we shall allow x to range over any real number. The set of points between two numbers a, b, with $b > a$, is called an *interval*. If both endpoints are included, it is called a *closed* interval; if neither endpoint is included, it is an *open* interval. That is, the set of x such that $1 \leq x \leq 5$ is a closed interval; the set of x such that $-1 < x < 4$ is an open interval. In general, a set which includes all its boundary points is called *closed*; a set with no boundary points is called *open*.

By a *function*, we mean a *rule* by which a variable x is transformed into some *unique* (single-valued) number, y. For example, consider

$$y = x^2$$

This function means: "Take any value of x and square it. The resulting value is y." This rule, or function, associates with every point along the real axis some number along the nonnegative real axis. The function $y = x^2$ represents the geometric shape of a parabola and is represented in Fig. 2-1a. An especially simple, though important function, comprises the equations of the form $y = mx + b$. Geome-

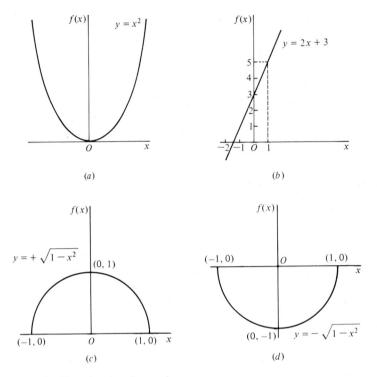

Figure 2-1 Four functions in x and y.

trically, these are straight lines with a vertical intercept (y intercept) b. The slopes of these lines are constant and equal to m. Consider, for example,

$$y = 2x + 3$$

When $x = 0$, $y = 3$. For each unit increase in x, y will increase by 2 units. Hence, the slope of this function is constant at $m = 2$. This function is plotted on Fig. 2-1b.

An important class of functions comprises the polynomials,

$$y = a_0 + a_1 x + a_2 x^2 + \cdots + a_n x^n$$

Functions of this type are called polynomials even if some of the a_i's are zero; for example, $y = x^n$ is still called a polynomial even though it has but one term. These functions in general wiggle around up to $n - 1$ times and then depart for plus or minus infinity. We shall explore their behavior in a while.

In contrast, consider the relationship

$$x^2 + y^2 = 1$$

The set of values of x and y which satisfy this equation correspond to the boundary of a circle in the xy plane with center at the origin and with radius 1. It is called the unit circle. However, this *implicit* function in x and y may not be written as

$$y = \pm\sqrt{1 - x^2}$$

and preserve the single-valuedness criterion which is part of the definition of a function. That is, for each $-1 < x < +1$, there are *two* values of y. The implicit function

$$x^2 + y^2 = 1$$

is equivalent to the *two* explicit functions,

$$y = +\sqrt{1 - x^2} \quad \text{and} \quad y = -\sqrt{1 - x^2}$$

as shown in Fig. 2-1, *c* and *d*.

Limits, Continuity

At one time, mathematicians spoke of "infinitesimals." This nomenclature has been replaced by the concept of a "limit." By the symbol

$$\lim_{x \to x_0} f(x) = A$$

we mean that as x *approaches* some value x_0, $f(x)$ becomes arbitrarily close to the value A. No matter how close to A, say within 0.0001, or 0.000001, you wish the function to be, it can be made to be that close or closer by selecting an x near x_0. This concept is expressed rigorously as:

"For any $\varepsilon > 0$, there exists a $\delta > 0$ such that if

$$|x - x_0| < \delta, \ |f(x) - A| < \varepsilon."$$

The *limit* of a function as $x \to x_0$ has no necessary connection with the value of the function *at* $x = x_0$. That is, it is one thing to assert that $\lim_{x \to x_0} f(x) = A$ and quite another to say that $f(x_0) = A$. The function need not even be defined at x_0; yet it may still have a limit as x *approaches* x_0.

When the *limit* of a function as $x \to x_0$ in fact *equals* the value of the function at x_0, the function is said to be *continuous at* x_0. That is, the function is continuous if

$$\lim_{x \to x_0} f(x) = f(x_0) \tag{2-1}$$

A formal definition of continuity is obtained by using the formal definition of a limit:

"The function $f(x)$ is continuous at x_0 if for every $\varepsilon > 0$, there exists a $\delta > 0$ such that if $|x - x_0| < \delta, \ |f(x) - f(x_0)| < \varepsilon."$

Example 1 Consider the function $y = 2x + 1$. As $x \to 1$, $y \to 3$. That is, the *limit* of $f(x) = 3$, as $x \to 1$. This can also be shown by demonstrating that $|f(x) - 3| < \varepsilon$, for *any* ε, if $|x - 1|$ is sufficiently small. We note that

$$|f(x) - 3| = |2x - 2| = 2|x - 1|$$

If we choose $\delta = \varepsilon/2$, then if $|(x - 1)| < \delta$,

$$2|x - 1| = |2x - 2| = |f(x) - 3| < 2\delta = \varepsilon$$

Hence, no matter how small ε is made, by choosing $\delta = \varepsilon/2$, $|x - 1| < \delta$ guarantees $|f(x) - 3| < \varepsilon$. Thus, by definition,

$$\lim_{x \to 1} (2x + 1) = 3$$

Another matter entirely is that $f(1) = 2(1) + 1 = 3$. In this case

$$\lim_{x \to 1} f(x) = f(1)$$

Because of this, the function $f(x) = 2x + 1$ is *continuous* at $x = 1$.

Example 2 Show that the function $y = x^2$ is continuous at $x = 2$. We first note that $f(2) = 2^2 = 4$. For any $\varepsilon > 0$, $|f(x) - 4| < \varepsilon$ is equivalent to $|x^2 - 4| < \varepsilon$, or $|x + 2||x - 2| < \varepsilon$. At points near $x = 2$, $|x + 2| \to 4$. Certainly, then, $|x + 2| < 5$. Then let $\delta = \varepsilon/5$. Then $|x - 2| < \delta$ implies $\varepsilon > 5|x - 2| > |x + 2||x - 2| = |f(x) - 4|$. Hence, there exists a $\delta > 0$ (in this case, say, $\delta = \varepsilon/5$), such that if x is within δ of $x_0 = 2$, ($|x - 2| < \delta$), then $f(x)$ is within ε of the value $4 = f(x)$, ($|f(x) - 4| < \varepsilon$), *and this holds for any $\varepsilon > 0$ whatsoever*. Hence,

$$\lim_{x \to 2} x^2 = 4 = f(2)$$

and thus x^2 is continuous at $x = 2$.

Example 3 In fact, the functions in the two examples above are continuous everywhere. As an example of a function which is not continuous everywhere, consider the step function depicted in Fig. 2-2a. This function is defined as

$$f(x) = \text{greatest integer in } x$$

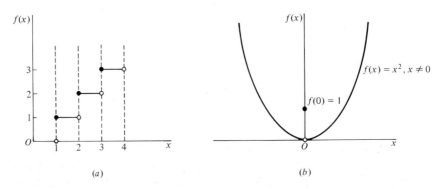

(a) (b)

Figure 2-2 (*a*) The step function: $f(x) =$ greatest integer in x. (*b*) A graph of function that is discontinuous at the origin.

For example, for $0 \le x < 1, f(x) = 0$ (note carefully the strict or weak inequalities); for $1 \le x < 2, f(x) = 1$; for $2 \le x < 3, f(x) = 2$, etc. Notice the "holes" on the right-hand side of each step: At the integer values $x = 1, 2, 3, \ldots$, the function jumps to the next integer value. The function is *defined* at $x = 1, 2, 3, \ldots$; for example, $f(1) = 1$, $f(2) = 2$, etc. However, if one approaches the integer values $x = 1, 2, 3$, from the left (denoted $x \to x_0^-$)

$$\lim_{x \to 1^-} f(x) = 0$$

$$\lim_{x \to 2^-} f(x) = 1$$

$$\cdots\cdots\cdots$$

From the right (denoted $x \to x_0^+$),

$$\lim_{x \to 1^+} f(x) = 1$$

$$\lim_{x \to 2^+} f(x) = 2$$

$$\cdots\cdots\cdots$$

In general, for integral values of x_0, $\lim_{x \to x_0} f(x) = f(x_0)$ only when x_0 is approached from the right. In this case, no unique number for $\lim_{x \to x_0} f(x)$ exists; hence, $f(x)$ is discontinuous at integral values of x.

Example 4 Consider the function $f(x)$ defined as

$$f(x) = \begin{cases} x^2 & \text{if } x \ne 0 \\ 1 & \text{if } x = 0 \end{cases}$$

This function is depicted in Fig. 2-2b. For all points except $x = 0, f(x)$ is the usual parabolic shape. For no particular reason, $f(0)$ is defined to be unity. Hence, the parabola has a hole at $x = 0$. In this case

$$\lim_{x \to 0} f(x) = 0$$

from either side of the origin. Since $f(0) = 1$,

$$\lim_{x \to 0} f(x) \ne f(0)$$

Hence, this function is discontinuous at the origin.

Example 5 Consider the hyperbolas defined by $y = 1/x$. This function exists in the strictly positive first quadrant and strictly negative third quadrant. Since $f(0)$ is undefined, this function cannot be continuous at $x = 0$.

PROBLEMS

1 Sketch the following functions:

    (a) $y = -2x + 1$
    (b) $y = 1/x$
    (c) $y = \sqrt{1-x}$ (For what values of x is this function defined?)
    (d) $y = |x|$ (absolute value of x)
    (e) $y = (x + 1)/(x - 1)$
    (f) $y = x$, if $x \geq 0$, $y = -x + 1$ if $x < 0$.

2 Show that the functions $1(a) - 1(e)$ are continuous for all values of x for which the function is defined. Show that the function in $1(f)$ is discontinuous at $x = 0$.

3 Does the existence of a "kink" or corner in a function (such as occurs in problem $1d$ at $x = 0$) imply that the function is discontinuous there?

4 For the function in problem $1e$, what is $\lim_{x \to \infty} f(x)$? (*Hint:* divide numerator and denominator through by x.)

2.2 DERIVATIVES

One of the most important mathematical concepts is the rate of change of a function. In economics, this concept shows up under the name "marginal." Marginal cost is the rate of change of total cost per increment of output. Marginal revenue is similarly the rate of change of total revenue. Geometrically, the marginal quantities are the slopes of the total quantities.

    Consider any function $y = f(x)$, as depicted in Fig. 2-3. At some point $x = x_0$, $f(x) = f(x_0)$. Suppose now that x is changed to $(x_0 + \Delta x)$. (Here, Δx is positive, but this is not a necessary restriction.) The new value of the function is given by $y + \Delta y = f(x_0 + \Delta x)$. The change in the functional value Δy is

$$\Delta y = f(x_0 + \Delta x) - f(x_0)$$

The *rate* of change of $f(x)$, per change in x, is

$$\frac{\Delta y}{\Delta x} = \frac{f(x_0 + \Delta x) - f(x_0)}{\Delta x} \tag{2-2}$$

Geometrically, $\Delta y/\Delta x$ is the slope of the chord CC passing through $f(x_0)$ and $f(x_0 + \Delta x)$, as seen in Fig. 2-3. Now, as Δx becomes smaller and smaller, the slope of the chord CC approaches the slope of the line TT which is tangent to the function at $f(x_0)$. The slope of this tangent line (if it exists) is written dy/dx. Therefore, assuming the limit exists (and is thus unique),

$$\frac{dy}{dx} = \lim_{\Delta x \to x_0} \frac{f(x_0 + \Delta x) - f(x_0)}{\Delta x} \tag{2-3}$$

This important limit, the limit of a *difference quotient*, is called the *derivative* of $f(x)$ at $f(x_0)$. It represents the slope of the curve at x_0.

    Before investigating the rules by which derivatives are found, let us investigate cases in which these limits do not exist. Consider the function $y = |x|$. For $x > 0$, this function is simply $y = x$; it has a constant slope of unity. For $x < 0$, the

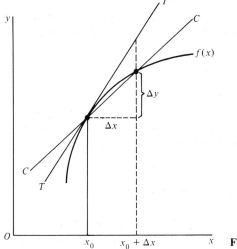

Figure 2-3 The derivative of a function.

function is given by $y = -x$; it has constant slope of *minus* one. At $x = 0$, the slope is undefined. The function has a "corner" there. It is *continuous*, but it is not *differentiable* there. If a function is to be differentiable at a point, it must be well defined there, and it must at least be continuous. However, these conditions alone are insufficient, as $y = |x|$ reveals. Simply stated, the difference quotient above must in fact possess a limit.

Differentiation of Polynomials

Let us find the derivative of $f(x) = x^2$. The difference quotient at any value of x is

$$\frac{\Delta y}{\Delta x} = \frac{f(x + \Delta x) - f(x)}{\Delta x} = \frac{(x + \Delta x)^2 - x^2}{\Delta x}$$

$$= \frac{2x\,\Delta x + (\Delta x)^2}{\Delta x} = 2x + \Delta x$$

Clearly, $\lim_{\Delta x \to 0} (\Delta y / \Delta x) = 2x$, hence

$$\frac{dy}{dx} = 2x$$

The slope of the parabola $y = x^2$ at any point equals twice the value of x. At $x = 0$, $dy/dx = 0$; i.e., the function is horizontal; at $x = -2$, $dy/dx = -4$, etc.

Now consider the polynomial $y = x^n$.

$$\frac{\Delta y}{\Delta x} = \frac{(x + \Delta x)^n - x^n}{\Delta x}$$

Expanding the numerator using the binomial theorem

$$\frac{\Delta y}{\Delta x} = \frac{\left[x^n + nx^{n-1} \, \Delta x + \frac{n(n-1)}{2} x^{n-2}(\Delta x)^2 + \cdots \right] - x^n}{\Delta x}$$

$$= nx^{n-1} + \frac{n(n-1)}{2} x^{n-1} \, \Delta x$$

$$+ \text{[terms in } (\Delta x)^2 \text{ and higher powers of } \Delta x]$$

As $\Delta x \to 0$, all terms except the first tend to 0. Thus

$$\frac{dy}{dx} = nx^{n-1} \tag{2-4}$$

It can be quickly verified that if $y = kx^n$ where k is any constant,

$$\frac{dy}{dx} = knx^{n-1} \tag{2-5}$$

Also, let $y = k_1 x^n + k_2 x^m$ where k_1 and k_2 are arbitrary constants. Then

$$\frac{dy}{dx} = k_1 nx^{n-1} + k_2 mx^{m-1}$$

The derivative of a sum is the sum of the derivatives. This property holds for any functions. Let us denote the derivative of functions $f(x)$, $g(x)$, and $h(x)$ as $f'(x)$ (read "f prime of x"), $g'(x)$, $h'(x)$. Suppose

$$y = f(x) \equiv g(x) + h(x)$$

Then
$$\frac{dy}{dx} = f'(x) \equiv g'(x) + h'(x)$$

The theorem extends to sums or differences of arbitrarily many terms.

The binomial theorem used in the above proof that for $y = x^n$, $dy/dx = nx^{n-1}$ in fact holds for *all* values of n, not merely positive integers. The value of n can be any real number. Thus, for example, if

$$y = \sqrt{x} = x^{1/2}$$

$$\frac{dy}{dx} = \frac{1}{2} x^{-1/2}$$

Likewise, for

$$y = \frac{1}{x^3} = x^{-3}$$

$$\frac{dy}{dx} = -3x^{-4}$$

When any function $y = f(x)$ is differentiated, its derivative, $f'(x)$, will again be some function of x. If $f'(x)$ is sufficiently "smooth" (i.e., differentiable), it too can be differentiated with respect to x. We write

$$f''(x) = \frac{df'(x)}{dx} = \frac{d}{dx}\frac{dy}{dx} = \frac{d^2y}{dx^2}$$

In fact, as long as succeeding derivatives are differentiable, they can be successively differentiated, producing higher-order derivatives.

The second derivative of $f(x)$ is the first derivative, or the rate of change, of the first derivative of $f(x)$. That is, just as $f'(x)$ indicates the slope of $f(x)$, $f''(x)$ gives the slope of $f'(x)$. Likewise, $f'''(x)$ gives the slope of $f''(x)$, $f^{(n)}(x)$ is the slope of $f^{(n-1)}(x)$, where $f^{(n)}(x)$ is the nth derivative of $f(x)$.

Example 1 Let $y = x^2$. Then $f'(x) = 2x$, $f''(x) = 2$, $f'''(x) = \cdots = f^{(n)}(x) = 0$. All derivatives of third order and higher are 0. The fact that $f''(x) > 0$ means that $f'(x)$ is always increasing; i.e., the slope of $y = x^2$ is always increasing. The student should check this against Fig. 2-1a.

Example 2 Let $y = 1/x = x^{-1}$. Then $dy/dx = -1/x^2 = -x^{-2}$, $d^2y/dx^2 = f''(x) = +2x^{-3}$, $f'''(x) = -6x^{-4}$, etc. Note that $f'(x) = dy/dx < 0$ always. This function is always *falling*, i.e., negatively sloped. From the expression for $f''(x)$, we can infer that for $x > 0$, the slope increases with increasing x, whereas for $x < 0$, the slope decreases as x increases.

PROBLEMS

1 Find the derivatives of the following functions by taking the limit of a difference quotient:
    (a) $y = 3x^2$ (b) $y = x^3$
    (c) $y = mx + b$ (d) $y = 1/x$
2 For each function, find dy/dx and d^2y/dx^2:
    (a) $y = 37x^4$ (b) $y = x^{a/b}$
    (c) $y = -x^{-2}$ (d) $y = x^3 - 1/x^2$
3 Sketch each of the functions in problems 1 and 2, indicating when the *functions* are rising or falling, and when the *slopes* are rising or falling, with increasing x.
4 Show that the circumference of a circle may be regarded as the rate of change of the area with respect to the radius. Interpret geometrically.

2.3 DIFFERENTIALS

Consider Fig. 2-4, largely a reproduction of Fig. 2-3. For any change in the variable x, Δx, the actual change in the functional value of $f(x)$ is, by definition, Δy. We may distinguish this from the change in y *measured up to the tangent line*. This

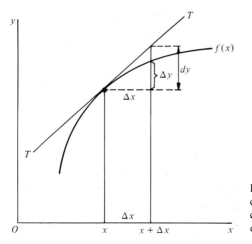

Figure 2-4 The distinction between the *actual* change in the function Δy and the differential change dy measured by the change in the height of the tangent line.

latter distance is defined to be dy. If dx is *any* change in x, then if $f'(x)$ represents the slope of the curve at the initial point,

$$dy = f'(x)\,dx = \frac{dy}{dx}\,dx$$

When we write lim $(\Delta y/\Delta x) = dy/dx$, we are asserting that the difference ε where

$$\frac{\Delta y}{\Delta x} - \frac{dy}{dx} = \varepsilon$$

tends to 0 as $\Delta x \to 0$. Multiplying both sides of this equation by Δx

$$\Delta y = \frac{dy}{dx}\,\Delta x + \varepsilon\,\Delta x$$

If we let $\Delta x = dx$,

$$\Delta y = dy + \varepsilon\,\Delta x \qquad (2\text{-}6)$$

This equation says that Δy and dy differ by an amount which is of "second-order smallness." The difference $dy - \Delta y = \varepsilon\,\Delta x$ tends to 0 much faster than Δx, since as Δx tends to 0, ε also tends to 0.

Example Let $y = x^2$. Then

$$\Delta y = (x + \Delta x)^2 - x^2 = 2x\,\Delta x + \Delta x^2$$

However, if $dx = \Delta x$,

$$dy = f'(x)\,dx = 2x\,\Delta x$$

Hence $\qquad\qquad \Delta y - dy = (\Delta x)^2$

When Δx is small (in particular, less than one in absolute value), $(\Delta x)^2$ is smaller than $|\Delta x|$. If, for example, $x = 2$, $\Delta x = .1$, $\Delta y - dy = .01$, one-tenth the amount of the change in x.

In general, the differential quantities dy are easier to calculate than the actual Δy. Hence, dy is often used as an empirical approximation to Δy. In an analytic sense, however, there is no need for dx or dy to be small, or infinitesimal. The dx's may range over any values whatsoever.

PROBLEMS

1 For each function below, find y, dy, and Δy. Show that $\Delta y - dy$ is of second-order smallness:

    (a) $y = x^3$
    (b) $y = 2x^2 + 3x$
    (c) $y = 1/x$
    (d) $y = x^n$ (use the binomial theorem)
    (e) $y = \sqrt{x}$

2.4 THE CHAIN RULE

Suppose now that in addition to the functional dependence $y = f(x)$, x is dependent upon some other variable t, say, $x = g(t)$. Then if t varies, x will in general vary and therefore so will y. Hence, y is functionally dependent upon t by the relation

$$y = f(x) = f(g(t)) = F(t) \tag{2-7}$$

The function $F(t)$ represents the "composite function" $f(g(t))$. Assuming that $f(x)$ and $g(t)$ are differentiable, the derivative $dy/dt = F'(t)$ is well defined. How is $F'(t)$ related to the derivatives of the original functions, $f(x)$ and $g(t)$? The answer is given by the *chain rule*:

$$\frac{dy}{dt} = F'(t) = \frac{dy}{dx}\frac{dx}{dt} = f'(x)g'(t) \tag{2-8}$$

There is a suggestion of canceling the dx's in the term

$$\frac{dy}{dx}\frac{dx}{dt}$$

It should remain a suggestion only. That procedure is as logically valid as canceling the 6s in

$$\frac{\cancel{6}4}{1\cancel{6}} = 4$$

Although it gives the correct result, the procedure is invalid because it is devoid of the implied functional dependences.

The chain rule is shown as follows. Changing t by Δt, x changes by Δx, y by Δy. Then

$$\Delta y = \frac{dy}{dx}\Delta x + \varepsilon \, \Delta x$$

However, using the same reasoning

$$\Delta x = \frac{dx}{dt}\Delta t + \zeta \, \Delta t$$

where $\zeta \to 0$ as $\Delta t \to 0$. Substituting this expression into the above,

$$\Delta y = \frac{dy}{dx}\frac{dx}{dt}\Delta t + \frac{dy}{dx}\zeta \, \Delta t + \varepsilon \, \Delta x$$

Dividing by Δt,

$$\frac{\Delta y}{\Delta t} = \frac{dy}{dx}\frac{dx}{dt} + \frac{dy}{dx}\zeta + \varepsilon \frac{\Delta x}{\Delta t}$$

If we now let $\Delta t \to 0$, $\Delta y / \Delta t \to dy/dt$, and since $\zeta \to 0$ and $\varepsilon \to 0$ as $\Delta t \to 0$,

$$\frac{dy}{dt} = \frac{dy}{dx}\frac{dx}{dt}$$

Example 1 Let $y = x^2$, $x = t + t^3$. Find dy/dt. This particular problem can be solved by direct substitution:

$$y = x^2 = (t + t^3)^2 = t^2 + 2t^4 + t^6$$

Therefore
$$\frac{dy}{dt} = 2t + 8t^3 + 6t^5$$

Using the chain rule to find dy/dt, we note

$$\frac{dy}{dx} = 2x \qquad \frac{dx}{dt} = 1 + 3t^2$$

Therefore
$$\frac{dy}{dt} = 2x(1 + 3t^2) = 2(t + t^3)(1 + 3t^2)$$

$$= 2t + 8t^3 + 6t^5$$

as before.

Example 2 Let $y = (ax + b)^n$. Find dy/dx. Suppose we let $u = ax + b$. Then $y = u^n$. Therefore,

$$\frac{dy}{dx} = \frac{dy}{du}\frac{du}{dx} = (nu^{n-1})a = an(ax + b)^{n-1}$$

The foregoing example shows a powerful use of the chain rule. Often very complicated expressions can be easily differentiated by a clever substitution and subsequent use of the chain rule.

Example 3 Let $y = \sqrt{1 - 3x^2}$. Find dy/dx. Here, we let $u = 1 - 3x^2$, noting that $du/dx = -6x$. Therefore, $y = u^{1/2}$, and

$$\frac{dy}{dx} = \frac{dy}{du}\frac{du}{dx} = \frac{1}{2}u^{-1/2}(-6x)$$

$$= \frac{-3x}{(1 - 3x^2)^{1/2}}$$

2.5 THE PRODUCT AND QUOTIENT RULES

The Product Rule

Consider a function such as $y = x^2(1 + x)^{1/2}$. This function cannot yet be differentiated with the tools at hand; it is the product of two functions. Here

$$f(x) = g(x)h(x) \qquad (2\text{-}9)$$

where in this case $g(x) = x^2$, $h(x) = (1 + x)^{1/2}$. Fortunately, an easy rule is available for derivatives of functions of the type (2-9). Let $y = f(x)$, $u = g(x)$, $v = h(x)$. Then

$$y = uv$$

If x changes by an amount Δx, by definition, u changes by Δu, v changes by Δv, and y changes by Δy. We have

$$y + \Delta y = (u + \Delta u)(v + \Delta v)$$

and thus

$$\Delta y = (u + \Delta u)(v + \Delta v) - uv$$

$$= u\,\Delta v + v\,\Delta u + \Delta u\,\Delta v$$

Dividing through by Δx,

$$\frac{\Delta y}{\Delta x} = u\frac{\Delta v}{\Delta x} + v\frac{\Delta u}{\Delta x} + \Delta u\frac{\Delta v}{\Delta x}$$

Taking limits as $\Delta x \to 0$, the last term tends to 0. Therefore,

$$\frac{dy}{dx} = u\frac{dv}{dx} + v\frac{du}{dx} \qquad (2\text{-}10)$$

The derivative of a product of two functions of x is the first times the derivative of the second, plus the second times the derivative of the first.

Example 1 Let $y = x^2(1 + x)^{1/2}$. Here, $u = x^2$, $v = (1 + x)^{1/2}$.

Therefore

$$\frac{dy}{dx} = x^2\frac{1}{2}(1 + x)^{-1/2} + (1 + x)^{1/2}(2x)$$

The Quotient Rule

Suppose $y = f(x) = g(x)/h(x) = u/v$. The derivative of this quotient can be found by taking a difference quotient as in the product rule derivation. However, note that

$$y = \frac{u}{v} = uv^{-1}$$

Now we can use the product rule directly:

$$\frac{dy}{dx} = u\frac{dv^{-1}}{dx} + v^{-1}\frac{du}{dx}$$

$$= -uv^{-2}\frac{dv}{dx} + \frac{1}{v}\frac{du}{dx}$$

$$= \frac{v\dfrac{du}{dx} - u\dfrac{dv}{dx}}{v^2} \tag{2-11}$$

Equation (2-11) is the most common form of this rule. The derivative of a quotient is the denominator times the derivative of the numerator, *minus* the numerator times the derivative of the denominator, all divided by the denominator squared.

Any student who has not already learned these rules must, unfortunately, memorize them. They are extremely useful and should be readily available.

Example 2 Let $y = x^2/\sqrt{1 + x^2}$. Find dy/dx. Here, $u = x^2$, $v = (1 + x^2)^{1/2}$. Hence,

$$\frac{dy}{dx} = \frac{(1 + x^2)^{1/2}(2x) - x^2\frac{1}{2}(1 + x^2)^{-1/2}(2x)}{(1 + x^2)}$$

The student should check that he or she understands where each term comes from.

2.6 IMPLICIT FUNCTIONS

Often, functions are encountered in which y is *not* written explicitly as a function of x, but is combined with x in various terms. For example, the unit circle is defined as $x^2 + y^2 = 1$. The slope is well defined at every point except $(1, 0)$ and $(-1, 0)$, where $dy/dx \to +\infty$. How can the slope be determined directly, without solving for x explicitly?

If we assume that there is *some* explicit function $y = f(x)$ associated with $x^2 + y^2 = 1$ (so that the expression dy/dx makes sense), the relation $x^2 + y^2 = 1$ can simply be differentiated term by term. (A more rigorous discussion of this process follows in Chap. 3.) The derivative of x^2 is $2x$; to differentiate y^2 with respect to x, let $z = y^2$ and use the chain rule

$$\frac{dz}{dx} = \frac{dy^2}{dx} = \frac{dz}{dy}\frac{dy}{dx} = 2y\frac{dy}{dx}$$

Hence, for $x^2 + y^2 = 1$, we have

$$2x + 2y\frac{dy}{dx} = 0$$

and thus

$$\frac{dy}{dx} = -\frac{x}{y} \qquad \text{for } y \neq 0$$

Example Suppose $y^3x^2 = 1$. Find dy/dx. We must use the product rule:

$$y^3 2x + x^2\left(3y^2\frac{dy}{dx}\right) = 0$$

$$\frac{dy}{dx} = -\frac{2y}{3x}$$

Notice that the derivatives of implicit functions will likely themselves be implicit functions.

2.7 ELASTICITY

A dimensionless variant of slope is the *percentage* change in the dependent variable due to a percentage change in the independent variable. This quantity is called the *elasticity* of the curve. Suppose $x = f(p)$ is a demand (or supply) curve, where $p = $ price and $x = $ quantity demanded. The elasticity of demand (or supply) is defined as

$$\varepsilon = \lim_{\Delta p \to 0} \frac{\Delta x/x}{\Delta p/p} = \lim_{\Delta p \to 0} \frac{p\,\Delta x}{x\,\Delta p} = \frac{p\,dx}{x\,dp} \tag{2-12}$$

If $|\varepsilon| > 1$, the curve is called *elastic;* if $0 < |\varepsilon| < 1$, the curve is called *inelastic.* Note that supply and demand curves are usually plotted with the *dependent* variable x on the *horizontal* axis. The "slope" dx/dp is thus the reciprocal of the usual slope.

Example 1 Let $x = ap^b$. Show that these functions exhibit constant elasticity $\varepsilon = b$. Using the definition (2-12),

$$\varepsilon = \frac{p\,dx}{x\,dp} = \frac{pbap^{b-1}}{ap^b} = b$$

These curves are either always elastic or always inelastic. If $b < 0$, these curves are downward-sloping for all p, and are used to represent demand curves. They belong to the class of functions called hyperbolas. If $b > 0$, these curves are upward-sloping and may represent supply curves.

Example 2 Consider the linear demand curves $x = a - bp$. Price varies between 0 and a/b. The elasticity at any point is

$$\varepsilon = \frac{p}{a - bp}(-b) = \frac{-bp}{a - bp} = \frac{-p}{\dfrac{a}{b} - p}$$

Clearly, when $p = 0, \varepsilon = 0$. As $p \to a/b, \varepsilon \to -\infty$. Also, $\varepsilon = -1$ when $p = a/2b$, the midpoint of the demand curve.

The elasticity of demand is related to the marginal-revenue curve. Total revenue is simply price times quantity, or

$$\text{TR} = px$$

Let us write the demand curve as $p = p(x)$, that is, price as a function of quantity. Then marginal revenue MR is defined as the rate of change in total revenue with respect to quantity, or

$$\text{MR} = \frac{d(\text{TR})}{dx}$$

Using the product rule

$$\text{MR} = p \cdot 1 + x \, dp/dx = p\left(1 + \frac{x \, dp}{p \, dx}\right)$$

$$= p(1 + 1/\varepsilon)$$

For demand curves, $\varepsilon < 0$. Hence, $\text{MR} > 0$ when $\varepsilon < -1$. Hence, for elastic demand curves, total revenue rises when quantity increases, i.e., when price falls. When demand is inelastic, i.e., when $-1 < \varepsilon < 0$, $\text{MR} < 0$. Total revenue falls when quantity increases, i.e., when price falls.

2.8 MAXIMA AND MINIMA

Probably the single most important application of the calculus in economics is its application to finding the maximum or minimum of functions. Most frequently, some postulate of maximizing behavior is made in economics—e.g., firms maximize "profits," consumers maximize "utility," etc. The calculus allows a detailed description of such points of "extrema."

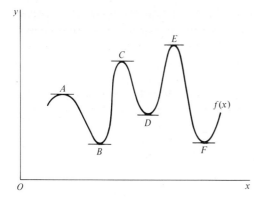

Figure 2-5 Relative minima and maxima (extrema).

Consider the rather squiggly function depicted in Fig. 2-5. Points A, B, C, D, E, and F are all points of *relative extrema*. In some neighborhood around these points, they all represent maximum or minimum values of $f(x)$. The adjective "relative" means that these are *local* extrema only, not the "global" maxima or minima over the whole range of x. These points all have one thing in common: the slope of $f(x)$ is 0, i.e., the function is horizontal at all these extrema. *A necessary condition for $f(x)$ to have a local maximum or minimum is that $dy/dx = f'(x) = 0$.*

Now consider a relative maximum, say point C. Immediately to the left of C, the function is rising; that is, $f'(x) > 0$, whereas to the right of C, $f'(x) < 0$. It is for this reason that we know $f'(x) = 0$ at point C. Moreover, we also know that the slope, $f'(x)$, is continually falling (going from $+$ to $-$) as we pass through C. Hence, $f''(x) \leq 0$ at C. We cannot be sure that $f''(x) < 0$ at C; $f''(x) = 0$ is a possibility. However, *if $f'(x) = 0$ at $x = x_0$ and if $f''(x_0) < 0$, then $f(x)$ has a relative maximum at $x = x_0$. If $f'(x_0) = 0$ and $f''(x_0) > 0$, $f(x)$ has a relative minimum.* If $f'(x_0) = 0$, $f''(x_0) = 0$, then the function may have either a maximum, minimum, or neither at that point.

Around the maximum points A, C, and E in Fig. 2-5, the function is said to be *concave downward*, or simply *concave*. Around the minimum points B, D, and F, the function is said to be *convex* (i.e., concave *upward*). For differentiable functions, concavity implies $f''(x) \leq 0$; that is, the slope, $f'(x)$, is continually nonincreasing. If $f''(x) < 0$, then concavity is implied, but concavity allows the possibility that $f''(x) = 0$. Similar remarks hold for convexity. If $f''(x) > 0$, then $f(x)$ is convex, but convexity also allows the possibility of $f''(x) = 0$. Example 2 below illustrates the possibilities allowed by $f''(x) = 0$.

Example 1 Consider $y = x^2$. Then $f'(x) = 2x$, $f''(x) = 2$. At $x = 0$, $f'(x) = 0$, $f''(x) > 0$. This function has a relative minimum at $x = 0$. (Check Fig. 2-1a.)

Example 2 Let $y = -x^4$. Then $f'(x) = -4x^3$, $f''(x) = 12x^2$. At $x = 0$, $f'(x) = f''(x) = 0$. However, this function *has* a relative maximum at $x = 0$, as a sketch of the curve quickly reveals. Likewise, $y = +x^4$ has a relative minimum at $x = 0$, with $f''(0) = 0$.

Example 3 Let $y = x^3$. Then $f'(0) = f''(0) = 0$. This function, the "cubic" function, is horizontal at $x = 0$, but it has neither a maximum nor a minimum at $x = 0$. The condition $f'(x) = 0$ is a *necessary* condition for a maximum or a minimum (a stationary value); however, $f''(x) < 0$, $f''(x) > 0$ (note the strict inequalities) are *sufficient* conditions for a relative maximum or minimum, respectively. But these strict inequalities for $f''(x)$ are not *implied by*, i.e., not necessary, conditions for a maximum or minimum.

Example 4 Consider a firm with a revenue function $R(x)$ and a cost function $C(x)$, both functions of output. If the firm maximizes profits,

$$\pi(x) = R(x) - C(x)$$

the first-order necessary conditions are

$$\pi'(x) = R'(x) - C'(x) = 0$$

This is the condition that the firm sets marginal revenue (MR) equal to marginal cost (MC). If the firm is a perfect competitor, it faces a fixed output price p. In that case, $R(x) = px$, and thus $R'(x) = p$. The first-order condition above therefore becomes

$$p - C'(x) = 0$$

That is, marginal revenue equals price here, which in turn equals marginal cost, $C'(x)$.

The condition that MR = MC is also consistent with *minimization* of profits. If we are to be sure that this is indeed a maximum and not a minimum, we need the sufficient second-order condition

$$\pi''(x) = R''(x) - C''(x) = MR'(x) - MC'(x) < 0$$

This second-order condition says that the marginal-revenue curve must have a lower slope than the marginal-cost curve. In the usual case, MR is downward-sloping; that is, $MR' < 0$, and MC is rising; that is, $MC' > 0$, and hence this sufficient condition is satisfied under these conditions. The "economic reasoning" behind this maximum condition is that as long as an addition to output will increase revenue (MR) by an amount greater than the cost of that additional output (MC), a profit-maximizing firm will produce that additional output. This process will terminate at a finite output only if, as output increases, the "net profitability," MR $-$ MC, eventually falls to 0. Hence, at the profit maximum, MR = MC, and, if profits are to decrease with still more output, $\pi''(x) = MR'(x) - MC'(x) < 0$ around the profit maximum.

Example 5 Suppose the consumers' demand curve is $x = 150 - p$, and the (total) cost function is $C = x^2/2$. Find the profit-maximizing price and quantity.

The profit function is

$$\pi(x) = px - \frac{x^2}{2} = (150 - x)x - \frac{x^2}{2} = 150x - \frac{3x^2}{2}$$

Therefore
$$\pi'(x) = 150 - 3x = 0$$
$$x = 50$$

Notice that we must express profits in terms of a single variable, in this case, x. The demand curve $x = 150 - p$ was used to write p in terms of x, or $p = 150 - x$. This is indeed a point of *maximum* profits, as the second-order conditions imply:

$$\pi''(x) = -3 < 0$$

The profit-maximizing *price* is derived from the demand curve:

$$p = 150 - 50 = 100$$

The analysis could have been carried out in terms of price:

$$\pi(p) = px - \frac{x^2}{2} = p(150 - p) - \frac{(150 - p)^2}{2}$$

$$= 150p - p^2 - \frac{(150 - p)^2}{2}$$

$$\pi'(p) = 150 - 2p - \frac{2(150 - p)(-1)}{2} = 0$$

$$= 300 - 3p = 0$$

Thus
$$p = 100$$

as before.

Example 6 A farmer has a length of fence P (perimeter) and wishes to enclose the largest rectangular area with it. Find the dimensions of the rectangle.

Let x = length of the rectangle. The width is therefore

$$w = \frac{P - 2x}{2}$$

The total area, $A(x)$, is thus

$$A(x) = \frac{x(P - 2x)}{2} = \frac{Px}{2} - x^2$$

Therefore,
$$A'(x) = \frac{P}{2} - 2x = 0$$

or
$$x = \frac{P}{4}$$

The width w is

$$w = \frac{[P - 2(P/4)]}{2} = \frac{P}{4} = x$$

For any given perimeter P the rectangle enclosing the largest area is a square, with each side $= P/4$.

Example 7 Let $A(x)$ be the average-cost curve of a firm, and $M(x) =$ marginal cost. Find the relation between these two important curves in economic theory.

The total-cost curve $T(x)$, by definition, is

$$T(x) \equiv A(x)x$$

Marginal cost is the rate of change of total cost with respect to output, or $T'(x)$. Thus, using the product rule,

$$M(x) = T'(x) = A(x) + xA'(x) \qquad (2\text{-}13)$$

This can be written

$$A'(x) = \frac{1}{x}[M(x) - A(x)]$$

If average-cost curve has a minimum, $A'(x) = 0$. At that point, necessarily (assuming $x > 0$), $M(x) = A(x)$; that is, marginal cost equals average cost. Also, if $A(x)$ is *falling* $[A'(x) < 0]$, then $M(x) < A(x)$, and if $A(x)$ is *rising*, $M(x) > A(x)$.

The relation written as

$$M(x) = A(x) + xA'(x)$$

shows the precise relation between the marginal and average curves, be they cost, product, or any other values.

PROBLEMS

1 Find the relative maxima (if any) and relative minima (if any) of the following functions. Identify each stationary value as one or the other, or neither.

(a) $y = 2x^2 - 3x + 5$ (b) $y = -3x^2 + 4x - 2$
(c) $y = 3$ (d) $y = 4x - 1/x$
(e) $y = x^3 - 12x^2 + 5$

2 A farmer's land is bordered on one side by a straight river. Find the dimensions of the largest plot which can be enclosed on three sides by a fence of length P, the fourth side being the river.

3 Consider the linear demand curves $x = a - bp$. Show that the maximum total expenditure occurs at the midpoint of this demand curve. What are the values of x, p, and MR there?

4 (a) A monopolist faces the demand curve $x = 100 - p/2$. The cost function is $C = x^2$. Find the output that maximizes this monopolist's profits. What are prices and profits at that output?

(b) Find the elasticity of demand at the profit-maximizing output.

5 (a) Now consider the monopolist of the previous question and suppose that a per-unit tax t is levied on output x. Find the profit-maximizing level of output, in terms of arbitrary levels of t.

(b) How will output change when t increases?

(c) What level of tax t should the government choose if it wishes to extract the maximum tax revenue from this monopolist?

6 Show that if the average-cost curve has a minimum, marginal cost must be rising in some neighborhood of that point.

7 Show that if the average-product curve for a factor of production has a maximum, it equals marginal product there. Show that at this maximum point, marginal product must be falling in some neighborhood of that point.

2.9 TWO IMPORTANT FUNCTIONS: $y = e^x$; $y = \log_e x$

1 The Function $y = e^x$

Suppose you put \$1 in a bank account which pays x percent interest over the year. At the end of the year, you will have an amount

$$y = (1 + x)$$

in the account. Suppose now the bank account pays x percent per year, *compounded semiannually*. In this case, the bank pays $(x/2)$ percent interest in the first half of the year, and $(x/2)$ percent on the increased amount in the second half. Therefore, after 6 months, the account would have

$$\left(1 + \frac{x}{2}\right)$$

and, with $(x/2)$ percent paid on this amount, after 1 year, the account would have in it,

$$y = \left(1 + \frac{x}{2}\right) + \left(1 + \frac{x}{2}\right)\frac{x}{2} = \left(1 + \frac{x}{2}\right)^2$$

Using similar reasoning, if interest is compounded *quarterly*, after 1 year, the account will have

$$y = \left(1 + \frac{x}{4}\right)^4$$

If the account is compounded n times during the year ($n = 365$ is common nowadays), the account will grow to

$$y = \left(1 + \frac{x}{n}\right)^n$$

What is the limit of this expression as $n \to \infty$? Let us approach the problem in two stages.

(*a*) Let $x = 1$. We then inquire as to

$$y = \lim_{n \to \infty} \left(1 + \frac{1}{n}\right)^n \tag{2-14}$$

Let us expand $(1 + 1/n)^n$ by the binomial theorem:

$$y_n = \left(1 + \frac{1}{n}\right)^n = 1^n + \frac{n \cdot 1^{n-1}(1/n)^1}{1!} + \frac{n(n-1)}{2!} 1^{n-2}\left(\frac{1}{n}\right)^2$$

$$+ \frac{n(n-1)(n-2)}{3!} 1^{n-3}\left(\frac{1}{n}\right)^3 + \cdots$$

$$= 1 + \frac{1}{1!} + \frac{1}{2!}\left(\frac{n-1}{n}\right) + \frac{1}{3!}\left(\frac{n-1}{n}\right)\left(\frac{n-2}{n}\right) + \cdots$$

Consider the limit of the terms $(n - k)/n$ as $n \to \infty$. Dividing numerator and denominator by n,

$$\frac{n-k}{n} = 1 - \frac{k}{n}$$

Clearly

$$\lim_{n \to \infty}\left(\frac{n-k}{n}\right) = 1 - \lim_{n \to \infty}\frac{k}{n} = 1$$

Moreover, any finite product of such terms tends to 1 as $n \to \infty$. Therefore,

$$y = \lim_{n \to \infty} y_n = \lim_{n \to \infty}\left(1 + \frac{1}{n}\right)^n = 1 + \frac{1}{1!} + \frac{1}{2!} + \frac{1}{3!} + \cdots$$

This infinite series converges to an important irrational number, known as e. To five decimal places,

$$e = 2.71828 \cdots$$

(b) Now let us return to the more general case of

$$\lim_{n \to \infty}\left(1 + \frac{x}{n}\right)^n$$

Make the substitution $m = n/x$. For fixed x, as $n \to \infty$, $m \to \infty$. Thus, the above expression becomes

$$\lim_{m \to \infty}\left(1 + \frac{1}{m}\right)^{mx} = \left[\lim_{m \to \infty}\left(1 + \frac{1}{m}\right)^m\right]^x = e^x$$

using the previous result and the algebra of exponents. Thus,

$$e^x = \lim_{n \to \infty}\left(1 + \frac{x}{n}\right)^n$$

Letting $z_n = [1 + (x/n)]^n$, expanding this expression by the binomial theorem, as before, yields

$$z_n = 1 + n\frac{x}{n} + \frac{n(n-1)}{2!}\left(\frac{x}{n}\right)^2 + \cdots$$

Using the same reasoning as in the case where $x = 1$,

$$\lim_{n \to \infty} z_n = e^x = 1 + x + \frac{x^2}{2!} + \frac{x^3}{3!} + \cdots \qquad (2\text{-}15)$$

Thus, the exponent e^x is representable by an infinite series. The *convergence* of infinite series to a finite sum is a much-explored aspect of mathematics. That the above series converges to the number e^x is evident from the derivation. Series which do not converge to finite sums (i.e., do not have a unique finite limit) are called *divergent*.

The function $y = e^x$ has an important property which will now be demonstrated. If we differentiate $y = e^x$, term by term (the reader will have to take our word that differentiating this particular series term by term is a valid procedure),

$$\frac{d}{dx} e^x = 0 + 1 + \frac{2x}{2!} + \frac{3x^2}{3!} + \frac{4x^3}{4!} + \cdots$$

$$= 1 + x + \frac{x^2}{2!} + \frac{x^3}{3!} + \cdots = e^x$$

This function is unchanged by differentiation; because of this feature, it occurs frequently in many applications of mathematics. The function $y = e^x$ is shown graphically in Fig. 2-6.

Consider now the derivative of

$$y = e^{ax}$$

where a is a constant. Letting $u = ax$ and using the chain rule,

$$\frac{dy}{dx} = \frac{dy}{du}\frac{du}{dx} = e^u(a) = ae^{ax}$$

Consider also

$$y = e^{x^n}$$

Letting $u = x^n$,

$$\frac{dy}{dx} = \frac{dy}{du}\frac{du}{dx} = e^{x^n}(nx^{n-1})$$

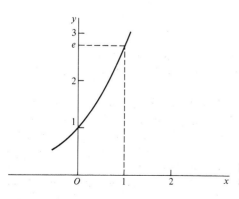

Figure 2-6 *The function* $y = e^x$. Note that at $x = 0$, $dy/dx = e^0 = 1$.

Let us now return to the original question of compound interest rates. Suppose \$1 is placed in an account which pays, say, 5 percent interest compounded every instant of the day. (Actually, daily compounding is minutely close to this limit.) After 1 year, the account will have in it

$$e^{.05} = 1 + .05 + \frac{(.05)^2}{2!} + \frac{(.05)^3}{3!} + \cdots$$

$$= 1.0513$$

Daily (continuous) compounding will convert 5 percent annual interest to the yearly equivalent of approximately 5.13 percent.

Suppose an amount P is invested at interest rate r, continuously compounded, for a period of t years. The future value FV is

$$FV = P(e^r)^t = Pe^{rt} \tag{2-16}$$

Also, the *present value* of an amount FV, at r percent is, by multiplying through by e^{-rt}

$$P = (FV)e^{-rt} \tag{2-17}$$

These formulas provide an analytically easy method of incorporating discounting into problems where time intervals are significant.

Example 1: Fisherian Investment† Suppose a crop is planted at time $t = 0$ and grows in *value* to $g(t)$ at time t. Suppose $g'(t) > 0$ and $g''(t) < 0$ so that the crop grows at a decreasing rate. What harvest time will maximize the present value of the crop?

The present value, assuming continuous discounting, is

$$P = g(t)e^{-rt}$$

To maximize P (wealth), set $dP/dt = 0$:

$$\frac{dP}{dt} = g(t)(-re^{-rt}) + g'(t)e^{-rt} = 0$$

Dividing by e^{-rt}

$$g'(t) = rg(t)$$

or
$$r = \frac{g'(t)}{g(t)} \tag{2-18}$$

The term $g'(t)/g(t)$ can be interpreted as the percent rate of growth. Wealth maximization therefore says that the crop should be harvested when the

---

† Irving Fisher, "The Theory of Interest," Augustus M. Kelley, New York, 1970. (First edition, The Macmillan Co., New York, 1930.)

percentage rate of growth of crop value equals the alternative earnings, measured by the interest rate. If $g(t)$ is known, the wealth-maximizing t can be obtained.

Example 2: The "Faustmann" Solution Suppose the crop in example 1 can be replanted immediately after each harvest. What harvest time maximizes the value of the land? The present value of the land, if a new crop is planted at t, $2t$, $3t$, etc., is

$$P = g(t)e^{-rt} + g(t)e^{-2rt} + g(t)e^{-3rt} + \cdots$$

Note that each term is the previous term multiplied by e^{-rt}. Using the formula for the sum of an infinite geometric series

$$P = \frac{g(t)e^{-rt}}{1 - e^{-rt}}$$

Using the quotient rule

$$\frac{dP}{dt} = \frac{(1 - e^{-rt})[-rg(t)e^{-rt} + e^{-rt}g'(t)] - g(t)e^{-rt}(+re^{-rt})}{(1 - e^{-rt})^2} = 0$$

Dividing by e^{-rt}, this is equivalent to

$$g'(t) = rg(t) + r\frac{g(t)e^{-rt}}{1 - e^{-rt}} \tag{2-19}$$

This equation says that the crop should be harvested when the growth in value of the crop equals the sum of the foregone annuity from the standing value of the crop and the annuity from the maximum value of the land, i.e., the annual land rent. This is the Fisherian solution with the addition of the opportunity cost of the land, expressed in terms of crop replanting.

This completes our brief discussion of $y = e^x$. We now turn to the inverse of the exponential function, the *logarithm*.

2. The Function $y = \log_e x$

The logarithm of a number a to the base b is defined as the number which, when b is raised to that power, results in a:

$$b^{\log_b a} = a$$

Before the age of computers, logarithms to the base 10 had wide empirical use. We shall be concerned here only with *logarithms to the base e*, called *natural logarithms*. The $\log_e x$ is sometimes denoted ln x; we shall, however, stick to $\log x$. Throughout this book, *log x means $\log_e x$*, that is, natural log of x. Thus, $\log x$ means

$$e^{\log x} = x$$

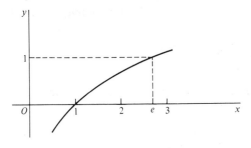

Figure 2-7 *The function* $y = \log x$. Note that at $x = 1$, $dy/dx = 1$. How is this curve related to $y = e^x$?

The rules of logarithms are easily derived using the laws of exponents. (See Fig. 2-7.) Letting $e^{\log a} = a$, $e^{\log b} = b$,

$$e^{\log a} \cdot e^{\log b} = e^{\log a + \log b} = ab$$

But by definition,

$$ab = e^{\log ab}$$

Hence

$$\log ab = \log a + \log b$$

Also

$$a^x = (e^{\log a})^x = e^{x \log a}$$

But again, by definition,

$$a^x = e^{\log a x}$$

Hence

$$\log a^x = x \log a$$

The equation $y = \log x$ means the same thing as $x = e^y$. If we differentiate $x = e^y$ implicitly with respect to x,

$$1 = e^y \frac{dy}{dx}$$

or

$$\frac{dy}{dx} = \frac{1}{e^y} = \frac{1}{x} \tag{2-20}$$

Thus, for $y = \log x$, $dy/dx = 1/x$.

Example 3 Let $y = \log ax$. Find dy/dx. By the laws of logarithms

$$y = \log ax = \log a + \log x$$

Since $\log a$ is a constant,

$$\frac{dy}{dx} = \frac{1}{x}$$

Example 4 Let $y = \log (a + bx)$. Find dy/dx. Using the chain rule, let $u = a + bx$. Then

$$\frac{dy}{dx} = \frac{dy}{du}\frac{du}{dx} = \left(\frac{1}{a + bx}\right)b = \frac{b}{a + bx}$$

Example 5 Let $y = a^x$. Find dy/dx. Take the log of both sides:

$$\log y = x \log a$$

Differentiating implicitly with respect to x,

$$\frac{1}{y}\frac{dy}{dx} = \log a$$

Thus

$$\frac{dy}{dx} = y \log a = a^x \log a$$

Example 6 Consider the demand curves $x = p^k, k < 0$. We previously showed that these curves exhibited constant elasticity. This can be demonstrated more quickly using logs:

$$\log x = \log (p^k) = k \log p$$

Taking the *differential* of both sides,

$$\frac{dx}{x} = k\frac{dp}{p}$$

Thus, the *percent* change in x is k times the *percent* change in price, i.e., k is the elasticity of demand. If the curve $x = p^k$ is plotted on log-log paper (graph paper with logarithmic intervals), the slope of the graph will be k, the elasticity.

PROBLEMS

1 Sketch the curve $y = e^{-x}$. What is the relationship of this curve to $y = e^x$, to $y = \log x$?

2. For each of the following functions, find dy/dx.

(a) $y = e^{-x}$ (b) $y = x \log x - x$

(c) $y = xe^x$ (d) $y = e^{(a + bx)}$

(e) $y = e^x \log x$ (f) $y = \log x^2$

(g) $y = (\log x)^2$ (*Hint:* Let $u = \log x$)   (h) $y = \log (\log x), x > 1$

3 Use the power series expansion of e^x to show that 6 percent interest compounded continuously is approximately 6.18 percent per annum.

4 Consider the wealth-maximizing times to harvest crops with or without replanting. Suppose seasonal factors do not permit replanting until after winter. Show that formulas (2-18) and (2-19) indicate that with replanting impossible, the crops will be left to grow larger than when replanting is possible. Explain in terms of opportunities forgone.

5 In this chapter, the formula for the sum of a geometric series was used. Letting $S_n = a + ar + ar^2 + \cdots + ar^{n-1}$, show that $S_n - rS_n = a - ar^n$, and, hence,

$$S_n = \frac{a - ar^n}{1 - r}$$

Show that if $|r| < 1$, the $\lim_{n \to \infty} S_n = a/(1 - r)$.

6 Consider an amount of money P invested at r percent annual interest, compounded continuously. Show that the number of years n it will take to double the initial investment, leaving the money in the account to accumulate compound interest, is approximately given by the formula

$$n = \frac{72}{r\%}$$

2.10 THE MEAN VALUE THEOREM

Consider Fig. 2-8a. A differentiable function $y = f(x)$ is shown between the values $x = a$ and $x = b$. Consider the chord joining the two points $(a, f(a))$ and $(b, f(b))$. The slope of this chord is

$$\frac{f(b) - f(a)}{b - a}$$

It is geometrically obvious (though it is not a proof) that at some point x^* between a and b, the slope of $f(x)$ is the same as the slope of this chord, or

$$f'(x^*) = \frac{f(b) - f(a)}{b - a}$$

This statement or the following equivalent one is called the *law of the mean*, or *the mean value theorem*: If $f(x)$ is differentiable on the interval $a \le x \le b$, then there exists an x^*, $a < x^* < b$, such that

$$f(b) = f(a) + (b - a)f'(x^*) \tag{2-21}$$

The reason why $f(x)$ has to be differentiable over the interval is exhibited in Fig. 2-8b. The mean value theorem is actually a special case of the more general result known as Taylor's theorem. It is to this more general problem that we now turn.

2.11 TAYLOR'S SERIES

It is often of great analytical convenience to approximate a function $f(x)$ by polynomials of the form

$$f(x) \approx f_n(x) = a_0 + a_1 x + a_2 x^2 + a_3 x^3 + \cdots + a_n x^n$$

In particular, let us approximate $f(x)$ around the point $x = 0$. What values of the

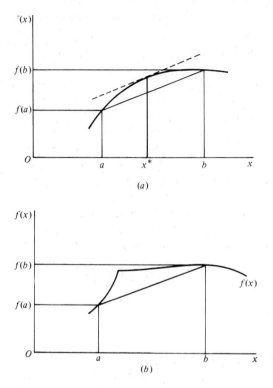

(a)

(b)

Figure 2-8 (*a*) The mean value theorem. (*b*) If $f(x)$ is not differentiable, the existence of x_0, $a < x_0 < b$, such that $f'(x_0) = [f(b) - f(a)]/(b - a)$ is not guaranteed.

coefficients $a_0, \ldots, a_n$ will best do this? To begin with, we should require $f_n(x) = f(x)$ at $x = 0$. Hence, we need to set

$$a_0 = f_n(0) = f(0)$$

Thus, the coefficient a_0 is determined in this fashion to be $f(0)$.

To approximate $f(x)$ even better, let us make the derivatives of $f(x)$ and $f_n(x)$ equal, at $x = 0$. We have

$$f'_n(x) = a_1 + 2a_2 x + 3a_3 x^2 + \cdots + na_n x^{n-1}$$

$$f''_n(x) = 2a_2 + 3 \cdot 2a_3 x + \cdots + n(n-1)x^{n-2}$$

$$\cdots\cdots\cdots\cdots\cdots\cdots\cdots\cdots\cdots\cdots\cdots\cdots$$

$$f_n^{(n)}(x) = n! \, a_n$$

Clearly, when $x = 0$, we get

$$a_1 = f'(0)$$

$$a_2 = \frac{f''(0)}{2!}$$

$$\cdots\cdots\cdots\cdots$$

$$a_n = \frac{f^{(n)}(0)}{n!}$$

Having thus determined the coefficients of $f_n(x)$ in this fashion, our approximating polynomial is

$$f_n(x) = f(0) + f'(0)x + \frac{f''(0)}{2!}x^2 + \frac{f'''(0)}{3!}x^3 + \cdots + \frac{f^{(n)}(0)}{n!}x^n \qquad (2\text{-}22)$$

An important class of functions comprises those for which $f_n(x)$ *converges* to $f(x)$, as $n \to \infty$, that is

$$f(x) = f(0) + f'(0)x + \frac{f''(0)}{2!}x^2 + \cdots \qquad (2\text{-}23)$$

These functions are called *analytic functions*. The power series representation (2-23) is called Maclaurin's series.

Suppose now we wish to approximate $f(x)$ at some arbitrary point $x = x_0$. In that case, write $f_n(x)$ in terms of powers of $(x - x_0)$:

$$f_n(x) = a_0 + a_1(x - x_0) + a_2(x - x_0)^2 + \cdots + a_n(x - x_0)^n$$

Using the same procedure as before, setting the derivatives of $f(x)$ equal to those of $f_n(x)$ at $x = x_0$, we determine

$$f(x) = f(x_0) + f'(x_0)(x - x_0) + \frac{f''(x_0)}{2!}(x - x_0)^2 + \cdots \qquad (2\text{-}24)$$

In this form, the power series is known as *Taylor's series*, or simply as a Taylor series. The Maclaurin series is a special case, where $x_0 = 0$.

Example 1 The series developed before, for e^x, is a convergent Taylor series expansion:

$$e^x = 1 + x + \frac{x^2}{2!} + \frac{x^3}{3!} + \cdots$$

Example 2 Find a Taylor series expansion for $\log(1 + x)$, around $x = 0$. (Assume convergence.)

We note:

$$f(0) = \log 1 = 0$$

$$f'(0) = \frac{1}{(1 + x)} = 1 \text{ at } x = 0$$

$$f''(0) = -(1 + x)^{-2} = -1 \text{ at } x = 0$$

$$f'''(0) = +2(1 + x)^{-3} = +2 \text{ at } x = 0$$

$$f^{iv}(0) = -3 \cdot 2(1 + x)^{-4} = -3! \text{ at } x = 0$$

$$\cdots \cdots \cdots \cdots \cdots \cdots \cdots \cdots \cdots$$

Hence $\quad \log(1 + x) = x - \frac{x^2}{2} + \frac{x^3}{3} - \frac{x^4}{4} + \cdots$

A most useful form of a Taylor series expansion for a finite power n is a Taylor series with Lagrange's form of the remainder. The finite power series can be made exact (under suitable continuity assumptions) if the last term is evaluated not at x_0, but at some point x^* between x and x_0:

$$f(x) = f(x_0) + f'(x_0)(x - x_0) + \frac{f''(x_0)}{2!}(x - x_0)^2 + \cdots + \frac{f^{(n)}(x^*)}{n!}(x - x_0)^n$$

$$(2\text{-}25)$$

where $x^* = x_0 + \theta(x - x_0)$, $0 \leq \theta \leq 1$.

Such an x^* between x and x_0 must exist, if $f^{(n+1)}(x)$ is continuous. Equation 2-25 is one variant of what is known as Taylor's theorem. (The variant is the particular form of the remainder, or last, term.) In this form, equation (2-25), the Taylor series expansion, is seen to be a generalization of the mean value theorem. To obtain the mean value theorem, merely terminate (2-25) at $f'(x^*)$.

Applications of Taylor's series: Derivation of the First- and Second-Order Conditions for a Maximum; Concavity and Convexity

Suppose $f(x)$ has a maximum at x_0. By definition

$$f(x_0) \geq f(x)$$

for all x in some neighborhood of x_0. Using the mean value theorem, i.e., a Taylor series terminated at the first-order term,

$$f(x_0) - f(x) = (x_0 - x)f'(x^*) \qquad (2\text{-}26)$$

for some x^* between x_0 and x. The left-hand side of (2-26) is nonnegative for x near x_0. Therefore, if x is to the left of x_0 (i.e., $x < x_0$), $f'(x^*) \geq 0$ necessarily, to make the product $(x_0 - x)f'(x^*) \geq 0$. For $x > x_0$, $f'(x^*) \leq 0$. Hence, $f'(x)$ is *positive* (or 0) to the left of x_0 and *negative* (or 0) to the right of x_0. If $f'(x)$ is continuous at x_0, then necessarily it passes through the value 0 at x_0; i.e.,

$$f'(x_0) = 0$$

Similar reasoning shows that $f'(x_0) = 0$ is also implied by a minimum at x_0. Let us now investigate the second-order conditions for a maximum. Consider a Taylor series expansion of $f(x)$ to the second-order term

$$f(x) = f(x_0) + f'(x_0)(x - x_0) + \frac{f''(x^*)}{2!}(x - x_0)^2$$

where, again, $x^* = x_0 + \theta(x - x_0)$, $0 \leq \theta \leq 1$. If $f(x)$ has a maximum at $x = x_0$, then $f'(x_0) = 0$. Hence, the preceding equation can be written

$$f(x) - f(x_0) = \tfrac{1}{2}f''(x^*)(x - x_0)^2 \qquad (2\text{-}27)$$

If $f(x)$ has a maximum at x_0, the left-hand side of (2-27), by definition, is nonpositive. Since $(x - x_0)^2 > 0$,

$$f''(x^*) \leq 0$$

By "squeezing" x closer and closer to x_0, we see that $f''(x) \leq 0$ for all points in some neighborhood of x_0; hence, at $x = x_0$

$$f''(x_0) \leq 0$$

A maximum point therefore implies $f''(x_0) \leq 0$. If, however, $f''(x_0) < 0$, then necessarily $f(x_0) > f(x)$. Thus, together with $f'(x_0) = 0, f''(x_0) < 0$ is sufficient for a maximum. Similar reasoning shows that at a *minimum* of $f(x), f''(x_0) \geq 0$; if $f''(x_0) > 0$, then a minimum is assured.

Concave and convex functions Consider the function depicted in Fig. 2-9a. This shape is called *strictly concave*. It can be described by indicating that for any two points $x = x_0$ and $x = x_1$, say $x_0 < x_1$, the function always lies above the chord joining $f(x_0)$ and $f(x_1)$. That is, suppose x is some intermediate point

$$x = \theta x_0 + (1 - \theta)x_1 \qquad 0 < \theta < 1$$

Then $f(x)$ is strictly concave if

$$f(x) > \theta f(x_0) + (1 - \theta)f(x_1)$$

If $0 \leq \theta \leq 1$ and

$$f(x) \geq \theta f(x_0) + (1 - \theta)f(x_1)$$

the function is called *weakly concave*, or simply concave. Convex functions are functions for which the chord connecting any two points on the function lies above the function; an example is shown in Fig. 2-9b. The terms *strictly* convex and *weakly* convex apply as for concave functions. The weak inequalities allow for straight-line segments in the function. The linear functions $f(x) = a + bx$ are both (weakly) concave *and* convex.

For differentiable functions, strict concavity can be described by saying that $f(x)$ always lies below the tangent line at any point. Consider Fig. 2-9a. Concavity

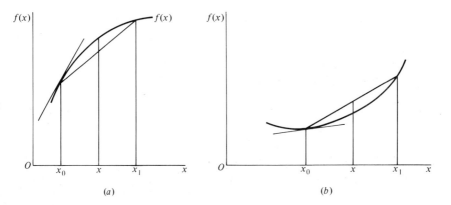

Figure 2-9 (a) A concave function. (b) A convex function.

can be interpreted as saying the slope of the tangent line is greater than that of the chord joining $f(x_0)$ and $f(x_1)$, if $x_1 > x_0$, i.e.,

$$f'(x_0) > \frac{f(x_1) - f(x_0)}{x_1 - x_0} \qquad \text{for } x_1 > x_0$$

If $x_1 < x_0$, the tangent line is less steep, or

$$f'(x_0) < \frac{f(x_1) - f(x_0)}{x_1 - x_0} \qquad \text{for } x_1 < x_0$$

In either case, if both sides are multiplied by $(x_1 - x_0)$ we get, for any $x = x_1$ (if $x_1 - x_0 < 0$, the inequality reverses sign),

$$f(x) < f(x_0) + f'(x_0)(x - x_0) \tag{2-28a}$$

or
$$f(x) - f(x_0) - f'(x_0)(x - x_0) < 0 \tag{2-28b}$$

For concavity (not *strict* concavity), a weak inequality is used in statements (2-28). Using a Taylor series expansion of $f(x)$ to two terms,

$$f(x) = f(x_0) + f'(x_0)(x - x_0) + \tfrac{1}{2}f''(x^*)(x - x_0)^2$$

Bringing the first two terms on the right to the other side, and using equation (2-28b), for concave functions

$$f''(x^*) < 0$$

since $(x - x_0)^2 > 0$. If x is squeezed towards x_0, we see that $f''(x_0) \le 0$, but $f''(x_0) < 0$ is not implied. If, however, $f''(x_0) < 0$, the function must be concave. Similarly, convexity of $f(x)$ at $x = x_0$ implies $f''(x_0) \ge 0$; if $f''(x_0) > 0$, then $f(x)$ is convex.

2.12 INTEGRATION

Indefinite Integrals

Up to now, we have been concerned with the *differential* calculus. That is, starting with some function $y = f(x)$, we inquired as to the properties of the derivatives of $f(x)$, and applied those properties to certain outstanding problems, e.g., the theory of maxima and minima. We now ask a different question: Suppose we are *given* the derivative $dy/dx = f'(x)$. What function $y = f(x)$ has $f'(x)$ as its derivative? For example, suppose we are told

$$\frac{dy}{dx} = 2x \tag{2-29}$$

From experience, we would know that

$$y = x^2 \qquad y = x^2 + 2 \qquad y = x^2 - 50,000$$

are all solutions to (2-29). The general "solution" to equation (2-29) is the class of equations

$$y = x^2 + c$$

where c is an arbitrary constant.

Equations of the form (2-29) in which dy/dx is a function of x (or is a function of x and y) are called *differential equations*. The process of solving these equations is called *integration*. We now turn our attention to this new technique, the *integral calculus*.

If $y = F(x)$ is a solution to $dy/dx = f(x)$, i.e.

$$\frac{dF(x)}{dx} = f(x)$$

$y = F(x)$ is called the *integral* of $f(x)$ with respect to x. If $F(x)$ is any solution to $dy/dx = f(x)$, the general solution is given by

$$y = F(x) + c$$

where c is an arbitrary *constant of integration*. Since $dy/dx = f(x)$

$$dy = f(x)\, dx \tag{2-30}$$

We now *integrate* both sides of this equation. This is written

$$\int dy = \int f(x)\, dx$$

The integral of the differential dy is, by definition, y. The integral of $f(x)\, dx$ is $F(x) + c$. Hence, we write the solution to equation (2-30) as

$$y = \int f(x)\, dx + c = F(x) + c$$

The term $\int f(x)\, dx + c$ is called an *indefinite* integral, since an arbitrary constant is used.

Although differentiation is usually straightforward (though possibly tedious), integration can be difficult or impossible with analytical methods. For example, the formula

$$\int x^n\, dx = \frac{x^{n+1}}{n+1} + c$$

might readily occur to the student, since

$$\frac{d\left(\dfrac{x^{n+1}}{n+1}\right)}{dx} = \frac{(n+1)x^n}{n+1} = x^n$$

However, it might take one some time to figure out that

$$\int \log x\, dx = x \log x - x + c$$

or that
$$\int x^2 e^x \, dx = x^2 e^x - 2xe^x + 2e^x + c$$

Some functions, in fact, do not even possess an analytic integral function. For example

$$\int e^{x^2} \, dx$$

cannot be written in terms of elementary functions (although note that $\int xe^{x^2} \, dx = \frac{1}{2}e^{x^2} + c$, as can be verified by differentiation of the latter term).

The Integral as the Area under a Curve

An important application of integration stems from its interpretation as the area under a curve. Consider Fig. 2-10, in which a marginal-cost function, $MC(x)$, is drawn. Consider the area beneath $MC(x)$ (down to the x axis), between $x = a$ and $x = b$. For any x between a and b, let us denote the area from a to x as

$$A_a^x$$

This is shown as the shaded area in Fig. 2-10.

If x is increased to $x + \Delta x$, the area increases by an amount ΔA, where

$$\Delta A = A_a^{x + \Delta x} - A_a^x$$

In the interval from x to $x + \Delta x$, there is some minimum value of $MC(x)$, MC_m, and some maximum value, MC_M. (In general, these do not have to be at the endpoints of the interval.) Clearly, therefore,

$$MC_m \, \Delta x \leq \Delta A \leq MC_M \, \Delta x$$

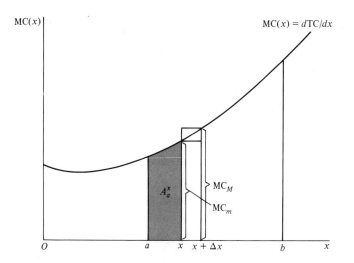

Figure 2-10 The integral of a function (marginal cost) as the area under the curve.

Dividing by Δx

$$\text{MC}_m \le \frac{\Delta A}{\Delta x} \le \text{MC}_M$$

If we now take a limit as $\Delta x \to 0$, MC_m and MC_M squeeze together to the limiting value, $\text{MC}(x)$. (Actually, Δx can be any interval which includes the value x.) Hence,

$$\lim_{\Delta x \to 0} \frac{\Delta A}{\Delta x} = \frac{dA}{dx} = \text{MC}(x)$$

But marginal cost, by definition, is the rate of change of total cost, $\text{TC}(x)$, as x changes; that is,

$$\text{MC}(x) = \frac{d\text{TC}(x)}{dx}$$

Since A_a^x and $\text{TC}(x)$ have the same derivative, they can differ by at most an arbitrary constant:

$$A_a^x = \text{TC}(x) + c \tag{2-31}$$

Here, the arbitrary constant of integration represents "fixed" costs, i.e., costs which do not change with output. Thus, $A(x)$ represents total *variable* costs.

Now consider the area *between* $x = a$ and $x = b$. When $x = a$,

$$A_a^x = A_a^a = 0$$

Then from (2-31),

$$A_a^a = 0 = \text{TC}(a) + c$$

and thus

$$c = -\text{TC}(a)$$

We can thus interpret A_a^x as the *change* in total costs by increasing output from a to x. In this calculation, fixed costs (the constant of integration) are irrelevant; the quantity cancels itself out in calculating total cost at x and subtracting total cost at a.

Total cost from a to b is

$$A_a^b = \int_a^b \text{MC}(x)\, dx \tag{2-32}$$

where the term $\int_a^b \text{MC}(x)\, dx$ means:

1. Find the integral function $\text{TC}(x)$ of $\text{MC}(x)$.
2. Substitute the value $x = b$ in $\text{TC}(x)$, then subtract TC evaluated at $x = a$.

The term (2-32) is called a definite integral. In general,

$$\int_a^b f(x)\, dx$$

gives the area under the curve $y = f(x)$ (to the x axis) between $x = a$ and $x = b$. Viewed in this manner, the area is an "infinite sum" of vertical strips of area of height $y = f(x)$. For this reason, an elongated "S" is the symbol for integration. Note that if $a > b$ and $f(x) > 0$, this integral will be negative.

Example 1 Find $\int_1^2 x^2 \, dx$. This integral represents the area under the parabola $y = x^2$, from $x = 1$ to $x = 2$. Performing the indicated operations

$$\int_1^2 x^2 \, dx = \left.\frac{x^3}{3}\right|_1^2 = \frac{8}{3} - \frac{1}{3} = \frac{7}{3}$$

Example 2 Find $\int_{-2}^1 4x^3 \, dx$.

$$\int_{-2}^1 4x^3 \, dx = \left. x^4 \right|_{-2}^1 = 1 - 16 = -15$$

This area is negative because for $x < 0$, $y = 4x^3$ is negative.

Example 3 Suppose a person receives a constant annual stream of income I. Find the present value of this *annuity*, at r percent annual interest, compounded continuously, from the present to T years in the future.

At any time t, the present value of the income stream is

$$Ie^{-rt}$$

Integrating (summing) this income stream from $t = 0$ to $t = T$

$$\int_0^T Ie^{-rt} \, dt$$

Performing the indicated operations

$$PV = \int_0^T Ie^{-rt} \, dt = I \int_0^T e^{-rt} \, dt = \left.\left(\frac{-I}{r}\right)e^{-rt}\right|_0^T = \frac{I}{r} - \left(\frac{I}{r}\right)e^{-rT}$$

Example 4 In the previous example, suppose the annuity lasts forever. What is its present value?

In the previous example, let $T \to \infty$. Then

$$PV = \frac{I}{r} - \lim_{T \to \infty} \frac{I}{r} e^{-rT} = \frac{I}{r}$$

since the exponential term tends to zero.

The chain rule is often useful for performing integration, as shown in example 5.

Example 5 Find $\int x\sqrt{1 + x^2}\, dx$.

Let $u = (1 + x^2)$. Then $du = 2x\, dx$. The integral above can thus be written

$$\frac{1}{2}\int (1 + x^2)^{1/2}(2x\, dx) = \frac{1}{2}\int u^{1/2}\, du = \frac{\frac{1}{2}u^{3/2}}{\frac{3}{2}}$$

$$= \tfrac{1}{3}(1 + x^2)^{3/2} + c$$

Example 6 Find $\int (1/x) \log x\, dx$.

Let $u = \log x$. Then $du = (1/x)\, dx$. Then

$$\int \frac{1}{x} \log x\, dx = \int u\, du = \frac{u^2}{2} = \frac{(\log x)^2}{2} + c$$

It can be appreciated that a certain amount of guesswork and fortuitous circumstances are needed for evaluating integrals. For this reason, tables of integrals are published. As previously mentioned, some integrals are extremely difficult or impossible to evaluate.

Because economists infrequently work with specific functional forms, an elaborate discussion of methods of integration is not in order. However, one technique which appears in the economics literature and is useful to know about is called *integration by parts*.

Recall the formula for the derivative of the product of two functions, $u(x) \cdot v(x)$, expressed in differential form:

$$d(uv) = u\, dv + v\, du$$

Rearranging

$$u\, dv = d(uv) - v\, du$$

Integrating both sides of this equation

$$\int u\, dv = uv - \int v\, du \tag{2-33}$$

It sometimes turns out that an integral can be cast into the form $\int u\, dv$, with the integral $\int v\, du$ a simpler form to integrate. Using the formula (2-33), the answer may be obtainable by performing the latter integration instead of the former.

Example 7 Find $\int \log x\, dx$.

Let us try $u = \log x$, $dv = dx$. Then $v = x + c$, $du = dx/x$. Using (2-33),

$$\int \log x\, dx = (\log x)(x + c) - \int (x + c)\frac{dx}{x}$$

$$= (x + c) \log x - \int dx - c \int \frac{dx}{x}$$

$$= (x + c) \log x - x - c \log x + K$$

where c and K are arbitrary constants. This expression can be combined into a simpler one, noting that the $c \log x$ term cancels:

$$\int \log x \, dx = x \log x - x + K$$

Example 8 Find $\int_0^1 xe^x \, dx$.

Let us try $u = x$, $dv = e^x \, dx$. Then $du = dx$, and $v = e^x$. (The constant of integration is not needed because this is a *definite* integral.) Integrating by parts

$$\int_0^1 xe^x \, dx = xe^x \bigg|_0^1 - \int_0^1 e^x \, dx = (e - 0) - e^x \bigg|_0^1 = e - (e - 1) = 1$$

Example 9 Suppose $p = p(x)$ is a demand curve, and let $p = p_0$ when $x = x_0$, $p = p_1$ when $x = x_1$. The integral

$$\int_{x_0}^{x_1} p \, dx$$

represents the area under the demand curve between x_0 and x_1. Integrating by parts, letting $u = p$, $dv = dx$,

$$\int_{x_0}^{x_1} p \, dx = px \bigg|_{x_0}^{x_1} - \int_{p_0}^{p_1} x \, dp$$

The area *under* the demand curve equals the change in total expenditure minus the (negative, if $p_1 < p_0$) area to the *left* of the demand curve. (Note that if $x_1 > x_0$, then $p_1 < p_0$ for downward-sloping demand curves, and, hence, $-\int_{p_0}^{p_1} x \, dp > 0$.)

PROBLEMS

1 Evaluate the following integrals:

(a) $\int xe^{x^2} \, dx$ (b) $\int x^2 e^{x^3} \, dx$

(c) $\int x^{n-1} e^{x^n} \, dx$ (d) $\int x \log x \, dx$

(e) $\int \log x^2 \, dx$

2 Consider the demand curve $x = p^{-2}$. Find the area under the demand curve and to the left of the demand curve, between $x = 2$ and $x = 4$.

3 Suppose an annuity lasts 5 years at 6 percent interest, compounded continuously:
(a) Find the present value if the annuity starts immediately.
(b) Find the present value if the annuity starts 4 years from now.
(c) Find the present value if the annuity starts T years from now and ends $T + 5$ years from now.

4 Suppose the marginal cost function is $MC(x) = 10 + 2x$. Find the total (variable?) costs of producing 100 units. Find the average cost curve, $AC(x)$, and discuss the relation of this $AC(x)$ to $MC(x)$.

2.13 DIFFERENTIAL EQUATIONS

In the preceding section we explored the problems of integrating expressions of the general form

$$\frac{dy}{dx} = f(x)$$

In general, however, the right-hand side will be a function not only of x, but also of y. For example, on the unit circle, $x^2 + y^2 = 1$, the slope can be expressed as

$$\frac{dy}{dx} = \frac{-x}{y}$$

We can express this dependence of dy/dx upon both x and y by writing

$$\frac{dy}{dx} = f(x, y) \tag{2-34}$$

Functions of two variables will be explored in the next chapter. We wish here to merely indicate how certain equations of the form (2-34) are solved, i.e., integrated.

Let us begin the discussion by considering the differential equation above, that is,

$$\frac{dy}{dx} = \frac{-x}{y} \tag{2-35}$$

This equation can be solved by separating the variables. We write

$$y\, dy = -x\, dx$$

Integrating both sides yields

$$\int y\, dy = -\int x\, dx + c$$

or

$$\frac{y^2}{2} = \frac{-x^2}{2} + c$$

In terms of a new constant r^2 where $r^2 = 2c$

$$x^2 + y^2 = r^2 \tag{2-36}$$

is the solution to the differential equation (2-35). (The constant of integration must be positive in this case, since $x^2 \geq 0$, $y^2 \geq 0$, hence, we can designate it as r^2.) Equation (2-36) represents all circles of radius r with center at the origin.

In this section we will merely indicate some special cases in which differential equations can be solved by separation of variables. These differential equations occasionally appear in economic models.

Example 1 Suppose $dy/dx = y/x$. Solve for the integral function, $y = F(x)$.
Separating variables, we have

$$\frac{dy}{y} = \frac{dx}{x}$$

Integrating both sides

$$\log y = \log x + \log c$$

Notice that we have written the constant of integration as "$\log c$." This loses no generality since $\log c$ takes on all real values. Then, using the rules of logarithms, the solution above can be written

$$\log y = \log cx$$

or

$$y = cx$$

Example 2 Suppose $dy/dx = -y/x$. Find $y = F(x)$.

Separating variables

$$\frac{dy}{y} = \frac{-dx}{x}$$

Integrating

$$\log y = -\log x + \log c = \log \frac{1}{x} + \log c$$

or

$$y = \frac{c}{x}$$

Example 3 Suppose $dy/dx = x^a y^b$. Find $y = F(x)$. Then,

$$y^{-b} \, dy = x^a \, dx$$

If $b \neq 1$ and $a \neq -1$, these terms integrate to powers of x or y:

$$\frac{y^{-b+1}}{-b+1} = \frac{x^{a+1}}{a+1} + c$$

One can solve for y by taking the $(-b+1)$st root of each side.

PROBLEMS

For each of the following equations, find the integral function $y = F(x)$.

1 $dy/dx = 2x/y$ 2 $dy/dx = 1/y$

3 $dy/dx = -1/y$ 4 $dy/dx = y/x^n,\ n \neq 1$

5 $dy/dx = x/y$ 6 $dy/dx = ye^x$

7 $dy/dx = y^2 xe^{x^2}$ 8 $dy/dx = y \log x$

SELECTED REFERENCES

Students should have any of the usual basic calculus texts available to them.

THREE

FUNCTIONS OF SEVERAL VARIABLES

3.1 FUNCTIONS OF SEVERAL VARIABLES

The mathematical examples in Chap. 1 involved only one decision variable. Most often, however, in economic theories, several decision variables are present, all of which simultaneously determine the value of some objective function. Consider, for example, the fundamental proposition in consumer theory that individuals desire many goods simultaneously. This postulate asserts that the satisfaction, or *utility*, derived from consuming some bundle of goods is some function of the consumption levels for each and every good in question. This is denoted mathematically as

$$U = f(x_1, x_2, \ldots, x_n)$$

where $x_1, x_2, \ldots, x_n$ are the levels of consumption of the n goods. In the theory of production, a function $y = f(L, K)$ is typically written (called the *production function*) which indicates that the level of output depends upon the levels of both labor and capital applied to production. The mathematical notation $y = f(x_1, \ldots, x_n)$ is simply a convenient shorthand to denote the inference of a unique value of some dependent variable y from the knowledge of the values of n *independent* variables, denoted $x_1, \ldots, x_n$. It is a generalization of the notion of a function of one variable, $y = f(x)$.

3.2 LEVEL CURVES: I

Consider a production function $y = f(L, K)$, where $y =$ output, $L =$ labor, and $K =$ capital services. The function f is the numerical rule by which levels of inputs are translated into a level of output. With only two independent variables, geometric representation of this function is possible. In Fig. 3-1, all points in the positive quadrant (i.e., points in the cartesian plane which correspond to positive values of L and K) represent possible input combinations. At each point in the plane, some unique value of the function $f(L, K)$ is implied. For example, at the points $A, B, C,$ and D, output y is, say, 5, whereas at E, $y = 10$, and at F, $y = 15$.

Economists often have occasion to connect up points for which the functional values are equal. For example, in Fig. 3-1, the smooth line drawn through the points $A, B, C,$ and D represents the locus of all points, i.e., the locus of all combinations of labor and capital, for which five units of output result. This curve, called an *isoquant* by economists, is called a *level curve* (in higher dimensions, a level *surface*) by mathematicians. It is a level curve because along such loci, the function (output, here) is neither increasing nor decreasing.† Another geometric representation of a function of two variables is given in Fig. 3-2.

This is a two-dimensional drawing of a three-dimensional picture. The L axis is perpendicular to the plane of this page. In this diagram, the value of the function y is plotted as the vertical distance above the LK plane. This generates a surface in three-dimensional space, whose height represents here the level of output produced. Constant output points of, say, five units would all lie in a horizontal plane (parallel to the LK plane) five units above the LK plane. The intersection of such a plane with the production surface would yield a curve in that surface all of whose points were five units above the LK axes. This level curve, or contour, would be another representation of the five-unit isoquant pictures in Fig. 3-1. In fact, the isoquants in Fig. 3-1 are really projections of the level curves of the surface depicted in Fig. 3-2 into the LK plane. Similar level curves are drawn for

---

† Those of you familiar with "contour maps" used in geological surveys (and hiking) will recognize those contours as the level curves of a function denoting the altitude of the terrain.

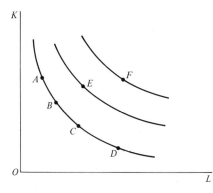

Figure 3-1 *Level Curves for a Production Function.* In this diagram, three separate level curves are drawn (out of the infinity of such curves that exist). Points $A, B, C,$ and D all represent combinations of labor and capital which yield the same output. They are therefore all on the same level curve, called, in production theory, an *isoquant*. Point E represents a higher level of output; point F a still higher output level.

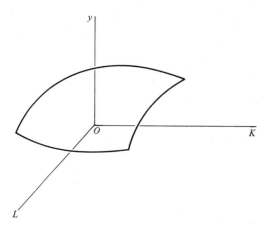

Figure 3-2 *A Three-Dimensional Represen-tation of a Function of Two Variables.* This figure depicts a two-dimensional surface in three-dimensional space. The level curves of Fig. 3-1 are projections of the intersection of horizontal planes (at some value of y) and this surface.

the theory of consumer behavior. In this context, the level curves represent loci of constant utilities and are called indifference curves. Since these curves play a central role in economic theory, we will have much to say about them in the course of this book.

This three-dimensional representation of a function of two variables, although difficult to draw, provides a useful visualization of the situation. The function is increasing, say, if it is rising vertically as one moves in a given direction, and a maximum of such a function is easily pictured as the " top of the hill." But needless to say, for more than two independent variables, such visual geometry becomes impossible, and, hence, algebraic methods become necessary.

3.3 PARTIAL DERIVATIVES

Consider a consumer's utility function, $U = f(x_1, \ldots, x_n)$, where, again, $x_1, \ldots, x_n$ represent the levels of consumption of n goods. If these x_i's are indeed " goods," i.e., they contribute positively to the consumer's welfare at the margin, then it would be convenient to be able to denote and analyze this effect mathematically. The statement that the *marginal utility* of some good x_i is positive means that if x_i is increased by some amount Δx_i, *holding the other goods* (the other x_i's) *constant,* the resulting change in total utility will be positive. This is exactly the same idea as taking derivatives in the calculus of one variable, with one important qualification: Since there are other variables present, we must specify in addition that these other variables are being held fixed at their previous levels. This type of derivative is called a *partial* derivative since it refers to changes in the function with respect to changes in only one of several variables. Partial derivatives are denoted with curled d's: $\partial y / \partial x_i$, instead of the ordinary d's used in the calculus of one variable.

As another example, consider a production function $y = f(L, K)$. The marginal product of, say, labor is the rate of change of output when the labor input is adjusted incrementally, for a specified, constant level of capital input. The marginal product of labor is thus the partial derivative of output with respect to labor (L). Likewise, the marginal product of capital is the partial derivative of $f(L, K)$ with respect to K.

Proceeding more formally, consider some function, $y = f(x_1, \ldots, x_n)$, evaluated at the point $x_1 = x_1^0, \ldots, x_n = x_n^0$. Consider how this function changes with adjustments in x_1 alone. We define the partial derivative of $f(x_1, \ldots, x_n)$ with respect to x_1 as:

$$\frac{\partial y}{\partial x_1} = \lim_{\Delta x_1 \to 0} \frac{\Delta f}{\Delta x_1}$$

$$= \lim_{\Delta x_1 \to 0} \frac{f(x_1^0 + \Delta x_1, x_2^0, \ldots, x_n^0) - f(x_1^0, \ldots, x_n^0)}{\Delta x_1} \tag{3-1}$$

The partial derivative, $(\partial f/\partial x_1)$, is evaluated at $x_1 = x_1^0, \ldots, x_n = x_n^0$ provided the limit exists. The student should note that the foregoing difference quotient is really an intuitive generalization from the difference quotient used to define the ordinary derivatives of functions of one variable. Analogously, we define:

$$\frac{\partial y}{\partial x_i} = \lim_{\Delta x_i \to 0} \frac{f(x_1^0, \ldots, x_i^0 + \Delta x_i, \ldots, x_n^0) - f(x_1^0, \ldots, x_n^0)}{\Delta x_i}$$

$$\text{where } i = 1, \ldots, n \tag{3-2}$$

We will use the notation $\partial y/\partial x_i$ and $\partial f/\partial x_i$ interchangeably.

When taking partial derivatives, the rule is simply to treat all other variables as constants. The ordinary rules of differentiation are then applied.

Example 1 Suppose a consumer's utility is given by the function

$$U(x_1, x_2) = x_1 \log x_2$$

The marginal utilities are the partial derivatives $\partial U/\partial x_1$, $\partial U/\partial x_2$. To find $\partial U/\partial x_1$, treat x_2 as constant:

$$\frac{\partial U}{\partial x_1} = \log x_2$$

Similarly, to find $\partial U/\partial x_2$, treat x_1 as a constant:

$$\frac{\partial U}{\partial x_2} = x_1 \frac{1}{x_2} = \frac{x_1}{x_2}$$

Example 2 Suppose a firm's production function is

$$y = L^\alpha K^\beta$$

where α, $\beta > 0$ are constants. The marginal products of labor and capital are, respectively,

$$\text{MP}_L = \frac{\partial y}{\partial L} = \alpha L^{\alpha-1} K^\beta$$

$$\text{MP}_K = \frac{\partial y}{\partial K} = L^\alpha \beta K^{\beta-1} = \beta L^\alpha K^{\beta-1}$$

The ordinary rules of differentiation, e.g., the product and quotient rules, apply to partial derivatives as well.

Example 3 Let $y = x_1 e^{x_1 + x_2^2}$.
Using the product rule,

$$\frac{\partial y}{\partial x_1} = x_1 e^{x_1 + x_2^2} + e^{x_1 + x_2^2} = e^{x_1 + x_2^2}(1 + x_1)$$

Also, using the chain rule as in differentiating $e^{a + x^2}$,

$$\frac{\partial y}{\partial x_2} = x_1 e^{x_1 + x_2^2}(2x_2) = 2x_1 x_2 e^{x_1 + x_2^2}$$

As with the case of ordinary derivatives, partial derivatives can be differentiated (partially!) again yielding *second partials.* However, a richer set of second derivatives exists for functions of several variables than for functions of one variable, because partials such as $\partial f/\partial x_1$ can be differentiated with respect to any of the n variables x_1 through x_n. We can denote "the partial derivative of $\partial f/\partial x_i$ with respect to x_j" as $\partial(\partial f/\partial x_i)\,\partial x_j$, or $\partial^2 f/\partial x_j\,\partial x_i$. Often, however, it is convenient to simply use subscripts to denote differentiation with respect to a variable. Following this tradition, we will write $\partial f/\partial x_i = f_i$, and for higher-order partials, subscripts read from left to right reflect the order of differentiation. That is, $f_{ij} = \partial^2 f/\partial x_j\,\partial x_i$, which, for utility functions, can be interpreted as the rate of change of the marginal utility of good i when the quantity of good j increases.

Example 4 Consider $U(x_1, x_2) = x_1 \log x_2$ again. We previously found

$$U_1 = \log x_2$$

$$U_2 = \frac{x_1}{x_2}$$

Therefore

$$U_{11} = \frac{\partial U_1}{\partial x_1} = 0$$

$$U_{12} = \frac{\partial U_1}{\partial x_2} = \frac{1}{x_2}$$

$$U_{21} = \frac{\partial U_2}{\partial x_1} = \frac{1}{x_2}$$

$$U_{22} = \frac{-x_1}{x_2^2}$$

Example 5 For the function $y = f(L, K) = L^\alpha K^\beta$, the first partials were found to be

$$f_L = \frac{\partial y}{\partial L} = \alpha L^{\alpha-1} K^\beta$$

$$f_K = \frac{\partial y}{\partial K} = \beta L^\alpha K^{\beta-1}$$

Hence
$$f_{LL} = \frac{\partial f_L}{\partial L} = \alpha(\alpha - 1) L^{\alpha-2} K^\beta$$

$$f_{LK} = \frac{\partial f_L}{\partial K} = \alpha L^{\alpha-1} \beta K^{\beta-1} = \alpha\beta L^{\alpha-1} K^{\beta-1}$$

$$f_{KL} = \frac{\partial f_K}{\partial L} = \beta(\alpha L^{\alpha-1}) K^{\beta-1} = \alpha\beta L^{\alpha-1} K^{\beta-1}$$

$$f_{KK} = \frac{\partial f_K}{\partial K} = \beta L^\alpha(\beta - 1) K^{\beta-2} = \beta(\beta - 1) L^\alpha K^{\beta-2}$$

Example 6 For $y = f(x_1, x_2) = x_1 e^{x_1 + x_2^2}$, we found

$$\frac{\partial y}{\partial x_1} = f_1 = e^{x_1 + x_2^2}(1 + x_1)$$

$$\frac{\partial y}{\partial x_2} = f_2 = 2x_1 x_2 e^{x_1 + x_2^2}$$

Thus
$$f_{11} = e^{x_1 + x_2^2} + (1 + x_1)e^{x_1 + x_2^2} = e^{x_1 + x_2^2}(2 + x_1)$$
$$f_{12} = e^{x_1 + x_2^2}(1 + x_1)2x_2 = 2(1 + x_1)x_2 e^{x_1 + x_2^2}$$
$$f_{21} = 2x_2(x_1 e^{x_1 + x_2^2} + e^{x_1 + x_2^2}) = 2(1 + x_1)x_2 e^{x_1 + x_2^2}$$
$$f_{22} = 2x_1[x_2 e^{x_1 + x_2^2}(2x_2) + e^{x_1 + x_2^2}] = 2x_1(1 + 2x_2^2)e^{x_1 + x_2^2}$$

Curiously enough, for each of these functions, $f_{12} = f_{21}$ (or, in the notation of the second example, $f_{LK} = f_{KL}$). The same "cross partial" derivative results no matter in which order the variables are differentiated. This occurrence in fact is general for all functions of several variables whose second partials are themselves continuous.

This invariance to the order of differentiation is one of the least intuitive theorems in elementary mathematics. It is sometimes known as Young's theorem. (Try asking some of your mathematician friends for an intuitive explanation of it!) The result accounts for some surprising relationships that appear in economics. Provided below is, in the author's opinion, the simplest explanation of invariance to the order of differentiation, for the case of functions in two variables. The generalization to n variables is routine. A rigorous discussion of the limit process is not given; hence, what follows is not a formal proof of the matter. It will do for our purposes, however.

Theorem Let $y = f(x_1, x_2)$ have second-order partials that exist and are continuous. Then $f_{12} = f_{21}$.

DISCUSSION. Consider a production function $y = f(L, K)$, where L and K are, respectively, the quantity of labor and capital used in the production process. If the theorem is to hold, then the answers to the following two questions should be identical:

1. How much, in the limit, does the marginal product of labor change when an extra unit of capital is added?
2. How much, in the limit, does the marginal product of capital change when one adds an extra unit of labor?

(Of course, both of these measurements must be made at the same point.) In Fig. 3-3, let

$$a = f(L^0, K^0)$$
$$b = f(L^0 + \Delta L, K^0)$$
$$c = f(L^0 + \Delta L, K^0 + \Delta K)$$
$$d = f(L^0, K^0 + \Delta K)$$

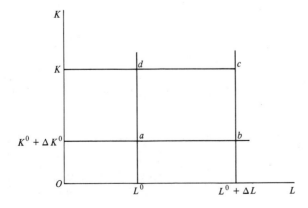

Figure 3-3 *Young's Theorem.* In this diagram, a, b, c, and d represent the *values* of $f(L, K)$ at the four corners of the rectangle.

That is, a, b, c, and d are the *values* of the function f (here, the levels of output) at the corners of the rectangle in the LK plane formed by the initial point L^0, K^0, and then changing L and K by amounts ΔL and ΔK, respectively, separately and then together.

Let us approximate the second-order partial derivatives by their second differences and see how they compare before any limits are taken. The marginal product of labor L evaluated at (L^0, K^0) is approximately

$$f_L(L^0, K^0) \approx \frac{f(L^0 + \Delta L, K^0) - f(L^0, K^0)}{\Delta L} = \frac{b - a}{\Delta L} \tag{3-3}$$

If the amount of capital K is now increased by some amount ΔK, the marginal product of labor, evaluated at $(L^0, K^0 + \Delta K)$ is

$$f_L(L^0, K^0 + \Delta K) \approx \frac{f(L^0 + \Delta L, K^0 + \Delta K) - f(L^0, K^0 + \Delta K)}{\Delta L}$$

$$= \frac{c - d}{\Delta L} \tag{3-4}$$

Then, f_{LK}, which measures the *change* in the marginal product of labor when an incremental amount of capital is added, can be found by taking the difference, per increment of capital, between the two marginal products of labor (3-3) and (3-4):

$$f_{LK} \approx \frac{1}{\Delta K}\left(\frac{c - d}{\Delta L} - \frac{b - a}{\Delta L}\right) = \frac{1}{\Delta K \, \Delta L}(c - d - b + a) \tag{3-5}$$

To find the other cross-partial f_{KL} we begin the process by first finding the marginal product of capital, and then asking how that value changes when the quantity of labor changes. Proceeding as before, the marginal product of capital evaluated at (L^0, K^0) is

$$f_K(L^0, K^0) \approx \frac{f(L^0, K^0 + \Delta K) - f(L^0, K^0)}{\Delta K} = \frac{d - a}{\Delta K} \tag{3-6}$$

Increasing the amount of labor to $L^0 + \Delta L$, the marginal product of capital is

$$f_K(L^0 + \Delta L, K^0) \approx \frac{f(L^0 + \Delta L, K^0 + \Delta K) - f(L^0 + \Delta L, K^0)}{\Delta K} = \frac{c - b}{\Delta K}$$

$$\tag{3-7}$$

Hence, the *change* in the marginal product of capital due to the change in labor is approximately

$$f_{KL} \approx \frac{1}{\Delta L}\left(\frac{c - b}{\Delta K} - \frac{d - a}{\Delta K}\right) = \frac{1}{\Delta L \, \Delta K}(c - b - d + a) \tag{3-8}$$

Notice that equations (3-5) and (3-8) are identical! That is, the second differences are the same, whether L or K is changed first. The remaining step (and it is a big step) in proving the theorem is to show that, under appropriate mathematical conditions on the function $f(L, K)$, the *limits* as $\Delta L \to 0$ and $\Delta K \to 0$, are the same, taken in either order. This step is omitted here. The argument is based on an application of the mean value theorem, and can be found in most elementary calculus texts.

In general, assuming the function is sufficiently well-behaved (no discontinuities in higher-order derivatives, etc.), the higher-order partial derivatives are also invariant to the order of differentiation. This is derived by simply applying Young's theorem over and over.

Example 7 Consider $y = f(x_1, x_2, x_3)$. Show that $f_{123} = f_{312} = f_{321}$, etc.
Applying Young's theorem to $f_1(x_1, x_2, x_3)$

$$f_{123} = f_{1(23)} = f_{1(32)} = f_{132}$$

However, $f_{13} = f_{31}$. Hence

$$f_{132} = f_{312}$$

Thus, $f_{123} = f_{312}$. Also, since $f_{3(12)} = f_{3(21)}$

$$f_{123} = f_{312} = f_{321}$$

In a similar fashion, for $y = f(x_1, \ldots, x_n)$

$$f_{ijk} = f_{jki}, \ldots$$

3.4 THE TOTAL DIFFERENTIAL OF A FUNCTION OF SEVERAL VARIABLES†

In the case of one variable, $y = f(x)$, one can write the *differential* expression

$$dy = f'(x)\, dx$$

The differential element dy measures the movement in y, measured along the line tangent to the function at some point x. The actual change in y, for some change in x, Δx, is given by

$$\Delta y = f(x + \Delta x) - f(x)$$

However, the difference between dy and Δy is of second-order smallness, i.e.,

$$\Delta y = f'(x)\, \Delta x + \varepsilon\, \Delta x$$

where $\varepsilon \to 0$ as $\Delta x \to 0$.

How does the concept of a total derivative generalize to the case of two variables? For $y = f(x_1, x_2)$, the generalization is

$$dy = f_1\, dx_1 + f_2\, dx_2 \tag{3-9}$$

---

† The student should review the section on total differentials in Chap. 2 if this concept is unfamiliar.

where $f_i = \partial f/\partial x_i$, $i = 1, 2$. The change dy is simply the sum of the movements in y due to changes in both x_1 and x_2.

As in the case of functions of one variable, a geometric interpretation can be given to the total differential (3-9). The function $f(x_1, x_2)$ can be thought of as ascribing a value to every point in the cartesian coordinate plane (x_1, x_2). If this plane is thought of as laid out horizontally (parallel to the earth's surface), and if the values of the function are plotted vertically above each point in that plane, then the function will be represented by a surface suspended in three-dimensional space. Assuming this surface has the requisite smoothness, at each point one can imagine a tangent *plane*. Then dy measures movements in y *measured up to the tangent plane*, due to changes in both x_1 and x_2. It does not reflect changes in the value of the *function* for changes in the independent variables. As before, Δy will denote changes in the function itself, while dy measures changes in y as we move along the plane tangent to the surface at some point.

Although equation (3-9) can be regarded simply as a *definition* of a total derivative, the expression can be motivated as follows. For finite changes Δx_1 and Δx_2 in x_1 and x_2, respectively, the change in the value of the function, Δy, is

$$\Delta y = f(x_1 + \Delta x_1, x_2 + \Delta x_2) - f(x_1, x_2) \tag{3-10}$$

We are now going to add 0 to this equation by both adding and subtracting the same term. (The reason for this contrivance will become clear shortly.) Hence,

$$\Delta y = f(x_1 + \Delta x_1, x_2 + \Delta x_2) - f(x_1, x_2 + \Delta x_2) + f(x_1, x_2 + \Delta x_2) - f(x_1, x_2)$$

The expression is similarly unchanged if the terms are grouped in pairs and each pair is multiplied by 1

$$\Delta y = \frac{f(x_1 + \Delta x_1, x_2 + \Delta x_2) - f(x_1, x_2 + \Delta x_2)}{\Delta x_1} \Delta x_1$$

$$+ \frac{f(x_1, x_2 + \Delta x_2) - f(x_1, x_2)}{\Delta x_2} \Delta x_2 \tag{3-11}$$

The expression (3-11) for Δy is now a weighted sum of two difference quotients. In the first term, x_2 is held constant (at the level $x_2 + \Delta x_2$) and x_1 is varied, whereas in the second term, x_1 is held constant and x_2 is varied. This is precisely the type of difference quotient used to define partial derivatives. Hence, assuming that all the appropriate limits exist, then as $\Delta x_1 \to 0$ and $\Delta x_2 \to 0$, the first difference quotient approaches f_1, while the second approaches f_2. As in the case of functions of one variable, the difference between y, as given by equation (3-10) or (3-11), and dy, as defined by (3-9), is of second-order smallness. That is,

$$\Delta y = f_1 \Delta x_1 + f_2 \Delta x_2 + \varepsilon_1 \Delta x_1 + \varepsilon_2 \Delta x_2$$

where $\varepsilon_1, \varepsilon_2 \to 0$ as $\Delta x_1, \Delta x_2 \to 0$. For movements *along* the tangent plane itself,

$$dy = f_1 \, dx_1 + f_2 \, dx_2$$

where dx_1 and dx_2 are arbitrary changes (not necessarily "small") in x_1 and x_2, respectively.

The generalization of equation (3-9) to the case of functions of several variables is straightforward. Using the same reasoning, the formula for the total differential of $y = f(x_1, \ldots, x_n)$ is†

$$dy = f_1 \, dx_1 + \cdots + f_n \, dx_n = \sum_{i=1}^{n} f_i \, dx_i \qquad (3\text{-}12)$$

Geometrically, equation (3-12) represents movements along a "hyperplane" tangent to an n-dimensional "surface" suspended in $(n + 1)$ space. The reason why algebraic analysis eventually supplants geometric reasoning is thus obvious.

The preceding analysis of the total differential is necessary for deriving the chain rule for functions of several variables. This is done in the next section; the chain rule is a tool of critical importance and, hence, must be thoroughly understood by the student.

PROBLEMS

1 For each of the following functions, find f_1, f_2, f_{12} and f_{21}. Verify that $f_{12} = f_{21}$ for these functions.
(a) $f(x_1, x_2) = x_1^2 x_2^3$ (b) $f(x_1, x_2) = (x_1 + x_2^2)/(x_1 + x_2)$
(c) $f(x_1, x_2) = x_2 \log x_1$ (d) $f(x_1, x_2) = x_1^2 e^{x_2}$
(e) $f(x_1, x_2) = x_1^{x_2}$

2 Find the total differential of the functions in problem 1.

3 Consider the function $y = x_1^2 + x_1 x_2 - x_2^2$. Show that the difference between dy and Δy is of second-order smallness, i.e., the difference involves the increment Δx raised to powers 2 and above.

4 Consider the production function $y = L^{1/3} K^{2/3}$, where L = labor, K = capital, and y = output. Suppose initially $L = 64$, $K = 27$. Suppose one unit of labor and two units of capital are added. By how much, approximately, will output increase? How much exactly? Which is an easier number to compute? Do you think it matters much which you use?

5 Let $y = L^\alpha K^{1-\alpha}$, where $0 < \alpha < 1$. Let $y' = \log y$, $L' = \log L$, $K' = \log K$.
(a) Show that this production function is linear in the logs of output, labor, and capital.
(b) Using logarithmic differentiation, show that for this production function, the percentage change in output due to small changes in the inputs is equal to the weighted sum of the percentage changes in labor and capital, the weights being α and $(1 - \alpha)$, respectively. In what sense is the relation you derive valid only for *small* changes?

3.5 THE CHAIN RULE‡

In economics, as well as most sciences one often encounters a sequence of functional relationships. For example, the output of a firm depends upon the input levels chosen by the firm, as specified in the production function. However, the input levels are determined, i.e., functionally related to the factor and output

---

† The summation sign $\sum_{i=1}^{n}$ means substitute successively the values 1 through n for i in the terms to the right of the summation sign, and then add up all n terms. It is a very useful, and, hence, very common shorthand.
‡ The student should review the section on the chain rule in Chap. 2, if this concept is unfamiliar.

prices. Hence, output is related, indirectly, to factor and output prices. It is therefore meaningful to inquire as to the changes in output that would follow a change in some price, i.e., a partial derivative of output with respect to that price. The chain rule is the mathematical device which expresses the partial derivative of the composite function in terms of the various partial derivatives of the individual functions in the functional sequence. We will now develop this idea more formally, for functions of several variables.

For functions of one variable, if

$$y = f(x) \text{ and } x = g(t)$$

then the functional dependence of y on t can be written

$$y = f(g(t)) = h(t)$$

Now
$$\Delta y = f'(x) \, \Delta x + \varepsilon \, \Delta x$$

and
$$\Delta x = g'(t) \, \Delta t + \zeta \, \Delta t$$

where $\varepsilon \to 0$ as $\Delta x \to 0$ and $\zeta \to 0$ as $\Delta t \to 0$. Combining these two expressions,

$$\Delta y = [f'(x) + \varepsilon][g'(t) \, \Delta t + \zeta \, \Delta t]$$

or
$$\Delta y = f'(x)g'(t) \, \Delta t + f'(x)\zeta \, \Delta t + g'(t)\varepsilon \, \Delta t + \varepsilon\zeta \, \Delta t$$

Dividing by Δt

$$\frac{\Delta y}{\Delta t} = f'(x)g'(t) + f'(x)\zeta + g'(t)\varepsilon + \varepsilon\zeta$$

Taking limits as $\Delta t \to 0$

$$\frac{dy}{dt} = f'(x)g'(t) = \frac{dy}{dx}\frac{dx}{dt} \tag{3-13}$$

since $\varepsilon, \zeta \to 0$ as $\Delta t \to 0$.

Suppose now that y is a function of two variables, $y = f(x_1, x_2)$. Suppose x_1 and x_2 are in turn functions of some other variable t. Let $x_1 = x_1(t), x_2 = x_2(t)$.† Then if t changes, so will, in general, x_1 and x_2 and, hence, also y. To express this functional dependence of y on t, we write $y = f(x_1(t), x_2(t)) = y(t)$. How can $y'(t)$ be expressed in terms of $f_1, f_2, x'_1(t)$ and $x'_2(t)$?

For given changes Δx_1 and Δx_2

$$\Delta y = f_1 \, \Delta x_1 + f_2 \, \Delta x_2 + \varepsilon_1 \, \Delta x_1 + \varepsilon_2 \, \Delta x_2 \tag{3-14}$$

where $\varepsilon_1, \varepsilon_2 \to 0$ as $\Delta x_1, \Delta x_2 \to 0$. However,

$$\Delta x_1 = x'_1(t) \, \Delta t + \zeta_1 \, \Delta t$$

$$\Delta x_2 = x'_2(t) \, \Delta t + \zeta_2 \, \Delta t$$

---

† Mathematicians frown on the use of the same symbol to denote a function and the value of that function. It will not get us into trouble, however, and it will reduce the number of symbols that the reader has to keep in mind.

Substituting these relations into (3-14)

$$\Delta y = f_1 x_1'(t)\,\Delta t + f_2\,x_2'(t)\,\Delta t + (f_1\zeta_1 + f_2\zeta_2 + \varepsilon_1 x_1' + \varepsilon_1\zeta_1 + \varepsilon_2 x_2' + \varepsilon_2\zeta_2)\,\Delta t$$

Dividing by Δt and taking limits,

$$\frac{dy}{dt} = f_1 x_1'(t) + f_2 x_2'(t) = \frac{\partial f}{\partial x_1}\frac{dx_1}{dt} + \frac{\partial f}{\partial x_2}\frac{dx_2}{dt} \tag{3-15}$$

Suppose now that x_1 and x_2 are themselves functions of several variables. For example, let $x_1 = g(r, s)$, $x_2 = h(r, s)$. In this case, $y = f(g(r, s), h(r, s)) = F(r, s)$, and we can only speak meaningfully of the *partial* derivatives of y with respect to r and s. The chain rule here is

$$\frac{\partial y}{\partial r} = f_1\frac{\partial g}{\partial r} + f_2\frac{\partial h}{\partial r} \tag{3-16}$$

with a similar expression holding with respect to the variable s. The only difference between (3-15) and (3-16) is that since r is one of several variables, the appropriate partial notation must be used.

The chain rule generalizes in a straightforward manner to the case where each independent variable is in turn a function of m other independent variables. Let

$$y = f(x_1, \ldots, x_n)$$

and let

$$x_i = g^i(t_1, \ldots, t_m) \qquad i = 1, \ldots, n$$

Then the chain rule is

$$\frac{\partial y}{\partial t_k} = \frac{\partial f}{\partial x_1}\frac{\partial x_1}{\partial t_k} + \cdots + \frac{\partial f}{\partial x_n}\frac{\partial x_n}{\partial t_k} \qquad k = 1, \ldots, m \tag{3-17}$$

This can also be written as

$$\frac{\partial y}{\partial t_k} = f_1 g_k^1 + \cdots + f_n g_k^n = \sum_{i=1}^{n} f_i g_k^i \qquad k = 1, \ldots, m \tag{3-18}$$

where the symbol g_k^i means $\partial g^i/\partial t_k$.

Example 1 Let $y = f(x_1, x_2)$, and let

$$x_1 = x_1^0 + h_1 t$$
$$x_2 = x_2^0 + h_2 t \tag{3-19}$$

where h_1 and h_2 are arbitrary constants. When $t = 0$, $x_1 = x_1^0$, $x_2 = x_2^0$. As t changes, x_1 and x_2 move along a straight line in the $x_1 x_2$ plane. This can be seen by eliminating t from these equations

$$x_2 = x_2^0 + \frac{h_2(x_1 - x_1^0)}{h_1} = \frac{h_2}{h_1}x_1 + \left(x_2^0 - x_1^0\frac{h_2}{h_1}\right) \qquad h_1 \neq 0 \tag{3-20}$$

This is the equation of a straight line with slope h_2/h_1, passing through the point (x_1^0, x_2^0).

Writing
$$y(t) = f(x_1^0 + h_1 t, x_2^0 + h_2 t)$$

is equivalent to saying that $f(x_1, x_2)$ is evaluated along the straight line (3-19), or, equivalently, (3-20). Using the chain rule

$$y'(t) = f_1 h_1 + f_2 h_2 \tag{3-21}$$

Example 2 Suppose $y = \log(x_1 + x_2)$, where $x_1 = t$, $x_2 = t^2$. This is equivalent to evaluating $\log(x_1 + x_2)$ along the parabola $x_2 = x_1^2$. Let us find dy/dt by direct substitution and by the chain rule.

(*i*) By direct substitution

$$y = \log(t + t^2)$$

Therefore
$$\frac{dy}{dt} = \frac{1}{t + t^2}(1 + 2t)$$

(*ii*) Using the chain rule,

$$\frac{dy}{dt} = f_1 \frac{dx_1}{dt} + f_2 \frac{dx_2}{dt}$$

$$= \frac{1}{x_1 + x_2} 1 + \frac{1}{x_1 + x_2} 2t$$

$$= \frac{1}{t + t^2}(1 + 2t)$$

as before.

Example 3 Suppose $y = x_1^2 e^{x_2}$, with $x_1 = \log t$, $x_2 = t^2$. Find dy/dt by (*i*) direct substitution, and by (*ii*) the chain rule.

(*i*) Substituting the expressions for x_1 and x_2, $y = (\log t)^2 e^{t^2}$. Using the product rule for differentiation

$$\frac{dy}{dt} = e^{t^2}(2 \log t)\frac{1}{t} + (\log t)^2 (2te^{t^2})$$

(*ii*) Using the chain rule

$$\frac{dy}{dt} = f_1 \frac{dx_1}{dt} + f_2 \frac{dx_2}{dt} = 2x_1 e^{x_2}\frac{1}{t} + x_1^2 e^{x_2}(2t)$$

$$= 2(\log t)e^{t^2}\frac{1}{t} + (\log t)^2 e^{t^2}(2t)$$

The final expressions are, as they must be, identical by either method.

Monotonic Transformations

A particular sequence of functional relationships which plays a prominent part in the theory of the consumer is a transformation of the *dependent* variable. Suppose a consumer's utility function is given by

$$U = U(x_1, x_2)$$

In the modern theory of the consumer, this utility, or preference, function is meant to merely *rank* various options, (x_1, x_2). The value of the function itself at some point is relevant only in regard to whether it is *greater* or *less* than at some other consumption point. The amount greater is of no significance unless one proposes to actually measure "utility" or happiness. We say that $U(x_1, x_2)$ is an *ordinal* ranking, not a cardinal function of alternatives.

This ordinality is given precise expression by saying that the utility function $V(x_1, x_2)$ given by

$$V(x_1, x_2) = F(U) = F(U(x_1, x_2))$$

where $F'(U) > 0$, conveys as much information as $U(x_1, x_2)$. The condition that $F'(U) > 0$ means that U and V always move in the same direction. The function V is called a *monotonically increasing* function of U. [If $F'(U) < 0$, V would be called monotonically decreasing.] Most often, the single term *monotonic* is used to mean *monotonically increasing*.

What the function F does is relabel the level curves of U, giving them new numbers, V. This is a different situation than previously where the independent variables were dependent on some other variable or variables. Here, the dependent variable U (in this case) is given a new value, $F(U) = V$. The function V is a function of the one variable U which in turn is a function of two variables, x_1 and x_2. We can thus ask, since V ultimately depends on *both* x_1 and x_2, how is $\partial V/\partial x_i$ related to $F(U)$ and $U(x_1, x_2)$? The answer is given in the following chain rule. We have

$$\Delta V = F'(U)\,\Delta U + \varepsilon\,\Delta U \qquad (3\text{-}22)$$

where $\varepsilon \to 0$ as $\Delta U \to 0$. However,

$$\Delta U = U_1\,\Delta x_1 + U_2\,\Delta x_2 + \varepsilon_1\,\Delta x_1 + \varepsilon_2\,\Delta x_2$$

Substituting this into (3-22)

$$\Delta V = F'(U)U_1\,\Delta x_1 + F'(U)U_2\,\Delta x_2 + [F'(U)](\varepsilon_1\,\Delta x_1 + \varepsilon_2\,\Delta x_2) + \varepsilon\,\Delta U$$

If only x_1 changes, that is, $\Delta x_2 = 0$, then dividing by Δx_1 and taking limits

$$\frac{\partial V}{\partial x_1} = F'(U)U_1 = \frac{dV}{dU}\frac{\partial U}{\partial x_1}$$

Similarly

$$\frac{\partial V}{\partial x_2} = F'(U)U_2 = \frac{dV}{dU}\frac{\partial U}{\partial x_2}$$

In general, suppose

$$y = f(x_1, \ldots, x_n)$$

and

$$z = F(y) = F(f(x_1, \ldots, x_n))$$

Then

$$\frac{\partial z}{\partial x_i} = F'(y)f_i \tag{3-23}$$

Example 4 Suppose $y = x_1 x_2$, and let $z = \log y$. Then applying (3-23)

$$\frac{\partial z}{\partial x_1} = \frac{1}{y}x_2 = \frac{1}{x_1}$$

and

$$\frac{\partial z}{\partial x_2} = \frac{1}{y}x_1 = \frac{1}{x_2}$$

These results can be checked by direct substitution. We have

$$z = \log y = \log(x_1 x_2) = \log x_1 + \log x_2$$

Thus

$$\frac{\partial z}{\partial x_1} = \frac{1}{x_1} \qquad \frac{\partial z}{\partial x_2} = \frac{1}{x_2}$$

Example 5 Let $y = x_2 + \log x_1$, $z = e^y$. Then applying (3-23)

$$\frac{\partial z}{\partial x_1} = e^y \frac{1}{x_1} = e^{x_2 + \log x_1} \frac{1}{x_1}$$

Using the definition of logs and rules of exponents

$$\frac{\partial z}{\partial x_1} = e^{x_2} e^{\log x_1} \frac{1}{x_1} = e^{x_2} x_1 \frac{1}{x_1} = e^{x_2}$$

Similarly,

$$\frac{\partial z}{\partial x_2} = e^y(1) = e^{x_2 + \log x_1} = x_1 e^{x_2}$$

By direct substitution,

$$z = e^{x_2 + \log x_1} = e^{x_2} e^{\log x_1} = x_1 e^{x_2}$$

from which the above partials directly follow.

Second Derivatives by the Chain Rule

Suppose that $y = f(x_1, x_2)$ and $x_1 = x_1(t)$, $x_2 = x_2(t)$. We need to find an expression for d^2y/dt^2, as this second derivative is important for analyzing the sufficient conditions under which a function of several variables achieves a maximum or a minimum position. Using the chain rule

$$\frac{dy}{dt} = f_1 \frac{dx_1}{dt} + f_2 \frac{dx_2}{dt}$$

Then, to find d^2y/dt^2, we have to differentiate this expression again. Do not forget, however, that f_1 and f_2 are themselves functions of x_1 and x_2, and, hence, functions of t. Then, using the product rule,

$$\frac{d^2y}{dt^2} = \frac{d}{dt}\frac{dy}{dt} = f_1\frac{d}{dt}\frac{dx_1}{dt} + \frac{dx_1}{dt}\frac{d}{dt}f_1(x_1(t), x_2(t)) + f_2\frac{d}{dt}\frac{dx_2}{dt}$$

$$+ \frac{dx_2}{dt}\frac{d}{dt}f_2(x_1(t), x_2(t))$$

Now use the chain rule to differentiate $f_1(x_1(t), x_2(t))$, etc., with respect to t. Noting that $\partial f_1/\partial x_1 = f_{11}$, etc.

$$\frac{d^2y}{dt^2} = f_1\frac{d^2x_1}{dt^2} + \frac{dx_1}{dt}\left(f_{11}\frac{dx_1}{dt} + f_{12}\frac{dx_2}{dt}\right)$$

$$+ f_2\frac{d^2x_2}{dt^2} + \frac{dx_2}{dt}\left(f_{21}\frac{dx_1}{dt} + f_{22}\frac{dx_2}{dt}\right)$$

Regrouping terms, and noting that $f_{12} = f_{21}$,

$$\frac{d^2y}{dt^2} = f_1\frac{d^2x_1}{dt^2} + f_2\frac{d^2x_2}{dt^2} + f_{11}\left(\frac{dx_1}{dt}\right)^2$$

$$+ 2f_{12}\frac{dx_1}{dt}\frac{dx_2}{dt} + f_{22}\left(\frac{dx_2}{dt}\right)^2 \tag{3-24}$$

Note that this expression is linear in the second derivatives of x_1 and x_2 with respect to t, and *quadratic* in the first derivatives of x_1 and x_2. The appropriate generalization to n variables, with $y = f(x_1, \ldots, x_n)$ and $x_i = x_i(t)$, $i = 1, \ldots, n$, is obtained in the same manner:

$$\frac{d^2y}{dt^2} = \sum_{i=1}^{n} f_i\frac{d^2x_i}{dt^2} + \sum_{i=1}^{n}\sum_{j=1}^{n} f_{ij}\frac{dx_i}{dt}\frac{dx_j}{dt} \tag{3-25}$$

Example 6 Let $y = f(x_1, x_2)$ and consider the straight lines $x_1 = x_1^0 + h_1 t$, $x_2 = x_2^0 + h_2 t$ once more. From equation (3-21),

$$y'(t) = f_1 h_1 + f_2 h_2$$

Therefore

$$y''(t) = \left(\frac{\partial f_1}{\partial x_1}\frac{dx_1}{dt} + \frac{\partial f_1}{\partial x_2}\frac{dx_2}{dt}\right)h_1 + \left(\frac{\partial f_2}{\partial x_1}\frac{dx_1}{dt} + \frac{\partial f_2}{\partial x_2}\frac{dx_2}{dt}\right)h_2$$

Since $\partial f_1/\partial x_1 = f_{11}$, etc., and $dx_i/dt = h_i$, this expression reduces to

$$y''(t) = f_{11}h_1^2 + 2f_{12}h_1 h_2 + f_{22}h_2^2 \tag{3-26}$$

For this "parameterization" of x_1 and x_2 in terms of t, $y''(t)$ is a "quadratic form" in h_1 and h_2.

Example 7 Let $y = f(x_1, x_2)$, and consider a monotonic transformation of y, $z = F(y) = F(f(x_1, x_2)) = g(x_1, x_2)$, with $F'(y) > 0$. How do the *second* partials of g compare with those of f?

From equation (3-23),

$$g_i = F'(y)f_i$$

Let us now differentiate this again, partially, with respect to x_j. Using the product rule for the right-hand side,

$$g_{ij} = F'(y)f_{ij} + f_i \frac{\partial F'(y)}{\partial x_j}$$

To evaluate this last term, keep in mind that $F'(y)$ is just some function of y, where $y = f(x_1, x_2)$ as before. Applying equation (3-23) to this last term

$$\frac{\partial F'(y)}{\partial x_j} = F''(y)f_j$$

Thus,
$$g_{ij} = F'(y)f_{ij} + f_i f_j F''(y) \tag{3-27}$$

Notice that g_{ij} and f_{ij} need not have the same sign. Although $F'(y) > 0$ is assumed, $F''(y) \gtrless 0$. Suppose $y = f(x_1, x_2) = x_1^2 x_2^2$, and let $z = g(x_1, x_2) = \log y$. Then, for example,

$$f_{11} = 2x_2^2 > 0$$

However
$$g(x_1, x_2) = \log(x_1^2 x_2^2) = 2 \log x_1 + 2 \log x_2$$

Then
$$g_{11} = \frac{-2}{x_1^2} < 0$$

Also
$$f_{12} = 4x_1 x_2$$

and
$$g_{12} \equiv 0$$

3.6 LEVEL CURVES: II

Consider again the representation of a function of two variables as presented in Fig. 3-1, with $y = f(L, K)$, a production function. The level curve representing, say, five units of output is simply $f(L, K) = 5$. In general, the level curves of some function $y = f(x_1, x_2)$ are defined by $f(x_1, x_2) = y_0$, where y_0 is some constant. How do we determine the curvature properties, such as the slope in the x_1, x_2 plane, or the convexity of that level curve?

The equation $f(x_1, x_2) = y_0$ represents one equation in two *unknowns*, x_1 and x_2. Under certain mathematical conditions (to be determined below) this equation can be solved for one of the unknowns in terms of the other, say

$$x_2 = x_2(x_1)$$

When this solution is substituted back into the equation from which it was derived, the *identity*

$$f(x_1, x_2(x_1)) \equiv y_0$$

results, by definition of a solution. In this identity, x_2 always adjusts to any value of x_1 so as to keep $f(x_1, x_2(x_1))$ always equal to y_0.

The slope of any level curve is simply the derivative dx_2/dx_1. But it is important to understand that this symbol, dx_2/dx_1, makes sense only if we have explicitly defined x_2 as a function of x_1, as we have, in fact, done above. It is nonsense to speak of derivatives unless one knows what function it is that is being differentiated. Since our function $x_2 = x_2(x_1)$ is well defined, dx_2/dx_1 can be found by differentiating the identity $f(x_1, x_2(x_1)) \equiv y_0$ with respect to x_1, using the chain rule. We therefore get

$$\frac{\partial f}{\partial x_1}\frac{dx_1}{dx_1} + \frac{\partial f}{\partial x_2}\frac{dx_2}{dx_1} \equiv \frac{\partial y_0}{\partial x_1} \equiv 0$$

or

$$f_1 + f_2\frac{dx_2}{dx_1} \equiv 0$$

Now assuming that $f_2 \neq 0$

$$\frac{dx_2}{dx_1} \equiv \frac{-f_1}{f_2} \tag{3-28}$$

The slope of a level curve at any point is the ratio of the first partials of the function $y = f(x_1, x_2)$, evaluated, of course, at some particular point on the level curve in question. The condition alluded to above that allows solution of $f(x_1, x_2) = y_0$ for $x_2 = x_2(x_1)$ can be seen to be simply that $f_2 \neq 0$. When $f_2 \neq 0$, at some point the derivative dx_2/dx_1 can be expressed in terms of the partials of the original function, and, hence, the equations $f(x_1, x_2) = y_0$ and $x_2 = x_2(x_1)$ are equivalent at such points. When $f_2 = 0$, the level curve becomes vertical and its derivative does not exist.

What is the meaning of $dx_2/dx_1 = -f_1/f_2$? Consider the production function $y = f(L, K)$ again. The level curves are the isoquants of this production function. In Fig. 3-4, consider a movement along an isoquant y_0, from A to B. This movement can be conceptually broken down into a vertical movement down to C, in which case only K is changed by an amount ΔK, and then a horizontal movement from C to B, in which only L changes, by an amount ΔL. The output change from A to C is approximately the marginal product of capital, evaluated at A, times the loss of capital, ΔK, or $f_K \Delta K$. In going from C to B, since labor is being added, the gain in output is approximately the marginal product of labor (evaluated at B) times the gain in labor, or $f_L \Delta L$. Since output is unchanged, by definition of an isoquant, from A to B, these quantities must add to 0, or

$$f_L \Delta L + f_K \Delta K = 0 \tag{3-29}$$

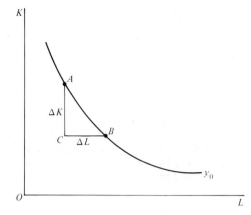

Figure 3-4 *Movement Along an Isoquant.* The move from A to B can be broken down into a decrease in K (A to C), then an increase in L (B to C) to achieve the same production level. Since y is constant, the *decrease* in output going from A to C ($-MP_K \Delta K$) equals the *increase* in output going from C to B ($MP_L \Delta L$). Thus $\Delta y = MP_L \Delta L + MP_K \Delta K = 0$.

In the limit, as the points A and B are brought closer and closer together, so that ΔL and $\Delta K \to 0$, equation (3-29) is simply an expression that the total differential of $y = f(L, K)$ equals 0, since y is unchanged, or

$$dy = f_L \ dL + f_K \ dK = 0 \qquad (3\text{-}30)$$

Now if and only if K can be expressed as a function of L or $K = K(L)$, as it always can if the isoquant is not vertical, then the total differential may be divided through by dL, yielding

$$f_L + f_K \frac{dK}{dL} = 0$$

or

$$\frac{dK}{dL} = -\frac{f_L}{f_K}$$

Thus equation (3-28), for production functions, measures the willingness of firms to substitute labor for capital, since it measures the ratio of the benefits of the additional labor, f_L, to the output lost due to using less capital, f_K.

In the theory of the consumer, the level curves of a utility function $U = U(x_1, x_2)$, the indifference curves, can be similarly analyzed. The slope of an indifference curve, which expresses the willingness of a consumer to make exchanges, is based on the ratio of perceived gains and losses from such an exchange. Following the above analysis, this slope, or exchange rate, dx_2/dx_1, is equal to $-U_1/U_2$, the ratio of marginal utility of good 1 to good 2. This ratio, since it expresses an evaluation of giving up some x_2 (a loss of $MU_2 \ dx_2$ or $U_2 \ dx_2$) in order to obtain some x_1 (a gain of $U_1 \ dx_1$) is called the marginal rate of substitution of x_1 for x_2. Since along an indifference curve $dU = 0$, $U_2 \ dx_2 = -U_1 \ dx_1$. Assuming $x_2 = x_2(x_1)$ is well defined, $dx_2/dx_1 = -U_1/U_2$, the ratio of perceived gains to losses, at the margin.

Convexity of the Level Curves

From the formula $dx_2/dx_1 = -f_1/f_2$, if the first partials are both positive, the level curves must be negatively sloped. In production theory, if the marginal products of each factor input are positive, then the isoquants will have a negative slope. An analogous statement concerning the marginal utilities and indifference curves holds for the consumer. Simply stated, a movement to the "northeast" from any factor-input combination, say, involves more of both factors. If the marginal products are positive, this must yield an increase in output, and, hence, the new point cannot lie along the same isoquant as the old. The willingness of consumers to make trade-offs—that is, to give up some of one good in order to get more of another good—is evidence that the level curves of utility function (the indifference curves) are negatively sloped. If they were positively sloped, consumers would have to be bribed by one good in order to consume some other good; indeed, one of the "goods" would really be a "bad," yielding negative utility at the margin.

However, in addition to asserting a negative slope of these level curves, economists also insist that these curves are convex to the origin, as shown in Fig. 3-1. Why do economists believe this, and how can we represent this convexity mathematically? Convexity of these level curves to the origin is a statement that the marginal value of either good (or factor) declines along that curve, as more of that good or factor is obtained, relative to the other. As x_1 is increased, say, the ratio $-f_1/f_2$ declines in absolute value, meaning that the benefits associated with having greater x_1, that is, f_1, are declining relative to the benefits of having some more x_2, measured by f_2 at the margin. The reason why economists believe this to be empirically correct is that the opposite assumption would imply that consumers would spend all of their income on one good, or that firms would hire only one factor of production. After all, if the marginal benefits of having x_1 rose the more x_1 one had, why would a person ever stop purchasing x_1 in favor of x_2 (assuming it was worthwhile to purchase some x_1 in the first place). We are assuming that the consumer or firm is a sufficiently small part of the market to have a negligible effect on the price of x_1. Convexity of the level curves is asserted because it is the only assertion about preferences or technology that is consistent with the simultaneous use of several goods or inputs, i.e., with the decision to *stop* utilizing some economic good at some point short of exhaustion of one's entire wealth.

Mathematically, convexity of the level curves can be represented, in two-dimensional space, by considering the curve $x_2 = x_2(x_1)$, the explicit function of the level curve. The negative slope of this curve is indicated by $dx_2/dx_1 < 0$; convexity by $d^2x_2/dx_1^2 > 0$. The positive second derivative means that the slope dx_2/dx_1 is increasing as x_1 increases, and this is precisely what is indicated by the level curves in Fig. 3-1. As x_1 (or L, there) increases, the slope becomes less and less negative, i.e., it increases. How do we express d^2x_2/dx_1^2 in terms of the partials of $f(x_1, x_2)$, from which the level curve is derived? As was seen above,

$$\frac{dx_2}{dx_1} = -\frac{f_1(x_1, x_2(x_1))}{f_2(x_1, x_2(x_1))} \tag{3-31}$$

Note, however, that we have explicitly indicated the independent variables x_1 and x_2 with the functional dependence of x_2 on x_1 also explicitly shown. To find d^2x_2/dx_1^2, we must differentiate the right-hand side of (3-31), using the quotient rule, and using the chain rule in the numerator and denominator. Hence,

$$\frac{d^2x_2}{dx_1^2} = -\left\{f_2\frac{d}{dx_1}[f_1(x_1, x_2(x_1))] - f_1\frac{d}{dx_1}[f_2(x_1, x_2(x_1))]\right\}\frac{1}{f_2^2}$$

$$= -\left[f_2\left(\frac{\partial f_1}{\partial x_1}\frac{dx_1}{dx_1} + \frac{\partial f_1}{\partial x_2}\frac{dx_2}{dx_1}\right)\right.$$

$$\left. -f_1\left(\frac{\partial f_2}{\partial x_1}\frac{dx_1}{dx_1} + \frac{\partial f_2}{\partial x_2}\frac{dx_2}{dx_1}\right)\right]\frac{1}{f_2^2}$$

$$= -\left[f_2\left(f_{11} + f_{12}\frac{dx_2}{dx_1}\right) - f_1\left(f_{21} + f_{22}\frac{dx_2}{dx_1}\right)\right]\frac{1}{f_2^2}$$

However, $dx_2/dx_1 = -f_1/f_2$. Substituting this into the last expression, and noting that $f_{12} = f_{21}$,

$$\frac{d^2x_2}{dx_1^2} = \left(-f_2 f_{11} + 2f_1 f_{12} - \frac{f_1^2 f_{22}}{f_2}\right)\frac{1}{f_2^2}$$

or
$$\frac{d^2x_2}{dx_1^2} = (-f_2^2 f_{11} + 2f_1 f_2 f_{12} - f_1^2 f_{22})\frac{1}{f_2^3} \tag{3-32}$$

Note that convexity of the level curve depends in a rather complicated manner on the first and second partials of $f(x_1, x_2)$. We shall have more to say about this expression and how it is generalized to more than two variables in Chap. 6. But note the following: Suppose $y = f(x_1, x_2)$ is a utility function. Then convexity of the indifference curves in no way implies, or is implied by, "diminishing marginal utility," that is, $f_{11} < 0$, $f_{22} < 0$. There is a cross effect f_{12} that must also be considered, and which can outweigh the effects, positive or negative, of the second partials f_{11} and f_{22}. Hence, diminishing marginal utility and convexity of indifference curves are two entirely independent concepts. And that is how it must be: Convexity of an indifference curve relates to how marginal evaluations change *holding utility* (the dependent variable) *constant*. The concept of diminishing marginal utility refers to changes in total utilities, i.e., movements from one indifference level to another. In addition, these changes in utility from one level curve to another have no *quantitative* significance; they merely ordinally rank the desirability of consumption bundles. We shall defer further discussion of these matters to Chap. 8, Utility Theory; it is hoped, however, that the student will understand the motivations for considering the mathematical tools developed.

PROBLEMS

1 Consider the following three utility functions:
(i) $U = x_1 x_2$ (ii) $V = x_1^2 x_2^2$ (iii) $W = \log x_1 + \log x_2$
   (a) Find the marginal utilities of x_1 and x_2 for each utility function.
   (b) Find the rates of change of marginal utility of one good with respect to a change in consumption of the other good for each utility function. Verify that, for these functions, the change in the marginal utility of one good due to a change in the other good is the same, no matter which good is chosen first.
   (c) Find the marginal rate of substitution of x_1 for x_2 for each utility function, and show that they are all identical.
   (d) From the above, which value, that derived in (b) or in (c), above, would you expect to play a positive role in the theory of consumer behavior?

2 Consider the two utility functions
(i) $U = x_1 e^{x_2}$ (ii) $V = x_2 + \log x_1$
   (a) Answer the same questions as in problem 1.
   (b) Verify that three of the four second partials of V are identically 0, whereas for U, those three are all $\neq 0$. Can it be that these two utility functions nonetheless imply identical behavior on the part of the consumer? (*Answer:* Yes! *Moral:* Beware of rates of change of marginal utilities.)

3 Consider the production function $y = L^\alpha K^{1-\alpha}$; where $L =$ labor, $K =$ capital, $y =$ output, and α is restricted to the values $0 < \alpha < 1$. (This type of production function is called *Cobb-Douglas.*)
   (a) Find the marginal products of labor and capital, MP_L and MP_K, respectively.
   (b) Find the rates of change of these marginal products due to changes in both labor and capital. Verify that the rate of change of MP_L with respect to K is the same as that of MP_K with respect to L.
   (c) Does the law of diminishing marginal productivity hold for this production function?

4 For the above production function, show that $f_L L + f_K K \equiv y$. (This is an example of Euler's theorem, which will be explored later.)

5 The theorem on invariance of second partials to the order of differentiation breaks down when the second partials are not continuous. Those students who know what *continuous* means to a mathematician should try to make up a function whose second partials *exist* but are not continuous.

6 Let $y = L^\alpha K^{1-\alpha}$ represent society's production function. Suppose L and K both grow at constant, though different, rates, i.e., let $L = L_0 e^{nt}$, $K = K_0 e^{mt}$, where t represents "time." Find dy/dt by direct substitution and by the chain rule.

7 Let $U = f(x_1, x_2)$ be a utility function, and let $V(x_1, x_2) = F(U)$, where $F'(U) > 0$. (V is a monotonic transformation of U.)
   (a) Show that $V_1/V_2 = U_1/U_2$.
   (b) Find V_{ij} in terms of U_{ij}, etc., $i, j = 1, 2$. Show that in general U_{ij} and V_{ij} need not have the same sign.

8 Consider the utility function $U = x_1^{1/3} x_2^{2/3}$. The demand curves associated with U are $x_1 = M/3p_1$, $x_2 = 2M/3p_2$, as will be shown later. Find the rates of change of U with respect to changes in each price and money income. Do the signs of these expressions agree with your intuition?

9 Let $y = f(x_1, x_2) \equiv g(x_1 - x_2)$. Let $u = x_1 - x_2$. Show that

$$\partial y/\partial u \equiv \partial y/\partial x_1 \equiv -\partial y/\partial x_2, \quad \partial^2 y/\partial u^2 \equiv \partial^2 y/\partial x_1^2 \equiv \partial^2 y/\partial x_2^2.$$

3.7 HOMOGENEOUS FUNCTIONS AND EULER'S THEOREM

In order to efficiently study the structure of many important economic models, it is necessary to first discuss an important class of functions known as *homogeneous* functions. The interest in these functions arose from a problem in the economic theory of distribution. The development of marginal productivity theory by Marshall and others led to the conclusion that factors of production would be paid the value of their marginal products. (This will be studied in the next and subsequent chapters in more detail.) Roughly speaking, factors would be hired until their contribution to the output of the firm just equaled the cost of acquiring additional units of that factor. Letting $y = f(x_1, x_2)$ be the firm's production function, and letting w_i denote the wage of factor x_i and p the price of the firm's output, the rule developed was that

$$pMP_i = pf_i = w_i$$

where $f_i = \partial f / \partial x_i$. But this analysis was developed in a "partial equilibrium" framework; that is, each factor was analyzed independently. The question then arose, how is it possible to be sure that the firm was capable of making these payments to both factors? All factor payments had to be derived from the output produced by the firm. Would enough output be produced (or perhaps would too much be produced, leaving the excess unclaimed) to be able to pay each unit of each factor the value of its marginal product?

A theorem developed by the great Swiss mathematician Euler (pronounced "Oiler"—for some reason this name is never anglicized) came to the rescue of this analysis. (It leads to other problems, but those will be deferred.) It turns out that if the production function exhibits constant returns to scale, then the sum of the factor payments will identically equal total output. Mathematically, if each factor x_i is paid $w_i = pf_i$, then the total payment to all x_i is $w_i x_i = pf_i x_i$. Total payments to both factors is thus

$$pf_1 x_1 + pf_2 x_2 = p(f_1 x_1 + f_2 x_2)$$

But, as we shall see, constant returns to scale production functions have the convenient property that, identically,

$$f_1 x_1 + f_2 x_2 \equiv y = f(x_1, x_2)$$

Hence, in this case,

$$w_1 x_1 + w_2 x_2 = pf_1 x_1 + pf_2 x_2 = p(f_1 x_1 + f_2 x_2) = py$$

or, total costs identically equal total revenues, and the product of the firm is exactly "exhausted" in making payments to all the factors.

How is the feature of *constant returns to scale* characterized? This means that if each factor is increased by the same proportion, output will increase by a like proportion. Mathematically, a production function $y = f(x_1, \ldots, x_n)$ exhibits constant returns to scale if

$$f(tx_1, \ldots, tx_n) \equiv tf(x_1, \ldots, x_n) \tag{3-33}$$

Note the identity sign: this proportionality of output and inputs must hold for all x_i's and all t. If, for example, all inputs are doubled, output will double, starting at any input combination.

The relation (3-33) is a special case of the more general mathematical notion of homogeneity of functions.

Definition A function $f(x_1, \ldots, x_n)$ is said to be homogeneous of degree r if, and only if,

$$f(tx_1, \ldots, tx_n) \equiv t^r f(x_1, \ldots, x_n) \tag{3-34}$$

That is, changing all arguments of the function by the same proportion t results in a change in the value of the function by an amount t^r, identically. Note again the identity sign—this is not an equation which holds only at one or a few points; the above relation is to hold for all $t, x_1, \ldots, x_n$. Constant returns to scale is the special case where a production function is homogeneous of degree one. Homogeneity of degree one is often called *linear homogeneity*.

Example 1 Consider the very famous Cobb-Douglas production function, $y = L^\alpha K^{1-\alpha} = f(L, K)$, where $L = $ labor, $K = $ capital. This production function is homogeneous of degree one; i.e., it exhibits constant returns to scale. Suppose labor and capital are changed by some factor t. Then,

$$f(tL, tK) \equiv (tL)^\alpha (tK)^{1-\alpha} \equiv t^\alpha L^\alpha t^{1-\alpha} K^{1-\alpha}$$

$$\equiv t^{\alpha+(1-\alpha)} L^\alpha K^{1-\alpha} \equiv t L^\alpha K^{1-\alpha} \equiv tf(L, K)$$

Output $f(L, K)$ is affected in exactly the same proportion, t, as are both inputs.

Consider now another important area in which the notion of homogeneity arises. In the theory of the consumer (also to be discussed later) individuals are presumed to possess demand functions for the goods and services they consume. If $p_1, \ldots, p_n$ represents the money prices of the goods $x_1, \ldots, x_n$ that a person actually consumes, and if M represents the consumer's money income, the ordinary demand curves are representable as

$$x_i = x_i^*(p_1, \ldots, p_n, M) \tag{3-35}$$

That is, the quantity consumed of any good x_i depends on its price p_i, all other relevant prices, and money income, M.

How would we expect the consumer to react to a proportionate change in *all* prices, with the same proportionate change in his or her money income? Although a formal proof must wait until a later chapter, we should expect *no change* in consumption under these conditions. Economists (for good reason) in general assert that it is only *relative* price changes, not absolute prices changes that matter in consumers' decisions.

What is being asserted here, mathematically? We are asserting homogeneity of degree zero of the above demand equations, i.e.,

$$x_i^*(tp_1, \ldots, tp_n, tM) \equiv t^0 x_i^*(p_1, \ldots, p_n, M) \equiv x_i^*(p_1, \ldots, p_n, M)$$

The functional value is to be unchanged by proportionate change in all the independent variables; this is precisely homogeneity of degree zero. The demands for goods and services are not to depend on the *absolute* levels of prices and income.† The theoretical reasons for asserting this proposition will become clearer in later chapters; our purpose here is only to illustrate and motivate the usefulness of the concept of homogeneity of functions.

Consider now the Cobb-Douglas production function again, $y = L^\alpha K^{1-\alpha} \equiv f(L, K)$. The marginal products of labor and capital are, respectively,

$$MP_L = f_L = \alpha L^{\alpha-1} K^{1-\alpha} = \alpha\left(\frac{K}{L}\right)^{1-\alpha}$$

$$MP_K = f_K = (1 - \alpha)L^\alpha K^{-\alpha} = (1 - \alpha)\left(\frac{K}{L}\right)^{-\alpha}$$

These marginal products exhibit a feature worth noting: They can be written as functions of the *ratios* of the two inputs. They are independent of the absolute value of either input. Only their proportion to one another counts.

Because of this dependence only on ratios, the marginal products of the Cobb-Douglas function are homogeneous of degree zero:

$$MP_L(tL, tK) = \alpha\left(\frac{tK}{tL}\right)^{1-\alpha} = \alpha\left(\frac{K}{L}\right)^{1-\alpha} = MP_L(L, K)$$

Similarly,

$$MP_K(tL, tK) = (1 - \alpha)\left(\frac{tK}{tL}\right)^{-\alpha} = (1 - \alpha)\left(\frac{K}{L}\right)^{-\alpha} = MP_K(L, K)$$

If labor and capital are changed, by the same proportion, say they are both doubled, the marginal products of labor and capital will be unaffected. Geometrically, changing each input by the same proportion means moving along a ray out of the origin, through the original point. At every point along any such ray, the marginal products of the Cobb-Douglas production function (and others?) are the same.

To what extent, if any, are these results peculiar to the Cobb-Douglas functions; i.e., to what extent do other functions exhibit the same or similar properties? Consider, first, any function $f(x_1, \ldots, x_n)$ which is homogeneous of degree zero. By definition,

$$f(tx_1, tx_2, \ldots, tx_n) \equiv f(x_1, x_2, \ldots, x_n)$$

Since this holds for *any* t, let $t = 1/x_1$. Then we have

$$f(x_1, x_2, \ldots, x_n) \equiv f\left(1, \frac{x_2}{x_1}, \ldots, \frac{x_n}{x_1}\right) \equiv g\left(\frac{x_2}{x_1}, \ldots, \frac{x_n}{x_1}\right)$$

---

† There was a time, in the macroeconomics literature, when this homogeneity of demand functions was denied, under the name "money illusion." It was asserted that a completely neutral inflation would lead an economy out of depression; that even though people were not in fact richer, a higher money income (together with proportionately higher money prices) would somehow make people "feel" richer, increasing their consumption expenditures. This line of argument has been largely abandoned.

Similarly, we could let $t = 1/x_i$. What the above shows is that *any* function which is homogeneous of degree zero is representable as a function of the *ratios* of the independent variables to any one such variable. Hence, that the marginal products of the Cobb-Douglas function were representable as functions of the capital-labor ratios is *not* peculiar to that production function; it will hold for any marginal product functions which are homogeneous of degree zero.

What, then, are the conditions that the marginal products be homogeneous of degree zero? The answer is given, in a more general form, by the following theorem:

Theorem 1 If $f(x_1, x_2, \ldots, x_n)$ is homogeneous of degree r, then the first partials $f_1, \ldots, f_n$ are homogeneous of degree $r - 1$.

PROOF By assumption, $f(tx_1, \ldots, tx_n) \equiv t^r f(x_1, \ldots, x_n)$. Since this is an identity, it is valid to differentiate both sides with respect to x_i

$$\frac{\partial f}{\partial (tx_i)} \frac{\partial (tx_i)}{\partial x_i} \equiv t^r \frac{\partial f}{\partial x_i}$$

However, $\partial(tx_i)/\partial x_i = t$. Dividing both sides of the identity by t therefore yields

$$\frac{\partial f}{\partial (tx_i)} \equiv t^{r-1} \frac{\partial f}{\partial x_i}$$

But this says that the function f_i, evaluated at $(tx_1, \ldots, tx_n)$ equals $t^{r-1} f_i(x_1, \ldots, x_n)$. Hence, f_i is homogeneous of degree $r - 1$.

If $y = f(x_1, \ldots, x_n)$ is any production function exhibiting constant returns to scale, the marginal products are homogeneous of degree zero. That is, the marginal products are the same at every point along any ray through the origin. The Cobb-Douglas function is thus only a special case of this theorem.

Homogeneity of any degree implies that the slopes of the level curves of the function are unchanged along any ray through the origin. This can be shown as follows: Let $y = f(x_1, \ldots, x_n)$ be a production function, for example, that is homogeneous of degree r. The slope of an isoquant in the x_i, x_j plane is

$$\frac{dx_j}{dx_i} = \frac{-f_i}{f_j}$$

But

$$\frac{f_i(tx_1, \ldots, tx_n)}{f_j(tx_1, \ldots, tx_n)} \equiv \frac{t^{r-1} f_i(x_1, \ldots, x_n)}{t^{r-1} f_j(x_1, \ldots, x_n)}$$

$$\equiv \frac{f_i(x_1, \ldots, x_n)}{f_j(x_1, \ldots, x_n)}$$

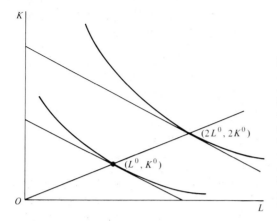

Figure 3-5 *Invariance of the Slope of Isoquants to a Proportionate Increase in Each Factor.* Consider any point (L^0, K^0). Suppose each input is doubled. If the production function is homogeneous of any degree, the slope of the isoquant, $-f_L/f_K$, will be the same at $(2L^0, 2K^0)$ as at (L^0, K^0). This property is known as *homotheticity*. The most general functions that exhibit this property can be written $F(f(x_1, \ldots, x_n))$ where $f(x_1, \ldots, x_n)$ is homogeneous of any degree and $F' \neq 0$.

Thus, the slope of any isoquant evaluated along a radial expansion of an initial point is identical to the slope at the original point. In other words, the ratios of the marginal products along any ray from the origin remain unchanged for homogeneous functions. The level curves are thus radial blowups or reductions of each other. This situation is depicted in Fig. 3-5.

The following describes a related class of production functions. Let $y = f(x_1, \ldots, x_n)$ be homogeneous of degree r, and let $z = F(y)$, where $F'(y) > 0$. $[F(y)$ is a monotonic transformation of y.] The function $z(x_1, \ldots, x_n)$ is called a *homothetic function*. It is easy to show that homothetic functions also preserve the property that slopes along a radial blowup remain unchanged; i.e., that the slopes of isoquants $z(tx_1, \ldots, tx_n)$ are the same as at $z(x_1, \ldots, x_n)$, and this is left to the student as an exercise. It is less than easy to show, but nonetheless true, that this is the most general class of production functions which have this property.†

Example 2 Consider the function $z = g(L, K) = F(y)$, where $y = L^\alpha K^{1-\alpha}$, and $F(y) = \log y$. Then

$$z = F(L^\alpha K^{1-\alpha}) \equiv \log L^\alpha K^{1-\alpha} \equiv \alpha \log L + (1 - \alpha) \log K$$

That is, the original function $L^\alpha K^{1-\alpha}$ is transformed by the function "F," in this case "log." We note that $F'(y) = 1/y > 0$, for positive L, K. Now $L^\alpha K^{1-\alpha}$ is homogeneous of degree 1, as noted before, but $\log (L^\alpha K^{1-\alpha})$ is *not* a homogeneous function:

$$g(tL, tK) \equiv \alpha \log tL + (1 - \alpha) \log tK$$

$$\equiv \alpha(\log t + \log L) + (1 - \alpha)(\log t + \log K)$$

$$\equiv \log t + \log L^\alpha K^{1-\alpha} \neq t^r g(L, K)$$

---

† See, e.g., F. W. McElroy, Returns to Scale, Euler's theorem, and the Form of Production Functions, *Econometrica*, **37**(2): 275–279 (1969).

However, $g(L, K) = \alpha \log L + (1 - \alpha)\log K$ is homothetic: The slope of a level curve is

$$\frac{-g_L}{g_K} = \frac{-\alpha/L}{(1 - \alpha)/K} = \frac{-\alpha}{1 - \alpha}\frac{K}{L}$$

As before, $-g_L/g_K$ is unaffected by changing K and L by a factor of t; the t's cancel in the expression K/L and, hence, the slope of the level curves of $\log L^\alpha K^{1-\alpha}$ are the same along any ray out of the origin. This function is *not* homogeneous but it *is* homothetic.

Suppose that instead of defining homothetic functions as $F(f(x_1, \ldots, x_n))$, where f is homogeneous of degree r, that instead we restrict f to be linearly homogeneous; i.e., homogeneous of degree 1. Though it might not seem so at first, this latter definition is just as general as the first definition; i.e., no functions are left out by so doing. The reason is that any homogeneous function of degree r can be converted to a linear homogeneous function by taking the rth root of $f(x_1, \ldots, x_n)$. Then, $[f(x_1, \ldots, x_n)]^{1/r}$ can be transformed by some function, F. Thus, since we can always consider F to be a composite of two transformations, the first of which takes the rth root of f, and the second, which operates on that, no generality is lost by defining homothetic functions as transformations of *linear* homogeneous functions.

Example 3 Let $y = f(x_1, x_2) = x_1 x_2$. Here, $f(x_1, x_2)$ is homogeneous of degree 2. Let

$$g(x_1, x_2) = F(f(x_1, x_2)) = \log(x_1 x_2) = \log x_1 + \log x_2$$

This function is homothetic but not homogeneous. How could $g(x_1, x_2)$ be constructed out of a *linear* homogeneous function? Let

$$g(x_1, x_2) = 2 \log(x_1 x_2)^{1/2}$$

Thus, $$g(x_1, x_2) = 2F(\phi(f(x_1, x_2)))$$

where ϕ means "take square root" and F is log, as before. Then the same function

$$g(x_1, x_2) = \log x_1 + \log x_2$$

is constructed as a transformation of the linear homogeneous function $(x_1 x_2)^{1/2}$.

We now prove the main theorem of this section.

Theorem 2 (Euler's theorem) Suppose $f(x_1, \ldots, x_n)$ is homogeneous of degree r. Then

$$\frac{\partial f}{\partial x_1} x_1 + \cdots + \frac{\partial f}{\partial x_n} x_n \equiv rf(x_1, \ldots, x_n)$$

Note the identity sign: this is not an equation; rather, it holds for all $x_1, \ldots,$ x_n. The two sides are algebraically identical.

PROOF By the definition of homogeneity,

$$f(tx_1, \ldots, tx_n) \equiv t^r f(x_1, \ldots, x_n)$$

Since this identity holds for all values of $x_1, \ldots, x_n$, and t, differentiate both sides with respect to t, using the chain rule:

$$\frac{\partial f}{\partial(tx_1)} \frac{\partial(tx_1)}{\partial t} + \cdots + \frac{\partial f}{\partial(tx_n)} \frac{\partial(tx_n)}{\partial t} \equiv rt^{r-1} f(x_1, \ldots, x_n)$$

However, $\partial(tx_i)/\partial t = x_i$, thus

$$\frac{\partial f}{\partial tx_1} x_1 + \cdots + \frac{\partial f}{\partial tx_n} x_n \equiv rt^{r-1} f(x_1, \ldots, x_n)$$

This relation is also an identity which holds for all t and all $x_1, \ldots, x_n$; in particular it must hold for $t = 1$. Putting $t = 1$ in the above identity results in Euler's theorem.

An important special case of homogeneity is that of homogeneity of degree 1, also called *linear homogeneity*. In this case, $r = 1$, and thus the Euler identity yields $\Sigma f_i x_i \equiv f(x_1, \ldots, x_n)$. This is precisely the property that was alluded to in the beginning of this section, concerning constant returns to scale and exhaustion of the product. When $r = 1$ (linear homogeneity), Euler's theorem says that the sum of the marginal products of each factor times the level of use of that factor exactly and identically adds up to total output. Thus, marginal productivity theory is consistent with itself in that case.

Another interesting case is when $f(x_1, \ldots, x_n)$ is homogeneous of degree zero. Then, Euler's theorem yields

$$\Sigma f_i x_i \equiv 0$$

This formula will be used in deriving some properties of demand functions for consumers and firms, both of which exhibit this type of homogeneity.

Example 4 Consider again the Cobb-Douglas function $y = L^\alpha K^{1-\alpha} = f(L, K)$. This function is homogeneous of degree 1, i.e., $r = 1$. We have $f_L = \alpha L^{-1} K^{1-\alpha}, f_K = (1-\alpha) L^\alpha K^{-\alpha}$. Then the left-hand side of the Euler identity becomes

$$f_L L + f_K K \equiv \alpha L^{-1} K^{1-\alpha} L + (1-\alpha) L^\alpha K^{-\alpha} K$$

$$\equiv \alpha L^\alpha K^{1-\alpha} + (1-\alpha) L^\alpha K^{1-\alpha}$$

$$\equiv (\alpha + 1 - \alpha) L^\alpha K^{1-\alpha} \equiv f(L, K)$$

Thus, $f_L L + f_K K$ is identically $L^\alpha K^{1-\alpha}$, the original production function.

Example 5 Let $y = x_1^{\alpha_1} x_2^{\alpha_2} = f(x_1, x_2)$. Then

$$f_1 = \alpha_1 x_1^{\alpha_1 - 1} x_2^{\alpha_2} \qquad f_2 = \alpha_2 x_1^{\alpha_1} x_2^{\alpha_2 - 1}$$

Then

$$f_1 x_1 + f_2 x_2 \equiv \alpha_1 x_1^{\alpha_1 - 1} x_2^{\alpha_2} x_1 + \alpha_2 x_1^{\alpha_1} x_2^{\alpha_2 - 1} x_2$$

$$\equiv \alpha_1 x_1^{\alpha_1} x_2^{\alpha_2} + \alpha_2 x_1^{\alpha_1} x_2^{\alpha_2}$$

$$\equiv (\alpha_1 + \alpha_2) x_1^{\alpha_1} x_2^{\alpha_2} \equiv (\alpha_1 + \alpha_2) f(x_1, x_2)$$

This function is homogeneous of degree $\alpha_1 + \alpha_2$; hence, that multiple appears on the right-hand side of the Euler identity.

Example 6 Consider a firm with a linear homogeneous production function, $y = f(L, K)$. By Euler's theorem

$$f_L L + f_K K \equiv y$$

Dividing by L and rearranging terms

$$f_K \frac{K}{L} \equiv \frac{y}{L} - f_L = \text{AP}_L - \text{MP}_L$$

Recall that if an average curve $A(x)$ is rising, then the associated marginal curve $M(x)$ lies *above* the average, i.e., $M(x) > A(x)$. Likewise, $A(x)$ is falling if and only if $M(x) < A(x)$. The above equation thus says that if the average product of labor is *rising*, the marginal product of capital f_K must be *negative*. Similar manipulation shows that if the average product of capital is rising, the marginal product of labor is negative. The stage of production where AP_L is rising is called *stage I; stage II* occurs when AP_L is falling but $\text{MP}_L > 0$; $\text{MP}_L < 0$ characterizes *stage III*. The above equation shows that for *linear homogeneous* production functions, stage I for labor is stage III for capital, and *vice versa*.

Example 7 Consider a two-good world with goods x_1 and x_2 which sell at prices p_1, p_2, respectively. Suppose that a consumer with money income M has the following demand function for x_1:

$$x_1 = \frac{M p_2}{p_1^2}$$

Show that the demand for this good is unaffected by a "balanced" or neutral inflation. Show also that Euler's theorem holds for this function.

Suppose money income M and both prices increase by the same proportion t. Then $x_1(tp_1, tp_2, tM) \equiv tM(tp_2/t^2 p_1^2) \equiv M p_2/p_1^2 \equiv x_1(p_1, p_2, M)$.

Hence, the consumer is unaffected by a change in absolute prices alone; i.e., this demand function is homogeneous of degree zero. Now,

$$\frac{\partial x_1}{\partial p_1} = \frac{-2Mp_2}{p_1^3}$$

$$\frac{\partial x_1}{\partial p_2} = \frac{M}{p_1^2}$$

$$\frac{\partial x_1}{\partial M} = \frac{p_2}{p_1^2}$$

Hence, $\quad \dfrac{\partial x_1}{\partial p_1} p_1 + \dfrac{\partial x_1}{\partial p_2} p_2 + \dfrac{\partial x_1}{\partial M} M \equiv \dfrac{-2Mp_2}{p_1^2} + \dfrac{Mp_2}{p_1^2} + \dfrac{Mp_2}{p_1^2} \equiv 0$

In many instances of dealing with homogeneous functions, what is desired is not Euler's theorem per se, but rather its converse. Suppose, for example, the product of a firm was exhausted for any input combination, i.e., we somehow knew that $\Sigma f_i x_i \equiv f(x_1, \ldots, x_n)$. Would this imply that the firm is linear homogeneous? The answer is in the affirmative.

Theorem 3 (The converse of Euler's theorem) Suppose

$$f_1 x_1 + \cdots + f_n x_n \equiv rf(x_1, \ldots, x_n)$$

for all $x_1, \ldots, x_n$. Then

$$f(tx_1, \ldots, tx_n) \equiv t^r f(x_1, \ldots, x_n)$$

that is, $f(x_1, \ldots, x_n)$ is homogeneous of degree r.

The proof of this theorem is given in the appendix to this chapter.

PROBLEMS

1 Show that the following functions are homogeneous and verify that Euler's theorem holds.
   (a) $f(x_1, x_2) = x_1 x_2^2$ (b) $f(x_1, x_2) = x_1 x_2 + x_2^2$
   (c) $f(x_1, x_2) = (x_1 + x_2)/(x_1^2 - 2x_2^2)$ (d) $f(x_1, x_2) = x_1^2/(x_1 x_2 - x_2^2)$
   (e) $f(x_1, x_2) = x_1$

2 Show that the following functions are *homothetic*.
   (a) $y = \log x_1 + \log x_2$ (b) $y = e^{x_1 x_2}$
   (c) $y = (x_1 x_2)^2 - x_1 x_2$ (d) $y = \log(x_1 x_2) + e^{x_1 x_2}$
   (e) $y = \log(x_1^2 + x_1 x_2)^2$

3 Let $f(x_1, x_2) = A(\alpha x_1^{-\rho} + (1 - \alpha)x_2^{-\rho})^{-1/\rho}$. Show that $f(x_1, x_2)$ is homogeneous of degree 1. (This production function is called a constant elasticity of substitution, or CES, production function.) Its properties will be investigated in Chap. 10.

4 Let $f(x_1, x_2) = F(h(x_1, x_2))$ where h is homogeneous of degree r and $F' > 0$ (f is a homothetic function). Show that the expansion paths of f are straight lines; i.e., that the level curves of f have the same slope along any ray out of the origin.

5 Let $f(x_1, x_2)$ be homogeneous of degree 1. Show that $f_{11} x_1 + f_{12} x_2 \equiv 0$ [by considering the homogeneity of $f_1(x_1, x_2)$].

6 Let $f(x_1, \ldots, x_n)$ be homogeneous of degree r in *the first k variables only*, i.e., $f(tx_1, \ldots, tx_k, x_{k+1}, \ldots, x_n) \equiv t^r f(x_1, \ldots, x_n)$. Show that

$$\sum_{i=1}^{k} f_i x_i \equiv rf(x_1, \ldots, x_n)$$

APPENDIX TO CHAPTER 3

We now present some additional theorems on homogeneous functions. We begin with the converse of Euler's theorem.

Theorem 3 (The Converse of Euler's Theorem) Suppose

$$f_1 x_1 + f_2 x_2 + \cdots + f_n x_n \equiv rf(x_1, \ldots, x_n)$$

for all $x_1, \ldots, x_n$. Then $f(tx_1, \ldots, tx_n) \equiv t^r f(x_1, \ldots, x_n)$; that is, $f(x_1, \ldots, x_n)$ is homogeneous of degree r.†

PROOF (To save notational clutter, we shall prove the case for a function of only two independent variables, x_1, x_2. The generalization to n variables is routine.)

Consider any arbitrary point (x_1^0, x_2^0). Construct the function

$$z = \phi(t) = f(tx_1^0, tx_2^0)$$

Differentiating with respect to t yields, using the chain rule,

$$\frac{dz}{dt} = \phi'(t) = x_1^0 f_1(tx_1^0, tx_2^0) + x_2^0 f_2(tx_1^0, tx_2^0) \qquad (3A-1)$$

By assumption, however, applying $f_1 x_1 + f_2 x_2 \equiv rf(x_1, x_2)$ at the point (tx_1^0, tx_2^0)

$$f_1(tx_1^0, tx_2^0)tx_1^0 + f_2(tx_1^0, tx_2^0)tx_2^0 \equiv rf(tx_1^0, tx_2^0) \qquad (3A-2)$$

By inspection of equations (3A-1) and (3A-2)

$$t\phi'(t) \equiv rf(tx_1^0, tx_2^0) \equiv r\phi(t) \qquad (3A-3)$$

---

† This theorem technically holds only for positive values of t. Consider the function $f(x_1, x_2) = (x_1^2 + x_2^2)^{3/2}$. Then $f(tx_1, tx_2) = |t|^3 f(x_1, x_2)$ since the square root is always taken as positive. This type of function would satisfy the proof of theorem 3; it however is not homogeneous for all values of t, but rather just for $t > 0$.

Equation (3A-3) is a differential equation that is easy to solve:† We have $z = \phi(t)$, $\phi'(t) = dz/dt$; hence (3A-3) is equivalent to

$$t \frac{dz}{dt} \equiv rz$$

Grouping each variable,

$$\frac{dz}{z} \equiv r \frac{dt}{t}$$

Integrating both sides yields

$$\int \frac{dz}{z} \equiv r \int \frac{dt}{t} + C'$$

where C' is the constant of integration. But $\int (dz/z) \equiv \log z$, $\int (dt/t) \equiv \log t$, and letting $C' \equiv \log C$ for convenience, the solution to (3A-3) is

$$\log z \equiv r \log t + \log C$$

or

$$\equiv \log Ct^r$$

Taking antilogs, the solution of the differential equation (3A-3) is

$$z \equiv \phi(t) \equiv Ct^r \tag{3A-4}$$

That this is a solution to equation (3A-3) can be verified by substituting this expression into that differential equation. The constant of integration can be evaluated by setting $t = 1$:

$$C \cdot 1^r = C = \phi(1) = f(x_1^0, x_2^0)$$

Hence, $\phi(t) = f(tx_1^0, tx_2^0) \equiv t^r f(x_1^0, x_2^0)$. But this is precisely the definition of homogeneity of degree r! Since (x_1^0, x_2^0) was any point in the $x_1 x_2$ plane, the theorem (the converse of Euler's theorem) is proven.

The following theorem discusses an easy but sometimes important special case of homogeneity—that of homogeneity of functions of only one variable.

Theorem 4 Suppose $y = f(x)$ is a function of one variable only, x. If $f(x)$ is homogeneous of degree r, then $f(x) \equiv kx^r$. That is, the simple polynomial x^r is the only possible functional form, for one variable, which is homogeneous of degree r.

PROOF From Euler's theorem

$$f'(x)x = rf(x)$$

or

$$\frac{dy}{dx} x = ry$$

---

† The interested student can review Sec. 2.13 for a review of these methods.

That is, all such homogeneous functions must satisfy this differential equation. We can therefore discover this class of functions by solving that equation and, it turns out, this is an easy differential equation to solve.

Collecting variables and integrating,

$$\frac{dy}{y} = r\frac{dx}{x}$$

$$\int \frac{dy}{y} = \log y, \int r\frac{dx}{x} = r \log x = \log x^r$$

Therefore,

$$\log y = \log x^r + \log k = \log kx^r$$

or, taking antilogs,

$$y = kx^r \qquad \text{Q.E.D.}$$

Consider again the definition of homogeneity

$$f(tx_1, \ldots, tx_n) \equiv t^r f(x_1, \ldots, x_n)$$

Is it possible to generalize this definition, replacing t^r by some more general function of t, say $\phi(t)$? That is, are there nonhomogeneous functions $f(x_1, \ldots, x_n)$ which satisfy

$$f(tx_1, \ldots, tx_n) \equiv \phi(t)f(x_1, \ldots, x_n) \tag{3A-5}$$

In fact, there are no such functions. That is, any function $f(x_1, \ldots, x_n)$ which satisfies equation (3A-5) is homogeneous of some degree, as the following *lemma* shows. We will have occasion to use this result in the next theorem, which is used in a later chapter.

Lemma Consider the class of functions $f(x_1, \ldots, x_n)$ such that

$$f(tx_1, \ldots, tx_n) \equiv \phi(t)f(x_1, \ldots, x_n) \tag{3A-5}$$

Then $\phi(t) = t^r$, for some value of r.

We will prove this for the case of two variables; the generalization to n variables is straightforward.

PROOF Differentiate equation (3A-5) with respect to t:

$$f_1(tx_1, tx_2)x_1 + f_2(tx_1, tx_2)x_2 \equiv \phi'(t)f(x_1, x_2) \tag{3A-6}$$

In fact, $\phi(t)$ can be given by setting x_1 and x_2 equal to some arbitrary numbers, e.g., $x_1 = x_2 = 1$. Then from equation (3A-5)

$$\phi(t) = \frac{f(t, t)}{f(1, 1)}$$

and from equation (3A-6)

$$\phi'(t) = \frac{f_1(t, t) + f_2(t, t)}{f(1, 1)}$$

Setting $t = 1$, one obtains

$$f_1 x_1 + f_2 x_2 \equiv \phi'(1)f \tag{3A-7}$$

Now $\phi'(1)$ is merely some constant. Whatever $\phi(t)$ is, its derivative, evaluated at $t = 1$, is some real number. But, using the converse of Euler's theorem (Theorem 3), equation (3A-7) says that $f(x_1, x_2)$ is homogeneous of degree $\phi'(1)$, or, $f(tx_1, tx_2) \equiv t^{\phi'(1)}f(x_1, x_2)$. Thus, no such generalization of the notion of homogeneity as indicated by equation (3A-5) is possible.

Consider now functions which are separable into the product of two functions, each a function of different variables:

Let $f(x_2, \ldots, x_n, y_1, \ldots, y_m) \equiv g(x_1, \ldots, x_n)h(y_1, \ldots, y_m)$. (The different variable names x and y are merely to aid in identification of the variables and the functions. There is no other significance to the distinction of x_i's and y_i's.) It will be convenient to simply designate the variables $x_1, \ldots, x_n$ simply as $\mathbf{x}$, and $y_1, \ldots, y_m$ as $\mathbf{y}$. This type of *vector* notation will be used occasionally throughout the book. Suppose $f(\mathbf{x}, \mathbf{y}) = g(\mathbf{x})h(\mathbf{y})$ is homogeneous of some degree r. What can be inferred about the functions $g(\mathbf{x})$ and $h(\mathbf{y})$?

Theorem 5 Let $f(\mathbf{x}, \mathbf{y}) \equiv g(\mathbf{x})h(\mathbf{y})$, where $\mathbf{x} = (x_1, \ldots, x_n)$ and $\mathbf{y} = (y_1, \ldots, y_m)$. Then $f(\mathbf{x}, \mathbf{y})$ is homogeneous of degree r in $(\mathbf{x}, \mathbf{y})$ if and only if $g(\mathbf{x})$ is homogeneous of some degree p and $h(\mathbf{y})$ is homogeneous of some degree $r - p$.

PROOF If $g(\mathbf{x})$ and $h(\mathbf{y})$ are homogeneous of degree p and $r - p$, respectively, then $g(t\mathbf{x}) = t^p g(\mathbf{x})$, $h(t\mathbf{y}) = t^{r-p}h(\mathbf{y})$. Then

$$f(t\mathbf{x}, t\mathbf{y}) \equiv g(t\mathbf{x})h(t\mathbf{y}) \equiv t^p g(\mathbf{x})t^{r-p}h(\mathbf{y}) \equiv t^r g(\mathbf{x})h(\mathbf{y})$$

Thus, the "if" part of the theorem is proven. Now consider the converse part. Let $f(\mathbf{x}, \mathbf{y})$ be homogeneous of some degree r. Then

$$g(t\mathbf{x})h(t\mathbf{y}) \equiv t^r g(\mathbf{x})h(\mathbf{y})$$

Rearranging
$$\frac{g(t\mathbf{x})}{g(\mathbf{x})} \equiv t^r \frac{h(\mathbf{y})}{h(t\mathbf{y})} \tag{3A-8}$$

Now the left-hand side of equation (3A-8) is a function of $\mathbf{x}$ and t only; it is independent of $\mathbf{y}$. The right-hand side, similarly, is independent of $\mathbf{x}$. But then the value of $g(t\mathbf{x})/g(\mathbf{x})$ cannot depend on $\mathbf{x}$ either, for if it did, the right-hand side would change value when $\mathbf{x}$ changed, which is impossible. Hence, $g(t\mathbf{x})/g(\mathbf{x})$ is a function of t only, i.e.,

$$\frac{g(t\mathbf{x})}{g(\mathbf{x})} \equiv \phi(t)$$

Or
$$g(t\mathbf{x}) \equiv \phi(t)g(\mathbf{x}) \tag{3A-9}$$

However, by the previous lemma, equation (3A-9) implies that $g(\mathbf{x})$ is homogeneous of some degree p. Using the exact same reasoning, $h(\mathbf{y})$ must also be homogeneous of some degree q. If $g(\mathbf{x})$ and $h(\mathbf{y})$ are both homogeneous, however, and $f(\mathbf{x}, \mathbf{y})$ is homogeneous of degree r, then clearly $q = r - p$, since

$$t^r f(\mathbf{x}, \mathbf{y}) \equiv f(t\mathbf{x}, t\mathbf{y}) \equiv g(t\mathbf{x})h(t\mathbf{y}) \equiv t^p g(\mathbf{x})t^q h(\mathbf{y})$$

$$\equiv t^{p+q}g(\mathbf{x})h(\mathbf{y}) \equiv t^{p+q}f(\mathbf{x}, \mathbf{y})$$

Hence $\qquad r = p + q \qquad$ Q.E.D.

Suppose now we are given some function $y = f(x_1, \ldots, x_n)$ which is homogeneous of degree r. Suppose some monotonic transformation is applied to $f(x_1, \ldots, x_n)$ yielding a new function $z = F(y) = F(f(x_1, \ldots, x_n)) = g(x_1, \ldots, x_n)$. Suppose this new function g is also homogeneous, of some degree s. What kinds of transformations F will produce this situation, i.e., what types of transformations will convert homogeneous functions into other homogeneous functions? The answer is given in the following theorem, a result we will have occasion to use in the sections on production functions.

Theorem 6 Let $z = g(x_1, \ldots, x_n) = F(f(x_1, \ldots, x_n)) = F(y)$, where f is homogeneous of degree r, g is homogeneous of degree s, and $F' \neq 0$. Then $F(y) = ky^{s/r}$ where k is an arbitrary constant. That is, f and g are simple powers of one another; no other transformation of a homogeneous function will result in another homogeneous function.

PROOF Clearly, if $F(y) = ky^{s/r}$, the theorem is satisfied. To show that this is the *only* functional form possible, apply Euler's theorem (again, for notational simplicity, we shall do the two-variable case only. The generalization to n variables is immediate)

$$sz = g_1 x_1 + g_2 x_2 = F'f_1 x_1 + F'f_2 x_2 = F'(y)ry$$

Rewriting, $\qquad \dfrac{s}{r} z = \dfrac{dz}{dy} y$

The most general functional form, $z = F(y)$, allowed by the conditions of the theorem is the solution to this differential equation. Grouping variables

$$\frac{dz}{z} = \frac{s}{r}\frac{dy}{y}$$

Integrating both sides yields

$$\int \frac{dz}{z} = \frac{s}{r}\int \frac{dy}{y} + \log k$$

or $\qquad\qquad \log z = \log y^{s/r} + \log k = \log ky^{s/r}$

where $\log k$ is the arbitrary constant of integration. Hence, taking antilogs

$$z = F(y) = ky^{s/r}$$

most general functional form of F which transforms one homogeneous into another.

REFERENCES

calculus text, students might find the following works useful:

thematical Analysis for Economists," Macmillan & Co., Ltd., London, 1938.
Martin's Press.
ial and Integral Calculus," 2d ed., Interscience Publishers, Inc., New York, This is a classic work.

FOUR

UNCONSTRAINED MAXIMA AND MINIMA: TWO INDEPENDENT VARIABLES

4.1 FIRST-ORDER NECESSARY CONDITIONS

Postulates of some sort of maximizing behavior lead naturally to the specification of mathematical models which involve the maximization of some function of several variables. Most often, this maximization takes place subject to test conditions specifying constraints on the movements of the variables in addition to the specifications of values of parameters. The well-known model of utility-maximization is an example of such a model: the consumer is asserted to maximize a utility function subject to the condition that he or she not exceed a given budgetary expenditure. There are some important examples, however, of *unconstrained* maximization, such as the model of a profit-maximizing firm (which will be dealt with below). Since the unconstrained case is simpler, we begin the analysis there.

In models with just one independent variable, the first-order condition necessary for $y = f(x)$ to attain a stationary value is $dy/dx = f'(x) = 0$. That is, the line tangent to the curve $f(x)$ must be horizontal at the stationary point. The term *stationary point* rather than *maximum* or *minimum* is appropriate at this juncture. The property of having a horizontal tangent line is common to the functions $y = x^2$, $y = -x^2$ and $y = x^3$ at the point $x = 0$, $y = 0$. The first function has a minimum at the origin, the second, a maximum, and the third, neither. However it is clear that if the slope of the tangent line is *not* 0 (horizontal), then the function certainly cannot have either a maximum or a minimum. Hence $f'(x) = 0$ is a *necessary* but not sufficient condition for $y = f(x)$ to have a maximum (or minimum) value.

Suppose now that y is a function of two variables, that is, $y = f(x_1, x_2)$. What are the analogous necessary conditions for a maximum of this function? Proceeding intuitively from the case of one variable, it must necessarily be the case that at the point in question, the tangent *plane* must be horizontal. In order for the tangent plane to be horizontal, the first partials $\partial f/\partial x_1$, $\partial f/\partial x_2$ must be 0; that is, the function must be level in the x_1 and x_2 directions.

Because intuition, especially about the second-order conditions for maximization is often unreliable, the above argument will now be developed more rigorously. Let $y = f(x_1, x_2)$, and suppose we wish to consider the behavior of this function at some point $\mathbf{x}^0 = (x_1^0, x_2^0)$.† Instead of working with the whole function, however, consider the function evaluated along any (differentiable) curve which passes through the point $\mathbf{x}^0$. The reason for doing this is that it will enable us to convert a problem in two variables to one involving one variable only, a problem we already know how to solve. All such curves can be represented parametrically by $x_1 = x_1(t)$, $x_2 = x_2(t)$, with $x_1 = x_1^0$, $x_2 = x_2^0$ at $t = 0$. That is, as t varies in value, x_1 and x_2 vary, and hence the pair $[x_1(t), x_2(t)]$, denoted $\mathbf{x}(t)$, traces out the locus of some curve in the x_1x_2 plane. [Setting $x_1(0) = x_1^0$, $x_2(0) = x_2^0$ merely ensures that the curve passes through (x_1^0, x_2^0) for *some* value of t.]

Example 1 This parametric representation of a curve in the x_1x_2 plane was developed in Chap. 3. Again, suppose

$$x_1 = x_1^0 + h_1 t$$
$$x_2 = x_2^0 + h_2 t$$

where h_1 and h_2 are arbitrary constants. Then these equations represent the straight lines in the $x_1 x_2$ plane which pass through (x_1^0, x_2^0). Any such line can be generated by appropriate choice of h_1 and h_2.

Example 2 Let

$$x_1 = x_1^0 + t$$
$$x_2 = x_2^0 e^t$$

This parameterization represents an exponential curve. When $t = 0$, $x_1 = x_1^0$, $x_2 = x_2^0$; hence the curve passes through (x_1^0, x_2^0).

Example 3 A parameterization which occurs frequently in the physical sciences is

$$x = a \cos \theta$$
$$y = a \sin \theta$$

where $0 \le \theta \le 2\pi$. This represents the equation of a circle in the xy plane, with radius a and center at the origin.

---

† We will often find it convenient to use the vector notation $\mathbf{x} = (x_1, \ldots, x_n)$ wherein the single symbol $\mathbf{x}$ denotes multidimensional value.

The function $f(x_1, x_2)$ evaluated along some differentiable curve $\mathbf{x}(t) = (x_1(t), x_2(t))$ is $y(t) = f(x_1(t), x_2(t))$. If $f(x_1, x_2)$ is to achieve a maximum value at $\mathbf{x} = \mathbf{x}^0$, the function evaluated along all such curves must necessarily have a maximum. Hence $y(t)$ must have a maximum (at $t = 0$) for all curves $\mathbf{x}(t)$. But the condition for this is simply $y'(t) = 0$. Using this chain rule the first-order conditions for a maximum are therefore

$$\frac{dy}{dt} = y'(t) = f_1 \frac{dx_1}{dt} + f_2 \frac{dx_2}{dt} = 0 \tag{4-1}$$

However, dy/dt must be 0 for *all* curves $(x_1(t), x_2(t))$ passing through $\mathbf{x}^0$; i.e., for *all* values of dx_1/dt and dx_2/dt. That is, it must be possible to put any values of dx_1/dt, dx_2/dt into this relationship and still obtain $dy/dt = 0$. The only way this can be guaranteed is if $f_1 = f_2 = 0$. Hence a necessary condition for $f(x_1, x_2)$ to be maximized at x_1^0, x_2^0 is that the first partials of that function must be 0 at this point. The above conditions are, of course, only necessary conditions for y to achieve a stationary point; only the second derivative of $y(t)$ reveals whether (x_1^0, x_2^0) is in fact a maximum, a minimum, or neither.

The generalization to the n variable case is direct, and the derivation is identical to the above. For $y = f(x_1, x_2, \ldots, x_n)$ to be maximized at $\mathbf{x}^0 = (x_1^0, \ldots, x_n^0)$ it is necessary that all the first partial derivatives equal 0; that is, $f_i = 0$, $i = 1, \ldots, n$.

4.2 SUFFICIENT CONDITIONS FOR MAXIMA AND MINIMA

For functions of one variable, $y = f(x)$, a sufficient condition for $f(x)$ to have a maximum at $x = x^0$ is that, together with $f'(x^0) = 0$, $f''(x^0) < 0$. The condition $f''(x^0) < 0$ expresses the notion that the slope is decreasing, e.g., as one walked over the top of a hill, the ground would be first rising, then level at the top, then falling. Alternatively, the function is called "concave downward," or simply, concave, if $f''(x) < 0$. If $f(x_1, x_2)$ has a maximum at $\mathbf{x}^0$, then $y(t) = f(x_1(t), x_2(t))$ has a maximum for all curves $\mathbf{x}(t)$. Hence it must be the case that at the maximum point, $d^2y/dt^2 = y''(t) \leq 0$ for all such curves.

The issues here are considerably more subtle than the student may perceive at this point, as the next section will demonstrate. Although $y''(t) \leq 0$ is *necessary* for a maximum, it is not sufficient. By expanding $f(x_1, x_2)$ by a Taylor series for functions of two (or, more generally, n variables), it can be shown that if $y''(t) < 0$ at $t = 0$ (the maximum point), then the function $f(x_1, x_2)$ is concave downwards at (x_1^0, x_2^0). Thus, in that case, a maximum will be achieved if $f_1 = f_2 = 0$. This analysis will be presented in the appendix to this chapter.

Let us then evaluate $y''(t)$. Using the chain and product rules on equation (4-1),

$$y'(t) = f_1 x_1'(t) + f_2 x_2'(t)$$

one obtains (this was derived explicitly in Chap. 3)

$$\frac{d^2y}{dt^2} = f_1 \frac{d^2x_1}{dt^2} + f_2 \frac{d^2x_2}{dt^2} + f_{11}\left(\frac{dx_1}{dt}\right)^2 + 2f_{12}\frac{dx_1}{dt}\frac{dx_2}{dt} + f_{22}\left(\frac{dx_2}{dt}\right)^2 \quad (4\text{-}2)$$

However, this is evaluated at $(x_1, x_2) = (x_1^0, x_2^0)$, a stationary point; hence $f_1 = f_2 = 0$. Letting $h_1 = dx_1/dt$, $h_2 = dx_2/dt$ for notational convenience, the condition that $d^2y/dt^2 < 0$ for all curves passing through (x_1^0, x_2^0) means that

$$f_{11}h_1^2 + 2f_{12}h_1h_2 + f_{22}h_2^2 < 0 \quad (4\text{-}3)$$

for all values of h_1 and h_2 (except $h_1 = h_2 = 0$). This inequality, since it must hold for all nontrivial h_1, h_2 (i.e., not both equal to 0), imposes restrictions on the signs and relative magnitudes of the second-order partials.

It is apparent from expression (4-3) that both f_{11} and f_{22} must be negative: Let $h_2 = 0$ and h_1 be any number and suppose f_{11} is positive. Then $d^2y/dt^2 = f_{11}h_1^2 > 0$, violating the sufficient conditions for a maximum. Interchanging all the subscripts gives the desired restriction on f_{22}, as the formulation is completely symmetrical. Thus, in order to have $d^2y/dt^2 < 0$ at $\mathbf{x}^0 = (x_1^0, x_2^0)$, it is necessary that

$$f_{11}(\mathbf{x}^0) < 0 \text{ and } f_{22}(\mathbf{x}^0) < 0$$

However, these conditions, which the student might have guessed at by considering the one-variable case, are *not*, by themselves, sufficient for $f(x_1, x_2)$ to have a maximum. We have yet to consider the role of the cross-partial f_{12} in this analysis. An additional restriction on the f_{ij}'s is required to ensure $d^2y/dt^2 < 0$ for all nontrivial h_1 and h_2. It can be derived by using the technique known as *completing the square*.

Consider the expression $x^2 + 2bx$. If the term b^2 is both added and subtracted, the identity $x^2 + 2bx \equiv (x + b)^2 - b^2$ results. Take equation (4-3) and factor out f_{11}:

$$f_{11}\left(h_1^2 + \frac{2f_{12}h_2}{f_{11}}h_1 + \frac{f_{22}}{f_{11}}h_2^2\right) < 0$$

The first two terms in the parentheses are quadratic in h_1 in the same sense as the algebraic example above. Completing the square in h_1 is accomplished by adding and subtracting $(f_{12}h_2/f_{11})^2$ in the parentheses. This yields

$$f_{11}\left[\left(h_1 + \frac{f_{12}h_2}{f_{11}}\right)^2 + \left(\frac{h_2}{f_{11}}\right)^2(f_{11}f_{22} - f_{12}^2)\right] < 0 \quad (4\text{-}4)$$

Since $f_{11} < 0$, in order to guarantee $d^2y/dt^2 < 0$, the square-bracketed term must be positive. However, the first term in the bracket is a squared term and hence is always positive anyway. In order to guarantee that $d^2y/dt^2 < 0$ *for all values of h_1 and h_2*, we must also require that the second term, in particular $f_{11}f_{22} - f_{12}^2$, be positive.

To sum up, then, suppose $f(x_1, x_2)$ has a stationary point at $\mathbf{x} = \mathbf{x}^0$, that is, the first-order necessary conditions for an extremum occur:

$$f_1(\mathbf{x}^0) = f_2(\mathbf{x}^0) = 0 \tag{4-5}$$

If, in addition,

$$f_{11} < 0 \quad \text{and} \quad f_{11}f_{22} - f_{12}^2 > 0 \quad \text{evaluated at } \mathbf{x}^0 \tag{4-6}$$

a maximum position is assured. Note that if (4-6) is satisfied, $f_{22} < 0$ is implied. It is also important to note that condition (4-6) imposes a restriction only on the relative magnitude of f_{12}; it does not imply anything about the sign of this second partial. The sign of f_{12} is thus irrelevant in determining whether a function has a maximum or minimum.

For $f(x_1(t), x_2(t))$ to achieve a *minimum* at $\mathbf{x}^0 = (x_1^0, x_2^0)$ the same first-order conditions (4-5) must, of course, be met. The analogous sufficient second-order conditions, i.e., guaranteeing $d^2y/dt^2 > 0$ are:

$$f_{11} > 0, f_{22} > 0 \quad \text{and} \quad f_{11}f_{22} - f_{12}^2 > 0 \tag{4-7}$$

where all partials are evaluated at $\mathbf{x}^0$. Note that the term $f_{11}f_{22} - f_{12}^2$ is positive for both minima and maxima. If this term is found to be negative, then the surface has a "saddle" shape at $\mathbf{x}^0$: it rises in one direction and falls in another, similar to the point in the center of a saddle.

One last precautionary note must be mentioned. These second-order conditions are *sufficient* conditions for a maximum or minimum; the strict inequalities (4-6) and (4-7) are *not* implied by maxima and minima. For example, the function $y = -x^4$ has a maximum at the origin, yet its second derivative is 0 there. Likewise $y = x^3$ has neither a maximum nor a minimum at $x = 0$, yet its second derivative is also 0 there. Hence, if one or more of the relations in (4-6) or (4-7) hold as *equalities*, the observer is unable at that juncture to determine the shape of the function at that point. The general rule, which will not be proved here, is, if $d^2y/dt^2 = 0$ for some $\mathbf{x}(t)$, one must calculate the higher-order derivatives d^3y/dt^3, d^4y/dt^4, etc. Then if the first occurrence of $d^ny/dt^n < 0$ for all curves $x(t)$ is an *even* order n, then the function has a maximum (minimum, if > 0) whereas if that first occurrence happens for an odd number n, neither a maximum nor a minimum is achieved. To make matters worse, however, there are functions, for example, $y = e^{-1/x^2}$ which have a minimum, say, at some point (here, $x = 0$), and yet the derivatives of all finite orders are 0 at that point (for this function, at $x = 0$). We shall ignore all such "nonregular" situations in which the ordinary sufficient conditions for an extremum do not hold; we will confine our attention only to "regular" extrema.

It can be shown that the second-order conditions (4-6) are sufficient for a function to be concave (downwards) at points other than a stationary value. Likewise, (4-7) guarantees that the function is convex (i.e., concave upwards) at any point. Proofs of these propositions will be deferred to the appendix.

Example 1 Suppose $f(x_1, x_2)$ has a maximum at some point. Then the sufficient second-order conditions are, again,

$$f_{11} h_1^2 + 2f_{12} h_1 h_2 + f_{22} h_2^2 < 0 \qquad (4\text{-}3)$$

for all nontrivial values of h_1 and h_2. Since this holds for *all* values of h_1 and h_2, suppose we let $h_1 = 1, h_2 = \pm 1$. Then this condition implies

$$f_{11} + f_{22} \pm 2f_{12} < 0 \qquad (4\text{-}8)$$

or
$$f_{11} + f_{22} < \mp 2f_{12}$$

Since f_{11} and f_{22} are both negative,

$$|f_{11} + f_{22}| > 2|f_{12}| \qquad (4\text{-}9)$$

is implied by the sufficient second-order conditions for a maximum.

Example 2 Suppose $f(x_1, x_2)$ is strictly concave at some point. The sufficient condition for concavity is again equation (4-3),

$$f_{11} h_1^2 + 2f_{12} h_1 h_2 + f_{22} h_2^2 < 0 \qquad (4\text{-}3)$$

Now let $h_1 = f_2, h_2 = -f_1$. Then (4-3) implies

$$f_{11} f_2^2 - 2f_{12} f_1 f_2 + f_{22} f_1^2 < 0 \qquad (4\text{-}10)$$

This was the condition developed in Chap. 3 [equation (3-32)] for the level curves to be convex to the origin. Hence concavity implies level curves having this property. The converse, however, is false.

PROBLEMS

1 For each of the following functions, find the stationary point and determine whether that point is a relative maximum, minimum, or saddle point of $f(x_1, x_2)$.

(a) $f(x_1, x_2) = x_1^2 - 4x_1 x_2 + 2x_2^2$

(b) $f(x_1, x_2) = -4x_1 - 6x_2 + x_1^2 - x_1 x_2 + 2x_2^2$

(c) $f(x_1 x_2) = 12x_1 - 4x_2 - 2x_1^2 + 2x_1 x_2 - x_2^2$

2 Using equation (4-3), show that the sufficient conditions for $f(x_1, x_2)$ to achieve a minimum at $\mathbf{x}^0$ are the relations (4-7).

3 Consider the production function $y = L^{\alpha} K^{\beta}$. Show that this function is strictly concave (downward) for all values of L and K if $0 < \alpha < 1, 0 < \beta < 1$ and if $\alpha + \beta < 1$. What shape does the function have for $\alpha + \beta = 1$?

4 Show that the production function $y = \log L^{\alpha} K^{\beta}$ is concave for all $\alpha, \beta > 0$.

5 Let $y = f(x_1, x_2)$ and let $z = F(y) = F(f(x_1, x_2)) = g(x_1, x_2)$. Show that if $F' > 0$, then g has a stationary point at (x_1^0, x_2^0) when and only when f is stationary there. Under what conditions will f have a maximum when and only when g has a maximum?

6 A monopolist produces y at cost $C(y)$, and sells this output in two separated markets, producing total revenues $\text{TR}(y) = \text{TR}^1(y_1) + \text{TR}^2(y_2)$, where $y = y_1 + y_2$.

(a) Show that the profit-maximizing monopolist will equate the marginal cost of production to the marginal revenues in each market.

(b) Assuming a regular maximum position, what conditions on the slopes of the marginal-revenue and marginal-cost curves are implied by profit-maximization?

(c) Using the equation $\text{MR} = p(1 + 1/\varepsilon)$ developed in Sec. 2.7, show that a discriminating monopolist will charge a higher price in the market whose demand is less elastic.

4.3 AN EXTENDED FOOTNOTE

In the previous section, sufficient conditions for the maximization of a function of two variables were derived via an artifact which reduced the problem to one dimension, or one variable. It is true that if a function has a maximum at some point, then all curves lying in the surface depicted by that function and passing through the maximum point must themselves have a maximum at that point. In that case, therefore, $y''(t) \leq 0$ for all such curves. Various plausible-sounding converses of this proposition, however, are *not* in general true. For example, suppose the function $f(x_1, x_2)$ possesses a maximum when evaluated along all possible polygonal curves, for any values of the coefficients $a_1, \ldots, a_n, b_1, \ldots, b_n$, for any finite n:

$$x_1 = x_1^0 + a_1 t + a_2 t^2 + \cdots + a_n t^n$$

$$x_2 = x_2^0 + b_1 t + b_2 t^2 + \cdots + b_n t^n$$

Even if $(x_1(t), x_2(t))$ has a maximum at $t = 0$ when evaluated along this wide range of curves, the function $f(x_1, x_2)$ itself need *not* have a maximum at x_1^0, x_2^0.

To illustrate this phenomenon, suppose the curves $(x_1(t), x_2(t))$ are limited to *straight lines* passing through (x_1^0, x_2^0). That is, consider the curves in the surface $y = f(x_1, x_2)$ formed by the intersection of that surface and vertical (perpendicular to the $x_1 x_2$ plane) planes. Then it is *not* the case that if all those curves have a maximum, then the function itself has a maximum, as the following counterexample, developed by the mathematician Peano shows: Consider the function

$$y = (x_2 - x_1^2)(x_2 - 2x_1^2)$$

depicted graphically in Fig. 4-1. This function has the value 0 along the curves $x_2 = x_1^2$, and along $x_2 = 2x_1^2$, both of which are parabolas in the $x_1 x_2$ space. In particular, $y = 0$ at the origin. The pluses and minuses shown in the diagram reflect the value of the function in the given section of the $x_1 x_2$ space. For any point below the lower parabola, $x_2 < x_1^2$ and hence $x_2 < 2x_1^2$ (the point is also below the upper parabola). Hence y is the product of two negative numbers and is thus positive. Likewise, above the upper parabola, $x_2 > 2x_1^2$, hence $x_2 > x_1^2$ and therefore $y = (+)(+) > 0$. In between the two parabolas, $x_2 > x_1^2$ but $x_2 < 2x_1^2$, hence $y = (+)(-) < 0$. Note now that any neighborhood containing the origin possesses both positive and negative values of y. Therefore, the function cannot

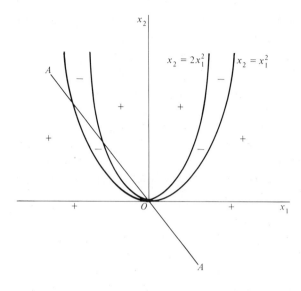

Figure 4-1 *The function $y = (x_2 - 2x_1{}^2)(x_2 - x_1{}^2)$*. This function exhibits the interesting property that when evaluated along all straight lines through the origin, the function has a minimum (of 0). However, the function itself clearly does *not* have either a minimum or a maximum at the origin since in any neighborhood of the origin, this function takes on both positive and negative values.

attain either a maximum or minimum at the origin. That is, since some values are greater than 0 and some less than 0 around the origin, neither a maximum or minimum can be achieved there. Rather, something analogous to a saddle point occurs. However, consider the function evaluated along any straight line through the origin, e.g., line AA in Fig. 4-1. After passing through the upper parabola, the function, along this line, changes from positive to 0 (at the origin) to positive again, implying that the origin is a minimum value of y, *evaluated along this* or any such line. However, the function itself, as we just have shown, does *not* have a minimum at the origin. Thus it is *not* the case that if a function attains a maximum (or minimum) evaluated along all straight lines going through some point that the function necessarily attains a maximum (minimum) there. It is possible to construct functions such that even if $y(t)$ has a maximum for all polygonal curves in the $x_1 x_2$ plane, the function itself does not have a maximum.† Exactly what class of functions $\mathbf{x}(t)$ for which a valid converse is obtainable seems to be unresolved.

4.4 AN APPLICATION OF MAXIMIZING BEHAVIOR: THE PROFIT-MAXIMIZING FIRM

The tools developed in the previous sections will now be applied to analyze the comparative statics of a profit-maximizing firm which sells its output y at constant unit price p, and purchases two inputs x_1 and x_2 at constant unit factor prices w_1 and w_2, respectively. That is, the firm in question is the textbook prototype, facing competitive input and output markets. The production process of the firm will be

---

† See H. Hancock, "Theory of Maxima and Minima," Dover Publications, Inc., New York, 1960.

summarized by the *production function,* $y = f(x_1, x_2)$. The production function will be interpreted here as a technological statement of the maximum output that can be obtained through the combining of two inputs, or factors, x_1 and x_2. The objective function of this firm is total revenue minus total cost (*profits*).†

We assert that the firm maximizes this function, i.e.,

$$\text{maximize} \qquad \pi = pf(x_1, x_2) - w_1 x_1 - w_2 x_2 \qquad \text{(4-11)}$$

The test conditions of this model are the particular values of the input prices w_1, w_2, and output price p. The objective of the model is to be able to state refutable propositions concerning observable behavior, e.g., changes in the levels of inputs used, as the test conditions change, i.e., as factor or output prices change.

The first-order conditions for profit-maximization are

$$\pi_1 = \frac{\partial \pi}{\partial x_1} = pf_1 - w_1 = 0 \qquad \text{(4-12a)}$$

and

$$\pi_2 = \frac{\partial \pi}{\partial x_2} = pf_2 - w_2 = 0 \qquad \text{(4-12b)}$$

Sufficient conditions for a maximum position are

$$\pi_{11} < 0 \qquad \pi_{22} < 0 \qquad \text{and} \qquad \pi_{11}\pi_{22} - \pi_{12}^2 > 0 \qquad \text{(4-13)}$$

Since $\pi_{ij} = pf_{ij}$, these second-order conditions reduce to

$$f_{11} < 0 \qquad f_{22} < 0 \qquad \text{(4-14)}$$

and

$$f_{11}f_{22} - f_{12}^2 > 0 \qquad \text{(4-15)}$$

What is the economic interpretation of these conditions? Equations (4-12) say that a profit-maximizing firm will employ resources up to the point where the marginal contribution of each factor to producing revenues pf_i, the value of the marginal product of factor i, is equal to the cost of acquiring additional units of that factor, w_i. These are *necessarily* implied by profit-maximization; however to ensure that the resulting factor employment pertains to *maximum* rather than minimum profits, conditions (4-14) and (4-15) are needed. Conditions (4-14) are a statement of the law of diminishing returns. That such a law is involved is easily seen. [Remember, though, conditions (4-13) are sufficient, not necessary—a maximum position is consistent with these relations holding as equalities.] Assuming it was worthwhile to hire one unit of that factor in the first place, if the value of the marginal product of that factor was increasing, the firm would hire that factor

---

† The student should be wary of the terms *firm* and *profits*. With regard to the former, the concept has not been defined here, and there is in fact, considerable debate in the profession as to exactly what firms are, why they exist at all, and what their boundaries are. With regard to profits, the model above leaves unspecified who has claims to the supposed excess of revenues over cost. Alternatively, if x_1 and x_2 are indeed the only two factors, in whose interest is it to maximize the expression in equation (4-11)? In spite of these shortcomings, since the model does yield refutable hypotheses, as we shall see shortly, it is potentially interesting. It might be referred to as a "black box" theory of the firm.

without bound, since the input would be generating more income than it was getting paid. Hence a finite maximum position is inconsistent with increasing marginal productivity.

However, diminishing marginal productivity in each factor does *not*, by itself, guarantee that a maximum profit position will be achieved. Condition (4-15) is also required. This relation, though less intuitive than diminishing marginal productivity, arises from the fact that changes in one factor affect the marginal products of the other factors as well as its own marginal product, and the overall effect on all marginal products must be akin to diminishing marginal productivity. Suppose, for example, that $f_{12} = f_{21} = \partial MP_1/\partial x_2 = \partial MP_2/\partial x_1$ is very large, in absolute terms, relative to $f_{11} = \partial MP_1/\partial x_1$ and $f_{22} = \partial MP_2/\partial x_2$. That is, suppose a change in x_1, say, affects the marginal product of factor 2 much more than the marginal product of factor 1. Then consider the consequences of an increase of one unit of x_1. In Fig. 4-2, if $f_{12} = f_{21} > 0$, MP_1 initially declines; however MP_2 shifts upward by a considerable amount, causing the firm to purchase many additional units of x_2. However, these additional units of x_2 have an effect on MP_1. Since $f_{12} = \partial MP_1/\partial x_2 > 0$, MP_1 also shifts up, by a relatively large amount. The final result, then, is that an increase in x_1 can lead to an *increase* in MP_1, if the cross-effects are large enough. Hence the original factor employment levels, though characterized by diminishing marginal productivity in each factor, do not, nonetheless describe a profit-maximum position, since it is clearly profitable in this case to increase the usage of both x_1 and x_2 together. In the case where f_{12} is negative and large relative to f_{11} and f_{22}, the analysis is similar. An increase in x_1 causes a relatively large fall in MP_2, a fall in x_2 and hence a relatively large *increase* in MP_1. (Remember, $\partial MP_1/\partial x_2 < 0$!) In this case, increasing one factor and decreasing the other (together) will increase profits.

Let us return now to the marginal relations (4-12). The purpose of formulating this model is not simply to assert the implied marginal reasoning; that is a

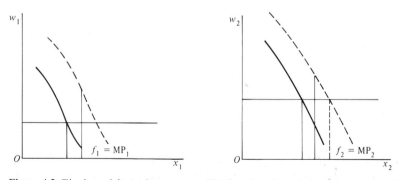

Figure 4-2 *The law of diminishing returns.* The fact that $f_{11} < 0$, $f_{22} < 0$ alone is *not* sufficient to guarantee a finite profit-maximum position. The cross-effects between the two factors must be considered. If x_1 is increased, MP_2 might shift out, say, a great deal, shifting MP_1 out resulting in a net *increase* in MP_1 even though $f_{11} = \partial MP_1/\partial x_1 < 0$. This will occur if f_{12} is large. Hence the condition $f_{11}f_{22} - f_{12}^2 \geq 0$ is also needed to achieve a finite profit maximum.

rather sterile endeavor. The purpose of this analysis is to be able to formulate refutable hypotheses as to how firms react to changes in the parameters they face; in particular, in this case, to changes in factor and output prices. To this end, we now consider the comparative statics of this model.

The first-order conditions in complete form are

$$pf_1(x_1, x_2) - w_1 = 0$$

$$pf_2(x_1, x_2) - w_2 = 0$$

These are two implicit relations in essentially five unknowns x_1, x_2, w_1, w_2, p. Under the "right" conditions (to be discussed below) it is possible to solve for two of these values in terms of the other three. In particular, we can solve for the choice functions

$$x_1 = x_1^*(w_1, w_2, p) \tag{4-16a}$$

and

$$x_2 = x_2^*(w_1, w_2, p) \tag{4-16b}$$

Equations (4-16) represent the factor-demand curves. These relations indicate the amount of each factor that will be hired, according to this model, as a function of the factor prices and product price; they are the choice functions of this model. Assuming that it is possible to solve for equations (4-16), it becomes meaningful to ask questions regarding the signs of the following six partial derivatives, which comprise the comparative statics of the profit-maximizing model:

$$\frac{\partial x_1^*}{\partial w_1} \quad \frac{\partial x_1^*}{\partial w_2} \quad \frac{\partial x_1^*}{\partial p} \quad \frac{\partial x_2^*}{\partial w_1} \quad \frac{\partial x_2^*}{\partial w_2} \quad \frac{\partial x_2^*}{\partial p} \tag{4-17}$$

These partials indicate the marginal changes in factor employment due to given price changes. It is important to keep in mind that in order to write down these relations and interpret them in some meaningful fashion, the explicit functions x_i^* must be well defined. Also note that the above factor-demand curves are not the marginal-product curves. The marginal-product functions f_1 and f_2 are expressed in terms of the factor inputs, while the factor demand curves are expressed in terms of prices, and dependent upon the behavioral assertion of the model.

Substituting equations (4-16) back into equations (4-12) produces the following *identities*:

$$pf_1(x_1^*(w_1, w_2, p), x_2^*(w_1, w_2, p)) - w_1 \equiv 0 \tag{4-18a}$$

and

$$pf_2(x_1^*(w_1, w_2, p), x_2^*(w_1, w_2, p)) - w_2 \equiv 0 \tag{4-18b}$$

Recall the monopolist-tax example of Chap. 1, where the solution $x = x^*(t)$ of the first-order relation (which set marginal revenue equal to marginal cost plus the tax) was then substituted back into that relation, yielding an *identity* in the tax rate t. For the same reasons, the relations (4-18) are identities in the prices w_1, w_2 and p. The factor-demand functions x_1^* and x_2^* are precisely those levels of x_1 and x_2 that the entrepreneur employs to keep the value of the marginal products of each factor equal to the wage of each factor, for any prices.

Hence, the assertion that the firm *always* obeys equations (4-12), for any prices converts those equations to the identities (4-18). Being identities, the relations (4-18) can be differentiated implicitly with respect to the various prices, producing relations which allow solutions for the partial derivatives (4-17). The general procedure is exactly the same as in the monopolist example. However, in this example, two first-order relations are present instead of only one, and that fact makes the algebra more difficult.

Before we do the differentiation, note that if the firm's production function were in fact known, then one could actually solve for the factor-demand curves explicitly. In that case we could know the *total* quantities involved in this model, a happy state of affairs. The factor-demand curves (4-16) could be differentiated directly to yield the partial derivatives (4-17). However, the economist is not likely to have this much information. Nonetheless, it is still possible to state refutable hypotheses concerning *marginal* quantities, through implicit differentiation of the identities (4-18).

Differentiating (4-18a) and (4-18b) partially, with respect to w_1, using the chain rule (remember that f_1 is a function of x_1 and x_2, which are in turn functions of w_1, w_2, and p, etc.),

$$p\frac{\partial f_1}{\partial x_1}\frac{\partial x_1^*}{\partial w_1} + p\frac{\partial f_1}{\partial x_2}\frac{\partial x_2^*}{\partial w_1} - 1 \equiv 0$$

$$p\frac{\partial f_2}{\partial x_1}\frac{\partial x_1^*}{\partial w_1} + p\frac{\partial f_2}{\partial x_2}\frac{\partial x_2^*}{\partial w_1} \equiv 0$$

Using subscript notation, these can be rewritten

$$pf_{11}\frac{\partial x_1^*}{\partial w_1} + pf_{12}\frac{\partial x_2^*}{\partial w_1} \equiv 1 \tag{4-19a}$$

$$pf_{21}\frac{\partial x_1^*}{\partial w_1} + pf_{22}\frac{\partial x_2^*}{\partial w_1} \equiv 0 \tag{4-19b}$$

Although the identities (4-19) look complicated, they are in fact a good deal simpler in form than (4-18). Whereas the first-order relations (4-18) are in general complicated algebraic expressions, (4-19a) and (4-19b) are simple *linear* relations in the unknowns $\partial x_1^*/\partial w_1$ and $\partial x_2^*/\partial w_1$. That is, (4-19a) and (4-19b) are of the same form as the elementary system of two simultaneous linear equations in two unknowns. The coefficients of the unknowns are the functions pf_{11}, pf_{12}, etc., but the system is still simple in that no products, or squares, etc., of the terms $\partial x_1^*/\partial w_1$, etc., are involved. And this is fortunate, since the goal of this analysis is to solve for those terms, i.e., find expressions for the partials of the form $\partial x_i^*/\partial w_j$.

To solve for $\partial x_1^*/\partial w_1$, for example, multiply (4-19a) by f_{22} and (4-19b) by f_{12}, and subtract (4-19b) from (4-19a). This yields, after some factoring (remember that $f_{12} = f_{21}$),†

$$p(f_{11}f_{22} - f_{12}^2)\frac{\partial x_1^*}{\partial w_1} = f_{22}$$

---

† In accordance with general custom, we will use the equality rather than the identity sign when the special emphasis is not required.

Now, if $f_{11}f_{22} - f_{12}^2 \neq 0$, that term can be divided on both sides,

yielding

$$\frac{\partial x_1^*}{\partial w_1} = \frac{f_{22}}{p(f_{11}f_{22} - f_{12}^2)} \tag{4-20a}$$

In like fashion, one obtains

$$\frac{\partial x_2^*}{\partial w_1} = \frac{-f_{21}}{p(f_{11}f_{22} - f_{12}^2)} \tag{4-20b}$$

To obtain the responses of the firm to changes in w_2, differentiate equations (4-18) with respect to w_2. Noting that w_2 enters only the second equation explicitly, the system of comparative statics relations becomes

$$pf_{11}\frac{\partial x_1^*}{\partial w_2} + pf_{12}\frac{\partial x_2^*}{\partial w_2} \equiv 0$$

$$pf_{21}\frac{\partial x_1^*}{\partial w_2} + pf_{22}\frac{\partial x_2^*}{\partial w_2} \equiv 1$$

Solving these equations as before yields

$$\frac{\partial x_1^*}{\partial w_2} = \frac{-f_{12}}{p(f_{11}f_{22} - f_{12}^2)} \tag{4-20c}$$

$$\frac{\partial x_2^*}{\partial w_2} = \frac{f_{11}}{p(f_{11}f_{22} - f_{12}^2)} \tag{4-20d}$$

Note that sufficient condition (4-15), $f_{11}f_{22} - f_{12}^2 > 0$ is enough to guarantee $f_{11}f_{22} - f_{12}^2 \neq 0$ and hence allow solution for these partials (4-20a–d). This is not mere coincidence; it is in fact an application of the "implicit function theorem" in mathematics, to be dealt with more generally in Chap. 5. The condition $f_{11}f_{22} - f_{12}^2 \neq 0$ is precisely the mathematical condition to allow solution (*locally*, not everywhere) for the factor-demand curves $x_i^*(w_1, w_2, p)$ in the first place. The relevance of that term is brought out in the solution for the partial derivatives above.

What refutable hypotheses emerge from the above analysis? Condition (4-15) implies that the denominators of (4-20a–d) are all positive. Condition (4-14), f_{11}, $f_{22} < 0$, (diminishing marginal productivity) makes the numerators of (4-20a) and (4-20d) negative. Hence, *the regular (sufficient) conditions for maximum profits imply that the factor-demand curves must be downward-sloping in their respective factor prices*. The model implies that changes in a factor price will result in a change in the usage of that factor in the opposite direction.

What about the cross-effects $\partial x_1^*/\partial w_2$, $\partial x_2^*/\partial w_1$? The most remarkable aspect of these two expressions is that they are always equal, by inspection of (4-20b) and (4-20c), noting that $f_{12} = f_{21}$. This *reciprocity relation*,

$$\frac{\partial x_1^*}{\partial w_2} = \frac{\partial x_2^*}{\partial w_1}$$

is representative of a number of such relations that appear in economics, as well as in the physical sciences, when maximizing principles are involved. As is obvious from the forms of these expressions, however, the reciprocity relations are no less intuitive than the mathematical theorem from which they originate—the invariance of cross-partial derivations to the order of differentiation.

Beyond the equality of these cross-effects, there is little else to say about them. The sign of f_{12} is not implied by the maximization hypothesis; hence the sign of $\partial x_i^*/\partial w_j$, $i \neq j$ is similarly not implied. No refutable proposition emerges about these terms from the profit-maximization model. All observed events relating, say, to the change in labor employment when the rental rate on capital increases are consistent with the above model.

Suppose now it is desired to find expressions relating to the effects of changes in the output price p. The procedure here is identical up through relations (4-18). Then, we differentiate those identities partially with respect to p, producing

$$pf_{11}\frac{\partial x_1^*}{\partial p} + pf_{12}\frac{\partial x_2^*}{\partial p} \equiv -f_1 \tag{4-21a}$$

$$pf_{21}\frac{\partial x_1^*}{\partial p} + pf_{22}\frac{\partial x_2^*}{\partial p} \equiv -f_2 \tag{4-21b}$$

remembering that the product rule is called for in differentiating the terms pf_1, pf_2. Solving these equations for $\partial x_1^*/\partial p$ and $\partial x_2^*/\partial p$ yields

$$\frac{\partial x_1^*}{\partial p} = \frac{-f_1 f_{22} + f_2 f_{12}}{p(f_{11} f_{22} - f_{12}^2)} \tag{4-22a}$$

$$\frac{\partial x_2^*}{\partial p} = \frac{-f_2 f_{11} + f_1 f_{12}}{p(f_{11} f_{22} - f_{12}^2)} \tag{4-22b}$$

It can be seen that no refutable implications emerge from these expressions. An increase in output price can lead to an increase or a decrease in the use of either factor, since the sign of f_{12} is unknown. (Note that if $f_{12} > 0$ is assumed, $\partial x_1^*/\partial p > 0$ and $\partial x_2^*/\partial p > 0$.) It is possible to show, however, that it cannot be the case that both $\partial x_1^*/\partial p < 0$ and $\partial x_2^*/\partial p < 0$ simultaneously. An increase in output price cannot lead to less use of both factors. The proof of this is left as an exercise.

The Supply Function

It is also possible to ask how *output* varies when a parameter changes. Since $y = f(x_1, x_2)$,

$$y^* = f(x_1^*, x_2^*)$$

where y^* is the profit-maximizing level of output.

The factor-demand curves are functions of the prices,

$$x_i = x_i^*(w_1, w_2, p) \qquad i = 1, 2$$

Substituting these functions into $f(x_1^*, x_2^*)$ yields

$$y^* \equiv f(x_1^*(w_1, w_2, p), x_2^*(w_1, w_2, p)) \equiv y^*(w_1, w_2, p) \qquad (4\text{-}23)$$

Equation (4-23) represents the supply function of this firm. It shows how output is related (1) to output price p, and (2) to the factor prices. Though the supply curve is commonly drawn only against output price p, factor prices must also enter the function, since factor costs obviously affect the level of output a firm will choose to produce.

How will output be affected by an increase in output price? To answer this, differentiate (4-23) with respect to p, using the chain rule

$$\frac{\partial y^*}{\partial p} \equiv \frac{\partial f}{\partial x_1} \frac{\partial x_1^*}{\partial p} + \frac{\partial f}{\partial x_2} \frac{\partial x_2^*}{\partial p}$$

or

$$\frac{\partial y^*}{\partial p} \equiv f_1 \frac{\partial x_1^*}{\partial p} + f_2 \frac{\partial x_2^*}{\partial p} \qquad (4\text{-}24)$$

Now, substitute equations (4-22) into this expression. This yields

$$\frac{\partial y^*}{\partial p} = \frac{-f_1^2 f_{22} + 2 f_{12} f_1 f_2 - f_2^2 f_{11}}{p(f_{11} f_{22} - f_{12}^2)} \qquad (4\text{-}25)$$

The denominator of this expression is positive by the sufficient second-order conditions. We also can infer, from equation (4-10), that the numerator is also positive. Therefore

$$\frac{\partial y^*}{\partial p} > 0 \qquad (4\text{-}26)$$

This says that the sufficient second-order conditions for profit maximum imply that the supply curve, as usually drawn, must be upward-sloping. It also provides an explanation as to why it cannot be the case that both $\partial x_1^*/\partial p$ and $\partial x_2^*/\partial p$ are negative. If p increases, output will increase. It is impossible, with positive marginal products, to produce more output with less of both factors.

It is also possible to derive some *reciprocity* relationships with regard to the output-supply and factor-demand functions. In particular, one can show

$$\frac{\partial y^*}{\partial w_i} \equiv \frac{-\partial x_i^*}{\partial p} \qquad i = 1, 2 \qquad (4\text{-}27)$$

The signs of these expressions are indeterminate; however this curious reciprocity result is valid. Its proof is left as an exercise.

4.5 THE LONG RUN AND THE SHORT RUN: AN EXAMPLE OF THE LE CHÂTELIER PRINCIPLE

It is commonplace to assert that certain factors of production are "fixed" over certain time intervals, e.g., that capital inputs cannot be varied over the short run. In fact, of course, these statements are incorrect; virtually anything can be changed, even quickly, if the benefits of doing so are great enough. Yet it does seem that certain inputs are more easily varied, i.e., less costly to vary than others. The extreme abstraction of this is to simply assert that for all intents and purposes, one factor is fixed. (A government edict fixing some level of input would suffice, if ignoring such edict carried with it a sufficiently long jail sentence.) How would a profit-maximizing firm react to changes in the wage of one factor x_1 when it found that it could not vary the level of x_2 employed? Would the factor-demand curve for x_1 be more elastic or less elastic than previously?

Suppose x_2 is held fixed at $x_2 = x_2^0$. The profit function then becomes

$$\max \pi = pf(x_1, x_2^0) - w_1 x_1 - w_2 x_2^0 .$$

In this case, there is only one decision variable: x_1. Hence the first-order condition for maximization is simply

$$\pi_1 = pf_1(x_1, x_2^0) - w_1 = 0 \tag{4-28}$$

and the sufficient second-order condition is

$$\pi_{11} = pf_{11} < 0 \tag{4-29}$$

We are dealing with a one-variable problem with, now, *four* parameters, w_1, w_2, p *and* x_2^0. The factor-demand curve, obtained from equation (4-28)

$$x_1 = x_1^S(w_1, p, x_2^0) \tag{4-30}$$

where x_1^S stands for short-run demand. Note, however, that w_2 does not enter this factor-demand curve. With x_2 fixed, $w_2 x_2^0$ is a fixed cost, and thus w_2 is irrelevant for the choice of x_1 in the short run. The slope of the short-run factor-demand curve is $\partial x_1^S / \partial w_1$. To obtain an expression for this partial, substitute, as before, x_1^S into equation (4-28), yielding the identity

$$pf_1(x_1^S, x_2^0) - w_1 \equiv 0$$

Differentiating this identity with respect to w_1 yields

$$pf_{11} \frac{\partial x_1^S}{\partial w_1} \equiv 1$$

or

$$\frac{\partial x_1^S}{\partial w_1} \equiv \frac{1}{pf_{11}} < 0 \tag{4-31}$$

Thus, the short-run factor-demand curve is downward-sloping. How does this slope compare with $\partial x_1^* / \partial w_1 = \partial x_1^L / \partial w_1$ (x_1^L for long-run demand) derived in (4-20a)? Taking the difference,

$$\frac{\partial x_1^L}{\partial w_1} - \frac{\partial x_1^S}{\partial w_1} = \frac{f_{22}}{p(f_{11} f_{22} - f_{12}^2)} - \frac{1}{pf_{11}}$$

Combining terms yields

$$\frac{\partial x_1^L}{\partial w_1} - \frac{\partial x_1^S}{\partial w_1} = \frac{f_{12}^2}{pf_{11}(f_{11} f_{22} - f_{12}^2)} < 0 \tag{4-32}$$

a determinately *negative* expression due to the second-order conditions (4-15) and (4-29). Since both $\partial x_1^L / \partial w_1$ and $\partial x_1^S / \partial w_1$ are negative, (4-32) says that the change in x_1 due to a change in its price is larger, in absolute value, when x_2 is variable (the long run) than when x_2 is fixed (the short run). This result is sometimes referred to as the "second law of demand." It is in agreement with intuition—if the price of labor, say, were to increase relative to capital's price, the firm would attempt to substitute out of labor. The degree to which it could do this, however, would be impaired if it could not at the same time increase the amount of capital employed. Hence the model implies that over longer periods of time, as the other factor becomes "unstuck," the demand for less-costly-to-change factor will become more elastic. Incidently, the usual factor-demand diagrams are drawn with the dependent variable x_1 on the *horizontal* axis; in that case the long-run factor-demand curves appear flatter than the short-run curves. Also note that this comparison makes sense only if the level of x_2 employed is the same in both cases. That is, the above is a local theorem, holding only at the point where the short- and long-run demand curves intersect, i.e., at the common value of x_2. It is not the case that all short-run factor-demand curves are less elastic than all long-run demands.

The result contained in this section is commonly believed to be empirically true, simply as a matter of assertion. It is interesting and noteworthy that this type of behavior is in fact mathematically implied by a maximization hypothesis. These types of relations are sometimes referred to as Le Châtelier effects, after the similar tendency of thermodynamic systems to exhibit the same types of responses. Some generalizations of this phenomenon and its relation to "envelope" theorems will be presented in Chap. 9.

To sum up, it has again been possible to state refutable propositions about some *marginal* quantities, in spite of the scarcity of information contained in the model. Should further information be used, e.g., the specific functional form of the production function, or, less grandiosely, independent measures of the sign of the cross-effect f_{12}, additional restrictions can be placed on the signs of the partial derivatives of the factor-demand curves.

The tools used in this analysis include the solution of simultaneous linear equations. For this reason, a short chapter on the theory of matrices and determinants is included next. It will be of great advantage to be able to have a general way of expressing the solutions of such equation systems, instead of laboriously working through each expression separately.

PROBLEMS

1 Show that no refutable implications emerge from the profit-maximization model with regard to the effects of changes in output-price on factor inputs. Show, however, that it cannot be the case that both factors decrease when output-price is increased.

2 Show that the rate of change of output with respect to a factor-price change is equal to the negative of the rate of change of that factor with respect to output price, i.e., equation (4-27).

3 (Very messy, but you should probably do this once in your life.) Consider the production function $y = x_1^{x_1} x_2^{x_2}$. Find the factor-demand curves and the comparative statics of a profit-maximizing firm with this production function. Be sure to review problem 3, Sec. 4.2, first. Show that for this firm, the sign of the cross-effect term, $\partial x_2^*/\partial w_1$ is negative.

4 There are several definitions of complementary and substitute factors in the literature, among which are:

(i) "Factor 1 is a substitute (complement) for factor 2 if the marginal product of factor 1 decreases (increases) as factor 2 is increased."

(ii) "Factor 1 is a substitute (complement) for factor 2 if the quantity of factor 1 employed increases when the price of factor 2 increases (decreases)."

(a) Show that both of these definitions are *symmetric*, i.e., if factor 1 is a substitute for factor 2, then factor 2 can't be a complement to factor 1.

(b) Show that these two definitions are equivalent in the two-factor profit-maximization model.

(c) Do you think that these two definitions will be equivalent in a model with three or more factors? Why?

5 Consider again problem 6, Sec. 4.2, wherein a monopolist sells his or her output in two separate markets. Suppose a per-unit tax t is placed on output sold in the first market.

(a) Show that an increase in t will reduce the output sold in market 1.

(b) What does the maximization hypothesis *alone* imply about the response of output in the second market to an increase in t?

(c) Suppose the output in market 2 were held fixed at the previously profit-maximizing level, by government regulation. Show that the response in output in market 1 to a tax increase is less in absolute terms in the regulated situation than in the unregulated situation. Provide an intuitive explanation for this.

6 The Le Châtelier results of Sec. 4.4 (also problem 5) hold, regardless of whether the two factors are complementary or substitutes. Explain the phenomenon intuitively for the case of complementary factors.

7 A monopolist sells his or her output in two markets, with revenue functions $R_1(y_1)$, $R_2(y_2)$, respectively. Total cost is a function of total output, $y = y_1 + y_2$. The same per-unit tax, t, is levied on output sold in *both* markets.

(a) Find $\partial y_1^*/\partial t$, $\partial y_2^*/\partial t$, and $\partial y^*/\partial t$ where y_i^* is the profit-maximizing level of output in market i, and $y^* = y_1^* + y_2^*$. Which, if any, of these partials have a sign implied by profit-maximization?

(b) Suppose output y_2 is held fixed. Find $(dy_1^*/dt)_{y_2}$. Does $(dy_1^*/dt)_{y_2}$ have a determinate sign?

4.6 ANALYSIS OF FINITE CHANGES: A DIGRESSION

The downward slope of the factor-demand curves can be derived without the use of calculus, on the basis of simple algebra. Suppose that at some factor-price vector (w_1^0, w_2^0), the input vector that maximizes profits is (x_1^0, x_2^0). This means that if some other input levels (x_1^1, x_2^1) were employed at the factor prices (w_1^0, w_2^0), profits would not be as high. Algebraically, then,

$$pf(x_1^0, x_2^0) - w_1^0 x_1^0 - w_2^0 x_2^0 \geq pf(x_1^1, x_2^1) - w_1^0 x_1^1 - w_2^0 x_2^1$$

However, there must be *some* factor-price vector (w_1^1, w_2^1) at which the input levels (x_1^1, x_2^1) would be the profit-maximizing levels to employ. Since (x_1^1, x_2^1) leads to maximum profits at (w_1^1, w_2^1), any other level of inputs, in particular (x_1^0, x_2^0) will not do as well. Hence,

$$pf(x_1^1, x_2^1) - w_1^1 x_1^1 - w_2^1 x_2^1 \geq pf(x_1^0, x_2^0) - w_1^1 x_1^0 - w_2^1 x_2^0$$

If these two inequalities are added together, all the production function terms cancel, leaving (after multiplication through by -1):

$$w_1^0 x_1^0 + w_2^0 x_2^0 + w_1^1 x_1^1 + w_2^1 x_2^1 \leq w_1^1 x_1^1 + w_2^0 x_2^2 + w_1^1 x_1^0 + w_2^1 x_2^0$$

If the terms on the right-hand side are brought over to the left, and the w_i's factored, the result is

$$w_1^0(x_1^0 - x_1^1) + w_2^0(x_2^0 - x_2^1) + w_1^1(x_1^1 - x_1^0) + w_2^1(x_2^1 - x_2^0) \leq 0$$

However, this can be factored again, using the terms $(x_1^0 - x_1^1)$, etc. [Note that $(x_1^0 - x_1^1) = -(x_1^1 - x_1^0)$, etc.], yielding

$$(w_1^0 - w_1^1)(x_1^0 - x_1^1) + (w_2^0 - w_2^1)(x_2^0 - x_2^1) \leq 0 \tag{4-33}$$

Suppose now that only one factor-price, say w_1, changed. Then equation (4-33) becomes

$$(w_1^0 - w_1^1)(x_1^0 - x_1^1) \leq 0$$

or

$$(\Delta w_1)(\Delta x_1) \leq 0 \tag{4-34}$$

Equation (4-34) says that the changes in factor utilization will move oppositely to changes in factor price, i.e., the law of demand applies to these factors. Note that if the profit-maximization point is unique, the weak inequalities can be replaced with strict inequalities.

This is the type of algebra which underlies the theory of revealed preference, to be discussed later. Curiously enough, the above type of analysis cannot be used to show the second law of demand, that (factor) demands will become more elastic as more factors are allowed to vary. As was stated in Sec. 4.4, that theorem was a strictly local phenomenon, holding only at a point. The above analysis, which makes use of finite changes, turns out to be insufficiently powerful to analyze the Le Châtelier effects, i.e., the *second* law of demand.

APPENDIX

TAYLOR SERIES FOR FUNCTIONS OF SEVERAL VARIABLES

In Chap. 2, we indicated that it is sometimes possible to represent a function of one variable x by an infinite power series

$$f(x) = f(x_0) + f'(x_0)(x - x_0) + \frac{f''(x_0)(x - x_0)^2}{2!} + \cdots \tag{4A-1}$$

It is, however, always possible to represent a function in a finite power series:

$$f(x) = f(x_0) + f'(x_0)(x - x_0) + \cdots + \frac{f^{(n)}(x^*)(x - x_0)^n}{n!} \tag{4A-2}$$

where x^* lies between x_0 and x, that is; $x^* = x_0 + \theta(x - x_0)$ where $0 \leq \theta \leq 1$. These formulas were used to derive the necessary and sufficient conditions for a maximum (or minimum) at $y = f(x)$.

Let us generalize these formulas to the case of, first, two independent variables; that is, $y = f(x_1, x_2)$. This is accomplished by an artifice similar to the derivation of the maximum conditions in the text. Consider $f(x_1, x_2)$ evaluated at some point $x^0 = (x_1^0, x_2^0)$, that is, $f(x_1^0, x_2^0)$. Let us now move to a new point, $(x_1^0 + h_1, x_2^0 + h_2)$, where we can consider $h_1 = \Delta x_1$, $h_2 = \Delta x_2$. If we let

$$y(t) = f(x_1^0 + h_1 t, x_2^0 + h_2 t) \tag{4A-3}$$

then when $t = 0$, $f(x_1, x_2) = f(x_1^0, x_2^0)$, and when $t = 1$, $f(x_1, x_2) = f(x_1^0 + h_1, x_2^0 + h_2)$. If h_1 and h_2 take on arbitrary values, any point in the $x_1 x_2$ plane can be reached. We can therefore derive a Taylor series for $f(x_1, x_2)$ by writing one for $y(t)$, around the point $t = 0$. In terms of finite sums

$$y(t) = y(0) + y'(0)t + \frac{y''(0)t^2}{2!} + \cdots + \frac{y^{(m)}(t^*)t^m}{m!} \tag{4A-4}$$

where $0 \leq |t^*| \leq |t|$. Setting $t = 1$, we have

$$y(1) = f(x_1^0 + h_1, x_2^0 + h_2)$$

$$y(0) = f(x_1^0, x_2^0)$$

$$y'(0) = f_1(x_1^0, x_2^0)h_1 + f_2(x_1^0, x_2^0)h_2$$

$$y''(0) = \sum_{i=1}^{2} \sum_{j=1}^{2} f_{ij}(x_1^0, x_2^0)h_i h_j$$

. . . .

Therefore, equation (4A-4) becomes

$$f(x_1^0 + h_1, x_2^0 + h_2) = f(x_1^0, x_2^0) + \Sigma f_i h_i + \frac{\Sigma\Sigma f_{ij} h_i h_j}{2!} + \cdots$$

$$+ \frac{\Sigma \cdots \Sigma f_{ij} \ldots (x_1^*, x_2^*) h_i h_j \cdots}{m!} \tag{4A-5}$$

where the last term is an m-sum of mth partials times a product of the appropriate m h_i's. The value of $x = (x_1, x_2)$ at which the last term is evaluated is some x^* between x and x^0, i.e., where

$$x_i^* = x_i^0 + \theta(x_i - x_i^0) \qquad i = 1, 2 \tag{4A-6}$$

with $0 \leq \theta \leq 1$. Formula (4A-5) generalizes in an obvious fashion to functions of n variables. Then the sums run from 1 through n instead of merely from 1 to 2.

The Maximum Conditions

First-order necessary conditions. We can derive the first-order conditions for maximizing $y = f(x_1, x_2)$ at x_1^0, x_2^0, by considering (4A-5) with the last term being the linear term. In that case, we have the mean value theorem for $f(x_1, x_2)$:

$$f(x_1^0 + h_1, x_2^0 + h_2) - f(x_1^0, x_2^0) = f_1(\mathbf{x}^*)h_1 + f_2(\mathbf{x}^*)h_2 \qquad (4A-7)$$

If $f(x_1, x_2)$ has a maximum at $f(x_1^0, x_2^0)$, then the left-hand side of equation (4A-5) is necessarily nonpositive (negative for a unique maximum) for all h_1, h_2 (not both 0). Letting $h_2 = 0$ first, we see that

$$f_1(x_1^*, x_2^*) \leq 0 \qquad h_1 > 0$$

and

$$f_1(x_1^*, x_2^*) \geq 0 \qquad h_1 < 0$$

This can happen (if f_1 is continuous) only if $f_1(x_1^0, x_2^0) = 0$. Similarly, we deduce $f_2 = 0$. This procedure generalizes to the case of n variables in an obvious fashion.

The second-order conditions; concavity. If $f(x_1, x_2)$ is a *concave* function at a stationary value, then $f(x_1, x_2)$ has a maximum there. A concave function of two (or n) variables is defined as in Chap. 2 for one variable. A function $f(x_1, x_2)$ is concave if it lies above (or on) the chord joining any two points. For differentiable functions, the function lies below (or on) the tangent plane. Letting

$$y(t) = f(x_1^0 + h_1 t, x_2^0 + h_2 t) \qquad (4A-3)$$

as before, and recalling equation (2-28) in Chap. 2, strict concavity implies

$$y(t) - y(0) - y'(0)t < 0 \qquad (4A-8)$$

for all h_1, h_2. Applying (4A-8) with $t = 1$, $x_i = x_i^0 + h_i$, $i = 1, 2$,

$$f(x_1, x_2) - f(x_1^0, x_2^0) - f_1(x_1^0, x_2^0)h_1 - f_2(x_1^0, x_2^0)h_2 < 0 \qquad (4A-9)$$

Taking the Taylor series expansion (4A-5) to the second-order term and rearranging slightly

$$f(x_1, x_2) - f(x_1^0, x_2^0) - f_1(x_1^0, x_2^0)h_1 - f_2(x_1^0, x_2^0)h_2 = \tfrac{1}{2} \sum_{i=1}^{2} \sum_{j=1}^{2} f_{ij}(x_1^*, x_2^*)h_i h_j$$

$$(4A-10)$$

From (4A-9)

$$\sum_{i=1}^{2} \sum_{j=1}^{2} f_{ij}(x_1^*, x_2^*)h_i h_j < 0 \qquad (4A-11)$$

for all h_i, h_j not both 0. Hence, strict concavity implies (4A-11). If the h_i's are made smaller and smaller, $f_{ij}(x_1^*, x_2^*)$ converges towards $f_{ij}(x_1^0, x_2^0)$. We can deduce that concavity at x_1^0, x_2^0 implies that

$$\sum_{i=1}^{2} \sum_{j=1}^{2} f_{ij}(x_1^0, x_2^0)h_i h_j \leq 0 \qquad (4A-12)$$

for all h_i, h_j, but *not* that this expression is *strictly* negative at (x_1^0, x_2^0). If this double sum is strictly negative, then $f(x_1, x_2)$ must be concave. Similar remarks hold for *convex* functions.

If $f(x_1, x_2)$ has an extremum at (x_1^0, x_2^0), then $f_1 = f_2 = 0$ there. Equation (4A-10) then reveals how the second partials are related to a maximum or minimum position. Again, all the results of this section generalize to functions of n variables by simply having the sums in expressions (4A-5), (4A-9), (4A-10), etc., run from 1 to n, instead of just from 1 to 2.

SELECTED REFERENCES

Allen, R. G. D.: "Mathematical Analysis for Economists," Macmillan & Co., Ltd., London, 1938. Reprinted by St. Martin's Press, Inc., New York.

Apostol, T.: "Mathematical Analysis," Addison-Wesley Publishing Co., Inc., Reading, Mass., 1957. A standard reference. Advanced.

Courant, R.: "Differential and Integral Calculus," 2d ed., Interscience Publishers, Inc., New York, 1936, vol. 1 and 2.

Hancock, H.: "Theory of Maxima and Minima," Ginn and Company, Boston, 1917. Reprinted by Dover Publications, Inc., New York, 1960. Difficult.

Panik, M. J.: "Classical Optimization: Foundations and Extensions," North-Holland Publishing Company, Amsterdam, 1976.

Samuelson, P. A.: "Foundations of Economic Analysis," Harvard University Press, Cambridge, Mass., 1947. The seminal work on comparative statics methodology.

CHAPTER FIVE

MATRICES AND DETERMINANTS

5.1 MATRICES

Most economic models involve the simultaneous interaction of several variables. We have seen, for the case of the profit-maximizing firm with two inputs, that the comparative statics of the model depended on solving two simultaneous linear equations. This occurrence is indeed general; for models with n variables, systems of n simultaneous linear equations need to be solved. For this reason, we shall take a short departure in this chapter and study the algebra of such systems. We will then show how this algebra can simplify the comparative statics of economic models.

Let us begin with the simplest system of simultaneous equations, two equations in two unknowns. Let us denote these equations as

$$a_{11}x_1 + a_{12}x_2 = b_1$$
$$a_{21}x_1 + a_{22}x_2 = b_2 \tag{5-1}$$

Notice the double-subscript notation for the coefficients. This permits easy identification of these numbers. The element a_{ij} appears in the ith *row* (horizontal) and jth *column* (vertical). Here, i and j take on the values $1, 2$; in general, they will run from 1 through n.

A very convenient notation that is extensively used in virtually all sciences involves separating out the coefficients (the a_{ij}'s) from the unknowns (the x_i's) and writing equations (5-1) thus:

$$\begin{pmatrix} a_{11} & a_{12} \\ a_{21} & a_{22} \end{pmatrix} \begin{pmatrix} x_1 \\ x_2 \end{pmatrix} = \begin{pmatrix} b_1 \\ b_2 \end{pmatrix} \tag{5-2}$$

This is known as *matrix notation*; the rectangular arrays of numbers are called *matrices* (plural of matrix). In general, the system of m equations in n unknowns

$$a_{11}x_1 + a_{12}x_2 + \cdots + a_{1n}x_n = b_1$$
$$a_{21}x_1 + a_{22}x_2 + \cdots + a_{2n}x_n = b_2 \qquad (5\text{-}3)$$
$$\cdots\cdots\cdots\cdots\cdots\cdots\cdots\cdots\cdots$$
$$a_{m1}x_1 + a_{m2}x_2 + \cdots + a_{mn}x_n = b_m$$

is written in matrix form as

$$\begin{pmatrix} a_{11} & a_{12} & \cdots & a_{1n} \\ a_{21} & a_{22} & \cdots & a_{2n} \\ \cdots & \cdots & \cdots & \cdots \\ a_{m1} & a_{m2} & \cdots & a_{mn} \end{pmatrix} \begin{pmatrix} x_1 \\ x_2 \\ \vdots \\ x_n \end{pmatrix} = \begin{pmatrix} b_1 \\ b_2 \\ \vdots \\ b_m \end{pmatrix} \qquad (5\text{-}4)$$

The system (5-4) is just another way of writing equations (5-3). This system involves "multiplication" of an $m \times n$ (m rows, n columns) matrix by an $n \times 1$ matrix, forming another $m \times 1$ matrix on the right-hand side. In general for any coefficient b_i from (5-3),

$$\sum_{j=1}^{n} a_{ij}x_j = b_i \qquad i = 1, \ldots, m \qquad (5\text{-}5)$$

Notice that to arrive at any particular b_i, the elements of the ith row of the (a_{ij}) matrix are multiplied, term by term with the elements of the (x_j) matrix, which consists of only one column, and those products are then summed. In this manner, general matrix multiplication is defined. Consider the matrix "product"

$$\begin{pmatrix} a_{11} & \cdots & a_{1n} \\ \cdots & \cdots & \cdots \\ a_{m1} & \cdots & a_{mn} \end{pmatrix} \begin{pmatrix} b_{11} & \cdots & b_{1r} \\ \cdots & \cdots & \cdots \\ b_{nr} & \cdots & b_{nr} \end{pmatrix} = \begin{pmatrix} c_{11} & \cdots & c_{1r} \\ \cdots & \cdots & \cdots \\ c_{m1} & \cdots & c_{mr} \end{pmatrix} \qquad (5\text{-}6)$$

or, simply, $$\mathbf{AB} = \mathbf{C}$$

Any element c_{ij} of the $\mathbf{C}$ matrix is defined to be

$$\sum_{k=1}^{n} a_{ik}b_{kj} = c_{ij} \qquad i = 1, \ldots, m, j = 1, \ldots, r \qquad (5\text{-}7)$$

That is, the element in the ith row and jth column of $\mathbf{C}$ is defined to be the sum of the products, term by term, of the elements in the ith row of $\mathbf{A}$ and the jth column of $\mathbf{B}$. This definition is therefore valid only if the number of *columns* of $\mathbf{A}$ equals the number of *rows* of $\mathbf{B}$. Otherwise, the definition yields nonsense.

Example 1

$$\begin{pmatrix} 2 & 1 & 0 \\ 3 & -1 & 1 \end{pmatrix} \begin{pmatrix} 1 & -1 \\ 2 & 0 \\ 0 & 2 \end{pmatrix} = \begin{pmatrix} 4 & -2 \\ 1 & -1 \end{pmatrix}$$

Here, a 2×3 matrix is multiplied by a 3×2 matrix. It results in a 2×2 matrix.

Example 2

$$\begin{pmatrix} 2 & 1 \\ -1 & 1 \end{pmatrix}\begin{pmatrix} 1 \\ 4 \end{pmatrix} = \begin{pmatrix} 6 \\ 3 \end{pmatrix}$$

A matrix with only one column is sometimes called a column vector or column matrix; a matrix with only one row is sometimes called a row vector or row matrix.

Example 3

$$(1 \quad 4)\begin{pmatrix} 2 & 1 \\ -1 & 1 \end{pmatrix} = (-2 \quad 5)$$

Notice that it *matters* if matrices are multiplied on the left or on the right; different matrices result.

Consider any two n vectors,

$$\mathbf{a} = (a_1, \ldots, a_n)$$
$$\mathbf{b} = (b_1, \ldots, b_n)$$

The scalar product $\mathbf{ab}$ (variously called the *dot product* or *inner product*, sometimes written $\mathbf{a} \cdot \mathbf{b}$) is defined to be

$$\mathbf{ab} = \sum_{i=1}^{n} a_i b_i$$

The matrix product $\mathbf{AB}$ can be seen to be defined in terms of the scalar product of the *row* vectors of $\mathbf{A}$ and *column* vectors of $\mathbf{B}$.

The algebra of matrices will be relegated to the appendix of this chapter. We are concerned here only with a way of systematically representing the solution of simultaneous equations.

5.2 DETERMINANTS, CRAMER'S RULE

Let us return to the two equation, two unknown system (5-1):

$$a_{11}x_1 + a_{12}x_2 = b_1$$
$$a_{21}x_1 + a_{22}x_2 = b_2 \tag{5-1}$$

To solve these equations for x_1, we multiply the first equation by a_{22} and the second equation by a_{12}, and subtract the second equation from the first:

$$(a_{11}a_{22} - a_{12}a_{21})x_1 = b_1 a_{22} - b_2 a_{12}$$

If $\qquad\qquad a_{11}a_{22} - a_{12}a_{21} \neq 0$

then $\qquad\qquad\qquad x_1 = \dfrac{b_1 a_{22} - b_2 a_{12}}{a_{11}a_{22} - a_{12}a_{21}}$ (5-8)

Similarly, to solve for x_2, multiply the first equation by a_{21} and the second by a_{11}, then subtract the first equation from the second:

$$(a_{11}a_{22} - a_{12}a_{21})x_2 = b_2 a_{11} - b_1 a_{21}$$

If, again $\qquad\qquad a_{11}a_{22} - a_{12}a_{21} \neq 0$

then $\qquad\qquad\qquad x_2 = \dfrac{b_2 a_{11} - b_1 a_{21}}{a_{11}a_{22} - a_{12}a_{21}}$ (5-9)

Let us now define something called a 2×2 *determinant*, or a *determinant of order 2*. Suppose

$$\begin{pmatrix} a & b \\ c & d \end{pmatrix}$$

is any *square*, 2×2 matrix. The determinant of this square matrix, written with straight vertical lines around the matrix, is defined to be

$$D_2 = \begin{vmatrix} a & b \\ c & d \end{vmatrix} = ad - bc$$ (5-10)

That is, the product of the upper right and lower left elements is subtracted from the product of the upper left and lower right elements.†

In terms of determinants, the solutions (5-8) and (5-9) can be written

$$x_1 = \frac{\begin{vmatrix} b_1 & a_{12} \\ b_2 & a_{22} \end{vmatrix}}{\begin{vmatrix} a_{11} & a_{12} \\ a_{21} & a_{22} \end{vmatrix}} \qquad x_2 = \frac{\begin{vmatrix} a_{11} & b_1 \\ a_{21} & b_2 \end{vmatrix}}{\begin{vmatrix} a_{11} & a_{12} \\ a_{21} & a_{22} \end{vmatrix}}$$

Notice that the determinant in the denominator of these expressions is the determinant of the matrix of coefficients, (a_{ij}). In the numerators, for the solution for x_1, the *first* column of the $|a_{ij}|$ determinant is replaced with the b_i's, whereas for x_2, the *second* column is replaced by the b_i's. This formula is known as *Cramer's rule*. It is the generalization of this rule to n variables that we shall investigate.

Notice that the solutions for x_1 and x_2 exist only if

$$|\mathbf{A}| = \begin{vmatrix} a_{11} & a_{12} \\ a_{21} & a_{22} \end{vmatrix} \neq 0$$

What is the geometric significance of this condition? Equations (5-1) represent two straight lines in the $x_1 x_2$ plane. These equations will not have any solution at

---

† Throughout this text, matrices and vectors will be indicated by boldface type. The determinant of a square matrix $\mathbf{A}$ will be indicated by the symbol $|\mathbf{A}|$ or A.

all if the lines are parallel; if the lines are not only parallel but coincident, an infinity (all points on the common line) of solutions result.

These two lines will be parallel if they have the same slope. Solving each equation for x_2, equations (5-1) are equivalent to

$$x_2 = -\frac{a_{11}}{a_{12}}x_1 + \frac{b_1}{a_{12}}$$

$$x_2 = -\frac{a_{21}}{a_{22}}x_1 + \frac{b_2}{a_{22}}$$

If the slopes are the same, then

$$\frac{a_{11}}{a_{12}} = \frac{a_{21}}{a_{22}}$$

or

$$|\mathbf{A}| = \begin{vmatrix} a_{11} & a_{12} \\ a_{21} & a_{22} \end{vmatrix} = a_{11}a_{22} - a_{12}a_{21} = 0$$

Hence the inability to solve equations (5-1) because $|\mathbf{A}| = 0$ occurs because the lines are parallel or coincident.

Consider now a system of three equations in three unknowns:

$$\begin{pmatrix} a_{11} & a_{12} & a_{13} \\ a_{21} & a_{22} & a_{23} \\ a_{31} & a_{32} & a_{33} \end{pmatrix} \begin{pmatrix} x_1 \\ x_2 \\ x_3 \end{pmatrix} = \begin{pmatrix} b_1 \\ b_2 \\ b_3 \end{pmatrix} \tag{5-11}$$

Define the determinant of order 3 as

$$D_3 = \begin{vmatrix} a_{11} & a_{12} & a_{13} \\ a_{21} & a_{22} & a_{23} \\ a_{31} & a_{32} & a_{33} \end{vmatrix} = a_{11} \begin{vmatrix} a_{22} & a_{23} \\ a_{32} & a_{33} \end{vmatrix} - a_{12} \begin{vmatrix} a_{21} & a_{23} \\ a_{31} & a_{33} \end{vmatrix}$$

$$+ a_{13} \begin{vmatrix} a_{21} & a_{22} \\ a_{31} & a_{32} \end{vmatrix} \tag{5-12}$$

The determinant D_3 is defined in terms of certain second-order determinants. All in all, six terms involving the products of three elements are involved, with particular signs. Notice that the determinant which is multiplied by a_{11} is that determinant which remains from D_3 when row 1 and column 1 are deleted. In like fashion, the determinant which is multiplied by a_{12} is that determinant which remains from D_3 when row 1 and column 2 are deleted (the row and column that a_{12} appears in), and similarly for the last determinant.

We define the *minor of a_{ij}* as that determinant which remains when row i and column j are deleted from the original determinant.

In the above definition of D_3, the elements of the first row are multiplied by their respective minors, but one such minor comes in with a negative sign.

Define the *cofactor of a_{ij}*, written A_{ij}, as $(-1)^{i+j}$ times the minor of a_{ij}. (Sometimes the term *signed cofactor* is used. This is redundant, though perhaps useful to emphasize the signing element $(-1)^{i+j}$.) In terms of cofactors, D_3 can be written

$$D_3 = a_{11}A_{11} + a_{12}A_{12} + a_{13}A_{13} \qquad (5\text{-}13)$$

Expanding this expression i.e., equation (5-12),

$$D_3 = a_{11}a_{22}a_{33} - a_{11}a_{23}a_{32} - a_{12}a_{21}a_{33} + a_{12}a_{23}a_{31} + a_{13}a_{21}a_{32}$$
$$- a_{13}a_{22}a_{31} \qquad (5\text{-}14)$$

In each triple, the three elements come from different rows and columns. No row or column is ever repeated. (If you are a chess player, the triples represent all possible ways three castles, or rooks can be placed on a 3×3 chessboard such that they cannot capture one another.) Equation (5-14) can be factored in another way, e.g.,

$$D_3 = -a_{12}(a_{21}a_{33} - a_{23}a_{31}) + a_{22}(a_{11}a_{33} - a_{13}a_{31})$$
$$- a_{32}(a_{11}a_{23} - a_{13}a_{21}) \qquad (5\text{-}15)$$

But this factorization can be written in terms of the elements and cofactors of column 2. By inspection, from (5-15)

$$D_3 = a_{12}A_{12} + a_{22}A_{22} + a_{32}A_{32} \qquad (5\text{-}16)$$

(Notice that A_{12} and A_{32} both have negative signing factors, since $(-1)^{1+2} = (-1)^{3+2} = -1$. This doesn't mean that A_{12} or A_{32} are necessarily negative; just that the *minors* of a_{12} and a_{32} are multiplied by -1.)

This algebra indicates that D_3 can be defined as the sum of the products of the elements of *any* row or *any* column times their respective cofactors. That is, D_3 can be written as:

$$D_3 = \sum_{j=1}^{3} a_{ij}A_{ij} = \sum_{i=1}^{3} a_{ij}A_{ij} \qquad (5\text{-}17)$$

In the first sum, the determinant is expanded using the elements and cofactors of row i; in the second sum, column j is used. Either way, the same number results. This result can be proved for determinants of order 3 by simply finding all six sums and verifying the result. More importantly, it is the generality of this result that is useful.

Determinants of higher order can be defined in terms of lower-order ones. That is,

$$D_4 = \begin{vmatrix} a_{11} & a_{12} & a_{13} & a_{14} \\ a_{21} & a_{22} & a_{23} & a_{24} \\ a_{31} & a_{32} & a_{33} & a_{34} \\ a_{41} & a_{42} & a_{43} & a_{44} \end{vmatrix} = a_{11}A_{11} + a_{12}A_{12} + a_{13}A_{13} + a_{14}A_{14}$$

where A_{ij} is the (signed) cofactor of element a_{ij}, that is, $(-1)^{i+j}$ times that third-order determinant that remains when row i and column j are deleted from D_4. The generalization of equation (5-17) will be stated now, without proof.

Theorem 1 Let D_n be any nth-order determinant of a square matrix $\mathbf{A} = (a_{ij})$. Then

$$D_n = \sum_{j=1}^{n} a_{ij} A_{ij} = \sum_{i=1}^{n} a_{ij} A_{ij} \tag{5-18}$$

where A_{ij} is the cofactor of element a_{ij}.

We shall now state and briefly sketch the proofs of the important elementary properties of determinants, culminating in Cramer's rule.

Theorem 2 If all the elements in any row (column) of D_n are 0, then $D_n = 0$.

PROOF Expanded D_n by that given row (column), and the sum of many 0's is 0.

Theorem 3 If D'_n is obtained from D_n by interchanging any two rows (columns) then $D'_n = -D_n$. A rigorous proof will not be given. However, it is clear that the same terms are involved in D'_n as in D_n since all the n-tuples are chosen with one element from each row and column, with no repeats. Only the signing factor $(-1)^{i+j}$ can be affected. If row 1 is interchanged, say, with row 2, then expanding D_n by the second row means that the signing factor will be $(-1)^{2+j}$ instead of $(-1)^{1+j}$. Hence, the sign of D_n will reverse. If row 1 and row 3 are interchanged, we can consider this as three separate steps: interchange rows 1 and 2, then 1 and 3, and then 3 and 2. This *odd* number of reversals changes the sign of D_n. The result in fact follows, as the theorem indicates, for an arbitrary interchange of rows, or an arbitrary interchange of columns.

Theorem 4 If D'_n is obtained from D_n by multiplying any row (column) by some scalar (number) k, then $D'_n = kD_n$.

PROOF Take that given row (column) and expand D_n by the cofactors of that row or column. Then k appears in each term, and, by factoring it out, the result is obtained.

Theorem 5 If D_n has 2 rows (columns) which are identical, then $D_n = 0$.

PROOF If any two rows, in particular the two identical ones are interchanged, then by Theorem 3 the value of the resulting determinant is opposite in sign but has the same absolute value as the original determinant. But since the determinant has exactly the same elements after interchange as before, the value of the determinant must be identical. The only value which satisfies this relationship of $D_n = -D_n$ is $D_n = 0$.

Corollary If one row (column) is proportional to another row (column) then $D_n = 0$.

PROOF Factor out the constant of proportionality and then use Theorem 5.

Theorem 6 Suppose each element of the kth row, a_{kj}, is equal to $a_{kj} = b_{kj} + c_{kj}$, the sum of two terms. Then let D'_n be the determinant formed by using the elements b_{kj} in the kth row and D''_n be the determinant formed using c_{kj} as elements in row k. Then $D_n = D'_n + D''_n$.

PROOF Expanding D_n by the elements and cofactors of row k,

$$D_n = (b_{k1} + c_{k1})A_{k1} + \cdots + (b_{kn} + c_{kn})A_{kn}$$

$$= \sum_{j=1}^{n} b_{kj} A_{kj} + \sum_{j=1}^{n} c_{kj} A_{kj} = D'_n + D''_n$$

Theorem 7 If D'_n is formed by adding, term by term, a multiple of any row (column) of D_n to another row (column) of D_n, then $D'_n = D_n$.

PROOF Consider for example the 3×3 determinant

$$D_3 = \begin{vmatrix} a_{11} & a_{12} & a_{13} \\ a_{21} & a_{22} & a_{23} \\ a_{31} & a_{32} & a_{33} \end{vmatrix}$$

Multiply the elements in row 1 by some number k and add this product, term by term, to row 2. Then

$$D'_3 = \begin{vmatrix} a_{11} & a_{12} & a_{13} \\ a_{21} + ka_{11} & a_{22} + ka_{12} & a_{23} + ka_{13} \\ a_{31} & a_{32} & a_{33} \end{vmatrix}$$

By Theorem 6

$$D'_3 = \begin{vmatrix} a_{11} & a_{12} & a_{13} \\ a_{21} & a_{22} & a_{23} \\ a_{31} & a_{32} & a_{33} \end{vmatrix} + k \begin{vmatrix} a_{11} & a_{12} & a_{13} \\ a_{11} & a_{12} & a_{13} \\ a_{31} & a_{32} & a_{33} \end{vmatrix}$$

By Theorem 5, this latter determinant equals 0. Thus $D'_3 = D_3$. The proof is general, of course, for any two rows (or columns), for any size determinant.

Theorem 8 If the elements of any row (column) are multiplied by the respective cofactors of some other row (column), the resulting sum is zero. This process is called *expansion by alien cofactors*.

PROOF This is equivalent to expanding a determinant which has two identical rows. Consider again the 3×3 determinant of the previous theorem. The theorem asserts, for example, that

$$a_{21} A_{11} + a_{22} A_{12} + a_{23} A_{13} = 0$$

This is the expansion of the determinant

$$\begin{vmatrix} a_{21} & a_{22} & a_{23} \\ a_{21} & a_{22} & a_{23} \\ a_{31} & a_{32} & a_{33} \end{vmatrix}$$

by row 1 or row 2. But this determinant is 0 by theorem 5. The generalization to any D_n is straightforward.

Theorem 9 (Cramer's rule) Consider a system of n linear equations in n unknowns,

$$\begin{pmatrix} a_{11} & \cdots & a_{1n} \\ \cdots\cdots\cdots \\ a_{n1} & \cdots & a_{nn} \end{pmatrix} \begin{pmatrix} x_1 \\ \vdots \\ x_n \end{pmatrix} = \begin{pmatrix} b_1 \\ \vdots \\ b_n \end{pmatrix}$$

If the determinant $|\mathbf{A}|$ of the coefficient matrix $\mathbf{A} = (a_{ij})$ is nonzero, then a unique solution exists for each x_i. In particular, the solution for each x_i may be expressed as the quotient of two determinants: the denominator is always the determinant $|\mathbf{A}|$, while the numerator is that determinant which is formed when column i in $|\mathbf{A}|$ is replaced by the column of b_i's. For example,

$$x_1 = \frac{\begin{vmatrix} b_1 & a_{12} & \cdots & a_{1n} \\ \cdots\cdots\cdots\cdots\cdots \\ b_n & a_{n2} & \cdots & a_{nn} \end{vmatrix}}{|\mathbf{A}|}$$

$$x_2 = \frac{\begin{vmatrix} a_{11} & b_1 & \cdots & a_{1n} \\ \cdots\cdots\cdots\cdots\cdots \\ a_{n1} & b_n & \cdots & a_{nn} \end{vmatrix}}{|\mathbf{A}|}$$

PROOF We shall demonstrate Cramer's rule for the three-equation case only. Consider such a system:

$$a_{11}x_1 + a_{12}x_2 + a_{13}x_3 = b_1$$
$$a_{21}x_1 + a_{22}x_2 + a_{23}x_3 = b_2 \tag{5-19}$$
$$a_{31}x_1 + a_{32}x_2 + a_{33}x_3 = b_3$$

In general, these equations are solved by multiplying through by various numbers, adding or subtracting one equation from another, etc. The theory of determinants gives us some handy numbers to work with.

Let us solve for x_1. Multiply the first equation through by A_{11}, the cofactor of a_{11}; multiply the second and third equations, respectively, by A_{21} and A_{31}. Then add the three resulting equations together. After factoring out the x_is, this yields

$$(a_{11}A_{11} + a_{21}A_{21} + a_{31}A_{31})x_1 + (a_{12}A_{11} + a_{22}A_{21} + a_{32}A_{31})x_2$$
$$+ (a_{13}A_{11} + a_{23}A_{21} + a_{33}A_{31})x_3 = b_1A_{11} + b_2A_{21} + b_3A_{31} \tag{5-20}$$

The first parentheses in (5-20) equals the determinant $|\mathbf{A}|$, since it is the sum of the elements in the first column of $|\mathbf{A}|$ times their respective cofactors. The second and third parentheses, however, represent an expansion by alien cofactors. There, the elements of the second or third column are multiplied by the cofactors of the first column, and summed. By Theorem 8, these terms sum to 0. Hence equation (5-20) reduces to

$$|\mathbf{A}|x_1 = b_1 A_{11} + b_2 A_{21} + b_3 A_{31}$$

If $|\mathbf{A}| \neq 0$,

$$x_1 = \frac{\begin{vmatrix} b_1 & a_{12} & a_{13} \\ b_2 & a_{22} & a_{23} \\ b_3 & a_{32} & a_{33} \end{vmatrix}}{|\mathbf{A}|} \tag{5-21}$$

In like fashion x_2 is obtained by multiplying equations 1, 2 and 3 in (5-19) by A_{12}, A_{22} and A_{32}, respectively, and summing. Then the coefficients of x_1 and x_3 are 0, and the b_i's multiply the respective cofactors of the second column. The same procedure obtains the general result, as stated in the theorem.

5.3 APPLICATION OF DETERMINANTS TO COMPARATIVE STATICS

The reason for studying determinants is not so much to actually solve given equations, but to be able to systematically write down the solutions to simultaneous linear equations. This need arises because the comparative statics of economic models involves simultaneous linear equations in the partial derivatives of choice variables with respect to parameters.

Consider again the profit-maximizing firm analyzed in Chap. 4, and recall equations (4-19):

$$pf_{11} \frac{\partial x_1^*}{\partial w_1} + pf_{12} \frac{\partial x_2^*}{\partial w_1} \equiv 1$$

$$pf_{21} \frac{\partial x_1^*}{\partial w_1} + pf_{22} \frac{\partial x_2^*}{\partial w_1} \equiv 0 \tag{4-19}$$

In matrix form these equations appear as

$$\begin{pmatrix} pf_{11} & pf_{12} \\ pf_{21} & pf_{22} \end{pmatrix} \begin{pmatrix} \dfrac{\partial x_1^*}{\partial w_1} \\ \dfrac{\partial x_2^*}{\partial w_1} \end{pmatrix} \equiv \begin{pmatrix} 1 \\ 0 \end{pmatrix} \tag{5-22}$$

Using Cramer's rule,

$$\frac{\partial x_1^*}{\partial w_1} = \frac{\begin{vmatrix} 1 & pf_{12} \\ 0 & pf_{22} \end{vmatrix}}{D} = \frac{pf_{22}}{D} \tag{5-23}$$

where $D = \begin{vmatrix} pf_{11} & pf_{12} \\ pf_{21} & pf_{22} \end{vmatrix}$

This is equation (4-20a), which was derived by algebraic manipulations. Notice that the term 1 on the right-hand side of (5-22) will always appear in column i, in the solution for $\partial x_i^*/\partial w_j$. If the numerator is expanded by that column, it is immediately apparent that equations (4-20a–d) can be written as

$$\frac{\partial x_i^*}{\partial w_j} = \frac{D_{ji}}{D} \qquad i, j = 1, 2 \tag{5-24}$$

where D_{ji} is the cofactor (signed, of course) of the element in the jth row and ith column. In this model, $D_{11} = pf_{22}, D_{22} = pf_{11}, D_{12} = D_{21} = -pf_{12}$. Notice, too, that $D = p^2(f_{11}f_{22} - f_{12}^2)$, and that $D > 0$, from the second-order conditions (4-15). This is in fact indicative of a trend; determinants will play a crucial role in the theory of maxima and minima.

In like fashion, equations (4-21), dealing with changes in the factor utilizations due to output-price changes, can be written

$$(pf_{ij}) \begin{pmatrix} \dfrac{\partial x_1^*}{\partial p} \\[2mm] \dfrac{\partial x_2^*}{\partial p} \end{pmatrix} \equiv \begin{pmatrix} -f_1 \\ -f_2 \end{pmatrix} \tag{5-25}$$

where the expression (pf_{ij}) stands for the 2×2 matrix in the left-hand side of (5-22). It is obvious from Cramer's rule that the solutions for $\partial x_1^*/\partial p$ and $\partial x_2^*/\partial p$ will involve the "off-diagonal" terms of pf_{12} and pf_{21}. Since the sign of these (equal) terms is not implied by maximization, we immediately suspect that no sign will emerge for $\partial x_1^*/\partial p$, etc., and hence no refutable hypotheses concerning the responses of inputs to output-price changes will emerge.

The two-factor profit-maximization firm is an example of a maximization model with two choice variables. The most general form of such models is†

maximize $\qquad\qquad f(x_1, x_2, \alpha) \tag{5-26}$

where the choice variables are x_1 and x_2 and α is a parameter, or perhaps a vector of parameters, $\alpha = (\alpha_1, \ldots, \alpha_m)$. The first-order necessary conditions implied by (5-26), usually called the *equilibrium conditions*, are

$$f_1(x_1, x_2, \alpha) = 0$$
$$f_2(x_1, x_2, \alpha) = 0 \tag{5-27}$$

---

† The function f here refers to the whole maximand, not just the production function part of the previous objective function.

The second-order sufficient conditions are

$$f_{11} < 0 \qquad f_{22} < 0 \qquad f_{11} f_{22} - f_{12}^2 > 0 \tag{5-28}$$

Equations (5-27) are two equations in three variables, x_1, x_2, and α. Under conditions we shall presently discuss, these equations can be solved for the explicit choice functions

$$x_1 = x_1^*(\alpha)$$

$$x_2 = x_2^*(\alpha) \tag{5-29}$$

It should always be remembered that equations (5-29) are the *simultaneous* solutions of (5-27). As the parameter α changes, *both* x_1 and x_2 will in general change. Substituting (5-29) back into (5-27) the identities from which the comparative statics are derivable are obtained:

$$f_1(x_1^*(\alpha), x_2^*(\alpha), \alpha) \equiv 0$$

$$f_2(x_1^*(\alpha), x_2^*(\alpha), \alpha) \equiv 0 \tag{5-30}$$

Differentiating this system with respect to α, the following system is obtained.

$$f_{11} \frac{\partial x_1^*}{\partial \alpha} + f_{12} \frac{\partial x_2^*}{\partial \alpha} + f_{1\alpha} \equiv 0$$

$$f_{21} \frac{\partial x_1^*}{\partial \alpha} + f_{22} \frac{\partial x_2^*}{\partial \alpha} + f_{2\alpha} \equiv 0 \tag{5-31}$$

In matrix form, this system is

$$\begin{pmatrix} f_{11} & f_{12} \\ f_{21} & f_{22} \end{pmatrix} \begin{pmatrix} \dfrac{\partial x_1^*}{\partial \alpha} \\ \dfrac{\partial x_2^*}{\partial \alpha} \end{pmatrix} \equiv \begin{pmatrix} -f_{1\alpha} \\ -f_{2\alpha} \end{pmatrix} \tag{5-32}$$

Solving by Cramer's rule,

$$\frac{\partial x_1^*}{\partial \alpha} = \frac{\begin{vmatrix} -f_{1\alpha} & f_{12} \\ -f_{2\alpha} & f_{22} \end{vmatrix}}{D} = \frac{-f_{1\alpha} f_{22}}{D} + \frac{f_{2\alpha} f_{12}}{D} \tag{5-33a}$$

and

$$\frac{\partial x_2^*}{\partial \alpha} = \frac{\begin{vmatrix} f_{11} & -f_{1\alpha} \\ f_{21} & -f_{2\alpha} \end{vmatrix}}{D} = \frac{-f_{2\alpha} f_{11}}{D} + \frac{f_{1\alpha} f_{21}}{D} \tag{5-33b}$$

where D is the determinant

$$D = \begin{vmatrix} f_{11} & f_{12} \\ f_{21} & f_{22} \end{vmatrix} = f_{11} f_{22} - f_{12}^2 > 0 \tag{5-34}$$

Equations (5-33) represent the most general comparative statics relations for unconstrained maximization models with two choice variables. Not surprisingly at this level of generality, no refutable hypotheses are implied. Certain information is available, though. The denominators D in equations (5-33) are positive. In addition, f_{11}, f_{22} are negative. This information is provided by the sufficient conditions for a maximum.

The other information that is available is provided by the actual structure of the model. Specifically, to be useful, a model will be constructed so that the effects of the parameters on the objective function, and hence the first-order equations will in general be known. That is, $f_{1\alpha}$ and $f_{2\alpha}$ will have an assumed sign, or else the model is simply not specified well enough to yield any results. In the profit-maximization model above, for the factor prices, (recall, f in that model designates only the production function, not the whole objective function)

$$f_{i\alpha} = \pi_{iw_i} = -1 \qquad i = 1, 2 \tag{5-35}$$

and

$$\pi_{1w_2} = \pi_{2w_1} = 0$$

The parameter w_1, for example, appears only in the first first-order equation, $\pi_1 = 0$. That is, $f_{2\alpha} \equiv 0$, in equations (5-31). For that reason, the term involving the cross-partial f_{12} in equation (5-33a) is 0. Since $\pi_{1w_1} = -1$, the result $\partial x_1^*/\partial w_1 < 0$ is obtained, for the profit-maximization model.

Similarly, for w_2, $f_{2\alpha} \equiv -1$, $f_{1\alpha} \equiv 0$. Hence, in equation (5-33b), the only remaining term on the right-hand side is $-f_{2\alpha}f_{11}/D$. From the second-order conditions, $\partial x_2^*/\partial w_2 < 0$ is implied.

The situation is different for the parameter p, output price. Output price enters *both* first-order equations (5-31). Therefore, the indeterminate cross-term f_{12} appears in the expressions for $\partial x_1^*/\partial p$ and $\partial x_2^*/\partial p$. As a result, no refutable hypotheses emerge for this parameter, with regard to each input.

The above analysis suggests that refutable comparative statics theorems will be forthcoming in a maximization model only if a given parameter enters one and only one first-order equation. This result, known as the *conjugate pairs theorem*, will be shown in greater generality in the next and succeeding chapters. From equations (5-33), if some parameter, α_i, enters only the ith first-order equation, then $\partial x_i^*/\partial \alpha_i$ and $f_{i\alpha_i}$ must have the same sign. This can be expressed as

$$f_{i\alpha_i} \frac{\partial x_i^*}{\partial \alpha_i} > 0 \tag{5-36}$$

Virtually all of the comparative statics results in economics are specific instances of equation (5-36), where some parameter α_i enters only the ith first-order equation.

5.4 THE IMPLICIT FUNCTION THEOREM

We have referred at several instances to the problem of "solving" the implicit equilibrium or choice relations, equations

$$f_1(x_1, x_2, \alpha) = 0$$

$$f_2(x_1, x_2, \alpha) = 0 \tag{5-37}$$

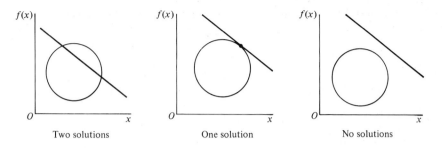

Two solutions   One solution   No solutions

Figure 5-1 In general, with nonlinear functions, no general assertions are possible regarding the number of solutions to n equations and n unknowns.

for the explicit relations

$$x_1 = x_1^*(\alpha)$$

$$x_2 = x_2^*(\alpha) \tag{5-38}$$

Sufficient conditions under which this procedure is valid are known as the *implicit function theorem*. One should be wary, incidentally, of a "nontheorem" which appears every now and then. This nontheorem asserts that if there are n equations and n unknowns, a unique solution results. This proposition is valid only in the case of *linear* equations whose coefficient matrix has a nonzero determinant. Figures 5-1a, b, and c demonstrate why the theorem cannot be applied to nonlinear functions.

The implicit function theorem is narrower in scope than the above nontheorem. Suppose equations (5-37) have a unique simultaneous solution at some point (x_1^0, x_2^0, α^0). Under what conditions can the implicit relations (5-37) be written as the explicit relations (5-38)?

To answer this, consider first the simplest case of one equation in two unknowns, e.g., the unit circle, depicted in Fig. 5-2,

$$x^2 + y^2 = 1 \tag{5-39}$$

For this function to be written as some explicit function, $y = f(x)$, a *unique y* must be associated with any x, around a certain point. Of course, (5-39) can be solved for y as

$$y = \pm(1 - x^2)^{1/2}$$

The function as written here is technically not a function at all; for each x, *two* values of y are given, instead of a unique y. However, such is not the case for solutions around individual points on the unit circle. Consider some point, A, $x = 1/\sqrt{2}, y = 1/\sqrt{2}$. In some *neighborhood* around $x = 1/\sqrt{2}$, a unique value of y is associated. That is, *around $x = 1/\sqrt{2}, y = 1/\sqrt{2}$*, the explicit functional relation

$$y = +(1 - x^2)^{1/2} \tag{5-40}$$

is valid. The implicit function (5-39) admits an explicit solution *around the point A*, not necessarily for all x.

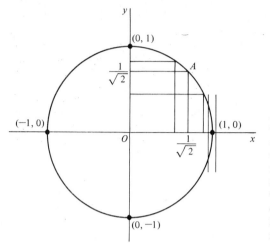

Figure 5-2 *The implicit function theorem.* Around any point where the circle is not vertical, a unique y exists for any x. However, around $x = +1$ or $x = -1$, *two* values of y are associated with any x, no matter how small the interval is made around that x value. If the function is *not* vertical, thus, an explicit solution $y = f(x)$ exists for an explicit relation $g(x,\ y) = 0$. However, $\partial g/\partial y \neq 0$ while sufficient, is not necessary.

The situation is different, however, at the intercepts of the unit circle and the x axis, the points $(-1, 0)$ and $(1, 0)$. At either of these two points, no matter how small the interval is made around the point, any value of x will be associated with *two* values of y. The implicit relation (5-39) does *not* admit of an explicit solution $y = f(x)$. An explicit solution of x on y, that is, $x = g(y)$ does exist—for any value of y around $(1, 0)$ or $(-1, 0)$, a unique value of x is implied [however, not at the points $(0, 1)$ and $(0, -1)$].

It can be seen that the reason why the implicit equation $x^2 + y^2 = 1$ does not admit of a unique solution $y = f(x)$ at $(1, 0)$ and $(-1, 0)$ is that at these points, the function *turns back* on itself. Moving counterclockwise around the circle, as y increases through the value 0, on the right hemicircle, x first increases and then decreases. (On the left hemicircle, moving clockwise, x decreases and then increases.) At the points $(1, 0)$ and $(-1, 0)$ the implicit function $x^2 + y^2 = 1$ is *vertical*, that is, $dy/dx \to \pm\infty$. As long as the function is not vertical, the implicit relation yields a well-defined explicit solution $y = f(x)$.

We can see how the analysis above relates to the ability to do comparative statics, in one-variable models. Consider one implicit choice equation, which might be the first-order equation of some objective function:

$$h(y,\ \alpha) = 0 \tag{5-41}$$

To find $\partial y/\partial \alpha$, an explicit solution of (5-41) must be assumed:

$$y = y^*(\alpha) \tag{5-42}$$

Substituting (5-42) into (5-41), the identity

$$h(y^*(\alpha),\ \alpha) \equiv 0 \tag{5-43}$$

results. Differentiating with respect to α,

$$h_y \frac{\partial y^*}{\partial \alpha} + h_\alpha \equiv 0 \tag{5-44}$$

In order to solve (5-44) for $\partial y^*/\partial\alpha$,

$$h_y \neq 0 \qquad\qquad (5\text{-}45)$$

must be assumed. This amounts to assuming that the function $h(y, \alpha)$ is not vertical (α plotted horizontally, y vertically).

In maximization models, the *sufficient* second-order conditions guarantee the existence of the explicit solutions (5-42). In these models, the implicit relation (5-41) is already the first partial of some objective function, $f(y, \alpha)$. That is, (5-41) is

$$f_y(y, \alpha) \equiv h(y, \alpha) = 0$$

The condition that $h_y \neq 0$ is guaranteed by the *sufficient* second-order condition for a maximum

$$f_{yy} \equiv h_y < 0$$

It should be noted that whereas $h_y \neq 0$ is sufficient to be able to write $y = y^*(\alpha)$, it is not necessary. There are some functions for which $h_y = 0$ at some point, and it is still possible to write $y = y^*(\alpha)$. For example, consider the function

$$y^3 - \alpha = 0$$

The solution to this equation, depicted in Fig. 5-3, is

$$y = \alpha^{1/3}$$

Although $dy/d\alpha \to \infty$ as $\alpha \to 0$, it is still the case that a unique y is associated with any α around $\alpha = 0$; the function, while vertical at $\alpha = 0$ does not turn back on itself there.

In models with two equations and two choice variables, the situation is algebraically more complicated, but conceptually similar. Consider the system (5-37) again, but let us just assume that these are just two equations in three unknowns,

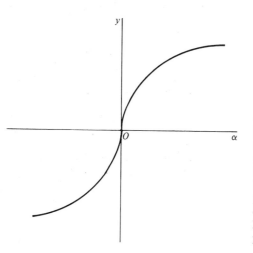

Figure 5-3 *The function $y = \alpha^{1/3}$.* This function illustrates why the condition $h_y < 0$ is sufficient but not necessary for writing an implicit function in explicit form. This function becomes vertical at the origin, yet it is still possible to define y as a single-valued function of α, because $\alpha^{1/3}$ does not turn back on itself. If $h_y \neq 0$, the explicit formulation is *always* possible; if $h_y = 0$, it *may* not be.

x_1, x_2, and α, without assuming for the moment that there exists an $f(x_1, x_2, \alpha)$ for which $f_1 = \partial f/\partial x_1, f_2 = \partial f/\partial x_2$. A *sufficient* condition that equations (5-37) admit the explicit solution (5-38) at some point is that neither of the explicit functions (5-38) become vertical, for any α, if α is one of many parameters. Let us try to solve for $\partial x_1^*/\partial\alpha$ and $\partial x_2^*/\partial\alpha$.

Differentiating equations (5-37), we get

$$\begin{pmatrix} \dfrac{\partial f_1}{\partial x_1} & \dfrac{\partial f_1}{\partial x_2} \\[2ex] \dfrac{\partial f_2}{\partial x_1} & \dfrac{\partial f_2}{\partial x_2} \end{pmatrix} \begin{pmatrix} \dfrac{\partial x_1^*}{\partial\alpha} \\[2ex] \dfrac{\partial x_2^*}{\partial\alpha} \end{pmatrix} = \begin{pmatrix} -f_{1\alpha} \\[2ex] -f_{2\alpha} \end{pmatrix} \tag{5-46}$$

A necessary and sufficient condition for solving for $\partial x_1^*/\partial\alpha$ and $\partial x_2^*/\partial\alpha$ uniquely is that the determinant

$$J = \begin{vmatrix} \dfrac{\partial f_1}{\partial x_1} & \dfrac{\partial f_1}{\partial x_2} \\[2ex] \dfrac{\partial f_2}{\partial x_1} & \dfrac{\partial f_2}{\partial x_2} \end{vmatrix} \neq 0 \tag{5-47}$$

This determinant, whose rows are the first partials of the equations to be solved, is called a *jacobian* determinant. If $J \neq 0$, the partials $\partial x_i^*/\partial\alpha$ are well defined, and in fact are so because the explicit equations $x_i = x_i^*(\alpha)$ are well defined. That is, $J \neq 0$ is precisely the sufficient condition which allows solution of the simultaneous equations (5-37) for the explicit equations (5-38). This is the generalization of relation (5-45) for one equation.

Condition (5-47) is implied by the *sufficient* second-order conditions for a maximum. In maximization models, $f_1(x_1, x_2, \alpha)$ and $f_2(x_1, x_2, \alpha)$ are $\partial f/\partial x_1$, $\partial f/\partial x_2$. Therefore, $\partial f/\partial x_1 = f_{11}$, etc., and the jacobian is

$$J = \begin{vmatrix} f_{11} & f_{12} \\ f_{12} & f_{22} \end{vmatrix}$$

From the sufficient second-order conditions, $J \neq 0$, since $J > 0$.

For models with n equations,

$$f_1(x_1, \ldots, x_n, \alpha) = 0$$
$$\cdots\cdots\cdots\cdots\cdots \tag{5-48}$$
$$f_n(x_1, \ldots, x_n, \alpha) = 0$$

a sufficient condition for explicit solutions

$$x_i = x_i^*(\alpha) \tag{5-49}$$

to exist at some point is that the jacobian of (5-48) be nonvanishing there:

$$
J = \begin{vmatrix} \dfrac{\partial f_1}{\partial x_1} & \cdots & \dfrac{\partial f_1}{\partial x_n} \\ \cdots\cdots\cdots\cdots \\ \dfrac{\partial f_n}{\partial x_1} & \cdots & \dfrac{\partial f_n}{\partial x_n} \end{vmatrix} \neq 0
\tag{5-50}
$$

PROBLEMS

1 Evaluate the following determinants

(a) $\begin{vmatrix} 1 & 2 \\ -1 & -3 \end{vmatrix}$ 　(b) $\begin{vmatrix} -2 & -1 \\ -4 & -3 \end{vmatrix}$

(c) $\begin{vmatrix} 1 & 2 & -1 \\ 0 & 1 & 1 \\ -1 & 0 & 1 \end{vmatrix}$ 　(d) $\begin{vmatrix} 0 & 1 & 1 \\ 1 & 0 & 1 \\ 1 & 1 & 0 \end{vmatrix}$

2 Suppose a square matrix is *triangular*, i.e., all elements below the diagonal are 0:

$$
A = \begin{pmatrix} a_{11} & a_{12} & \cdots & a_{1n} \\ 0 & a_{22} & \cdots & a_{2n} \\ \cdots\cdots\cdots\cdots\cdots \\ 0 & 0 & \cdots & a_{nn} \end{pmatrix}
$$

Show that $|A| = a_{11} a_{22} \cdots a_{nn}$, the product of the diagonal elements.

3 Consider the system of n equations in n unknowns

$$
Ax = b
$$

where the vector b consists of 0's in all entries except a one in some row j. Assuming $|A| \neq 0$, show that the solutions can be represented as

$$
x_i = \frac{A_{ji}}{|A|} \qquad i, j = 1, \ldots, n
$$

where A_{ji} is the cofactor of element a_{ji}.

4 Consider a firm which hires two inputs x_1 and x_2 at factor prices w_1 and w_2 respectively. If this firm is one of many identical firms, then in the long run, the profit-maximizing position will be at the minimum of its average-cost curve. Analyze the comparative statics of this firm in the long run by asserting the behavioral postulate'

minimize 　　　　　　　 $AC = \dfrac{w_1 x_1 + w_2 x_2}{f(x_1, x_2)}$

where $y = f(x_1, x_2)$ is the firm's production function.

　(a) Show that the first-order necessary conditions for min AC are $w_i - AC^* f_i = 0, i = 1, 2$, where AC^* is min AC. Interpret.

　(b) Show that the sufficient second-order conditions for min AC are the same as for profit-maximization in the short-run (fixed-output price), that is

$$
f_{11} < 0 \qquad f_{22} < 0 \qquad f_{11} f_{22} - f_{12}^2 > 0
$$

(*Hint:* in differentiating the product $AC^* f_i$, remember that $\partial AC^*/\partial x_i = 0$ by the first-order conditions.)

(c) Find all partials of the form $\partial x_i^*/\partial w_j$. (Remember that w_1 and w_2 appear in AC.) Show that $\partial x_i^*/\partial w_i < 0$ is *not* implied by this model, nor is $\partial x_i^*/\partial w_j = \partial x_j^*/\partial w_i$.

(d) Show that $f_1 x_1^* + f_2 x_2^* = y^*$. Is this Euler's theorem? (If it is, you have just proved that all production functions are linear homogeneous!)

5 Consider a firm with the production function $y = f(x_1, x_2)$, which sells its output in a competitive output market at price p. It is, however, a monopsonist in the input market, i.e., it faces rising factor-supply curves, in which the unit factor prices w_1 and w_2 rise with increasing factor usage, that is, $w_1 = k_1 x_1$, $w_2 = k_2 x_2$. The firm is asserted to be a profit-maximizer.

(a) How might one represent algebraically a decrease in the supply of factor 1?

(b) If the supply of x_1 decreases, will the use of factor one decrease? Demonstrate.

(c) What will happen to the usage of factor 2 if the supply of x_1 decreases?

(d) Explain, in about one sentence, why factor-demand curves for this firm do *not* exist.

(e) Suppose the government holds the firm's use of x_2 constant, at the previous profit-maximizing level. If the supply of x_1 decreases, will the use of x_1 change by more or less, absolutely, than previously?

APPENDIX

SIMPLE MATRIX OPERATIONS

A matrix, again, is any rectangular array of numbers:

$$\mathbf{A} = \begin{pmatrix} a_{11} & \cdots & a_{1n} \\ \cdots\cdots\cdots\cdots \\ a_{m1} & \cdots & a_{mn} \end{pmatrix}$$

This matrix has m rows and n columns. Suppose some other matrix $\mathbf{B}$ has n rows and r columns ($\mathbf{B}$ must have the same number of rows as $\mathbf{A}$ has columns):

$$\mathbf{B} = \begin{pmatrix} b_{11} & \cdots & b_{1r} \\ \cdots\cdots\cdots\cdots \\ b_{n1} & \cdots & b_{nr} \end{pmatrix}$$

The matrix product $\mathbf{C} = \mathbf{AB}$ is defined to be the $m \times r$ matrix

$$\begin{pmatrix} c_{11} & \cdots & c_{1r} \\ \cdots\cdots\cdots\cdots \\ c_{m1} & \cdots & c_{mr} \end{pmatrix} = \begin{pmatrix} a_{11} & \cdots & a_{1n} \\ \cdots\xrightarrow{\hspace{1cm}}\cdots \\ a_{m1} & \cdots & a_{mn} \end{pmatrix} \begin{pmatrix} b_{11} & \cdots & b_{1r} \\ \cdots\downarrow\cdots \\ b_{n1} & \cdots & b_{nr} \end{pmatrix}$$

where any element c_{ij} of $\mathbf{C}$ is defined to be

$$c_{ij} = \sum_{k=1}^{n} a_{ik} b_{kj}$$

Schematically, each element of any *row* of $\mathbf{A}$ is multiplied, term by term, by the elements of some *column* of $\mathbf{B}$ (as shown by the direction of the arrows above) and the result is summed. Note that while the product $\mathbf{AB}$ may be well defined, $\mathbf{BA}$ may not be, since the number of columns in the left-hand matrix must equal the number of rows in the right-hand matrix in a matrix product. In general, even for square matrices, *matrix multiplication is not commutative*, i.e., in general

$$\mathbf{AB} \neq \mathbf{BA}$$

The associative and distributive laws do hold, however. If $\mathbf{A}$ is $m \times n$, $\mathbf{B}$ is $n \times r$, $\mathbf{C}$ is $r \times p$, then $\mathbf{ABC}$ is $m \times p$ and the following laws are valid:

Associative Law $(\mathbf{AB})\mathbf{C} = \mathbf{A}(\mathbf{BC})$

If $\mathbf{A}$ is $m \times n$, $\mathbf{B}$ and $\mathbf{C}$ are $n \times p$, then:

Distributive Law $\mathbf{A}(\mathbf{B} + \mathbf{C}) = \mathbf{AB} + \mathbf{AC}$

For the associative law, we simply note

$$\sum_{h=1}^{r} \sum_{k=1}^{n} (a_{ik} b_{kh}) c_{hj} = \sum_{k=1}^{n} \sum_{h=1}^{r} a_{ik}(b_{kh} c_{hj})$$

For the distributive law

$$\sum_{k=1}^{n} a_{ik}(b_{kj} + c_{kj}) = \sum_{k=1}^{n} a_{ik} b_{kj} + \sum_{k=1}^{n} a_{ik} c_{kj}$$

The *transpose* of any matrix, $\mathbf{A}'$, is the matrix $\mathbf{A}$ with its rows and columns interchanged. That is,

$$(a_{ij})' = (a_{ji})$$

The transpose of a product is the product of the transposed matrices, in the reverse order:

$$(\mathbf{AB})' = \mathbf{B}'\mathbf{A}'$$

To prove this, let c_{ij} be an element of $(\mathbf{AB})'$. By definition,

$$c_{ij} = \sum_{k=1}^{n} a_{jk} b_{ki}$$

An element of $\mathbf{B}'\mathbf{A}'$ is

$$\sum_{k=1}^{n} b_{ki} a_{jk}$$

identical to the former sum.

A matrix is called *symmetric* if it equals its transpose, that is,

$$\mathbf{A} = \mathbf{A}'$$

That is, for every element a_{ij}, $a_{ij} = a_{ji}$. The rows and columns can be interchanged leaving the same matrix. This is a very important class of matrices in economics. The matrices encountered in maximization models are the second partials of some objective function, $f(x_1, \ldots, x_n)$. By Young's theorem, $f_{ij} = f_{ji}$. Hence, these matrices are symmetric.

The Rank of a Matrix

Consider an $m \times n$ matrix (a_{ij}) and consider each of its rows, A_1, ..., A_m, separately. Each row i,

$$A_i = (a_{i1}, \ldots, a_{in}) \qquad i = 1, \ldots, m$$

represents a point in euclidean n-space. It is important to discuss the "dimensionality" of these m points; i.e., do they all lie on a single line (one dimension), a plane, (two dimensions) etc.? Algebraically, if these m vectors lie in an m-dimensional space, then it is not possible to write any vector A as a linear combination of the others. In other words, if

$$k_1 A_1 + \cdots + k_m A_m = 0$$

where the k_i are scalars (ordinary numbers), then all the k_i's must be zero. In this case, A_1, ..., A_m are said to be *linearly independent*.

For any given matrix A, the maximum number of linearly independent row vectors in A is called the *rank of* A. If A has m rows and n columns, and $n > m$, then the maximum possible rank of A is m. It is not obvious, but true that the number of linearly independent *column* vectors of A equals the number of linearly independent *row* vectors. Thus the rank of a matrix is the maximum number of linear independent vectors in A, formed from either the rows or the columns of A.

Example 1 The vectors $A_1 = (1, 0, 0)$, $A_2 = (0, 1, 0)$, $A_3 = (0, 0, 1)$ are linearly independent.

$$k_1 A_1 + k_2 A_2 + k_3 A_3 = (k_1, k_2, k_3) = 0$$

if and only if $k_1 = k_2 = k_3 = 0$. The matrix

$$A = \begin{pmatrix} 1 & 0 & 0 \\ 0 & 1 & 0 \\ 0 & 0 & 1 \end{pmatrix}$$

therefore has rank 3.

Example 2 Let $A_1 = (1, 1, 0)$, $A_2 = (1, 0, 1)$, $A_3 = (1, -1, 2)$. These vectors are linearly *dependent*. Here, $A_3 = 2A_2 - A_1$, or

$$A_1 - 2A_2 + A_3 = 0$$

Any one of these vectors can be written as a linear combination of the other two, but not less than two. The matrix

$$A = \begin{pmatrix} 1 & 1 & 0 \\ 1 & 0 & 1 \\ 1 & -1 & 2 \end{pmatrix}$$

therefore has rank 2.

A set of m linearly independent vectors $\mathbf{A}_1, \ldots, \mathbf{A}_m$ is said to form a *basis* for euclidean m-space. Any vector $\mathbf{b}$ in that space can be written as a linear combination of $\mathbf{A}_1, \ldots, \mathbf{A}_m$, that is,

$$\mathbf{b} = \sum_{i=1}^{m} k_i \mathbf{A}_i$$

where the k_i's are scalars.

Consider a system of n equations in n unknowns,

$$\begin{pmatrix} a_{11} & \cdots & a_{1n} \\ \cdots \cdots \cdots \cdots \\ a_{n1} & \cdots & a_{nn} \end{pmatrix} \begin{pmatrix} x_1 \\ \vdots \\ x_n \end{pmatrix} = \begin{pmatrix} b_1 \\ \vdots \\ b_n \end{pmatrix}$$

or, in matrix notation, $\mathbf{Ax} = \mathbf{b}$. If the rank of $\mathbf{A}$ is less than n, then some row of $\mathbf{A}$ is a linear combination of the other rows. But this is the procedure for solving the above system for the x's. If rank $(\mathbf{A}) < n$, then at least one equation is derivable from the others, i.e., there are really less than n independent equations in n unknowns. In this case, no unique solution exists. We saw in the chapter that simultaneous equations admitted a unique solution if the determinant of $\mathbf{A}$, $|\mathbf{A}|$, was nonzero. An important result of matrix theory is thus:

Theorem If $\mathbf{A}$ is a square $n \times n$ matrix, then the rank of $\mathbf{A}$ is n if and only if $|\mathbf{A}| \neq 0$.

This algebra is the basis of the nonvanishing jacobian determinant of the implicit function theorem. Briefly, if rank $(\mathbf{A}) < n$, then some row (or column) is a linear combination of the other rows (columns). By repeated application of the corollary to theorem 5 in the chapter proper, $|\mathbf{A}| = 0$. Conversely, if $|\mathbf{A}| = 0$, some row of $\mathbf{A}$ is either 0 or a linear combination of the other rows, and hence $\mathbf{A}_1, \ldots, \mathbf{A}_n$ are linearly dependent. A more formal proof of this part can be found in any standard linear algebra text.

A square $n \times n$ matrix $\mathbf{A}$ that has a rank n is called *nonsingular*. If rank$(\mathbf{A}) < n$, $\mathbf{A}$ is called *singular*.

The Inverse of A Matrix

In ordinary arithmetic, the inverse of a number x is its reciprocal, $1/x$. The inverse of a number x is that number y which makes the product $xy = 1$. In matrix algebra, the unity element for square $n \times n$ matrices is the *identity matrix* $\mathbf{I}$, where

$$\mathbf{I} = \begin{pmatrix} 1 & 0 & \cdots & 0 \\ 0 & 1 & \cdots & 0 \\ 0 & \cdots & \cdots & 1 \end{pmatrix}$$

That is, $\mathbf{I}$ is a square $n \times n$ matrix with 1's on the main diagonal, and 0's elsewhere.

Formally, if (a_{ij}) is the identity matrix, then $a_{ij} = 1$ if $i = j$, $a_{ij} = 0$ if $i \neq j$. It can be verified that for any square matrix **A**,

$$\mathbf{AI} = \mathbf{IA} = \mathbf{A}$$

Thus the identity matrix **I** corresponds to the number 1 in ordinary arithmetic.

Is there a *reciprocal* matrix **B**, for some matrix **A** such that

$$\mathbf{AB} = \mathbf{I}$$

If so, we call **B** the *inverse* of **A**, denoted $\mathbf{A}^{-1}$.

The problem of finding the inverse of a matrix is equivalent to solving

$$\mathbf{Ax} = \mathbf{b}$$

for a unique **x**, where **A** is an $n \times n$ square matrix. If $\mathbf{A}^{-1}$ exists, multiply the above by $\mathbf{A}^{-1}$ on the left, yielding

$$\mathbf{x} = \mathbf{A}^{-1}\mathbf{b}$$

This is the simultaneous solution for **x**. This solution exists if and only if $|\mathbf{A}| \neq 0$. This is correspondingly the condition that $\mathbf{A}^{-1}$ exists, that is, **A** must be nonsingular, or have rank n.

Assuming $|\mathbf{A}| \neq 0$, consider the following matrix, **A*** called the *adjoint* of **A**:

$$\mathbf{A}^* = \begin{pmatrix} A_{11} & A_{21} & \cdots & A_{n1} \\ A_{12} & A_{22} & \cdots & A_{n2} \\ \cdots\cdots\cdots\cdots\cdots \\ A_{1n} & A_{2n} & \cdots & A_{nn} \end{pmatrix}$$

The adjoint, **A***, is formed from the cofactors of the a_{ij}'s, *transposed*. Consider the matrix product **AA***:

$$\begin{pmatrix} a_{11} & \cdots & a_{1n} \\ \cdots\cdots\cdots \\ a_{n1} & \cdots & a_{nn} \end{pmatrix} \begin{pmatrix} A_{11} & \cdots & A_{n1} \\ \cdots\cdots\cdots \\ A_{1n} & \cdots & A_{nn} \end{pmatrix} = \begin{pmatrix} |\mathbf{A}| & \cdots & \cdots & \cdots & 0 \\ \vdots & \ddots & & & \vdots \\ \vdots & & |\mathbf{A}| & & \vdots \\ \vdots & & & \ddots & \vdots \\ 0 & \cdots & \cdots & \cdots & |\mathbf{A}| \end{pmatrix} = |\mathbf{A}|\mathbf{I}$$

Any element of **AA*** off the main diagonal is formed by the product of the elements of some row of **A** and the cofactors of some other row; these products sum to zero by the theorem on alien cofactors. The diagonal elements of **AA***, however, are formed from the sums of products of a row of **A** and the cofactors of that row; this sums to $|\mathbf{A}|$. Hence,

$$\mathbf{AA}^* = |\mathbf{A}|\mathbf{I}$$

The inverse of **A**, $\mathbf{A}^{-1}$ is thus $(1/|\mathbf{A}|)\mathbf{A}^*$, or

$$\mathbf{A}^{-1} = \begin{pmatrix} \dfrac{A_{11}}{|\mathbf{A}|} & \cdots & \dfrac{A_{n1}}{|\mathbf{A}|} \\ \cdots\cdots\cdots\cdots\cdots \\ \dfrac{A_{1n}}{|\mathbf{A}|} & \cdots & \dfrac{A_{nn}}{|\mathbf{A}|} \end{pmatrix}$$

By inspection, it can be seen that if $AA^{-1} = I$, then $A^{-1}A = I$ also; that is, the left or right inverse of A is the same A^{-1}. Also, A^{-1} is unique. Suppose there exists some B such that

$$AB = I$$

Multiplying on the left by A^{-1},

$$A^{-1}AB = IB = B = A^{-1}$$

It is also true that

$$(AB)^{-1} = B^{-1}A^{-1}$$

The proof of this is left as an exercise.

Orthogonality

Two vectors are called orthogonal if their scalar product is 0.

Example 1 The vectors $E_1 = (1, 0, 0)$, $E_2 = (0, 1, 0)$ and $E_3 = (0, 0, 1)$ are all mutually orthogonal.

Example 2 Let $a = (2, -1, 1)$, $b = (-1, -1, 1)$. Then $ab = 0$; thus a and b are orthogonal.

Orthogonal vectors must be linearly independent. Suppose a square matrix A is made up of row vectors $a_1, \ldots, a_n$ which are mutually orthogonal, and whose euclidean "length" is unity:

$$\|a_i\| = \sum_{j=1}^{n} a_{ij}^2 = 1$$

A is called an *orthogonal* matrix. It can be quickly verified that the transpose of A, A', is the inverse of A, i.e.,

$$A'A = I$$

PROBLEMS

1 Find the rank of the following matrices. For which does $|A| \neq 0$?

$$A = \begin{pmatrix} -1 & 1 & 2 \\ 1 & -1 & -2 \\ -2 & 2 & 4 \end{pmatrix} \quad B = \begin{pmatrix} 1 & 0 & -1 \\ -1 & 1 & 1 \\ 1 & -1 & -1 \end{pmatrix} \quad C = \begin{pmatrix} -1 & 0 & 1 \\ 1 & -1 & 1 \\ 0 & -1 & 3 \end{pmatrix}$$

2 Prove that $(AB)^{-1} = B^{-1}A^{-1}$, if A and B are two square nonsingular matrices.

3 Prove that $(A^{-1})^{-1} = A$, that is, the inverse of the inverse is the original matrix.

4 Show that $(A')^{-1} = (A^{-1})'$, i.e., the transpose of the inverse is the inverse of the transpose.

5 Show that if $\mathbf{A}$ is $n \times n$, and $\mathbf{h}$ is an $n \times 1$ column vector, then

$$\mathbf{h'Ah} = \sum_{j=1}^{n} \sum_{i=1}^{n} a_{ij} h_i h_j$$

The expression $\mathbf{h'Ah}$ is called a quadratic form. These expressions appear in the theory of maxima and minima.

6 Show that if $\mathbf{h'Ah} < 0$ for any vectors $\mathbf{h} \neq \mathbf{0}$, then (among other things) the diagonal elements of $\mathbf{A}$ are all negative; that is, $a_{ii} < 0$, $i = 1, \dots, n$.

7 Prove that if $\mathbf{A}$ is an orthogonal matrix, $\mathbf{A'A} = \mathbf{I}$; that is, $\mathbf{A'} = \mathbf{A}^{-1}$.

8 Prove that if the rows of a square matrix $\mathbf{A}$ are orthogonal and have unit length, the columns likewise have these properties.

SELECTED REFERENCES

The implicit function theorem can be found in any advanced calculus text. Classic references are:

Apostol, T.: "Mathematical Analysis," Addison-Wesley Publishing Co., Inc., Reading, Mass., 1957.
Courant, R.: "Differential and Integral Calculus," 2d ed., Interscience Publishers, Inc., New York, 1936, vol. 1 and 2.

Matrices and determinants are the subject of any linear, or matrix, algebra text. Perhaps the clearest and most useful for economists is:

Hadley, G.: "Linear Algebra," Addison-Wesley Publishing Co., Inc., Reading, Mass., 1961.
Samuelson, P. A.: "Foundations of Economic Analysis," Harvard University Press, Cambridge, Mass., 1947. The first systematic exposition of the application of the implicit function theorem in economic methodology.

CONSTRAINED AND UNCONSTRAINED MAXIMA AND MINIMA OF FUNCTIONS OF SEVERAL VARIABLES

6.1 UNCONSTRAINED MAXIMA AND MINIMA

In Chap. 4 we considered the necessary and sufficient conditions for $y = f(x_1, x_2)$ to have a maximum at some point. How do those conditions generalize to the case of n variables, $y = f(x_1, \ldots, x_n)$?

First-Order Necessary Conditions

As was noted in Chap. 4, the necessary first-order conditions for $y = f(x_1, \ldots, x_n)$ to have a stationary value is that all the first partials of f equal zero; that is, $f_i = 0$, $i = 1, \ldots, n$, at the point in question.

> **Example 1** Consider the profit-maximizing firm which employs n factors of production. The objective function is
>
> $$\pi = pf(x_1, \ldots, x_n) - \sum_{i=1}^{n} w_i x_i$$
>
> where $y = f(x_1, \ldots, x_n)$ is the production function. The first-order necessary conditions are
>
> $$\pi_i = pf_i - w_i = 0 \qquad i = 1, \ldots, n$$

The firm equates the value of marginal product to the wage at every margin, i.e., for every factor input. This is a straightforward generalization of the two-variable case.

Second-Order Sufficient Conditions

Using a Taylor series approach, as was done in the Appendix to Chap. 4, it can be shown that a sufficient condition for $y = f(x_1, \ldots, x_n)$ to have a maximum at some stationary value is that for all curves, $y(t) = f(x_1(t), \ldots, x_n(t))$, $y''(t) < 0$. Using the chain rule, this sufficient condition is

$$\frac{d^2 y}{dt^2} = \sum_{i=1}^{n} \sum_{j=1}^{n} f_{ij} \frac{dx_i}{dt} \frac{dx_j}{dt} < 0 \qquad (6\text{-}1)$$

for all dx_i/dt, dx_j/dt not all equal to 0.

A square matrix (a_{ij}) which has the property that

$$\sum_{i=1}^{n} \sum_{j=1}^{n} a_{ij} h_i h_j < 0 \qquad (6\text{-}2)$$

for all nontrivial (not all 0) h_i, h_j is said to be *negative definite*. (If the strict inequality is replaced by " ≤ 0," the matrix is called *negative semidefinite*.) Similarly, (a_{ij}) positive definite (semidefinite) means that the sum in (6-2) is strictly positive (nonnegative) for all nontrivial h_i, h_j. Thus, if at a point where $f_i = 0$, $i = 1, \ldots, n$, the matrix of second partials of f (called the *hessian* matrix) is negative definite, then $f(x_1, \ldots, x_n)$ has a maximum there. If the hessian matrix is positive definite there, a minimum exists. If the hessian is negative semidefinite, then f definitely does *not* have a minimum, but it is not possible to say whether f has a maximum or some sort of saddle point at the stationary value. An expression of the form (6-2), in matrix form $\mathbf{h'Ah}$, is called a *quadratic form*.

Geometrically, negative definiteness of the hessian matrix

$$\mathbf{H} = \begin{pmatrix} f_{11} & \cdots & f_{1n} \\ \cdots\cdots\cdots\cdots \\ f_{n1} & \cdots & f_{nn} \end{pmatrix}$$

ensures that the function f will be *concave* (downwards). If $\mathbf{H}$ is positive definite, f is convex.

Example 2 Consider the function $y = (x_2 - x_1^2)(x_2 - 2x_1^2)$ depicted in Fig. 4-1 of Chap. 4. This is a function which has a minimum at the origin when evaluated along all straight lines through the origin, yet the function itself does *not* have a minimum there. The hessian matrix of second partials is

$$\mathbf{H} = \begin{pmatrix} 24x_1^2 - 6x_2 & -6x_1 \\ -6x_1 & 2 \end{pmatrix}$$

At the origin, this matrix is

$$\mathbf{H} = \begin{pmatrix} 0 & 0 \\ 0 & 2 \end{pmatrix}$$

This matrix is clearly positive semidefinite:

$$Q = \sum_{j=1}^{2} \sum_{i=1}^{2} f_{ij} h_i h_j = 2h_2^2 \geq 0$$

When $h_1 =$ anything, $h_2 = 0$, this quadratic form $Q = 0$; when $h_2 \neq 0, Q > 0$.

In the two-variable case, $y = f(x_1, x_2)$, the sufficient second-order conditions for a maximum, (6-1), imply that $f_{11} < 0, f_{22} < 0$ and $f_{11} f_{22} - f_{12}^2 > 0$, as was shown in Chap. 4. Note that this last expression can be stated as the determinant of the cross-partials of the objective function,

$$\begin{vmatrix} f_{11} & f_{12} \\ f_{21} & f_{22} \end{vmatrix} > 0$$

Note also that the conditions $f_{11}, f_{22} < 0$ relate to the diagonal elements of that determinant. The theory of determinants allows a very simple statement of the sufficient second-order conditions for $y = f(x_1, \ldots, x_n)$ to have a maximum. First, consider the following construction:

Definition Let A_n be some nth-order determinant. By a "principal minor of order k" of A_n we mean that determinant that remains of A_n when any $n - k$ rows and the *same numbered columns* are eliminated from A_n.

For example, if some row, row i, is eliminated, then to form a principal minor of order $n - 1$, *column i* must be eliminated. Since there are n choices of rows (and their corresponding columns) to eliminate, there are clearly n principal minors of order $n - 1$ of A_n. If, say, rows 1 and 3 and columns 1 and 3 are eliminated, then a principal minor or order $n - 2$ remains. There are $\binom{n}{2} = n(n-1)/2!$ of these, and in general $\binom{n}{k} = n!/k!(n-k)!$ principal minors of order k [or order $(n-k)$]. Note that the first-order principal minors of A_n are simply the diagonal elements of A_n, and the second-order principal minors are the set of 2×2 determinants that look like

$$\begin{vmatrix} a_{ii} & a_{ij} \\ a_{ji} & a_{jj} \end{vmatrix}$$

The resemblance of this determinant to the 2×2 determinant of cross-partials of a function $f(x_1, x_2)$ provides the motivation for the following theorem.

Theorem Consider a function $y = f(x_1, \ldots, x_n)$ which has a stationary value at $\mathbf{x} = \mathbf{x}^0$. Consider the hessian matrix of cross-partials of f, (f_{ij}). Then if all of the principal minors of $|(f_{ij})|$ of order k have sign $(-1)^k$, for all $k = 1, \ldots, n$ ($k = n$ yields the whole determinant, $|f_{ij}|$) at $\mathbf{x} = \mathbf{x}^0$, then $f(x_1, \ldots, x_n)$ has a maximum at $\mathbf{x} = \mathbf{x}^0$. If all the principal minors of $|(f_{ij})|$ are positive, for all $k = 1, \ldots, n$, at $\mathbf{x} = \mathbf{x}^0$, then $f(x_1, \ldots, x_n)$ has a minimum value at $\mathbf{x} = \mathbf{x}^0$. If any of the principal minors has a sign strictly opposite to that stated above, the function has a saddle point at $\mathbf{x} = \mathbf{x}^0$. If some or all of the principal minors are 0 and the rest have the appropriate sign given in the above conditions, then it is not possible to indicate the shape of the function at $\mathbf{x} = \mathbf{x}^0$. (This corresponds to the 0 second-derivative situation in the calculus of functions of one variable.)

The theorem as stated above is the form in which we shall actually use the result. However, it is somewhat overstated. Consider the "naturally ordered" principal minors of an $n \times n$ hessian,

$$|f_{11}| \qquad \begin{vmatrix} f_{11} & f_{12} \\ f_{21} & f_{22} \end{vmatrix} \qquad \begin{vmatrix} f_{11} & f_{12} & f_{13} \\ f_{21} & f_{22} & f_{23} \\ f_{31} & f_{32} & f_{33} \end{vmatrix} \qquad \cdots$$

Recall that in the two-variable case, $f_{11} < 0$ and $f_{11} f_{22} - f_{12}^2 > 0$ implies $f_{22} < 0$. In fact, if all of these naturally ordered principal minors have the appropriate sign for a maximum or minimum of $f(x_1, \ldots, x_n)$, then all of the other principal minors have the appropriate sign. Thus, the theorem as stated is in some sense "too strong;" i.e., more is assumed that is necessary, but we shall need the sufficient condition that *all* principal minors of order k have sign $(-1)^k$ for a maximum, or that they are *all* positive for a minimum.

There are several inelegant proofs of this theorem, one by completing a rather gigantic square *á la* the proof used in Chap. 4, and an elegant proof based on matrix theory, a proof which is beyond the level of this book.† Hence, no proof will be offered. It is hoped that the discussion of the two-variable case will have at least made the theorem not implausible.

Example 3 Consider the profit-maximizing firm with n factors of production. The objective function, again, is

maximize $\qquad \pi = pf(x_1, \ldots, x_n) - \Sigma w_i x_i$

The first-order conditions, again, are

$$\pi_i = pf_i - w_i = 0 \qquad i = 1, \ldots, n \tag{6-3}$$

These equations represent n equations in the n decision variables $x_1, \ldots, x_n$

---

† See George Hadley, "Linear Algebra," Addison Wesley Publishing Co., Inc., Reading, Mass., 1961.

and $n + 1$ parameters $w_1, \ldots, w_n, p$. If the jacobian determinant is nonzero, i.e.,

$$J = \left| \frac{\partial \pi_i}{\partial x_j} \right| \neq 0 \qquad (6\text{-}4)$$

then at this stationary value, these equations can be solved for the explicit choice functions, i.e., the factor-demand curves,

$$x_i = x_i^*(w_1, \ldots, w_n, p) \qquad i = 1, \ldots, n \qquad (6\text{-}5)$$

The sufficient conditions for a maximum are that the principal minors of $(\pi_{ij}) = (pf_{ij})$ alternate in sign, i.e., have sign $(-1)^k$, $k = 1, \ldots, n$. Since $p > 0$, this is equivalent to saying that the principal minors of the matrix of second partials of the production function,

$$\begin{vmatrix} f_{11} & f_{12} & \cdots & f_{1n} \\ f_{21} & f_{22} & \cdots & f_{2n} \\ \cdots & \cdots & \cdots & \cdots \\ f_{n1} & f_{n2} & \cdots & f_{nn} \end{vmatrix}$$

alternate in sign. Specifically, this means that, among other things, the diagonal terms are all negative, that is, $f_{ii} < 0$, $i = 1, \ldots, n$. This says that there is diminishing marginal productivity in each factor. In addition, all $n(n-1)/2$ second-order determinants

$$\begin{vmatrix} f_{ii} & f_{ij} \\ f_{ji} & f_{jj} \end{vmatrix} > 0, \qquad i, j = 1, \ldots, n, \quad i \neq j$$

The "own-effects" dominate cross-effects in the sense that $f_{ii} f_{jj} - f_{ij}^2 > 0$, i, $j = 1, \ldots, n$, $i \neq j$. Then there are all the remaining principal minors to consider; these are not easily given intuitive explanations.

The second-order conditions say that in a neighborhood of a maximum point, the objective function (in this example, this is equivalent to the production function) must be concave (downwards). The conditions $f_{ii} < 0$ ensure that the function is concave in all the two-dimensional planes whose axes are y and some x_i. The second-order principal minors relate to concavity in all possible three-dimensional subspaces y, x_i, x_j. But concavity in all of these lower-order dimensions is not sufficient to guarantee concavity in higher dimensions; hence, all the orders of principal minors, including the whole hessian determinant itself, must be checked for the appropriate sign.

In terms of solving for the factor-demand curves, the *sufficient* second-order conditions guarantee that this is possible. The nth-order principal minor, i.e., the determinant of the entire (π_{ij}) matrix has sign $(-1)^n \neq 0$ by these sufficient conditions. But this determinant is precisely the jacobian of the system (6-3); hence, applying the implicit function theorem, the choice functions (6-5) are derivable from (6-3).

Substituting the choice functions (6-5) back into (6-3) yields the identities:

$$pf_i(x_1^*, \ldots, x_n^*) - w_i \equiv 0, \qquad i = 1, \ldots, n \qquad (6\text{-}6)$$

To find the responses of the system to a change in some factor price w_j, differentiate (6-6) with respect to w_j. This yields the system of equations:

$$pf_{11} \frac{\partial x_1^*}{\partial w_j} + \cdots + pf_{1n} \frac{\partial x_n^*}{\partial w_j} \equiv 0$$

$$pf_{j1} \frac{\partial x_1^*}{\partial w_j} + \cdots + pf_{jn} \frac{\partial x_n^*}{\partial w_j} \equiv 1$$

$$pf_{n1} \frac{\partial x_1^*}{\partial w_j} + \cdots + pf_{nn} \frac{\partial x_n^*}{\partial w_j} \equiv 0$$

In matrix notation, this system is written:

$$\begin{pmatrix} pf_{11} & \cdots & pf_{1n} \\ \cdots & \cdots & \cdots \\ pf_{n1} & \cdots & pf_{nn} \end{pmatrix} \begin{pmatrix} \dfrac{\partial x_1^*}{\partial w_j} \\ \cdots \\ \dfrac{\partial x_n^*}{\partial w_j} \end{pmatrix} \equiv \begin{pmatrix} 0 \\ \vdots \\ 1 \\ \vdots \\ 0 \end{pmatrix} \qquad (6\text{-}7)$$

where the 1 on the right-hand side appears in row j. Solving for $\partial x_i^*/\partial w_j$ by Cramer's rule involves putting the right-hand column in column i of the $|(pf_{ij})|$ determinant, in the numerator, i.e.,

$$\frac{\partial x_i^*}{\partial w_j} = \frac{\begin{vmatrix} pf_{11} & 0 & pf_{1n} \\ \vdots & 1 & \vdots \\ pf_{n1} & 0 & pf_{nn} \end{vmatrix}}{H} \qquad (6\text{-}8)$$

where $H = |pf_{ij}|$, the jacobian determinant of second partials of π. Expanding the numerator by the cofactors of column i,

$$\frac{\partial x_i^*}{\partial w_j} = \frac{H_{ji}}{H} \qquad (6\text{-}9)$$

where H_{ji} is the cofactor of the element in row j and column i of H.

In general, H has sign $(-1)^n$ by the sufficient second-order conditions for a maximum. For $i \neq j$, however, the sign of H_{ij} is not implied by the maximum conditions. Thus, in general, no refutable implications emerge for the response of any factor to a change in the price of some *other* factor. However, when $i = j$,

$$\frac{\partial x_i^*}{\partial w_i} = \frac{H_{ii}}{H} \qquad (6\text{-}10)$$

The cofactor H_{ii} is a principal minor; by the maximum conditions it has sign $(-1)^{n-1}$, i.e., opposite to the sign of H. Thus,

$$\frac{\partial x_i^*}{\partial w_i} = \frac{H_{ii}}{H} < 0 \qquad i = 1, \dots, n \tag{6-11}$$

As in the two-factor case, the model does yield a refutable hypothesis concerning the slope of each factor-demand curve. The response of any factor to a change in its *own* price is in the opposite direction to the change in its price.

Finally, from the symmetry of H, from equation (6-9),

$$\frac{\partial x_i^*}{\partial w_j} = \frac{H_{ji}}{H} = \frac{H_{ij}}{H} = \frac{\partial x_j^*}{\partial w_i} \tag{6-12}$$

The reciprocity conditions thus generalize in a straightforward fashion to the n-factor case.

Since the parameter p enters each first-order equation (6-3), no refutable hypotheses emerge for the responses of factor inputs to output price changes. The matrix system of comparative statics relations obtained from differentiating (6-3) with respect to p are (compare equations (4-21), Chap. 4):

$$\begin{pmatrix} pf_{11} & \cdots & pf_{1n} \\ \cdots\cdots\cdots\cdots \\ pf_{n1} & \cdots & pf_{nn} \end{pmatrix} \begin{pmatrix} \dfrac{\partial x_1^*}{\partial p} \\ \cdots \\ \dfrac{\partial x_n^*}{\partial p} \end{pmatrix} = \begin{pmatrix} -f_1 \\ \vdots \\ -f_n \end{pmatrix} \tag{6-13}$$

Solving by Cramer's rule for $\partial x_i^*/\partial p$,

$$\frac{\partial x_i^*}{\partial p} = -\sum_{j=1}^{n} \frac{f_j H_{ji}}{H} \gtreqless 0 \tag{6-14}$$

It can be shown that if p increases, then at least one factor must increase, but this is precious little information.

Finally, the supply function of this competitive firm is defined as

$$y = f(x_1^*(\mathbf{w}, p), \dots, x_n^*(\mathbf{w}, p)) = y^*(w_1, \dots, w_n, p)$$

where $\mathbf{w}$ is the vector of factor prices $(w_1, \dots, w_n)$. It can be shown that

$$\frac{\partial y^*}{\partial p} > 0 \tag{6-15}$$

and
$$\frac{\partial y^*}{\partial w_i} = -\frac{\partial x_i^*}{\partial p} \qquad i = 1, \dots, n \tag{6-16}$$

We shall leave these results to a later chapter, as they are difficult to obtain by the present methods and outrageously simple by methods involving what is known as the *envelope theorem*, which will be discussed later.

6.2 THE THEORY OF CONSTRAINED MAXIMA AND MINIMA: FIRST-ORDER NECESSARY CONDITIONS

In most of the maximization problems encountered in economics, a separate, additional equation appears which constrains the values of the decision variables to some subspace of all real values, i.e., some subspace of what is referred to as euclidean n-space. For example, in the theory of the consumer, individuals are posited to maximize a utility function, $U(x_1, x_2)$, subject to a constraint which dictates that the consumer not exceed a certain total budgetary expenditure. This problem can be stated more formally as,

maximize $$U(x_1, x_2) = U \tag{6-17}$$

subject to $$p_1 x_1 + p_2 x_2 = M \tag{6-18}$$

where x_1 and x_2 are the amounts of two goods consumed, p_1 and p_2 their respective prices, and M is total money income. This problem can be solved simply by solving for one of the decision variables, say x_2, from the constraint, and inserting that solution into the objective function. In that case, an unconstrained problem of one less dimension results: From (6-18),

$$x_2(x_1) = \frac{-p_1}{p_2} x_1 + \frac{M}{p_2} \tag{6-19}$$

Since once x_1 is known, x_2 is known also from the above, the problem reduces to maximizing $U(x_1, x_2(x_1))$ over the one decision variable x_1. This yields

$$\frac{dU}{dx_1} = \frac{\partial U}{\partial x_1} + \frac{\partial U}{\partial x_2}\frac{dx_2}{dx_1}$$

$$= U_1 + U_2 \frac{-p_1}{p_2} = 0$$

or $$\frac{U_1}{U_2} = \frac{p_1}{p_2} \tag{6-20}$$

This is the familiar tangency condition that the marginal rate of substitution $(-U_1/U_2$, the rate at which a consumer is *willing* to trade off x_2 for $x_1)$ is equal to the opportunity to do so in the market $(-p_1/p_2$, the slope of the budget line). The condition is illustrated in Fig. 6-1. Under the right curvature conditions on the utility function (to be guaranteed by the appropriate second-order conditions), point A clearly represents the maximum achievable utility if the consumer is constrained to consume some consumption bundle along the budget line MM.

The more general constrained maximum problem,

maximize $$f(x_1, \ldots, x_n) = y$$

subject to $$g(x_1, \ldots, x_n) = 0$$

can be solved in the same way, i.e., by direct substitution, reducing the problem to

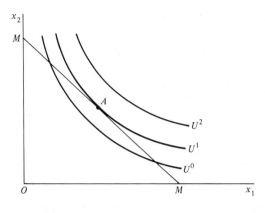

Figure 6-1 *Utility maximization.* In this diagram, three indifference levels are drawn, with $U^2 > U^1 > U^0$. The line MM represents a consumer's budget constraint. The constrained utility maximum occurs at point A, where the indifference curve is tangent to (has the same slope as) the budget constraint. The second-order conditions for a maximum say that the level curves of the utility function, i.e., the indifference curves, must be convex to the origin; i.e., the utility function must be "quasi-concave" (in addition to strictly increasing).

an unconstrained one in $n - 1$ dimensions. However, a highly elegant solution which preserves the symmetry of the problem, known as the method of Lagrange multipliers (after the French mathematician Lagrange), will be given instead. The proof proceeds along the lines developed earlier for unconstrained maxima.

Consider the behavior of the function $f(x_1, \ldots, x_n)$ along some differentiable curve $\mathbf{x}(t) = (x_1(t), \ldots, x_n(t))$; that is, consider $y(t) = f(x_1(t), \ldots, x_n(t))$. If $y'(t) = 0$ and $y''(t) < 0$ for every feasible curve $\mathbf{x}(t)$, then $f(x_1, \ldots, x_n)$ has a maximum at that point. However, in this case, $\mathbf{x}(t)$ cannot represent *all* curves in n-space. Only those curves which lie in the constraint are admissible. This smaller family of curves comprises those curves for which $g(x_1(t), \ldots, x_n(t)) \equiv 0$. Notice the identity sign—we mean to ensure that $g(x_1, \ldots, x_n)$ is 0 *for every point along a given curve* $\mathbf{x}(t)$, not just for some points. The problem can be stated as follows:

maximize $\qquad\qquad f(x_1(t), \ldots, x_n(t)) = y(t) \qquad\qquad\qquad$ (6-21)

subject to $\qquad\qquad g(x_1(t), \ldots, x_n(t)) \equiv 0 \qquad\qquad\qquad$ (6-22)

Setting $y'(t) = 0$ yields

$$f_1 \frac{dx_1}{dt} + \cdots + f_n \frac{dx_n}{dt} = 0 \qquad\qquad (6\text{-}23)$$

for all values of the dx_i/dt which satisfy the constraint. What restriction does $g(x_1(t), \ldots, x_n(t))$ place on these values? Differentiating g with respect to t yields

$$g_1 \frac{dx_1}{dt} + \cdots + g_n \frac{dx_n}{dt} \equiv 0 \qquad\qquad (6\text{-}24)$$

In the unconstrained case, the expression (6-23) was zero for *all* dx_i/dt; hence, in that case $f_i = 0$, $i = 1, \ldots, n$, was necessary for a maximum. Here, however, (6-23) *and* (6-24) must hold simultaneously. Hence, the values of dx_i/dt are not completely unrestricted. However, assuming $f_1 \neq 0$, we can write, from (6-23),

$$\frac{dx_1}{dt} = -\frac{f_2}{f_1} \frac{dx_2}{dt} - \cdots - \frac{f_n}{f_1} \frac{dx_n}{dt} \qquad\qquad (6\text{-}25)$$

Similarly, from (6-24), if $g_1 \neq 0$,

$$\frac{dx_1}{dt} = -\frac{g_2}{g_1}\frac{dx_2}{dt} - \cdots - \frac{g_n}{g_1}\frac{dx_n}{dt} \tag{6-26}$$

Subtracting (6-26) from (6-25) yields, after factoring,

$$\left(\frac{f_2}{f_1} - \frac{g_2}{g_1}\right)\frac{dx_2}{dt} + \cdots + \left(\frac{f_n}{f_1} - \frac{g_n}{g_1}\right)\frac{dx_n}{dt} = 0 \tag{6-27}$$

and, what is more, this expression must be 0 for *all* $dx_2/dt, \ldots, dx_n/dt$. By eliminating one of the dx_i/dt's, the remaining dx_i/dt's can have unrestricted values. If $f_1 \neq 0$, $g_1 \neq 0$, then for any values whatsoever of $dx_2/dt, \ldots, dx_n/dt$, a judicious choice of dx_1/dt will allow (6-23) and (6-24) to hold. But since (6-27) holds for any values at all of $dx_2/dt, \ldots, dx_n/dt$, it must be true that the coefficients in parentheses are all 0; i.e., $f_i/f_1 = g_i/g_1$, $i = 2, \ldots, n$. In the case where all of the f_i, g_i are not 0, these conditions can be expressed simply as

$$\frac{f_i}{f_j} = \frac{g_i}{g_j} \qquad i, j = 1, \ldots, n \tag{6-28}$$

These $n - 1$ conditions say that the level curves of the objective function have to be parallel to the level curves of the constraint. This is the familiar tangency condition, illustrated by the utility maximization problem above. The $n - 1$ conditions (6-28) and the constraint (6-22) itself constitute the complete set of first-order conditions for a constrained maximum problem with one constraint. Of course, these first-order conditions are necessary for any stationary value—maximum, minimum, or saddle shape.

The above conditions can be given an elegant and useful formulation by constructing a new function $\mathscr{L}$ called a lagrangean, where

$$\mathscr{L} = f(x_1, \ldots, x_n) + \lambda g(x_1, \ldots, x_n)$$

The variable λ is simply a new, independent variable and is called a Lagrange multiplier.† Note that $\mathscr{L}$ always equals f for values of $x_1, \ldots, x_n$ which satisfy the constraint. Thus, $\mathscr{L}$ can be expected to have a stationary value when f does. Indeed, taking the partials of $\mathscr{L}$ with respect to $x_1, \ldots, x_n$ and λ and setting them equal to 0 yields

$$\mathscr{L}_1 = f_1 + \lambda g_1 = 0$$
$$\cdots\cdots\cdots\cdots\cdots$$
$$\mathscr{L}_n = f_n + \lambda g_n = 0$$
$$\mathscr{L}_\lambda = g(x_1, \ldots, x_n) = 0 \tag{6-29}$$

---

† It is of no consequence whether one writes $\mathscr{L} = f + \lambda g$ or $\mathscr{L} = f - \lambda g$; this merely changes the sign of the Lagrange multiplier.

Eliminating λ from the first n equations of (6-29) (by bringing λg_i over to the right-hand side and dividing one equation by another) yields

$$\frac{f_i}{f_j} = \frac{g_i}{g_j}$$

precisely the first-order conditions for a constrained maximum. Hence, the lagrangean function provides an easy mnemonic for writing the first-order conditions for constrained-maximum problems. However, we shall see that this is a most useful construction for the second-order conditions also, and in the theory of comparative statics. It will turn out that the lagrange multiplier λ often has an interesting economic interpretation.

> **Example** Consider again the utility-maximization problem analyzed at the beginning of this section. The lagrangean for this problem is
>
> $$\mathscr{L} = U(x_1, x_2) + \lambda(M - p_1 x_1 - p_2 x_2)$$
>
> Differentiating $\mathscr{L}$ with respect to x_1, x_2 and λ yields
>
> $$\mathscr{L}_1 = U_1 - \lambda p_1 = 0 \tag{6-30a}$$
>
> $$\mathscr{L}_2 = U_2 - \lambda p_2 = 0 \tag{6-30b}$$
>
> $$\mathscr{L}_\lambda = M - p_1 x_1 - p_2 x_2 = 0 \tag{6-30c}$$
>
> The partial $\mathscr{L}_\lambda$ is simply the budget constraint again since $\mathscr{L}$ is linear in λ. The variable λ can be eliminated from (6-30a) and (6-30b) by bringing $\lambda p_1, \lambda p_2$ over to the right-hand side and then dividing one equation by the other. This yields $U_1/U_2 = p_1/p_2$, the tangency conditions (6-20) arrived at by direct substitution.

There are many problems in economics in which more than one constraint appears. For example, a famous general-equilibrium model is that of the "small country" which maximizes the value of its output with fixed world prices, subject to constraints which say that the amount of each of several factors of production used cannot exceed a given amount. The general mathematical structure of maximization problems with r constraints is

maximize $\qquad\qquad f(x_1, \ldots, x_n) = y \tag{6-31}$

subject to $\qquad\qquad g^1(x_1, \ldots, x_n) = 0$

$$\cdots\cdots\cdots\cdots\cdots\cdots$$

$$g^r(x_1, \ldots, x_n) = 0 \tag{6-32}$$

These are r equations where, of necessity, $r < n$. (Why?)

The first-order conditions for this problem can be found by generalizing the Lagrange multiplier method derived above. Multiplying each constraint by its own Lagrange multiplier λ^j, form the lagrangean

$$\mathscr{L} = f(x_1, \ldots, x_n) + \lambda^1 g^1(x_1, \ldots, x_n) + \cdots + \lambda^r g^r(x_1, \ldots, x_n) \tag{6-33}$$

Then the first partials of $\mathscr{L}$ with respect to the $n + r$ variables x_i, λ^j give the correct first-order conditions:

$$\mathscr{L}_i = f_i + \lambda^1 g_i^1 + \cdots + \lambda^r g_i^r = 0 \qquad i = 1, \ldots, n \qquad (6\text{-}34)$$

$$\mathscr{L}_j = g^j = 0 \qquad j = 1, \ldots, r \qquad (6\text{-}35)$$

where g_i^j means $\partial g^j / \partial x_i$. The proof of this can be obtained only by more advanced methods; it is given in the next section.

6.3 CONSTRAINED MAXIMIZATION WITH MORE THAN ONE CONSTRAINT: A DIGRESSION†

Consider the maximization problem

maximize $\qquad\qquad f(x_1, \ldots, x_n) = y$

subject to $\qquad\qquad g^1(x_1, \ldots, x_n) = 0$

$$\cdots\cdots\cdots\cdots\cdots\cdots$$

$$g^r(x_1, \ldots, x_n) = 0$$

Letting $x_i = x_i(t)$, $i = 1, \ldots, n$, as before, the first-order conditions for a maximum (or any stationary value) are

$$\frac{dy}{dt} = f_1 \frac{dx_1}{dt} + \cdots + f_n \frac{dx_n}{dt} = 0 \qquad (6\text{-}36)$$

for any $dx_1/dt, \ldots, dx_n/dt$ satisfying

$$g_1^1 \frac{dx_1}{dt} + \cdots + g_n^1 \frac{dx_n}{dt} = 0$$

$$\cdots\cdots\cdots\cdots\cdots\cdots\cdots$$

$$g_1^r \frac{dx_1}{dt} + \cdots + g_n^r \frac{dx_n}{dt} = 0 \qquad (6\text{-}37)$$

where $g_i^j = \partial g^j / \partial x_i$.

For any function $y = f(x_1, \ldots, x_n)$, the *gradient* of f, written $\mathbf{V}f$, is a vector composed of the first partials of f:

$$\mathbf{V}f = (f_1, \ldots, f_n)$$

The differential of f can be written

$$dy = \mathbf{V}f\, d\mathbf{x}$$

where $d\mathbf{x} = (dx_1, \ldots, dx_n)$. Along a level surface, $dy = 0$, and hence $\mathbf{V}f$ is orthogonal to the direction of the tangent hyperplane. The gradient of f, $\mathbf{V}f$, thus represents the direction of maximum increase of $f(x_1, \ldots, x_n)$.

† In order to understand this section, the student must be familiar with some concepts of linear algebra, such as rank of a matrix, etc., developed in the Appendix to Chapter 5. I am indebted to Mr. Ron Heiner for demonstrating this approach to the problem to me.

Note that equation (6-36) is the scalar product of the gradient of f, $\mathbf{Vf}$, and the vector $\mathbf{h} = (h_1, \ldots, h_n) = (dx_1/dt, \ldots, dx_n/dt)$. Likewise, equations (6-37) are the scalar products of the gradients of the g^j functions, $\mathbf{Vg}^j$, and $\mathbf{h}$. Let $\mathbf{Vg}$ denote the $r \times n$ matrix whose rows are, respectively, $\mathbf{Vg}^1, \ldots, \mathbf{Vg}^r$. Then equations (6-36) and (6-37) can be written, respectively,

$$\mathbf{Vf} \cdot \mathbf{h} = 0 \qquad (6\text{-}38)$$

for all $\mathbf{h} \neq 0$ satisfying

$$(\mathbf{Vg})\mathbf{h} = \mathbf{0} \qquad (6\text{-}39)$$

Assume now that the matrix $\mathbf{Vg}$ has rank r, equal to the number of constraints. This says that the constraints are independent, i.e., there are no redundant constraints. If the rank of $\mathbf{Vg}$ was less than r, say $r - 1$, then one constraint could be dropped and the subspace in which the dx_i/dt could range over would not be affected. It is as if a ration-point constraint were imposed with the ration prices proportional to the original money prices. In that case, the additional rationing constraint would either be redundant to or inconsistent with the original budget constraint.

Assuming rank $\mathbf{Vg} = r$, the rows of $\mathbf{Vg}$, that is, the gradient vectors $\mathbf{Vg}^j = (g_1^j, \ldots, g_n^j)$, $j = 1, \ldots, r$, form a basis for an r-dimensional subspace E_r of E_n, euclidean n-space. From (6-39), the admissible vectors $\mathbf{h}$ are all orthogonal to E_r; hence, they must all lie in the remaining $n - r$ dimensional space, E_r'. However, from (6-38), $\mathbf{Vf}$ is orthogonal to all those $\mathbf{h}$'s, and hence to E_r'. Hence, $\mathbf{Vf}$ must lie in E_r. Since the vectors $\mathbf{Vg}^j$ form a basis for E_r, $\mathbf{Vf}$ can be written as a unique linear combination of those vectors, or

$$\mathbf{Vf} = \lambda^1 \mathbf{Vg}^1 + \cdots + \lambda^r \mathbf{Vg}^r \qquad (6\text{-}40)$$

However, this is equivalent to setting the partial derivatives of the lagrangean expression $\mathscr{L} = f - \Sigma \lambda^j g^j$ with respect to $x_1, \ldots, x_n$ equal to 0.

6.4 SECOND-ORDER CONDITIONS

In the past two sections, the first-order necessary conditions for a function to achieve a stationary value subject to constraints were derived. Those conditions are implied whenever the function has a maximum, a minimum, or a saddle shape (a minimum in some directions and a maximum in others). We now seek to state sufficient conditions under which the type of stationary position can be specified. The discussion will be largely limited to the two-variable case, with the general theorems stated at the end of this section.

Consider the two-variable problem,

maximize $\qquad\qquad f(x_1, x_2) = y$

subject to $\qquad\qquad g(x_1, x_2) = 0$

The lagrangean function is $\mathscr{L}(x_1, x_2, \lambda) = f(x_1, x_2) + \lambda g(x_1, x_2)$. The first-order conditions are, again,

$$\frac{dy}{dt} = f_1 \frac{dx_1}{dt} + f_2 \frac{dx_2}{dt} = 0 \tag{6-41}$$

for all dx_1/dt, dx_2/dt satisfying

$$g_1 \frac{dx_1}{dt} + g_2 \frac{dx_2}{dt} \equiv 0 \tag{6-42}$$

These conditions imply that $\mathscr{L}_1 = f_1 + \lambda g_1 = 0$, $\mathscr{L}_2 = f_2 + \lambda g_2 = 0$. Sufficient conditions for these equations to represent a relative *maximum* are that $d^2 y/dt^2 < 0$, for all dx_1/dt, dx_2/dt satisfying (6-42). Similarly, $d^2 y/dt^2 > 0$ under those conditions implies a *minimum*. How can these conditions be put into a more useful form? Differentiating (6-41) again with respect to t, the sufficient second-order condition is

$$\frac{d^2 y}{dt^2} = f_1 \frac{d^2 x_1}{dt^2} + f_2 \frac{d^2 x_2}{dt^2} + f_{11} \left(\frac{dx_1}{dt}\right)^2$$

$$+ 2f_{12} \frac{dx_1}{dt} \frac{dx_2}{dt} + f_{22} \left(\frac{dx_2}{dt}\right)^2 < 0 \tag{6-43}$$

subject to

$$g_1 \frac{dx_1}{dt} + g_2 \frac{dx_2}{dt} \equiv 0 \tag{6-42}$$

Since (6-42) is an identity, differentiate it again with respect to t, remembering that g_1 and g_2 are functions of $x_1(t)$, $x_2(t)$. This yields

$$g_1 \frac{d^2 x_1}{dt^2} + g_2 \frac{d^2 x_2}{dt^2} + g_{11} \left(\frac{dx_1}{dt}\right)^2 + 2g_{12} \frac{dx_1}{dt} \frac{dx_2}{dt} + g_{22} \left(\frac{dx_2}{dt}\right)^2 \equiv 0 \tag{6-44}$$

Now multiply (6-44) through by λ, the Lagrange multiplier, and add to equation (6-43). Since this amounts to adding 0,

$$\frac{d^2 y}{dt^2} = (f_1 + \lambda g_1) \frac{d^2 x_1}{dt^2} + (f_2 + \lambda g_2) \frac{d^2 x_2}{dt^2} + (f_{11} + \lambda g_{11}) \left(\frac{dx_1}{dt}\right)^2$$

$$+ 2(f_{12} + \lambda g_{12}) \frac{dx_1}{dt} \frac{dx_2}{dt} + (f_{22} + \lambda g_{22}) \left(\frac{dx_2}{dt}\right)^2 < 0 \tag{6-45}$$

subject to (6-42). However, from the first-order conditions, $\mathscr{L}_1 = f_1 + \lambda g_1 = 0$, $\mathscr{L}_2 = f_2 + \lambda g_2 = 0$. Also, $f_{11} + \lambda g_{11}$ is simply $\mathscr{L}_{11}$, and likewise $\mathscr{L}_{12} = f_{12} + \lambda g_{12}$, etc. If we may simplify the notation a bit and write $h_1 = dx_1/dt$, $h_2 = dx_2/dt$, then the sufficient second-order conditions for a maximum are that

$$\mathscr{L}_{11} h_1^2 + 2\mathscr{L}_{12} h_1 h_2 + \mathscr{L}_{22} h_2^2 < 0 \tag{6-46}$$

for all h_1, h_2 not both equal to 0, such that

$$g_1 h_1 + g_2 h_2 \equiv 0 \tag{6-47}$$

For the case of n variables and one constraint, the derivations proceed along similar lines, producing

$$\sum_{i=1}^{n} \sum_{j=1}^{n} \mathcal{L}_{ij} h_i h_j < 0 \qquad (6\text{-}48)$$

for all h_i, h_j such that

$$\sum_{i=1}^{n} g_i h_i \equiv 0 \qquad (6\text{-}49)$$

In this case the matrix of terms $(\mathcal{L}_{ij})$ is said to be *negative definite subject to constraint*.

Equations (6-46) and (6-47) can be combined into one useful expression: From (6-47),

$$h_2 = -h_1 \frac{g_1}{g_2}$$

Substituting this into (6-46) yields

$$\mathcal{L}_{11} h_1^2 + 2\mathcal{L}_{12} h_1 \left(-h_1 \frac{g_1}{g_2} \right) + \mathcal{L}_{22} \left(-h_1 \frac{g_1}{g_2} \right)^2 < 0$$

Or, by multiplying by g_2^2,

$$(\mathcal{L}_{11} g_2^2 - 2\mathcal{L}_{12} g_1 g_2 + \mathcal{L}_{22} g_1^2) h_1^2 < 0 \qquad (6\text{-}50)$$

for any value of $h_1 \neq 0$. This implies that the expression in the parentheses must itself be < 0. How can that expression be conveniently remembered? It turns out, fortuitously, that the expression in parentheses in (6-50) is precisely the negative of the determinant

$$D = \begin{vmatrix} \mathcal{L}_{11} & \mathcal{L}_{12} & g_1 \\ \mathcal{L}_{21} & \mathcal{L}_{22} & g_2 \\ g_1 & g_2 & 0 \end{vmatrix} \qquad (6\text{-}51)$$

as can be immediately verified by expansion of D. Hence, *a sufficient condition for $f(x_1, x_2)$ to have a maximum subject to $g(x_1, x_2) \equiv 0$ is, together with the first-order relations, that $D > 0$.* Likewise, for relative minimum subject to constraint, the sufficient second-order condition is that $D < 0$. Also, $D = 0$ corresponds to the case where the second derivatives $d^2 y/dt^2 = 0$, hence no statement can be made regarding the type of stationary value in question.

Note that $\partial^2 \mathcal{L}/\partial x_1 \, \partial \lambda \equiv \mathcal{L}_{1\lambda} \equiv g_1 \equiv \mathcal{L}_{\lambda 1}$ and $\mathcal{L}_{2\lambda} \equiv \mathcal{L}_{\lambda 2} \equiv g_2$, and $\mathcal{L}_{\lambda\lambda} = 0$, since λ enters the lagrangean $\mathcal{L} = f + \lambda g$ linearly. Hence, D is simply the determinant of the matrix of cross-partials of $\mathcal{L}$ with respect to x_1, x_2 and λ, that is,

$$D = \begin{vmatrix} \mathcal{L}_{11} & \mathcal{L}_{12} & \mathcal{L}_{1\lambda} \\ \mathcal{L}_{21} & \mathcal{L}_{22} & \mathcal{L}_{2\lambda} \\ \mathcal{L}_{\lambda 1} & \mathcal{L}_{\lambda 2} & \mathcal{L}_{\lambda\lambda} \end{vmatrix}$$

For the n-variable case, the situation is more complicated, but the rules are analogous to the unconstrained case. The lagrangean is $\mathscr{L} = f(x_1, \ldots, x_n) + \lambda g(x_1, \ldots, x_n)$. Consider the matrix of cross-partials of $\mathscr{L}$ with respect to $x_1, \ldots, x_n$ and λ, noting, as before, that $\mathscr{L}_{i\lambda} = g_i$, $\mathscr{L}_{\lambda\lambda} = 0$:

$$
\mathbf{H} = \begin{pmatrix}
\mathscr{L}_{11} & \cdots & \mathscr{L}_{1n} & g_1 \\
\cdots\cdots\cdots\cdots\cdots\cdots\cdots\cdots \\
\mathscr{L}_{n1} & \cdots & \mathscr{L}_{nn} & g_n \\
g_1 & \cdots & g_n & 0
\end{pmatrix}
$$

This matrix is commonly referred to as a "bordered hessian" matrix, noting how the first partials of the constraint function g *border* the cross-partials of $\mathscr{L}$ with respect to $x_1, \ldots, x_n$.

Consider the following construction: By a "*border-preserving* principal minor of order k" of the above matrix, we mean that determinant that remains when any $n - k$ rows and the same numbered columns are deleted, *with the special added proviso that the border itself not be deleted.* Hence, the deletions that can occur must only come from rows 1 through n, not row or column $n + 1$. (Note that a border-preserving principal minor of order k is a $(k + 1) \times (k + 1)$ determinant.)

The second-order sufficient conditions are then:

Theorem Together with the first-order condition $\mathscr{L}_i = 0$, $i = 1, \ldots, n$ and $\mathscr{L}_\lambda = g = 0$, if all the border-preserving principal minors of H of order k have sign $(-1)^k$, $k = 2, \ldots, n$, then a maximum position is obtained. If all the border-preserving principal minors are negative, $k = 2, \ldots, n$, then a minimum is obtained.†

Suppose, even more generally, that there are r constraints involved. The lagrangean function is $\mathscr{L} = f(x_1, \ldots, x_n) + \sum_{j=1}^r \lambda_j g^j(x_1, \ldots, x_n)$. The bordered hessian matrix of this lagrangean is

$$
\mathbf{H} = \begin{pmatrix}
\mathscr{L}_{11} & \cdots & \mathscr{L}_{1n} & g_1^1 & \cdots & g_1^r \\
\cdots\cdots\cdots\cdots\cdots\cdots\cdots\cdots\cdots \\
\mathscr{L}_{n1} & \cdots & \mathscr{L}_{nn} & g_n^1 & \cdots & g_n^r \\
g_1^1 & \cdots & g_n^1 & 0 & \cdots & 0 \\
\cdots\cdots\cdots\cdots\cdots\cdots\cdots\cdots \\
g_1^r & \cdots & g_n^r & 0 & \cdots & 0
\end{pmatrix}
$$

The sufficient conditions here state that for a *minimum*, the border-preserving principal minors of order $k > r$ (which again must involve deletions only from rows 1 through n) have sign $(-1)^r$, where r is the number of (independent) constraints. For a *maximum*, the border-preserving principal minors of order $k > r$ alternate in sign, beginning with $(-1)^{r+1}$, the second of opposite sign, etc. These principal minors must be of order greater than r, because, as inspection of H

---

† In fact, if only the "naturally ordered" principal minors have this property, then *all* of the border-preserving principal minors have that property.

reveals (note the $r \times r$ matrix of 0's in the lower right), a determinant involving fewer than r rows and columns from rows and columns 1 through n must equal 0. Note again that with r bordering rows, a border-preserving principal minor of order k has $k + r$ rows and columns. An alternative presentation of the second-order conditions is given in Table 6-1. In this table, $m \geq 2r + 1$ is the size of the whole determinant.

Example Consider again the basic consumer theory model, maximize $U(x_1, x_2)$ subject to $p_1 x_1 + p_2 x_2 = M$. (See Fig. 6-1 again.) Assuming more is preferred to less, the ordinal indifference levels must be indexed such that $U^2 > U^1 > U^0$. The condition that a point of tangency of an indifference curve and the budget constraint actually represent a maximum rather than a minimum of utility subject to constraint is clearly that the indifference curves have the shape indicated, i.e., convex to the origin. This convexity is a statement of the law of diminishing marginal rate of substitution of x_2 for x_1 along an indifference curve. We previously showed, in Chap. 3, that this convexity to the origin is expressible as [see Sec. 3.6, equation (3-32)]

$$\frac{d^2 x_2}{dx_1^2} \equiv [-U_2^2 U_{11} + 2U_{12} U_1 U_2 - U_1^2 U_{22}] \frac{1}{U_2^3} > 0 \qquad (6\text{-}52)$$

If this is to be positive, the square-bracketed term must be positive, assuming that $U_2 > 0$, i.e., the consumer is not sated in good 2. But by inspection, the term in brackets is equal to the following determinant, which must therefore itself be positive:

$$D' = \begin{vmatrix} U_{11} & U_{12} & -U_1 \\ U_{21} & U_{22} & -U_2 \\ -U_1 & -U_2 & 0 \end{vmatrix} > 0 \qquad (6\text{-}53)$$

However, from the first-order conditions for utility maximization (6-30), $U_1 = \lambda p_1$, $U_2 = \lambda p_2$. Substituting this into D' and then dividing the last row and column by λ (and, hence, D' by λ^2, which is positive), the condition $D' > 0$ is equivalent to

$$D = \begin{vmatrix} U_{11} & U_{12} & -p_1 \\ U_{21} & U_{22} & -p_2 \\ -p_1 & -p_2 & 0 \end{vmatrix} > 0 \qquad (6\text{-}54)$$

Table 6-1 Second-order conditions: Sign of all size $m \times m$ (border-preserving) principal minors

		Constraints	
Condition	0	1	r
Maximum	$(-1)^m$	$(-1)^{m-1}$	$(-1)^{m-r}$
	$m = 1, \ldots, n$	$m = 3, \ldots, n+1$	$m = 1 + 2r, \ldots, n+r$
Minimum	$(-1)^0 = +1$	$(-1)^1 = -1$	$(-1)^r$

But D is seen to be the determinant of the bordered hessian matrix, the cross-partials of $\mathscr{L}$ with respect to x_1, x_2 and λ. This is in accordance with the general theorem of this section.

The second-order conditions for constrained maximization are algebraic statements of the geometric property of convexity to the origin, as exhibited by indifference curves. This type of convexity is actually referred to as *quasi-concavity*, which means, more precisely, that if a straight line joins any two points on a level curve of the function (say, an indifference curve), then the function lies "above" that chord, i.e., the chord cuts through only higher-valued points than the two end points (the consumption bundles lying along any chord joining two points on an indifference curve are preferred to the two end points).† Clearly, concavity, in which a chord joining *any* two points lies below the function is a stronger condition than quasi-concavity (which specifies that the two points must lie on a level curve) and, hence, concavity implies quasi-concavity, but not the reverse.

6.5 GENERAL METHODOLOGY

In Chap. 5, we considered the general economic model which was characterized by being an *unconstrained* maximization. Let us now explore models which have a constraint as an added feature.

Consider some economic agent that behaves in accordance with the following general model.

maximize $$f(x_1, x_2, \alpha) = y \tag{6-55}$$

subject to $$g(x_1, x_2, \alpha) = 0 \tag{6-56}$$

where x_1 and x_2 are the decision variables and α is some parameter (or vector of parameters) over which the agent has no control. What will be the response to autonomous changes in the environment, i.e., to changes in the parameter α?

The first-order conditions for a maximum are derived by setting the partials of the lagrangian function $\mathscr{L} = f(x_1, x_2, \alpha) + \lambda g(x_1, x_2, \alpha)$, with respect to x_1, x_2 and λ, equal to zero:

$$\begin{aligned}
\mathscr{L}_1 &= f_1(x_1, x_2, \alpha) + \lambda g_1(x_1, x_2, \alpha) = 0 \\
\mathscr{L}_2 &= f_2(x_1, x_2, \alpha) + \lambda g_2(x_1, x_2, \alpha) = 0 \\
\mathscr{L}_\lambda &= g(x_1, x_2, \alpha) = 0
\end{aligned} \tag{6-57}$$

† Strictly speaking, the function is strictly or nonstrictly quasi-concave if, respectively, the chord lies *entirely* in higher-valued points, or whether some points along the chord have equal value to the end points (e.g., if an indifference curve had a "flat" section).

Equations (6-57) represent three equations in the four unknowns x_1, x_2, λ, and α. Assuming the implicit function theorem (as was discussed above) is applicable, these equations can be solved, in principle at least, for the choice functions

$$x_1 = x_1^*(\alpha)$$
$$x_2 = x_2^*(\alpha) \tag{6-58}$$
$$\lambda = \lambda^*(\alpha)$$

Substituting these values back into equations (6-57) from which they were derived yields the *identities*.

$$f_1(x_1^*, x_2^*, \alpha) + \lambda^* g_1(x_1^*, x_2^*, \alpha) \equiv 0$$
$$f_2(x_1^*, x_2^*, \alpha) + \lambda^* g_2(x_1^*, x_2^*, \alpha) \equiv 0 \tag{6-59}$$
$$g(x_1^*, x_2^*, \alpha) \equiv 0$$

Since we are interested in *changes* in the x_i^*'s (i.e., marginal values) as α changes, we differentiate (6-59) with respect to α, using the chain rule. The first equation then yields

$$f_{11}\frac{\partial x_1^*}{\partial \alpha} + f_{12}\frac{\partial x_2^*}{\partial \alpha} + f_{1\alpha} + \lambda^* g_{11}\frac{\partial x_1^*}{\partial \alpha} + \lambda^* g_{12}\frac{\partial x_2^*}{\partial \alpha} + \lambda^* g_{1\alpha} + g_1\frac{\partial \lambda^*}{\partial \alpha} \equiv 0$$

However, noting that $\mathscr{L}_{11} = f_{11} + \lambda^* g_{11}$, ..., this equation can be more conveniently written

$$\mathscr{L}_{11}\frac{\partial x_1^*}{\partial \alpha} + \mathscr{L}_{12}\frac{\partial x_2^*}{\partial \alpha} + g_1\frac{\partial \lambda^*}{\partial \alpha} \equiv -\mathscr{L}_{1\alpha} \tag{6-60}$$

Similarly, differentiating the second and third equations of (6-59) yields

$$\mathscr{L}_{21}\frac{\partial x_1^*}{\partial \alpha} + \mathscr{L}_{22}\frac{\partial x_2^*}{\partial \alpha} + g_2\frac{\partial \lambda^*}{\partial \alpha} \equiv -\mathscr{L}_{2\alpha} \tag{6-61}$$

$$g_1\frac{\partial x_1^*}{\partial \alpha} + g_2\frac{\partial x_2^*}{\partial \alpha} \equiv -g_\alpha \tag{6-62}$$

In matrix notation, this system of three linear equations can be written

$$\begin{pmatrix} \mathscr{L}_{11} & \mathscr{L}_{12} & g_1 \\ \mathscr{L}_{21} & \mathscr{L}_{22} & g_2 \\ g_1 & g_2 & 0 \end{pmatrix} \begin{pmatrix} \dfrac{\partial x_1^*}{\partial \alpha} \\ \dfrac{\partial x_2^*}{\partial \alpha} \\ \dfrac{\partial \lambda^*}{\partial \alpha} \end{pmatrix} = \begin{pmatrix} -\mathscr{L}_{1\alpha} \\ -\mathscr{L}_{2\alpha} \\ -g_\alpha \end{pmatrix} \tag{6-63}$$

Notice that the coefficient matrix on the left of (6-63) is the matrix of second partials of the lagrangian function. In unconstrained maximization models, this coefficient matrix was the matrix of second partials of the objective function. The manipulation of the model is formally identical in the constrained and unconstrained cases; the only difference is the conditions imposed on the principal minors of the coefficient matrix by the sufficient second-order conditions.

The reason why the coefficient matrix comes out to be the second partials of $\mathscr{L}$ is that identities (6-59) are precisely the first partials of $\mathscr{L}$,

$$\mathscr{L}_1(x_1^*, x_2^*, \lambda^*, \alpha) \equiv 0$$

$$\mathscr{L}_2(x_1^*, x_2^*, \lambda^*, \alpha) \equiv 0 \tag{6-64}$$

$$\mathscr{L}_\lambda(x_1^*, x_2^*, \alpha) \equiv 0$$

(Notice that λ^* does not appear in $\mathscr{L}_\lambda = g(x_1^*, x_2^*, \alpha) \equiv 0$.) Differentiating the first identity with respect to α yields

$$\mathscr{L}_{11}\frac{\partial x_1^*}{\partial \alpha} + \mathscr{L}_{12}\frac{\partial x_2^*}{\partial \alpha} + \mathscr{L}_{1\lambda}\frac{\partial \lambda^*}{\partial \alpha} + \mathscr{L}_{1\alpha} \equiv 0$$

This is precisely equation (6-60), noting again that $\mathscr{L}_{1\lambda} = g_1$. In like fashion, equations (6-61) and (6-62) are derivable directly from $\mathscr{L}_2 = 0$, $\mathscr{L}_\lambda = 0$.

Since the jacobian determinant J needed to ensure solution of equations (6-57) for the explicit choice functions (6-58) is formed from the matrix of first partials of (6-57), J is in fact the determinant of second partials of the lagrangian $\mathscr{L}$ with respect to x_1, x_2 and λ, that is, the determinant of the coefficient matrix in (6-63). This determinant is denoted by H below. The *sufficient* second-order conditions imply, among other things, that this determinant is nonzero, and thus the explicit relations (6-58) are valid. And this determinant forms the denominator in the solution by Cramer's rule for $\partial x_i^*/\partial \alpha$ and $\partial \lambda^*/\partial \alpha$. Let us now proceed, in the same manner as for the unconstrained models.

Solving for $\partial x_1^*/\partial \alpha$ by Cramer's rule,

$$\frac{\partial x_1^*}{\partial \alpha} = \frac{\begin{vmatrix} -\mathscr{L}_{1\alpha} & \mathscr{L}_{12} & g_1 \\ -\mathscr{L}_{2\alpha} & \mathscr{L}_{22} & g_2 \\ -g_\alpha & g_2 & 0 \end{vmatrix}}{H} = -\frac{\mathscr{L}_{1\alpha}H_{11}}{H} - \frac{\mathscr{L}_{2\alpha}H_{21}}{H} - \frac{g_\alpha H_{31}}{H} \tag{6-65}$$

where H is the bordered hessian determinant of the coefficient matrix. Solutions for $\partial x_2^*/\partial \alpha$ and $\partial \lambda^*/\partial \alpha$ are, likewise

$$\frac{\partial x_2^*}{\partial \alpha} = \frac{\begin{vmatrix} \mathscr{L}_{11} & -\mathscr{L}_{1\alpha} & g_1 \\ \mathscr{L}_{21} & -\mathscr{L}_{2\alpha} & g_2 \\ g_1 & -g_\alpha & 0 \end{vmatrix}}{H} \tag{6-66}$$

$$\frac{\partial \lambda^*}{\partial \alpha} = \frac{\begin{vmatrix} \mathscr{L}_{11} & \mathscr{L}_{12} & -\mathscr{L}_{1\alpha} \\ \mathscr{L}_{21} & \mathscr{L}_{22} & -\mathscr{L}_{2\alpha} \\ g_1 & g_2 & -g_\alpha \end{vmatrix}}{H} \tag{6-67}$$

It is clear that at this level of generality, no prediction as to the sign of $\partial x_i^*/\partial \alpha$ or $\partial \lambda^*/\partial \alpha$ is forthcoming. There simply is not enough information in the system. All we know is that the denominators in these expressions are positive, but we have no information regarding the numerators. The signs of the off-diagonal cofactors are not implied by the maximum conditions.

Suppose now that the parameter α did not appear in either the second or third first-order relations (6-57). Then $\mathcal{L}_{2\alpha} = 0$ and $g_\alpha = 0$, and

$$\frac{\partial x_1^*}{\partial \alpha} = \frac{-\mathcal{L}_{1\alpha}\begin{vmatrix} \mathcal{L}_{22} & g_2 \\ g_2 & 0 \end{vmatrix}}{H} = \frac{+\mathcal{L}_{1\alpha}g_2^2}{H} \tag{6-68}$$

The partial $\partial x_1^*/\partial \alpha$ now has a predictable sign: Since $H > 0$ and $H_{11} < 0$, by the second-order conditions (here, $H_{11} = -g_2^2 < 0$ always), $\partial x_1^*/\partial \alpha$ will have the same sign as the direction of "disturbance" of the first equation. That is, if an increase in α has the effect of shifting the marginal curve $\mathcal{L}_1$ to the right ($\mathcal{L}_{1\alpha} > 0$), then the response will be to increase the utilization of x_1. Hence, if it is possible to make statements like, "an increase in income will *shift* a demand curve to the right," or "a change in technology will lower (shift down) such and such marginal-cost curve," then if that income or technology parameter enters only one first-order relation, it will in general be possible to predict the algebraic sign of the partial derivative of the associated variable (the one for which that first-order equation is the first partial of the lagrangian). More succinctly, if α enters the *i*th first-order equation only, then $\partial x_i^*/\partial \alpha$ and $\mathcal{L}_{i\alpha}$ have the same sign, or

$$\frac{\partial x_i^*}{\partial \alpha}\mathcal{L}_{i\alpha} > 0 \tag{6-69}$$

This result holds for the case of n variables as well as for just two variables; its precise statement is given in the problems following. The result follows because of the conditions on the principal minors imposed by the second-order conditions for a constrained maximum (or minimum).

In the case of $\partial \lambda^*/\partial \alpha$, however, a sign is *never* implied by the sufficient second-order conditions alone, no matter how the parameter α enters the first-order equations. Suppose, for example, α enters only the constraint, i.e., the third first-order equation. Then $-\mathcal{L}_{1\alpha} = -\mathcal{L}_{2\alpha} = 0$, and

$$\frac{\partial \lambda^*}{\partial \alpha} = \frac{-g_\alpha H_{33}}{H} = \frac{-g_\alpha}{H}(\mathcal{L}_{11}\mathcal{L}_{22} - \mathcal{L}_{12}^2) \gtrless 0 \tag{6-70}$$

The cofactor H_{33}, while a principal minor, is not a *border-preserving* principal minor. The border row and column of H are deleted when forming H_{33}. Hence, no sign is implied for $\partial \lambda^*/\partial \alpha$. If α enters any of the other equations, then the off-diagonal cofactors H_{31} and H_{32} will enter the expressions. These expressions are likewise not signed by the maximum conditions.

6.6 THE ENVELOPE THEOREM

One of the most important analytic devices we shall encounter throughout this book is called *the envelope theorem*. It concerns the rate of change of the objective function itself when a parameter changes.

Unconstrained Maxima

Consider first a model consisting of an unconstrained maximum:

maximize $\qquad\qquad\qquad y = f(x_1, \ldots, x_n, \alpha)$ $\qquad\qquad\qquad$ (6-71)

The first-order conditions are

$$f_i(x_1, \ldots, x_n, \alpha) = 0 \qquad i = 1, \ldots, n \qquad\qquad (6\text{-}72)$$

Assuming the sufficient second-order conditions hold, these equations are solved for the choice functions

$$x_i = x_i^*(\alpha) \qquad i = 1, \ldots, n \qquad\qquad (6\text{-}73)$$

Let us now substitute these choices, (6-73), into the objective function:

$$y^* = f(x_1^*(\alpha), \ldots, x_n^*(\alpha), \alpha) = \phi(\alpha) \qquad\qquad (6\text{-}74)$$

The function $\phi(\alpha)$ is called the *indirect objective function*. It represents the maximum value of y for any α, since the x_i's which maximize y for given α are substituted into $y = f(x_1, \ldots, x_n)$.

How does y^*, or $\phi(\alpha)$ change when α changes? Differentiating (6-74) with respect to α,[†]

$$\frac{\partial y^*}{\partial \alpha} = \frac{\partial \phi}{\partial \alpha} = \sum f_i \frac{\partial x_i^*}{\partial \alpha} + f_\alpha$$

However, $\qquad\qquad\qquad f_i = 0 \qquad i = 1, \ldots, n$

from the first-order relations (6-72). Therefore

$$\frac{\partial y^*}{\partial \alpha} = \frac{\partial \phi}{\partial \alpha} = f_\alpha \qquad\qquad (6\text{-}75)$$

This equation says that at any given $(x_1^*, \ldots, x_n^*)$, the rate of change of the *maximum* value of y with respect to a parameter (i.e., allowing the x_i's to "adjust" to the parameter change) is equal to the rate of change of y when all the x_i's are fixed, that is, f_α. This phenomenon will be dealt with in more detail in Chap. 9. The student should not confuse this with the Le Châtelier effects of Chap. 3. There, in certain models, when some variable in the objective function was held fixed, the absolute response of *another variable* to a change in a parameter *declined* (or in any event, changed) when some other variable was held fixed. In equation

---

[†] The notation $\partial\phi/\partial\alpha$ is used instead of $\phi'(\alpha)$ in case α represents only one of several parameters.

(6-75), it is the value of the objective function itself that is being observed. The value of the objective function is what it is, at any given x_i's. The rate of change of y with respect to α is the same in the limit, i.e., at the margin, whether or not the x_i's are fixed, since the x_i's are already at their y-maximizing values. We shall see, however, in Chap. 9 that the second derivatives of y with respect to α *do* change when the x_i's are the choice functions $x_i^*(\alpha)$ instead of fixed at given values.

Example Consider the profit-maximizing firm, with objective function

$$\text{maximize} \qquad \pi = pf(x_1, \ldots, x_n) - \sum w_i x_i \qquad (6\text{-}76)$$

The first-order conditions for a maximum are

$$\pi_i = pf_i - w_i = 0 \qquad i = 1, \ldots, n \qquad (6\text{-}77)$$

Assuming the sufficient second-order conditions hold, equations (6-77) are solved for

$$x_i = x_i^*(w_1, \ldots, w_n, p) \qquad i = 1, \ldots, n \qquad (6\text{-}78)$$

The *maximum* value of profits for any factor and output prices is given by

$$\pi^* = pf(x_1^*, \ldots, x_n^*) - \sum w_i x_i^* \qquad (6\text{-}79)$$

How does π^* change when, say, w_j changes?

$$\frac{\partial \pi^*}{\partial w_j} = p \sum_{i=1}^{n} f_i \frac{\partial x_i^*}{\partial w_j} - x_j^* - \sum_{i=1}^{n} w_i \frac{\partial x_i^*}{\partial w_j}$$

where the product rule has been used on the term $w_j x_j^*$. Combining terms,

$$\frac{\partial \pi^*}{\partial w_j} = \sum_{i=1}^{n} (pf_i - w_i) \frac{\partial x_i^*}{\partial w_j} - x_j^* = -x_j^* \qquad (6\text{-}80)$$

using equations (6-77). Note that if all the x_i's are held fixed,

$$\frac{\partial \pi}{\partial w_j} = -x_j$$

Hence, at $x_i = x_i^*$, $i = 1, \ldots, n$

$$\frac{\partial \pi^*}{\partial w_j} = \frac{\partial \pi}{\partial w_j} \qquad (6\text{-}81)$$

In like fashion, one finds

$$\frac{\partial \pi^*}{\partial p} = \frac{\partial \pi}{\partial p} = f(x_1^*, \ldots, x_n^*) = y^* \qquad (6\text{-}82)$$

Equations (6-80) and (6-82) can be used to derive the reciprocity conditions of this model in one step. Keeping equations (6-78) in mind, (6-80) and (6-82) can be differentiated again:

$$\pi_{w_j w_i}^* = \frac{-\partial x_j^*}{\partial w_i}$$

However $\qquad\qquad \pi^*_{w_j w_i} = \pi^*_{w_i w_j}$

Therefore $\qquad \pi^*_{w_j w_i} = \dfrac{-\partial x^*_j}{\partial w_i} = \dfrac{-\partial x^*_i}{\partial w_j} = \pi^*_{w_i w_j}$ $\qquad$ (6-83)

Thus, the reciprocity condition $\partial x^*_i / \partial w_j = \partial x^*_j / \partial w_i$ is seen to result from Young's theorem (invariance of second partials to the order of differentiation) applied to the indirect objective function! Additionally,

$$\pi^*_{w_i p} = -\frac{\partial x^*_i}{\partial p}$$

But also $\qquad\qquad \pi^*_{p w_i} = \dfrac{\partial y^*}{\partial w_i}$

Hence $\qquad\qquad \dfrac{\partial y^*}{\partial w_i} = -\dfrac{\partial x^*_i}{\partial p}$ $\qquad$ (6-84)

These derivations are valid only because of equations (6-78). That is, the expression $\partial y / \partial p$ is gibberish; y is itself not a function of p. However, y^* *is* a function of p (through the demand curves). The fact that y^* (*not* y) and $-x^*_i$ (*not* $-x_i$) are functions of the parameters allows these expressions to be differentiated again.

Constrained Maxima

Consider now a model of the form

maximize $\qquad\qquad f(x_1, \ldots, x_n, \alpha) = y$

subject to $\qquad\qquad g(x_1, \ldots, x_n, \alpha) = 0$

The lagrangian is $\mathcal{L} = f + \lambda g$. Setting the first partials of $\mathcal{L}$ equal to 0,

$$\mathcal{L}_i = f_i + \lambda g_i = 0 \qquad i = 1, \ldots, n \qquad (6\text{-}85)$$

$$\mathcal{L}_\lambda = g = 0 \qquad\qquad\qquad\qquad (6\text{-}86)$$

Solving these equations for

$$x_i = x^*_i(\alpha) \qquad i = 1, \ldots, n$$

$$\lambda = \lambda^*(\alpha)$$

we define

$$y^* = f(x^*_1, \ldots, x^*_n, \alpha) = \phi(\alpha) \qquad (6\text{-}87)$$

as before. Here, y^* is the maximum value of y for any α, for x_i's which satisfy the constraint.

How does y^* change when α changes? Differentiating (6-87) with respect to α

$$\frac{\partial y^*}{\partial \alpha} = \frac{\partial \phi}{\partial \alpha} = \sum f_i \frac{\partial x^*_i}{\partial \alpha} + f_\alpha \qquad (6\text{-}88)$$

Here, however, $f_i \neq 0$. Differentiating the constraint

$$g(x_1^*(\alpha), \ldots, x_n^*(\alpha), \alpha) \equiv 0$$

with respect to α,

$$\sum g_i \frac{\partial x_i^*}{\partial \alpha} + g_\alpha \equiv 0 \tag{6-89}$$

Multiply equation (6-89) by λ, and add to equation (6-88). (This adds zero to that expression.) Then

$$\frac{\partial y^*}{\partial \alpha} = \sum f_i \frac{\partial x_i^*}{\partial \alpha} + f_\alpha + \sum \lambda g_i \frac{\partial x_i^*}{\partial \alpha} + \lambda g_\alpha$$

$$= \sum (f_i + \lambda g_i) \frac{\partial x_i^*}{\partial \alpha} + f_\alpha + \lambda g_\alpha$$

Using the first-order conditions (6-85),

$$\frac{\partial y^*}{\partial \alpha} = f_\alpha + \lambda g_\alpha = \mathscr{L}_\alpha \tag{6-90}$$

where $\mathscr{L}_\alpha$ is the partial derivative of the lagrangian function with respect to α, holding the x_i's fixed. Thus, in evaluating the response of the objective function to a change in a parameter in a *constrained* maximization model, the lagrangian function plays an analogous role to the objective function in an unconstrained model. Equation (6-90) is a statement of the envelope theorem for models with one constraint; the result generalizes in an obvious way for models with more than one constraint: For

maximize $\qquad f(x_1, \ldots, x_n, \alpha) = y$

subject to $\qquad g^j(x_1, \ldots, x_n, \alpha) = 0 \qquad j = 1, \ldots, r$

$$\frac{\partial y^*}{\partial \alpha} = \frac{\partial \mathscr{L}}{\partial \alpha} = f_\alpha + \sum_{j=1}^r \lambda^j \frac{\partial g^j}{\partial \alpha} \tag{6-91}$$

where $\mathscr{L}$ is the lagrangian $f + \sum \lambda^j g^j$. The proof of (6-91) is left as an exercise.

The second-order effects of α on y^* are left for Chap. 9. The results of this section will, however, be applied in the next two chapters.

PROBLEMS

1 Consider the constrained maximum problem

maximize $\qquad f(x_1, \ldots, x_n, \alpha_1, \ldots, \alpha_m) = y$

subject to $\qquad g(x_1, \ldots, x_n, \alpha_1, \ldots, \alpha_m) = 0$

Prove that if some parameter α_i enters the ith first-order relation and that equation only, then $\mathscr{L}_{i\alpha_i}(\partial x_i^*/\partial \alpha_i) > 0$.

2 Prove the same result if there is more than one constraint.

3 Show that diminishing marginal utility in each good neither implies nor is implied by convexity of the indifference curves.

4 Find the maximum or minimum values of the following functions $f(x_1, x_2)$ subject to the constraints $g(x_1, x_2) = 0$, by the method of direct substitution and by Lagrange multipliers. Be sure to check the second-order conditions to see if a maximum or minimum (if either) is, achieved.

  (a) $f(x_1, x_2) = x_1 x_2$; $g(x_1, x_2) = 2 - (x_1 + x_2)$.
  (b) $f(x_1, x_2) = x_1 + x_2$; $g(x_1, x_2) = 1 - x_1 x_2$.
  (c) $f(x_1, x_2) = x_1 x_2$; $g(x_1, x_2) = M - p_1 x_1 - p_2 x_2$, where p_1, p_2 and M are parameters.
  (d) $f(x_1, x_2) = p_1 x_1 + p_2 x_2$; $g(x_1, x_2) = U^0 - x_1 x_2$.

5 Show that the second-order conditions for Problems 4(a) and 4(b) are equivalent; also that the second-order conditions for Problems 4(c) and 4(d) are equivalent.

SELECTED REFERENCES

Allen, R. G. D.: "Mathematical Analysis for Economists," Macmillan & Co., Ltd., London, 1938.

Apostol, T.: "Mathematical Analysis," Addison-Wesley Publishing Company Inc., Reading, Mass., 1957.

Courant, R.: "Differential and Integral Calculus" (Trans.), Interscience Publishers, Inc., New York, 1947.

Hadley, G.: "Nonlinear and Dynamic Programming," Addison-Wesley Publishing Company, Inc., Reading, Mass., 1964.

Hancock, H.: "Theory of Maxima and Minima," Ginn and Company, Boston, Mass., 1917. Reprinted by Dover Publications, Inc., New York, 1960.

Panik, M. J.: "Classical Optimization: Foundations and Extensions," North-Holland Publishing Company, Amsterdam, 1976.

Samuelson, P. A.: "Foundations of Economic Analysis," Harvard University Press, Cambridge, Mass., 1947.

CHAPTER SEVEN

THE DERIVATION OF COST FUNCTIONS

7.1 THE COST FUNCTION

We begin this chapter with a discussion of a mathematical construct which has been an important part of the economics literature relating to firm and industry behavior, the *cost function* of a profit- (wealth-) maximizing firm. Specifically, we would like to determine the properties of a function which specifies the total cost of producing any given level of output. Since total costs will obviously be affected by the prices of the inputs that the firm hires, the cost function will be written

$$C = C^*(y, w_1, \ldots, w_n) \tag{7-1}$$

where y is the output level and $w_1, \ldots, w_n$ are the prices of the factors $x_1, \ldots, x_n$, respectively. (The factor prices are assumed here to be constant, for convenience.)

The existence of a function as specified above, however, must be predicated on assertions concerning the behavior of firms. If, for example, firms acted randomly, then there would be no unique cost associated with a given output level and factor-price vector. Even without the assumption of randomness, there are multiple ways in which a firm could combine given inputs, many of which would produce different levels of output. Each of these different input arrangements would produce a different level of cost, and hence a function such as equation (7-1) would not be well defined. Thus, in order to be able to assert the existence of a well-defined cost function, it is necessary, at the very least, to have previously asserted a *theory* of the firm. In doing so, we explicitly recognize that the cost of production depends on what the firm's owners or managers intend to do (the theoretical assertions) and what their constraints are (the test conditions, such as the production function itself, the rules of contracting, and, in some contexts, the factor prices). A wealth-maximizing firm is apt to have a different cost function than a "socialist cooperative" type of firm, which seeks to maximize, say, output per laborer in the firm. Not only are the objective functions of these two firm types different (different behavioral assertions), but if the latter firm is located, say, in Yugoslavia and the former in the United States, the property rights and contracting rules are likely to differ. Thus, even with identical production functions, the cost functions of these firms would differ. And even though production functions might be regarded as strictly technological relationships (a matter of some dispute since legal frameworks and contracting costs affect output levels), the cost function can never be so regarded. The cost function always depends on the objectives of the firm.

We shall tentatively assert that the predominant firm behavior can be characterized as *wealth-maximizing*, and we will derive the cost functions of a firm on this basis. Wealth-maximization and the implied resulting cost function are merely assertions. Their usefulness depends on the degree to which refutable propositions emerge from this theory. Even if confirmed, those refutable propositions may also be derivable from other hypotheses about firm behavior, and hence we should not expect to be able to "prove" that firms maximize wealth.

Consider, then, the assertion that firms maximize the quantity π, where

$$\pi = pf(x_1, \ldots, x_n) - \sum_{i=1}^{n} w_i x_i \tag{7-2}$$

This quantity, π, is of course not *wealth*, which is a stock concept. Rather, π is the *flow* quantity *profits*. The present, or capitalized value of π is wealth. In our present model, in which costs of adjustment do not appear, maximizing π necessarily maximizes wealth. How is the cost function (7-1), $C = C^*(y, w_1, \ldots, w_n)$ to be derived? Note that output y is entered as a *parameter* in the cost function. However, the profit-maximizing firm treats y as a decision variable, not as a parameter. That is, output is jointly determined along with inputs as a function of factor and output prices. The factor-demand curves for the profit-maximizing firm are $x_i = x_i^*(w_1, \ldots, w_n, p)$. Nowhere does y enter as an argument in these functions. Rather, $y = y^*(w_1, \ldots, w_n, p)$ defines the *supply curve* of such a firm. This latter function shows how much output will be produced for various output (and also input) prices. The cost function specified in equation (7-1) implies that we can observe changes in cost C when an experimental condition, output, is varied autonomously, *holding factor prices constant*. But a profit-maximizing firm never varies output autonomously; output y is changed only when some factor price or output price changes. Hence, the model specified as equation (7-2), maximization of profits, cannot be directly used to derive the cost function of a firm.

Cost functions must be derived from models in which output y enters as a parameter, i.e., as some test condition. That is, we have to assert that a firm is behaving in a particular way, with regard to the production of some arbitrary level of output y_0, where the subscript is added to indicate that this is a parametric value. If, however, it is asserted that the firm in question is a wealth- or profit-maximizer, then it necessarily follows that such a firm must produce any given level of output at the *minimum possible cost*. For any given output, total revenue, py, is fixed. The difference between total revenue and total cost can be a maximum only if the total cost of producing that output level is as small as possible. Hence, the only assertion concerning cost which is consistent with profit-maximizing behavior is,

minimize
$$C = \sum_{i=1}^{n} w_i x_i \qquad (7\text{-}3a)$$

subject to
$$f(x_1, \ldots, x_n) = y_0 \qquad (7\text{-}3b)$$

where, again, y_0 is a parametrically assigned output level. Assuming that $f(x_1, \ldots, x_n)$ is sufficiently well behaved mathematically so that the first- and second-order conditions for a constrained minimum are valid, this model will yield, by solution of the first-order lagrangian equations, the *observable* relations

$$x_i = x_i^*(w_1, \ldots, w_n, y_0) \qquad i = 1, \ldots, n \qquad (7\text{-}4)$$

Equations (7-4) would be the factor-demand curves of a profit-maximizing firm only if that firm were really operating under a constraint which held output constant. It must be noted that these demand curves are *not* the same relations derived in Chap. 4, for a profit-maximizing firm, that is, $x_i = x_i^*(w_1, \ldots, w_n, p)$. These factor demands are functions of output *price* in addition to factor prices; the factor-demand relations (7-4) are functions of output *level* (and factor prices). They are different functions, since they involve different independent variables. It must always be kept in mind which function—i.e., which underlying model—is being considered.

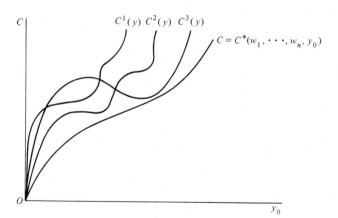

Figure 7-1 The cost function is the minimum cost associated with any output level y_0 and factor prices $w_1, \ldots, w_n$. It is the only cost that is relevant to the behavior of the wealth-maximizing firms. Other behavioral postulates might imply differing cost structures, such as the functions $C^1(y)$, $C^2(y)$ and $C^3(y)$ illustrated above.

The purpose for specifying these relations is to define the *indirect cost function* (generally referred to as simply the *cost function*)

$$C = \sum_{i=1}^{n} w_i x_i^*(w_1, \ldots, w_n, y_0) = C^*(w_1, \ldots, w_n, y_0) \tag{7-5}$$

The cost function $C^*(w_1, \ldots, w_n, y_0)$ is constructed by substituting those values of the inputs at which the cost of producing y_0 is minimized into the general expression for total cost, $\sum w_i x_i$. Hence, C^* must be the minimum cost associated with the parametric values $w_1, \ldots, w_n, y_0$ (see Fig. 7-1).

7.2 MARGINAL COST

The marginal cost of a given output level is, loosely speaking, the rate of change of total cost with respect to a change in output. That is, marginal cost is the response of the firm measured by total cost (an event) to a change in a test condition (the level of output). It is tempting to define marginal cost MC as simply

$$MC = \frac{\partial C}{\partial y} = \frac{\partial(\sum w_i x_i)}{\partial y}$$

To do so, however, would be to ignore the discussion of the previous section on the meaning of a cost function.

As written above, $cost = C = \sum w_i x_i$, is *not* a function of output y. It is a function of the inputs $x_1, \ldots, x_n$, and factor prices $w_1, \ldots, w_n$ only. It makes no sense mathematically to differentiate a function with respect to a nonexistent argument. The mathematics is telling us something: The cost function has not yet been adequately defined.

As indicated in the last section, there are many ways of combining inputs, and only one of those ways is relevant to us here. Only the *cost-minimizing* combination of inputs that produces a given level of output y_0 is relevant. Additionally, marginal cost is not just some arbitrary increase in total cost that results from an increase in output level; it is the *minimum* increase in cost associated with an increase in output level. Since the function $C^*(w_1, \ldots, w_n, y_0)$ defined in equation (7-5) gives these minimum costs at any output (and factor-price) levels, marginal cost is properly defined in terms of C^* as

$$MC = \frac{\partial C^*(w_1, \ldots, w_n, y_0)}{\partial y_0} \tag{7-6}$$

This partial derivative, being well defined, also shows what is being held constant—the *ceteris paribus* conditions—when a marginal-cost schedule is drawn. As commonly drawn (see Fig. 7-2) in two dimensions, the marginal-cost function depends on the values of the factor prices, i.e., MC can shift up or down

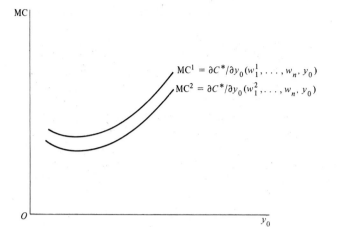

MC

$$MC^1 = \partial C^*/\partial y_0(w_1^1, \ldots, w_n, y_0)$$
$$MC^2 = \partial C^*/\partial y_0(w_1^2, \ldots, w_n, y_0)$$

O y_0

Figure 7-2 *The Marginal-Cost Function* The marginal-cost function, being the partial derivative of $C^*(w_1, \ldots, w_n, y_0)$ with respect to output y_0 is itself a function of those same arguments $w_1, \ldots, w_n, y_0$. Shown above are two marginal-cost functions, for two different values of w_1^1. It is not possible to determine from the above graph whether $w_1^1 \lessgtr w_1^2$.

when a factor price changes. A change in factor price represents a shift in the MC curve in Fig. 7-2 only because MC there has been drawn as a function of y_0 only, holding all the w_i's constant. It is also possible to draw MC as a function of, say, w_1, holding y_0, w_2, ..., w_n constant, resulting in such a curve as is drawn in Fig. 7-3. This curve has no common name, but, as we shall see later, its slope, $\partial MC/\partial w_1$, can be either positive or negative, i.e., its sign is not implied by wealth-maximization. On this graph, changes in y_0, as well as the other factor prices, would *shift* the curve. In the next few sections we will explore the implications of wealth-maximization and cost-minimization on these marginal-cost functions. In addition, we shall discuss the relationships between marginal and average cost.

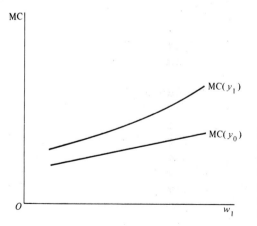

MC

$MC(y_1)$

$MC(y_0)$

O w_1

Figure 7-3 *Marginal Cost as a Function of a Factor Price for specific levels of output* This curve, which has no common name, is drawn simply to illustrate the many-dimensional aspect of marginal cost. Its slope, $\partial MC/\partial w_1$, shown as positive here, is in fact indeterminate.

7.3 AVERAGE COST

A frequently discussed function, the *average-cost function* AC is defined as

$$AC = \frac{C^*(w_1, \ldots, w_n, y_0)}{y_0} = AC^*(w_1, \ldots, w_n, y_0) \tag{7-7}$$

Again, AC must be defined in terms of the *minimum* cost achievable at any output and factor-price level, as given by $C^*(w_1, \ldots, w_n, y_0)$. As with the marginal-cost function, a behavioral postulate is a logical necessity for a proper definition of the average-cost functions. Since AC^* is a function of factor prices and output, the partial derivatives $\partial AC^*/\partial w_i$, $i = 1, \ldots, n$ and $\partial AC^*/\partial y_0$ are well defined. That is, we can meaningfully inquire as to the changes in average cost when output and factor prices vary. In the usual diagram, Fig. 7-4, average cost is plotted against output y_0. Its familiar U shape is *not* implied solely by cost minimization, as we shall see later. Changes in factor price will shift the average cost as drawn in Fig. 7-4. As will be shown later, an increase in a factor price can only increase a firm's average costs (Though this is not true for marginal costs!), as a moment's reflection clearly reveals. Otherwise, a firm could always make a larger profit by agreeing to pay more to some factors of production, say, labor. This would be readily agreed upon. Clearly, all empirical evidence refutes this particular harmony of interests. At some point, firms must begin to run short of revenues and regard increasing factor costs as profit-lowering.

7.4 A GENERAL RELATIONSHIP BETWEEN AVERAGE AND MARGINAL COSTS

By definition

$$AC^* \equiv \frac{C^*(w_1, \ldots, w_n, y_0)}{y_0} \tag{7-8}$$

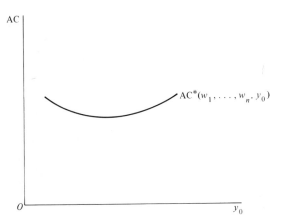

AC

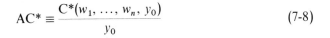

$AC^*(w_1, \ldots, w_n, y_0)$

O

y_0

Figure 7-4 *The average-cost function* The average-cost function is drawn in its usually assumed U-shape form. Since y_0 is the only parameter allowed to vary, changes in factor prices will shift this curve. In fact, $\partial AC^*/\partial w_i > 0$, for all factor prices, i.e., an increase in a factor price must increase a firm's average cost at that output level. It would be possible to plot AC^* explicitly against, say w_1 holding $w_2, \ldots, w_n$ and y_0 constant. That curve would necessarily have a positive slope.

Since this is a mathematical identity, it is valid to differentiate both sides with respect to any of the arguments. Differentiating with respect to y_0 yields (using the quotient rule on the right-hand side)

$$\frac{\partial AC^*}{\partial y_0} \equiv \frac{[y_0(\partial C^*/\partial y_0) - C^*]}{y_0^2}$$

Noting that $\partial C^*/\partial y_0 \equiv MC^*$, and rearranging terms slightly, gives

$$MC^* \equiv AC^* + \frac{\partial AC^*}{\partial y_0} y_0 \tag{7-9}$$

This is a general relation between marginal and average quantities. (It holds as well for average and marginal products, etc.) It is useful for understanding the nature of these magnitudes.

Marginal cost is *not* the cost of producing the " last " unit of output. The cost of producing the last unit of output is the same as the cost of producing the first or any other unit of output and is, in fact, the *average* cost of output. Marginal cost (in the finite sense) is the increase (or decrease) in cost resulting from the production of an extra increment of output, which is not the same thing as the " cost of the last unit." The decision to produce additional output entails the greater utilization of factor inputs. In most cases (the exception being firms whose productive process is characterized by constant returns to scale, i.e., linear homogeneity), this greater utilization will involve losses (or possibly gains) in input efficiency. When factor proportions and intensities are changed, the marginal productivities of the factors change because of the law of diminishing returns, therefore affecting the per unit cost of output. The effects of these complicated interrelationships are summarized in equation (7-9) above. Note what the equation says: Marginal cost is equal to average cost plus an adjustment factor. This latter effect is the *damage* (or gain, in the case of falling marginal costs) to all the factors of production caused by the increase in output, which causes the cost for each unit of output to increase (or decrease, for falling MC), or $\partial AC^*/\partial y_0$, multiplied by the number of units involved, y_0. That is to say, marginal cost differs from average cost by the per-unit effect on costs of higher output, multiplied by the number of units so affected (total output). The very reason why marginal quantities are usually more useful concepts than average quantities is that the average quantities ignore, whereas the marginal quantities have incorporated within them, the interrelationships of all the relevant economic variables, in this case, the factor inputs.

7.5 THE COST-MINIMIZATION PROBLEM

We now turn explicitly to the mathematical model from which all cost curves for wealth-maximizing firms are derived:

minimize
$$C = \sum_{i=1}^{n} w_i x_i \tag{7-10}$$

subject to $\qquad\qquad f(x_1, \ldots, x_n) = y_0$ $\qquad\qquad$ (7-11)

where the w_i's are unit (constant) factor prices, $f(x_1, \ldots, x_n)$ is the production function of the firm, and y_0 is a parametric value of output. This model, referred to as the cost-minimization model, asserts that firms will minimize the total cost, $\sum w_i x_i$, of producing any arbitrarily specified output level. Let us develop the empirical implications of this assertion.

To keep things manageable, we will develop the two-variable case of this model first. That is, assume that the firm employs two factors, x_1 and x_2, only. Since this is a problem of constrained minimization, form the lagrangian function

$$\mathscr{L} = w_1 x_1 + w_2 x_2 + \lambda[y_0 - f(x_1, x_2)] \qquad (7\text{-}12)$$

where λ is the Lagrange multiplier. Differentiating $\mathscr{L}$ with respect to x_1, x_2, and λ yields the first-order conditions for a minimum:

$$\mathscr{L}_1 = w_1 - \lambda f_1 = 0 \qquad (7\text{-}13a)$$

$$\mathscr{L}_2 = w_2 - \lambda f_2 = 0 \qquad (7\text{-}13b)$$

$$\mathscr{L}_\lambda = y_0 - f(x_1, x_2) = 0 \qquad (7\text{-}13c)$$

The sufficient second-order condition for an interior minimum is that the following bordered hessian determinant be *negative* (this determinant is, of course, simply the determinant of the matrix formed by the second partials of the lagrangian $\mathscr{L}$ with respect to x_1, x_2, and λ):

$$\Delta = \begin{vmatrix} -\lambda f_{11} & -\lambda f_{12} & -f_1 \\ -\lambda f_{21} & -\lambda f_{22} & -f_2 \\ -f_1 & -f_2 & 0 \end{vmatrix} < 0 \qquad (7\text{-}14)$$

The elements of this determinant are, row by row, the *first* partials of the first-order equations (7-13), which makes them the second partials of the lagrangian function $\mathscr{L}$.

These algebraic conditions for a minimum can be interpreted geometrically. In Fig. 7-5, the level curve $f(x_1, x_2) = y_0$, the constraint in the cost-minimization problem, defines a locus of input combinations which yield the output y_0. Economists call these level curves *isoquants*. (See Chap. 3 for additional review.) The slope of these isoquants at any point is, again, found by differentiating the identity $f(x_1, x_2(x_1)) \equiv y_0$ implicitly with respect to x_1. This yields

$$f_1 + f_2 \frac{dx_2}{dx_1} \equiv 0$$

or $\qquad\qquad\qquad\qquad \dfrac{dx_2}{dx_1} \equiv -\dfrac{f_1}{f_2} \qquad\qquad\qquad (7\text{-}15)$

assuming $f_2 \neq 0$, i.e., that the isoquant is not vertical at this point. The slope of the isoquant is the negative ratio of the marginal products of input 1 to input 2. Thus, $-f_1/f_2$ defines a particular *direction* in the x_1, x_2 plane.

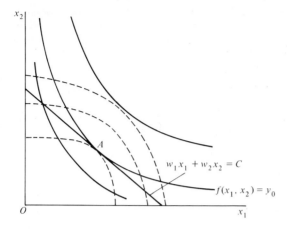

Figure 7-5 *The Tangency Solution to the Cost-minimization Problem* Assuming that marginal products are positive, i.e., that output increases as one increases either input (movement in a "north-easterly" direction), production isoquants must be convex-to-the-origin in order that a tangency point be a *minimum* cost for a specified output. If the isoquants were shaped like the dotted curves here, A would clearly represent a maximum cost, i.e., the most inefficient way to produce output y_0.

On the other hand, the objective function $C = w_1 x_1 + w_2 x_2$ also defines a direction. For any specific value of C, say C_0, the objective function is a linear curve, i.e., a straight line in the $x_1 x_2$ plane. Its slope is $dx_2/dx_1 = -w_1/w_2$.

If λ is eliminated from equations (7-13a) and (7-13b), by moving λf_1 and λf_2 to the right-hand side and dividing one equation by the other, one gets

$$\frac{w_1}{w_2} = \frac{f_1}{f_2} \tag{7-16}$$

That is, the ratio of wages equals the ratio of marginal products for the two factors. This is a straightforward application of the maximization theorems presented in Chap. 6. That this tangency is necessary for a minimum-cost solution is evident from Fig. 7-5. Lower costs are associated with *isocost* lines (i.e., curves of equal cost, $C = w_1 x_1 + w_2 x_2$) that are closer to the origin. The minimum-cost problem says: Pick the isocost line which has slope $-w_1/w_2$ closest to the origin, but which still allows output y_0 to be achieved. The furthest point toward the origin that $C = w_1 x_1 + w_2 x_2$ can be pushed and still make contact with the isoquant $f(x_1, x_2) = y_0$ is clearly the tangency point A.

What about the second-order conditions (7-14)? These conditions relate to the curvature of the isoquants. If the isoquants were shaped like the broken curves in Fig. 7-5, i.e., concave-to-the-origin, or quasi-convex, the tangency would clearly not represent a minimum-cost solution. Costs could be lowered by proceeding to where such an isoquant intersected one of the axes. This would not be a tangency solution but, rather, a "corner solution."

There is a major empirical reason for believing that production isoquants are not shaped like the broken curves in Fig. 7-5, but rather are convex to the origin as originally drawn, and as implied by the second-order conditions (7-14). The empirical reason for believing in such convexity of the isoquants is that if they were otherwise, we would observe firms employing only one factor of production. With isoquants concave to the origin in all dimensions, the minimum-cost

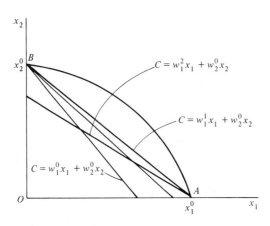

Figure 7-6 *The Empirical Implications of Quasi-convex Production Functions* With the isoquants concave-to-the-origin and wages given by w_1^0 and w_2^0, the minimum-cost solution is at point B, where only x_2 is hired. The demand for x_1 is 0. As w_1 is lowered, the cost line pivots around B, the intersection with x_1 axis moving outward toward A. When A is reached, a multiple solution exists; the firm is indifferent between hiring x_1^0 of x_1, or x_2^0 of x_2. When w_1 is now made arbitrarily smaller, the demand for x_2 falls to 0, and the demand for x_1 jumps discontinuously to x_1^0. The demand for x_1 remains constant at x_1^0 for all further lowering of its wage, w_1. The demand curve for x_1 is thus vertical at that level.

solution would be at the intersection of the isoquant with one axis. (In an unlikely case, two or more such intersections could occur at the same cost, providing multiple solutions.) Since wealth-maximizing firms are cost-minimizers, only one factor, that which gave the minimum-cost solution, would be hired. Additionally, consider how the solution would change if a factor price changed. In Fig. 7-6, as the factor price w_1 is lowered from its original value of w_1^0, the minimum-cost solution remains at corner B, with the firm showing no response to the increased factor price. It hires x_2^0 amount of x_2. Then, at some critical value of w_1, say w_1^1, the isocost line would cut through both corners; i.e., both intersections of the isoquant with the axes. The firm would then be indifferent to hiring x_2^0 of x_2 or x_1^0 of x_1; i.e., the firm's costs are identical with corner A and corner B. As soon as w_1 is lowered below w_1^1, even just a trifle, the firm would suddenly switch over completely to x_1 at the level x_1^0 given by the intersection at A. The firm would show no response to further lowering of w_1. This scenario implies that the demand curves for the two factors will be in vertical sections as depicted in Fig. 7-7. There will be no response to some factor-price changes, and violent responses (when the firm switches corners) to others. Now we simply do not see this combined intransigence and discontinuous hiring of factors in the real world. Rather, firms respond gradually to factor-price changes, with larger responses accompanying larger price changes. This observed behavior is inconsistent with isoquants which are concave to the origin and hence we can assert with confidence the quasi-concavity of production functions. Indeed, as mentally changing the slope of the isocost line in Fig. 7-5 will indicate, factor-price changes will imply continuous, or smooth responses in factor hiring for the case of convex-to-the-origin isoquants.

One might believe on *intuitive* or *introspective* grounds that isoquants are convex to the origin. It may be plausible to the reader that along any isoquant, the slope $-f_1/f_2$ decreases in absolute value as more x_1 is hired. That is, the marginal product of x_1 relative to that of x_2 falls as more x_1 is hired. This is often called the

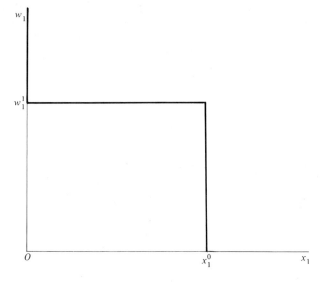

Figure 7-7 *The Demand for* x_1, *if isoquants were concave to the origin* The reason for rejecting concave-to-the-origin isoquants is that they imply empirical behavior inconsistent with the facts. In particular, such firms would show no response to factor-price changes except at critical wage levels (here, w_1^1). The demand curve would consist of two vertical sections. This behavior is not observed by real-world firms.

"law of diminishing marginal technical rate of substitution." It is not the same as the law of diminishing returns, discussed earlier in Chap. 3, which asserts $f_{ii} < 0$. *Neither one of these two "laws" implies the other.*

If all this is plausible to you, all well and good. But intuition is *not* a good enough reason for believing in the convexity of isoquants. None of us has ever seen an isoquant, and we are not ever likely to do so. The only reason for believing, with some confidence, in such convexity is that the reverse situation implies firm behavior which is inconsistent with the facts of the empirical world, i.e., the situation of intransigence and discontinuous response to factor-price changes.

Having established that an interior tangency point is the only sensible solution to the cost-minimization problem; i.e., not in contradiction with the facts, and obvious as it may be from the geometry of Fig. 7-2 that the tangency point A is the minimum-cost solution, it is still interesting and useful to go on to ask: what is it about the decision-making process of the firm that leads to this type of solution? That is, what does such a solution (a tangency) imply about the nature of minimum-cost decision making? To answer this question, it is necessary to examine again the meanings of the slopes of level curves, in this case $-f_1/f_2$ and $-w_1/w_2$. (The reader should review, if necessary, the sections of Chap. 3 dealing with level curves and surfaces.)

In Fig. 7-8, consider point A' on the isoquant $f(x_1, x_2) = y_0$. The cost lines $C = w_1 x_1 + w_2 x_2$ have a slope $-w_1/w_2$ which is less in absolute value than the

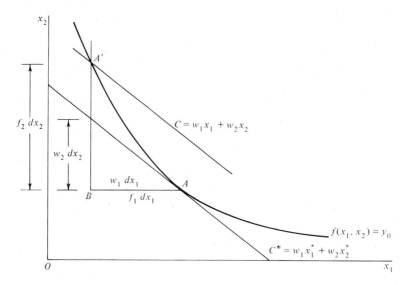

Figure 7-8 *Tangency and Non-tangency Points* It is obvious from the geometry that A' cannot be a minimum-cost solution. In terms of the economics of cost-minimizing firms, however, point A' indicates that the firm's *willingness* to trade away some x_2 to get some x_1, as measured by the slope of the isoquant at A', is unequal to the firm's *opportunities* for doing so, as measured by the isocost line $C = w_1 x_1 + w_2 x_2$. At point A', the value, internally, to the firm of additional units of x_1 is measured by f_1/f_2, the slope of the isoquant at A'. This internal value is greater than the market cost of exchanging some x_2 to get more x_1, or w_1/w_2. It therefore is cost-saving to move from A' to A. Similar reasoning would apply if A' were to the right of A; then, x_2 would be the desirable factor at market prices.

slope of $f(x_1, x_2) = y_0$ at A', $(-f_1/f_2)$. Suppose the firm decided to produce the same output y_0 at point A, hiring more x_1 by an amount dx_1, and less x_2 by an amount dx_2. We can view the move from A' to A conceptually as one from A' to B, and then B to A. The decrease in output caused by hiring less x_2 is the marginal product of x_2, MP_2, which is approximately f_2 evaluated at A, multiplied by the decrease in x_2, or $f_2 \, dx_2$. In Fig. 7-8, this is the decline in output due to a movement from A' to B. In moving from B to A, x_1 is increased by an amount dx_1, and that extra x_1 has a marginal product approximately equal to f_1 evaluated at A, and hence the gain in output going from B to A is $f_1 \, dx_1$. Since the output at A is the same as the output at A', both being y_0, it must be the case that $f_1 \, dx_1 + f_2 \, dx_2 = 0$. If the point A' is moved arbitrarily close to A, so that the approximation becomes better and better, this simply becomes the statement that along any level curve, the total differential $dy = f_1 \, dx_1 + f_2 \, dx_2$ equals 0. Assuming x_2 can be written as a function of x_1, the slope of the isoquant again is $dx_2/dx_1 = -f_1/f_2$. But we can now understand what this relationship means to a firm. The slope of an isoquant represents how much x_2 can be given up, per unit x_1 added, in order to keep output constant. This output-preserving ratio of inputs must equal the ratio of the gain in output $(\text{MP}_1 = f_1)$ to the loss in output $(\text{MP}_2 = f_2)$

that occurs per unit changes in the inputs. *This slope, f_1/f_2, therefore measures the value of x_1 to the firm, internally, in terms of x_2.*

Suppose, for example, that the marginal product of x_1 is 10, while the marginal product of x_2 is 5. Then $f_1/f_2 = 2$. Then clearly for "small" changes at least, it will be possible to decrease x_2 by 2 units for every unit of increased x_1. The ratio f_1/f_2, equal to 2 here, measures the rate at which one factor x_2 can be displaced by additions of the other factor x_1 keeping output constant. It is the marginal technical rate of substitution.

Now consider point A' again in Fig. 7-8. Suppose that $w_1/w_2 = 1$; that is, the slope of the isocost line equals -1. This means that the factor market allows input x_1 to be substituted for input x_2 at equal cost. That is, for every added unit of x_1, exactly one unit of x_2 has to be given up in order to maintain the same expenditure level. But we have seen, in our numerical example, that the firm can give up *two* units of x_2, add one unit of x_1, and have the same output. Therefore, a savings of the cost of one unit of x_2 is obtained by moving toward A. Hence, A' cannot be a minimum-cost solution.

In general, the slope of the isoquant measures the firm's *willingness* to trade one input for the other (substitute x_1 for x_2). The slope of the isocost lines represents the *opportunities* afforded by the factor market for doing so. When the firm is willing to trade one factor for another at terms of trade different from the factor market, cost saving is possible. This is the meaning of a tangency solution. It doesn't matter if the original point is to the left or right of A on the isoquant $f(x_1, x_2) = y_0$. In a more general sense, the gains from exchange (exchange with a general market at fixed prices as well as exchange with other individuals) are not exhausted unless one's *willingness* to trade, e.g., as measured by a firm's output-preserving marginal rate of factor substitution, equals the available *opportunities* for such trading, e.g., as measured by the cost of exchanging one factor for another. For firms, such efficient factor combinations are summarized by the condition that $f_1/f_2 = w_1/w_2$.

7.6 THE FACTOR-DEMAND CURVES

Let us now return to the first-order equations (7-13), which are, again

$$w_1 - \lambda f_1 = 0 \qquad (7\text{-}13a)$$

$$w_2 - \lambda f_2 = 0 \qquad (7\text{-}13b)$$

$$y_0 - f(x_1, x_2) = 0 \qquad (7\text{-}13c)$$

The sufficient second-order condition is that the determinant of the matrix of second partials of $\mathscr{L}$ with respect to x_1, x_2, and λ, which is in fact the matrix formed by the first partials of (13a), (13b), and (13c) with respect to those variables (these equations already being the first partials of $\mathscr{L}$), be negative.

This determinant, again, is

$$\Delta = \begin{vmatrix} -\lambda f_{11} & -\lambda f_{12} & -f_1 \\ -\lambda f_{21} & -\lambda f_{22} & -f_2 \\ -f_1 & -f_2 & 0 \end{vmatrix} < 0 \qquad (7\text{-}14)$$

The implicit function theorem, discussed in Chap. 6, says that if the determinant of the first partials of a system of equations is nonzero, those equations can be solved, locally (in principle—not, perhaps, easily) for those variables being differentiated as explicit functions of the remaining variables (here the parameters) of the system. The determinant Δ is such a determinant and is nonzero, in fact negative, by the sufficient second-order conditions. Hence, equations (7-13) can be solved for x_1, x_2, and λ in terms of the parameters w_1, w_2, and y_0, yielding

$$x_1 = x_1^*(w_1, w_2, y_0) \qquad (7\text{-}17a)$$

$$x_2 = x_2^*(w_1, w_2, y_0) \qquad (7\text{-}17b)$$

$$\lambda = \lambda^*(w_1, w_2, y_0) \qquad (7\text{-}17c)$$

Equations (7-17a) and (7-17b) represent the factor-demand curves *when output is held constant*, previously discussed as equations (7-4). Note the parameter y_0 in these equations. If, say, x_1 is plotted on a two-dimensional graph with its wage represented on the other axis, the resulting plot will be a curve [actually, a one-dimensional projection of equation (7-17a)] along which w_2 and y_0 are constant. These curves, therefore, do not represent the factor-demand curves of a firm engaged in unrestricted profit-maximization, in which case output would be variable, and output *price* (for the competitive case) would be parametric.

Interpretation of the Lagrange Multiplier

Equation (7-17c) gives λ as a function of w_1, w_2 and y_0. But what is λ? This new variable was concocted as an artifice—as a convenient way of stating a constrained minimization problem. Does λ have any meaningful economic interpretation? Indeed, we can show that λ, or more correctly $\lambda^*(w_1, w_2, y_0)$ is identically the marginal-cost function of the firm!

The first clue to this interpretation of λ can be gleaned from the first-order equations (7-13). Solving for λ yields

$$\lambda = \frac{w_1}{f_1} = \frac{w_2}{f_2} \qquad (7\text{-}18)$$

Also, by multiplying (7-13a) by x_1, (7-13b) by x_2, and adding, one obtains

$$\lambda f_1 x_1 + \lambda f_2 x_2 = w_1 x_1 + w_2 x_2$$

Factoring out λ, and noting that $w_1 x_1 + w_2 x_2 = C$,

$$\lambda = \frac{C}{f_1 x_1 + f_2 x_2}$$

Note the "units" of w_1/f_1 and w_2/f_2. Say that, for example, x_1 is "labor," x_2 is "capital." The wage rate w_1 is measured in dollars per laborer; the marginal product of labor has units output per laborer. Hence, the expression w_1/f_1 has the units dollars per output, since the labor units cancel. The measure dollars per output in fact comprises the units of marginal cost, though it also comprises the units of average cost.

What, then, is the meaning of the following extended equality?

$$\lambda = \frac{w_1}{f_1} = \frac{w_2}{f_2} = \frac{C}{f_1 x_1 + f_2 x_2} \qquad (7\text{-}19)$$

The firm is at its cost-minimizing input mix. Suppose it were to increase its input of x_1, say, labor, by a small amount Δx_1. The total cost would rise by an amount $(w_1)(\Delta x_1)$. Output would also rise, by an amount $(MP_1)(\Delta x_1) = (f_1)(\Delta x_1)$. Hence, $\lambda = w_1/f_1 = (w_1)(\Delta x_1)/(f_1)(\Delta x_1)$ represents the incremental cost of increasing output through the use of one input, here x_1, or labor. Similarly, $\lambda = w_2/f_2 = (w_2)(\Delta x_2)/(f_2)(\Delta x_2)$ represents the incremental cost of additional output when the other input, x_2, say capital, is increased. The equality of these two incremental costs, as indicated by equation (7-18) means that a necessary condition for cost-minimization is that the incremental cost of additional output must be the same *at all margins*, i.e., for each independent decision variable. This common incremental cost of output is the *marginal cost of output*. Equation (7-18) says that the firm is indifferent, at the margin, to hiring additional labor or capital—the net costs of doing so are identical for each input.

This is, of course, what must be true at a minimum-cost point. For suppose that the firm could achieve a lower incremental cost of output by hiring labor, say, than capital. In that case, total costs could clearly be lowered by shifting resources away from capital and toward labor. Only when costs are equalized at all the margins can a minimum-cost solution be achieved. And this common marginal cost is equal to λ.

What about the last equality in equation (7-19), $\lambda = C/(f_1 x_1 + f_2 x_2)$? This is a rather more difficult expression to interpret. Consider that $\lambda = w_1/f_1 = w_1 x_1/f_1 x_1$. Whereas w_1/f_1 refers explicitly to *per-unit* changes in input 1, $w_1 x_1/f_1 x_1$ applies that marginal-factor cost $(w_1 x_1)$ and benefits $(f_1 x_1)$ to the total input level. Likewise, $\lambda = w_2 x_2/f_2 x_2$, the cost of all units of factor 2 per marginal contribution of that factor multiplied by the total factor usage, is also marginal cost, since the incremental costs must be the same at every margin. Then, by elementary algebra,†

$$\lambda = \frac{w_1 x_1}{f_1 x_1} = \frac{w_2 x_2}{f_2 x_2} = \frac{w_1 x_1 + w_2 x_2}{f_1 x_1 + f_2 x_2}$$

---

† It is valid to add the numerators and denominators, respectively, of fractions which are equal. Thus, if $a/b = c/d$ (implying $ad = bc$), then $a/b = c/d = (a + c)/(b + d)$, as can be quickly verified.

This expression says that not only is marginal cost the same at every margin, it is also the same if a combination of *both* (*every*, in the multifactor case) factors is changed. Marginal cost is the same at "either or both" margins.

The foregoing was intended as an intuitive explanation of why the function $\lambda = \lambda^*(w_1, w_2, y_0)$ might reasonably be regarded as the marginal-cost function. While intuitively plausible (and ultimately sound), the approach is deficient in terms of our original definition of marginal cost. Specifically

$$MC = \frac{\partial C^*}{\partial y_0}$$

where $C^*(w_1, w_2, y_0)$ is the (indirect) cost function. It remains to be proved explicitly that $\lambda^* \equiv \partial C^*/\partial y_0$. We shall now do so.

By definition

$$C^* = w_1 x_1^*(w_1, w_2, y_0) + w_2 x_2^*(w_1, w_2, y_0) \tag{7-20}$$

That is, the minimum cost for any output level y_0 (and factor prices w_1, w_2) is obtained by substituting into the expression for total cost, $C = w_1 x_1 + w_2 x_2$, the values of the inputs that are derived from the cost-minimization problem. These are the relations $x_i = x_i^*(w_1, w_2, y_0)$, $i = 1, 2$ (equations 7-17a,b). Thus, differentiating C^* partially with respect to y_0,

$$\frac{\partial C^*}{\partial y_0} = w_1 \frac{\partial x_1^*}{\partial y_0} + w_2 \frac{\partial x_2^*}{\partial y_0} \tag{7-21}$$

However, from the first-order relations, $w_1 = \lambda^* f_1$, $w_2 = \lambda^* f_2$. Substituting these values into equation (7-21), and factoring out λ^*,

$$\frac{\partial C^*}{\partial y_0} = \lambda^*\left(f_1 \frac{\partial x_1^*}{\partial y_0} + f_2 \frac{\partial x_2^*}{\partial y_0}\right) \tag{7-22}$$

If in fact $\lambda^* = \partial C^*/\partial y_0$, the term in parentheses in equation (7-22) must equal 1. How can this be shown? Consider the last equation of the first-order conditions (actually the constraint):

$$y_0 - f(x_1, x_2) = 0$$

When the solutions to the first-order relations, the factor-demand curves holding output constant, equations (7-17a,b) are substituted back into those first-order conditions, the equations (7-13) become identities. In particular,

$$y_0 - f(x_1^*(w_1, w_2, y_0), x_2^*(w_1, w_2, y_0)) \equiv 0$$

That is, x_1^* and x_2^* *always* lie on the isoquant of output level y_0 for any w_1, w_2 and any y_0, precisely because x_1^* and x_2^* are the solutions of equations which say, among other things: output is held to y_0.

Hence, we can differentiate this identity with respect to y_0:

$$1 - f_1 \frac{\partial x_1^*}{\partial y_0} - f_2 \frac{\partial x_2^*}{\partial y_0} \equiv 0$$

or
$$f_1 \frac{\partial x_1^*}{\partial y_0} + f_2 \frac{\partial x_2^*}{\partial y_0} \equiv 1$$

This is precisely what was needed. The term in the parentheses in equation (7-22) equals 1, and therefore,

$$\lambda^* \equiv \frac{\partial C^*}{\partial y_0} \qquad (7\text{-}23)$$

That $\lambda^* \equiv \partial C^*/\partial y_0$ is in fact a simple consequence of the envelope theorem derived in the last chapter. Recall the general-maximum problem with, for simplicity here, one constraint:

maximize $\qquad f(x_1, \ldots, x_n, \alpha_1, \ldots, \alpha_m) = y$

subject to $\qquad g(x_1, \ldots, x_n, \alpha_1, \ldots, \alpha_m) = 0$

The lagrangian for this problem is

$$\mathscr{L} = f(\mathbf{x}, \boldsymbol{\alpha}) + \lambda g(\mathbf{x}, \boldsymbol{\alpha})$$

The envelope theorem says that

$$\frac{\partial y^*}{\partial \alpha_i} = \frac{\partial \mathscr{L}}{\partial \alpha_i} = f_{\alpha_i} + \lambda^* g_{\alpha_i}$$

That is, the rate of change of the indirect objective function in which all the x_i's can adjust to changes in a parameter is in fact equal to the rate of change of the lagrangian function (which numerically equals the objective function since the constraint equals 0) with respect to that parameter, *holding all the x_i's fixed.*

Applying this theorem to the problem at hand,

minimize $\qquad\qquad C = w_1 x_1 + w_2 x_2$

subject to $\qquad y_0 - f(x_1, x_2) = 0$

we have $\qquad \mathscr{L} = w_1 x_1 + w_2 x_2 + \lambda(y_0 - f(x_1, x_2))$

Here, the parameter y_0 enters only the constraint, hence

$$\frac{\partial C^*}{\partial y_0} = \frac{\partial \mathscr{L}}{\partial y_0} = \lambda = \lambda^*$$

The Lagrange multiplier was introduced as an artifice for writing, in a convenient manner, the first- and second-order conditions for a constrained-maximum problem. We see here, however, that the Lagrange multiplier can have interesting economic interpretations. This fact greatly enhances the value of lagrangian methods. As we shall see, these multipliers, more often than not, provide useful formulas and insights for analyzing economic problems.

7.7 COMPARATIVE STATICS RELATIONS

It is now time to inquire as to the response of cost-minimizing firms to changes in the parameters they face. Specifically, how does such a firm react to an increase or decrease in a factor price? Will more or less input be used when its own or some other input's price increases? How will marginal and average cost be affected? Will the firm increase or decrease its output if competitive pressures force it to remain at the minimum point on its average-cost curve?

The format for investigating these questions is, again,

minimize
$$C = w_1 x_1 + w_2 x_2$$

subject to
$$f(x_1, x_2) = y_0$$

where w_1 and w_2 are the factor prices and y_0 is a parametrically determined level of output. The lagrangian is

$$\mathscr{L} = w_1 x_1 + w_2 x_2 + \lambda(y_0 - f(x_1, x_2))$$

Differentiating with respect to x_1, x_2, and λ yields the first-order conditions for constrained minimization:

$$w_1 - \lambda f_1 = 0 \tag{7-13a}$$

$$w_2 - \lambda f_2 = 0 \tag{7-13b}$$

$$y_0 - f(x_1, x_2) = 0 \tag{7-13c}$$

The sufficient second-order conditions are, again

$$\Delta = \begin{vmatrix} -\lambda f_{11} & -\lambda f_{12} & -f_1 \\ -\lambda f_{21} & -\lambda f_{22} & -f_2 \\ -f_1 & -f_2 & 0 \end{vmatrix} < 0 \tag{7-14}$$

These relations were given verbal interpretation in the previous sections.

If the production function $y = f(x_1, x_2)$ were actually known, then equations (7-13) could be used directly to characterize the least-cost solution. Everything about the firm would be completely known, including the *total* amounts of each factor that would be used at any input level, and all the changes that might come about because of a change in a parameter. However, economists are not generally blessed with this kind of information. Rather, we *assert* that some sort of production relationship $y = f(x_1, x_2)$ exists, with quasi-concave properties [summarized as the inequality $\Delta < 0$, equation (7-14)]. We then inquire as to *changes* in response to parameter changes, i.e., we limit the analysis to *marginal* quantities. This is accomplished by using the methodology of comparative statics outlined earlier.

Equations (7-13) represent three equations in six variables x_1, x_2, λ, w_1, w_2, and y_0. As long as certain mathematical conditions exist, namely that $\Delta \neq 0$, these equations can be solved, in principle yielding the relations already discussed:

$$x_1 = x_1^*(w_1, w_2, y_0) \tag{7-17a}$$

$$x_2 = x_2^*(w_1, w_2, y_0) \tag{7-17b}$$

$$\lambda = \lambda^*(w_1, w_2, y_0) \tag{7-17c}$$

The new variable λ is identified as marginal cost.

The comparative statics of this model can be summarized as the determination of the signs of the nine partial derivatives:

$$\frac{\partial x_i^*}{\partial w_j} \qquad i, j = 1, 2$$

$$\frac{\partial x_i^*}{\partial y_0} \qquad i = 1, 2$$

$$\frac{\partial \lambda^*}{\partial w_i} \qquad i = 1, 2$$

$$\frac{\partial \lambda^*}{\partial y_0} \tag{7-24}$$

We seek to determine, first, the extent to which the constrained-minimum hypothesis generates (qualitative) information about these marginal quantities. It will also be shown that some relationships exist among these partials, and that expressions can be derived which may be useful if empirical information is used in addition to the minimization hypothesis.

The first step in comparative statics analysis, of course, is to substitute the solutions (7-17) into the first-order equations (7-13), from which they were solved. This yields the *identities*

$$w_1 - \lambda^*(w_1, w_2, y_0) f_1(x_1^*(w_1, w_2, y_0), x_2^*(w_1, w_2, y_0)) \equiv 0 \tag{7-25a}$$

$$w_2 - \lambda^*(w_1, w_2, y_0) f_2(x_1^*(w_1, w_2, y_0), x_2^*(w_1, w_2, y_0)) \equiv 0 \tag{7-25b}$$

$$y_0 - f(x_1^*(w_1, w_2, y_0), x_2^*(w_1, w_2, y_0)) \equiv 0 \tag{7-25c}$$

These are identities because the solutions to equations (7-13) are substituted into the equations from which they were solved. The economic significance of this step is that now it is being asserted that whatever the factor prices and output level may be, the firm will always instantaneously adjust the factor inputs (its decision variables) to those levels which will minimize the total cost of that output level. The *identities* (7-25) tell us that we have asserted that we will never observe the firm to be in any other than a cost-minimizing configuration. Having built in this strong assertion, it is then possible to alter the parameters and observe the resulting changes in the x_i's. These changes are observed mathematically by differentiating the identities (7-25) with respect to a parameter and solving for the relevant partial derivatives contained in the list (7-24).

Let us begin the formal analysis by observing the cost-minimizing reaction to a change in w_1, the price of factor 1. Differentiating the identities (7-25) with respect to w_1 yields, using the product rule for $\lambda^* f_1$ and $\lambda^* f_2$, along with the chain rule,

$$1 - \lambda^* f_{11} \frac{\partial x_1^*}{\partial w_1} - \lambda^* f_{12} \frac{\partial x_2^*}{\partial w_1} - f_1 \frac{\partial \lambda^*}{\partial w_1} \equiv 0 \qquad (7\text{-}26a)$$

$$- \lambda^* f_{21} \frac{\partial x_1^*}{\partial w_1} - \lambda^* f_{22} \frac{\partial x_2^*}{\partial w_1} - f_2 \frac{\partial \lambda^*}{\partial w_1} \equiv 0 \qquad (7\text{-}26b)$$

$$- f_1 \frac{\partial x_1^*}{\partial w_1} \quad - f_2 \frac{\partial x_2^*}{\partial w_1} \qquad\qquad \equiv 0 \qquad (7\text{-}26c)$$

These relations can be more clearly summarized using matrix notation. Since (7-26) represents three *linear* equations (actually, identities) in the three unknowns $\partial x_1^*/\partial w_1$, $\partial x_2^*/\partial w_1$, and $\partial \lambda^*/\partial w_1$, (7-26) becomes

$$\begin{pmatrix} -\lambda^* f_{11} & -\lambda^* f_{12} & -f_1 \\ -\lambda^* f_{21} & -\lambda^* f_{22} & -f_2 \\ -f_1 & -f_2 & 0 \end{pmatrix} \begin{pmatrix} \dfrac{\partial x_1^*}{\partial w_1} \\[2mm] \dfrac{\partial x_2^*}{\partial w_1} \\[2mm] \dfrac{\partial \lambda^*}{\partial w_1} \end{pmatrix} = \begin{pmatrix} -1 \\ 0 \\ 0 \end{pmatrix} \qquad (7\text{-}27)$$

One need only solve (7-27) for the marginal quantities. Using Cramer's rule,

$$\frac{\partial x_1^*}{\partial w_1} = \frac{\begin{vmatrix} -1 & -\lambda^* f_{12} & -f_1 \\ 0 & -\lambda^* f_{22} & -f_2 \\ 0 & -f_2 & 0 \end{vmatrix}}{\Delta} = -\frac{\Delta_{11}}{\Delta} \qquad (7\text{-}28a)$$

In like fashion, replacing the second and third column of Δ with the right-hand column vector $(-1, 0, 0)$ for the numerator of Cramer's rule, one gets

$$\frac{\partial x_2^*}{\partial w_1} = \frac{-\Delta_{12}}{\Delta} \qquad (7\text{-}28b)$$

$$\frac{\partial \lambda^*}{\partial w_1} = \frac{-\Delta_{13}}{\Delta} \qquad (7\text{-}28c)$$

where Δ_{ij} is the (signed) cofactor of the element in the ith row and jth column of the determinant Δ.

These solutions are only valid if $\Delta \neq 0$. Otherwise, the above partials are undefined. The mathematics indicates that in order for these partials to exist, the solutions (7-17) must first be well defined. The implicit function theorem of Chap. 6 indicates that these solutions are valid if the determinant of first partials of (7-13) is nonzero. This determinant is exactly Δ, and the *sufficient* second-order condition for constrained minimization says that in fact $\Delta < 0$. Hence, under these assumptions, the solutions (7-28) are valid expressions.

What can be said of the sign of these partials? As just noted, the denominators of these expressions, Δ, are all negative. The cofactor Δ_{11} is a border-preserving principle minor and is negative under the minimization hypothesis. Indeed, by inspection,

$$\Delta_{11} = \begin{vmatrix} -\lambda^* f_{22} & -f_2 \\ -f_2 & 0 \end{vmatrix} = -f_2^2 < 0$$

Hence, the qualitative result $\partial x_1^* / \partial w_1 < 0$, is demonstrable.

The cofactor Δ_{12} is *not* a border-preserving principle minor; in general, its sign will not be known, and, hence, the sign of $\partial x_2^* / \partial w_1$ will not be determinate. However, in the *two-variable case only*, *assuming positive marginal products*,

$$\Delta_{12} = (-1)^{1+2} \begin{vmatrix} -\lambda^* f_{21} & -f_2 \\ -f_1 & 0 \end{vmatrix} = +f_1 f_2 > 0$$

Hence, *for the two-variable case only,*

$$\frac{\partial x_2^*}{\partial w_1} > 0$$

The fact that it must happen that $\partial x_2^* / \partial w_1 > 0$ for the two-factor case is easily explainable. Suppose w_1 falls. The firm will then hire more x_1. If the firm also hired more x_2, then output would have to rise, given the assumption of positive marginal products. And marginal products will be positive as long as factor prices w_1 and w_2 are positive. If x_1 increases, then if output is to be held constant, x_2 must decrease. This relationship, however, need not hold for more than two factors. Some other factor (or both) must decline, but not necessarily one or the other.

Finally,

$$\Delta_{13} = \begin{vmatrix} -\lambda^* f_{21} & -\lambda^* f_{22} \\ -f_1 & -f_2 \end{vmatrix} = \lambda^* (f_{21} f_2 - f_{22} f_1) \gtrless 0$$

Hence, $\partial \lambda^* / \partial w_1 \gtrless 0$.

Similar relationships can be derived for the responses to a change in w_2. In that case, the minus one appears in the *second* row of the right-hand side of the matrix equation, since w_2 appears only in the second first-order relation:

$$\begin{pmatrix} -\lambda^* f_{11} & -\lambda^* f_{12} & -f_1 \\ -\lambda^* f_{21} & -\lambda^* f_{22} & -f_2 \\ -f_1 & -f_2 & 0 \end{pmatrix} \begin{pmatrix} \dfrac{\partial x_1^*}{\partial w_2} \\ \dfrac{\partial x_2^*}{\partial w_2} \\ \dfrac{\partial \lambda^*}{\partial w_2} \end{pmatrix} = \begin{pmatrix} 0 \\ -1 \\ 0 \end{pmatrix} \tag{7-29}$$

Again solving by Cramer's rule,

$$\frac{\partial x_1^*}{\partial w_2} = \frac{-\Delta_{21}}{\Delta} \tag{7-30a}$$

$$\frac{\partial x_2^*}{\partial w_2} = \frac{-\Delta_{22}}{\Delta} \tag{7-30b}$$

$$\frac{\partial \lambda^*}{\partial w_2} = \frac{-\Delta_{23}}{\Delta} \tag{7-30c}$$

The cofactor Δ_{22} is a border-preserving principle minor; it must be negative by the sufficient second-order conditions. In fact, by inspection, $\Delta_{22} = -f_1^2 < 0$. Hence, the refutable hypothesis, $\partial x_2^*/\partial w_2 < 0$, can be asserted for these relations. The cofactor Δ_{12} on inspection also has a determinate sign. In fact, by the symmetry of the determinant Δ, $\Delta_{12} = \Delta_{21} = f_1 f_2 > 0$. Again, that $\partial x_1^*/\partial w_2 > 0$ for this model is *not* generalizable to the n-factor case. With more than two factors present, the numerator for $\partial x_2^*/\partial w_1$, or $\partial x_1^*/\partial w_2$ will be an $n \times n$ off-diagonal cofactor. Its sign will be indeterminate.

What is curious, however, is that like the profit-maximization model, the reciprocity relation

$$\frac{\partial x_1^*}{\partial w_2} = \frac{\partial x_2^*}{\partial w_1} \tag{7-31}$$

is valid, since on comparing equations (7-28b) and (7-30a) we note that $\Delta_{12} = \Delta_{21}$. This is a different result than that obtained for unconstrained profit-maximization. In that earlier model, the x_i's were functions of factor prices and output *price;* that is, $x_i = x_i^*(w_1, w_2, p)$. Here, the factors are functions of the output level, y_0: $x_i = x_i^*(w_1, w_2, y_0)$. These are two different functions. (We have used the same notation "x_i^*" for both in spite of this to avoid notational clutter.) The results are therefore different.

Finally, we have $\partial \lambda^*/\partial w_2 \gtrless 0$, as we had before, since $\Delta_{23} \gtrless 0$, being an off-diagonal (and non-border-preserving) cofactor. We shall defer explanation of this sign indeterminacy until after the following discussion with respect to parametric output level changes.

How does the firm react to an autonomous shift in output? Differentiating the identities (7-25) with respect to y_0, noting that y_0 appears only in the third identity (7-25c),

$$
\begin{pmatrix}
-\lambda^* f_{11} & -\lambda^* f_{12} & -f_1 \\
-\lambda^* f_{21} & -\lambda^* f_{22} & -f_2 \\
-f_1 & -f_2 & 0
\end{pmatrix}
\begin{pmatrix}
\dfrac{\partial x_1^*}{\partial y_0} \\[2mm]
\dfrac{\partial x_2^*}{\partial y_0} \\[2mm]
\dfrac{\partial \lambda^*}{\partial y_0}
\end{pmatrix}
=
\begin{pmatrix}
0 \\
0 \\
-1
\end{pmatrix}
\tag{7-32}
$$

Solving via Cramer's rule yields

$$\frac{\partial x_1^*}{\partial y_0} = \frac{\begin{vmatrix} 0 & -\lambda^* f_{12} & -f_1 \\ 0 & -\lambda^* f_{22} & -f_2 \\ -1 & -f_2 & 0 \end{vmatrix}}{\Delta} = \frac{-\Delta_{31}}{\Delta} \lessgtr 0 \tag{7-33a}$$

Similarly

$$\frac{\partial x_2^*}{\partial y_0} = \frac{-\Delta_{32}}{\Delta} \lessgtr 0 \tag{7-33b}$$

$$\frac{\partial \lambda^*}{\partial y_0} = \frac{-\Delta_{33}}{\Delta} \lessgtr 0 \tag{7-33c}$$

Consider this last relationship, $\partial \lambda^*/\partial y_0$, that is, $\partial MC/\partial y_0$. This expression gives the slope of the marginal-cost function. The numerator, Δ_{33}, is the determinant

$$\Delta_{33} = \begin{vmatrix} -\lambda^* f_{11} & -\lambda^* f_{12} \\ -\lambda^* f_{12} & -\lambda^* f_{22} \end{vmatrix}$$

(noting that $f_{12} = f_{21}$). Hence, $\Delta_{33} = \lambda^{*2}(f_{11} f_{22} - f_{12}^2)$. This looks like an expression we have encountered previously: to be exact, in the profit-maximization model. There, the term $(f_{11} f_{22} - f_{12}^2)$ appeared in the denominator of the comparative statics relations. The sign of this expression was asserted to be positive by the sufficient second-order relations for profit-maximization. Why, then, can we not assert from equation (7-33c) that $\partial MC/\partial y_0 > 0$, i.e., the marginal-cost curve is upward-sloping, since it appears that $\Delta_{33} > 0$?

In fact, in the case where these cost curves refer to a firm which is also achieving maximum profits (i.e., the firm is reaching an interior solution to the profit-maximization problem), the marginal-cost function is indeed upward-sloping. However, profit-maximization is *not* implied by cost-minimization. Cost-minimization is a much weaker hypothesis, both in terms of the implied behavior of firms, and, equivalently, from the mathematical conditions the cost-minimization hypothesis entails on the curvature properties of the production function. For profit-maximization, the production function must be strictly concave (downwards). Strict concavity, while sufficient for cost-minimization, is not necessary. The second-order conditions for cost-minimization require only *quasi-concavity*, i.e., convexity of the level curves (the isoquants, here) to the origin.

That this is a weaker condition can be readily seen. Consider the production function $y = x_1 x_2$, shown in Fig. 7-9. This production function is homogeneous of degree 2. Its level curves are rectangular hyperbolas, and clearly, a cost-minimization solution will exist for all factor prices. But will a finite profit-maximum point ever be achieved (with constant factor profits)? When both input levels are doubled, output will increase by a factor of four. Costs, $C = w x_1 + w_2 x_2$, will only double, however. Hence, this firm's marginal- and average-cost functions must always be declining (this will be given a rigorous proof below). Therefore, a profit-maximizing point cannot ever be achieved. This firm would make ever-increasing profits, the larger output it produced. The

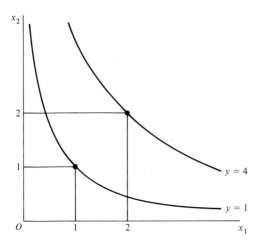

Figure 7-9 *The Production Function* $y = x_1 x_2$
The level curves of this production function are clearly convex, being rectangular hyperbolas. A cost-minimization solution will necessarily exist for all factor-price combinations. However, for example, when $x_1 = x_2 = 2$, $y = 4$, whereas when $x_1 = x_2 = 4$, $y = 16$. Revenues will always increase twice as fast as costs, and hence no profit-maximum point can exist. The marginal- and average-cost functions are always falling here. Profit-maximization is a much stronger assertion than cost-minimization, i.e., the former places much stronger restrictions on the shape of the production function than does cost-minimization.

second-order conditions for profit-maximization immediately reveal this situation:

$$f_{11}f_{22} - f_{12}^2 = 0 \cdot 0 - 1^2 = -1 < 0$$

The profit-maximization hypothesis places much stronger restrictions on the shape of the production function than does cost-minimization. Quasi-concavity, while implied by concavity, does not itself imply concavity.

Consider now expressions (7-33a) and (7-33b). These expressions say that if the output level is raised, the factor input levels can either increase or decrease. The situation is analogous to the somewhat more familiar case of inferior goods in consumer theory (to be discussed formally in the next chapter). There, when income rises, it is commonly believed that for many individuals, the quantity of hamburger, for example, will *decrease*, not increase. Hamburger is often regarded as an "inferior good." In the same manner, factors of production can be inferior.

Consider the case, perhaps, of unskilled labor. Suppose a firm wished to dig one or two ditches. In all likelihood, it would hire a worker or two and some shovels. However, if the firm intended to dig several city blocks' worth of drainage ditches, it would undoubtedly hire some mechanical diggers (backhoes) and some skilled operators. It might reduce its demand for unskilled labor, perhaps even to 0.

Thus, it is reasonable to be unable to predict the sign of $\partial x_i^*/\partial y_0$. No refutable hypothesis concerning output effects emerges strictly from the minimization hypothesis. A negative or a positive sign for $\partial x_i^*/\partial y_0$ is consistent with the model.

It should be pointed out, however, that a factor which is in use cannot be inferior over the whole range of output. That is, it must have been the case that $\partial x_i^*/\partial y_0 > 0$ at some lower levels of output, else the factor would not ever be employed in the first place. Remember that these comparative statics relations are *local*, not global, results.

There is one set of relationships concerning output effects which are not intuitively, or even geometrically, obvious. Note again the equations

$$\frac{\partial \lambda^*}{\partial w_1} = \frac{-\Delta_{13}}{\Delta} \qquad (7\text{-}28c)$$

$$\frac{\partial x_1^*}{\partial y_0} = \frac{-\Delta_{31}}{\Delta} \qquad (7\text{-}33a)$$

$$\frac{\partial \lambda^*}{\partial w_2} = \frac{-\Delta_{23}}{\Delta} \qquad (7\text{-}30c)$$

$$\frac{\partial x_2^*}{\partial y_0} = \frac{-\Delta_{32}}{\Delta} \qquad (7\text{-}33b)$$

The symmetry of the determinant Δ immediately indicates that

$$\frac{\partial \lambda^*}{\partial w_i} \equiv \frac{\partial x_i^*}{\partial y_0} \qquad i = 1, 2 \qquad (7\text{-}34)$$

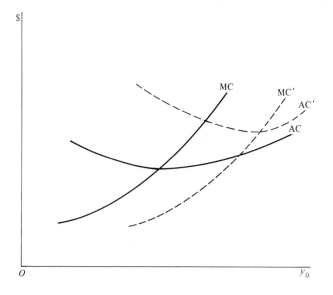

Figure 7-10 *Changes in the Marginal- and Average-cost Curves when the Price of an Inferior Factor Changes* When the price of an inferior factor increases, the marginal-cost curve of the firm shifts *down*, the average-cost curve shifts up. With any increase in factor costs, unit cost of production must increase. The firm will never regard an increase in factor costs as beneficial. However, if the factor is inferior, the *marginal* cost of output declines.

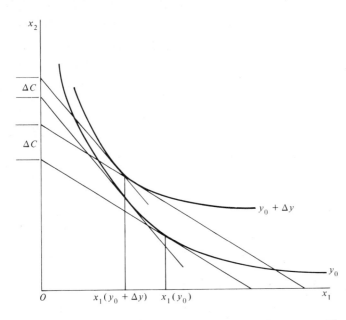

Figure 7-11 *The Effects of a Decline in the Unit-Cost Inferior Factor* The factor x_1 is inferior, as an increase in output from y_0 to $y_0 + \Delta y$ reduces the demand for x_1. At any level of x_1, as amounts of x_2 are increased (vertical movements), the isoquants become flatter. We can arbitrarily define the units such that $w_2 = 1$. Then vertical movements can be identified as marginal costs, since the intercepts of the isocost lines with the vertical axis are $x_2 = C/w_2 = C$. Since the isoquants converge as x_1 is decreased, when x_1 is inferior, the marginal cost of expanding output from y_0 to $y_0 + \Delta y$ is less, when less x_1 is used, that is, as w_1 is raised.

That is, the rate of change of the marginal-cost function with respect to a factor price is equal to (and therefore of the same sign as) the magnitude of the output effect for that factor. But output effects can be negative as well as positive. This leads to the strange result that the marginal-cost curve, as commonly drawn (see Fig. 7-10) against output, will shift *down* when the wage of an inferior factor *increases*. If, say, $\partial x_1^* / \partial y_0 < 0$, then x_1 is an inferior factor (less is used as output rises). If w_1 increases, the marginal-cost curve will actually *fall*, i.e., shift down along the whole range where x_1 is inferior.

How can we explain this result? Consider Fig. 7-11. What happens when a cost-minimizing firm experiences an increase in a factor price (holding output constant)? The firm, of course, substitutes away from that factor. However, if x_1 is inferior, then for any level of x_1, increases in x_2 will result in new isoquant levels which are flatter than the previous, lower one at that level of x_1. That is, since parallel shifts in the isocost line result in tangencies to the left of the original one, then the isoquants directly vertical from the original tangency must have a lower absolute slope. This means that the distance between isoquants representing successive output levels *narrows* as x_1 is reduced. Hence, an increase in w_1, which reduces x_1, *reduces* the cost of additional output.

Envelope Results

The reciprocity conditions $\partial x_i^*/\partial w_j = \partial x_j^*/\partial w_i$ and $\partial \lambda^*/\partial w_i = \partial x_i^*/\partial y_0$ can be given a simpler and more powerful proof and interpretation by use of the envelope theorem presented in the last chapter. Recall again that for the general constrained maximum (or minimum) problem,

maximize $\qquad\qquad\qquad f(x_1, x_2, \alpha) = y$

subject to $\qquad\qquad\qquad g(x_1, x_2, \alpha) = 0$

where α represents one or more parameters, that $\partial y^*/\partial \alpha = \partial \mathscr{L}/\partial \alpha$; that is, the rate of change of the maximum value of f for any α, with respect to α, allowing the decision variables x_1 and x_2 to "adjust" via $x_1 = x_1^*(\alpha)$, $x_2 = x_2^*(\alpha)$, is the same as the partial derivative of the lagrangian $\mathscr{L} = f(x_1, x_2, \alpha) + \lambda g(x_1, x_2, \alpha)$ with respect to α, *holding the x_i's fixed.* We have already used this theorem to show that λ is interpretable as marginal cost [see equation (7-23)].

The cost-minimization problem

minimize $\qquad\qquad\qquad C = w_1 x_1 + w_2 x_2$

subject to $\qquad\qquad\qquad f(x_1, x_2) = y_0$

has as its lagrangian

$$\mathscr{L} = w_1 x_1 + w_2 x_2 + \lambda(y_0 - f(x_1, x_2))$$

The envelope theorem thus says that

$$\frac{\partial C^*}{\partial w_1} = \frac{\partial \mathscr{L}}{\partial w_1} = x_1 = x_1^*(w_1, w_2, y_0) \qquad\qquad (7\text{-}35)$$

and similarly for x_2. Also, as was shown before, (equation (7-23)), $\partial C^*/\partial y_0 = \partial \mathscr{L}/\partial y_0 = \lambda^*(w_1, w_2, y_0)$. Equation (7-35) is often referred to as Shephard's lemma; it is an important part of the duality theory of cost and production functions to be discussed in Chap. 10.

Although we have already proved the envelope theorem, it is perhaps wise to repeat the procedure in connection with equation (7-35). Differentiating $C^* = w_1 x_1^* + w_2 x_2^*$ with respect to w_1, remembering that x_1^* and x_2^* are themselves functions of w_1,

$$\frac{\partial C^*}{\partial w_1} = x_1^* + w_1 \frac{\partial x_1^*}{\partial w_1} + w_2 \frac{\partial x_2^*}{\partial w_1}$$

Using the first-order conditions $w_1 = \lambda f_1$, $w_2 = \lambda f_2$, and factoring out λ,

$$\frac{\partial C^*}{\partial w_1} = x_1^* + \lambda^* \left(f_1 \frac{\partial x_1^*}{\partial w_1} + f_2 \frac{\partial x_2^*}{\partial w_1} \right)$$

Consider now the constraint identity $f(x_1^*, x_2^*) \equiv y_0$. Differentiating this identity with respect to w_1 yields

$$f_1 \frac{\partial x_1^*}{\partial w_1} + f_2 \frac{\partial x_2^*}{\partial w_1} \equiv 0$$

But this is precisely the expression in parentheses in the earlier equation; hence, as the envelope theorem indicated,

$$\frac{\partial C^*}{\partial w_1} \equiv x_1^*(w_1, w_2, y_0) \qquad (7\text{-}35)$$

We also showed previously that

$$\frac{\partial C^*}{\partial y_0} \equiv \lambda^*(w_1, w_2, y_0) \qquad (7\text{-}23)$$

Now $C^*(w_1, w_2, y_0)$ is twice differentiable, assuming the production function is well behaved, i.e., that a smooth interior solution to the cost-minimization problem obtains. But observe the cross-partials of $C^*(w_1, w_2, y_0)$: Since $C_{w_1}^* \equiv x_1^*(w_1, w_2, y_0)$, C_{w_1, w_2}^* is simply $\partial x_1^*/\partial w_2$, that is,

$$C_{w_1, w_2}^* \equiv \frac{\partial x_1^*}{\partial w_2}$$

However, $C_{w_1, w_2}^* \equiv C_{w_2, w_1}^*$, since partial derivatives can be taken without regard to order. But $C_{w_2, w_1}^* \equiv \partial x_2^*/\partial w_1$. Hence (almost) trivially,

$$C_{w_2, w_1}^* \equiv \frac{\partial x_2^*}{\partial w_1} \equiv \frac{\partial x_1^*}{\partial w_2} \equiv C_{w_1, w_2}^*$$

which was equation (7-31).

Likewise, since $\partial C^*/\partial y_0 \equiv C_{y_0}^* = \lambda^*(w_1, w_2, y_0)$,

$$C_{y_0, w_1}^* \equiv \frac{\partial \lambda^*}{\partial w_1}$$

But $C_{y_0, w_1}^* \equiv C_{w_1, y_0}^* \equiv \partial x_1^*/\partial y_0$. Thus,

$$\frac{\partial \lambda^*}{\partial w_1} \equiv \frac{\partial x_1^*}{\partial y_0}$$

which was equation (7-34). Similar reasoning of course shows that $\partial \lambda^*/\partial w_2 \equiv \partial x_2^*/\partial y_0$.

This is a very powerful, yet simple, way of regarding reciprocity conditions. (Perhaps it is powerful precisely because of its simplicity.) Reciprocity conditions are simply the statement that the cross-partials of the cost function are invariant to the order of differentiation. The reciprocity conditions appear, however, only because the first partials of $C^*(w_1, w_2, y_0)$ have the peculiarly simple forms $\partial C^*/\partial w_i = x_i^*$, $\partial C^*/\partial y_0 \equiv \lambda^*$. These simple first partials occur because the lagrangian $\mathcal{L} = w_1 x_1 + w_2 x_2 + \lambda(y_0 - f(x_1, x_2))$ is in fact *linear* in the parameters w_1, w_2, y_0. When such linearity of the lagrangian occurs, reciprocity conditions will appear. These results and more envelope phenomena will be discussed in further detail in later sections.

Example Consider the production function $y = x_1 x_2^2$. This function exhibits increasing returns to scale and thus a finite profit maximum would not be reached with constant prices. However, there is still a cost-minimizing input combination for any given output level y_0. Let us find the constant-output factor-demand curves.

minimize
$$C = w_1 x_1 + w_2 x_2$$

subject to
$$x_1 x_2^2 = y_0$$

The lagrangian is

$$\mathscr{L} = w_1 x_1 + w_2 x_2 + \lambda(y_0 - x_1 x_2^2)$$

Differentiating with respect to x_1, x_2, and λ,

$$\mathscr{L}_1 = w_1 - \lambda x_2^2 = 0$$

$$\mathscr{L}_2 = w_2 - 2\lambda x_1 x_2 = 0$$

$$\mathscr{L}_\lambda = y_0 - x_1 x_2^2 = 0$$

Combining the first two expressions,

$$\frac{w_1}{w_2} = \frac{x_2}{2x_1}$$

or
$$x_2 = \frac{2w_1 x_1}{w_2}$$

Now substitute this expression for x_2 into the production function:

$$x_1 \left(\frac{2w_1 x_1}{w_2} \right)^2 = y_0$$

or
$$\frac{4x_1^3 w_1^2}{w_2^2} = y_0$$

Solving for x_1,

$$x_1^* = 4^{-1/3} w_1^{-2/3} w_2^{2/3} y_0^{1/3}$$

In like fashion one obtains, from the first-order tangency condition,

$$x_1 = \frac{w_2 x_2}{2w_1}$$

Substituting this into the production function yields

$$\frac{w_2 x_2}{2w_1} x_2^2 = y_0$$

or
$$x_2^* = 2^{1/3} w_1^{1/3} w_2^{-1/3} y_0^{1/3}$$

Note that x_1^* and x_2^* are multiplicatively separable in the factor prices and output. Also, x_1^* and x_2^* are homogeneous of degree zero in w_1 and w_2. The cost function is obtained by substituting x_1^* and x_2^* into $C = w_1 x_1 + w_2 x_2$:

$$C^* = w_1 4^{-1/3} w_1^{-2/3} w_2^{2/3} y_0^{1/3} + w_2 2^{1/3} w_1^{1/3} w_2^{-1/3} y_0^{1/3}$$

$$= k w_1^{1/3} w_2^{2/3} y_0^{1/3}$$

where $k = 4^{-1/3} + 2^{1/3} = 2^{-2/3} + 2^{1/3} = 2^{1/3}(2^{-1} + 2^0) = \frac{3}{2}(2^{1/3})$. Note that C^* is homogeneous of degree 1 in w_1 and w_2, a general property of cost functions. Note also that

$$\frac{\partial C^*}{\partial w_1} = \frac{1}{3} k w_1^{-2/3} w_2^{2/3} y_0^{1/3} \equiv x_1^*$$

and

$$\frac{\partial C^*}{\partial w_2} = \frac{2}{3} k w_1^{1/3} w_2^{-1/3} y_0^{1/3} \equiv x_2^*$$

These envelope properties are shown for the general case in equation (7-35).

7.8 ELASTICITIES; FURTHER PROPERTIES OF THE FACTOR-DEMAND CURVES

The properties of the factor-demand curves $x_i = x_i^*(w_1, w_2, y_0)$ and the marginal cost curve $\lambda = \lambda^*(w_1, w_2, y_0)$ are often stated in terms of dimensionless elasticity expressions, instead of using the slopes (partial derivatives) directly. In particular, one can define the elasticities of demand as

$$\varepsilon_{ij} = \lim_{\Delta w_j \to 0} \frac{\dfrac{\Delta x_i}{x_i}}{\dfrac{\Delta w_j}{w_j}}$$

where ε_{ij} thus represents the (limit of the) percentage change in a factor usage x_i (holding output constant) due to a given percentage change in some factor price w_j. When $i = j$, this is called the *own-elasticity* of factor demand; when $i \neq j$, this is called a *cross-elasticity*.

Taking limits, and simplifying the compound fraction,

$$\varepsilon_{ij} = \frac{w_j}{x_i^*} \frac{\partial x_i^*}{\partial w_j} \qquad i, j = 1, 2 \tag{7-36}$$

This is the definition we will use throughout. In like fashion, one can define the *output elasticity* of factor demand as the percentage change in the utilization of a factor per percentage change in output† (holding factor prices constant),

or
$$\varepsilon_{iy_0} = \lim_{\Delta y \to 0} \frac{\frac{\Delta x_i}{x_i}}{\frac{\Delta y}{y}} = \frac{y_0}{x_i^*} \frac{\partial x_i^*}{\partial y_0} \tag{7-37}$$

Elasticities are dimensionless expressions, as can be seen by inspection. To a mathematician, they are logarithmic derivatives: For example, consider the function $x_i = x_i^*(w_1, w_2, y_0)$. Define $x_i' = \log x_i$, $w_j' = \log w_j$. Then by the chain rule,

$$\frac{\partial x_i'}{\partial w_j'} = \frac{dx_i'}{dx_i} \frac{\partial x_i^*}{\partial w_j} \frac{dw_j}{dw_j'}$$

$$= \frac{1}{x_i^*} \frac{\partial x_i^*}{\partial w_j} e^{w_j'}$$

$$= \frac{w_j}{x_i^*} \frac{\partial x_i^*}{\partial w_j}$$

remembering that the definition of a logarithm is $e^{\log x} \equiv x$. Many economists feel more comfortable speaking about elasticities; others prefer the slopes (partial derivatives) directly. It is probably a matter of taste.

Homogeneity

The demand curves $x_i = x_i^*(w_1, w_2, y_0)$ are homogeneous of degree zero in factor prices, or, for the two-factor case, in w_1 and w_2. That is, $x_i^*(tw_1, tw_2, y_0) \equiv x_i^*(w_1, w_2, y_0)$. Holding output y_0 constant, a proportional change in all factor prices leaves the input combination unchanged. This is really another way of saying that only changes in *relative* prices, not absolute prices, affect behavior.

If the cost-minimizing firm faced factor prices tw_1, tw_2, the problem would be to

minimize $\qquad tw_1 x_1 + tw_2 x_2$

subject to $\qquad f(x_1, x_2) = y_0$

Since $tw_1 x_1 + tw_2 x_2 = t(w_1 x_1 + w_2 x_2)$ is a very simple monotonic transformation of the objective function, we should expect no substantial changes in the

---

† Note that the output elasticity is *not* $[(\Delta y/y)/(\Delta x_i/x_i)]$, or $(x_i/y)(\partial y/\partial x_i) = (1/AP_i)MP_i$. This latter expression, though well-defined, is not a measure of the responsiveness of factor demand to output changes. And it is most certainly *not* the reciprocal of ε_{iy_0} above: ε_{iy_0} can be positive or negative (for the case of inferior factors); $(x_i/y)(\partial y/\partial x_i)$ is necessarily positive as long as the marginal product of x_i is positive.

first-order equations. Forming the lagrangian $\mathcal{L} = t(w_1 x_1 + w_2 x_2) + \lambda(y_0 - f(x_1, x_2))$, the first-order equations for a constrained minimum are

$$\mathcal{L}_1 = tw_1 - \lambda f_1 = 0 \tag{7-38a}$$

$$\mathcal{L}_2 = tw_2 - \lambda f_2 = 0 \tag{7-38b}$$

$$\mathcal{L}_\lambda = y_0 - f(x_1, x_2) = 0 \tag{7-38c}$$

Eliminating the Lagrange multiplier from (7-38a) and (7-38b),

$$\frac{tw_1}{tw_2} = \frac{w_1}{w_2} = \frac{f_1}{f_2}$$

Thus the same tangency condition emerges for factor prices (tw_1, tw_2) as for (w_1, w_2). The isoquant must have slope w_1/w_2, for any value of t. And output, meanwhile, is still constrained to be at level y_0. Hence the identical solution to the cost-minimization problem (in terms of the x_i's) emerges for factor prices (tw_1, tw_2) as for (w_1, w_2); hence the solutions $x_i = x_i^*(w_1, w_2, y_0)$ are unchanged when (w_1, w_2) are replaced by (tw_1, tw_2). Thus $x_i^*(w_1, w_2, y_0) \equiv x_i^*(tw_1, tw_2, y_0)$, or the factor-demand curves (holding output constant) are homogeneous of degree zero in the factor prices. This result is perfectly general for the n-factor case; $x_i^*(w_1, \ldots, w_n, y_0) \equiv x_i^*(tw_1, \ldots, tw_n, y_0)$, $i = 1, \ldots, n$.

Clearly, however, *something* must be changed when factor prices are multiplied by some common scalar. What *is* changed is total cost, and therefore marginal and average costs also. If factor prices are doubled, the input combination will remain the same, but the nominal cost of purchasing that input combination will clearly double. Total cost $C = C^*(w_1, w_2, y_0)$ is homogeneous of degree one in factor prices. Total cost $C^*(w_1, w_2, y_0) \equiv w_1 x_1^* + w_2 x_2^*$, a linear function of the x_i^*'s. When factor prices are changed by some multiple t, the x_i^*'s are unchanged, and hence

$$C^*(tw_1, tw_2, y_0) \equiv tw_1 x_1^*(tw_1, tw_2, y_0) + tw_2 x_2^*(tw_1, tw_2, y_0)$$

$$\equiv tw_1 x_1^*(w_1, w_2, y_0) + tw_2 x_2^*(w_1, w_2, y_0)$$

$$\equiv t[w_1 x_1^*(w_1, w_2, y_0) + w_2 x_2^*(w_1, w_2, y_0)]$$

$$\equiv tC^*(w_1, w_2, y_0)$$

Again, this result is perfectly general for the n-factor case; the cost function is homogeneous of degree one in factor prices.

Since total costs increase or decrease by whatever scalar multiple factor prices are changed by, marginal and average costs are similarly affected. Since

$$AC \equiv \frac{C^*(w_1, w_2, y_0)}{y_0} \tag{7-39}$$

$$AC(tw_1, tw_2, y_0) \equiv C^*(tw_1, tw_2, y_0) \frac{1}{y_0}$$

$$\equiv tC^*(w_1, w_2, y_0) \frac{1}{y_0}$$

$$\equiv tAC(w_1, w_2, y_0)$$

Similarly, since $MC \equiv \lambda^*(w_1, w_2, y_0)$, from the first-order equations

$$\lambda^*(tw_1, tw_2, y_0) \equiv \frac{tw_i}{f_i(x_1^*, x_2^*)} \qquad i = 1, 2$$

The factor inputs x_i^* are unchanged by the multiplication of factor prices by t. Hence only the numerator of the above fraction is affected, in a simple linear fashion, and hence

$$\lambda^*(tw_1, tw_2, y_0) \equiv t\lambda^*(w_1, w_2, y_0) \tag{7-40}$$

or the marginal-cost function is homogeneous of degree one in factor prices.

It should be carefully noted that all of the above homogeneity results are completely independent of any homogeneity of the production function itself. These results are derivable for any cost-minimizing firm. Nowhere was any assumption about the homogeneity of the production function implied or used; therefore these results hold for *any* production function for which a cost-minimizing tangency solution is achieved.

Euler relations Since the factor-demand curve $x_i = x_i^*(w_1, w_2, y_0)$ is homogeneous of degree zero in w_1, w_2, by Euler's theorem

$$\frac{\partial x_i^*}{\partial w_1} w_1 + \frac{\partial x_i^*}{\partial w_2} w_2 \equiv 0 \cdot x_i^* \equiv 0 \qquad i = 1, 2 \tag{7-41}$$

This relation can be stated neatly in terms of elasticities. Dividing (7-41) by x_i^*

$$\frac{w_1}{x_i^*} \frac{\partial x_i^*}{\partial w_1} + \frac{w_2}{x_i^*} \frac{\partial x_i^*}{\partial w_2} \equiv 0 \qquad i = 1, 2$$

or

$$\varepsilon_{i1} + \varepsilon_{i2} \equiv 0 \qquad i = 1, 2 \tag{7-42}$$

using the definitions of elasticities and cross-elasticities given in equation (7-36). More generally, for the n-factor case, the factor demands $x_i^*(w_1, \ldots, w_n, y_0)$ are homogeneous of degree zero in $w_1, \ldots, w_n$. Similar reasoning yields

$$\varepsilon_{i1} + \varepsilon_{i2} + \cdots + \varepsilon_{in} \equiv 0 \qquad i = 1, \ldots, n$$

or

$$\sum_{j=1}^{n} \varepsilon_{ij} \equiv 0 \qquad i = 1, \ldots, n \tag{7-43}$$

For any factor, holding output constant, the sum of its own elasticity of demand plus its cross-elasticities with respect to all other factor prices, sums identically to zero.

Another relationship concerning cross-elasticities can be derived using the reciprocity relations $\partial x_i^* / \partial w_j \equiv \partial x_j^* / \partial w_i$. This reciprocity relation can be converted into elasticities as follows. Each side will be multiplied by 1 in a complicated way (the asterisks are omitted to save notational clutter):

$$\frac{x_i \, w_j}{x_i \, w_j} \frac{\partial x_i}{\partial w_j} \equiv \frac{x_j \, w_i}{x_j \, w_i} \frac{\partial x_j}{\partial w_i}$$

Rearranging terms yields

$$\frac{x_i}{w_j} \left(\frac{w_j}{x_i} \frac{\partial x_i}{\partial w_j} \right) \equiv \frac{x_j}{w_i} \left(\frac{w_i}{x_j} \frac{\partial x_j}{\partial w_i} \right)$$

or

$$(w_i x_i)\varepsilon_{ij} \equiv (w_j x_j)\varepsilon_{ji}$$

Dividing through by total cost $C = \sum_{i=1}^{n} w_i x_i$,

$$\kappa_i \varepsilon_{ij} \equiv \kappa_j \varepsilon_{ji} \qquad i, j = 1, \ldots, n \tag{7-44}$$

where $\kappa_i = w_i x_i / C$ represents the share of total cost accounted for by factor x_i.

Never forget, incidentally, what is being held constant here. These elasticities and shares refer to constrained cost-minimization, i.e., output-held-constant factor curves. Slightly different relationships are derivable for, e.g., the profit-maximizing (unconstrained) firm.

The reciprocity relations in terms of elasticities, equations (7-44) can be substituted into equations (7-43) to yield new interdependencies of the cross-elasticities. Substituting (7-44) into (7-43),

$$\sum_{j=1}^{n} \varepsilon_{ij} \equiv \sum_{j=1}^{n} \frac{\kappa_j}{\kappa_i} \varepsilon_{ji} \equiv 0$$

Multiplying through by κ_i yields

$$\sum_{j=1}^{n} \kappa_j \varepsilon_{ji} \equiv \kappa_1 \varepsilon_{1i} + \kappa_2 \varepsilon_{2i} + \cdots + \kappa_n \varepsilon_{ni} \equiv 0 \qquad i = 1, \ldots, n \tag{7-45}$$

The difference between (7-43) and (7-45) is that in this last relation (7-45), the elasticities being considered are those between the various factors and *one particular factor price*, whereas in equation (7-43), the elasticities all pertain to the relationship of one particular factor x_i to all factor prices. In the former case, the shares are not involved, the relationship being derived directly from Euler's equation; in the latter case of how all factors relate to a given price change, the shares of cost allocated to those factors do play a part.

Equation (7-45) can also be derived by a different route. Consider the production function constraint $f(x_1^*, x_2^*) \equiv y_0$. Differentiating with respect to some factor price w_i

$$f_1 \frac{\partial x_1^*}{\partial w_i} + f_2 \frac{\partial x_2^*}{\partial w_i} \equiv 0$$

From the first-order relations $w_j = \lambda f_j$, this is equivalent to

$$w_1 \frac{\partial x_1^*}{\partial w_i} + w_2 \frac{\partial x_2^*}{\partial w_i} \equiv 0 \tag{7-46}$$

Note in equation (7-46) that the terms refer to the change in the various factors with respect to the same factor price, w_i. If this expression is now manipulated in a manner similar to the derivation of equation (7-44), equation (7-45) results.

Output Elasticities

The output elasticities are related to one another also, as can be seen by differentiating the production constraint $f(x_1^*, x_2^*) \equiv y_0$ with respect to y_0:

$$f_1 \frac{\partial x_1^*}{\partial y_0} + f_2 \frac{\partial x_2^*}{\partial y_0} \equiv 1$$

Again using the first-order relations $w_i = \lambda f_i$,

$$\frac{w_1}{\lambda} \frac{\partial x_1^*}{\partial y_0} + \frac{w_2}{\lambda} \frac{\partial x_2^*}{\partial y_0} \equiv 1$$

To convert these terms to elasticities, multiply the first by $(y_0/y_0)(x_1^*/x_1^*)$, that is, by unity, in that fashion. Do the same for the second term, using x_2^* instead of x_1^*. This yields

$$\frac{w_1 x_1^*}{\lambda y_0} \left(\frac{y_0}{x_1^*} \frac{\partial x_1^*}{\partial y_0} \right) + \frac{w_2 x_2^*}{\lambda y_0} \left(\frac{y_0}{x_2^*} \frac{\partial x_2^*}{\partial y_0} \right) \equiv 1$$

or

$$\kappa_1' \varepsilon_{1y_0} + \kappa_2' \varepsilon_{2y_0} \equiv 1 \tag{7-47}$$

where the "weights" κ_i' are the total cost of each factor divided by marginal cost times output. This result generalizes easily to the n-factor case:

$$\sum \kappa_i' \varepsilon_{iy_0} \equiv 1 \tag{7-48}$$

where $\kappa_i' = w_i x_i / \lambda y_0$.

It should be noted that these weights, κ_i', do not themselves sum to unity, and hence equation (7-48) should not properly be called a *weighted average* of the output elasticities. In fact, $\sum \kappa_i' = (\sum w_i x_i)/\lambda y_0 = (1/\lambda)(C^*/y_0) = AC/MC$. In a special case, therefore, the weights do sum to 1—when marginal cost λ equals average cost. This situation will occur when a firm is operating at the minimum point on its average-cost curve, i.e., where marginal cost intersects average cost. Thus we could say that for a firm in long-run competitive equilibrium, the weighted average of the output elasticities of all factors sums to unity, where the weights are the share of total cost spent on that particular factor.

7.9 THE AVERAGE-COST CURVE

Consider now the average-cost curve (AC) of a firm employing two variable inputs x_1 and x_2, at factor prices w_1 and w_2, respectively. By definition

$$AC = \frac{C^*(w_1, w_2, y_0)}{y_0} = \frac{1}{y_0}(w_1 x_1^* + w_2 x_2^*) \tag{7-49}$$

How is average cost affected by a change in a factor price, say w_1? Can average cost ever fall in response to an increase in factor price? In this case, intuition proves correct—increased factor costs can only increase overall average cost. If this were otherwise, firms could always make larger profits by contracting for higher wage payments. This behavior is not commonly observed.

We can demonstrate the positive relationship between AC and w_1 as follows. Differentiating (7-49) with respect to w_1 yields

$$\frac{\partial AC}{\partial w_1} = \frac{1}{y_0}\left(x_1^* + w_1 \frac{\partial x_1^*}{\partial w_1} + w_2 \frac{\partial x_2^*}{\partial w_1}\right)$$

noting the use of the product rule on the term $w_1 x_1^*$. Using the first-order relations, $w_i = \lambda^* f_i$

$$\frac{\partial AC}{\partial w_1} = \frac{x_1^*}{y_0} + \frac{\lambda^*}{y_0}\left(f_1 \frac{\partial x_1^*}{\partial w_1} + f_2 \frac{\partial x_2^*}{\partial w_1}\right)$$

However, differentiation of the constraint identity, $f(x_1^*, x_2^*) \equiv y_0$, with respect to w_1 [see equation (7-26c)] yields $f_1(\partial x_1^*/\partial w_1) + f_2(\partial x_2^*/\partial w_1) \equiv 0$. Hence, the expression in parentheses above vanishes, leaving

$$\frac{\partial AC}{\partial w_1} = \frac{x_1^*}{y_0} > 0$$

In general, by similar reasoning

$$\frac{\partial AC}{\partial w_i} = \frac{x_i^*}{y_0} \qquad i = 1, \ldots, n \tag{7-50}$$

for firms with any number of factors. For positive input and output levels (the only relevant ones), therefore, average cost must move in the same direction as factor prices.

Equation (7-50) is intuitively sensible from the definition of AC directly. Average cost is a linear function of the w_i's: $AC = (x_1^*/y_0)w_1 + (x_2^*/y_0)w_2$. If w_1 changes to $w_1 + \Delta w_1$, at the margin, the change in AC will just be the multiple of w_1, (x_1^*/y_0), that is, $(x_1^*/y_0)\Delta w_1$. For finite movements, x_1^*/y_0 and x_2^*/y_0 also change, but *at the margin*, the instantaneous rate of change of AC is simply x_1^*/y_0 (before x_1^* can change).

This is actually another simple application of the envelope theorem. Since $AC = C^*/y_0$,

$$\frac{\partial AC}{\partial w_1} = \frac{1}{y_0}\frac{\partial C^*}{\partial w_1}$$

However, by the envelope theorem, recalling the lagrangian $\mathscr{L} = w_1 x_1 + w_2 x_2 + \lambda(y_0 - f(x_1, x_2))$

$$\frac{\partial C^*}{\partial w_1} = \frac{\partial \mathscr{L}}{\partial w_1} = x_1^*$$

Hence

$$\frac{\partial AC}{\partial w_1} = \frac{x_1^*}{y_0}$$

7.10 ANALYSIS OF FIRMS IN LONG-RUN COMPETITIVE EQUILIBRIUM

The foregoing analysis can be modified and extended to analyze a well-known situation in economics. Consider a price-taking firm in a competitive industry composed of a large number of identical firms. Suppose also that entry into this industry is very easy, i.e., the costs of entry are low. What will the behavior of firms in this industry be, i.e., how will such firms respond to changes in factor prices, or other parameters which might appear? (See also Chap. 5, problem 4.)

Under conditions of immediate entry of new firms into an industry in which positive profits appear, output price must immediately be driven down to the point of minimum average cost for all firms. Any response the firm makes to some parameter change must take into account the prospect of instantaneous adjustment of output price to minimum average cost. In this case, profit-maximizing behavior will be equivalent to each firm minimizing its average cost, since at any other point, the firm would cease to exist.

Let us now investigate how the location of the minimum AC point is affected by a change in a factor price. The point of minimum average cost occurs when

$$MC(w_1, w_2, y_0) = AC(w_1, w_2, y_0) \tag{7-51}$$

The question being asked is, how does the output level y_0 associated with minimum average cost change, when a factor price changes? A functional dependence of y_0 on factor prices w_1, w_2 is being asserted. Where does this functional relationship come from? Equation (7-51) represents an implicit function of y_0, w_1, and w_2. Assuming the sufficient conditions for the implicit function theorem are valid, (7-51) can be solved for one variable in terms of the remaining two; in particular

$$y_0 = y_0^*(w_1, w_2) \tag{7-52}$$

We can now derive $\partial y_0^*/\partial w_i$ by implicit differentiation. Substituting (7-52) back into (7-51), one gets the *identity*

$$MC(w_1, w_2, y_0^*(w_1, w_2)) \equiv AC(w_1, w_2, y_0^*(w_1, w_2)) \tag{7-53}$$

This relation is an identity because output level y_0 is posited to always adjust via equation (7-52) to any change in w_1 or w_2 so as to keep the firm at minimum average cost. Differentiating this identity with respect to, say, w_1,

$$\frac{\partial MC}{\partial w_1} + \frac{\partial MC}{\partial y_0}\frac{\partial y_0^*}{\partial w_1} \equiv \frac{\partial AC}{\partial w_1} + \frac{\partial AC}{\partial y_0}\frac{\partial y_0^*}{\partial w_1}$$

However, at minimum average cost, $\partial AC/\partial y_0 = 0$, from the first-order conditions for a minimum. Hence, solving for $\partial y_0^*/\partial w_1$

$$\frac{\partial y_0^*}{\partial w_1} = \frac{1}{\dfrac{\partial MC}{\partial y_0}}\left[\frac{\partial AC}{\partial w_1} - \frac{\partial MC}{\partial w_1}\right] \tag{7-54}$$

with a similar expression holding for $\partial y_0^*/\partial w_2$.

Equation (7-54) admits of an easy interpretation. It says that if, say, w_1 increases, the minimum average-cost point will shift to the right (i.e., the minimum AC output level will increase) if the AC curve shifts up by more than the marginal-cost curve. (Note that we know that $\partial MC/\partial y_0 > 0$ at minimum AC.) This is geometrically obvious. Consider Fig. 7-12. The marginal-cost curve always cuts through the AC curve from below, at the point of minimum average cost. When w_1, say, increases, average cost must shift up by some amount [equation (7.50)]. If marginal cost shifts by less than the shift in average cost, the point of minimum average cost will clearly move to the right. And, of course, if marginal cost actually shifts down when w_1 increases (indicating that x_1 is an inferior factor), then the new MC curve must necessarily intersect the new (raised) AC curve to the right of, i.e., at a higher output level than, the old minimum AC point.

Equation (7-54) can be used to relate the output level changes directly to the output elasticities of factor demand. From equation (7-50),

$$\frac{\partial AC}{\partial w_1} = \frac{x_1^*}{y_0}$$

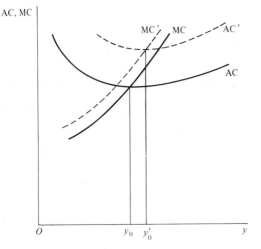

Figure 7-12 Shifts in the MC and AC curves when a factor price changes.

and from (7-34),

$$\frac{\partial MC}{\partial w_1} = \frac{\partial x_1^*}{\partial y_0}$$

Substituting these values into equation (7-54),

$$\frac{\partial y_0^*}{\partial w_1} = \frac{1}{\dfrac{\partial MC}{\partial y_0}} \left(\frac{x_1^*}{y_0} - \frac{\partial x_1^*}{\partial y_0} \right)$$

Factoring out x_1^*/y_0,

$$\frac{\partial y_0^*}{\partial w_1} = \frac{\dfrac{x_1^*}{y_0}}{\dfrac{\partial MC}{\partial y_0}} (1 - \varepsilon_{1y_0}) \tag{7-55}$$

where $\varepsilon_{iy_0} = (y_0/x_i)(\partial x_i/\partial y_0)$ is the output elasticity of factor i, as defined in equation (7-37).

The output effects of changing factor prices on firms in long-run competitive equilibrium can be read out of equations (7-54) and (7-55). If a factor price, say, w_1, rises, then if factor 1 is output elastic ($\varepsilon_{1y_0} > 1$), all the firms will wind up producing less output. Minimum average costs (and thus the product price) increase, but the marginal-cost curve shifts up even more. Hence, less total output is sold, since the product-demand curve is downward-sloping.† If factor 1 is output inelastic (but not inferior) ($0 \le \varepsilon_{1y_0} < 1$), the marginal-cost curve will shift up by less than the average curve, since by equation (7-55), $\partial y_0^*/\partial w_1 > 0$. Finally, if factor 1 is inferior ($\varepsilon_{1y_0} < 0$), then the marginal-cost curve shifts *down* when w_1 increases, average cost still shifts upward, and hence $\partial y_0^*/\partial w_1 > 0$.

PROBLEMS

1 Explain why cost functions are not just technological data. Why does cost depend on the objectives of the firm and the system of laws under which the firm operates?

2 Are convex (to the origin) isoquants postulated because of empirical reasons or because they make the second-order conditions for constrained cost-minimization valid for interior solutions?

3 What is the difference between the factor-demand curves obtained in this chapter, i.e. from cost-minimization, and those obtained earlier from the profit-maximization model? What observable (in principle) differences are there between the two?

4 Discuss the relationships between the following definitions of complementary factors:

    (i) $f_{ij} > 0$ (ii) $(\partial x_i/\partial w_j)_{w_i,\, p} < 0$ (iii) $(\partial x_i/\partial w_j)_{w_i,\, y_0} < 0$

---

† A paradoxical implication of this result is that an increase in a factor price can actually stimulate the entry of new firms into the industry, depending on the elasticity of output (product) demand. With all firms contracting, if total quantity demanded at the new price = min AC is greater than total y_0 for all firms, the slack will be taken up by new firms.

where $f(x_1, x_2)$ is a production function for a competitive firm, and where the parameters outside the parentheses indicate that those parameters are to be held constant.

5 Consider the profit-maximizing firm with two inputs. This model can be treated as the *constrained maximum problem*,

maximize $$py - w_1 x_1 - w_2 x_2$$

subject to $$y = f(x_1, x_2)$$

Using the lagrangian

$$\mathcal{L} = py - w_1 x_1 - w_2 x_2 + \lambda[f(x_1, x_2) - y]$$

(*a*) Show that if the profit maximum is conceived to be achieved in two steps: first hold y constant and maximize over x_1 and x_2 (as functions of y), and then maximize over the variable y, the lagrangian is

$$\mathcal{L} = \max_{y} \left(py - \min_{x_1, x_2}\{(w_1 x_1 + w_2 x_2) + \lambda[y - f(x_1, x_2)]\} \right)$$

(*b*) Show, therefore, that profit-maximization implies cost-minimization at the profit-maximizing level of output.

(*c*) Derive the comparative statics of this model treating y, x_1, and x_2 as independent variables subject to a constraint. Note that the reciprocity condition $\partial y^*/\partial w_i = -\partial x_i^*/\partial p$ and the supply slope $\partial y^*/\partial p > 0$ are more easily derived than in the original unconstrained format.

6 Consider the production function $y = x_1^{\alpha_1} x_2^{\alpha_2}$. Show that the constant-output factor-demand functions have the form

$$x_i^* = k_i\, w_i^{-\alpha_j/(\alpha_1 + \alpha_2)} w_j^{\alpha_j/(\alpha_1 + \alpha_2)} y_0^{1/(\alpha_1 + \alpha_2)} \qquad i \neq j$$

Show that the cost function has the form

$$C^* = (k_1 + k_2) w_1^{\alpha_1/(\alpha_1 + \alpha_2)} w_2^{\alpha_2/(\alpha_1 + \alpha_2)} y_0^{1/(\alpha_1 + \alpha_2)}$$

and that $\partial C^*/\partial w_i \equiv x_i^*$.

7 Suppose a production function $y = f(L, K)$ is linear homogeneous.

(*a*) Show that

$$f_{LL} L + f_{LK} K \equiv 0$$

$$f_{KL} L + f_{KK} K \equiv 0$$

(*b*) Show that

$$f_{LL} L^2 = f_{KK} K^2$$

(*c*) If the law of diminishing returns applies to both factors, show that the factors are technical complements; i.e., the marginal product of either factor rises when more of the other factor is applied.

(*d*) Show that if the marginal products are positive, the isoquants must be downward-sloping.

(*e*) Show that

$$\Delta = -\lambda \begin{vmatrix} f_{LL} & f_{LK} & f_L \\ f_{KL} & f_{KK} & f_K \\ f_L & f_K & 0 \end{vmatrix}$$

where Δ is defined as in equation (7-14), and λ is marginal cost.

(*f*) Show that $\Delta = \lambda(y^2/K^2)f_{LL} = \lambda(y^2/L^2)f_{KK}$ if $f(L, K)$ is homogeneous of degree one. Show, therefore, that there can be no "stage I" or "stage III" of the production process if the isoquants are convex to the origin.

SELECTED REFERENCES

Alchian, A. A.: Costs and Outputs in M. Abramovitz (ed.), "The Allocation of Economic Resources," Stanford University Press, Stanford, 1959.

Allen, R. G. D.: "Mathematical Economics," Macmillan & Co., Ltd., London, 1956.

Coase, R. H.: The Nature of the Firm, *Economica*, (N.S.), **4,** 331–351, 1937. Reprinted in American Economic Association, "Readings in Price Theory," Richard D. Irwin, Chicago, 1952.

Hicks, J. R.: "Value and Capital," 2d ed., Clarendon Press, Oxford, 1946.

Samuelson, Paul A.: "Foundations of Economic Analysis," Harvard University Press, Cambridge, Mass., 1948.

Shephard, Ronald W.: "Cost and Production Functions," Princeton University Press, Princeton, N.J., 1953; also the revised version of this book which has become a classic, "Cost and Profit Functions," Princeton University Press, Princeton, N.J., 1970.

THE DERIVATION OF CONSUMERS' DEMAND FUNCTIONS

8.1 INTRODUCTORY REMARKS: THE BEHAVIORAL POSTULATES

In this chapter we shall analyze one other fundamental problem in economics, that of the derivation of a consumer's demand function from the behavioral postulate of maximizing utility. The central theme of this discussion will be to study the structure of models of consumer behavior in order to discover what, if any, refutable hypotheses can be derived. Thus, our analysis is mainly methodological: We wish to find out, in particular, what it is about the postulate of utility maximization subject to constraints that either leads to or fails to generate refutable hypotheses.

The behavioral assertion we shall study is that a consumer engages in some sort of constrained maximizing behavior, the objective of which is to

$$\text{maximize} \qquad U(x_1, x_2, \ldots, x_n) \qquad (8\text{-}1)$$

where $x_1, \ldots, x_n$ represents the goods which the consumer actually consumes, and $U(x_1, \ldots, x_n)$ represents the consumer's own subjective evaluation of the satisfaction, or utility, derived from consuming those commodities. However, we live in a world of scarcity, and as such consumers are faced with making choices concerning the levels of consumption they will undertake. The consequences of scarcity can be summarized by saying that consumers face a budget constraint, assumed to be linear:

$$\text{Budget constraint} \qquad \sum p_i x_i = M \qquad (8\text{-}2)$$

where p_i represents the unit price of commodity x_i, and M is the total budget per time period of the consumer. The classical problem in the theory of the consumer is thus stated as

maximize $$U(x_1, \ldots, x_n)$$

subject to $$\sum p_i x_i = M \qquad (8\text{-}3)$$

The hypothesis (8-3) is often referred to as *rational* behavior, or as what a rational consumer would do. If this were so, then another theory would have to be developed for *irrational* consumers, i.e., consumers who did not obey (8-3). (The question of how these irrational consumers might behave has never been seriously studied, probably for good reason.) Also, utility maximization has been attacked on various introspective grounds, largely having to do with whether people are capable of performing the intricate calculations necessary to achieve a maximum of utility. And, finally, it might be argued by some that since utility is largely unmeasurable, any analysis based on maximizing some unmeasurable quantity is doomed to failure.

All the above criticisms are largely irrelevant. The purpose of formulating these models is to derive refutable hypotheses. In this context, behavior indicated by (8-3) is *asserted* to be true, for all consumers. That is, (8-3) is our basic behavioral postulate. Refutation of (8-3) can come about only if the theorems derived from it are demonstrably shown to be false, on the basis of empirical evidence. This is not a postulate for rational consumers; it is for *all* consumers. If some consumers are found whose actions clearly contradict the implications of (8-3), the proper response is not to accuse them of being irrational; rather, it is our theory which must be accused of being false.†

This admittedly extreme view of the role of theorizing is not lightly taken. The reason is that the *stupidity* hypothesis, and the *disequilibrium* or *slow adjustment* hypotheses are consistent with all observable behavior, and therefore are unable to generate refutable implications. Anything in the world can be explained on the basis that the participants are stupid, or ill-informed, or slow to react, or are somehow in disequilibrium, without theories to describe the above alleged phenomena. These terms are metaphors for a lack of useful theory or the failure to adequately specify the additional constraints on consumers' behavior. We therefore stick our necks out and assert, boldly, that all consumers maximize some utility function subject to constraints, most commonly (though not exclusively, especially if non-price or rationing conditions are imposed) a linear budget constraint of the form (8-2) above. The theory is to be rejected only on the basis of its having been falsified by facts.

---

† A study of chronic psychotics at a New York State mental institution, people whom society has pronounced *irrational* in some sense, showed that psychotics obey the law of demand, i.e., they too buy less when prices are raised, etc. See Battalio, *et al.*, A Test of Consumer Demand Theory Using Observations of Individual Purchases, *Western Economic Journal*, December 1973, pp. 411–428.

We have alluded to the concept of a utility function in earlier chapters; let us now investigate such functions more closely. A utility function is a summary of some aspects of a given individual's tastes, or preferences, regarding the consumption of various bundles of goods. The early marginalists perceived this function as indicating a *cardinal* measure of satisfaction, or utility, received by a consumer upon consumption of goods and services. That is, a steak might have yielded some consumer 10 "utiles," a potato 5 utiles, and hence one steak gave twice the satisfaction of one potato. The total of utiles for all goods consumed was a measure of the overall welfare of the individual.

Toward the end of the nineteenth century, perhaps initially from introspection, the concept of utility as a *cardinal* measure of some inner level of satisfaction was discarded. More importantly, though, economists, particularly Pareto, became aware that no refutable implications of cardinality were derivable that were not also derivable from the concept of utility as a strictly *ordinal* index of preferences. As we shall see presently, all of the known implications of the utility-maximization hypothesis are derivable from the assumption that consumers are merely able to *rank* all commodity bundles, without regard to the intensity of satisfaction gained by consuming a particular commodity bundle. This is by no means a trivial assumption. We assert that all consumers, when faced with a choice of consuming two or more bundles of goods, $\mathbf{x}^1 = (x_1^1, \ldots, x_n^1), \ldots,$ $\mathbf{x}^k = (x_1^k, \ldots, x_n^k)$, can rank all of these bundles of goods in terms of their desirability to that consumer. More specifically, for any two bundles of goods $\mathbf{x}^i$ and $\mathbf{x}^j$, we assert that any consumer can decide among the following three mutually exclusive situations:

1. $\mathbf{x}^i$ is preferred to $\mathbf{x}^j$
2. $\mathbf{x}^j$ is preferred to $\mathbf{x}^i$
3. $\mathbf{x}^i$ and $\mathbf{x}^j$ are equally preferred

Only one category can apply at any one time; if that category should change, we would say that the consumer's tastes, or preferences, have changed. In the important case 3, above, we say that the consumer is indifferent between $\mathbf{x}^i$ and $\mathbf{x}^j$.

The cardinalists wanted to go much farther than this. They wanted to be able to place some psychological measure of the degree to which the consumer was better off if he or she consumed $\mathbf{x}^i$ rather than $\mathbf{x}^j$, in situation 1, above. Such a measure might be useful to, say, psychologists studying human motivation; to economists, it turns out that no additional refutable implications are forthcoming from such knowledge. Hence, cardinality as a feature of utility has been discarded.

The utility function is thus constructed simply as an index. The utility index is to become larger when a more preferred bundle of goods is consumed. Letting $U(\mathbf{x}) = U(x_1, \ldots, x_n)$ designate such an index, for cases 1, 2, and 3, above, $U(\mathbf{x})$ must have the properties, respectively,

1. $U(\mathbf{x}^i) > U(\mathbf{x}^j)$
2. $U(\mathbf{x}^j) > U(\mathbf{x}^i)$
3. $U(\mathbf{x}^i) = U(\mathbf{x}^j)$

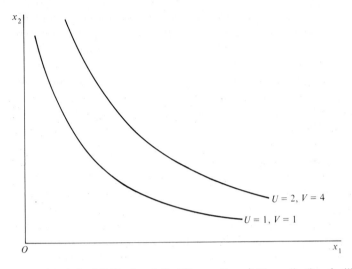

Figure 8-1 *Ordinal Utility Levels (Indifference Curves)* The ordinality of utility functions is expressed by asserting that relabeling the values of the indifference contours of utility functions has no effect on the behavior of consumers.

How is the ordinality of $U(x_1, \ldots, x_n)$ expressed? Consider Fig. 8-1, in which two level curves, or indifference surfaces, are drawn for $U = U(x_1, x_2)$. The inner curve is defined as $U(x_1, x_2) = 1$; the other indifference curve is the locus $U(x_1, x_2) = 2$. Suppose, now, instead of this U index, we decided to label these two loci by the square of U or, by $V = U^2$. Then these two indifference curves, in terms of V units, would have utilities of one and four, respectively. Or, one could consider a third index $W = \log U$, in which the "W-utiles" would be 0 and log 2, respectively. Ordinality means that any one of these utility functions is as good as the other, i.e., they all contain the same information, since they all preserve the *ranking*, though not the cardinal difference, between different indifference levels. In general, starting with any given utility function $U = U(x_1, \ldots, x_n)$, consider any monotonic transformation of U, that is, let $V = F(U(x_1, \ldots, x_n))$ where $dV/dU = F'(U) > 0$. Then V and U always move in the same direction; the V index is merely a relabeling of the U index which preserves the rank ordering of the indifference levels. To say that utility is an ordinal concept is therefore to say that the utility function is arbitrary up to any monotonic (i.e., monotonically increasing) transformation. We shall check and see that all implications regarding observable phenomena that are derivable from asserting the existence of $U(x_1, \ldots, x_n)$ are also derivable from $V = F(U(x_1, \ldots, x_n))$ where $F' > 0$, and vice-versa. Ordinality means that $F(U(x_1, \ldots, x_n))$ conveys the identical information concerning a consumer's preferences as does $U(x_1, \ldots, x_n)$.

The assertion that consumers possess utility functions is a statement that people do in fact have preferences.† How these preferences come to be, and why

---

† The mere existence of preferences, however, may not be enough to guarantee the existence of utility functions. See Chap. 11.

they might differ among people of different countries or ethnic groups, is a discipline outside of economics. These are certainly interesting questions. They are also exceedingly difficult to grapple with. The specialty of economics arose precisely because it was fruitful in many problems to ignore the origins of individuals' tastes and explain certain events on the basis of changes in opportunities, assuming that individuals' tastes remained constant in the interim.

Merely to assert that individuals have tastes or preferences is, however, to assert very little. In order to derive refutable implications from utility analysis, certain other restrictions must be placed on the utility function. To begin with, we shall assume that the utility function is mathematically well behaved, that is, it is sufficiently smooth to be differentiated as often as necessary. This postulate is questioned by some who note that commodity bundles invariably come in discrete packages (except perhaps for liquids, such as water or gasoline), and also, for the case of services, such as visits to the doctor, the units are often difficult to define. We note these objections and then ask, what is to be gained in our analysis by explicitly recognizing the discrete nature of many goods? In most problems, very little is gained, and it is costly in terms of complexity to fully account for discreteness. Again recall the role of assumptions in economic analysis: assumptions are made because there is a trade-off between precision and tractability, or usefulness of theories. It is nearly always impossible to fully characterize any real-world object; simplifying assumptions are therefore a necessary ingredient in any useful theory. Hence, differentiability of utility functions is simply assumed.

In what class of problems is differentiability least likely to be a critical assumption? When consumers either singly or in groups make repeated purchases of a given item, we can convert the analysis from the discrete items to time (flow) rates of consumption. Instead of, say, noting that a consumer purchased one loaf of bread on Monday, another on Friday and another the following Tuesday, we can speak of an average rate of consumption of bread of seven-fourths loaves per week. There is no reason why the average consumption per week, or other time unit, cannot be any real number, thus allowing differentiability of the consumer's utility function. We can speak of continuous *services of goods*, even if the goods themselves are purchased in discrete units.

Assuming consumers possess differentiable utility functions $U = U(x_1, \ldots, x_n)$, the following properties of those functions are asserted. These are not intended to represent a minimum set of mutually exclusive properties; rather, they are the important features of utility functions which are the basis of the neoclassical paradigm of consumer-choice theory.

I Nonsatiation, or "More is preferred to less" All goods which the consumer chooses to consume at positive prices have the property that, other things being equal, more of any good is preferred to less of it. The mathematical translation of this postulate is that if $x_1, \ldots, x_n$ are the goods consumed, the marginal utility of any good x_i is positive, or $U_i = \partial U/\partial x_i > 0$. Increasing any x_i, holding the other goods constant, always leads to a preferred position, i.e., the utility index increases.

II Substitution The consumer, at any point, is willing to give up some of one good to get an additional increment of some other good. This postulate is related to postulate I. The notion of trade-offs is perhaps the critical concept in all of economics. How do we describe the notion of trade-offs mathematically? The reasoning is analogous to that used in the definition of isoquants in the chapter on costs. Consider Fig. 8-2.

The *maximum* amount a consumer will give up of one commodity, say, x_2, to get one unit of x_1 is that amount which will leave the consumer indifferent between the new and the old situation. Starting at point A, the consumer is willing to give up a maximum of two units of x_2, say, to get one unit of x_1. The trade-offs for any consumer are hence defined by the loci of points which are indifferent to the initial point. These curves are the consumer's *indifference curves;* since the consumer is indifferent to all points on the curve, $U(x_1, \ldots, x_n) = U^0 = $ constant for all such points.

The slope of the indifference curve represents the trade-offs a consumer is willing to make. In Fig. 8-2, the slope $= -2$(approximately) at point A; at point B the slope $= -1$, indicating that the consumer will swap x_2 and x_1 one-for-one at that point.

For the case of two commodities, the indifference curves are the level curves of the utility function $U = U(x_1, x_2)$, defined as $U(x_1, x_2) = U^0$. Defining

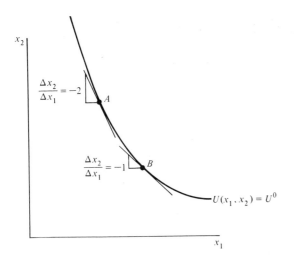

Figure 8-2 *Value, in Economics, Means Exchange Value* The value of any commodity is the maximum amount of some other good that an individual is willing to part with in order to gain an extra unit of the good in question. In the limit (i.e., at the margin) the value of x_1 is therefore given by the slope of the indifference curve through that point. At point A, the marginal value of x_1 is the absolute slope of the level curve [indifference curve $U(x_1, x_2) = U^0$], called the marginal rate of substitution of x_1 for x_2, and is equal to two units of x_2 there. At point B, the marginal value of x_1 is one unit of x_2.

$x_2 = x_2(x_1, U^0)$ from this relation as before, the slope of the indifference curves at any point, using the chain rule, is found by differentiating the identity $U(x_1, x_2(x_1, U^0)) \equiv U^0$ with respect to x_1:

$$U_1 + U_2 \frac{\partial x_2}{\partial x_1} \equiv 0$$

and thus

$$\frac{\partial x_2}{\partial x_1} \equiv \frac{-U_1}{U_2}$$

By postulate I above, U_1 and U_2 are both positive. Hence, $\partial x_2 / \partial x_1 < 0$, or the slope of the indifference curves is negative. For the n-good case,

$$\frac{\partial x_i}{\partial x_j} = \frac{-U_j}{U_i} < 0$$

A negative slope means precisely that the consumer is willing to make trade-offs. The substitution postulate means that the indifference curves are negatively sloped, a situation implied by the postulate that "more is preferred to less." If the indifference curves were positively sloped, consumers would not be trading-off one good to get some of another; rather, the situation would be better characterized by that of bribing the consumer with more of one good in order to accept more of the other. One of the goods must actually be a "bad," with negative marginal utility. Only then can $-U_j/U_i$ be positive; only then would a consumer be indifferent between two consumption bundles, one of which contained more of each item than the other.

The substitution postulate is an explicit denial of the "priority of needs" fallacy. Politicians and pressure groups are forever urging that we "rearrange our priorities," i.e., devote more resources to the goods they value more highly than others. While it is useful for such groups to talk of "needs" and "priorities," it is fallacious for economists to do so. The notion of a trade-off is inconsistent with one good being "prior" to another in consumption.

The ultimate reason for rejecting the notion of priority of some goods over others is by appeal to the empirical facts, however, and not from logic. "Nonpriority" is an empirical assertion. How could one test for it? Consider a consumer who, by all reasonable measures, is considered to be rather poor. Suppose he or she is made even poorer by taxation or appropriation of some of his or her income. As income is lowered, if this consumer held the consumption of all goods except one constant and reduced some other good to zero, and then repeated the process for the other goods, we would have to conclude that such behavior indicated that some goods were prior to others, in fulfilling the person's desires. However, it is unlikely that we should find such individuals. In all likelihood, all people, even very poor people, when faced with a reduction of income will tend to spread out the reduction amongst several goods, rather than merely consuming only less clothing, say, or only less shelter. Real-world behavior is consistent with $U_i > 0$, $i = 1, \ldots, n$ for the goods actually consumed by a given individual.

The notion of substitution and trade-offs provide the critical underpinnings of the concept of *value* in economics. It is only by what people are willing to give up in order to get more of some other good that value can be meaningfully measured. In Fig. 8-2, the consumer at A is willing to give up 2 units of x_2 to get 1 unit of x_1; we conclude from this that the consumer *values* x_1 at 2 units of x_2, or that he or she values x_2 at $\frac{1}{2}$ unit of x_1. This value, indicated by the slope of the indifference curve at some point, is called the marginal rate of substitution (MRS) of x_1 for x_2; it is the marginal value of x_1 in terms of x_2.

The last postulate economists make regarding utility functions is a restriction on the behavior of these marginal values. Specifically, it is asserted that:

III Along any indifference surface, the marginal value of any good decreases as more of that good is consumed This says that

$$\left(\frac{\partial^2 x_j}{\partial x_i^2}\right)_{U^0} > 0 \qquad i, j = 1, \ldots, n$$

We shall show, however, that this generalization of diminishing marginal rate of substitution, while implied by the second-order conditions for maximization of utility subject to a budget constraint, is insufficient in itself to guarantee an interior constrained maximum. The condition required is that the indifference surfaces (actually, "hypersurfaces" in n-dimensions) be convex to the origin, analogous to the convexity of the two-dimensional indifference curves. Mathematically, this is the condition of "quasi-concavity" of the utility function explored in Chap. 6. Its algebraic formulation, none too intuitive, is that the border-preserving principal minors of the bordered hessian below alternate in sign:

$$H = \begin{vmatrix} U_{11} & \cdots & U_{1n} & U_1 \\ U_{21} & \cdots & U_{2n} & U_2 \\ \cdots\cdots\cdots\cdots\cdots\cdots\cdots \\ U_{n1} & \cdots & U_{nn} & U_n \\ U_1 & \cdots & U_n & 0 \end{vmatrix} \tag{8-4}$$

The border-preserving principal minors of order 2 in H above have the form

$$H_2^{ij} = \begin{vmatrix} U_{ii} & U_{ij} & U_i \\ U_{ji} & U_{jj} & U_j \\ U_i & U_j & 0 \end{vmatrix} = -(U_{ii}U_j^2 - 2U_{ij}U_iU_j + U_{jj}U_i^2)$$

In Chaps. 3 and 6 we found

$$\frac{d^2 x_2}{dx_1^2} = \frac{d(-U_1/U_2)}{dx_1}$$

$$= \frac{-1}{U_2^3}(U_{11}U_2^2 - 2U_{12}U_1U_2 + U_{22}U_1^2)$$

The bordered Hessian H_2^{ij} above is precisely a generalization of this to the case of n goods, wherein all goods except x_i and x_j are held constant. $H_2^{ij} > 0$ then says that in that x_i, x_j (hyper)plane, at stipulated values of the x_k's, $k \neq i, j$, the MRS of x_i for x_j decreases, or $\partial^2 x_j / \partial x_i^2 > 0$. If this diminishing MRS holds for *every* pair of goods x_i and x_j, $i, j = 1, \ldots, n$, this says only that all the border-preserving principal minors of order two are positive; this is insufficient information from which to infer anything about the higher-order minors or H itself. Hence the notion that the indifference hypersurface is convex to the origin is a much stronger assumption, in an n-good world, than simply diminishing MRS between any pair of goods, other goods held constant. Only in the case of only two goods, wherein there are no other goods to be held constant, is quasi-concavity equivalent to diminishing MRS.

All the above postulates can be summarized as saying that we assert that all consumers possess utility functions $U = U(x_1, \ldots, x_n)$ which are differentiable everywhere, and which are strictly increasing $(U_i > 0, i = 1, \ldots, n)$ and strictly quasi-concave. The adjective "strictly" is used to denote that there are no flat portions of the indifference curves anywhere; this guarantees uniqueness of all our solutions.

These mathematical restrictions are asserted not merely because they guarantee an interior solution to the constrained utility-maximization problem, which they do, but more fundamentally, because such restrictions are believed to be confirmed by data involving real people. To deny these postulates is to assert strange behavior. As in the case of factor demands discussed in an earlier chapter, the assumption that, for example, indifference curves are concave to the origin implies that consumers will spend all of their budget on one good. A corner solution is achieved, point B in Fig. 8-3. At certain prices, only x_1 will be consumed. Then, as p_1 is increased past a certain level, the consumer suddenly switches over entirely to x_2. This inflexible and then erratic behavior is hard (impossible?) to find in the real world; it is for that reason and that reason only that the assumption of quasi-concavity is made.

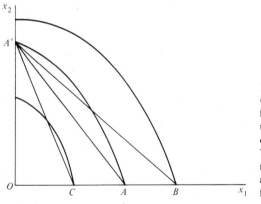

Figure 8-3 *Nonquasi-concave Indifference Curves* As p_1 increases, the budget line shifts from $A'B$ to $A'A$ to $A'C$. The maximum utility point will change suddenly from lying on the x_1 axis, to lying on the x_2 axis at A'. This behavior is not observed; for that reason it is asserted that indifference surfaces are convex to the origin, i.e., the utility function is quasi-concave.

8.2 UTILITY MAXIMIZATION

Let us now begin our analysis of the problem at hand, stated in relations (8-3),

maximize $\qquad\qquad\qquad U(x_1, \ldots, x_n)$

subject to $\qquad\qquad\qquad \sum p_i x_i = M$

We will, for simplicity, consider the two-variable case only, in the formal analysis, and briefly sketch the generalizations to n variables.

Suppose, then, the consumer consumes two goods, x_1 and x_2, in positive amounts. These goods are purchased in a competitive market at constant unit prices p_1 and p_2, respectively. The consumer comes to the market with an amount of money income, M. Under the assumption of nonsatiation, the consumer will spend all of his or her income M on x_1 and x_2, since M itself does not appear in the utility function. Income M is useful only for the purchase of x_1 and x_2, as expressed by writing the utility function as $U = U(x_1, x_2)$.

We assert that the consumer (i.e., all consumers) act to

maximize $\qquad\qquad\qquad U = U(x_1, x_2)$

subject to $\qquad\qquad p_1 x_1 + p_2 x_2 = M \qquad\qquad\qquad$ (8-5)

A necessary consequence of this behavior is that the first partials of the following lagrangian equal zero:

$$\mathscr{L} = U(x_1, x_2) + \mu(M - p_1 x_1 - p_2 x_2) \qquad\qquad (8\text{-}6)$$

where μ is the Lagrange multiplier. Hence

$$\mathscr{L}_1 = U_1 - \mu p_1 = 0 \qquad\qquad\qquad (8\text{-}7a)$$

$$\mathscr{L}_2 = U_2 - \mu p_2 = 0 \qquad\qquad\qquad (8\text{-}7b)$$

$$\mathscr{L}_\mu = M - p_1 x_1 - p_2 x_2 = 0 \qquad\qquad (8\text{-}7c)$$

The sufficient second-order condition for this constrained maximum is that the bordered hessian determinant of the second partials of $\mathscr{L}$ be positive:

$$D = \begin{vmatrix} \mathscr{L}_{11} & \mathscr{L}_{12} & \mathscr{L}_{1\mu} \\ \mathscr{L}_{21} & \mathscr{L}_{22} & \mathscr{L}_{2\mu} \\ \mathscr{L}_{\mu 1} & \mathscr{L}_{\mu 2} & \mathscr{L}_{\mu\mu} \end{vmatrix} = \begin{vmatrix} U_{11} & U_{12} & -p_1 \\ U_{21} & U_{22} & -p_2 \\ -p_1 & -p_2 & 0 \end{vmatrix} > 0 \qquad (8\text{-}8)$$

We will, of course, assume that D is strictly greater than zero; only $D \geq 0$ is implied by the maximization hypothesis.

Thus far we have accomplished little. Most of the terms in equations (8-7) and (8-8) are unobservable, containing the derivatives of an ordinal utility function. As we have repeatedly emphasized, the only propositions of interest are those which may lead to refutable hypotheses; in order to do so, all terms must be capable of being observed. Thus the objects of our inquiry are the demand functions which are implied by the system of equations (8-7). These three equations contain six separate terms: x_1, x_2, μ, p_1, p_2, and M. Under the conditions specified by the implicit function theorem, that the jacobian determinant formed by the first partials of these equations ($\mathscr{L}_1 = 0$, $\mathscr{L}_2 = 0$ and $\mathscr{L}_\mu = 0$) is not equal to zero, this system can be solved, in principal, for the variables x_1, x_2, and μ in terms of the remaining three, p_1, p_2, and M. In fact, this jacobian is simply the determinant D above, in equation (8-8). Each row of D consists of the first partials of the corresponding first-order equation in (8-7). Since the system of equations (8-7) is itself the first partials of $\mathscr{L}$, the jacobian determinant consists of the second partials of $\mathscr{L}$, with respect to x_1, x_2, and μ. The *sufficient* second-order conditions guarantee that $D \neq 0$ (in fact, $D > 0$), hence in this case we can write,

$$x_1 = x_1^*(p_1, p_2, M) \tag{8-9a}$$

$$x_2 = x_2^*(p_1, p_2, M) \tag{8-9b}$$

$$\mu = \mu^*(p_1, p_2, M) \tag{8-9c}$$

Equations (8-9) are the *simultaneous* solution of equations (8-7). Note the parameters involved: prices and money income. Equations (8-9a) and (8-9b) indicate the chosen levels of consumption for any given set of prices and money income. Hence, these equations represent what are commonly referred to as the *money-income-held-constant* demand curves. The phrase "money income held constant" is somewhat of a misnomer. Money income M is simply one of the three parameters upon which demand depends. The phrase arose from the usual graphical treatment of these demand curves in which p_1, say, is plotted vertically and x_1 is plotted on the horizontal axis, as in Fig. 8-4. In this usual graph, since only two dimensions are available, only the parameter p_1 is varied, and p_2 and M are held fixed at some levels p_2^0 and M^0. Thus this graph really represents a projection of the function $x_1 = x_1^*(p_1, p_2, M)$ onto a plane parallel to the x_1, p_1 axes, at some fixed levels of p_2 and M. Because these two-dimensional graphs obscure the other

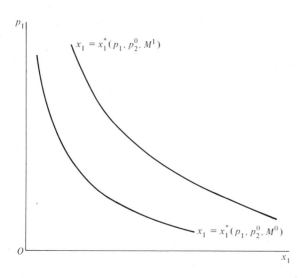

p_1

$x_1 = x_1^*(p_1, p_2^0, M^1)$

$x_1 = x_1^*(p_1, p_2^0, M^0)$

O

x_1

Figure 8-4 *The Money-income-held-constant Demand Curve* The notion that "money income is held constant" is simply a way of stating that in fact x_1 is a function not only of p_1, against which it is plotted, but also p_2 and M. What is being held constant is merely a convention as to which variables are chosen to be plotted. In the usual case, depicted here, where x_1 is plotted against its price p_1, changes in M result in a different projection of the demand curve $x_1^*(p_1, p_2, M)$, and hence the drawn demand curve in the figure shifts.

variables in the demand curve, one has to specify what they are; e.g., in this case they are p_2 and M. These *ceteris paribus* (other things held fixed) conditions are simply another way of indicating exactly what variables are present in the demand function. "Movements along" the demand curve $x_1 = x_1^*(p_1, p_2, M)$ simply refer to the response of quantity x_1 to changes in its own price p_1 where "shifts in the demand curve" represent responses to either p_2 or M. But it all depends on which variables are chosen to be graphed.

Although the marginal relations from which they are solved are not observable, the demand relations (8-9a) and (8-9b) relate to observable variables, and hence are potentially interesting.

If the demand functions (8-9a) and (8-9b) are substituted into $U(x_1, x_2)$, one obtains the *indirect utility function*

$$U^*(p_1, p_2, M) \equiv U(x_1^*(p_1, p_2, M), x_2^*(p_1, p_2, M)) \tag{8-10}$$

Note that U^* is a function only of the parameters: prices and money income. The function $U^*(p_1, p_2, M)$ gives the maximum value of utility for any given prices and money income p_1, p_2, M, since it is precisely those quantities x_1 and x_2 that maximize utility subject to the budget constraint that are substituted into $U(x_1, x_2)$.

Let us now investigate the first-order marginal relations (8-7). In so doing, we can discover some aspects of the nature of maximizing behavior and some of the properties of the demand relations (8-9a) and (8-9b). The first proposition is one alluded to earlier, that no assumption of cardinality is necessary for the derivation of the demand curves $x_i^*(p_1, p_2, M)$; the same demand curves will occur if the indifference levels are relabeled by some monotonic transformation of $U(x_1, x_2)$.

Proposition 1 The demand curves implied by the assertion

maximize $\qquad\qquad\qquad\qquad U(x_1, x_2)$

subject to $\qquad\qquad\qquad\quad p_1 x_1 + p_2 x_2 = M$

are identical to those derived when $U(x_1, x_2)$ is replaced by $V(x_1, x_2) = F(U(x_1, x_2))$, where $F'(U) > 0$.

PROOF Consider how the demand curves are in fact derived. The two demand curves $x_1^*(p_1, p_2, M)$ and $x_2^*(p_1, p_2, M)$ are derived from a tangency condition and the budget constraint. The tangency condition is obtained by eliminating the Lagrange multiplier μ from equations (8-7a) and (8-7b), or

$$\frac{U_1}{U_2} = \frac{p_1}{p_2} \tag{8-11}$$

(This is the condition that would be obtained without the use of lagrangian methods.) This equation, and the budget constraint

$$M - p_1 x_1 - p_2 x_2 = 0$$

are the two equations whose solutions are the demand curves above. How are these equations affected by replacing $U(x_1, x_2)$ by $V(x_1, x_2) = F(U(x_1, x_2))$, that is, by relabeling the indifference map, but preserving the rank ordering? Instead of (8-11) we get

$$\frac{V_1}{V_2} = \frac{p_1}{p_2} \tag{8-12}$$

However, $V_1 = F'(U)U_1$, $V_2 = F'(U)U_2$, and therefore

$$\frac{V_1}{V_2} = \frac{F'U_1}{F'U_2} = \frac{U_1}{U_2} = \frac{p_1}{p_2}$$

Since V_1/V_2 is identically U_1/U_2 everywhere, the equations used to solve for the demand curves are unchanged by such a transformation of U. That is, the solutions of (8-11) and the budget constraint are identical to the solutions of (8-12) and the budget constraint.

We are not quite done, however. It remains to be shown that $V_1/V_2 = p_1/p_2$ is indeed a point of *maximum*, rather than minimum utility subject to constraint. That is, one must check that the consumer will actually set $V_1/V_2 = p_1/p_2$. We suspect that if $F' < 0$, then V_1/V_2 would still equal U_1/U_2, but $V_1/V_2 = p_1/p_2$ would not be a tangency relating to *maximum* utility, since with $F' < 0$, increases in both x_1 and x_2, which would increase U, will *decrease* V. Hence we must check to see if the second-order conditions are satisfied by $F(U(x_1, x_2))$, given $F' > 0$.

Since $V_1 = F'(U)U_1$, using the product and chain rules, $V_{11} = F'U_{11} + U_1 F''U_1$, and in general

$$V_{ij} = F'U_{ij} + F''U_i U_j \tag{8-13}$$

Hence the second-order condition for $V(x_1, x_2)$ is

$$
D' = \begin{vmatrix} V_{11} & V_{12} & -p_1 \\ V_{21} & V_{22} & -p_2 \\ -p_1 & -p_2 & 0 \end{vmatrix}
$$

$$
= \begin{vmatrix} F'U_{11} + F''U_1^2 & F'U_{12} + F''U_1 U_2 & -p_1 \\ F'U_{21} + F''U_1 U_2 & F'U_{22} + F''U_2^2 & -p_2 \\ -p_1 & -p_2 & 0 \end{vmatrix} > 0 \tag{8-14}
$$

Is (8-14) equivalent to (8-8)? Noting that $p_1 = U_1/\mu$, $p_2 = U_2/\mu$,

$$
D' = \frac{1}{\mu} \begin{vmatrix} F'U_{11} + F''U_1^2 & F'U_{12} + F''U_1 U_2 & -p_1 \\ F'U_{21} + F''U_1 U_2 & F'U_{22} + F''U_2^2 & -p_2 \\ -U_1 & -U_2 & 0 \end{vmatrix}
$$

If the last row is multiplied by $F''U_2$ and then added to the second row, the value of the determinant is unaffected. But this operation has the effect of eliminating the terms $F''U_1 U_2$ and $F''U_2^2$ from the first and second elements in row two. Also, if row three is multiplied by $F''U_1$, and row three is added to row one, the terms $F''U_1^2$ and $F''U_1 U_2$ are eliminated there. Reassembling the last row to the prices,

$$D' = \begin{vmatrix} F'U_{11} & F'U_{12} & -p_1 \\ F'U_{21} & F'U_{22} & -p_2 \\ -p_1 & -p_2 & 0 \end{vmatrix}$$

Now factor out F' from the first two rows.

$$D' = (F')^2 \begin{vmatrix} U_{11} & U_{12} & \dfrac{-p_1}{F'} \\ U_{21} & U_{22} & \dfrac{-p_2}{F'} \\ -p_1 & -p_2 & 0 \end{vmatrix}$$

Multiplying the last column by F', and dividing by same out front,

$$D' = F' \begin{vmatrix} U_{11} & U_{12} & -p_1 \\ U_{21} & U_{22} & -p_2 \\ -p_1 & -p_2 & 0 \end{vmatrix} = F'D$$

Hence D', the bordered hessian associated with $V(x_1, x_2) = F(U(x_1, x_2))$, is identically D, the bordered hessian for $U(x_1, x_2)$ multiplied by F'. Since $F' > 0$, D' and D have the same sign, and therefore $F(U(x_1, x_2))$ achieves a maximum whenever $U(x_1, x_2)$ does, and vice versa. This completes the proof of proposition 1.

The demand curves are independent of any monotonic transformation of the utility function; i.e., they are independent of any relabeling of the indifference map. This proposition simply reinforces the notion that it is only *exchange values* that matter. Along any indifference curve, the slope measures the trade-offs a consumer is willing to make with regard to giving up one commodity to get more of another. These marginal evaluations of goods are the only operational measures of value; it matters not one whit whether that indifference curve is labeled as 10 utiles or 10,000 or 10^{10} utiles. It is the *slope*, and only the slope, of that level curve that matters for value and exchange, not some index of "satisfaction" associated with any given consumption bundle. In fact, it is impossible to tell whether a consumer is pleased or displeased to consume a given commodity bundle. If those are the only goods over which he or she has to make decisions, the *exchange* values do not in any way reflect whether the consumer is ecstatic or miserable with his or her lot.

The above derivation also makes clear why the concept of *diminishing marginal utility* is irrelevant in modern economics. With strictly ordinal utility, the rate at which marginal utility changes with respect to commodity changes depends on the particular index ranking used. Consider the relation between V_{ij} and U_{ij}:

$$V_{ij} = F'U_{ij} + F''U_i U_j \qquad (8\text{-}15)$$

Now $F' > 0$ is assumed, and U_i and U_j are positive by nonsatiation. However, F'' can be positive or negative; for example, if $F(U) = \log U$, $F' > 0$ and $F'' < 0$; if $F(U) = e^U$, $F' > 0$, $F'' > 0$. Suppose $U_{ij} < 0$. Then if V is chosen so that $F'' > 0$, it is possible that $V_{ij} > 0$. Similarly, if $U_{ij} > 0$, there is some monotonic transformation which would make $V_{ij} < 0$, by having F'' sufficiently negative. Hence U_{ij} and V_{ij} (which include the case U_{ii} and V_{ii}) need not have the same sign, and yet the identical demand curves are implied for each utility function! Thus a given set of observable demand relations is consistent with a utility function exhibiting diminishing marginal utility and some monotonic transformation of it exhibiting increasing marginal utility. Hence, the rate of increase or decrease of marginal utility carries no observable implications.

In a similar vein, economists once defined complementary or substitute goods in terms of marginal utilities as follows: Two goods were called complements if consuming more of one raised the marginal utility of the other; and vice versa for substitutes. For example, it was argued that increasing one's consumption of pretzels raised the marginal utility of beer, hence beer and pretzels were complements. The algebra above shows why this reasoning is fallacious. The term being considered in this definition is $\partial U_i / \partial x_j = U_{ij} = U_{ji}$. But if $U_{ij} > 0$, say, some monotonic transformation of U, $F(U)$, with $F'' < 0$ can produce a new utility function with $\partial V_i / \partial x_j = V_{ij} < 0$, opposite to U_{ij}, and yet imply the same *observable* behavior, summarized in the demand relations. Hence this definition is incapable of categorizing observable behavior and is thus useless.

We now come to the second proposition concerning the demand curves which can be inferred directly from the first-order relations (8-7):

Proposition 2 The demand curves $x_i = x_i^*(p_1, p_2, M)$ are homogeneous of degree zero in p_1, p_2, and M. That is, $x_i^*(tp_1, tp_2, tM) \equiv x_i^*(p_1, p_2, M)$.

PROOF Suppose all prices and money income are multiplied by some factor t. Then the utility maximum problem becomes

maximize
$$U(x_1, x_2)$$

subject to
$$tp_1 x_1 + tp_2 x_2 = tM$$

But this "new" budget constraint is clearly equivalent to the old one, $p_1 x_1 + p_2 x_2 = M$. Hence the first- and second-order equations are identical for these two problems, and thus the demand curves derived from this one, being solutions of those same first-order equations, are unchanged.

The meaning of this proposition is that it is only *relative* prices that matter to consumers, not absolute prices, or absolute money-income levels. This simply reinforces the tangency condition $U_1 / U_2 = p_1 / p_2$. It is the price *ratios* and the ratios of income to prices which determine marginal values and exchanges. Again, as mentioned earlier in the chapter on cost, some economists in the 1930s argued that consumers and producers would react to changes in nominal price levels even if real (relative) price levels remained unchanged. This concept, called money illusion, has been largely discarded. It was a denial of the homogeneity of demand curves.

Interpretation of the Lagrange Multiplier

Let us now consider the meaning of the Lagrange multiplier μ. From the first-order relations

$$\mu^* = \frac{U_1}{p_1} = \frac{U_2}{p_2}$$

Also, by multiplying (8-7a) by x_1^*, (8-7b) by x_2^* and adding,

$$U_1 x_1^* + U_2 x_2^* = \mu^*(p_1 x_1^* + p_2 x_2^*) = \mu^* M$$

Hence
$$\mu^* = \frac{U_1}{p_1} = \frac{U_2}{p_2} = \frac{U_1 x_1^* + U_2 x_2^*}{M} \qquad (8\text{-}16)$$

These relations provide an important clue to the interpretation of μ^*. At any given consumption point, a certain amount of additional utility U_1 can be gained by consuming an additional increment of x_1. However, the marginal cost of this extra x_1 is p_1. Hence the marginal utility per dollar expenditure on x_1 is U_1/p_1. Similarly, the marginal utility per dollar expenditure on x_2 is U_2/p_2. What the first equalities in (8-16) therefore say is that at a constrained maximum, the marginal utility per dollar must be the same at "both margins," i.e., for x_1 and x_2. If $U_1/p_1 > U_2/p_2$, say, the consumer could increase his or her utility with the same budget expenditure simply by reallocating expenditures from x_2 to x_1.

What of the third equality in (8-16)? This relation says that the marginal utility per dollar must occur when the incremental expenditure is spread out over both commodities, as when it is spent at either margin. It is an envelope-related phenomenon, exhibiting the property that the rate of change of the objective function with respect to a parameter is the same, whether or not the decision variables adjust to that change. The rate of change of utility with respect to income is the same at each margin, and at all margins simultaneously.

Thus far, however, we have not shown mathematically what has been inferred on the basis of intuition. To say that μ^* is the marginal utility of money income is to say that $\mu^* = \partial U^*/\partial M$, where again

$$U^*(p_1, p_2, M) = U(x_1^*(p_1, p_2, M), x_2^*(p_1, p_2, M)) \qquad (8\text{-}10)$$

This can be shown directly. Differentiating (8-10),

$$\frac{\partial U^*}{\partial M} \equiv \frac{\partial U}{\partial x_1} \frac{\partial x_1^*}{\partial M} + \frac{\partial U}{\partial x_2} \frac{\partial x_2^*}{\partial M}$$

$$\equiv U_1 \frac{\partial x_1^*}{\partial M} + U_2 \frac{\partial x_2^*}{\partial M} \qquad (8\text{-}17)$$

Using the first-order relations (8-7), $U_1 = \mu^* p_1$, $U_2 = \mu^* p_2$,

$$\frac{\partial U^*}{\partial M} \equiv \mu^* \left(p_1 \frac{\partial x_1^*}{\partial M} + p_2 \frac{\partial x_2^*}{\partial M} \right) \tag{8-18}$$

Now consider the budget constraint $p_1 x_1 + p_2 x_2 = M$. When the demand curves are substituted back into this equation, one gets the identity

$$p_1 x_1^* + p_2 x_2^* \equiv M$$

Differentiating with respect to M yields

$$p_1 \frac{\partial x_1^*}{\partial M} + p_2 \frac{\partial x_2^*}{\partial M} \equiv 1 \tag{8-19}$$

But this is precisely the expression in parentheses in equation (8-18), above. Hence, substituting (8-19) into (8-18) yields

$$\mu^* \equiv \frac{\partial U^*}{\partial M} \tag{8-20}$$

What we have just done is in fact merely a rederivation of the envelope theorem for the utility-maximization problem. Using the envelope theorem, recalling that the lagrangian $\mathscr{L} = U(x_1, x_2) + \mu(M - p_1 x_1 - p_2 x_2)$,

$$\frac{\partial U^*}{\partial M} = \frac{\partial \mathscr{L}}{\partial M} = \mu^*$$

Nonsatiation implies that $\mu^* = \partial U^* / \partial M > 0$.

Example Consider the utility function $U = x_1 x_2$. The level curves of this utility function are the rectangular hyperbolas $x_1 x_2 = U^0 = $ constant. What are the money-income demand curves associated with this utility function? The lagrangian for this problem is

$$\mathscr{L} = x_1 x_2 + \mu(M - p_1 x_1 - p_2 x_2)$$

The first-order equations are thus

$$\mathscr{L}_1 = x_2 - \mu p_1 = 0$$
$$\mathscr{L}_2 = x_1 - \mu p_2 = 0$$
$$\mathscr{L}_\mu = M - p_1 x_1 - p_2 x_2 = 0$$

The demand curves are the simultaneous solutions of these equations. Before proceeding, let us check the second-order determinant. Noting that $U_{11} = U_{22} = 0$, $U_{12} = U_{21} = 1$,

$$D = \begin{vmatrix} 0 & 1 & -p_1 \\ 1 & 0 & -p_2 \\ -p_1 & -p_2 & 0 \end{vmatrix} = 2p_1 p_2 > 0$$

The second-order condition is satisfied since both prices are assumed to be positive.

Returning to the first-order equations, eliminate μ from the first two equations:

$$x_2 = \mu p_1, \qquad x_1 = \mu p_2$$

Dividing

$$\frac{x_2}{x_1} = \frac{p_1}{p_2}$$

or

$$p_2 x_2 = p_1 x_1$$

This equation says, incidentally, that the total amount spent on x_1, $(p_1 x_1)$, always equals the amount spent on x_2, $(p_2 x_2)$, at any set of prices. We should thus expect the demand curves to be unitary elastic. (Why?)

The relation $p_2 x_2 = p_1 x_1$ is derived solely from the tangency condition $U_1/U_2 = p_1/p_2$, not at all from the budget constraint. This equation therefore holds for all possible income levels. It is the locus of all points (x_1, x_2) where the slopes of the level curves are equal to $-p_1/p_2$. Hence, $p_2 x_2 = p_1 x_1$ represents what is called the *income-consumption* path, shown in Fig. 8-5. The income-consumption path, one of the so-called Engel curves, illustrates how a consumer would respond to changes in income, holding prices constant. Rewriting the present equation slightly as $x_2 = (p_1/p_2)x_1$, we see that the income-consumption path is a straight line, or ray, emanating from the origin. [The point $(0, 0)$ obviously satisfies the equation, and x_2 is a linear function of x_1.] The slope of this line is p_1/p_2. Since the income-consumption path is a straight line, by an easy exercise in similar triangles, a given percentage increase in money income M leads to that same percentage increase in the

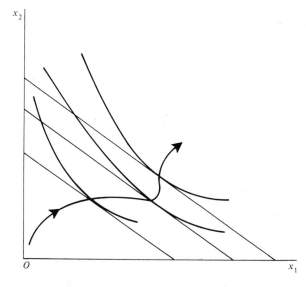

Figure 8-5 *The Income-Consumption Path* The income-consumption path is the locus of all tangencies of the indifference curves to various budget constraints. That is, it is the locus of points (x_1, x_2) such that $U_1/U_2 = p_1/p_2$, where the slope of the indifference curve equals the slope of the budget constraint. This equation is independent of money income M; hence it represents the solutions of the first-order equations that correspond to all values of M. As M is increased, the implied consumption bundle moves in the direction of the arrow along the curve, reaching higher indifference levels for higher M.

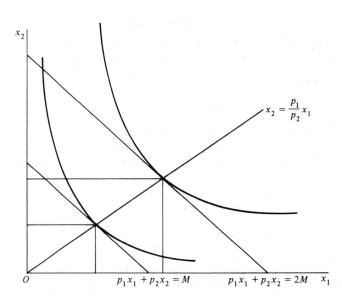

Figure 8-6 *The Income-Consumption Path for the Utility Function $U = x_1 x_2$* The income-consumption path is the solution of the tangency condition $U_1/U_2 = p_1/p_2$. For the utility function $U = x_1 x_2$, $U_1 = x_2$, $U_2 = x_1$, thus the income-consumption path is $x_2/x_1 = p_1/p_2$, or $x_2 = (p_1/p_2)x_1$. This is represented geometrically as a straight line emanating from the origin. Doubling M will move the budget constraint twice as far from the origin as previously; when this is done for this utility function, clearly the consumption of x_1 and x_2 will exactly double. Hence, we expect to find demand curves with unitary income elasticities for this utility function.

consumption of both commodities (see Fig. 8-6). We therefore expect to find that the demand curves derived from this utility function ($U = x_1 x_2$) possess unitary income elasticity as well as unitary price elasticity. In order to derive the demand curves, the budget constraint must be brought in. The demand curves, we recall, are the simultaneous solutions of the tangency condition $U_1/U_2 = p_1/p_2$ and the budget constraint $p_1 x_1 + p_2 x_2 = M$. Since the former gives $p_2 x_2 = p_1 x_1$, substitute this into the budget equation, yielding

$$p_1 x_1 + (p_1 x_1) = M$$

or

$$2p_1 x_1 = M$$

Therefore

$$x_1 = x_1^* = \frac{M}{2p_1}$$

is the implied demand curve for x_1. In similar fashion,

$$x_2 = x_2^* = \frac{M}{2p_2}$$

is the implied demand curve for x_2.

Let us check the properties of these demand curves. We note, first, $\partial x_1^* / \partial p_1 = -M/2p_1^2 < 0$, $\partial x_2^* / \partial p_2 = -M/2p_2^2 < 0$; the demand curves are downward-sloping. The cross effects are both 0; since x_1^* is not a function of p_2, and x_2^* is not a function of p_1, $\partial x_1^* / \partial p_2 = \partial x_2^* / \partial p_1 = 0$. This is a very unusual property for the money-income demand curves. In general, $\partial x_i^* / \partial p_j \neq \partial x_j^* / \partial p_i \neq 0$, $i \neq j$.

The price elasticity of each demand curve is given by

$$\varepsilon_{ii} = \frac{p_i}{x_i^*} \frac{\partial x_i^*}{\partial p_i}$$

Thus, for $x_1^* = M/2p_1$, $\partial x_1^* / \partial p_1 = -M/2p_1^2$. However,

$$p_1/x_1^* = p_1/(M/2p_1) = 2p_1^2/M.$$

Hence,

$$\varepsilon_{11} = \frac{p_1}{x_1^*} \frac{\partial x_1^*}{\partial p_1} = \frac{2p_1^2}{M} \frac{-M}{2p_1^2} = -1$$

with a similar result for ε_{22}. As indicated earlier, the price elasticities of demand are indeed equal to 1, as expected, since total expenditures $p_1 x_1$ and $p_2 x_2$ are the same for all prices.

Regarding the income elasticities,

$$\varepsilon_{1M} = \frac{M}{x_1^*} \frac{\partial x_1^*}{\partial M}$$

Here, $\partial x_1^* / \partial M = 1/2p_1$, $M/x_1 = M/(M/2p_1) = 2p_1$. Hence, $\varepsilon_{1M} = 1$ as expected from the linearity of the income-consumption path. Similar algebra shows that $\varepsilon_{2M} = 1$ also.

8.3 THE RELATIONSHIP BETWEEN THE MAXIMUM-UTILITY MODEL AND THE COST-MINIMIZATION MODEL

In the previous chapter we studied the problem,

minimize $\qquad\qquad C = w_1 x_1 + w_2 x_2$

subject to $\qquad\qquad f(x_1, x_2) = y_0$

where $y = f(x_1, x_2)$ was a production function, and w_1 and w_2 were the factor prices. Consider now a problem mathematically identical to this, that of minimizing the cost, or expenditure, of achieving a given utility level U^0, or

minimize $\qquad\qquad M = p_1 x_1 + p_2 x_2$

subject to $\qquad\qquad U(x_1, x_2) = U^0 \qquad\qquad\qquad (8\text{-}21)$

where p_1 and p_2 are the prices of the two consumer goods x_1 and x_2, respectively, and $U = U(x_1, x_2)$ is a utility function. The entire analysis of the previous chapter applies to this cost-minimization problem. The only changes are in the interpretation of the variables; the mathematical structure is the same.

The first-order conditions for this problem are given by setting the partials of the appropriate lagrangian equal to 0:

$$\mathcal{L} = p_1 x_1 + p_2 x_2 + \lambda(U^0 - U(x_1, x_2))$$

$$\mathcal{L}_1 = p_1 - \lambda U_1 = 0 \tag{8-22a}$$

$$\mathcal{L}_2 = p_2 - \lambda U_2 = 0 \tag{8-22b}$$

$$\mathcal{L}_\lambda = U^0 - U(x_1, x_2) = 0 \tag{8-22c}$$

The sufficient second-order condition for a constrained minimum is that the determinant Δ be negative:

$$\Delta = \begin{vmatrix} -\lambda U_{11} & -\lambda U_{12} & -U_1 \\ -\lambda U_{21} & -\lambda U_{22} & -U_2 \\ -U_1 & -U_2 & 0 \end{vmatrix} < 0 \tag{8-23}$$

Assuming (8-22) and (8-23) hold, demand curves of the following type are implied, as simultaneous solutions to the first-order relations (8-22):

$$x_1 = x_1^*(p_1, p_2, U^0) \tag{8-24a}$$

$$x_2 = x_2^*(p_1, p_2, U^0) \tag{8-24b}$$

Also, an equation for λ^* is determined:

$$\lambda = \lambda^*(p_1, p_2, U^0) \tag{8-24c}$$

What is the relation between the demand curves (8-24), derived from cost-minimization, $x_i = x_i^*(p_1, p_2, U^0)$, $i = 1, 2$, and the demand curves (8-9), derived from utility-maximization, $x_i = x_i^*(p_1, p_2, M)$, $i = 1, 2$? To avoid notational confusion, let us refer to the demand relations (8-9) as

$$x_i = x_i^M(p_1, p_2, M) \qquad i = 1, 2 \tag{8-9}$$

and the others as

$$x_i = x_i^U(p_1, p_2, U^0) \qquad i = 1, 2 \tag{8-24}$$

Consider the first-order relations (8-22a) and (8-22b). Eliminating λ yields

$$\frac{p_1}{p_2} = \frac{U_1}{U_2}$$

This is the same tangency condition as that derived in the utility-maximization problem. In both cases, the budget line must be tangent to the indifference curve. In fact, consider Fig. 8-7. In the utility-maximization problem, given parametric prices and money income M some maximum level of utility U^* will be achieved, at, say, point A, where the consumer will consume x_1^* and x_2^* amounts of x_1 and x_2, respectively.

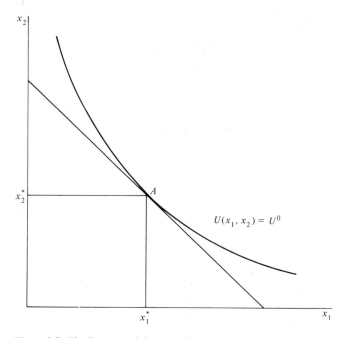

Figure 8-7 *The Tangency Solution to Both the Cost-minimization* and *Utility-maximization Problems*
If $U(x_1, x_2)$ is maximized subject to $p_1 x_1 + p_2 x_2 = M$, some level of utility U^* will be achieved at point A. If now U^* is set equal to U^0, and the consumer minimizes the cost of achieving $U^* = U^0$, the point A will again be achieved. However, the comparative statics of the two problems differs, because the parameters of each problem are not identical (see Fig. 8-8a and b).

Suppose now the indifference level U^* were specified in advance; that is, $U^* = U^0$, and the consumer minimized the cost of achieving $U^* = U^0$, with the same prices. Then, clearly, the consumer would wind up at the same A, consuming the package (x_1^*, x_2^*). But the comparative statics of the two problems are *not* the same! The adjustments to price changes are different because different things are being held constant. Consider Fig. 8-8. In the case $x_i = x_i^M(p_1, p_2, M)$, as p_1, say, is lowered, the budget line MM' swings out along the x_1 axis to MM'' to a new, higher intercept, as depicted in panel (*a*). This increases the achieved utility level to U^{**}. However, in the cost-minimization problem [panel (*b*)], if p_1 is lowered, the level of U is parametric: it is held fixed at U^0. It is the achieved minimum budget M^* that decreases, as the new tangency at A'' is reached, at the new expenditure level M^{**}.

Whereas the demand curves (8-9), $x_i = x_i^M(p_1, p_2, M)$ are called the "*money income* held constant" demand curves, the demand curves (8-24), $x_i = x_i^U(p_1, p_2, U^0)$ are called the "*real income* held constant," or "income-compensated" demand curves. These latter curves hold utility, or "real" income, constant; they are mathematically equivalent to the "output held constant" factor demands of the previous chapter.

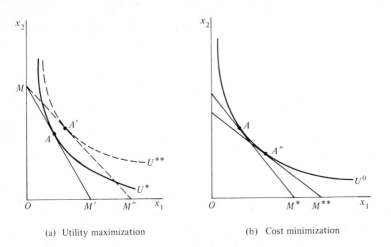

(a) Utility maximization   (b) Cost minimization

Figure 8-8 *Utility-maximization; Cost-minimization* The comparative statics of the cost-minimization problem differs from the statics of the utility-maximization problem in that different parameters are held constant when a price changes. When p_1 changes, say, lowers, in the utility-maximization problem (Fig. 8-8a), the horizontal intercept, which equals M/p_1, shifts to the right, to keep M constant. A new tangency, A', on a higher utility level is implied. In the cost-minimization problem (Fig. 8-8b), as p_1 lowers, the utility level is held constant at U^0, and, hence, the tangency point slides along $U(x_1, x_2) = U^0$ to point A'', where a new, lower expenditure level M^{**} is achieved.

Finally, we note from (8-7a) and (8-7b),

$$\mu = \frac{U_1}{p_1} = \frac{U_2}{p_2}$$

However, from (8-22a) and (8-22b),

$$\lambda = \frac{p_1}{U_1} = \frac{p_2}{U_2}$$

Hence, at any tangency point, for the proper U^* and M^*,

$$\lambda^* = \frac{1}{\mu^*} \tag{8-25}$$

In the production scenario, λ^* is the marginal cost of *output*. Here, in utility analysis, it is the (unobservable) marginal cost of *utility*. It is the reciprocal of μ^*, the marginal utility of money income, as the units of each term would indicate.

The student is warned, however, not to simply regard $\partial M^*/\partial U^0 = 1/(\partial U^*/\partial M)$ as trivial. These partials cannot simply be inverted; $\partial M^*/\partial U^0$ and $\partial U^*/\partial M$ refer to two separate problems. It is a matter of some curiosity that the simple relation (8-25) holds.

The fundamental contribution to the theory of the consumer, known as the Slutsky equation (developed by E. Slutsky in 1915), relates the rates of change of consumption with respect to price changes when money income is held constant, to the corresponding change when real income, or utility, is held constant. That is, a relationship is given between $\partial x_i^M / \partial p_j$ and $\partial x_i^U / \partial p_j$. This relationship will be derived in the next section.

We must first demonstrate that the second-order conditions for the utility maximization and cost minimization problems are identical. This fact is visually obvious from Fig. 8-7. Clearly, interior solutions to both problems require that the indifference curves be convex to the origin, at all levels. Therefore, we should be able to show that the determinant D given in (8-8) is positive if and only if Δ, given in (8-23), is negative. This is a useful exercise in determinants, and is needed for our derivation of the Slutsky equation; hence, we do it here: Recall that†

$$\Delta = \begin{vmatrix} -\lambda U_{11} & -\lambda U_{12} & -U_1 \\ -\lambda U_{21} & -\lambda U_{22} & -U_2 \\ -U_1 & -U_2 & 0 \end{vmatrix} \tag{8-23}$$

From the first-order relations of the cost-minimization problem (8-22), $U_1 = p_1/\lambda$, $U_2 = p_2/\lambda$. Making this substitution, and multiplying the first two rows by -1 [and, hence, Δ by $(-1)^2 = 1$],

$$\Delta = \begin{vmatrix} \lambda U_{11} & \lambda U_{12} & \dfrac{p_1}{\lambda} \\[2ex] \lambda U_{21} & \lambda U_{22} & \dfrac{p_2}{\lambda} \\[2ex] -\dfrac{p_1}{\lambda} & -\dfrac{p_2}{\lambda} & 0 \end{vmatrix}$$

Now, multiply the last row and the last column by λ, and then divide rows 1 and 2 by λ. This again leaves Δ unchanged, hence,

$$\Delta = \begin{vmatrix} U_{11} & U_{12} & \dfrac{p_1}{\lambda} \\[2ex] U_{21} & U_{22} & \dfrac{p_2}{\lambda} \\[2ex] -p_1 & -p_2 & 0 \end{vmatrix}$$

Now multiply the last column by $-\lambda$, or, equivalently, by $-1/\mu$. Then

$$\Delta = (-\mu) \begin{vmatrix} U_{11} & U_{12} & -p_1 \\ U_{21} & U_{22} & -p_2 \\ -p_1 & -p_2 & 0 \end{vmatrix} = -\mu D \tag{8-26}$$

That is, we have shown that Δ, the bordered hessian determinant for the cost-minimization problem, is identically the bordered hessian D for the utility-

---

† We shall temporarily leave off the *'s from λ and μ for notational ease.

maximization problem, multiplied by $-\mu$. By nonsatiation, $\mu > 0$, and hence $\Delta < 0$ if and only if $D > 0$. Thus, the second-order conditions of our two problems are entirely equivalent; if one is satisfied, so is the other. The above proof is easily generalized to the case of n goods, though the algebra is a trifle messier. For either cost-minimization or utility-maximization, the utility functions must be quasi-concave.

Let us recall the comparative statics of the cost-minimization problem. As was shown in the previous Chap., differentiating the first-order conditions (8-22) with respect to p_1 yields the comparative statics equations

$$
\begin{vmatrix}
-\lambda U_{11} & -\lambda U_{12} & -U_1 \\
-\lambda U_{21} & -\lambda U_{22} & -U_2 \\
-U_1 & -U_2 & 0
\end{vmatrix}
\begin{pmatrix}
\dfrac{\partial x_1^U}{\partial p_1} \\[2ex]
\dfrac{\partial x_2^U}{\partial p_1} \\[2ex]
\dfrac{\partial \lambda^*}{\partial p_1}
\end{pmatrix}
=
\begin{pmatrix}
-1 \\
0 \\
0
\end{pmatrix}
$$

Using Cramer's rule, we find, again,

$$
\frac{\partial x_1^U}{\partial p_1} = \frac{-\Delta_{11}}{\Delta} \tag{8-27a}
$$

$$
\frac{\partial x_2^U}{\partial p_1} = \frac{-\Delta_{12}}{\Delta} \tag{8-27b}
$$

Similarly, differentiation with respect to p_2 yields

$$
\frac{\partial x_1^U}{\partial p_2} = \frac{-\Delta_{21}}{\Delta} = \frac{\partial x_2^U}{\partial p_1} \tag{8-27c}
$$

$$
\frac{\partial x_2^U}{\partial p_2} = \frac{-\Delta_{22}}{\Delta} \tag{8-27d}
$$

These expressions are now interpretable as the pure substitution effects of price changes. Again, since the x_i^U's are the x_i's which minimize the cost of staying on some utility level U^0, the response to price changes hold utility constant while preserving the condition that the MRS equal the price ratio.

We showed above that $\Delta = -\mu D = (-1/\lambda)D$. It is useful to relate the cofactors Δ_{11}, etc., to the corresponding cofactors D_{11}, etc., of D, since then we shall be able to relate the comparative statics of the *money-income*-held-constant demand curves, $x_i^M(p_1, p_2, M)$, whose expressions will involve the determinant D and its cofactors, to the *compensated* demand curves $x_i^U(p_1, p_2, U^0)$.

By inspection of the determinant D, equation (8-8),

$$
D_{11} = \begin{vmatrix} U_{22} & -p_2 \\ -p_2 & 0 \end{vmatrix} = -p_2^2
$$

Similarly, $D_{12} = D_{21} = +p_1 p_2$, and $D_{22} = -p_1^2$. By inspection of Δ,

$$\Delta_{11} = \begin{vmatrix} -\lambda U_{22} & -U_2 \\ -U_2 & 0 \end{vmatrix} = -U_2^2$$

Since $U_2 = \mu p_2$,

$$\Delta_{11} = -\mu^2 p_2^2 = \mu^2 D_{11} \tag{8-28a}$$

Similarly

$$\Delta_{12} = \Delta_{21} = +U_1 U_2 = \mu^2 p_1 p_2 = \mu^2 D_{12} \tag{8-28b}$$

and

$$\Delta_{22} = -\mu^2 p_1^2 = \mu^2 D_{22} \tag{8-28c}$$

Hence, the pure substitution effects can be written in terms of the D determinant as

$$\frac{\partial x_1^U}{\partial p_1} = \frac{-\Delta_{11}}{\Delta} = \frac{-\mu^2 D_{11}}{-\mu D} = \frac{\mu D_{11}}{D} \tag{8-29a}$$

Similarly

$$\frac{\partial x_1^U}{\partial p_2} = \frac{\partial x_2^U}{\partial p_1} = \frac{-\Delta_{12}}{\Delta} = \frac{\mu D_{12}}{D} \tag{8-29b}$$

and

$$\frac{\partial x_2^U}{\partial p_2} = \frac{-\Delta_{22}}{\Delta} = \frac{\mu D_{22}}{D} \tag{8-29c}$$

8.4 THE SLUTSKY EQUATION: THE COMPARATIVE STATICS OF THE UTILITY-MAXIMIZATION MODEL

We shall now derive the fundamental relationship between the money-income demand curve, $x_i = x_i^M(p_1, p_2, M)$, derived from utility-maximization, and the real-income, or compensated demand curve, $x_i = x_i^U(p_1, p_2, U^0)$, derived from cost-minimization. Let us analyze the comparative statics of the utility-maximization problem. The first-order equations, in identity form, are, again,

$$U_1(x_1^M, x_2^M) - \mu^* p_1 \equiv 0$$
$$U_2(x_1^M, x_2^M) - \mu^* p_2 \equiv 0$$
$$M - p_1 x_1^M - p_2 x_2^M \equiv 0 \tag{8-7}$$

How will the consumer react, first, to a change in his or her money income M, prices being held constant? Differentiating these identities with respect to M, noting that M itself appears only in the third equation, the following system of equations is found:

$$U_{11} \frac{\partial x_1^M}{\partial M} + U_{12} \frac{\partial x_2^M}{\partial M} - p_1 \frac{\partial \mu^*}{\partial M} \equiv 0 \tag{8-30a}$$

$$U_{21} \frac{\partial x_1^M}{\partial M} + U_{22} \frac{\partial x_2^M}{\partial M} - p_2 \frac{\partial \mu^*}{\partial M} \equiv 0 \tag{8-30b}$$

$$1 - p_1 \frac{\partial x_1^M}{\partial M} - p_2 \frac{\partial x_2^M}{\partial M} \equiv 0 \tag{8-30c}$$

In matrix form, this system of equations is:

$$
\begin{pmatrix}
U_{11} & U_{12} & -p_1 \\
U_{21} & U_{22} & -p_2 \\
-p_1 & -p_2 & 0
\end{pmatrix}
\begin{pmatrix}
\dfrac{\partial x_1^M}{\partial M} \\[6pt]
\dfrac{\partial x_2^M}{\partial M} \\[6pt]
\dfrac{\partial \mu^*}{\partial M}
\end{pmatrix}
\equiv
\begin{pmatrix}
0 \\
0 \\
-1
\end{pmatrix}
\tag{8-30}
$$

The coefficient matrix is, again, the second partials of the lagrangian function $\mathscr{L} = U + \mu(M - p_1 x_1 - p_2 x_2)$ and the right-hand coefficients are the negative first partials of the first-order equations with respect to the parameter in question, here M, as the general methodology indicates. Solving this system by using Cramer's rule yields

$$
\frac{\partial x_1^M}{\partial M} = \frac{\begin{vmatrix} 0 & U_{12} & -p_1 \\ 0 & U_{22} & -p_2 \\ -1 & -p_2 & 0 \end{vmatrix}}{D} = \frac{-D_{31}}{D}
\tag{8-31a}
$$

and similarly

$$
\frac{\partial x_2^M}{\partial M} = \frac{-D_{32}}{D}
\tag{8-31b}
$$

$$
\frac{\partial \mu^*}{\partial M} = \frac{-D_{33}}{D}
\tag{8-31c}
$$

In none of these instances can a definitive sign be given. The denominators D are positive, by the sufficient second-order conditions. However, inspection reveals

$$
D_{31} = -p_2 U_{12} + p_1 U_{22} \gtrless 0
$$

and likewise

$$
D_{32} = p_2 U_{11} - p_1 U_{21} \gtrless 0
$$

Also,

$$
D_{33} = U_{11} U_{22} - U_{12}^2 \gtrless 0
$$

because D_{33} is not a *border-preserving* principal minor.

What equations (8-31a) and (8-31b) say, not surprisingly, is that convexity of the indifference curves is insufficiently strong to rule out the possibility of inferior goods. That is, it is entirely possible to have $\partial x_1^M/\partial M < 0$ or $\partial x_2^M/\partial M < 0$, as Fig. 8-9 shows. It is *not* possible, however, for both x_1 and x_2 to be inferior. If that were so, more income would result in reduced purchases of both x_1 and x_2, violating the postulate that more is preferred to less. On a more formal level, the

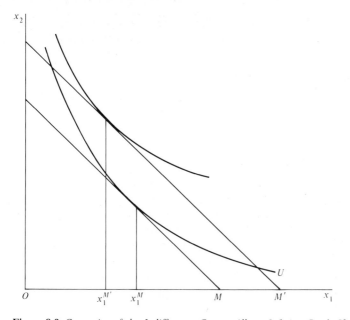

Figure 8-9 *Convexity of the Indifference Curves Allows Inferior Goods* If money income is raised from M to M', the consumption of one good, say x_1, can decrease. A common example is the case of hamburger. As incomes rise, say, as students leave college and acquire jobs, hamburger is often replaced by steak. A word of warning: inferiority is a "local" concept. A good cannot be inferior over the whole range of consumption, or else it would never have been consumed in positive amounts in the first place!

third equation in the comparative statics system, equation (8-30c), the differentiated budget constraint, says that $p_1\, \partial x_1^M/\partial M + p_2\, \partial x_2^M/\partial M = 1 > 0$. Since the prices p_1 and p_2 are both positive, it cannot be that $\partial x_1^M/\partial M < 0$ *and* $\partial x_2^M/\partial M < 0$. Also, inferiority is of necessity a *local* concept. Goods cannot be inferior over the whole range of consumption, or else they would never be consumed in positive amounts in the first place!

Let us now differentiate the first-order equations (8-7) with respect to the prices, in particular, p_1. This operation will yield the rates of change of consumption of any good with respect to a change in one price, holding all other prices and money income constant. Performing the indicated operation,

$$U_{11}\frac{\partial x_1^M}{\partial p_1} + U_{12}\frac{\partial x_2^M}{\partial p_1} - p_1\frac{\partial \mu^*}{\partial p_1} - \mu^* \equiv 0 \qquad (8\text{-}32a)$$

$$U_{21}\frac{\partial x_1^M}{\partial p_1} + U_{22}\frac{\partial x_2^M}{\partial p_1} - p_2\frac{\partial \mu^*}{\partial p_1} \equiv 0 \qquad (8\text{-}32b)$$

$$-p_1\frac{\partial x_1^M}{\partial p_1} - x_1^M - p_2\frac{\partial x_2^M}{\partial p_1} \equiv 0 \qquad (8\text{-}32c)$$

where the product rule has been used to differentiate $-\mu^* p_1$ and $-p_1 x_1^M$ (partially) with respect to p_1. In matrix form, this system of equations is

$$
\begin{pmatrix}
U_{11} & U_{12} & -p_1 \\
U_{21} & U_{22} & -p_2 \\
-p_1 & -p_2 & 0
\end{pmatrix}
\begin{pmatrix}
\dfrac{\partial x_1^M}{\partial p_1} \\[2ex]
\dfrac{\partial x_2^M}{\partial p_1} \\[2ex]
\dfrac{\partial \mu^*}{\partial p_1}
\end{pmatrix}
\equiv
\begin{pmatrix}
\mu^* \\
0 \\
x_1^M
\end{pmatrix}
\qquad (8\text{-}32)
$$

It is apparent right here that no comparative statics results will be forthcoming from this model; i.e., no definitive sign for $\partial x_i^M/\partial p_1$ or $\partial \mu^*/\partial p_1$ is implied by utility-maximization. The reason is that there are two nonzero entries in the right-hand side column. This means that knowledge of the signs of *two* cofactors in a given column of D will have to be determined; since only one can be a border-preserving principal minor (whose sign *is* known), at least one must be an off-diagonal cofactor, whose sign and size is indeterminate from the maximization hypothesis alone.

Solving via Cramer's rule,

$$
\frac{\partial x_1^M}{\partial p_1} = \frac{\begin{vmatrix} \mu^* & U_{12} & -p_1 \\ 0 & U_{22} & -p_2 \\ x_1^M & -p_2 & 0 \end{vmatrix}}{D} = \frac{\mu^* D_{11}}{D} + \frac{x_1^M D_{31}}{D} \qquad (8\text{-}33a)
$$

Likewise, putting $(\mu^*, 0, x_1^M)$ into the second and third columns, respectively, in the numerator,

$$
\frac{\partial x_2^M}{\partial p_1} = \frac{\mu^* D_{12}}{D} + \frac{x_1^M D_{32}}{D} \qquad (8\text{-}33b)
$$

$$
\frac{\partial \mu^*}{\partial p_1} = \frac{\mu^* D_{13}}{D} + \frac{x_1^M D_{33}}{D} \qquad (8\text{-}33c)
$$

The determinant D_{11} is a border-preserving principal minor and is negative by the second-order conditions. Actually, by inspection, $D_{11} = -p_2^2 < 0$, quite apart from the second-order conditions. The determinant D_{33} is on-diagonal; however, it is not border-preserving; hence its sign is unknown. All the other cofactors are off-diagonal and are thus of indeterminate sign.

The interest in equations (8-33a) and (8-33b) stems from the interpretation of the individual terms in the expression. Recall equation (8-29a) and (8-29b). In fact, the first term on the right-hand side of equations (8-33a) and (8-33b) are the pure substitution effects of a change in price, as derived from the cost-minimization model. Consider also equations (8-31a) and (8-31b), relating to the income effects. These expressions are, respectively, precisely the second terms of the above equations multiplied by the term $-x_1^M$. Hence, equations (8-33a) and (8-33b) can be written

$$\frac{\partial x_1^M}{\partial p_1} = \frac{\partial x_1^U}{\partial p_1} - x_1^M \frac{\partial x_1^M}{\partial M} \tag{8-34a}$$

$$\frac{\partial x_2^M}{\partial p_1} = \frac{\partial x_2^U}{\partial p_1} - x_1^M \frac{\partial x_2^M}{\partial M} \tag{8-34b}$$

The equations for the response of the money-income-held-constant demand curves to price changes, when written in this form, are known as the *Slutsky equations*. Similar expressions can be written with respect to changes in p_2, and are left as an exercise for the student:

$$\frac{\partial x_1^M}{\partial p_2} = \frac{\partial x_1^U}{\partial p_2} - x_2^M \frac{\partial x_1^M}{\partial M} \tag{8-34c}$$

$$\frac{\partial x_2^M}{\partial p_2} = \frac{\partial x_2^U}{\partial p_2} - x_2^M \frac{\partial x_2^M}{\partial M} \tag{8-34d}$$

In general (and this result is, in fact, a general result for the case of n goods),

$$\frac{\partial x_i^M}{\partial p_j} = \frac{\partial x_i^U}{\partial p_j} - x_j^M \frac{\partial x_i^M}{\partial M} \qquad i, j = 1, \ldots, n \tag{8-34}$$

The Slutsky equation shows that the response of a utility-maximizing consumer to a change in price can be split up, conceptually, into two parts: first, a pure substitution effect, or a response to a price change holding the consumer on the original indifference surface, and second, a pure income effect, wherein income is changed, holding prices constant, to reach a tangency on the new indifference curve. This result can be most easily seen with the aid of Fig. 8-10.

Suppose a consumer with preferences given by the indifference curves shown in Fig. 8-10 initially faces the budget constraint MM, and achieves maximum utility at point A, consuming x_1^0 amount of x_1. Suppose p_1 is lowered. The budget line will pivot to the right, producing a new utility maximum at point B. The total change in consumption of x_1 is $x_1^M - x_1^0$. This amount, however, is partitionable into

$$x_1^M - x_1^0 = \left(x_1^U - x_1^0 \right) + \left(x_1^M - x_1^U \right)$$

The first term, $x_1^U - x_1^0$, is a change in x_1, holding utility constant. The tangency point C occurs at the new, lower, p_1, but at a reduced budget level represented by the budget constraint $M''M''$. Point C is the combination of x_1 and x_2 that minimizes the cost of achieving the old utility level at the new prices (i.e., new price p_1 of x_1). Hence, the change $x_1^U - x_1^0$ is a pure substitution effect, and would be generated by the cost-minimization problem.

The remaining part of the total change, $x_1^M - x_1^U$, is generated by a parallel shift of the budget equation from $M''M''$ to MM'. Since prices are held constant, this is a pure income effect.

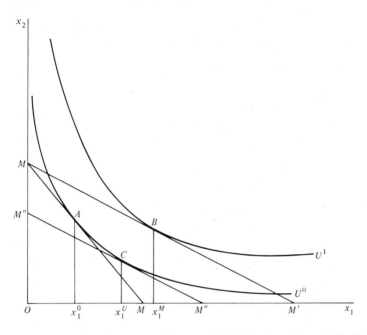

Figure 8-10 *The Substitution and Income Effects of a Price Change* This diagram relates to finite movements in the consumption of x_1 due to a finite change in p_1. It is therefore not directly comparable with the Slutsky equation, which deals with instantaneous rates of change. However, the income and substitution effects of a price change are easily seen in the above well-known diagram. The original tangency is at A, on budget line MM. When p_1 is lowered, the horizontal intercept increases, and the budget line pivots to MM', yielding a new tangency at B. The total change in consumption of x_1 is $x_1^M - x_1^0$. This amount can be attributed to $x_1^U - x_1^0$, a pure substitution effect obtained by sliding the budget line around the indifference curve U^0 until it is parallel to the budget line MM', reflecting the new prices. Since utility is held constant, this is indeed a pure substitution effect. The remaining part, $x_1^M - x_1^U$, of the total change in x_1 is attributable to a parallel shift in the budget line from $M''M''$ to MM'. This is a pure income effect since prices are held constant.

The above graphical exposition of the Slutsky equation, although useful, is not an exact description of equation (8-34). The Slutsky equation is a statement about various partial derivatives, i.e., rates of change at some point, rather than a description of finite movements. More precisely, equation (8-34) is a relationship between $\partial x_i^M/\partial p_j$, the *uncompensated* rate of change of x_i, to $\partial x_i^U/\partial p_j$, the *compensated* rate of change. It is a relationship between the equations (8-9) and (8-24). The Slutsky equations are sometimes written

$$\left(\frac{\partial x_i}{\partial p_j}\right)_M = \left(\frac{\partial x_i}{\partial p_j}\right)_U - x_j \left(\frac{\partial x_i}{\partial M}\right)_p$$

where the parameters outside the parentheses indicate the *ceteris paribus* conditions, i.e., what is being held constant. This representation is satisfactory, but it obscures the source of these partial derivatives. As has been constantly stressed, the notation dy/dx, $\partial f/\partial x_1$, etc., makes sense only if well-specified functions $y = f(x)$, $y = f(x_1, x_2, \ldots)$ etc., exist (and are differentiable). It is nonsense to write derivative-type expressions when the implied functional dependence is lacking. The Slutsky equation should be regarded as a relationship between two different conceptions of a demand function:

$$x_i = x_i^M(p_1, p_2, M) \tag{8-9}$$

and
$$x_i = x_i^U(p_1, p_2, U) \tag{8-24}$$

Each equation is a solution of a well-defined system of equations stemming from an optimization hypothesis; in the case of equation (8-9), from utility-maximization, and in the case of equation (8-24), from cost-minimization. The Slutsky equation shows that these two equations are related in an interesting manner.

Let us examine the Slutsky equation again and see why it makes sense. We have

$$\frac{\partial x_i^M}{\partial p_j} = \frac{\partial x_i^U}{\partial p_j} - x_j^M \frac{\partial x_i^M}{\partial M}$$

When a price changes, the consumer begins to substitute away from the good becoming relatively higher-priced. However, the price change also changes the opportunity set of the consumer. If the price p_j falls, the consumer can achieve certain consumption levels previously outside his or her former budget constraint. This is like a gain in income. However, what determines the size and sign of this income effect? If p_j *decreases*, an effect similar to an *increase* in income is produced. Both produce larger opportunities. Price increases and income decreases are similarly related. Hence, it is plausible that the income term in the Slutsky equation be entered with a negative sign. The negative sign indicates that the implied change in income is in the opposite direction to the price change.

What about the multiplier x_j^M, in the income term? What is its meaning and/or function? Suppose the commodity whose price has changed is salt. Salt is a very minor part of most people's budget. Hence, the income effect of a price change in salt should be small, even for large price changes. Suppose, however, the price of petroleum changes. Petroleum products may occupy a large part of our budgets, especially of those people who commute by car, or heat their homes with oil. These income effects can be expected to be large. It is plausible, therefore, to "weight" the income effect $\partial x_i^M/\partial M$ by the amount of the good x_j whose price has changed. If the price of Rolls Royces increases, the effect on my consumption of that and other goods is negligible. Change the price of something I consume intensively and my *real* income, or utility, is apt to change considerably.

In the case where $i = j$, the Slutsky equation takes the form

$$\frac{\partial x_i^M}{\partial p_i} = \frac{\partial x_i^U}{\partial p_i} - x_i^M \frac{\partial x_i^M}{\partial M} \tag{8-35}$$

The important question, again, is, what refutable hypothesis emerges from this analysis? Can anything be said of the sign of $\partial x_i^M/\partial p_i$? Strictly speaking, no.

However, we know that $\partial x_i^U / \partial p_i < 0$. If x_i is not an inferior good, that is, if $\partial x_i^M / \partial M \geq 0$, then $\partial x_i^M / \partial p_i < 0$ necessarily. This proposition is nontautological only if an independent measure of inferiority (i.e., not based on the Slutsky equation) is available.

It is conceivable, though not likely, that $\partial x_i^M / \partial p_i > 0$, the so-called *Giffen good* case. Do not make the mistaken assumption that because something is mathematically possible, it is therefore likely to be observed in the real world. The refutable proposition $\partial x_i^M / \partial p_i < 0$ cannot be inferred from utility-maximization alone; it is not on that account less usable. Utility-maximization is a hypothesis concerning individual preferences for more rather than less, and provides probably the most successful framework for analyzing economic problems.†

The Slutsky Equation in Elasticity Form

The Slutsky equation can be written in terms of dimensionless elasticity coefficients.‡ First, multiply the entire equation through by p_j / x_i. Then we have

$$\frac{p_j}{x_i} \frac{\partial x_i^M}{\partial p_j} = \frac{p_j}{x_i} \frac{\partial x_i^U}{\partial p_j} - \frac{p_j x_j}{x_i} \frac{\partial x_i^M}{\partial M}$$

The first two expressions are already elasticities; the income term can be made one by multiplying it by M/M, that is, by 1, yielding

$$\varepsilon_{ij}^M = \varepsilon_{ij}^U - \kappa_j \varepsilon_{iM} \tag{8-36}$$

where ε_{ij}^M = elasticity of response of x_i to change in p_j, holding money income constant

ε_{ij}^U = elasticity of response of x_i to change in p_j, holding utility constant

$\kappa_j = p_j x_j / M$, the share of the consumer's budget spent on good j

ε_{iM} = income elasticity of good i

The difference between the (cross) elasticities of the uncompensated and compensated demand curves depends on the size of the income elasticity of the good and the importance of the good whose price has changed, measured by the share of the consumer's budget spent on the good whose price has changed.

> **Example** We previously showed that the money-income demand curves implied by the utility function $U = x_1 x_2$ were $x_1^M = M/2p_1, x_2^M = M/2p_2$. Let us find the compensated demand curves $x_1^U(p_1, p_2, U^0), x_2^U(p_1, p_2, U^0)$ and show that the relationship between x_1^M and x_1^U, etc., is as given by the Slutsky equation.

---

† There are "general equilibrium" reasons for not believing that $\partial x_i^M / \partial p_i > 0$. If p_i falls, the consumers of x_i experience a gain in wealth; however, the current owners and sellers of x_i experience a wealth loss. Since at any time the quantity bought equals the quantity sold, the overall income effects of price changes are apt to be small.

‡ To save notational clutter, we will leave off the superscripts for x_i when it is not needed.

The compensated demand curves are solutions to the model,

minimize $\qquad\qquad\qquad M = p_1 x_1 + p_2 x_2$

subject to $\qquad\qquad U(x_1, x_2) = x_1 x_2 = U^0$

The lagrangian is

$$\mathscr{L} = p_1 x_1 + p_2 x_2 + \lambda(U^0 - x_1 x_2)$$

producing the first-order equations

$$\mathscr{L}_1 = p_1 - \lambda x_2 = 0$$

$$\mathscr{L}_2 = p_2 - \lambda x_1 = 0$$

$$\mathscr{L}_\lambda = U^0 - x_1 x_2 = 0$$

The conditions $\mathscr{L}_1 = \mathscr{L}_2 = 0$ yield the tangency condition $U_1/U_2 = \lambda x_2/\lambda x_1 = p_1/p_2$, or

$$p_1 x_1 = p_2 x_2$$

The same tangency condition is obtained for the cost-minimization model as for utility-maximization. The constraint, however, is not the budget equation, but rather the constant utility equation $x_1 x_2 = U^0$. Combining the tangency and constant-utility condition yields

$$x_1 \frac{p_1 x_1}{p_2} = U^0$$

or $\qquad\qquad\qquad x_1 = x_1^U = \left(\frac{p_2 U^0}{p_1}\right)^{1/2}$

Similarly $\qquad\qquad\qquad x_2^U = \left(\frac{p_1 U^0}{p_2}\right)^{1/2}$

We note in passing that, as required by the second-order conditions,

$$\frac{\partial x_1^U}{\partial p_1} = -\frac{1}{2}(p_2 U^0)^{1/2} p_1^{-3/2} < 0$$

$$\frac{\partial x_2^U}{\partial p_2} = -\frac{1}{2}(p_1 U^0)^{1/2} p_2^{-3/2} < 0$$

Also, the reciprocity condition $\partial x_1^U/\partial p_2 = \partial x_2^U/\partial p_1$ holds:

$$\frac{\partial x_1^U}{\partial p_2} = \frac{1}{2}(U^0)^{1/2}(p_1 p_2)^{-1/2} = \frac{\partial x_2^U}{\partial p_1}$$

The cost, or expenditure function, is given by $M^* = p_1 x_1^U + p_2 x_2^U = 2(p_1 p_2 U^0)^{1/2}$. The Slutsky equation is a relationship which holds at any particular point of tangency with a budget line and an indifference curve. Thus, the terms $\partial x_i^M/\partial p_j$ and $\partial x_i^U/\partial p_j$ must be evaluated at the same point.

Since x_i^M and x_i^U are functions of different variables, M and U, respectively, we have to make sure the same point is being considered, such that $x_1^M(p_1, p_2, M) = x_1^U(p_1, p_2, U^0)$, and $x_2^M(p_1, p_2, M) = x_2^U(p_1, p_2, U^0)$. This is most easily handled via the indirect utility function $U^* = x_1^M x_2^M = M^2/4p_1 p_2$. This can be viewed as relating, at given prices, the utility levels to money-income levels. If utility is maximized subject to a given budget M, then minimizing cost subject to being on the indifference level $U^0 = M^2/4p_1 p_2$ will lead to the same consumption bundle for this utility function. We note also, that this is the same relationship as was given by the expenditure function $M^* = 2(p_1 p_2 U^0)^{1/2}$.

Let us now evaluate the partial derivatives in a Slutsky equation:

$$\frac{\partial x_1^M}{\partial p_1} = \frac{\partial x_1^U}{\partial p_1} - x_1 \frac{\partial x_1^M}{\partial M}$$

Here, $\partial x_1^M/\partial p_1 = -M/2p_1^2$,

$$\frac{\partial x_1^M}{\partial M} = \frac{1}{2p_1}$$

$$x_1 \frac{\partial x_1^M}{\partial M} = \frac{M}{2p_1} \frac{1}{2p_1} = \frac{M}{4p_1^2}$$

and $\partial x_1^U/\partial p_1 = -\frac{1}{2}(p_2 U^0)^{1/2} p_1^{-3/2}$. The money-income level M corresponding to U^0 is given by either the expenditure or indirect utility function, as $U^0 = M^2/4p_1 p_2$. Thus, at any given point,

$$\frac{\partial x_1^U}{\partial p_1} = -\frac{1}{2} p_2^{1/2} p_1^{-3/2} \frac{M}{2} p_1^{-1/2} p_2^{-1/2}$$

$$= \frac{-M}{4p_1^2}$$

Hence

$$\frac{-M}{2p_1^2} \equiv \frac{-M}{4p_1^2} - \frac{M}{4p_1^2}$$

$$\equiv \frac{-M}{2p_1^2}$$

as required.

Instant Slutsky Equation

The Slutsky equation was derived via the traditional methods of comparative statics. The procedure is somewhat tedious and long, an unfortunate requisite for doing that derivation correctly. However, a much shorter route is available by way of the more modern envelope analysis. The new method is perhaps more revealing than the old.

We start off with a money-income demand curve, $x_1 = x_1^M(p_1, p_2, M)$. When p_1 changes, p_2 and M are typically held constant, producing a change in utility, since, as will be shown, $\partial U^*/\partial p_i = -\mu^* x_i^M < 0$. (When p_1, for example, is lowered, the opportunity set of the consumer expands, hence the attained utility increases.) Suppose, now, when p_1 changes, M is also changed to the minimum amount necessary to keep utility constant. That is, define the function $M = M^*(p_1, p_2, U^0)$ such that M^* is exactly that minimum money-income level that keeps $U = U^0$ when p_1 (or any other price) changes. Then, by definition, if $x_1^U(p_1, p_2, U^0)$ is the utility-held-constant demand curve,

$$x_1^U(p_1, p_2, U^0) \equiv x_1^M(p_1, p_2, M^*(p_1, p_2, U^0))$$

This is an identity—it defines $x_1^U(p_1, p_2, U^0)$. Differentiate both sides with respect to p_1, say, using the chain rule on the right-hand side:

$$\frac{\partial x_1^U}{\partial p_1} \equiv \frac{\partial x_1^M}{\partial p_1} + \frac{\partial x_1^M}{\partial M} \frac{\partial M^*}{\partial p_1}$$

What is $\partial M^*/\partial p_1$? The function $M^*(p_1, p_2, U^0)$ is the minimum cost, or expenditure, of achieving utility level U^0 (at given prices). M^* is therefore simply the (indirect) cost or expenditure function from the cost-minimization problem

minimize $\qquad\qquad M = p_1 x_1 + p_2 x_2$

subject to $\qquad U^0 - U(x_1, x_2) = 0$

the lagrangian of which is $\mathcal{L} = p_1 x_1 + p_2 x_2 + \lambda(U^0 - U(x_1, x_2))$. By the envelope theorem,

$$\frac{\partial M^*}{\partial p_1} = \frac{\partial \mathcal{L}}{\partial p_1} = x_1^* = x_1^U = x_1^M$$

at any given point. Substituting this into the above equation yields,

$$\frac{\partial x_1^U}{\partial p_1} \equiv \frac{\partial x_1^M}{\partial p_1} + x_1^M \frac{\partial x_1^M}{\partial M}$$

This is precisely the Slutsky equation (8-34a)! (Note that here $\partial x_1^U/\partial p_1$ appears alone on the left-hand side; we have merely rearranged the terms.)

This proof is perfectly general. For n goods,

$$x_i^U(p_1, \ldots, p_n, U^0) \equiv x_i^M(p_1, \ldots, p_n, M^*(p_1, \ldots, p_n, U^0))$$

where $M^*(p_1, \ldots, p_n, U^0)$ is the minimum cost of achieving utility level U^0 at given prices. By the envelope theorem from the cost-minimization problem, $\partial M^*/\partial p_j = x_j^U = x_j^M$ at a given point. Thus

$$\frac{\partial x_i^U}{\partial p_j} \equiv \frac{\partial x_i^M}{\partial p_j} + \frac{\partial x_i^M}{\partial M} \frac{\partial M^*}{\partial p_j}$$

$$\equiv \frac{\partial x_i^M}{\partial p_j} + x_j^M \frac{\partial x_i^M}{\partial M} \qquad \text{QED}$$

The Slutsky equation can be derived in this fashion by starting with the compensated demand curve $x_i^U(p_1, \ldots, p_n, U^0)$ and using it to derive the uncompensated demand curve $x_i^M(p_1, \ldots, p_n, M)$. Specifically, if some p_j changes, change U^0 also by that *maximum* amount consistent with holding money income M constant. That is, define $U^0 = U^*(p_1, \ldots, p_n, M)$ to be the maximum achievable utility level for a given budget M, at given prices. Then U^* is simply the indirect utility function of the utility-maximization problem: max $U(x_1, \ldots, x_n)$ subject to $\sum p_i x_i = M$. The associated lagrangian is $\mathscr{L} = U(x_1, \ldots, x_n) + \mu(M - \sum p_i x_i)$. By the envelope theorem, $\partial U^*/\partial p_j = \partial \mathscr{L}/\partial p_j = -\mu^* x_j^M$.

By definition, then,

$$x_i^M(p_1, \ldots, p_n, M) \equiv x_i^U(p_1, \ldots, p_n, U^*(p_1, \ldots, p_n, M)) \qquad (8\text{-}37)$$

A similar procedure to the above, together with an extra step, yields the Slutsky equation. This derivation is left to the student as an exercise.

8.5 ELASTICITY FORMULAS FOR MONEY-INCOME-HELD-CONSTANT AND REAL-INCOME-HELD-CONSTANT DEMAND CURVES

Certain useful relations concerning the various elasticities of demand are derivable from the utility-maximization model. In general, they stem from either of two sources:

1. The homogeneity of the demand curves in prices and money income
2. The budget constraint.

1 Homogeneity We know that $x_1^M(p_1, p_2, M)$ and $x_2^M(p_1, p_2, M)$ are homogeneous of degree zero in prices and money income. Thus, by Euler's theorem, for x_1^M,

$$\frac{\partial x_1^M}{\partial p_1} p_1 + \frac{\partial x_1^M}{\partial p_2} p_2 + \frac{\partial x_1^M}{\partial M} M \equiv 0$$

Dividing this expression by x_1^M yields

$$\varepsilon_{11}^M + \varepsilon_{12}^M + \varepsilon_{1M} \equiv 0$$

Similarly

$$\varepsilon_{21}^M + \varepsilon_{22}^M + \varepsilon_{2M} \equiv 0$$

In general, for the case of n goods, with $x_i = x_i^M(p_1, \ldots, p_n, M)$,

$$\varepsilon_{i1}^M + \varepsilon_{i2}^M + \cdots + \varepsilon_{in}^M + \varepsilon_{iM} \equiv 0 \qquad (8\text{-}38)$$

2 The budget constraint

(a) *Income elasticities* Differentiate the budget constraint with respect to M:

$$p_1 \frac{\partial x_1^M}{\partial M} + p_2 \frac{\partial x_2^M}{\partial M} \equiv 1$$

This expression is equivalent to

$$\frac{p_1 x_1}{M}\left(\frac{M}{x_1}\frac{\partial x_1^M}{\partial M}\right) + \frac{p_2 x_2}{M}\left(\frac{M}{x_2}\frac{\partial x_2^M}{\partial M}\right) \equiv 1$$

or
$$\kappa_1 \varepsilon_{1M} + \kappa_2 \varepsilon_{2M} \equiv 1$$

In general, for the case of n goods,

$$\kappa_1 \varepsilon_{1M} + \cdots + \kappa_n \varepsilon_{nM} \equiv 1 \tag{8-39}$$

The weighted sum of the income elasticities of all goods equals one. The weights are the shares of income spent on each good; the shares themselves sum to one.

(b) *Price elasticities*   Now differentiate the budget identity $p_1 x_1^M + p_2 x_2^M \equiv M$ with respect to p_1:

$$x_1^M + p_1 \frac{\partial x_1^M}{\partial p_1} + p_2 \frac{\partial x_2^M}{\partial p_1} \equiv 0$$

This is equivalent to

$$\frac{p_1 x_1^M}{M}\left(\frac{p_1}{x_1^M}\frac{\partial x_1^M}{\partial p_1}\right) + \frac{p_2 x_2^M}{M}\left(\frac{p_1}{x_2^M}\frac{\partial x_2^M}{\partial p_1}\right) \equiv -\frac{p_1 x_1^M}{M}$$

or
$$\kappa_1 \varepsilon_{11}^M + \kappa_2 \varepsilon_{21}^M = -\kappa_1$$

In general, for n goods, using the same technique,

$$\kappa_1 \varepsilon_{1j}^M + \cdots + \kappa_n \varepsilon_{nj}^M \equiv -\kappa_j \tag{8-40}$$

The weighted sum of the elasticities for all goods with respect to the price of a certain good sums to the negative of the share of the budget spent on the good in question. The weights are again the shares of the budget spent on each good. Note a difference between (8-38) and (8-40): Equation (8-38) relates to *one* good and *all* prices (and money income), whereas equation (8-40) relates to *all* goods and *one* price change.

The compensated demand curves $x_i^U(p_1, p_2, U^0)$ have slightly different elasticity properties. These properties are again derived from two sources: homogeneity and the constraint equation, in this case $U(x_1, x_2) = U^0$.

1 Homogeneity   The demand curves $x_1^U(p_1, p_2, U^0)$, $x_2^U(p_1, p_2, U^0)$ are homogeneous of degree zero in the prices only. If prices are both doubled, say, since relative prices are unaffected, the tangency point remains the same. Hence, for x_1^U, by Euler's theorem,

$$\frac{\partial x_1^U}{\partial p_1} p_1 + \frac{\partial x_1^U}{\partial p_2} p_2 \equiv 0$$

Dividing by x_1^U yields,

$$\varepsilon_{11}^U + \varepsilon_{12}^U \equiv 0$$

where

$$\varepsilon_{ij}^U = \frac{p_j}{x_i^U} \frac{\partial x_i^U}{\partial p_j}$$

is the (cross) elasticity of compensated demand of good i with respect to the price p_j of good j. For the case of n goods, using the same technique, one finds

$$\varepsilon_{i1}^U + \varepsilon_{i2}^U + \cdots + \varepsilon_{in}^U \equiv 0 \tag{8-41}$$

2 The constraint $U(x_1^U, x_2^U) \equiv U^0$ Differentiate this identity with respect to p_1, say:

$$U_1 \frac{\partial x_1^U}{\partial p_1} + U_2 \frac{\partial x_2^U}{\partial p_1} \equiv 0$$

From the first-order conditions for cost-minimization, $U_1 = p_1/\lambda$, $U_2 = p_2/\lambda$, hence (after multiplying by λ),

$$p_1 \frac{\partial x_1^U}{\partial p_1} + p_2 \frac{\partial x_2^U}{\partial p_1} \equiv 0$$

This is almost the same relation as derived above in equation (8-41); it in fact is derivable from that equation by noting that for compensated demand curves, $\partial x_i^U/\partial p_j = \partial x_j^U/\partial p_i$. Converting this expression to elasticities gives

$$\frac{p_1 x_1^U}{M} \left(\frac{p_1}{x_1^U} \frac{\partial x_1^U}{\partial p_1} \right) + \frac{p_2 x_2^U}{M} \left(\frac{p_1}{x_2^U} \frac{\partial x_2^U}{\partial p_1} \right) \equiv 0$$

or

$$\kappa_1 \varepsilon_{11}^U + \kappa_2 \varepsilon_{21}^U \equiv 0$$

In general, for the n-good case $x_i^U(p_1, p_2, \ldots, p_n, U^0)$,

$$\kappa_1 \varepsilon_{1j}^U + \kappa_2 \varepsilon_{2j}^U + \cdots + \kappa_n \varepsilon_{nj}^U \equiv 0 \tag{8-42}$$

Note the difference between (8-41) and (8-42): In equation (8-41), only one demand relationship $x_i^U(p_1, \ldots, p_n, U^0)$ is being considered, and the cross-effects of that good and all other prices are related. In (8-42), the response of all goods to a given price change are related. The identities (8-38) through (8-42) are the elasticity formulas commonly encountered in the theory of the consumer.

Return a moment to the derivation of equation (8-41) or (8-42). From the homogeneity of degree zero of the compensated demand curves $x_i = x_i^U(p_1, \ldots, p_n, U^0)$ with respect to prices, from Euler's theorem,

$$p_1 \frac{\partial x_i^U}{\partial p_1} + \cdots + p_n \frac{\partial x_i^U}{\partial p_n} \equiv 0$$

Letting $s_{ij} = \partial x_i^U/\partial p_j$, the pure substitution effect on x_i of a change in p_j, we have

$$p_1 s_{i1} + p_2 s_{i2} + \cdots + p_n s_{in} \equiv 0$$

However, for compensated changes $s_{ij} = s_{ji}$. Hence, also,

$$p_1 s_{1i} + p_2 s_{2i} + \cdots + p_n s_{ni} \equiv 0$$

These results are known as Hicks' *third law*. (The first two are, respectively, $s_{ij} = s_{ji}$, $s_{ii} < 0$). The law can be stated succinctly as

$$\sum_{i=1}^{n} p_i s_{ij} = \sum_{j=1}^{n} p_j s_{ij} = 0 \tag{8-43}$$

8.6 CONCLUDING REMARKS: SPECIAL CASES

We have shown how the behavioral assertion of utility maximization leads to certain propositions which are, at least in principle, refutable. Specifically, the proposition that if a good is noninferior, then if its price is lowered, more will be consumed, is implied by utility-maximization. In addition, the income-compensated demands $x_i^U(p_1, \ldots, p_n, U^0)$ have the property of negative slope in their own price, and also possess the reciprocity properties $\partial x_i^U / \partial p_j = \partial x_j^U / \partial p_i$. In addition, the elasticity properties (8-38)–(8-42) are implied.

Let us now explore some special cases. In the example worked out earlier for the utility function $U = x_1 x_2$, certain special results were obtained, in particular, $\partial x_i^M / \partial p_j = \partial x_j^M / \partial p_i = 0$, together with unitary price and income elasticities. In general, what types of utility functions yield these properties?

Consider first the unusual case $\partial x_i^M / \partial p_j = \partial x_j^M / \partial p_i$. This condition always holds for the *compensated* demands, but not generally for the *uncompensated* demands x_i^M. If this does hold, then, using the Slutsky equation,

$$\frac{\partial x_i^M}{\partial p_j} = \frac{\partial x_i^U}{\partial p_j} - x_j^M \frac{\partial x_i^M}{\partial M} = \frac{\partial x_j^U}{\partial p_i} - x_i^M \frac{\partial x_j^M}{\partial M} = \frac{\partial x_j^M}{\partial p_i}$$

However, $\partial x_i^U / \partial p_j = \partial x_j^U / \partial p_i$ always. Hence, we are left with

$$x_j^M \frac{\partial x_i^M}{\partial M} = x_i^M \frac{\partial x_j^M}{\partial M} \tag{8-44}$$

Multiplying this equation through by $M/(x_i^M x_j^M)$ yields

$$\varepsilon_{iM} = \frac{M}{x_i^M} \frac{\partial x_i^M}{\partial M} = \frac{M}{x_j^M} \frac{\partial x_j^M}{\partial M} = \varepsilon_{jM}$$

Thus, all pairs of goods for which $\partial x_i^M / \partial p_j = \partial x_j^M / \partial p_i$ have equal income elasticities. Suppose this is true of all commodities consumed. Then, using equation (8-39) that the weighted sum of income elasticities sums to unity, denoting the common value of the income elasticities as ε_M,

$$\kappa_1 \varepsilon_M + \cdots + \kappa_n \varepsilon_M = \varepsilon_M(\kappa_1 + \cdots + \kappa_n) = 1$$

Thus, $\varepsilon_{1M} = \cdots = \varepsilon_{nM} = \varepsilon_M = 1$, since the shares $\kappa_i = p_i x_i / M$ sum to unity.

What types of utility functions possess unitary income elasticities for all goods? Recall Fig. 8-6 for the specific case of $U = x_1 x_2$. The income elasticities were unity because the income-consumption paths, the locus of all possible tangency points, was a straight line out of the origin. This is the property of homotheticity, of which the homogeneous function $U = x_1 x_2$ is a particular case.

Mathematically, consider equation (8-44) once more. This equation is equivalent to:

$$\frac{\partial \left(x_j^M / x_i^M \right)}{\partial M} = 0 \tag{8-45}$$

For, using the quotient rule,

$$\left(x_i^M \frac{\partial x_j^M}{\partial M} - x_j^M \frac{\partial x_i^M}{\partial M} \right) \left(\frac{1}{x_i^M} \right)^2 = 0$$

Since x_i^M is presumed positive, equation (8-44) results. Equation (8-45) says that the ratio of consumption of x_j to x_i is the same at all income levels. This ratio, x_j/x_i, is simply the slope of the ray from the origin through (x_i, x_j). To say that this ray has constant slope in the x_i, x_j plane, for all pairs of goods, is to say that the utility function is homothetic. The reasoning can be reversed, using equation (8-45) as a definition of homotheticity to show that homothetic utility functions imply demand curves that have unitary income elasticities and exhibit the property that $\partial x_i^M / \partial p_j = \partial x_j^M / \partial p_i$. Any one of these three statements implies the other two; they are all equivalent.

We shall explore some properties of special utility functions in a later chapter. Since utility functions are not in themselves observable, these exercises have limited applicability, save as a convenient way of summarizing various properties, e.g., unitary income elasticities. A more important question, however, stems from the attempt to estimate consumer-demand functions with various assumed functional forms. It then becomes important to check that the empirical functions are consistent with utility theory, in order to strengthen the plausibility of the results.

Consider now one last special case that appears in the literature on general equilibrium. Assume that, instead of the consumer bringing an amount of money income M to the market to purchase goods and services, the consumer comes to the market with initial endowments of $n + 1$ goods $x_0^0, x_1^0, \ldots, x_n^0$. The market sets prices of $p_0, p_1, \ldots, p_n$ for these goods, and the consumer maximizes utility subject to the constraint that the value of the goods purchased equal the value of the initial endowment, i.e.,

maximize $\qquad\qquad U(x_0, x_1, \ldots, x_n)$

subject to $\qquad\qquad p_0 x_0^0 + \cdots + p_n x_n^0 = p_0 x_0 + \cdots + p_n x_n$

that is, $\qquad\qquad$ subject to $\displaystyle\sum_{i=0}^{n} p_i x_i^0 = \sum_{i=0}^{n} p_i x_i$

The first-order conditions are obtained by setting the partials of the lagrangian equal to 0:

$$\mathscr{L} = U(x_0, \ldots, x_n) + \mu\left(\sum p_i x_i^0 - \sum p_i x_i\right)$$

$$\mathscr{L}_0 = U_0 - \mu p_0 = 0$$

$$\mathscr{L}_1 = U_1 - \mu p_1 = 0$$

$$\cdots\cdots\cdots\cdots\cdots\cdots$$

$$\mathscr{L}_n = U_n - \mu p_n = 0$$

$$\mathscr{L}_\mu = \sum p_i^0 x_i^0 - \sum p_i x_i = 0$$

These first-order equations are solved for the demand functions:

$$x_i = x_i^M(p_0, \ldots, p_n, x_0^0, \ldots, x_n^0) \qquad i = 0, \ldots, n \qquad (8\text{-}46)$$

This situation is depicted in Fig. 8-11. It is apparent, using reasoning similar to that used before, that these demand functions are homogeneous of degree zero in the $n + 1$ prices $p_0, \ldots, p_n$. It is customary to choose one commodity and set its price equal to one. This commodity, say x_0, is called the numeraire; it is the commodity in terms of which all prices are quoted. The situation being described

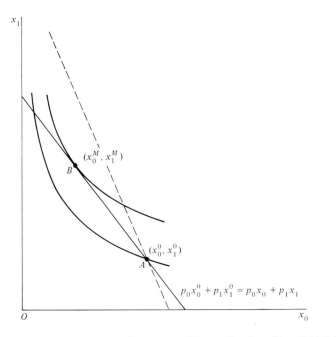

Figure 8-11 *General Equilibrium Demand Curves* Starting with an initial endowment (x_0^0, x_1^0) (point A), and prices indicated by the budget line, a consumer will maximize utility at point B, (x_0^M, x_1^M). The consumer will have sold x_0, the numeraire, and purchased x_1, but winding up with still positive amounts of each. An increase in the numeraire price (or a decrease in p_1) will rotate the budget line clockwise through A, producing a gain in real income over the previous situation.

is one of barter. If one of the goods is, say, gold, it may turn out that in addition to its amenity values (for which it enters the utility function, being useful in jewelry, dentistry, etc.), this commodity will also serve as a medium of exchange, being the commodity for which transactions costs are least. This model is incapable of predicting which commodity, if any, will be so chosen, but we can designate x_0 as that commodity which is the numeraire, and set $p_0 = 1$. The remaining prices p_1, ..., p_n then become *relative* prices.

Similar results are obtained in this model as in the standard utility-maximization problem. The endowment of the numeraire, x_0^0, serves the same function as M, the money income of the consumer. The compensated-demand curves $x_i = x_i^U(p_1, \ldots, p_n, U^0)$ are derivable from

minimize
$$x_0^0 = \sum_{i=0}^{n} p_i x_i - \sum_{i=1}^{n} p_i x_i^0$$

subject to
$$U(x_0, \ldots, x_n) = U^0$$

Note that the implied compensated-demand curves are *not* functions of the initial endowments, which enter the objective functions as constants and drop out upon differentiation. Once the utility level U^0 is specified, the original endowment is irrelevant—the demands are determined by tangency and the utility level U^0.

The indirect "endowment function" (formerly cost, or expenditure function) is given by

$$x_0 = x_0^*(p_1, \ldots, p_n, x_0^0, \ldots, x_n^0) = \sum_{i=0}^{n} p_i x_i^U - \sum_{i=1}^{n} p_i x_i^0 \tag{8-47}$$

Thus, by the envelope theorem,

$$\frac{\partial x_0^*}{\partial p_i} \equiv (x_i^U - x_i^0) \tag{8-48}$$

We can use these results to derive the implied Slutsky equation for this general equilibrium system. Proceeding as before, starting with the ordinary demand curves

$$x_i^M(p_1, \ldots, p_n, x_0^0, \ldots, x_n^0) \qquad i = 0, \ldots, n$$

define x_0^* to be the minimum x_0^0 to keep $U(x_0, \ldots, x_n) = U^0$. Then x_0^* is just the indirect function (8-47) above. Thus, by definition,

$$x_i^U(p_1, \ldots, p_n, x_0^0, \ldots, x_n^0) \equiv x_i^M(p_1, \ldots, p_n, x_0^*, x_1^0, \ldots, x_n^0)$$

Differentiating with respect to some p_j,

$$\frac{\partial x_i^U}{\partial p_j} \equiv \frac{\partial x_i^M}{\partial p_j} + \frac{\partial x_i^M}{\partial x_0^0} \frac{\partial x_0^*}{\partial p_j}$$

Using equation (8-48) and rearranging,

$$\frac{\partial x_i^M}{\partial p_j} = \frac{\partial x_i^U}{\partial p_j} - (x_j^M - x_j^0) \frac{\partial x_i^M}{\partial x_0^0} \tag{8-49}$$

Thus, the Slutsky equation has the same form as previously, with the important exception that the *income* effect, $\partial x_i^M / \partial x_0^0$, is weighted by the *change* in the consumption of x_j, $(x_j^M - x_j^0)$. If the amount of x_j was unchanged after going to the market, that is, $x_j^M = x_j^0$, there would be no income effect at all. Also, if, say, some price p_j goes up, then while formerly this acted as a decrease in real income, if the consumer is a net *seller* of x_j, this income effect is positive, i.e., it raises his or her real income. Of course, at any given point, $x_i^M = x_i^U$.

Slutsky versus Hicks Compensations

Although we have been referring to equation (8-35) as the Slutsky equation, this version was in fact first introduced by J. R. Hicks in "Value and Capital" (1937), based on Pareto's discussion of the phenomenon. Slutsky compensated the consumer in a slightly different form: after a price change, instead of adjusting M to return the consumer to the original indifference curve, Slutsky gave the consumer enough income to purchase the original bundle of goods. This is in fact more than $M^*(p_1, \ldots, p_n, U^0)$, the minimum M to return the consumer to the original utility level. How does this affect the Slutsky equation? Surprisingly, not at all. In the limit (at the margin, that is), the Hicks and Slutsky compensations are identical.

Consider Fig. 8-12. The original tangency is at (x_1^0, x_2^0). Suppose p_1 is lowered. Then compensating á la Hicks leads to a new level of x_1, x_1^U, at a new tangency of the same indifference curve U^0, and a new budget line. Compensation according to Slutsky, however, places the new budget line through (x_1^0, x_2^0) at the new prices. *Whether the prices* are raised or lowered (the diagram is for p_1 lowered, relative to p_2), the consumer can achieve a higher level of utility, say U^s (for Slutsky). If x_1 is a normal good, this will raise the consumption of x_1. Hence, the Slutsky demand curve x_1^s while equal to the Hicks curve at x_1^0, x_2^0, lies to the right of x_1^U for p_1 not equal to the original price. Assuming that $x_1^U(p_1, p_2, U^0)$ and $x_1^s(p_1, p_2, x_1^0, x_2^0)$ are both differentiable, the diagram clearly indicates that the two have a point of tangency at (x_1^0, x_2^0). But this says that the slopes of the two demand curves are equal there, or

$$\frac{\partial x_1^U}{\partial p_1} = \frac{\partial x_1^s}{\partial p_1}$$

This result is perfectly general; using similar reasoning,

$$\frac{\partial x_i^U}{\partial p_j} = \frac{\partial x_i^s}{\partial p_j}$$

If x_i is inferior rather than normal, a tangency still occurs, but with the Slutsky demand curve to the left of the Hicksian curve.

An algebraic proof of the above follows trivially from the general equilibrium variant of the Slutsky equation, (8-49),

$$\frac{\partial x_i^M}{\partial p_j} = \frac{\partial x_i^U}{\partial p_j} - (x_j^M - x_j^0) \frac{\partial x_i^M}{\partial x_j^0}$$

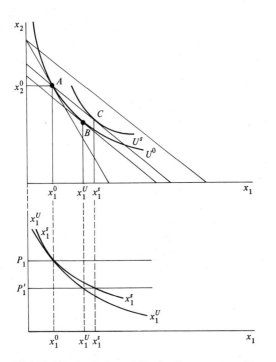

Figure 8-12 *The Hicks and Slutsky Compensations* The consumer starts at point (x_1^0, x_2^0). When p_1 is lowered, compensating according to Hicks leads to the new tangency B where $x_1 = x_1^U$. If a Slutsky compensation is made through the original point A, a new tangency on a higher indifference level, at point C, is attained. If x_1 is a normal good, the Slutsky demand, x_1^s, is greater than x_1^U. The same situation $(x_1^s > x_1^U)$ occurs if the price change is in the other direction. The consumer can always achieve a higher indifference level by moving away, i.e., adjusting to the price change. Hence, $x_1^s = x_1^s$ at x_1^0, but $x_1^s > x_1^U$ everywhere else. Hence, x_1^s and x_1^U are tangent at x_1^0, i.e., they have the same slope there, or $\partial x_1^s / \partial p_1 = \partial x_1^U / \partial p_1$.

A Slutsky compensation is equivalent to starting the consumer off at $x_i = x_i^0$, $i = 1, \ldots, n$. In this case, there is no income effect, and $\partial x_i^M / \partial p_j \equiv \partial x_i^s / \partial p_j$ by definition, and, hence, $\partial x_i^s / \partial p_j \equiv \partial x_i^U / \partial p_j$. Note, however, in the figure, that the Slutsky demand curve is more concave than the Hicks curve. The second derivatives are not equal, and, in fact, for normal goods, $\partial^2 x_i^s / \partial p_i^2 \geq \partial^2 x_i^U / \partial p_i^2$. This was first brought out by A. Wald and J. Mosak, who resolved the conflict between the Hicks and Slutsky variants of compensation.† What Mosak showed was that if p_j changed by an amount Δp_j, the difference between the Hicksian demand and the Slutsky demand was of second-order smallness, i.e., it involved powers of Δp of order two and higher.

---

† See J. Mosak, On the Interpretation of the Fundamental Equation of Value Theory, in O. Lange et al. (eds.), "Studies in Mathematical Economics and Econometrics," University of Chicago Press, Chicago, 1942.

The importance of this result is that in general it will not matter much which type of compensation is used, if the price change is not too large. Although the Hicks compensation is probably neater from the standpoint of the mathematical theory, this compensation will not be easy to observe. The Slutsky compensation, on the other hand, is calculable on the basis of simple arithmetic. Using the Wald-Mosak result, we can be assured that the compensations will not be very different, and that the easily observed Slutsky compensation is a good approximation to the "ideal" compensation á la Hicks.

This issue comes into play in the definition of index numbers. The Laspeyres index, used by the United States and other countries to define the consumer price index, is essentially a Slutsky compensation. The price index indicates the amount of dollars needed in the current year to purchase *the original consumption bundle* in the base year. Substitution away from that original basket of goods is not considered (a feature which biases the CPI upward, i.e., it exaggerates the impact of price changes by not allowing the consumer to adjust to the change). However, for small relative price changes, the bias should not be much worse, since the Slutsky compensation is a good approximation to the Hicksian compensation, which a "true" price index would try to calculate.

PROBLEMS

1 What is the difference, in a many-commodity model, between diminishing marginal rate of substitution between any pair of commodities, and quasi-concavity of the utility function? Which is a more restrictive concept?

2 Why does the proposition " More is preferred to less " imply downward-sloping indifference curves?

3 What dependence, if any, does the homogeneity of degree zero of the money-income-held-constant demand curves have on the homogeneity of the consumer's utility function?

4 Show that the marginal utility of money income, μ^*, is homogeneous of degree *minus one*. (*Hint:* Use equation (8-16).

5 Consider the utility functions of the form, $U = x_1^{\alpha_1} x_2^{\alpha_2}$. Show that the implied demand curves are,

$$x_1^M = \frac{\alpha_1}{(\alpha_1 + \alpha_2)} \frac{M}{p_1}$$

$$x_2^M = \frac{\alpha_2}{(\alpha_1 + \alpha_2)} \frac{M}{p_2}$$

Find μ^* and $U^*(x_1^M, x_2^M)$, and verify that $\mu^* = \partial U^*/\partial M$.

6 Prove the elasticity formulas (8-38), (8-39), (8-40), (8-41) and (8-42) for the n commodity case.

7 Is it possible to define complements in consumer theory, by saying that the marginal utility of x_i increases when more x_j is consumed? (*Hint:* What mathematical term is being defined, and is it invariant to a monotonic transformation?)

8 Substitutes can be defined by the sign of the *gross* (including income effects) cross-effects of prices on quantities, or the *net* effect (i.e., *not* including income effects). That is, one may define " x_i is a substitute for x_j " if:

(*i*) $\quad \dfrac{\partial x_i^M}{\partial p_j} > 0 \qquad$ or

(ii) $\dfrac{\partial x_i^U}{\partial p_j} > 0$

(with the reverse sign on the inequality for "complements".)

(a) Which term is likely to be the more observable (empirically)?

(b) Are these terms invariant to a monotonic transformation of the utility function?

(c) According to the above definitions, if x_i is a substitute for x_j, is x_j necessarily a substitute for x_i?

9 Considering Hicks' "third law," and the above definition (ii) of substitutes and complements, show that there is a tendency toward substitution of commodities in the sense that

$$\sum_{i \neq j} p_i s_{ij} = \sum_{j \neq i} p_j s_{ij} > 0$$

10 Describe the effects of a monotonic transformation of the utility function on:

(a) The rate of change of the marginal utility of one good with respect to a change in another good.

(b) The law of diminishing marginal utility.

(c) The slopes of demand curves.

(d) The values of income elasticities.

(e) The homogeneity of the demand functions.

(f) The size and sign of the marginal utility of income.

11 For the utility-maximization model, show that

$$\frac{\partial x_1^M}{\partial M} = \frac{-1}{\mu^*} \left(\frac{\partial \mu^*}{\partial p_1} + x_1^M \frac{\partial \mu^*}{\partial M} \right)$$

where μ^* is the marginal utility of money income.

12 Suppose a consumer will have income x_1^0 this year and x_2^0 next year. He or she consumes x_1 this year and x_2 next year, being able to borrow and lend at interest rate r. Assume the consumer maximizes the utility of consumption over these two years.

(a) Derive the comparative statics for this problem. Will an increase in this year's income necessarily lead to an increase in consumption this year?

(b) Prove that the consumer will be better off (worse off) if the interest rate rises if he or she was a net saver (dissaver) this year.

13 Consider the utility-maximization problem, max $U(x_1, x_2)$ subject to $p_1 x_1 + p_2 x_2 = 1$ where prices have been "normalized" by setting $M = 1$. Let $U^*(p_1, p_2)$ be the indirect utility function, and μ be the Lagrange multiplier.

(a) Show that $\mu^* = (\partial U/\partial x_1)x_1^* + (\partial U/\partial x_2)x_2^*$

(b) Show that $\partial U^*/\partial p_1 = -\mu^* x_1^*$, $\partial U^*/\partial p_2 = -\mu^* x_2^*$

(c) Show that $\mu^* = -[(\partial U^*/\partial p_1)p_1 + (\partial U^*/\partial p_2)p_2]$

(d) Prove that if $U(x_1, x_2)$ is homogeneous of degree r in (x_1, x_2), then $U^*(p_1, p_2)$ is homogeneous of degree $-r$ in (p_1, p_2).

14 Consider the class of utility functions which are "additively separable," i.e., $U(x_1, x_2) \equiv U^1(x_1) + U^2(x_2)$. (These utility functions are thought by some to be relevant to problems involving intertemporal choice.)

(a) Find the first- and second-order conditions for utility-maximization for these utility functions. Show that diminishing marginal utility in at least one good is implied.

(b) Show that if there is diminishing marginal utility in each good, then both goods are "normal," i.e., not inferior.

15 Using the envelope theorem, show that

(a) $\partial U^*/\partial p_i = -\mu^* x_i^M$ where $U^* = U(x_1^M, x_2^M)$.

(b) Show, therefore, that

$$\partial(\mu^* x_i^M)/\partial p_j = \partial(\mu^* x_j^M)/\partial p_i$$

(c) If you didn't do it that way, prove the result in problem 11 via the envelope theorem.

16 The "real income," or "utility held constant" demand curves are written

$$x_1 = x_1^U(p_1, p_2, U^0)$$

Suppose now, when p_1 changes, U^0 is also adjusted to that maximum amount achievable so as to keep money income M constant, i.e.,

$$U^0 = U^*(p_1, p_2, M)$$

is that functional relationship which keeps M constant by adjusting utility, when p_1 or p_2 changes. Thus, the money-income-held-constant demand curves can be written

$$x_1^M(p_1, p_2, M) \equiv x_1^U(p_1, p_2, U^*(p_1, p_2, M))$$

(a) Show that the income effect on x_1 is proportional to the "utility effect" on x_1, i.e., the change in x_1^U when U is changed, the factor of proportionality being the marginal utility of money income.

(b) Show that

$$\frac{\partial x_1^M}{\partial p_2} \equiv \frac{\partial x_1^U}{\partial p_2} - x_2 \frac{\partial x_1^M}{\partial M}$$

(This is an alternative derivation of the Slutsky equation to that given in the text.)

17 In a leading economics text, the following form of the "law of diminishing marginal rate of substitution" is given: The more of one good a consumer has, holding the *quantities* of all other goods constant, the smaller the marginal evaluation of that good becomes in terms of all other goods, i.e. the indifference curves become less steep. (Sketch this condition graphically.)

(a) This is a postulate about the slopes of indifferences curves, i.e., about the term $(-U_1/U_2)$. What is the sign, according to this postulate, of $\partial(-U_1/U_2)/\partial x_1$, $\partial(-U_1/U_2)/\partial x_2$?

(b) Show that this postulate implies that the indifference curves are convex to the origin.

(c) Suppose this postulate is violated for good 2. Show that x_1 is an inferior good. Show that if the postulate is violated for good 1 also, then the indifference curves are *concave* to the origin.

(d) Show that the above postulate rules out inferior goods (for the two-good case).

(e) Show that in part (c), in which the indifference curves are still assumed to be convex to the origin, the marginal evaluation of x_2 *increases* the more it is consumed relative to x_1. Explain intuitively.

(f) Show that in a three-good world, the above postulate is insufficiently strong to imply indifference curves which are convex to the origin.

18 An historically important class of utility functions includes those functions which exhibit vertically parallel indifference curves, i.e., with x_1 on the horizontal axis and x_2 on the vertical axis, the slopes of *all* indifference curves are the same at any given level of x_1. For these utility functions:

(a) Prove graphically and algebraically that the income effect on x_1 equals 0.

(b) Show that the "ordinary" demand curve for x_1, $x_1^M(p_1, p_2, M)$ and the compensated demand curve for x_1, $x_1^U(p_1, p_2, U)$ are identical by showing that at any point, the slopes of x_1^M and x_1^U are the same, and that the shifts in x_1^M and x_1^U are the same with respect to a change in p_2, the price of the second good.

(c) Consider the utility function $U = x_2 + \log x_1$. Show that this function has vertically parallel indifference curves.

(d) For $U = x_2 + \log x_1$, show also that the price-consumption path with respect to changes in p_1 are horizontal; i.e., that the amount of x_2 consumed is independent of the price of good 1.

19 Suppose a consumer's utility is a function of *income* Y and leisure L; that is, $U = U(Y, L)$. Suppose income is related to the wage rate w by

$$Y = (24 - L)w$$

That is, income equals the number of hours worked, $(24 - L)$, times the wage rate. Why is the wage rate the price of leisure?

(a) Derive the Slutsky equation for this model and illustrate the income and substitution effects of a change in wage rate on the amount of leisure consumed.

(b) In "ordinary" utility theory, if a good is known to be noninferior, then, necessarily, $\partial x_i^M / \partial p_i < 0$. Here, in order to assert $\partial L^* / \partial w < 0$, where L^* is the utility-maximizing level of leisure, *nonsuperiority* of leisure must be asserted. Demonstrate this and explain why this case is different from the usual situation.

SELECTED REFERENCES

Alchian, A. A.: The Meaning of Utility Measurement, *American Economic Review*, **43**: 26–50, March 1953.

Becker, G. S.: Irrational Behavior and Economic Theory, *Journal of Political Economy*, **70**: 1–13, 1962.

———: A Theory of the Allocation of Time, *Economic Journal*, **75**: 493–517, 1965.

Debreu, G.: "Theory of Value," Cowles Foundation Monograph 17, John Wiley & Sons, Inc., New York, 1959. The seminal work in the formal, abstract approach to economic theory. Get out your old topology notes first.

Friedman, M.: The Marshallian Demand Curve, in "Essays in Positive Economics," University of Chicago Press, Chicago, 1953. Debatable, to say the least, but important in terms of the issues analyzed.

Georgescu-Roegen, N.: The Pure Theory of Consumer Behavior, *Quarterly Journal of Economics*, **50**: 545–593, 1936.

Hicks, J. R.: "Value and Capital," 2d ed., Oxford University Press, London, 1946.

———: "A Revision of Demand Theory," Oxford University Press, London, 1956.

Lancaster, K. J.: A New Approach to Consumer Theory, *Journal of Political Economy*, **74**: 132–157, April 1966.

Marshall, A.: "Principles of Economics," 8th ed., Macmillan & Co., Ltd., London, 1920.

Mosak, J. L.: On the Interpretation of the Fundamental Equation in Value Theory, in O. Lange, F. McIntyre, and T. O. Yntema (eds.), "Studies in Mathematical Economics and Econometrics in Memory of Henry Schultz," University of Chicago Press, Chicago, 1942.

Samuelson, P. A.: "Foundations of Economic Analysis," Harvard University Press, Cambridge, Mass., 1947.

Slutsky, E.: Sulla Teoria del Bilancio del Consumatore, *Giornale degli Economisti*, **51**: 19–23, 1915. Translated as On the Theory of the Budget of the Consumer, in "Readings in Price Theory," G. Stigler and K. Boulding (eds.), Richard D. Irwin, Inc., Homewood, Ill., 1952

Wold, H., and L. Jureen: "Demand Analysis," John Wiley & Sons, Inc., New York, 1953.

CHAPTER NINE

THE COMPARATIVE STATICS OF MAXIMIZATION MODELS

9.1 PROFIT-MAXIMIZATION

In this chapter we shall discuss some general results pertaining to models in which a specific objective function is asserted to be maximized (or minimized; minimization can be accomplished by maximizing the negative of an objective function, hence no generality is lost by considering maximization only). In a later chapter we shall discuss nonmaximization models, in which the equilibrium equations, i.e., those implicit equations relating the decision variables and the parameters, are not the first partials of some objective or lagrangian function. The most common example of such nonmaximization models is the familiar three-equation macromodel involving, for example, income, price level, interest rate, and consumption. Often, maximizing behavior is implicit in the construction of the individual equations in the model; e.g., some sort of wealth-maximization is commonly the basis of the consumption function, which relates consumption to income. However, the consumption function itself is not the first partial derivative of a lagrangian function which generates all the equations of the macromodel.

The purpose of the present analysis is to discover what mathematical structures of models involving an explicit objective function lead to refutable hypotheses. More specifically, since no quantitative data on the size of various variables will be present in our analysis, we wish to determine what types of model structures imply a definitive sign pattern for the responses of decision variables to changes in various parameters. If the structural equations of a model imply a set of choice functions $x_i = x_i^* (\alpha_1, \ldots, \alpha_m)$, where the α_i's are parameters, or test conditions, under what mathematical conditions can one determine the sign of some (or all) $\partial x_i^*/\partial \alpha_j$? We have already investigated these matters somewhat (Chap. 6). In this chapter a more general and more elegant discussion will be given. We shall find that the functional forms for which refutable hypotheses emerge are indeed limited but still a useful enough set of structures to be worthy of study.

We shall begin by considering once more the model:

maximize $$\pi = pf(x_1, x_2) - w_1 x_1 - w_2 x_2$$

where $y = f(x_1, x_2) = $ production function of firm
  $w_1, w_2 = $ factor prices of x_1, x_2, respectively
    $p = $ output-price

The first-order conditions for a maximum are, again

$$\pi_1 = pf_1 - w_1 = 0 \tag{9-1a}$$

$$\pi_2 = pf_2 - w_2 = 0 \tag{9-1b}$$

from which the factor-demand curves

$$x_1 = x_1^*(w_1, w_2, p) \tag{9-2a}$$

$$x_2 = x_2^*(w_1, w_2, p) \tag{9-2b}$$

are derived by simultaneous solution of (9-1a) and (9-1b). It bears repeating that maximizing profits is not an observable event. There is no way to look at a corporate balance sheet, say, and conclude from it alone that the firm is indeed maximizing profits. Similarly, the marginal relations (9-1) are not observable unless the production function $y = f(x_1, x_2)$ is known. As a matter of empirical reality, the production function will not be known (or at least not known in sufficient detail to permit direct observation of a firm's setting the value of the marginal product of each factor equal to its respective wage). The choice or demand functions here [equations (9-2)], however, merely relate the quantities of each factor purchased (an observable event, at least in principle) to the prices of each factor and output-price (likewise observable quantities). Hence, the implied demand functions, though derived from nonobservable concepts, are themselves observable. And if it turns out, as it does in this case, that certain restrictions on the demand functions, namely, $\partial x_i^*/\partial w_i < 0, i = 1, 2$, are implied by the maximization hypothesis, then the model is potentially interesting and useful. We say potentially interesting because the implications may turn out to be refuted by facts. If it turns out that when a factor price is raised relative to another price, the firm indeed reduces its purchases of that factor, the profit-maximization hypothesis is *confirmed;* i.e., it is found to be consistent with the facts. It is not proved, however. Some other behavior hypothesis also consistent with negatively sloping demand functions could be the "true" behavioral postulate. On the other hand, if it is found that when a factor price increases, the firm clearly and unambiguously raises its purchase of that factor, the profit-maximization theory is refuted, i.e., disproved.

Let us now rederive the comparative statics of the profit-maximization model

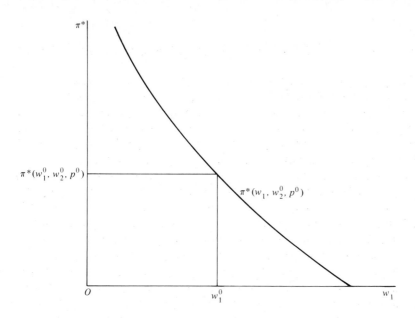

Figure 9-1 The profit function $\pi^*(w_1, w_2, p)$ plotted against various values of w_1. The profit function is negatively sloped in w_1 because, by the envelope theorem, $\partial\pi^*/\partial w_1 = -x_1^* < 0$. Clearly, as any factor price is increased, the firm must make lower, rather than higher, profits.

in a new way, in which the general structure of comparative-statics relations is more clearly exposed. The indirect profit function (hereafter referred to as simply the *profit function*) $\pi^*(w_1, w_2, p)$ is defined as

$$\pi^*(w_1, w_2, p) \equiv pf\left(x_1^*(w_1, w_2, p), x_2^*(w_1, w_2, p)\right)$$

$$- w_1 x_1^*(w_1, w_2, p) - w_2 x_2^*(w_1, w_2, p) \qquad (9\text{-}3)$$

Consider now Fig. 9-1, in which π^*, profits, is plotted against various values of w_1, holding w_2 and p constant at values w_2^0 and p^0. Note first that π^* is negatively sloped with regard to w_1. Why? By the envelope theorem,

$$\frac{\partial\pi^*}{\partial w_1} = -x_1^* < 0$$

since $x_1^* > 0$. Clearly, as any factor price is increased, the firm will make lower profits. At every point along this curve, some values of x_1^* and x_2^* are implied, though they are not drawn in. The value of x_1^*, however, is represented geometrically by the (negative) slope of the π^* curve in the π^*w_1 plane. In fact, $\pi^*(w_1, w_2^0, p^0)$ is convex (downward) in w_1. We know from earlier analysis that $\partial x_1^*/\partial w_1 < 0$. But since $\partial\pi^*/\partial w_1 = -x_1^*$,

$$-\frac{\partial x_1^*}{\partial w_1} = +\frac{\partial^2\pi^*}{\partial w_1^2} > 0 \qquad (9\text{-}4)$$

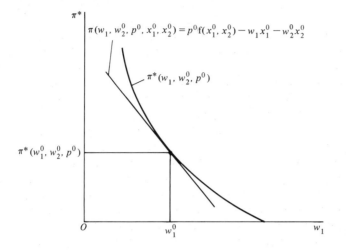

$$\pi(w_1, w_2^0, p^0, x_1^0, x_2^0) = p^0 f(x_1^0, x_2^0) - w_1 x_1^0 - w_2^0 x_2^0$$

$$\pi^*(w_1, w_2^0, p^0)$$

$$\pi^*(w_1^0, w_2^0, p^0)$$

Figure 9-2 The profit function $\pi^*(w_1, w_2^0, p^0)$ and the profit function $\pi(w_1, w_2^0, p^0, x_1^0, x_2^0)$, where x_1^0 and x_2^0 are those levels which maximize profits when $w_1 = w_1^0$.

This suggests that the comparative-statics relations are directly related to the curvature properties of the indirect objective function (here the profit function). The statement that $\partial x_i^*/\partial w_i < 0$ is equivalent to stating that $\pi^*(w_1, w_2, p)$ is convex in at least the w_1, w_2 directions. Perhaps the general shape of $\pi^*(w_1, w_2, p)$ will reveal the comparative statics of this model. Indeed it does, as we now demonstrate.

Consider now Fig. 9-2. The profit function $\pi^*(w_1, w_2, p)$ is drawn in as in Fig. 9-1 with w_1 on the horizontal axis, holding w_2 and p constant throughout at $w_2 = w_2^0$, $p = p^0$. Consider the value of π^* at $w_1 = w_1^0$. Some values of x_1^* and x_2^* are implied, given by

$$x_1^0 = x_1^*(w_1^0, w_2^0, p^0) \qquad x_2^0 = x_2^*(w_1^0, w_2^0, p^0)$$

Suppose now that w_1 is changed but that x_1 and x_2 are held fixed at $x_1 = x_1^0$, $x_2 = x_2^0$. Then, as w_1 moves away from w_1^0, the "wrong" x_i's will be employed by the firm; i.e., factor levels will be other than those which would maximize profits at the new level of w_1. Profits will therefore be lower than if the x_i^*'s adjusted to the new w_1 according to the factor-demand equations $x_i^*(w_1, w_2^0, p^0)$, $i = 1, 2$. This situation is depicted in Fig. 9-2. The constrained-profit function

$$\pi(w_1, w_2^0, p^0, x_1^0, x_2^0) = p^0 f(x_1^0, x_2^0) - w_1 x_1^0 - w_2^0 x_2^0 \qquad (9\text{-}5)$$

shows the level of profits for given w_2^0 and p^0, holding $x_1 = x_1^0$, $x_2 = x_2^0$. In this particular case, $\pi(w_1, w_2^0, p^0, x_1^0, x_2^0)$ is clearly a linear function, since everything other than the linear term $x_1^0 w_1$ on the right-hand side of (9-5) is constant. But this π function, (9-5), is equal to $\pi^*(w_1, w_2^0, p^0)$ at the one point at which x_1 and x_2 are in fact the profit-maximizing input levels; this is at $w_1 = w_1^0$, by which $x_1^0 = x_1^*(w_1^0,$

w_2^0, p^0) and $x_2^0 = x_2^*(w_1^0, w_2^0, p^0)$ were determined in the first place. At all other values of w_1, $\pi < \pi^*$. Hence,

$$\pi(w_1, w_2^0, p^0, x_1^0, x_2^0) \leq \pi^*(w_1, w_2^0, p^0) \tag{9-6}$$

with the equality holding when $w_1 = w_1^0$. But observe the geometric consequences of this in Fig. 9-2. π^* always lies above π, except at w_1^0, where $\pi^* = \pi$. Assuming π^* and π are both differentiable, this means that π^* and π are tangent to each other at $w_1 = w_1^0$. Tangency means that π^* and π have the same slope at w_1^0. This is precisely the envelope theorem, $\partial \pi^*/\partial w_1 = \partial \pi/\partial w_1$. The reason why this result (that the rate of change of the indirect objective function with respect to a parameter change is independent of any adjustment of the decision variables to the parameter change) is called an envelope theorem is now apparent. The profit function $\pi^*(w_1, w_2^0, p^0)$ is an envelope curve lying above all direct profit functions $\pi(w_1, w_2^0, p^0, x_1^0, x_2^0)$ but tangent to π at one particular point. At a different value of w_1, say w_1^1, there will be different implied profit-maximizing levels of inputs $x_i^1 = x_i^*(w_1^1, w_2^0, p^0)$, and then π^* will be tangent to the implied $\pi(w_1, w_2^0, p^0, x_1^1, x_2^1)$ at some other point $w_1 = w_1^1$. But the π^* function will lie above all such direct profit functions, tangent to each at one point. It is an envelope of all the direct profit functions since π^* alone represents the *maximum* level of profits for any set of parameter values. Obviously, we need not consider changes in the parameter w_1 only; the same reasoning applies to w_2 and p also.

However, we have more information than merely equality of slope at $w = w_1$ in Fig. 9-2. Since π^* is everywhere above π (except at $w_1 = w_1^0$), $\pi^*(w_1, w_2^0, p^0)$ must be more convex (or less concave) than $\pi(w_1, w_2^0, p^0, x_1^0, x_2^0)$. In this particular case, π is linear, and thus $\pi^*(w_1, w_2^0, p^0)$ must be convex in w_1, or $\partial^2\pi^*/\partial w_1^2 \geq 0$. This follows directly from tangency of π^* to π. But this is precisely the proposition that factor demands are downward-sloping, since $\partial^2\pi^*/\partial w_1^2 = -\partial x_1^*/\partial w_1 \geq 0$. Hence, it is possible to make inferences about the comparative statics of the profit-maximization model on the basis of some simple geometry of tangency points.

Let us derive these properties formally, without the appeal to visual geometry. Let $\pi^*(w_1, w_2, p)$ be the profit function for any values of w_1, w_2, and p. Define the new function representing the (negative) difference between $\pi^*(w_1, w_2, p)$, the *maximum* level of profits, and any other level of profits as

$$z = F(x_1, x_2, w_1, w_2, p) \equiv [pf(x_1, x_2) - w_1 x_1 - w_2 x_2] - \pi^*(w_1, w_2, p)$$

$$\equiv \pi(x_1, x_2, w_1, w_2, p) - \pi^*(w_1, w_2, p) \tag{9-7}$$

The function $F(x_1, x_2, w_1, w_2, p)$ is to be considered as a function of five independent variables, x_1, x_2, w_1, w_2, and p. What values can $z = F(x_1, x_2, w_1, w_2, p)$ take on? Since π^* is the maximum value of π, $z = \pi - \pi^* \leq 0$, with equality holding only when $x_1 = x_1^*(w_1, w_2, p)$ and $x_2 = x_2^*(w_1, w_2, p)$. Thus, F is negative whenever $x_i \neq x_i^*$, $i = 1, 2$, and $F = 0$ when $x_i = x_i^*$, $i = 1, 2$. *This says that $F(x_1, x_2, w_1, w_2, p)$ has a maximum (of 0) when $x_i = x_i^*(w_1, w_2, p)$, $i = 1, 2$.* At an interior maximum, the first partials of F with respect to all five "variables" are all 0, and if the sufficient second-order conditions are assumed, the matrix of second partials is negative definite; i.e., the principal minors of order k have sign $(-1)^k$. Let us write down these first- and second-order conditions. Note that $\pi^*(w_1, w_2, p)$ is not a function of x_1 or x_2. Thus,

$$F_{x_1} = \frac{\partial \pi}{\partial x_1} = pf_1 - w_1 = 0 \tag{9-8a}$$

$$F_{x_2} = \frac{\partial \pi}{\partial x_2} = pf_2 - w_2 = 0 \tag{9-8b}$$

These relations are merely the original first-order equations (9-1). Now differentiate with respect to w_1, w_2, and p:

$$F_{w_1} = \frac{\partial \pi}{\partial w_1} - \frac{\partial \pi^*}{\partial w_1} = 0 \tag{9-9a}$$

$$F_{w_2} = \frac{\partial \pi}{\partial w_2} - \frac{\partial \pi^*}{\partial w_2} = 0 \tag{9-9b}$$

$$F_p = \frac{\partial \pi}{\partial p} - \frac{\partial \pi^*}{\partial p} = 0 \tag{9-9c}$$

However, $\partial \pi / \partial w_1 = -x_1$ (remember that x_1 and x_2 are held constant here; π, not π^* is being differentiated). Similarly, $\partial \pi / \partial w_2 = -x_2$, $\partial \pi / \partial p = f(x_1, x_2) = y$. Then equations (9-9) become

$$F_{w_1} = -x_1 - \frac{\partial \pi^*}{\partial w_1} = 0 \tag{9-10a}$$

$$F_{w_2} = -x_2 - \frac{\partial \pi^*}{\partial w_2} = 0 \tag{9-10b}$$

$$F_p = y - \frac{\partial \pi^*}{\partial p} = 0 \tag{9-10c}$$

Equations (9-10) or, for that matter, (9-9) are simply the envelope theorem. This alternative proof of the envelope theorem is perhaps more revealing than the previous derivation in Chap. 6; here, the geometric property of an envelope is more clearly seen. We are merely stating that $\pi^*(w_1, w_2, p)$ must be an envelope curve to all possible direct profit functions $\pi(x_1, x_2, w_1, w_2, p)$.

Equations (9-10) mean that $\partial \pi^* / \partial w_i = -x_i^*$. That is, since the maximum value of F occurs when $x_i = x_i^*(w_1, w_2, p)$, the derivatives in equations (9-10) must be evaluated at that point. Thus, equations (9-10) can be written

$$F_{w_1} = -x_1 + x_1^*(w_1, w_2, p) = 0 \tag{9-11a}$$

$$F_{w_2} = -x_2 + x_2^*(w_1, w_2, p) = 0 \tag{9-11b}$$

$$F_p = y - y^*(w_1, w_2, p) = 0 \tag{9-11c}$$

where, of course, $y^*(w_1, w_2, p) = f(x_1^*, x_2^*)$.

However, we can do even better than this. Consider the second-order conditions: the principal minors of order k of the 5×5 determinant of second partials of $F(x_1, x_2, w_1, w_2, p)$ have sign $(-1)^k$, or 0; that is, the matrix $\mathbf{H}$ must be negative semidefinite:

$$
H = \left|
\begin{array}{cc:ccc}
F_{x_1 x_1} & F_{x_1 x_2} & F_{x_1 w_1} & F_{x_1 w_2} & F_{x_1 p} \\
F_{x_2 x_1} & F_{x_2 x_2} & F_{x_2 w_1} & F_{x_2 w_2} & F_{x_2 p} \\
\hdashline
F_{w_1 x_1} & F_{w_1 x_2} & F_{w_1 w_1} & F_{w_1 w_2} & F_{w_1 p} \\
F_{w_2 x_1} & F_{w_2 x_2} & F_{w_2 w_1} & F_{w_2 w_2} & F_{w_2 p} \\
F_{p x_1} & F_{p x_2} & F_{p w_1} & F_{p w_2} & F_{p p}
\end{array}
\right|
\tag{9-12}
$$

The determinant H has been partitioned into essentially an upper left-hand corner, which relates to the original decision variables x_1 and x_2 only, and a lower right-hand portion, which involves the second partials with respect only to the parameters w_1, w_2, and p.

Let us fill in the values of this determinant given the profit-maximization model. From equations (9-8), $F_{x_i x_j} = p f_{ij}$. Thus, the upper left portion of H is simply the second partials of the production function. More interestingly, using equations (9-11), we have

$$
F_{w_1 w_1} = \frac{\partial[-x_1 + x_1^*(w_1, w_2, p)]}{\partial w_1}
$$

But x_1 is *not* a function of w_1; only x_1^* is a function of w_1 (and w_2 and p also). Hence,

$$
F_{w_1 w_1} = \frac{\partial x_1^*}{\partial w_1}
$$

In general,

$$
F_{w_i w_j} = \frac{\partial x_i^*}{\partial w_j} \qquad F_{w_i p} = \frac{\partial x_i^*}{\partial p} \qquad F_{p w_i} = \frac{-\partial y^*}{\partial w_i} \qquad F_{p p} = \frac{-\partial y^*}{\partial p}
$$

The determinant H thus becomes

$$
H = \left|
\begin{array}{cc:ccc}
p f_{11} & p f_{12} & -1 & 0 & f_1 \\
p f_{21} & p f_{22} & 0 & -1 & f_2 \\
\hdashline
-1 & 0 & \dfrac{\partial x_1^*}{\partial w_1} & \dfrac{\partial x_1^*}{\partial w_2} & \dfrac{\partial x_1^*}{\partial p} \\
0 & -1 & \dfrac{\partial x_2^*}{\partial w_1} & \dfrac{\partial x_2^*}{\partial w_2} & \dfrac{\partial x_2^*}{\partial p} \\
f_1 & f_2 & -\dfrac{\partial y^*}{\partial w_1} & -\dfrac{\partial y^*}{\partial w_2} & -\dfrac{\partial y^*}{\partial p}
\end{array}
\right|
\tag{9-13}
$$

Let us designate this determinant by its component submatrices as

$$|\mathbf{H}| = H = \begin{vmatrix} \mathbf{F}_{xx} & \mathbf{F}_{x\alpha} \\ \mathbf{F}_{\alpha x} & \mathbf{F}_{\alpha\alpha} \end{vmatrix} \tag{9-14}$$

where $\mathbf{F}_{xx}$ refers to the 2×2 matrix of pf_{ij}'s in the upper left corner of H, $\mathbf{F}_{\alpha\alpha}$ designates the 3×3 matrix of terms $\partial x_i^*/\partial w_j$, $\partial x_i^*/\partial p$, etc. [the partial derivatives of the choice functions $x_1^*(w_1, w_2, p)$, $x_2^*(w_1, w_2, p)$, and $y^*(w_1, w_2, p)$] and $\mathbf{F}_{x\alpha}$ and $\mathbf{F}_{\alpha x}$ those 2×3 and 3×2 matrices of mixed partials of choice variables and parameters. We shall have little occasion to consider these last two submatrices.

The comparative-statics relations forthcoming in this model can be read directly out of this matrix. First, since all the entries are second partials of some objective function, the matrix is symmetric; i.e., an element a_{ij} in row i, column j, is equal to a_{ji}, the element in row j, column i. From the lower right matrix $\mathbf{F}_{\alpha\alpha}$ we therefore obtain, almost trivially, the reciprocity conditions

$$\frac{\partial x_1^*}{\partial w_2} = \frac{\partial x_2^*}{\partial w_1} \quad \text{and} \quad \frac{\partial x_i^*}{\partial p} = -\frac{\partial y^*}{\partial w_i} \quad i = 1, 2$$

These results are obtained without the complicated manipulations involved in the implicit-function-theorem approach to comparative statics, where Cramer's rule is used to solve for the above partial derivatives. In addition, the direct dependence of these reciprocity conditions on the theorem of invariance of cross-partials to the order of differentiation is clearly seen: reciprocity *is* the theorem on invariance of cross-partials.

What do the second-order conditions for maximizing $z = F(x_1, x_2, w_1, w_2, p) \equiv \pi(x_1, x_2, w_1, w_2, p) - \pi^*(w_1, w_2, p)$ imply? If the whole matrix $\mathbf{H}$ is negative semidefinite, then $\mathbf{F}_{xx}$ and $\mathbf{F}_{\alpha\alpha}$ must be so also. This is easily seen: all diagonal elements must be negative (strictly speaking, nonpositive) and all 2×2 principal minors are ≥ 0. But the determinant of $\mathbf{F}_{xx}$ is one of those second-order principal minors. Likewise, the determinant $|\mathbf{F}_{\alpha\alpha}|$ is one of the third-order principal minors [whose sign is therefore $(-1)^3 < 0$]. Also, the principal minors of $|\mathbf{F}_{\alpha\alpha}|$ of order 2 are some of the principal minors of order 2 of the whole determinant H, and the principal minors of order 1 of $|\mathbf{F}_{\alpha\alpha}|$, the diagonal elements of $|\mathbf{F}_{\alpha\alpha}|$, are clearly diagonal elements of H. In other words, the principal minors of H include all the principal minors of $|\mathbf{F}_{\alpha\alpha}|$; therefore, since $\mathbf{H}$ is negative semidefinite, $\mathbf{F}_{\alpha\alpha}$ must be also.

The remaining comparative-statics theorems for the profit-maximizing firm can now be read at a glance from equation (9-13), in particular from the subdeterminant $|\mathbf{F}_{\alpha\alpha}|$ (the last three rows and columns). Since the diagonal elements must be negative, by the sufficient second-order conditions, $\partial x_1^*/\partial w_1 < 0$, $\partial x_2^*/\partial w_2 < 0$, $\partial y^*/\partial p > 0$. The direct dependency of these results on the second-order conditions for maximization is clearly exhibited here. In addition to these qualitative relations, the second-order principal minors give us the result

$$\frac{\partial x_1^*}{\partial w_1} \frac{\partial x_2^*}{\partial w_2} - \left(\frac{\partial x_1^*}{\partial w_2}\right)^2 \geq 0 \tag{9-15}$$

This situation is described by saying that the direct effects outweigh the cross-effects. This property of maximizing systems was first encountered in the discussion in Chap. 4, concerning the derivation of the second-order conditions. This was illustrated with reference to the law of diminishing returns (diminishing marginal product), wherein it was shown that diminishing returns in each factor were not sufficient to guarantee a maximum position. In addition to that, the condition $f_{11}f_{22} - f_{12}^2 > 0$ had to hold; this was in effect saying that the cross-effects of increased use of one factor on the other could not be powerful enough to counteract the diminishing marginal product in each factor.

In addition to equation (9-15) for the factor demands, for mixed demand and supply,

$$\frac{\partial x_i^*}{\partial w_i}\left(-\frac{\partial y^*}{\partial p}\right) - \frac{\partial x_i^*}{\partial p}\left(-\frac{\partial y^*}{\partial w_i}\right) \geq 0 \qquad i = 1, 2 \qquad (9\text{-}16)$$

The behavior of the quantities $\partial y^*/\partial p$ and $\partial y^*/\partial w_i$ is similar to that of the factor demands, but since the x_i's are inputs and y is output, a negative sign for the derivatives of y^* is needed to preserve exact symmetry. Finally, the whole 3×3 determinant $|\mathbf{F}_{\alpha\alpha}|$ must be nonpositive; it is not easy to interpret this condition intuitively, except again to indicate the general nature of direct effects outweighing cross-effects.

A way of characterizing these results geometrically is to say that $\pi^*(w_1, w_2, p)$ is convex in the factor prices w_1 and w_2 and convex in the output-price p. We in fact know that π^* can only be weakly convex, not strictly convex, from the homogeneity properties of π^*. Since the factor demands are homogeneous of degree zero, they are unaffected by scalar multiplication of all prices, or

$$\pi^*(tw_1, tw_2, tp) \equiv tpf(x_1^*, x_2^*) - tw_1 x_1^* - tw_2 x_2^* \equiv t\pi^*(w_1, w_2, p)$$

Thus, π^* is necessarily homogeneous of degree 1 in all prices. This being the case, π^* has linear elements; i.e., it is conical in shape, having straight sides along rays from the origin. Hence, it cannot be the case that $|\mathbf{F}_{\alpha\alpha}| < 0$, since this would imply *strict* concavity.

That $|\mathbf{F}_{\alpha\alpha}| = 0$ can be seen by application of Euler's theorem. Multiply column 1 of $|\mathbf{F}_{\alpha\alpha}|$ by w_1, column 2 by w_2, and column 3 by p. Then

$$|\mathbf{F}_{\alpha\alpha}| = \frac{1}{w_1 w_2 p} \begin{vmatrix} \dfrac{\partial x_1^*}{\partial w_1} w_1 & \dfrac{\partial x_1^*}{\partial w_2} w_2 & \dfrac{\partial x_1^*}{\partial p} p \\[2mm] \dfrac{\partial x_2^*}{\partial w_1} w_1 & \dfrac{\partial x_2^*}{\partial w_2} w_2 & \dfrac{\partial x_2^*}{\partial p} p \\[2mm] -\dfrac{\partial y^*}{\partial w_1} w_1 & -\dfrac{\partial y^*}{\partial w_2} w_2 & -\dfrac{\partial y^*}{\partial p} p \end{vmatrix}$$

Now add columns 1 and 2 to column 3. This does not change the value of the determinant. But $x_1^*(w_1, w_2, p)$, $x_2^*(w_1, w_2, p)$, and the supply function $y^*(w_1, w_2, p)$ are all homogeneous of degree zero in the prices, and this latter manipulation of the determinant therefore yields, by Euler's theorem, 0s in column 3. Hence, $|\mathbf{F}_{\alpha\alpha}| = 0$.

The Le Châtelier Principle

We have previously encountered the proposition that in the long run, i.e., when all factors of production can freely adjust to changes in parameter values, the factor-demand curves are more elastic than in the short run, when some factors are held fixed at their previous levels. Remembering, of course, that " fixed " is really short-hand for "costly to change," we see that the envelope analysis of the preceding pages affords an illuminating look at this proposition.

Consider Fig. 9-3. As in Fig. 9-2, the profit function $\pi^*(w_1, w_2^0, p^0)$ is plotted against various values of w_1. At $w_1 = w_1^0$, the factor-demand levels $x_1^0 = x_1^*(w_1^0, w_2^0, p^0)$ and $x_2^0 = x_2^*(w_1^0, w_2^0, p^0)$ are obtained. Holding x_1 and x_2 fixed at $x_1 = x_1^0$ and $x_2 = x_2^0$, we draw the constrained-profit function $\pi(w_1, w_2^0, p^0, x_1^0, x_2^0) = p^0 f(x_1^0, x_2^0) - w_1 x_1^0 - w_2^0 x_2^0$. This function is, again, linear in w_1 and tangent

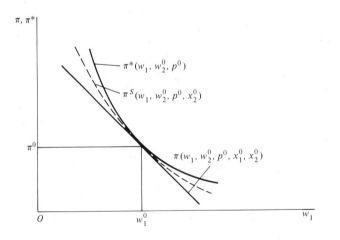

Figure 9-3 The Le Châtelier principle seen as an envelope phenomenon. At wage $w_1 = w_1^0$, factor levels $x_1^0 = x_1^*(w_1^0, w_2^0, p^0)$ and $x_2^0 = x_2^*(w_1^0, w_2^0, p^0)$ are used, generating profits of $\pi^0 = \pi^*(w_1^0, w_2^0, p^0)$. If both x_1 and x_2 are held fixed at x_1^0 and x_2^0, then as w_1 is changed, profits π will be less than maximum profits π^*. If only one input, say x_2, is held fixed at x_2^0, then for $w_1 \neq w_1^0$, profits π^S will be greater than π (when both inputs were held fixed), but π^S will be less than π^*, where no constraints are placed on input levels. Since this occurs at wages $w_1 > w_1^0$ and $w_1 < w_1^0$, the triple tangency depicted above must occur, assuming all three profit functions are differentiable. This implies that the slope of all three profit functions (in the w_1 direction) are equal; that is, $\partial \pi^*/\partial w_1 = \partial \pi^S/\partial w_1 = \partial \pi/\partial w_1 = -x_1^0$. But, clearly, π^* is the most convex; i.e., its second derivative is greatest. But $\partial^2 \pi^*/\partial w_1^2 = -\partial x_1^*/\partial w_1$, $\partial^2 \pi^S/\partial w_1^2 = -\partial x_1^S/\partial w_1$, and $\partial^2 \pi/\partial w_1 = 0$; hence $-\partial x_1^*/\partial w_1 \geq -\partial x_1^S/\partial w_1 \geq 0$ or $\partial x_1^*/\partial w_1 \leq \partial x_1^S/\partial w_1 \leq 0$, a statement that the fewer the constraints placed on the system the greater the absolute response of a factor to a change in its price will be.

to π^* at $w_1 = w_1^0$, since at that particular wage, the "correct," i.e., profit-maximizing levels, of inputs are used. At all other values of w_1, $\pi < \pi^*$; hence, assuming differentiability of π and π^*, a tangency situation is implied.

Suppose now that instead of holding *both* x_1 and x_2 fixed at $x_1 = x_1^0$ and $x_2 = x_2^0$, a new profit function π^S (for short run) is defined which holds only x_2 fixed at $x_2 = x_2^0$ but allows x_1 (but only x_1) to adjust to changes in w_1. Then a demand curve of the following form is implied by profit maximization:

$$x_1 = x_1^S(w_1, w_2, p, x_2^0) \tag{9-17}$$

Note that x_2^0 enters as a parameter; x_2 is fixed at $x_2 = x_2^0 = x_2^*(w_1^0, w_2^0, p^0)$. Only x_1 is a decision variable here; hence, there is only one choice function or, in this case, factor-demand curve, given by (9-17).

Where will $\pi^S(w_1, w_2^0, p^0, x_2^0)$ lie in relation to π^* and π? Again, at $w_1 = w_1^0$, the correct levels of x_1 and x_2 will be utilized; hence, at $w_1 = w_1^0$, $\pi^S = \pi^* = \pi$. At other values of w_1, π^S must clearly be less than π^*, since again $\pi^*(w_1, w_2^0, p^0)$ represents the maximum attainable profits when no constraints are placed on the firm's decisions. However, for the same types of reasons, at $w_1 \neq w_1^0$, $\pi^S > \pi$, since in evaluating π, *both* inputs are held fixed at $x_1 = x_1^0$ and $x_2 = x_2^0$ instead of just one. As a simple matter of logic, constraints on a system which is maximizing some entity can only lower the value of the objective function; the more binding constraints there are the lower the value of the objective function. Hence, for all $w_1 \neq w_1^0$, $\pi < \pi^S < \pi^*$, and at $w_1 = w_1^0$, $\pi = \pi^S = \pi^*$. Hence, the function π^S must lie in between π and π^*, and the three curves must be tangent at $w_1 = w_1^0$, as depicted in Fig. 9-3.

The analytical consequences of this triple tangency are similar to before. Since the slopes in the w_1 direction are all equal, at $w = w_1^0$,

$$\pi_{w_1} = \pi_{w_1}^S = \pi_{w_1}^* = -x_1^*(w_1, w_2^0, p^0)$$
$$= -x_1^S(w_1, w_2^0, p^0, x_2^0)$$

However, π^* is the most convex, followed by π^S, and then π (which is linear), and thus

$$\pi_{w_1 w_1}^* \geq \pi_{w_1 w_1}^S \geq \pi_{w_1 w_1} = 0 \tag{9-18}$$

But since $\pi_{w_1}^* = -x_1^*(w_1, w_2^0, p^0)$, as before,

$$\pi_{w_1 w_1}^* = -\frac{\partial x_1^*}{\partial w_1} \tag{9-19}$$

Similarly, since $\pi_{w_1}^S = x_1^S(w_1, w_2^0, p^0, x_2^0)$,

$$\pi_{w_1 w_1}^S = -\frac{\partial x_1^S}{\partial w_1} \tag{9-20}$$

From equation (9-18), therefore,

$$\frac{\partial x_1^*}{\partial w_1} \leq \frac{\partial x_1^S}{\partial w_1} \tag{9-21}$$

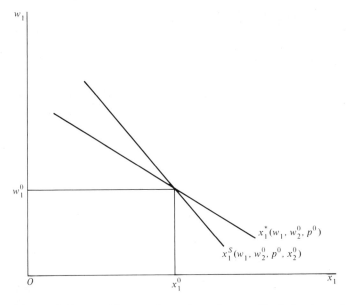

Figure 9-4 Short- and long-run factor-demand curves. The factor-demand curves $x_1^*(w_1, w_2^0, p^0)$, the long-run factor demand for x_1, and $x_1^S(w_1, w_2^0, p^0, x_2^0)$, the short-run demand, in which x_2 is held fixed at x_2^0, are in fact the (negative) second derivatives of their respective profit functions. Since π^S is less convex than π^*, its second (partial) derivative, $-\partial x_1^S/\partial w_1$, is less than $-\partial x_1^*/\partial w_1$, the second partial derivative of π^*. In the above diagram, x_1^S is the steeper curve, but this occurs because x_1, the dependent variable, is plotted on the horizontal axis. In fact, the above curve shows that $|\partial x_1^*/\partial w_1| > |\partial x_1^S/\partial w_1|$; that is, the response of a factor to a change in its price is greater (in absolute value) when there are fewer constraints on the other factors.

Equation (9-21) is depicted in Fig. 9-4 (remember that in the usual factor-demand diagrams the dependent variable x_1 is plotted on the *horizontal* axis) in which the long-run demand curve $x_1^*(w_1, w_2^0, p^0)$ is more elastic (has a flatter ordinary slope at $x_1 = x_1^0$, $w_1 = w_1^0$) than the short-run curve $x_1^S(w_1, w_2^0, p^0, x_2^0)$.

We see that the Le Châtelier principle, which indicates that a maximizing system will react to a change in a parameter value so as to minimize the impact of that "shock," is in fact an envelope phenomenon. In this model, the Le Châtelier principle says simply that as more factors are held fixed, then as a wage is changed, profits will be successively lower. Since this occurs for wages above and below the "correct" wage (at which the profit-maximizing inputs are used), the geometric translation of this addition of constraints to the system (in the form of holding decision variables fixed) is to make the profit function less convex (or more concave). Since the slope of the profit function in this particular model is the (negative) factor-demand function, this decreased convexity is equivalent to decreased absolute slope of the demand function. This is the familiar proposition that long-run factor demands are more elastic than short-run demands. The fact that the Le Châtelier principle translates into factor demands in the first place, though, depends upon the peculiarity of the profit-maximization model. Since

$\pi = pf(x_1, x_2) - w_1 x_1 - w_2 x_2$, $\partial \pi^* / \partial w_i = -x_i^*$; that is, the decision variables happen to be first partials of the profit function with respect to their prices. Unless this duality feature is present, the envelope theorems will not lead to simple or useful propositions like those in the profit-maximization model.

Another model in which this feature is present is the cost-minimization model, from which the compensated or (in the case of production) constant-output-demand curves are derived. Before proceeding to the general analysis, we shall investigate this useful model.

9.2 COST-MINIMIZATION

Let us return now to the mathematical model described in detail in Chap. 7:

minimize $\qquad\qquad p_1 x_1 + p_2 x_2 = C$

subject to $\qquad\qquad f(x_1, x_2) = y$

where we now denote the prices of x_1 and x_2 as p_1 and p_2, respectively. As we showed earlier, this model can be given (at least) two interpretations. If $y = f(x_1, x_2)$ is a production function relating factor inputs x_1 and x_2 to output y, and if p_1 and p_2 are factor prices, this model yields factor-demand curves in which output y is parametric. These constant-output demands can be substituted into the objective function to yield the various cost functions of the firm. On the other hand, if $y = f(x_1, x_2)$ is conceived of as a utility function for two consumer goods, x_1 and x_2, whose prices are p_1 and p_2, respectively, the model yields demand curves in which utility y is parametric (or held constant). These are the income-compensated demands of consumer theory, and form, through the Slutsky equation, the basis of refutable propositions concerning the behavior of consumers. We shall investigate this model again, now, in order to illustrate the derivation of comparative-statics relations from the general envelope properties of the indirect objective function, here the cost function.

The lagrangian for the above model is

$$\mathcal{L} = p_1 x_1 + p_2 x_2 + \lambda(y - f(x_1, x_2))$$

yielding the first-order relations for constrained minimum,

$$\mathcal{L}_1 = p_1 - \lambda f_1 = 0 \qquad \mathcal{L}_2 = p_2 - \lambda f_2 = 0 \qquad \mathcal{L}_\lambda = y - f(x_1, x_2) = 0$$
$$(9\text{-}22)$$

Again, the quantity y is a parameter here, not a decision variable. The second-order condition is that the determinant of the second partials of $\mathcal{L}$ be negative:

$$\Delta = \begin{vmatrix} -\lambda f_{11} & -\lambda f_{12} & -f_1 \\ -\lambda f_{21} & -\lambda f_{22} & -f_2 \\ -f_1 & -f_2 & 0 \end{vmatrix} < 0 \qquad (9\text{-}23)$$

The implied choice (demand) functions are obtained from simultaneous solution of equations (9-22):

$$x_1 = x_1^*(p_1, p_2, y) \tag{9-24a}$$

$$x_2 = x_2^*(p_1, p_2, y) \tag{9-24b}$$

$$\lambda = \lambda^*(p_1, p_2, y) \tag{9-24c}$$

The cost, or expenditure, function is found by substituting the cost-minimizing values of the decision variables, given by equations (9-24a) and (9-24b), into the objective function

$$C^*(p_1, p_2, y) \equiv p_1 x_1^*(p_1, p_2, y) + p_2 x_2^*(p_1, p_2, y)$$

The cost function $C^*(p_1, p_2, y)$ gives the minimum cost for any set of prices p_1, p_2 and output y. Let us hold p_2 fixed throughout this discussion at $p_2 = p_2^0$ and y fixed at $y = y^0$. When $p_1 = p_1^0$, the variables x_1, x_2, and λ take on the values

$$x_1^0 = x_1^*(p_1^0, p_2^0, y^0) \tag{9-25a}$$

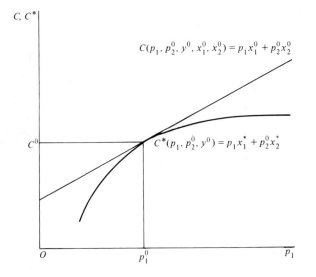

Figure 9-5 The cost function $C^*(p_1, p_2^0, y^0)$ for varying p_1, holding p_2 and y fixed, and the cost function $C(p_1, p_2^0, y^0, x_1^0, x_2^0)$, in which x_1 and x_2 are held fixed at $x_1^0 = x_1^*(p_1^0, p_2^0, y^0)$ and $x_2^0 = x_2^*(p_1^0, p_2^0, y^0)$. $C(p_1, p_2^0, y^0, x_1^0, x_2^0) = p_1 x_1^0 + p_2 x_2^0$ is clearly linear in p_1; that is, geometrically it is a straight line. At $p_1 = p_1^0$, $C = C^*$ since x_1^0 and x_2^0 are precisely those quantities which minimize total cost subject to constraint. For $p_1 \neq p_1^0$, $C^* < C$, since then the "wrong" x_i's are employed for C, whereas C^* is the *minimum* cost, calculated by using whatever x_1^* and x_2^* are appropriate. But since $C^* = C$ at $p_1 = p_1^0$ and $C^* < C$ in the neighborhood around p_1^0, C^* must be tangent to C at p_1^0; also, C^* must be concave in p_1, since $C = p_1 x_1^0 + p_2^0 x_2^0$ is linear in p_1. We therefore have, from tangency, $C_{p_1} = C_{p_1}^* = x_1^* = x_1^0$ and, from concavity in p_1, $C_{p_1 p_1}^* = \partial x_1^*/\partial p_1 \leq 0$.

$$x_2^0 = x_2^*(p_1^0, p_2^0, y^0) \tag{9-25b}$$

$$\lambda^0 = \lambda^*(p_1^0, p_2^0, y^0) \tag{9-25c}$$

The associated value of cost C^* is $C^0 = C^*(p_1^0, p_2^0, y^0)$. As in the profit-maximization model, let us plot cost against various values of p_1 (hold p_2 and y fixed throughout). This situation is depicted in Fig. 9-5. At $p_1 = p_1^0$, $C^* = C^0$. Suppose now that x_1 and x_2 are held fixed at $x_1 = x_1^0$ and $x_2 = x_2^0$. Then this cost function C for various p_1 is

$$C = p_1 x_1^0 + p_2^0 x_2^0 = C(p_1, p_2^0, y^0, x_1^0, x_2^0)$$

This is a linear function of p_1, the vertical intercept being $p_2^0 x_2^0$. Its slope is given by

$$C_{p_1} = \frac{\partial C}{\partial p_1} = x_1^0 \tag{9-26}$$

Clearly, $C_{p_1 p_1} = 0$. Suppose now that x_1 and x_2 are *not* held fixed but vary in accordance with the demand functions (9-24). In this case, the cost function $C^*(p_1, p_2^0, y^0)$ will be plotted out as p_1 varies. C^* is the minimum cost for any p_1, p_2, y; therefore at all $p_1 \neq p_1^0$, $C^* < C$ (assuming C^* represents a unique minimum). And at $p_1 = p_1^0$, $C^* = C^0$, since there the "correct," i.e., cost-minimizing, variables x_1 and x_2 are utilized. Assuming C^* is differentiable, $C^*(p_1, p_2^0, y^0)$ must be tangent to $C(p_1, p_2^0, y^0, x_1^0, x_2^0)$ at $p_1 = p_1^0$, $C^* = C^0$. However, it is also apparent, since $C^* < C$ for values of p_1 to either side of p_1^0, that $C^*(p_1, p_2^0, y^0)$ must be concave (downward) in p_1, that is, that

$$\frac{\partial^2 C^*}{\partial p_1^2} \leq 0 \tag{9-27}$$

Given the tangency, however, $C^*(p_1, p_2^0, y^0)$ and $C(p_1, p_2^0, y^0, x_1^0, x_2^0)$ must have the same slope in the p_1 direction, i.e.,

$$\frac{\partial C^*}{\partial p_1} = \frac{\partial C}{\partial p_1} = x_1^0 = x_1^*(p_1, p_2^0, y^0)$$

evaluated at $p_1 = p_1^0$. This, of course, is the basic envelope theorem, which says that the rate of change of the objective function with respect to some parameter is the same whether or not the decision variables are allowed to adjust to the change in parameter values. The reason for this is apparent in the tangency point in Fig. 9-5.

However, we also have concavity of C^* in the p_1 direction. Hence, from equation (9-27),

$$\frac{\partial^2 C^*}{\partial p_1^2} = \frac{\partial x_1^*}{\partial p_1} \leq 0 \tag{9-28}$$

Thus, as in the case of the profit-maximizing firm, the law of demand for constant output or for the income-compensated (utility-held-constant) demand curves of consumer theory is also seen to be a consequence of the curvature properties of the indirect objective function. Of course, in the same manner, one can show that $\partial^2 C^*/\partial p_2^2 = \partial x_2^*/\partial p_2 \le 0$.

Le Châtelier Phenomena

Using reasoning analogous to that used in the profit-maximization model, consider a cost function defined when only x_2 is held fixed at $x_2 = x_2^0 = x_2^*(p_1^0, p_2^0, y^0)$ but where x_1 is allowed to vary in accordance with the implied demand curve

$$x_1 = x_1^S(p_1, p_2^0, y^0, x_2^0)$$

where the superscript S again stands for short run. Then, as depicted in Fig. 9-6, the cost function $C^S(p_1, p_2^0, y^0, x_2^0)$ must also be tangent to C^* and C at $p_1 = p_1^0$, but for $p_1 \ne p_1^0$, C^S must lie in between C and C^*, or $C^* < C^S < C$. Since this occurs for values of p_1 less than and greater than p_1^0, C^S is concave but not as concave as C^*. Hence,

$$C^*_{p_1 p_1} \le C^S_{p_1 p_1} \le C_{p_1 p_1} = 0 \tag{9-29}$$

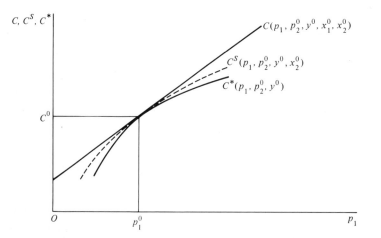

Figure 9-6 Short- and long-run total cost functions. Using reasoning similar to that in Fig. 9-5, the more things held constant, the greater the level of minimum cost will be, at $p_1 \ne p_1^0$. At $p_1 = p_1^0$, the correct x_i's, x_1^0 and x_2^0, are used by construction, and hence $C = C^S = C^*$. The function $C^S(p_1, p_2^0, y^0, x_2^0)$ is that minimum cost achievable when only x_1 is allowed to adjust to changes in p_1 but x_2 is held fixed at x_2^0. Thus, for $p_1 \ne p_1^0$, $C^* < C^S < C$, producing the triple tangency depicted above. But, also, clearly C^* is the most concave in p_1, then C^S, and last C, which is linear. Thus, $C^*_{p_1 p_1} \le C^S_{p_1 p_1} \le C_{p_1 p_1} = 0$. Since $C^S_{p_1} = x_1^S$, this concavity relation yields $\partial x_1^*/\partial p_1 \le \partial x_1^S/\partial p_1$; that is, the absolute response of a factor or good to a change in its own price, holding output (or utility) constant, will be greater the fewer constraints are placed on the system. This result, sometimes known as *the second law of demand* is a mathematical consequence of the maximization hypothesis in this model. The result translates loosely into the proposition that long-run demand curves of this type are more elastic than short-run demand curves at any given point.

Since $C^*_{p_1} = C^S_{p_1}$ due to tangency, $C^S_{p_1} = x^S_1(p_1, p^0_2, y^0, x^0_2)$. Thus, from equation (9-29), since $C^S_{p_1 p_1} = \partial x^S_1 / \partial p_1$,

$$\frac{\partial x^*_1}{\partial p_1} \le \frac{\partial x^S_1}{\partial p_1} \tag{9-30}$$

or the long-run demand for constant output (or utility) is more elastic than the corresponding short-run curve, in which the other decision variable is held fixed. As the minimum system becomes more constrained, the ability of that system to respond to changes in the environment (the parameters) becomes reduced. The absolute response of a variable to a change in its own price is largest when the firm or consumer can move out of or into the other variable.

All the above results—the negative slope of the demand curves and the Le Châtelier effects—are consequences of a peculiar situation that the first partials of the indirect objective function with respect to various parameters are precisely the original decision variables. Only for this reason does the curvature of the indirect objective function (here, the cost function, in the previous example, the profit function), given by its second partials relate in a simple way to the slopes of the demand functions. Only because the demand function is itself the *first* partial of C^* or π^* are the signs of the second partials of C^* or π^* (the first partials of x^*_i, for each model) easily interpretable. This unusual property is not present in many models (particularly the utility-maximization model, for which reason no refutable propositions emerge from the maximization hypothesis alone), but it occurs often enough to be useful.

We shall explore the general situation in the next section. First, let us analyze the cost-minimization model more formally, without appeal to the visual geometry of the model. Consider a new function F, defined as the difference between any given cost level and the minimum cost, or

$$z = F(x_1, x_2, p_1, p_2, y) \equiv C(x_1, x_2, p_1, p_2, y) - C^*(p_1, p_2, y) \tag{9-31}$$

where $C(x_1, x_2, p_1, p_2, y) \equiv p_1 x_1 + p_2 x_2$. This function is to be considered as dependent upon the five independent "variables," x_1, x_2, p_1, p_2, and y. For values of these variables which satisfy the constraint $f(x_1, x_2) = y$ (actually, only x_1, x_2, and y are constrained by this relation), it must be the case that $F \ge 0$, since C^* is the minimum cost, whereas C is any other cost. However, $C = C^*$ when $x_1 = x^*_1(p_1, p_2, y)$, $x_2 = x^*_2(p_1, p_2, y)$ given by equations (9-24). This means that F has a minimum value (of 0) at $x_i = x^*_i(p_1, p_2, y)$, $i = 1, 2$, subject to the constraint $f(x_1, x_2) = y$. In other words, solution of the original cost-minimization problem implies the solution of:

minimize $\quad F(x_1, x_2, p_1, p_2, y) \equiv C(x_1, x_2, p_1, p_2, y) - C^*(p_1, p_2, y)$

subject to $\quad\quad f(x_1, x_2) = y$

The lagrangian for this problem is

$$\mathscr{L}' = C(x_1, x_2, p_1, p_2, y) - C^*(p_1, p_2, y) + \lambda(y - f(x_1, x_2)) \tag{9-32}$$

Notice that $\mathscr{L}' = \mathscr{L} - C^*$, where $\mathscr{L}$ is the original lagrangian expression for the cost-minimization problem. It is not, in fact, comparisons of C^* and C, the direct cost function, that are relevant for comparative statics but comparisons of C^* and $\mathscr{L}$, the lagrangian expression, in *constrained*-minimization (or maximization) problems. The constraint always being satisfied, $y - f(x_1, x_2) \equiv 0$, and hence the value of C is the same as the value of $\mathscr{L}$. However, the curvature properties of the two functions are not the same.

Taking the first partials of $\mathscr{L}'$ [equation (9-32)] with respect to all five "variables" and the Lagrange multiplier λ, we have

$$\mathscr{L}'_{x_1} = C_{x_1} - \lambda f_1 = p_1 - \lambda f_1 = 0 \tag{9-33a}$$

$$\mathscr{L}'_{x_2} = C_{x_2} - \lambda f_2 = p_2 - \lambda f_2 = 0 \tag{9-33b}$$

$$\mathscr{L}'_{p_1} = C_{p_1} - C^*_{p_1} = x_1 - C^*_{p_1} = 0 \tag{9-33c}$$

$$\mathscr{L}'_{p_2} = C_{p_2} - C^*_{p_2} = x_2 - C^*_{p_2} = 0 \tag{9-33d}$$

$$\mathscr{L}'_y = \lambda - C^*_y = 0 \tag{9-33e}$$

$$\mathscr{L}'_\lambda = y - f(x_1, x_2) = 0 \tag{9-33f}$$

Equations (9-33a), (9-33b), and (9-33f) are the three first-order equations of the original problem; not surprisingly, since this new problem is dependent upon prior solution of that problem, the first-order equations of this new problem include the former first-order equations. Equations (9-33c) to (9-33e) are the envelope theorem. They say that the rate of change of minimum cost with respect to a factor price is equal to the level of that factor, at the given prices, i.e.,

$$\frac{\partial C^*}{\partial p_i} = x_i = x_i^*(p_1, p_2, y)$$

also $$\frac{\partial C^*}{\partial y} = MC = \lambda = \lambda^*(p_1, p_2, y)$$

That is, the Lagrange multiplier is equal to marginal cost, or, more precisely, the Lagrange multiplier function λ^* is the marginal cost function, the first partial of C^* with respect to output (or utility), expressed as a function of prices and output (utility).

However, since $C - C^*$ has a constrained minimum, the border-preserving principal minors of the second partials of $\mathscr{L}'$ (the bordered hessian of $C - C^*$) must all be negative (including H itself). This bordered hessian is, by differentiating equations (9-33) with respect to all six variables, in order, and noting that since x_i and p_j are independent variables here, $\partial x_i / \partial p_j = 0$, but $C^*_{p_i p_j} = \partial x_i^* / \partial p_j$, etc.,

$$H = \begin{vmatrix} -\lambda f_{11} & -\lambda f_{12} & 1 & 0 & 0 & -f_1 \\ -\lambda f_{21} & -\lambda f_{22} & 0 & 1 & 0 & -f_2 \\ 1 & 0 & -\dfrac{\partial x_1^*}{\partial p_1} & -\dfrac{\partial x_1^*}{\partial p_2} & -\dfrac{\partial x_1^*}{\partial y} & 0 \\ 0 & 1 & -\dfrac{\partial x_2^*}{\partial p_1} & -\dfrac{\partial x_2^*}{\partial p_2} & -\dfrac{\partial x_2^*}{\partial y} & 0 \\ 0 & 0 & -\dfrac{\partial \lambda^*}{\partial p_1} & -\dfrac{\partial \lambda^*}{\partial p_2} & -\dfrac{\partial \lambda^*}{\partial y} & 1 \\ -f_1 & -f_2 & 0 & 0 & 1 & 0 \end{vmatrix} \tag{9-34}$$

Among these border-preserving minors is the one found by deleting rows and columns 3, 4, and 5; this yields the second-order condition for the original cost-minimization problem, $\Delta < 0$, given in equation (9-23).

The comparative statics of the cost-minimization model are given by the principal minors of the subdeterminant below and to the right of the partitions in H; call this submatrix $\mathbf{H}_{\alpha\alpha}$. The border-preserving principal minors of $|\mathbf{H}_{\alpha\alpha}|$ are all border-preserving principal minors of H; they are all nonpositive whichever matrix they are derived from.

Consider the 3×3 border-preserving principal minors of $|\mathbf{H}_{\alpha\alpha}|$, e.g.,

$$\begin{vmatrix} -\dfrac{\partial x_1^*}{\partial p_1} & -\dfrac{\partial x_1^*}{\partial y} & 0 \\ -\dfrac{\partial \lambda^*}{\partial p_1} & -\dfrac{\partial \lambda^*}{\partial y} & 1 \\ 0 & 1 & 0 \end{vmatrix} \leq 0 \tag{9-35}$$

As indicated, this determinant is nonpositive by the second-order conditions for a constrained minimum. Expanding this determinant by the last row quickly yields

$$\frac{\partial x_1^*}{\partial p_1} \leq 0 \tag{9-36}$$

In a similar fashion, the border-preserving principal minor involving $\partial x_2^*/\partial p_2$ yields

$$\frac{\partial x_2^*}{\partial p_2} \leq 0 \tag{9-37}$$

A term that cannot be signed is $\partial \lambda^*/\partial y$, the rate of change of marginal cost with respect to output. As explained earlier in the chapter on cost, level curves, e.g. isoquants which are convex-to-the-origin in no way implies concavity or non-concavity of the objective function. Quasi-concavity is a feature of the level surfaces of a function; nothing is implied by the shape of those level curves with regard to how fast or slow the function changes from one such level to another. Hence, the cost function associated with a production or utility function can exhibit either increasing or decreasing marginal costs.

Consider now the determinant $|\mathbf{H}_{\alpha\alpha}|$ itself:

$$
|\mathbf{H}_{\alpha\alpha}| = \begin{vmatrix} -\dfrac{\partial x_1^*}{\partial p_1} & -\dfrac{\partial x_1^*}{\partial p_2} & -\dfrac{\partial x_1^*}{\partial y} & 0 \\[2mm] -\dfrac{\partial x_2^*}{\partial p_1} & -\dfrac{\partial x_2^*}{\partial p_2} & -\dfrac{\partial x_2^*}{\partial y} & 0 \\[2mm] -\dfrac{\partial \lambda^*}{\partial p_1} & -\dfrac{\partial \lambda^*}{\partial p_2} & -\dfrac{\partial \lambda^*}{\partial y} & 1 \\[2mm] 0 & 0 & 1 & 0 \end{vmatrix} \le 0 \tag{9-38}
$$

Let us quickly evaluate this determinant by expanding by the last row:

$$
|\mathbf{H}_{\alpha\alpha}| = (-1)^{4+3} D_{43} = - \begin{vmatrix} -\dfrac{\partial x_1^*}{\partial p_1} & -\dfrac{\partial x_1^*}{\partial p_2} & 0 \\[2mm] -\dfrac{\partial x_2^*}{\partial p_1} & -\dfrac{\partial x_2^*}{\partial p_2} & 0 \\[2mm] -\dfrac{\partial \lambda^*}{\partial p_1} & -\dfrac{\partial \lambda^*}{\partial p_2} & 1 \end{vmatrix}
$$

Expanding this latter determinant by the last column yields

$$
|\mathbf{H}_{\alpha\alpha}| = -(-1)^{3+3} \begin{vmatrix} -\dfrac{\partial x_1^*}{\partial p_1} & -\dfrac{\partial x_1^*}{\partial p_2} \\[2mm] -\dfrac{\partial x_2^*}{\partial p_1} & -\dfrac{\partial x_2^*}{\partial p_2} \end{vmatrix} \le 0
$$

or

$$
-|\mathbf{H}_{\alpha\alpha}| = \frac{\partial x_1^*}{\partial p_1}\frac{\partial x_2^*}{\partial p_2} - \left(\frac{\partial x_1^*}{\partial p_2}\right)^2 \ge 0 \tag{9-39}
$$

noting that $\partial x_1^*/\partial p_2 = \partial x_2^*/\partial p_1$, by symmetry of $\mathbf{H}_{\alpha\alpha}$. In fact, $|\mathbf{H}_{\alpha\alpha}| = 0$, from the homogeneity of degree zero of the constant output (utility) demand curves: multiply the first column of the determinant immediately above (9-39) by p_1, the second column by p_2, and add column 1 to column 2. By Euler's theorem, the second column vanishes, and hence $|\mathbf{H}_{\alpha\alpha}| = 0$.

Equations (9-36), (9-37), and (9-39) suggest that $C^*(p_1, p_2, y)$ may be weakly concave in the prices p_1 and p_2. Indeed, this is so, as can be seen directly from the definition of quasi-convexity of $C - C^*$. Since $C - C^*$ is convex subject to constraint, the constraint being $y - f(x_1, x_2) = 0$, so is any subsystem of $C - C^*$ when one or more variables are held constant. That is, $C - C^*$ is a function of the five variables, x_1, x_2, p_1, p_2, and y. It is quasi-convex [convex subject to the constraint $y - f(x_1, x_2) = 0$] in all five of these variables. But then, if, say, x_1 and x_2 are held constant, $C - C^*$ must be quasi-convex in the remaining variables, p_1, p_2, and y. A function could not possibly be, say, convex in some variables but suddenly become concave in all variables when additional dimensions are included. Indeed, this is the geometric meaning of the conditions on all the (border-preserving) principal minors of lower order than the whole determinant in the second-order conditions for (constrained) maximization or minimization. Each order of principal minor is a check on the concavity (or convexity) of the function when various variables are held constant.

The matrix of second partials of $C - C^*$ when x_1 and x_2 are held constant is simply the unbordered part $\mathbf{H}_{\alpha\alpha}$, or

$$
\begin{pmatrix}
-\dfrac{\partial x_1^*}{\partial p_1} & -\dfrac{\partial x_1^*}{\partial p_2} & -\dfrac{\partial x_1^*}{\partial y} \\[2mm]
-\dfrac{\partial x_2^*}{\partial p_1} & -\dfrac{\partial x_2^*}{\partial p_2} & -\dfrac{\partial x_2^*}{\partial y} \\[2mm]
-\dfrac{\partial \lambda^*}{\partial p_1} & -\dfrac{\partial \lambda^*}{\partial p_2} & -\dfrac{\partial \lambda^*}{\partial y}
\end{pmatrix}
\tag{9-40}
$$

We denote these terms by a_{ij}; quasi-convexity says that

$$
\sum_{i=1}^{3} \sum_{j=1}^{3} a_{ij} h_i h_j \geq 0
\tag{9-41}
$$

for all values of h_i, h_j, $i, j = 1, 2, 3$, which also satisfy the constraint

$$
0 \cdot h_1 + 0 \cdot h_2 + 1 \cdot h_3 = 0
\tag{9-42}
$$

The coefficients $(0, 0, 1)$ in the above constraint on the h_i's are the first partials of the constraint $y - f(x_1, x_2) = 0$ with respect to p_1, p_2, and y, respectively. (These coefficients form the last row of $\mathbf{H}_{\alpha\alpha}$.) But, clearly then, the constraint (9-42) says only that $h_3 = 0$ and that h_1 and h_2 can take on any values whatsoever. Using this in equation (9-41) gives

$$
\sum_{i=1}^{2} \sum_{j=1}^{2} a_{ij} h_i h_j \geq 0
\tag{9-43}
$$

for any values of h_1 and h_2. But this says precisely that the submatrix of (9-40) consisting of its first two rows and columns, the elements of which are the terms $-\partial x_i^* / \partial p_j$, is convex. Its diagonal elements are therefore nonnegative, i.e.,

$$
-\frac{\partial x_i^*}{\partial p_i} \geq 0 \quad \text{or} \quad \frac{\partial x_i^*}{\partial p_i} \leq 0 \quad i = 1, 2
$$

and

$$
\frac{\partial x_1^*}{\partial p_1} \frac{\partial x_2^*}{\partial p_2} - \left(\frac{\partial x_1^*}{\partial p_2}\right)^2 \geq 0
$$

In fact, we know that this (negative submatrix) $(\partial x_i^* / \partial p_j)$ is not *strictly* concave from the homogeneity of degree zero of $x_i^*(p_1, p_2, y)$ in the prices.

The above analysis is perfectly general; the same results are obtained for systems of n goods or factors. The cost or expenditure function $C^*(p_1, \ldots, p_n, y)$ has the property of being concave (weakly) in all prices $p_1, \ldots, p_n$. Since $\partial C^*/\partial p_i \equiv x_i^*$, the matrix of pure substitution terms $(\partial x_i^*/\partial p_j)$ is thus weakly concave. The implications of this concavity are that the diagonal elements are nonpositive, i.e.,

$$\frac{\partial x_i^*}{\partial p_i} \leq 0$$

and that the principal minors of order k have sign $(-1)^k$ or zero.

In addition to the above qualitative information on the signs of the first partials of the demand functions, the symmetry of $\mathbf{H}_{\alpha\alpha}$ yields the reciprocity relations derived earlier in the chapter on cost. Since C is linear in the original parameters, the second partials of C with respect to prices and output are 0, and thus $\mathbf{H}_{\alpha\alpha}$ consists of the second partials of $-C^*(p_1, p_2, y)$. Using the envelope theorem as before gives

$$C_{p_i}^* = x_i^*, \qquad C_y^* = \lambda^*$$

Therefore,

$$C_{p_i p_j}^* = \frac{\partial x_i^*}{\partial p_j} = \frac{\partial x_j^*}{\partial p_i} = C_{p_j p_i}^*$$

and

$$C_{p_i y}^* = \frac{\partial x_i^*}{\partial y} = \frac{\partial \lambda^*}{\partial p_i} = C_{y p_i}^*$$

Again, reciprocity is seen to occur as a direct result of the invariance of second partials to the order of differentiation; in particular, the appealing relations above occur because the first partials of the indirect objective function are precisely the original decision variables. This unusual situation occurs in only a few economic models—enough, perhaps, to render them interesting. We now turn to the general comparative statics of maximization systems.

9.3 THE COMPARATIVE STATICS OF MAXIMIZATION SYSTEMS

In the previous two sections we examined two important special cases of economic systems in which an objective function is asserted to be maximized (or minimized, in the case of the cost problem). Let us now examine the general structure of these maximization models in order to discover the structures which allow the derivation of refutable hypotheses in such models. We shall perform the analysis for models involving n decision variables $x_1, \ldots, x_n$, denoted simply as $\mathbf{x}$, and m parameters $\alpha_1, \ldots, \alpha_m$, denoted simply as $\boldsymbol{\alpha}$. A single side constraint will be imposed on these variables. This will allow sufficient generality to derive all results.

The general model is:

maximize $$y = f(\mathbf{x}, \boldsymbol{\alpha})$$

subject to $$g(\mathbf{x}, \boldsymbol{\alpha}) = 0 \tag{9-44}$$

The first-order conditions are found by differentiating the implied lagrangian with respect to the x_i's and λ:

$$\mathscr{L} = f(\mathbf{x}, \boldsymbol{\alpha}) + \lambda g(\mathbf{x}, \boldsymbol{\alpha})$$

$$\mathscr{L}_1 = f_1 + \lambda g_1 = 0$$

$$\mathscr{L}_n = f_n + \lambda g_n = 0 \tag{9-45a}$$

$$\mathscr{L}_\lambda = g = 0 \tag{9-45b}$$

The sufficient second-order conditions for a constrained maximum are that the principal minors of the bordered hessian matrix of second partials of $\mathscr{L}$ have sign $(-1)^k$, where $k =$ number of $\mathbf{x}$ rows and columns (1 less than the size of the whole determinant, here); $k = 2, \ldots, n$.

$$H = \begin{vmatrix} \mathbf{f_{xx}} + \lambda \mathbf{g_{xx}} & \mathbf{g_x} \\ \mathbf{g_x} & 0 \end{vmatrix} \tag{9-46}$$

The above determinant H has $n + 1$ rows and columns. The first n rows and columns, denoted by $\mathbf{f_{xx}} + \lambda \mathbf{g_{xx}}$, consist of the second partial derivatives of the lagrangian $\mathscr{L}$. That is, the element in the ith row and jth column is $\mathscr{L}_{ij} = f_{ij} + \lambda g_{ij}$. Bordering this matrix is the row (and column) of first partials g_1, $\ldots, g_n$ of the constraint $g(\mathbf{x}, \boldsymbol{\alpha})$ with respect to the x_i's. These elements can also be viewed as $\mathscr{L}_{i\lambda} = \mathscr{L}_{\lambda i} = g_i$. Thus, e.g., the border-preserving principal minors of order 2, formed by striking $n - 2$ of rows 1 to n and the same numbered column, are all positive, etc.

The choice functions which indicate the responses of the system to changes in the test conditions or environment, i.e., the parameters, are found, in principle, by simultaneous solution of equations (9-45), yielding

$$x_i = x_i^*(\boldsymbol{\alpha}) \qquad i = 1, \ldots, n \tag{9-47}$$

and $$\lambda = \lambda^*(\boldsymbol{\alpha}) \tag{9-48}$$

Relations (9-47) and (9-48) are all potentially interesting, assuming that the parameters $\boldsymbol{\alpha}$ are in principle observable. The Lagrange multiplier λ will not in general be an observable variable, though its value may be derivable from other variables in the model, e.g., by differentiating the cost function with respect to output in the previous cost model.

It bears repeating that it is *not* relations (9-45) which are the goal of this analysis but the choice functions (9-47). Equations (9-45) in economics are statements of the form "marginal benefits equal marginal costs," where the particular "benefits" and "costs" are specified in the model. These marginal relations are (it is hoped) intuitively appealing. However, they are generally also vacuous in themselves, because usually economists will not have sufficient information about the functional forms of the f and g functions to be able to observe or test (9-45) directly. Since the marginal relations (9-45) will not in general be observable, neither will their solutions, the choice function (9-47). However, curiously (and fortunately) enough, although the "total" relations (9-47) may be unobservable, the maximization or other quantitative hypothesis may under certain circumstances be sufficient to imply a sign for the slopes of the choice function in certain directions, i.e., their partial derivatives. Thus, whereas economists may lack sufficient knowledge to predict the total demand for some good, say bread, the response of consumers to an increase in the price of bread, assuming the other parameters remain constant, may nonetheless be implied. We say that economists make predictions about *marginal* quantities rather than *total* quantities. This is the essence of the theory of comparative statics; it is a nontrivial happenstance that such marginal quantities are often predictable. Without it, the general theory of choice would be doomed to failure for lack of sufficient information about behavior.

Let us see how all this comes about. The indirect objective function $\phi(\alpha)$ is defined as the maximum value of $f(\mathbf{x}, \alpha)$ for given values of the parameters α for values of $\mathbf{x}$ which also satisfy the constraint $g(\mathbf{x}, \alpha) = 0$. Mathematically,

$$\phi(\alpha) \equiv f(\mathbf{x}^*(\alpha), \alpha) \tag{9-49}$$

where the $\mathbf{x}^*(\alpha)$ are given by equations (9-47). Consider now a new objective function,

$$z = F(\mathbf{x}, \alpha) = f(\mathbf{x}, \alpha) - \phi(\alpha) \tag{9-50}$$

defined over the $n + m$ variables $x_1, \ldots, x_n, \alpha_1, \ldots, \alpha_m$. Since $\phi(\alpha)$ is the maximum value of $f(\mathbf{x}, \alpha)$ for given α, $f(\mathbf{x}, \alpha) \leq \phi(\alpha)$. And when $\mathbf{x} = \mathbf{x}^*(\alpha)$, $\phi(\alpha) = f(\mathbf{x}, \alpha)$, by definition. Thus, assuming the maximum is unique, when $\mathbf{x} \neq \mathbf{x}^*(\alpha)$, $F(\mathbf{x}, \alpha) < 0$ and when $\mathbf{x} = \mathbf{x}^*(\alpha)$, $F(\mathbf{x}, \alpha) = 0$. This means that $F(\mathbf{x}, \alpha)$ has a maximum value (of 0) when $\mathbf{x} = \mathbf{x}^*(\alpha)$, subject to the constraint $g(\mathbf{x}, \alpha) = 0$.

We can thus state this new primal-dual problem as

$$\max_{\mathbf{x}, \alpha} z = F(\mathbf{x}, \alpha) = f(\mathbf{x}, \alpha) - \phi(\alpha) \tag{9-51}$$

subject to $$g(\mathbf{x}, \alpha) = 0$$

As indicated, this maximization is to take place over the $n + m$ variables $(\mathbf{x}, \alpha)$. Here, the α's are not treated as parameters but as independent variables. The lagrangian for this problem is

$$\mathcal{L}^* = f(\mathbf{x}, \alpha) - \phi(\alpha) + \lambda g(\mathbf{x}, \alpha) \tag{9-52}$$

Note that $\mathcal{L}^* = \mathcal{L} - \phi(\alpha)$ and that $\mathcal{L}^* = 0$ when $\mathbf{x} = \mathbf{x}^*(\alpha)$. In constrained-maximization problems, the original lagrangian expression is fundamentally related to the indirect objective function. The lagrangian technique, at first merely an artifice for deriving maximization conditions, is, in addition, a critical construction in comparative statics analysis.

When (9-52) is differentiated with respect to the x_i's and α_j's, the first-order conditions for the problem (9-51) are

$$\mathscr{L}^*_{x_i} = f_{x_i} + \lambda g_{x_i} = 0 \qquad i = 1, \ldots, n \tag{9-53a}$$

$$\mathscr{L}^*_{\alpha_j} = f_{\alpha_j} + \lambda g_{\alpha_j} - \phi_{\alpha_j} = 0 \qquad j = 1, \ldots, m \tag{9-53b}$$

$$\mathscr{L}^*_{\lambda} = g(\mathbf{x}, \boldsymbol{\alpha}) = 0 \tag{9-53c}$$

These conditions hold when $\mathbf{x} = \mathbf{x}^*(\boldsymbol{\alpha})$. Equations (9-53a) and (9-53c) are simply the first-order conditions for the original, or primal, problem; these conditions must hold if $F(\mathbf{x}, \boldsymbol{\alpha})$ is to have a constrained maximum. Equations (9-53b), on the other hand, represent the envelope theorem. At $\mathbf{x} = \mathbf{x}^*(\boldsymbol{\alpha})$, the rate of change of the indirect objective function $\phi(\boldsymbol{\alpha})$ with respect to some parameter α_j, that is, ϕ_{α_j}, in which the x_i's are allowed to adjust to the changes in α_j is equal to the rate of change of the original lagrangian $\mathscr{L} = f + \lambda g$ with respect to that α_j, holding the x_i's constant. This situation was depicted earlier in Figs. 9-2 and 9-5 for the profit-maximization and constrained-cost-minimization problems. The indirect objective function $\phi(\boldsymbol{\alpha})$ is an envelope curve to all possible direct lagrangian functions. The tangency of $\phi(\boldsymbol{\alpha})$ and $\mathscr{L}(\mathbf{x}, \boldsymbol{\alpha})$ implies that $\phi_{\alpha_j} = \mathscr{L}_{\alpha_j} = f_{\alpha_j} + \lambda g_{\alpha_j}$. Equations (9-53b), the envelope theorem, are in fact derivable from equations (9-53a) and (9-53c), for example, by the methods used in Chap. 6. Hence, the $n + m + 1$ equations (9-53) cannot all be independent; they cannot in fact have dimensionality exceeding $n + 1$.

The second-order conditions for this primal-dual problem (9-51) are that the matrix of second partials of $\mathscr{L}^*$ with respect to $\mathbf{x}$ and $\boldsymbol{\alpha}$,

$$\mathscr{L}^* = \begin{pmatrix} \mathscr{L}^*_{\mathbf{xx}} & \mathscr{L}^*_{\mathbf{x\alpha}} \\ \mathscr{L}^*_{\alpha\mathbf{x}} & \mathscr{L}^*_{\alpha\alpha} \end{pmatrix}$$

is negative (semi-) definite subject to constraint, i.e., that

$$\sum_{i=1}^{n+m} \sum_{j=1}^{n+m} \mathscr{L}^*_{ij} h_i h_j \le 0 \tag{9-54a}$$

for all values of $h_1, \ldots, h_{n+m}$ which satisfy

$$\sum_{i=1}^{n+m} g_i h_i = 0 \tag{9-54b}$$

In these expressions, the subscripts refer to partial differentiation with respect to the x_i's and α_j's; the sum runs from 1 to $n + m$ to indicate that [in (9-54a), for example] all $(n + m)^2$ second partials of $\mathscr{L}^*$ are involved. Specifically, these expressions can be broken down into their component parts of x_i's and α_j's:

$$\sum_{i=1}^{n+m} \sum_{j=1}^{n+m} \mathcal{L}_{ij}^* h_i h_j = \sum_{i=1}^{n} \sum_{j=1}^{n} \mathcal{L}_{x_i x_j}^* h_i h_j$$

$$+ 2 \sum_{i=1}^{n} \sum_{j=1}^{m} \mathcal{L}_{x_i \alpha_j}^* h_i h_{n+j}$$

$$+ \sum_{i=1}^{m} \sum_{j=1}^{m} \mathcal{L}_{\alpha_i \alpha_j}^* h_{n+i} h_{n+j} \le 0 \qquad (9\text{-}55a)$$

for all h_i, h_j which satisfy

$$\sum_{i=1}^{n+m} g_i h_i = \sum_{i=1}^{n} g_{x_i} h_i + \sum_{j=1}^{m} g_{\alpha_j} h_{n+j} = 0 \qquad (9\text{-}55b)$$

These second-order conditions include those for the original maximization problem. Since equations (9-55) are to hold for all such values of the h's, let $\mathbf{h} = (h_1, \ldots, h_n, h_{n+1}, \ldots, h_{n+m}) = (h_1, \ldots, h_n, 0, \ldots, 0)$, that is, let $h_j = 0$ for all the h_j's that are attached to any second partial of $\mathcal{L}^*$ with respect to an α_j. Then equations (9-55) become

$$\sum_{i=1}^{n} \sum_{j=1}^{n} \mathcal{L}_{x_i x_j}^* h_i h_j \le 0 \qquad (9\text{-}56a)$$

subject to

$$\sum_{i=1}^{n} g_{x_i} h_i = 0 \qquad (9\text{-}56b)$$

precisely the second-order conditions for the primal problem.

The above analysis shows that if the whole matrix $\mathcal{L}^*$ is negative (semi-) definite subject to constraint, the square portion $\mathcal{L}_{xx}^*$ in the upper left corner must be so also, the constraint being that part of $g(\mathbf{x}, \boldsymbol{\alpha}) = 0$ which applies only to the x_i's, that is, equation (9-56b). Even more interestingly, the matrix in the lower right of $\mathcal{L}^*$, $\mathcal{L}_{\alpha\alpha}^*$, the matrix of second partials of $\mathcal{L}^*$ with respect to the α_i's only, must similarly be negative (semi-) definite subject to constraint. If we let $\mathbf{h} = (h_1, \ldots, h_n, h_{n+1}, \ldots, h_{n+m}) = (0, \ldots, 0, h_{n+1}, \ldots, h_{n+m})$, that is, set the h_i's that are attached to any second partial of $\mathcal{L}^*$ involving an x_i equal to 0, equations (9-55) become

$$\sum_{j=1}^{m} \sum_{i=1}^{m} \mathcal{L}_{\alpha_i \alpha_j}^* h_{n+i} h_{n+j} \le 0 \qquad (9\text{-}57a)$$

for all h_{n+i}, h_{n+j} satisfying

$$\sum_{i=1}^{m} g_{\alpha_i} h_{n+i} = 0 \qquad (9\text{-}57b)$$

In determinant form, equations (9-57) say that the border-preserving principal minors of order k of the following bordered hessian determinant have sign $(-1)^k$ or 0:

$$H_{\alpha\alpha} = \begin{vmatrix} \mathcal{L}_{\alpha\alpha}^* & \mathbf{g}_\alpha \\ \mathbf{g}_\alpha & 0 \end{vmatrix} \qquad (9\text{-}58)$$

where $\mathscr{L}^*_{\alpha\alpha}$ is the $m \times m$ matrix of second partials of $\mathscr{L}^*$ with respect to the α_i's, and $\mathbf{g}_\alpha = (g_{\alpha_1}, \ldots, g_{\alpha_m})$. A determinant of this form occurred in the cost-minimization problem of the previous section in equation (9-38).

These conditions place restrictions on the comparative-statics choice functions (9-47) and (9-48). Let us evaluate the terms in $\mathscr{L}^*_{\alpha\alpha}$.

Differentiating equation (9-53b) with respect to some α_i gives

$$\mathscr{L}^*_{\alpha_i\alpha_j} = f_{\alpha_i\alpha_j} + \lambda g_{\alpha_i\alpha_j} - \phi_{\alpha_i\alpha_j} \tag{9-59}$$

However, when $\mathbf{x} = \mathbf{x}^*(\boldsymbol{\alpha})$, $\lambda = \lambda^*(\boldsymbol{\alpha})$

$$\mathscr{L}^*_{\alpha_i} \equiv f_{\alpha_i}(\mathbf{x}^*, \boldsymbol{\alpha}) + \lambda^*(\boldsymbol{\alpha})g_{\alpha_i}(\mathbf{x}^*, \boldsymbol{\alpha}) - \phi_{\alpha_i}(\boldsymbol{\alpha}) \equiv 0$$

Differentiating this identity with respect to some α_j yields

$$\sum_{k=1}^n \frac{\partial f_{\alpha_i}}{\partial x_k}\frac{\partial x_k^*}{\partial \alpha_j} + f_{\alpha_i\alpha_j} + \lambda^* \sum_{k=1}^n \frac{\partial g_{\alpha_i}}{\partial x_k}\frac{\partial x_k^*}{\partial \alpha_j} + \lambda^* g_{\alpha_i\alpha_j} + g_{\alpha_i}\frac{\partial \lambda^*}{\partial \alpha_j} - \phi_{\alpha_i\alpha_j} \equiv 0$$

Notice that three of these terms constitute exactly $\mathscr{L}^*_{\alpha_i\alpha_j}$ in equation (9-59). Subtracting these terms from equation (9-59) (which doesn't change the value of $\mathscr{L}^*_{\alpha_i\alpha_j}$ since these terms sum to zero) leads to

$$\mathscr{L}^*_{\alpha_i\alpha_j} = -\left[\sum_{k=1}^n \left(\frac{\partial f_{\alpha_i}}{\partial x_k} + \lambda^*\frac{\partial g_{\alpha_i}}{\partial x_k}\right)\frac{\partial x_k^*}{\partial \alpha_j} + g_{\alpha_i}\frac{\partial \lambda^*}{\partial \alpha_j}\right]$$

or, more simply,

$$\mathscr{L}^*_{\alpha_i\alpha_j} = -\sum_{k=1}^n \mathscr{L}_{\alpha_i x_k}\frac{\partial x_k^*}{\partial \alpha_j} - g_{\alpha_i}\frac{\partial \lambda^*}{\partial \alpha_j} \qquad i, j = 1, \ldots, m \tag{9-60}$$

Equations (9-60) are expressions involving the partial derivatives of the choice functions (9-47) and (9-48). The conditions on the bordered hessian determinants of these terms, (9-58), place restrictions on the size and sign of these terms and also constitute the known implications of the maximization hypothesis.

It is obvious from the complexity of the expressions (9-60) that at this level of generality, no refutable implications of the maximization hypothesis will be forthcoming. In order to derive meaningful theorems in economics (or for that matter in any other science in which the system behaves in accordance with constrained maximization), additional restrictions on the functional forms of the objective function and constraint(s) will have to be specified. In the profit-maximization and cost-minimization models discussed earlier, the $\mathscr{L}^*_{\alpha_i\alpha_j}$ relations reduced to exactly one term, the rest being 0. In those two models, the price parameters entered the model in the form $\sum \alpha_i x_i$, in the objective function only. Hence, $g_{\alpha_i} \equiv 0$, and, therefore, $\partial g_{\alpha_i}/\partial x_k \equiv 0$. What's more, since $f_{\alpha_i} = x_i$, $f_{\alpha_i x_k} = 0$ when $k \neq i$, and $f_{\alpha_i x_i} = 1$. Hence, in those models, $\mathscr{L}^*_{\alpha_i\alpha_j} = -\partial x_i^*/\partial \alpha_j$. Thus, the terms in the $\mathscr{L}_{\alpha\alpha}$ matrix consisted of only the partial derivatives of the choice functions (9-47), and refutable implications were derivable.

It is thus apparent that, at the very least, refutable comparative-statics theorems are likely to be derivable from maximization models only if the $\mathscr{L}^*_{\alpha_i\alpha_j}$

expressions boil down to exactly one term. If two terms are left in $\mathscr{L}^*_{\alpha_i\alpha_j}$, the model will at best imply a sign for the sum of two partial derivatives of the choice functions. This may be useful information, but economists are most often concerned with the effects on a single variable when a parameter changes, not, for example, with the fact that the sum of the demands for capital and labor will be reduced when wages increase, etc. Let us investigate these matters in greater detail.

Reciprocity Relations

Due to the invariance of second partials to the order of differentiation, $\mathscr{L}^*_{\alpha_i\alpha_j} = \mathscr{L}^*_{\alpha_j\alpha_i}$. From equation (9-60), then, the general form of all reciprocity relations in these models is

$$\sum_{k=1}^{n} \mathscr{L}^*_{\alpha_i x_k} \frac{\partial x^*_k}{\partial \alpha_j} + g_{\alpha_i} \frac{\partial \lambda^*}{\partial \alpha_j} = \sum_{k=1}^{n} \mathscr{L}^*_{\alpha_j x_k} \frac{\partial x^*_k}{\partial \alpha_i} + g_{\alpha_j} \frac{\partial \lambda^*}{\partial \alpha_i} \tag{9-61}$$

In models with no constraints, i.e., unconstrained-maximization problems like the profit-maximization model above, equation (9-61) becomes

$$\sum_{k=1}^{n} f_{\alpha_i x_k} \frac{\partial x^*_k}{\partial \alpha_j} = \sum_{k=1}^{n} f_{\alpha_j x_k} \frac{\partial x^*_k}{\partial \alpha_i} \tag{9-62}$$

In the case where each parameter α_k enters one and only one first-order equation (the kth, by definition of α_k), $f_{\alpha_i x_k} = 0$ for $i \neq k$, and thus equation (9-62) becomes

$$f_{\alpha_i x_i} \frac{\partial x^*_i}{\partial \alpha_j} = f_{\alpha_j x_j} \frac{\partial x^*_j}{\partial \alpha_i} \tag{9-63}$$

In models where the parameters enter in the form of a linear expression $\sum_{i=1}^{n} \alpha_i x_i$, $f_{\alpha_i x_i} \equiv 1$, $i = 1, \ldots, n$, and then

$$\frac{\partial x^*_i}{\partial \alpha_j} = \frac{\partial x^*_j}{\partial \alpha_i} \tag{9-64}$$

A relation like (9-64) will occur in unconstrained problems only when each parameter enters one and only one first-order relation and when those parameters shift those first-order relations at the same rate, i.e., when $f_{\alpha_i x_i} = f_{\alpha_j x_j}$, since $f_{\alpha_i x_i} = \partial f_{x_i}/\partial \alpha_i$, etc.

A similar situation occurs in constrained problems when the parameters in question do not enter the constraint. Then, $g_{\alpha_i} \equiv 0,$ $i = 1, \ldots, m$, and hence $\partial g_{\alpha_i}/\partial x_k \equiv 0$. Thus, equation (9-61) again reduces to (9-62), and the ensuing analysis applies. Suppose now that some parameter α_i appears in the objective function only and in only one first-order relation $\mathscr{L}^*_{x_i} = \mathscr{L}_{x_i} = 0$. And suppose a parameter α_j enters the constraint equation only. Then equation (9-61) becomes

$$f_{\alpha_i x_i} \frac{\partial x^*_i}{\partial \alpha_j} = \sum_{k=1}^{n} \lambda^* g_{\alpha_j x_k} \frac{\partial x^*_k}{\partial \alpha_i} + g_{\alpha_j} \frac{\partial \lambda^*}{\partial \alpha_i}$$

Suppose, in addition, $g_{\alpha_j} = $ constant [as in the cost-minimization problem, where

y^0, output (or utility), enters as $y^0 - f(x_1, \ldots, x_n) = 0$ (do not confuse this f function with the objective function above) and hence $g_{y^0} \equiv 1$]. Then $g_{\alpha_j x_k} = 0$, $k = 1, \ldots, n$, and the above equation becomes

$$f_{\alpha_i x_i} \frac{\partial x_i^*}{\partial \alpha_j} = g_{\alpha_j} \frac{\partial \lambda^*}{\partial \alpha_i}$$

In the cost-minimization problem, where $\alpha_i = p_i$ (some price) and $\alpha_j = y^0$ (output), $f_{\alpha_i x_i} = 1$, and $g_{\alpha_j} = 1$. Hence (and in general when $f_{\alpha_i x_i} = g_{\alpha_j}$), in these special cases,

$$\frac{\partial x_i^*}{\partial \alpha_j} = \frac{\partial \lambda^*}{\partial \alpha_i} \tag{9-65}$$

In the cost-minimization problem, this was the relationship $\partial MC/\partial p_i = \partial x_i^*/\partial y^0$.

What emerges from this analysis is that the reciprocity conditions encountered in some of the elementary economic models occur only because of some highly unusual functional forms. Unusual or not from a mathematical standpoint, in the empirical process of building scientific models, it is these functional forms which are often formulated precisely because they are so useful.

Qualitative Results

The determinantal conditions (9-58), in conjunction with equations (9-60), are, again, too general to be usefully applied, even though they are in principle refutable, since they imply restrictions on observable quantities. To accomplish this, however, would require knowledge of the values of the various cross-partials of f and g, information which is not generally available. When can refutable hypotheses be derived without such detailed information on the functions in the model?

In models with no constraints, the second-order conditions state that the matrix of terms $\mathcal{L}_{\alpha_i \alpha_j}^* = -\sum_{k=1}^{n} f_{\alpha_i x_k} (\partial x_k^*/\partial \alpha_j)$ is negative semidefinite. In particular, this implies that the diagonal terms of that matrix are nonpositive, i.e.,

$$-\sum_{k=1}^{n} f_{\alpha_i x_k} \frac{\partial x_k^*}{\partial \alpha_i} \leq 0 \tag{9-66}$$

If, however, a given parameter α_i enters only one first-order relation $f_{x_i} = 0$, then all but one term in equation (9-66) are 0, yielding,

$$f_{\alpha_i x_i} \frac{\partial x_i^*}{\partial \alpha_i} \geq 0 \tag{9-67}$$

In this case, the decision variable will move in the same direction as the effect on the first-order relation of that parameter. For example, in the profit-maximization model with $\pi = pf(x_1, \ldots, x_n) - \sum w_i x_i$, $\pi_{x_i} = pf_i - w_i$, and increasing the wage w_i tends to decrease π_{x_i}, since $\pi_{x_i w_i} = \pi_{w_i x_i} = -1$. Hence, the partial derivative $\partial x_i^*/\partial w_i \leq 0$, that is, the law of factor demand for profit-maximizing firms.

In addition to the implications of the negativity of the diagonal terms of $\mathcal{L}_{\alpha\alpha}^*$, the other determinantal conditions, e.g., that the second-order principal minors be positive, or $\mathscr{L}^*_{\alpha_i\alpha_i}\mathscr{L}^*_{\alpha_j\alpha_j} - (\mathscr{L}^*_{\alpha_i\alpha_j})^2 \geq 0$, also imply restrictions on the choice functions. However, these restrictions will be very difficult to observe directly, even in models as simple as the profit-maximization model. In that model, for example, this condition says that $(\partial x_i^*/\partial w_i)(\partial x_j^*/\partial w_j) - (\partial x_i^*/\partial w_j)^2 \geq 0$, or that direct effects outweigh, in the above sense, the cross-effects. But such propositions in fact have limited empirical applicability.

A similar, though more complex, analysis applies to constrained-maximization problems. The determinantal conditions (9-57) are, again,

$$\sum_{j=1}^{m} \sum_{i=1}^{m} \mathscr{L}^*_{\alpha_i\alpha_j} h_{n+i} h_{n+j} \leq 0 \tag{9-57a}$$

for all h_{n+i}, h_{n+j} satisfying

$$\sum_{i=1}^{m} g_{\alpha_i} h_{n+i} = 0 \tag{9-57b}$$

where $\mathscr{L}^*_{\alpha_i\alpha_j}$ is given as

$$\mathscr{L}^*_{\alpha_i\alpha_j} = -\sum_{k=1}^{n} \mathscr{L}_{\alpha_i x_k} \frac{\partial x_k^*}{\partial \alpha_j} - g_{\alpha_i} \frac{\partial \lambda^*}{\partial \alpha_j} \tag{9-60}$$

Suppose now that the parameters can be divided into two groups, $\alpha_1, \ldots, \alpha_r$, which appear only in the objective function $f(\mathbf{x}, \boldsymbol{\alpha})$, and $\alpha_{r+1}, \ldots, \alpha_m$, which appear only in the constraint $g(\mathbf{x}, \boldsymbol{\alpha})$. Then, if $h_{n+r+1}, \ldots, h_{n+m}$ are all set equal to 0, equation (9-57b) will be satisfied and equation (9-57a) will become

$$\sum_{i=1}^{r} \sum_{j=1}^{r} \mathscr{L}^*_{\alpha_i\alpha_j} h_{n+i} h_{n+j} \leq 0 \tag{9-68}$$

for *all* values of h_{n+i}, h_{n+j}, $i, j = 1, \ldots, r$. That is, if this type of partitioning of the parameters is possible, the model will behave in the same manner as an unconstrained maximum: the matrix of terms $\mathscr{L}^*_{\alpha_i\alpha_j}$ with respect to those parameters which appear in the objective function only will be negative semidefinite. In fact, notice the effect of this partition on $\mathscr{L}^*_{\alpha_i\alpha_j}$, $i, j = 1, \ldots, r$. Since α_i, $i = 1, \ldots, r$, does not appear in the constraint equation, $g_{\alpha_i} \equiv 0$, $i = 1, \ldots, r$, and likewise $\partial g_{\alpha_i}/\partial x_k \equiv 0$, $i = 1, \ldots, r$. Hence,

$$\mathscr{L}^*_{\alpha_i\alpha_j} = -\sum_{k=1}^{n} f_{\alpha_i x_k} \frac{\partial x_k^*}{\partial \alpha_j} \qquad i, j = 1, \ldots, r \tag{9-69}$$

an expression almost exactly like equation (9-66) for unconstrained-maximization models.

A similar analysis follows. The diagonal terms of this $r \times r$ matrix are nonpositive, i.e.,

$$-\sum_{k=1}^{n} f_{\alpha_i x_k} \frac{\partial x_k^*}{\partial \alpha_i} \leq 0 \qquad i = 1, \ldots, r \tag{9-70}$$

and the principal minors alternate in sign. If a parameter α_i appears only in the *i*th first-order relation, that is, $\mathscr{L}_{x_i} = f_{x_i}(\mathbf{x}, \alpha_i) + \lambda g_{x_i}(\mathbf{x}) = 0$, so that $f_{x_i \alpha_k} = 0$, $k \neq i$, then equation (9-70) becomes

$$f_{\alpha_i x_i} \frac{\partial x_i^*}{\partial \alpha_i} \geq 0 \qquad (9\text{-}71)$$

the same as equation (9-67) for unconstrained models. Useful comparative-statics relations concerning the parameters appearing in the constraint will not in general be available.

The above situation is precisely that encountered in the cost-minimization problem. There, the prices entered only the objective function, whereas the output parameter entered only the constraint. And, since the objective function had the peculiarly simple form $M = \sum p_i x_i$, with $M_{p_i x_i} = 1$, the matrix (9-68) reduced to the terms $\partial x_i / \partial p_j$, which, as we showed earlier, was negative semidefinite, with $\partial x_i / \partial p_i \leq 0$, etc. The output parameter y entered the constraint only; no refutable propositions were derivable for the sign of the output effects $\partial x_i / \partial y$, $i = 1, \ldots, n$.

Le Châtelier Effects

We shall finish off this chapter with a discussion of the general structure of effects due to the imposition of additional constraints on the variables. These Le Châtelier effects, named after Le Châtelier, who analyzed the effects of additional constraints on thermodynamic systems, were exhibited in the previous models as the result that long-run demands in certain models were more elastic than the corresponding short-run demands. The short run was defined as a situation in which one or more variables was to be held constant at the level appropriate to some maximum point, as the parameters, prices, changed from those values which produced that maximum point.

Consider Fig. 9-7. The indirect objective function to our constrained-maximization problem is now denoted $^1\phi(\boldsymbol{\alpha})$, the preceding superscript indicating that there is one constraint, in this case the original binding constraint, on the decision variables, for illustration only. Since only one variable can be plotted on a given axis, $^1\phi(\boldsymbol{\alpha})$ is plotted against some α_i, a representative parameter. At the vector of parameter values $\boldsymbol{\alpha} = \boldsymbol{\alpha}^0$ (where $\alpha_i = \alpha_i^0$), the objective function takes on the values $^1\phi(\boldsymbol{\alpha}^0) = f(x^*(\boldsymbol{\alpha}^0), \boldsymbol{\alpha}^0)$. The function $^1\phi(\boldsymbol{\alpha})$ has no determinate shape at this level of generality; it has been drawn concave around $\alpha_i = \alpha_i^0$ for illustration only.

Suppose now another, *just binding* constraint $h(\mathbf{x}, \boldsymbol{\alpha}) = 0$ is added to the model. The phrase *just binding* means that the addition of this constraint does not displace the original solution $\mathbf{x}^0 = \mathbf{x}^*(\boldsymbol{\alpha}^0)$. An example of this in the previous models was holding one factor of production fixed at the previously determined profit-maximizing or cost-minimizing level. Then, when the other factor's price varied, the response of the variable factors was different. But it is impossible to compare a short-run factor-demand curve at one value of x_i and its long-run demand at some other value. These comparisons are valid only at a given point, e.g., the intersection of the short- and long-run curves in Fig. 9-4. It is not the case

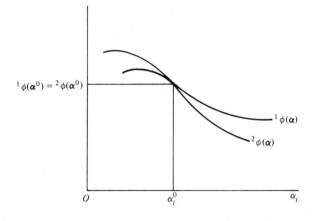

Figure 9-7 The indirect objective functions $^1\phi(\alpha)$ and $^2\phi(\alpha)$, the latter being the maximum value of $f(\mathbf{x}, \alpha)$ when an additional constraint $h(\mathbf{x}, \alpha)$ is added to the model, maximize $f(\mathbf{x}, \alpha)$ subject to $g(\mathbf{x}, \alpha) = 0$. The new constraint $h(\mathbf{x}, \alpha)$ is added to avoid disturbing the original solution $\mathbf{x}^0 = \mathbf{x}^*(\alpha^0)$, that is, by requiring $h(\mathbf{x}^0, \alpha^0) = 0$. This is akin to holding capital fixed at the previously determined profit-maximizing level and *then* changing a factor price. By this construction, $^1\phi(\alpha^0) = {}^2\phi(\alpha^0)$. However, for $\alpha \neq \alpha^0$, $^2\phi(\alpha) \leq {}^1\phi(\alpha)$ since additional restraints on the decision variables can only lower the maximum value of the objective function. Since $^2\phi(\alpha^0) = {}^1\phi(\alpha^0)$ and $^2\phi(\alpha_i) \leq {}^1\phi(\alpha_i)$ to either side of α_i^0, $^2\phi(\alpha)$ must be tangent to $^1\phi(\alpha)$ but must also be more concave in α_i (and the other parameters) than $^1\phi(\alpha)$. Since the slopes are equal, $^2\phi_{\alpha_i}(\alpha^0) = {}^1\phi_{\alpha_i}(\alpha^0)$, and from concavity $^2\phi_{\alpha_i\alpha_i}(\alpha^0) \leq {}^1\phi_{\alpha_i\alpha_i}(\alpha^0)$, among the other conditions for concavity in all the remaining parameters.

that all long-run factor demands in the previous models are more elastic than all short-run demand curves; the Le Châtelier effects are local relations holding only at one point. Hence, in our general discussion, the original model, maximize $f(\mathbf{x}, \alpha^0)$ subject to $g(\mathbf{x}, \alpha^0) = 0$, is solved, resulting in the solution values $\mathbf{x}^0 = \mathbf{x}^*(\alpha^0)$. Now, a new constraint, $h(\mathbf{x}, \alpha) = 0$, is added to the problem, *such that* $h(\mathbf{x}^0, \alpha^0) = 0$. By requiring $h(\mathbf{x}^0, \alpha^0) = 0$, we know that the addition of this constraint does not alter the original solution of the model since that solution value is not constrained at all by $h(\mathbf{x}, \alpha) = 0$. However, the comparative statics of the model *does* change. As any α_i moves away from α_i^0, the new constraint will in general become binding. Thus, for example, if capital is held fixed at some previously profit-maximizing level, then as the wage of labor changes, the response in terms of labor utilized will be different (smaller, in absolute terms) than if capital were allowed to vary, for profit-maximizing firms.

In Fig. 9-7, in addition to the original indirect objective function $^1\phi(\alpha)$, the indirect objective function $^2\phi(\alpha)$ for the amended model:

maximize $\qquad\qquad\qquad\qquad f(\mathbf{x}, \alpha)$

subject to $\qquad\qquad g(\mathbf{x}, \alpha) = 0 \qquad h(\mathbf{x}, \alpha) = 0 \qquad\qquad$ (9-72)

has been plotted. This indirect objective function is labeled $^2\phi(\alpha)$ to indicate that there are now *two* constraints in the model. Since $h(\mathbf{x}^0, \alpha^0) = 0$, $^1\phi(\mathbf{x}^0,$

$\alpha^0) = {}^2\phi(\mathbf{x}^0, \alpha^0)$; that is, the two objective functions have the same value at $\alpha = \alpha^0$. However, if $\alpha \neq \alpha^0$, ${}^2\phi(\alpha) \leq {}^1\phi(\alpha)$. The addition of a constraint on the x_i's can only reduce the maximum value of $f(\mathbf{x}, \alpha)$, since fewer choices are available for the values of the decision variables. If both ${}^1\phi(\alpha)$ and ${}^2\phi(\alpha)$ are differentiable, the situation ${}^2\phi(\alpha^0) = {}^1\phi(\alpha^0)$ and ${}^2\phi(\alpha) \leq {}^1\phi(\alpha)$ for $\alpha \neq \alpha^0$ must result in a tangency of ${}^2\phi(\alpha)$ and ${}^1\phi(\alpha)$ at $\alpha = \alpha^0$, as depicted in Fig. 9-7. The consequences of this tangency are:

1. ${}^2\phi(\alpha^0) = {}^1\phi(\alpha^0)$ [by construction: the additional constraint is just binding, that is, $h(\mathbf{x}^0, \alpha^0) = 0$].
2. ${}^2\phi_{\alpha_i}(\alpha^0) = {}^1\phi_{\alpha_i}(\alpha^0)$, $i = 1, \ldots, m$ [the slopes of ${}^1\phi(\alpha)$ and ${}^2\phi(\alpha)$ are equal in all directions at $\alpha = \alpha^0$, since the surfaces ${}^1\phi(\alpha)$ and ${}^2\phi(\alpha)$ are tangent].
3. ${}^2\phi_{\alpha_i\alpha_i} \leq {}^1\phi_{\alpha_i\alpha_i}$. In any given α_i direction, the function ${}^2\phi(\alpha)$ is more concave, as depicted in Fig. 9-7, or less convex than ${}^1\phi(\alpha)$.

Condition 3 in fact only partially characterizes this increased concavity of ${}^2\phi(\alpha)$ compared with ${}^1\phi(\alpha)$. In m dimensions, concavity is a statement that the matrix of second partials is negative semidefinite. Condition 3 is part of a statement that ${}^2\phi(\alpha)$ is more concave than ${}^1\phi(\alpha)$, subject to constraint, i.e., that ${}^2\phi(\alpha) - {}^1\phi(\alpha)$ is itself concave. The Le Châtelier effects are consequences of the concavity of ${}^2\phi(\alpha) - {}^1\phi(\alpha)$. Let us now demonstrate these conditions analytically.

The first-order conditions for the model with two constraints, (9-72), are found by differentiating the lagrangian ${}^2\mathscr{L} = f(\mathbf{x}, \alpha) + \lambda_1 g(\mathbf{x}, \alpha) + \lambda_2 h(\mathbf{x}, \alpha)$ with respect to the x_i's and λ's, yielding

$$f_i + \lambda_1 g_i + \lambda_2 h_i = 0 \qquad i = 1, \ldots, n$$

$$g(\mathbf{x}, \alpha) = 0 \qquad h(\mathbf{x}, \alpha) = 0 \tag{9-73}$$

The solutions of (9-73) are

$$x_i = {}^2x_i^*(\alpha) \qquad i = 1, \ldots, n$$

$$\lambda_1 = {}^2\lambda_1^*(\alpha) \qquad \lambda_2 = {}^2\lambda_2^*(\alpha) \tag{9-74}$$

where, again, the preceding superscript indicates the number of constraints in the model. At this point, we shall drop the asterisks from the variables to save notational clutter. All values of the x_i's will be presumed to satisfy the respective models. The partial derivatives of these choice functions will be denoted ${}^2(\partial x_i/\partial\alpha_j)$; those relating to the original model will be denoted ${}^1(\partial x_i/\partial\alpha_j)$, etc.

Let us investigate this solution, (9-74), more closely. The solution of the model without $h(\mathbf{x}, \alpha) = 0$, equations (9-47), will be denoted $x_i = {}^1x_i(\alpha)$, $i = 1, \ldots, n$, and $\lambda = \lambda_1 = {}^1\lambda_1(\alpha)$. At $\alpha = \alpha^0$, $\mathbf{x} = \mathbf{x}^0 = {}^1\mathbf{x}(\alpha^0)$, $\lambda = {}^1\lambda = {}^1\lambda^0$. These values were derived from equations (9-45),

$$f_i + \lambda_1 g_i = 0 \qquad i = 1, \ldots, n$$

$$g(\mathbf{x}, \alpha) = 0$$

But the same values of $\mathbf{x}$ and λ_1 result from the first-order equations (9-73) by construction, i.e., because we have constructed $h(\mathbf{x}, \boldsymbol{\alpha}) = 0$ such that $h(\mathbf{x}^0, \boldsymbol{\alpha}^0) = 0$. Since $f_i + \lambda_1 g_i + \lambda_2 h_i = 0$, and $f_i + \lambda_1 g_i = 0$, $i = 1, \ldots, n$, it must be the case that $\lambda_2 = 0$ at the solution point, that is, $\lambda_2(\boldsymbol{\alpha}^0) = 0$. This is in accordance with our understanding of the meaning of Lagrange multipliers: these multipliers measure the marginal cost in terms of the restrictions on attainable values of the objective function due to the imposition of a constraint. Since the constraint $h(\mathbf{x}, \boldsymbol{\alpha})$ is nonbinding at $\boldsymbol{\alpha} = \boldsymbol{\alpha}^0$, that is, ${}^2\phi(\boldsymbol{\alpha}^0) = {}^1\phi(\boldsymbol{\alpha}^0)$, the marginal cost of this constraint, in terms of units of $f(\mathbf{x}, \boldsymbol{\alpha})$ forgone, is 0 at that one point. What, then, is the rate of change of ${}^2\phi(\boldsymbol{\alpha})$ with respect to a change in some α_i? By the envelope theorem,

$$ {}^2\phi_{\alpha_i} = {}^2\mathscr{L}_{\alpha_i} = f_{\alpha_i} + \lambda_1 g_{\alpha_i} + \lambda_2 h_{\alpha_i} = f_{\alpha_i} + \lambda_1 g_{\alpha_i} = {}^1\phi_{\alpha_i} \qquad (9\text{-}75) $$

since $\lambda_2 = 0$. Hence, ${}^2\phi(\boldsymbol{\alpha})$ and ${}^1\phi(\boldsymbol{\alpha})$ have the same slope at $\boldsymbol{\alpha} = \boldsymbol{\alpha}^0$, as depicted by the tangency point in Fig. 9-7.

Now consider the second-order changes. When $\boldsymbol{\alpha} \neq \boldsymbol{\alpha}^0$, ${}^2\phi(\boldsymbol{\alpha}) \leq {}^1\phi(\boldsymbol{\alpha})$. In some neighborhood around $\boldsymbol{\alpha}^0$, these functions can be approximated by a Taylor series carried to second-order terms, yielding

$$ {}^2\phi(\boldsymbol{\alpha}^0) + \sum_{i=1}^{m} {}^2\phi_{\alpha_i}(\boldsymbol{\alpha}^0) h_i + \frac{1}{2} \sum_{i=1}^{m} \sum_{j=1}^{m} {}^2\phi_{\alpha_i \alpha_j}(\boldsymbol{\alpha}^0) h_i h_j \leq $$

$$ {}^1\phi(\boldsymbol{\alpha}^0) + \sum_{i=1}^{m} {}^1\phi_{\alpha_i}(\boldsymbol{\alpha}^0) h_i + \frac{1}{2} \sum_{i=1}^{m} \sum_{j=1}^{m} {}^1\phi_{\alpha_i \alpha_j}(\boldsymbol{\alpha}^0) h_i h_j \qquad (9\text{-}76) $$

where $h_i = \alpha_i - \alpha_i^0$. However, ${}^2\phi(\boldsymbol{\alpha}^0) = {}^1\phi(\boldsymbol{\alpha}^0)$ by construction, and, from equation (9-75), since $\lambda_2 = 0$, ${}^2\phi_{\alpha_i}(\boldsymbol{\alpha}^0) = {}^1\phi_{\alpha_i}(\boldsymbol{\alpha}^0)$. Equation (9-76) can thus be written

$$ \sum\sum ({}^2\phi_{\alpha_i \alpha_j} - {}^1\phi_{\alpha_i \alpha_j}) h_i h_j \leq 0 \qquad (9\text{-}77) $$

for all values of h_i, h_j. This is condition 3 above: the hessian matrix of second partials of ${}^2\phi(\boldsymbol{\alpha}) - {}^1\phi(\boldsymbol{\alpha})$ is negative semidefinite, or since ${}^2\phi(\boldsymbol{\alpha}) \leq {}^1\phi(\boldsymbol{\alpha})$, ${}^2\phi(\boldsymbol{\alpha}) - {}^1\phi(\boldsymbol{\alpha})$ is a concave (perhaps only weakly concave) function of the α_i's. This is a rather surprising result. The functions ${}^1\phi(\boldsymbol{\alpha}) - f(\mathbf{x}, \boldsymbol{\alpha})$ and ${}^2\phi(\boldsymbol{\alpha}) - f(\mathbf{x}, \boldsymbol{\alpha})$ are merely quasi-concave; their difference, however, is concave.

Let us now apply equation (9-77) to the comparative statics of the two models. Note first that from the definitions of the lagrangians for the primal-dual problems,

$$ {}^1\mathscr{L}^*(\mathbf{x}, \boldsymbol{\alpha}) = f(\mathbf{x}, \boldsymbol{\alpha}) - {}^1\phi(\boldsymbol{\alpha}) + \lambda_1 g(\mathbf{x}, \boldsymbol{\alpha}) \qquad (9\text{-}52) $$

and
$$ {}^2\mathscr{L}^*(\mathbf{x}, \boldsymbol{\alpha}) = f(\mathbf{x}, \boldsymbol{\alpha}) - {}^2\phi(\boldsymbol{\alpha}) $$
$$ + \lambda_1 g(\mathbf{x}, \boldsymbol{\alpha}) + \lambda_2 h(\mathbf{x}, \boldsymbol{\alpha}) \qquad (9\text{-}78) $$

$$ {}^1\mathscr{L}^*(\mathbf{x}, \boldsymbol{\alpha}) - {}^2\mathscr{L}^*(\mathbf{x}, \boldsymbol{\alpha}) = {}^2\phi(\boldsymbol{\alpha}) - {}^1\phi(\boldsymbol{\alpha}) - \lambda_2 h(\mathbf{x}, \boldsymbol{\alpha}) $$

When $\mathbf{x} = \mathbf{x}^*$,

$$ {}^1\mathscr{L}^*(\mathbf{x}, \boldsymbol{\alpha}) - {}^2\mathscr{L}^*(\mathbf{x}, \boldsymbol{\alpha}) \equiv {}^2\phi(\boldsymbol{\alpha}) - {}^1\phi(\boldsymbol{\alpha}) \qquad (9\text{-}79) $$

Thus, $^2\phi_{\alpha_i\alpha_j} - {}^1\phi_{\alpha_i\alpha_j}$ can be calculated from the primal-dual lagrangians. From equation (9-60),

$$ {}^1\mathscr{L}^*_{\alpha_i\alpha_j} = - \sum_{k=1}^{n} {}^1\mathscr{L}_{\alpha_i x_k} \, {}^1\!\left(\frac{\partial x_k}{\partial \alpha_j}\right) - g_{\alpha_i} \, {}^1\!\left(\frac{\partial \lambda_1}{\partial \alpha_j}\right) \tag{9-80} $$

In like fashion, for the model with two constraints, one finds

$$ {}^2\mathscr{L}^*_{\alpha_i\alpha_j} = - \sum_{k=1}^{n} {}^2\mathscr{L}_{\alpha_i x_k} \, {}^2\!\left(\frac{\partial x_k}{\partial \alpha_j}\right) - g_{\alpha_i} \, {}^2\!\left(\frac{\partial \lambda_1}{\partial \alpha_j}\right) - h_{\alpha_i} \, {}^2\!\left(\frac{\partial \lambda_2}{\partial \alpha_j}\right) \tag{9-81} $$

Now
$$ {}^2\mathscr{L}_{\alpha_i x_k} = \frac{\partial f_{\alpha_i}}{\partial x_k} + \lambda_1 \frac{\partial g_{\alpha_i}}{\partial x_k} + \lambda_2 \frac{\partial h_{\alpha_i}}{\partial x_k} $$

However, $\lambda_2 = 0$, since $h(\mathbf{x}, \boldsymbol{\alpha})$ is just binding. Therefore,

$$ {}^2\mathscr{L}_{\alpha_i x_k} = \frac{\partial f_{\alpha_i}}{\partial x_k} + \lambda_1 \frac{\partial g_{\alpha_i}}{\partial x_k} = {}^1\mathscr{L}_{\alpha_i x_k} \tag{9-82} $$

Although $\lambda_2 = 0$, $\partial\lambda_2/\partial\alpha_j \neq 0$ in general. When $\boldsymbol{\alpha}$ departs from $\boldsymbol{\alpha}^0$, the constraint $h(\mathbf{x}, \boldsymbol{\alpha})$ becomes binding and then $\lambda_2 \neq 0$. Thus, λ_2 is not constant at zero; that is, $\partial\lambda_2/\partial\alpha_j \neq 0$. Equation (9-77) now becomes, using equations (9-79) to (9-82),

$$ \sum_{i=1}^{m} \sum_{j=1}^{m} \left(\sum_{k=1}^{n} \left\{ \left(\frac{\partial f_{\alpha_i}}{\partial x_k} + \lambda_1 \frac{\partial g_{\alpha_i}}{\partial x_k} \right) \left[{}^2\!\left(\frac{\partial x_k}{\partial \alpha_j}\right) - {}^1\!\left(\frac{\partial x_k}{\partial \alpha_j}\right) \right] \right\} \right. $$
$$ \left. + g_{\alpha_i}\left[{}^2\!\left(\frac{\partial \lambda_1}{\partial \alpha_j}\right) - {}^1\!\left(\frac{\partial \lambda_1}{\partial \alpha_j}\right) \right] + h_{\alpha_i}\, {}^2\!\left(\frac{\partial \lambda_2}{\partial \alpha_j}\right) \right) h_i h_j \leq 0 \tag{9-83} $$

for any values of h_i, h_j.

Equation (9-83) gives the general structure of the change in the choice functions due to the imposition of an additional, just binding constraint for differentiable maximization systems. Again, it is nothing more than the statement that the matrix of differences $({}^1\mathscr{L}^*_{\alpha_i\alpha_j} - {}^2\mathscr{L}^*_{\alpha_i\alpha_j})$ is negative semidefinite. The usual Le Châtelier effects are consequences of the negativity of the diagonal terms of this matrix, that is, ${}^1\mathscr{L}^*_{\alpha_i\alpha_i} \leq {}^2\mathscr{L}^*_{\alpha_i\alpha_i}$, with the strict inequality generally assumed. For example, for the profit-maximizing firm, if the new (and only) constraint is $x_n = x_n^0$ (note that $\partial f_{\alpha_i}/\partial x_k = 0$, $i \neq k$, and $\partial f_i/\partial\alpha_i = -1$) and $h_{\alpha_i} \equiv 0$ (prices don't enter the new constraint), a diagonal term of (9-83) is $-[{}^1(\partial x_i/\partial w_i) - {}^0(\partial x_i/\partial w_i)] \leq 0$, precisely the statement (9-21) that long-run factor demands are more elastic than short-run demands. The same analysis applies to the cost-minimization model, though the inequality in (9-83) must be reversed since this is a minimization rather than a maximization model. Since the prices there do not enter the constraint, and since $-\partial f_{\alpha_i}/\partial x_k = 1$ if $i = k$ and 0 otherwise, the same result follows. In addition, however, a definitive result emerges for the slope of the marginal cost function. Although it is not possible to state, from cost-minimization alone, whether marginal cost rises or falls with increased output, the term $\partial\lambda_1/\partial y$ is a diagonal term of $\mathscr{L}^*_{\alpha_i\alpha_j}$; the above analysis therefore shows that marginal cost must be rising faster or falling slower when additional constraints are placed on the decision variables.

The remaining Le Châtelier effects are those relating to the alternation in sign of the principal minors of $(^1\mathscr{L}^*_{\alpha_i\alpha_j} - {}^2\mathscr{L}^*_{\alpha_i\alpha_j})$. For example, for the profit-maximizing firm,

$$\left[{}^1\!\left(\frac{\partial x_i}{\partial w_i}\right) - {}^0\!\left(\frac{\partial x_i}{\partial w_i}\right)\right]\left[{}^1\!\left(\frac{\partial x_j}{\partial w_j}\right) - {}^0\!\left(\frac{\partial x_j}{\partial w_j}\right)\right] \geq \left[{}^1\!\left(\frac{\partial x_i}{\partial w_j}\right) - {}^0\!\left(\frac{\partial x_i}{\partial w_j}\right)\right]^2$$

with a similar result holding for the constant output demands.

Although we have derived these results for a model with one constraint and then added a second, the results are perfectly general. It is possible to start with r constraints ($r < n$, the number of decision variables) (why?) and add an $(r + 1)$st. The identical results emerge with the appropriate changes in some of the functions. If the constraints are denoted $g^1(\mathbf{x}, \boldsymbol{\alpha}) = 0, \ldots, g^r(\mathbf{x}, \boldsymbol{\alpha}) = 0$, then

$$^r\mathscr{L}_{\alpha_i x_k} = \frac{\partial f_{\alpha_i}}{\partial x_k} + \sum_{j=1}^{r} \lambda_j \frac{\partial g^j_{\alpha_i}}{\partial x_k}$$

and the same analysis follows.

PROBLEMS

1 Explain why, in maximization models, if a parameter enters the constraint, qualitative comparative-statics results regarding that parameter will not in general be forthcoming.

2 Show from profit-maximization that $\partial y^*/\partial p > \partial y^s/\partial p$, where y^s is the short-run supply curve in which one factor is held fixed.

3 Show that although it is not possible to sign $\partial \lambda^*/\partial y_0$ in the cost-minimization model, it is nonetheless true that

$$\frac{\partial \lambda^s}{\partial y_0} > \frac{\partial \lambda^*}{\partial y_0}$$

i.e., marginal cost rises faster or falls slower when a factor is held fixed than when all factors are variable. (λ^s refers to the short-run marginal cost function.)

4 Show that the marginal utility of money income rises faster or falls slower when all consumption levels are variable than when one or more goods are held fixed in consumption.

5 Consider the problem of firms in long-run equilibrium again, in which the behavioral assertion is:

minimize
$$\text{AC} = \frac{w_1 x_1 + w_2 x_2}{y}$$

where $y = f(x_1, x_2)$ is the production function.

    (a) Show that $\partial(x_i^*/y^*)/\partial w_i < 0$, $i = 1, 2$.

    (b) Show that $\varepsilon_{iw_i} < \varepsilon_{yw_i}$; that is, the elasticity of factor demand is less than the elasticity of output with respect to a factor price.

    (c) Show that $\partial(x_i^*/y^*)\,\partial w_j = \partial(x_j^*/\partial y^*)/\partial w_i$.

    (d) Show that $\partial(x_1^*/x_2^*)/\partial w_1 < 0$ (for the two-factor case).

6 Consider a firm which produces two outputs, x_1 and x_2, using one input, v. The firm's technology is given by the function $f(x_1, x_2) = v$. (This function gives the amount of v necessary to produce any combination of x_1 and x_2; for a fixed v its graph is the production possibility curve.) Suppose the firm is a price taker and faces output-prices p_1 and p_2 and input-price w. Assume the firm's objective is to maximize profits:

$$\pi = p_1 x_1 + p_2 x_2 - wv$$

(a) Derive the first-order conditions and interpret.

(b) Derive the second-order conditions.

(c) Define the *profit function* as that function giving maximal profits for any level of prices:

$$\pi^*(p_1, p_2, w) = p_1 x_1^* + p_2 x_2^* - wv^*$$

Show that $\partial \pi^* / \partial p_1 = x_1^*$ and $\partial \pi^* / \partial w = -v^*$. What are x_1^* and v^*?

(d) Show that $\partial x_1^* / \partial w = -\partial v^* / \partial p_1$.

(e) Show that the output supply curves are upward-sloping and the factor-demand curve is downward-sloping.

7 Consider a profit-maximizing firm employing two factors. Define the short run as the condition where the firm behaves as if it were under a total expenditure constraint; i.e., in the short run, *total expenditures are fixed* (at the long-run profit-maximizing level). The long run is the situation where no additional constraints are placed on the firm.

(a) Are these short-run demands necessarily downward-sloping?

(b) Show that the short-run factor-demand curves for this model are not necessarily less elastic than the long-run factor-demand curves. Why does this anomalous result arise for this model?

(c) Show that if a factor is *inferior* in terms of its response to a change in total expenditure, the long-run factor demand is necessarily more elastic than the short-run demand for that factor.

BIBLIOGRAPHY

Samuelson, P. A.: The Le Chatelier Principle in Linear Programming, *RAND Corporation Monograph*, August 4, 1949 (chap. 43 in "Scientific Papers").

————: An Extension of the Le Chatelier Principle, *Econometrica*, April 1960, pp. 368–379 (chap. 42 in "Scientific Papers").

————: Structure of a Minimum Equilibrium System, in R. W. Pfouts (ed.), "Essays in Economics and Econometrics: A Volume in Honor of Harold Hotelling," The University of North Carolina Press, Chapel Hill, 1960 (chap. 44 in "Scientific Papers").

These three articles have all been reprinted in J. Stiglitz (ed.): "The Collected Scientific Papers of Paul A. Samuelson," The M.I.T. Press, Cambridge, Mass., 1966.

————: "Foundations of Economic Analysis," Harvard University Press, Cambridge, Mass., 1947.

Silberberg, E.: A Revision of Comparative Statics Methodology in Economics, or, How to Do Economics on the Back of an Envelope, *Journal of Economic Theory*, **7**: 159–172, February 1974.

————: The Le Chatelier Principle as a Corollary to a Generalized Envelope Theorem, *Journal of Economic Theory*, **3**: 146–155, June 1971.

TEN

COST AND PRODUCTION FUNCTIONS: SPECIAL TOPICS

10.1 HOMOGENEOUS AND HOMOTHETIC PRODUCTION FUNCTIONS†

An interesting and important class of production functions is the homothetic production functions, of which the homogeneous functions are a subset. A production function is homogeneous of degree r if when all inputs are increased (decreased) by the same proportion, output increases (decreases) by the rth power of that increase. Formally, if $f(x_1, \ldots, x_n)$ is homogeneous of degree r,

$$f(tx_1, \ldots, tx_n) \equiv t^r f(x_1, \ldots, x_n)$$

Several properties of homogeneous functions in general were noted in an earlier chapter, especially Euler's theorem, already used extensively in other contexts. In addition, the geometric property that

$$\frac{f_i(tx_1, \ldots, tx_n)}{f_j(tx_1, \ldots, tx_n)} \equiv \frac{f_i(x_1, \ldots, x_n)}{f_j(x_1, \ldots, x_n)}$$

i.e., that the slopes of the level curves are the same along every point of a given ray out of the origin was proved using the homogeneity of degree $r - 1$ of the first partials f_i and f_j.

However, homogeneous functions are not the only functions with this geome-

---

† The student may wish to review the sections in Chap. 3 on homogeneity.

tric property. Consider any monotonic transformation $F(z)$ of a homogeneous production function $z = f(x_1, \ldots, x_n)$. That is, consider $y = H(x_1, \ldots, x_n) = F(f(x_1, \ldots, x_n))$, where $F'(z) > 0$. The requirement that $F'(z) > 0$ ensures that z and y move in the same direction; e.g., when z increases, y must increase. The slope of a level curve $H(x_1, \ldots, x_n) = y_0$ in the $x_i x_j$ plane is

$$\frac{H_i}{H_j} = \frac{F'(z)f_i}{F'(z)f_j} = \frac{f_i}{f_j}$$

But we already know that f_i/f_j is invariant under a radial expansion. Hence the function $H(x_1, \ldots, x_n) = F(f(x_1, \ldots, x_n))$ also exhibits this property.

The class of functions $y = H(x_1, \ldots, x_n) = F(f(x_1, \ldots, x_n))$ where $F' \neq 0$ and $f(x_1, \ldots, x_n)$ is a homogeneous function is called the *homothetic functions*. In fact, no generality is lost if $f(x_1, \ldots, x_n)$ is restricted to *linear* homogeneous functions, i.e., functions homogeneous of degree 1. The reason is that if $f(x_1, \ldots, x_n)$ is homogeneous of degree r, then $[f(x_1, \ldots, x_n)]^{1/r}$ is homogeneous of degree 1:

$$[f(tx_1, \ldots, tx_n)]^{1/r} \equiv [t^r f(x_1, \ldots, x_n)]^{1/r} \equiv t[f(x_1, \ldots, x_n)]^{1/r}$$

Taking the rth root of f can be incorporated into the monotonic transformation $y = F(z)$. That is, $F(z)$ can be itself thought of as a composite function, the first part of which is taking the rth root of $f(x_1, \ldots, x_n)$ and the second part whatever transformation yields $H(x_1, \ldots, x_n)$. Hence we can define as the class of homothetic functions all functions $H(x_1, \ldots, x_n) \equiv F(f(x_1, \ldots, x_n))$ where $f(x_1, \ldots, x_n)$ is homogeneous of degree 1 and $F' \neq 0$.

The statement that the slopes of the level curves are invariant under radial expansion or contraction of the original point, i.e., when $x_1, \ldots, x_n$ is replaced by $tx_1, \ldots, tx_n$, can be expressed another way. The slope of the level curve (surface) at any point is H_i/H_j. This is just another function of the x_i's; that is, define

$$\frac{H_i}{H_j} \equiv h_{ij}(x_1, \ldots, x_n)$$

The function $h_{ij}(x_1, \ldots, x_n)$ designates the (negative) slope of the level surface of H in the $x_i x_j$ plane. This slope is unchanged under $x_1, \ldots, x_n \to tx_1, \ldots, tx_n$. But this is simply a statement that $h_{ij}(x_1, \ldots, x_n)$ is homogeneous of degree zero, that is, that $h_{ij}(tx_1, \ldots, tx_n) \equiv h_{ij}(x_1, \ldots, x_n)$. It can in fact be shown by more advanced methods that homotheticity can be defined in this manner also; i.e., if $h_{ij}(x_1, \ldots, x_n)$ is homogeneous of degree zero for all $x_i x_j$ planes, then $H(x_1, \ldots, x_n)$ must have the form $H(x_1, \ldots, x_n) \equiv F(f(x_1, \ldots, x_n))$, where $f(x_1, \ldots, x_n)$ is homogeneous of degree 1 and $F' \neq 0$.

Example Consider the production function $y = H(x_1, x_2) = x_1 x_2 + x_1^2 x_2^2$. This function is not homogeneous, as can readily be verified. It is homothetic, however, since $H(x_1, x_2) \equiv z + z^2$, where $z = x_1 x_2$. That is, $H(x_1, x_2) \equiv F(f(x_1, x_2))$, where $F(z) = z + z^2$. Note that $F'(z) = 1 + 2z \neq 0$, since production is presumed to be nonnegative. The slope of a level curve of $H(x_1, x_2)$ is

$$-\frac{H_1}{H_2} = -\frac{x_2 + 2x_1 x_2^2}{x_1 + 2x_1^2 x_2}$$

$$= -\frac{x_2(1 + 2x_1 x_2)}{x_1(1 + 2x_1 x_2)} = -\frac{x_2}{x_1}$$

Note that $F'(z) = 1 + 2x_1 x_2$ appears in the numerator and denominator. Hence, $H_1 / H_2 = h_{12}(x_1, x_2) = x_2/x_1$. The function h_{12} is clearly homogeneous of degree zero: $h_{12}(tx_1, tx_2) \equiv tx_2/tx_1 \equiv x_2/x_1 \equiv h_{12}(x_1, x_2)$. Thus, the level curves of $x_1 x_2 + x_1^2 x_2^2$ have the same slope at all points along any given ray out of the origin.

Still another way to express homotheticity is to state that the output elasticities for all factors are equal at any given point. That is, $\varepsilon_{1y_0} = \varepsilon_{2y_0} = \cdots = \varepsilon_{ny_0}$. This is clear from the geometry of straight-line expansion paths. Consider Fig. 10-1. Any increase, say, in output from y_0 to y_0' will result in a new tangency point B along a straight line through the origin and the former tangency point A. The triangles OAx_1^0 and $OB(tx_1^0)$ are similar; hence, x_1 increases by $OB/OA \equiv t$. But, clearly, x_2 increases by $OB/OA \equiv t$ also, for the same reason. Hence for homothetic production functions, output elasticities are equal in all factors.

This result can be shown algebraically by noting that a straight-line expansion path implies that the ratio x_j/x_i, the slope of the ray out to that point in the $x_i x_j$ plane, is the same for any output level as long as factor prices are held constant. That is,

$$\frac{\partial(x_j^*/x_i^*)}{\partial y_0} \equiv 0$$

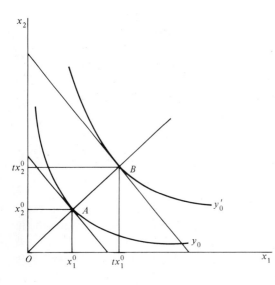

Figure 10-1 Homothetic production functions. The level curves of homothetic production functions are all radial expansions of one another; i.e., at the intersections of any ray out of the origin and the level curves, the slopes are all the same. Put another way, if output is increased autonomously, i.e., holding factor prices constant, the new tangency point will lie along the ray projecting the old tangency point from the origin. By similar triangles, it is clear that x_1 increases in the same proportion t as x_2 does when y_0 is increased.

Using the quotient rule and multiplying through by x_i^2 yields

$$x_i^* \frac{\partial x_j^*}{\partial y_0} - x_j^* \frac{\partial x_i^*}{\partial y_0} \equiv 0$$

After multiplication by y_0 and division by $x_i^* x_j^*$ this leads to

$$\frac{y_0}{x_j^*} \frac{\partial x_j^*}{\partial y_0} \equiv \frac{y_0}{x_i^*} \frac{\partial x_i^*}{\partial y_0}$$

or
$$\varepsilon_{j y_0} \equiv \varepsilon_{i y_0} \qquad i, j = 1, \ldots, n \tag{10-1}$$

The value of this common output elasticity can be found by applying equation (7-48). Since $\varepsilon_{i y_0} = \varepsilon_{j y_0} = \varepsilon_{y_0}$, say, this constant can be removed from the summation, yielding

$$\varepsilon_{y_0} \sum \kappa_i' = 1$$

However,

$$\sum \kappa_i' = \frac{\sum w_i x_i}{(MC) y_0} = \frac{AC}{MC}$$

Thus
$$\varepsilon_{y_0} = \frac{MC}{AC} \tag{10-2}$$

The common value of output elasticity, for homothetic functions, is the ratio of marginal to average cost. Therefore, for firms with increasing average costs, the factors are all output-elastic; that is, $\varepsilon_{y_0} = \varepsilon_{i y_0} > 1$ for all factors; for firms with declining (average) cost, factors are all output-inelastic. Also, if the firm is at the minimum point of its AC curve, the output elasticities of its factors are all unity if the production function is homothetic.

10.2 THE COST FUNCTION: FURTHER PROPERTIES

We have already shown that $C^*(w_1, w_2, y_0)$ is homogeneous of degree 1 in w_1 and w_2, or, more generally, for the n-factor firm, $C^*(w_1, \ldots, w_n, y_0)$ is homogeneous of degree 1 in $w_1, \ldots, w_n$. Again, since $C^* = \sum w_i x_i^*(w_1, \ldots, w_n, y_0)$, and since the $x_i^*(w_1, \ldots, w_n, y_0)$'s are homogeneous of degree zero in $w_1, \ldots, w_n$,

$$C^*(tw_1, \ldots, tw_n, y_0) \equiv \sum tw_i x_i^*(tw_1, \ldots, tw_n, y_0)$$

$$\equiv t \sum w_i x_i^*(w_1, \ldots, w_n, y_0)$$

$$\equiv tC^*(w_1, \ldots, w_n, y_0)$$

Suppose in addition that the production function $y = f(x_1, \ldots, x_n)$ is homogeneous of some degree $r > 0$ in $x_1, \ldots, x_n$. In this case, we shall demonstrate that the cost function can be partitioned into

$$C^*(w_1, \ldots, w_n, y_0) \equiv y_0^{1/r} A(w_1, \ldots, w_n) \tag{10-3}$$

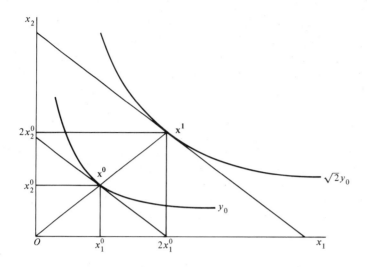

Figure 10-2 A production function homogeneous of degree $1/2$. When input levels x_1^0, x_2^0 are doubled, say, output increases by the factor $2^{1/2} = \sqrt{2}$. However, since $C = w_1 x_1 + w_2 x_2$, cost doubles; that is, $C(x^0) = \frac{1}{2}C(x^1)$. This means that a doubling of cost is accompanied by a $\sqrt{2}$-fold increase in y_0, that is, cost and output are related as $C = A y_0^2$. The constant of proportionality is constant only in that it does not involve y_0, output. It *is* a function of factor prices; that is, $A = A(w_1, w_2)$.

where it is to be noted that the function $A(w_1, \ldots, w_n)$ is a function of factor prices only. In the case where $r = 1$, that is, $f(x_1, \ldots, x_n)$ exhibits constant returns to scale,

$$C^*(w_1, \ldots, w_n, y_0) \equiv y_0 \, AC(w_1, \ldots, w_n) \tag{10-4}$$

where $A(w_1, \ldots, w_n)$ becomes the average cost function AC. But average cost $AC(w_1, \ldots, w_n)$ is a function of factor prices only, i.e., independent of output level. This is of course as it must be; if a firm exhibits constant returns to scale, $AC = MC = $ constant, i.e., a function of factor prices only at every level of output. This result and others below are often referred to as the *Samuelson-Shephard duality theorem*.

We shall prove some of these results for the case of differentiable functions. For simplicity, we shall deal with functions of only two variables, i.e., the two-factor case. The generalizations to n factors are straightforward and are left as exercises for the student. We shall drop the subscript 0 for output y, still remembering, however, that y is a parameter in the cost-minimization model.

Equation (10-3) is intuitively plausible. Consider Fig. 10-2. Suppose the firm is initially at point x^0 utilizing inputs $x^0 = (x_1^0, x_2^0)$. Some level of cost $C(x^0)$ would exist. Suppose now both inputs were doubled, to $(2x_1^0, 2x_2^0) = x^1$. Then since the production function is homothetic (indeed, homogeneous), the new cost-minimizing tangency will lie on a ray from the origin extending past the original point x^0 to point x^1 at twice the input levels. At x^1, the cost $C(x^1)$ is clearly twice $C(x^0)$ since both inputs have exactly doubled while factor prices remain the same.

Hence, $C(\mathbf{x}^1) = 2C(\mathbf{x}^0)$. However, y_0, output at $\mathbf{x}^0$, has grown only to $2^{1/2}y_0 = \sqrt{2}\,y_0$, since the production function is homogeneous of degree $\frac{1}{2}$. This means that, holding factor prices constant, cost and output are related in the proportion $C = Ay_0^2$, since a doubling, say, of cost is accompanied by an increase of output of the factors of $\sqrt{2}$. The proportionality constant A, in fact, must be dependent on factor prices; that is, $A = A(w_1, w_2)$. For a different slope of the isocost line, the proportionality constant will be different; however, cost and output will still have the general relation (10-3).

The above reasoning cannot be applied to general nonhomogeneous functions. (It can be applied in a more complicated fashion, and we shall do so, to general homothetic functions.) If the production function is nonhomothetic, a given increase in output is not related to a simple proportionate expansion of all inputs. Instead, the ratios of one factor to another will change. Hence, the cost function will necessarily be a more complicated function than (10-3), wherein factor prices and output are all mixed together and not separable into two parts, one related to output and the other to factor prices.

In proving (10-3), we shall use the following relationship, already discussed in the first discussion of interpreting λ, the Lagrange multiplier of the constrained cost-minimization problem, as marginal cost. Since $C^* \equiv w_1 x_1^* + w_2 x_2^*$, then since $w_1 = \lambda^* f_1$, $w_2 = \lambda^* f_2$,

$$C^* \equiv \lambda^*(f_1 x_1^* + f_2 x_2^*)$$

However, for homogeneous functions, $f_1 x_1 + f_2 x_2 \equiv ry$, where r is the degree of homogeneity. Hence for homogeneous functions,

$$C^* \equiv \lambda^* ry \tag{10-5a}$$

or

$$\frac{C^*}{y} \equiv r\frac{\partial C^*}{\partial y} \tag{10-5b}$$

The question now is: What general functional form $C^*(w_1, w_2, y)$ has the property of obeying equations (10-5), which says that average cost C^*/y is proportional to marginal cost, the factor of proportionality being the constant r. This question is answered by integrating the partial differential equation (10-5).

Rearranging the terms in (10-5b) yields

$$\frac{\partial C^*}{C^*} \equiv \frac{1}{r}\frac{\partial y}{y} \tag{10-6}$$

The differential notation ∂C^* is used rather than dC^* to remind us that in that differentiation w_1 and w_2 were being held constant. Integrating both sides of (10-6) gives

$$\int \frac{\partial C^*}{C^*} \equiv \frac{1}{r}\left(\int \frac{\partial y}{y}\right) + K(w_1, w_2) \tag{10-7}$$

As in all integrations, an arbitrary constant appears. However, since this was a *partial* differential equation with respect to y, the constant term can include any arbitrary function of the variables held constant in the original differentiation, i.e., the factor prices here. In fact, the theory of partial differential equations assures us that the inclusion of an arbitrary function in the integration constant of the variable held fixed in the partial differentiation yields the general solution to the partial differential equation.

Performing the indicated integration in equation (10-7) yields

$$\log C^* = \frac{1}{r} \log y + \log A(w_1, w_2) \tag{10-8}$$

Here, we have written the constant term $K(w_1, w_2)$ as $\log A(w_1, w_2)$. There is no loss of generality involved, since any real number is the logarithm of some positive number. This manipulation, however, permits us to rewrite (10-8) as

$$\log C^* \equiv \log \left[y^{(1/r)} A(w_1, w_2) \right] \tag{10-9}$$

since the logarithm of a product is the sum of the individual logarithms and $\log a^b \equiv b \log a$. Since the above logarithms are equal (identical, in fact), their antilogarithms are equal; i.e.,

$$C^* \equiv y^{(1/r)} A(w_1, w_2) \tag{10-10}$$

which was to be proved.

That (10-10) is a solution of the partial differential equation (10-5) can be seen by substitution:

$$\lambda = \frac{\partial C^*}{\partial y} = \frac{1}{r} y^{[(1/r)-1]} A(w_1, w_2)$$

Substituting this into the right-hand side of equation (10-5a) yields

$$\frac{1}{r} y^{[(1/r)-1]} Ary \qquad \text{or} \qquad y^{(1/r)} A$$

But this is identically the left-hand side, C^*. By definition, since the substitution of the form $C^* = y^{(1/r)} A(w_1, w_2)$ into the equation $C^* = \lambda^* ry$ makes that equation an identity, $C^* = y^{(1/r)} A(w_1, w_2)$ is a solution of (10-5). And, it is the most general solution of (10-5) because of the inclusion of the arbitrary *function* $A(w_1, w_2)$ as the constant of integration. It is also clear that the integration constant must be positive; otherwise positive outputs would be associated with imaginary (involving $\sqrt{-1}$) costs.

To recapitulate, what has been shown is that if the production function is homogeneous of any degree r $(r > 0)$, then costs, output, and factor prices are related in the multiplicatively separable fashion $C^* = y^{(1/r)} A(w_1, w_2)$. Equivalently, for homogeneous production functions, average costs are always proportional to marginal costs, the factor of proportionality being the degree of homogeneity r; that is, $C^*/y \equiv r \, \partial C^*/\partial y$.

Either equation (10-5) or (10-10) can be used to show the relationship of the degree of homogeneity to the slope of the marginal and average cost functions.

From (10-10),

$$\mathrm{MC} = \frac{\partial C^*}{\partial y} = \frac{1}{r} y^{[(1/r)-1]} A(w_1, w_2)$$

and thus

$$\frac{\partial \mathrm{MC}}{\partial y} = \frac{1}{r}\left(\frac{1}{r} - 1\right) y^{[(1/r)-2]} A(w_1, w_2)$$

By inspection, if $r < 1$, $\partial \mathrm{MC}/\partial y > 0$; that is, for a homogeneous production function exhibiting decreasing returns to scale, marginal costs (not surprisingly) are always increasing. Similarly, if $r > 1$, $\partial \mathrm{MC}/\partial y < 0$; that is, falling marginal costs are associated with homogeneous production functions exhibiting increasing returns to scale. Lastly, if $r = 1$, the constant-returns-to-scale case, marginal cost is constant and equal to $A(w_1, w_2)$ for all levels of output.

Alternatively, from (10-5b), if $r > 1$, say, AC > MC. Since marginal cost is always below average cost, AC must always be falling, with similar reasoning holding for $r < 1$ and $r = 1$. Also, differentiating (10-5a) partially with respect to y yields

$$\frac{\partial C^*}{\partial y} \equiv \lambda^* \equiv r\left(\lambda^* + y\frac{\partial \lambda^*}{\partial y}\right)$$

Solving for $\partial \lambda^*/\partial y$, that is, $\partial \mathrm{MC}/\partial y$ gives

$$\frac{\partial \mathrm{MC}}{\partial y} \equiv \frac{1}{ry}\mathrm{MC}(1 - r) \tag{10-11}$$

from which the above results can be read directly.

Homothetic Functions

Let us now consider the functional form of the cost function associated with the general class of homothetic production functions, $y = F(f(x_1, x_2))$, where $f(x_1, x_2)$ is homogeneous of degree 1, and $F'(z) > 0$, where $z = f(x_1, x_2)$. Proceeding as before, we have

$$C^* \equiv w_1 x_1^* + w_2 x_2^*$$
$$\equiv \lambda^*(F'(z)f_1)x_1^* + \lambda^*(F'(z)f_2)x_2^*$$
$$\equiv \lambda^* F'(z)(f_1 x_1^* + f_2 x_2^*)$$

or

$$C^* \equiv \lambda^* F'(z)z \tag{10-12}$$

using Euler's theorem. Now y is a monotonic transformation of z; that is, $F'(z) > 0$. This means that if z were plotted against y, the resulting curve would always be upward-sloping. Under these conditions, a unique value of y will be associated with any value of z; that is, the function $y = F(z)$ is "invertible" to $z = F^{-1}(y)$. The situation is the same as expressing demand curves as $p = p(x)$ (price as a function of quantity) instead of the more common $x = x(p)$ (quantity as a function of price). Thus we can write

$$C^* \equiv \lambda^* F'(F^{-1}(y))[F^{-1}(y)]$$

or, combining all the separate functions of y,

$$C^* \equiv \lambda^* G(y) \tag{10-13}$$

That is, for homothetic functions, the cost function can be written as marginal cost times some function of y only, $G(y)$. If the homothetic function were in fact homogeneous of some degree r, then $G(y) = ry$, a particularly simple form, as indicated in equation (10-5a). As before, the question is: What general functional form of $C^*(w_1, w_2, y)$ satisfies the partial differential equation (10-13)? That is, what restrictions on the form of $C^*(w_1, w_2, y)$ are imposed by the structure (10-13)?

This question is answered as before by integrating the differential equation (10-13). Separating the y terms and remembering that $\lambda^* = \partial C^*/\partial y$, we have

$$\frac{\partial C^*}{C^*} \equiv \frac{\partial y}{G(y)} \tag{10-14}$$

The critical thing to notice about (10-14) is that the right-hand side is a function of y only. We shall assume that some integral function of $1/G(y)$ exists, and we shall designate that integral function as $\log J(y)$. Also, an arbitrary constant of integration must appear, and, as in the homogeneous case, this constant is not really a constant but an arbitrary *function* of the remaining variables, w_1 and w_2, which are treated as constants when the cost function is differentiated partially with respect to y. This constant function will be designated $\log A(w_1, w_2)$. Thus, integrating (10-14) gives

$$\int \frac{\partial C^*}{C^*} \equiv \int \frac{\partial y}{G(y)} + \log A(w_1, w_2)$$

which yields

$$\log C^* \equiv \log J(y) + \log A(w_1, w_2)$$

Using the rules of logarithms and taking antilogarithms, we have

$$C^* \equiv J(y)A(w_1, w_2) \tag{10-15}$$

What equation (10-15) says is that for homothetic productions, the cost function can be written as the product of two functions: a function of output y and another function of factor prices only. $C^*(w_1, w_2, y)$ is said to be multiplicatively separable in y and the factor prices.

That C^* should have this form is entirely reasonable. Recall that a homothetic function is simply a monotonic function of a linear homogeneous function. It is as if the isoquants of a linear homogeneous (constant-returns-to-scale) production function were relabeled through some technological transformation, represented by $F(z)$. But it is only a transformation of output values, not a change in the shapes of the isoquants themselves. Since the cost function for a linear homogeneous production function can be written $C^* = yA(w_1, w_2)$ and one gets a homo-thetic function by operating on output y alone, not surprisingly the only change induced in the cost function is the replacement of y by some more complicated function of y, designated $J(y)$ in equation (10-15).

The correctness of (10-15) as a solution to (10-13) can be checked heuristically as follows. When this form, $C^* = J(y)A(w_1, w_2)$, is substituted into (10-13), the right-hand side must be identically C^*. Performing the indicated operations gives $\lambda^* = J'(y)A(w_1, w_2)$, and thus

$$C^* = J'(y)A(w_1, w_2) \times \text{ some function of } y$$

and (10-15) is therefore of the requisite form.

10.3 THE DUALITY OF COST AND PRODUCTION FUNCTIONS

At this juncture let us recapitulate the analysis of production and cost functions. The starting point of the analysis was the assumption of a well-defined quasi-concave production function, i.e., one whose isoquants are convex to the origin. We asserted that the firm would always minimize the total factor cost of produc-ing any given output level, as this was the only postulate consistent with wealth or profit maximization. The first-order conditions of the implied constrained-mini-mization problem were then solved, in principle, for the factor-demand relations $x_i = x_i^*(w_1, w_2, y)$, along with the Lagrange multiplier (identified as marginal cost) $\lambda = \lambda^*(w_1, w_2, y)$. The comparative-statics relations were developed via the implicit-function theorem yielding certain sign restrictions on some of the partial derivatives of the above demand relations, namely, $\partial x_i^*/\partial w_i < 0$.

These demand relations were then substituted into the expression for total cost, $C = w_1 x_1 + w_2 x_2$, yielding the total cost function

$$C^*(w_1, w_2, y) = w_1 x_1^* + w_2 x_2^*$$

It was shown via the envelope theorem that $\partial C^*/\partial w_i = x_i^*$, $\partial C^*/\partial y = \lambda^*$. Also, certain properties of the cost function regarding homogeneity and functional form were derivable from assumptions about the production function.

We now pose a new question. We have seen how it is possible to derive cost functions from production functions. Is it possible, and if so, how, to derive production functions from cost functions? That is, suppose one were given a cost function which satisfied the properties implied by the usual analysis of production functions. Is it possible to identify with that cost function some unique production function which would generate that cost function? The answer in general is yes; there is, in fact, a duality between production and cost functions: the existence of one implies, for well-behaved functions, the unique existence of the other. We shall now investigate these matters.

A critical step in the construction of the cost function was inverting the solution of the first-order relations $w_i - \lambda f_i = 0$, $y - f(x_1, x_2) = 0$ to obtain the demand relations $x_i = x_i^*(w_1, w_2, y)$. The uniqueness of these solutions is guaranteed by the sufficient second-order conditions for constrained minimum, which in turn guarantees that the jacobian matrix of the first-order equations, i.e., the cross-partials of the lagrangian $\mathscr{L}$, has nonzero determinant. These sufficient second-order conditions also imply that $\partial x_i^*/\partial w_i < 0$, $i = 1,\ 2$. However, $x_i^* = \partial C^*/\partial w_i$. Hence,

$$\frac{\partial x_i^*}{\partial w_i} = \frac{\partial^2 C}{\partial w_i^2} < 0 \tag{10-16}$$

That is, the cost function has the property that the second partials with respect to the factor prices are negative. As was shown in the previous chapter, the cost functions for any well-behaved production function are weakly concave in the factor prices. Again, for the two-factor case, $C^*(w_1, w_2, y)$ is linear homogeneous in w_1, w_2. Thus, as shown earlier in a different manner, since $x_i^*(w_1, w_2, y)$ is a first partial of C^* with respect to a factor price, x_i^* is homogeneous of degree zero in w_1, w_2. Hence by Euler's theorem,

$$\frac{\partial x_1^*}{\partial w_1} w_1 + \frac{\partial x_1^*}{\partial w_2} w_2 \equiv 0$$

Similarly

$$\frac{\partial x_2^*}{\partial w_1} w_1 + \frac{\partial x_2^*}{\partial w_2} w_2 \equiv 0$$

Eliminating w_1 and w_2 (noting that $\partial x_1^*/\partial w_2 = \partial x_2/\partial w_1^* = C_{12}^*$, $C_{ii}^* = \partial x_i^*/\partial w_i$) reveals that

$$C_{11}^* C_{22}^* - C_{12}^{*2} = 0 \tag{10-17}$$

The determinant of the cross-partials of C^* with respect to the factor prices equals 0. Since $C_{11}^*, C_{22}^* < 0$, this guarantees that C^* is at least weakly concave in w_1 and w_2. In fact, C^* cannot be strongly concave in w_1 and w_2 because it is linearly homogeneous in w_1 and w_2; that is, radial expansions of w_1 and w_2 produce *linear* expansions of C^*. This result in fact generalizes to the case of n factors using the methodology of the previous chapter.

Consider now the problem of constructing a production function from a cost function. Before proceeding, we would check to see whether in fact the given $C^*(w_1, w_2, y)$ exhibited "weak" concavity in w_1 and w_2 and linear homogeneity in w_1 and w_2. Assume that these conditions are met. Then the implied factor demands are

$$x_1^*(w_1, w_2, y) = \frac{\partial C^*}{\partial w_1} \qquad x_2^*(w_1, w_2, y) = \frac{\partial C^*}{\partial w_2}$$

However, x_1^* and x_2^* are homogeneous of degree zero in w_1 and w_2; hence they can be written

$$x_1^*(w_1, w_2, y) \equiv x_1^*\left(1, \frac{w_2}{w_1}, y\right) \equiv g_1(w, y)$$

$$x_2^*(w_1, w_2, y) \equiv x_2^*\left(1, \frac{w_2}{w_1}, y\right) \equiv g_2(w, y) \tag{10-18}$$

where $w = w_2/w_1$. But (10-18) represents two equations in the four variables x_1, x_2, w, and y. Under the mathematical conditions that the jacobian of these equations is nonzero, i.e., that

$$J = \begin{vmatrix} g_{1w} & g_{1y} \\ g_{2w} & g_{2y} \end{vmatrix} \neq 0$$

these equations can be used to eliminate the variable w. This will leave one equation in x_1, x_2, and y, say

$$g(x_1, x_2, y) = 0$$

Solving this equation for $y = f(x_1, x_2)$ yields the production function.

How stringent is the assumption that the above jacobian determinant be nonzero? The partials g_{1w} and g_{2w} are essentially the slopes of the factor-demand relations (a reciprocal slope in the case of g_{1w}) with respect to changes in *relative* prices. In particular, using the chain rule leads to

$$\frac{\partial x_1^*}{\partial w_1} = \frac{\partial x_1^*}{\partial w}\frac{\partial w}{\partial w_1} = \frac{\partial g_1}{\partial w}\left(-\frac{w_2}{w_1^2}\right) < 0$$

and hence $g_{1w} = -(w_1^2/w_2)(\partial x_1^*/\partial w_1) > 0$. Similarly,

$$\frac{\partial x_2^*}{\partial w_2} = \frac{\partial x_2^*}{\partial w}\frac{\partial w}{\partial w_2} = g_{2w}\frac{1}{w_1}$$

and hence

$$g_{2w} = w_1\frac{\partial x_2^*}{\partial w_2^*} < 0$$

If both factors are normal, as would be the case for homothetic production functions, then $g_{1y}, g_{2y} > 0$ and J has the sign pattern

$$\begin{vmatrix} + & + \\ - & + \end{vmatrix} > 0$$

implying that $J > 0$, and thus $J \neq 0$. In the nonhomothetic case, it would be pure coincidence if $J = 0$; hence it is not implausible to assert $J \neq 0$. Hence in general we shall expect to find a unique production function associated with any well-specified cost function. This is not to say that it will be *easy* to find either the production function or the cost function from the other. In general, the equations to be solved, i.e., the first-order relations in the case of deriving the cost functions or equations (10-18) in the case of deriving the production function, will be complicated nonlinear functions. But we can be assured that the functions exist, in principle, and that they are unique.

Example We previously have found the cost function associated with a Cobb-Douglas production function. It had the same multiplicatively separable form. Let us see how equations (10-18) can be used to reverse the process.

Suppose C^* is given to us or estimated econometrically as

$$C^* = y^k w_1^\alpha w_2^{1-\alpha} \tag{10-19}$$

where $0 < \alpha < 1$ (to ensure that $C_1^* = x_1^* > 0, C_2^* = x_2^* > 0, C_{11}^*, C_{22}^* < 0$) and the exponents of w_1 and w_2 sum to unity (to ensure C^* homogeneous of degree 1 in w_1 and w_2). The parameter k can take on unrestricted positive values. What production function will generate this cost function?

By the envelope theorem (Shephard's lemma) $\partial C^*/\partial w_i = x_i^*$. Hence

$$x_1^* = y^k \alpha w_1^{\alpha-1} w_2^{1-\alpha} = \alpha y^k \left(\frac{w_2}{w_1}\right)^{1-\alpha}$$

Similarly
$$x_2^* = y^k (1 - \alpha) w_1^\alpha w_2^{-\alpha} = (1 - \alpha) y^k \left(\frac{w_2}{w_1}\right)^{-\alpha}$$

Letting $w = w_2/w_1$, let us eliminate this variable. The asterisks are redundant here and will be dropped to save notational clutter. It will be easiest if we take logarithms of both sides of the equation. Then

$$\log x_1 = \log \alpha + k \log y + (1 - \alpha) \log w$$

$$\log x_2 = \log (1 - \alpha) + k \log y - \alpha \log w$$

Multiply the first equation by α and the second by $1 - \alpha$, and add:

$$\alpha \log x_1 + (1 - \alpha) \log x_2 = \alpha \log \alpha + (1 - \alpha) \log (1 - \alpha) + k \log y$$

or
$$\log x_1^\alpha x_2^{1-\alpha} = \log \alpha^\alpha (1 - \alpha)^{1-\alpha} y^k$$

Taking antilogarithms and rearranging slightly, we get

$$y = K x_1^{\alpha/k} x_2^{(1-\alpha)/k} \tag{10-20}$$

where $K = [1/\alpha^\alpha (1 - \alpha)^{1-\alpha}]^{1/k}$. Equation (10-20) is the production function associated with the cost function (10-19). As expected, it is of the Cobb-Douglas, or multiplicatively separable, type, and is homogeneous of degree $1/k$, since C^* was homogeneous of degree k in y.

The Importance of Duality

The duality of cost and production functions is important for reasons other than mathematical elegance. Economists will have occasion to estimate factor-demand and cost functions. There are basically two ways to approach this problem. One way is to estimate, by some procedure, the underlying production function for some activity and to then calculate, by inverting the implied first-order relations, the factor-demand curves (holding output constant). The cost function can then be calculated also. This, however, is a very arduous procedure. Production functions are largely unobservable. The data points will represent a sampling of input and output levels that will have taken place at different times, as factor or output prices changed. And of what use is knowledge of the production function itself? Largely, it is to derive implications regarding factor usage and cost considerations when various parameters, e.g., factor and output-prices, change.

It would seem to make more sense to start with estimating the cost functions or the factor-demand curves directly; i.e., some functional form of the cost function could be asserted, say a logarithmic linear function, and costs could be estimated directly. However, this procedure would always be subject to the criticism that the estimated cost or demand functions were beasts without parents; i.e., they were derived for fictitious, or nonexistent, production processes. And that would be a serious criticism indeed.

However, the duality results of the previous sections rescue this simpler approach. We can be assured that if a cost function satisfies some elementary properties, i.e., linear homogeneity and concavity in the factor prices, then there in fact is some real, unique underlying production function. Thus, the cost function will be more plausible.

Moreover, the cost function may be easier to estimate, econometrically, than the production function. The cost function is a function of factor prices and output levels, all of which are potentially observable, possibly easily so. What is more, once estimated, the cost function can be used to derive directly the constant-output factor-demand curves using the relation $x_i^* = \partial C^*/\partial w_i$. Thus, the simpler approach of estimating cost functions is apt to be more useful than the more complicated procedure of estimating production functions. The duality results assure us that procedure is in fact theoretically sound.

10.4 ELASTICITY OF SUBSTITUTION; THE CONSTANT-ELASTICITY-OF-SUBSTITUTION (CES) PRODUCTION FUNCTION

Neoclassical production theory recognizes the possibility of substituting one factor of production for another. The existence of more than one point on an isoquant is equivalent to such an assertion. However, we have not yet considered any quantitative measurement of the degree to which one factor can in fact be so substituted for another.

Consider a production function with L-shaped isoquants, represented in Fig. 10-3. This function can be written algebraically as $y = \min [(x_1/a_1), (x_2/a_2)]$, where a_1 and a_2 are constants. This function describes an activity for which no effective substitution is possible. For any wage ratio, the cost-minimizing firm will always operate at the elbow of the isoquants. The marginal product of each factor is 0 unless it is combined in a fixed proportion with the other input. (For this reason, this production function is described as one of *fixed coefficients.*)

How shall the degree of substitutability of one factor for another be described? Consider the Cobb-Douglas production function $y = x_1^\alpha x_2^{1-\alpha}$, where, say, x_1 is labor and x_2 is capital. A cost-minimizing firm satisfies the first-order conditions of the lagrangian

$$\mathcal{L} = w_1 x_1 + w_2 x_2 + \lambda(y - f(x_1, x_2))$$

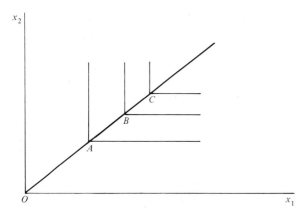

Figure 10-3 The fixed-coefficient production function. This production function is given by $y = \min(x_1/a_1, x_2/a_2)$, where a_1 and a_2 are parameters. No substitution among the factors is worthwhile: the marginal products of x_1 or x_2 are 0 at all points except along the ray out of the origin through the corners of the production function. Although extensively used in input-output analysis and short-term forecasting models, it is doubtful that this is a useful way to look at the real world.

or, in this case,

$$w_1 - \lambda \alpha x_1^{\alpha-1} x_2^{1-\alpha} = 0 \tag{10-21a}$$

$$w_2 - \lambda(1 - \alpha)x_1^{\alpha} x_2^{-\alpha} = 0 \tag{10-21b}$$

$$y - x_1^{\alpha} x_2^{1-\alpha} = 0 \tag{10-21c}$$

Upon division, equations (10-21a) and (10-21b) yield

$$\frac{x_2}{x_1} = \frac{1 - \alpha}{\alpha} \frac{w_1}{w_2} \tag{10-22}$$

This expression can also be derived from the constant-output factor-demand curves derived earlier:

$$x_1^* = \left(\frac{\alpha}{1 - \alpha}\right)^{1-\alpha} \left(\frac{w_2}{w_1}\right)^{1-\alpha} y \tag{10-23a}$$

$$x_2^* = \left(\frac{\alpha}{1 - \alpha}\right)^{-\alpha} \left(\frac{w_2}{w_1}\right)^{-\alpha} y \tag{10-23b}$$

Equation (10-22) says that for this production function, the capital-labor ratio is (1) independent of the level of output, and (2) a function only of the *ratio* of the wage rates (rental rate on capital to the labor wage rate). (We shall shortly consider the generality of this situation.)

We can therefore conceive of the capital-labor ratio as a simple function of the wage ratio. If we let $u = x_2/x_1$, $w = w_2/w_1$ for notational ease, equation (10-22) becomes

$$u = \frac{k}{w} \tag{10-24}$$

where $k = (1 - \alpha)/\alpha$. How does x_2/x_1 vary when w_2/w_1 varies? From equation (10-24),

$$\frac{du}{dw} = -\frac{k}{w^2} \tag{10-25}$$

where the expression is negative, as expected. Although this actual rate of change in the capital-labor ratio is a measure of substitutability, a more frequent measure is the dimensionless elasticity analog,

$$\sigma = -\frac{du/u}{dw/w} = -\frac{w}{u}\frac{du}{dw} \tag{10-26}$$

the (roughly) percentage change in the input ratio per percentage change in factor prices. A minus sign is added to make the measure positive. This measure σ is called the *elasticity of substitution*. Applying equation (10-26) to the Cobb-Douglas case gives

$$\sigma = \frac{w}{u}\frac{k}{w^2} = \frac{w^2}{k}\frac{k}{w^2} = 1$$

Thus, the elasticity of substitution for a Cobb-Douglas production is constant along the whole range of any isoquant and equal to 1.

The Cobb-Douglas production function $y = x_1^\alpha x_2^{1-\alpha}$ is a special case of production functions which exhibit constant elasticity of substitution (CES) along any isoquant. We shall investigate these important functions, deriving their functional form and other properties. These functions have wide application in empirical work on production processes.

The concept of the elasticity of substitution is not dependent on the behavioral assertion of cost-minimization. The concept can as easily be described as the percentage change in the input ratio per percentage change in the marginal rate of substitution (MRS) since the cost-minimizing firm always sets $w_1/w_2 = f_1/f_2 = \text{MRS}$. Thus we can write, as an alternative definition,

$$\sigma = -\frac{f_1/f_2}{x_1/x_2}\frac{d(x_1/x_2)}{d(f_1/f_2)} \tag{10-27}$$

(Note that we are considering the inverse ratios x_1/x_2 instead of x_2/x_1, etc. As we shall shortly see, this is of no consequence.) Let us evaluate this expression. Along any isoquant, $y = y_0$, and hence $x_2 = x_2(x_1)$. Then $dx_2/dx_1 = -f_1/f_2$. Keeping in mind that along an isoquant $x_2 = x_2(x_1)$, we can write (10-27) (using the chain rule) as

$$\sigma = -\frac{f_1 x_2}{f_2 x_1}\frac{d(x_1/x_2)/dx_1}{\dfrac{d(f_1/f_2)}{dx_1}}$$

Evaluating the terms in the second fraction yields

$$\frac{d(x_1/x_2)}{dx_1} = \left(x_2 - x_1\frac{dx_2}{dx_1}\right)\frac{1}{x_2^2}$$

$$= \left(x_2 + x_1\frac{f_1}{f_2}\right)\frac{1}{x_2^2}$$

$$= \frac{1}{f_2 x_2^2}(f_1 x_1 + f_2 x_2)$$

Similarly, $d(f_1/f_2)/dx_1$ is simply $-d^2x_2/dx_1^2$, since $dx_2/dx_1 = -f_1/f_2$. From Chap. 3,

$$-\frac{d^2x_2}{dx_1^2} = \frac{1}{f_2^3}(f_2^2 f_{11} - 2f_1 f_2 f_{12} + f_1^2 f_{22})$$

Combining these expressions leads to

$$\sigma = -\frac{f_1 x_2\ f_2^3}{f_2 x_1\ f_2 x_2^2\,(f_2^2 f_{11} - 2f_1 f_2 f_{12} + f_1^2 f_{22})}\ \frac{f_1 x_1 + f_2 x_2}{}$$

or

$$\sigma = -\frac{f_1 f_2(f_1 x_1 + f_2 x_2)}{x_1 x_2(f_2^2 f_{11} - 2f_1 f_2 f_{12} + f_1^2 f_{22})} \tag{10-28}$$

This rather cumbersome expression for σ can be drastically simplified in the important special case of linear homogeneous production functions. First, the numerator immediately becomes $f_1 f_2\, y$, upon application of Euler's theorem. For the denominator, since $f(x_1, x_2)$ is homogeneous of degree 1, f_1 and f_2 are homogeneous of degree zero. Hence, applying Euler's theorem to f_1 and f_2, we have

$$f_{11} x_1 + f_{12} x_2 \equiv 0 \qquad \text{or} \qquad f_{11} = -f_{12}\frac{x_2}{x_1}$$

Similarly

$$f_{22} = -f_{12}\frac{x_1}{x_2}$$

Making these substitutions leads to

$$x_1 x_2(f_2^2 f_{11} - 2f_1 f_2 f_{12} + f_1^2 f_{22})$$

$$= -x_1 x_2 f_{12}\left(f_2^2\frac{x_2}{x_1} + 2f_1 f_2 + f_1^2\frac{x_1}{x_2}\right)$$

$$= -f_{12}(f_2^2 x_2^2 + 2f_1 f_2 x_1 x_2 + f_1^2 x_1^2)$$

$$= -f_{12}(f_1 x_1 + f_2 x_2)^2 = -f_{12} y^2$$

Therefore, for linear homogeneous production functions

$$\sigma = -\frac{f_1 f_2 y}{-f_{12} y^2} = \frac{f_1 f_2}{y f_{12}} \tag{10-29}$$

a drastic simplification of equation (10-28) indeed.

A curiosity concerning equations (10-28) and (10-29) is that they are symmetric between x_1 and x_2. That is, the identical expression results when the subscripts are interchanged. Thus we can speak of the elasticity of substitution between x_1 and x_2 rather than the elasticity of substitution of x_2 for x_1, or of x_1 for x_2. It does not matter whether x_2/x_1 is related to f_2/f_1 or x_1/x_2 is related to f_1/f_2 by derivatives in σ. The formula is the same either way.

Formula (10-29) can be related to the expression for the rate of change of one factor with respect to another. Recalling equation (7-28b) on the comparative statics of cost-minimization, we have

$$\frac{\partial x_2^*}{\partial w_1} = -\frac{\Delta_{12}}{\Delta}$$

where

$$\Delta = \begin{vmatrix} -\lambda^* f_{11} & -\lambda^* f_{12} & -f_1 \\ -\lambda^* f_{21} & -\lambda^* f_{22} & -f_2 \\ -f_1 & -f_2 & 0 \end{vmatrix}$$

Thus

$$\frac{\partial x_1^*}{\partial w_2} = \frac{f_1 f_2}{\lambda^* (f_{11} f_2^2 - 2f_{12} f_1 f_2 + f_{22} f_1^2)}$$

which, for linear homogeneous production functions, becomes (as before, dropping the asterisks to remove clutter)

$$\frac{\partial x_1}{\partial w_2} = \frac{f_1 f_2 x_1 x_2}{\lambda y^2 f_{12}}$$

or

$$\frac{y\lambda}{x_1 x_2} \frac{\partial x_1}{\partial w_2} = \frac{f_1 f_2}{y f_{12}} = \sigma$$

Noting that $\lambda = w_2 / f_2$, we can write this as

$$\frac{y}{f_2 x_2} \frac{w_2}{x_1} \frac{\partial x_1}{\partial w_2} = \sigma$$

When we let $\kappa_i = f_i x_i / y$ ($\kappa_1 + \kappa_2 = 1$, by Euler's theorem) and denote the cross-elasticity of demand by ε_{12}, we have

$$\varepsilon_{12} = \kappa_2 \sigma \tag{10-30}$$

Thus, the elasticity of substitution is related in this simple fashion to the cross-elasticity of (constant-output) factor demand. And, of course,

$$\sigma = \frac{1}{\kappa_2} \varepsilon_{12} = \frac{1}{\kappa_1} \varepsilon_{21}$$

Knowledge of σ at any point would undoubtedly be a useful technological datum for empirical work. Beyond the strictly qualitative results of comparative statics, measurement of the degree of responsiveness to changes in parameters is an essential part of any science. Hence, it would be useful to be able to estimate a quantity like σ. A useful first approximation in so doing is to assume that the production process is linear homogeneous and exhibits *constant* elasticity of substitution everywhere. That is, σ is the same at all factor combinations. What would such production functions look like? We have already shown that the Cobb-Douglas function has the property $\sigma = 1$ everywhere. What about other values of σ?

Return to equation (10-26), $\sigma = -(w/u)(du/dw)$, where $u = x_2 / x_1$, $w = w_2 / w_1$.

Strictly speaking, we should in general write

$$\sigma = -\frac{w}{u}\frac{\partial u}{\partial w}$$

since in general $u = x_2/x_1$ will not be a function of the wage ratio w_2/w_1 only but will also depend on the output level y. However, consider the case first of homothetic production functions. The cost function for all homothetic production functions can be written

$$C^* = J(y)A(w_1, w_2) \tag{10-31}$$

where $A(w_1, w_2)$ is linear homogeneous. (Any cost function is linear homogeneous in the factor prices.) Using the envelope theorem (Shephard's lemma), we have

$$x_1 = J(y)A_1(w_1, w_2) \tag{10-32a}$$

$$x_2 = J(y)A_2(w_1, w_2) \tag{10-32b}$$

where $A_1 = \partial A/\partial w_1$, etc. Since A_1 and A_2 are first partials of a linear homogeneous function, they are homogeneous of degree zero in w_1 and w_2. But then

$$A_1(w_1, w_2) = A_1\left(1, \frac{w_2}{w_1}\right) = B_1(w)$$

and so forth, and therefore we can write

$$x_1 = J(y)B_1(w) \tag{10-33a}$$

$$x_2 = J(y)B_2(w) \tag{10-33b}$$

(In fact, only the factor demands of homothetic production functions have this functional form.) Dividing equation (10-33b) by (10-33a) gives

$$u = \frac{x_2}{x_1} = \frac{B_2(w)}{B_1(w)} = B(w)$$

That is, for all homothetic production functions, the ratio of factor inputs is a function of the ratio of wage rates only, not at all a function of output y. This of course is geometrically obvious, since the isoquants of homothetic production functions are merely radial blowups of each other. Hence, in formula (10-26) it is valid, for homothetic production functions, to write $\sigma = -(w/u)(du/dw)$ since u is indeed some well-defined function of w only.

Suppose now, maintaining the assumption of homotheticity, that σ is constant everywhere. The class of homothetic functions having constant elasticity of substitution consists of those which satisfy the differential equation

$$-\frac{w}{u}\frac{du}{dw} = \sigma = \text{constant}$$

Let us solve this differential equation. Rearranging variables gives

$$\frac{du}{u} = -\sigma\frac{dw}{w}$$

Integrating both sides and denoting the arbitrary constant of integration as log c, we have

$$\log u = -\sigma \log w + \log c = \log cw^{-\sigma}$$

or
$$u = cw^{-\sigma} = c\left(\frac{1}{w}\right)^{\sigma} \qquad (10\text{-}34)$$

where, of necessity, $c > 0$. Thus, all such production functions must have the property that the capital-labor ratio is proportional to the wage ratio raised to some power, that power being the negative of the elasticity of substitution. What production functions satisfy (10-34)? For cost-minimizing firms, $1/w = w_1/w_2 = f_1/f_2 = -\partial x_2/\partial x_1$, the slope of an indifference curve at some arbitrary output level y. Rewriting (10-34) in terms of the original variables yields

$$\frac{x_2}{x_1} = c\left(\frac{f_1}{f_2}\right)^{\sigma}$$

or, taking roots, $(k = c^{1/\sigma})$
$$\left(\frac{x_2}{x_1}\right)^{1/\sigma} = -k\frac{\partial x_2}{\partial x_1}$$

Now k is any positive number. We can, for convenience, write $k = (1 - \alpha)/\alpha$, where $0 < \alpha < 1$. As α varies between 0 and 1, k varies from 0 to ∞, so no generality is lost. Separating variables gives

$$\alpha\frac{\partial x_1}{x_1^{1/\sigma}} = -\frac{(1 - \alpha)\,\partial x_2}{x_2^{1/\sigma}} \qquad (10\text{-}35)$$

We have to distinguish two cases now when integrating this expression. When $\sigma = 1$, logarithms will be involved, whereas when $\sigma \neq 1$, the integrals will be simple polynomials.

Case 1 Let $\sigma = 1$. Integrating both sides of (10-35) yields

$$\alpha\int\frac{\partial x_1}{x_1} = -(1 - \alpha)\left(\int\frac{\partial x_2}{x_2}\right) + \log g(y)$$

The arbitrary constant of integration can in general be any function of y, since y was held constant in determining the slope $\partial x_2/\partial x_1$. Again, since equation (10-35) is really a *partial* differential equation, the arbitrary constant of integration can involve any function of the variable or variables held constant, in this case output y. For convenience, we have denoted this constant of integration log $g(y)$. Performing the indicated operations, we have

$$\alpha \log x_1 = -(1 - \alpha)\log x_2 + \log g(y)$$

or
$$g(y) = x_1^{\alpha} x_2^{1-\alpha}$$

Up to this point, the only assumption about the form of the production function we have made is that it is homothetic. Indeed, assuming $g(y)$ is monotonic, we can write

$$y = F(x_1^{\alpha} x_2^{1-\alpha}) \qquad (10\text{-}36)$$

where F is the inverse function of g; that is, if $z = g(y)$, $y = g^{-1}(z) = F(z) = F(x_1^\alpha x_2^{1-\alpha})$. Equation (10-36) has the required form for homotheticity, being a function of a linear homogeneous function. If now we insist that $y = f(x_1, x_2) = F(x_1^\alpha x_2^{1-\alpha})$ be homogeneous of some degree s, then by theorem 6 of Chap. 3, $F(z) = kz^s$, or

$$f(x_1, x_2) = kx_1^{\alpha_1}x_2^{\alpha_2} \tag{10-37}$$

where $\alpha_1 = \alpha s$, $\alpha_2 = (1 - \alpha)s$, and thus $\alpha_1 + \alpha_2 = s$. If $f(x_1, x_2)$ is to be linear homogeneous, with $\sigma = 1$, then

$$f(x_1, x_2) = kx_1^\alpha x_2^{1-\alpha} \tag{10-38}$$

Equations (10-36) to (10-38) represent the general functional forms of production functions which exhibit constant elasticity of substitution equal to unity everywhere ($\sigma = 1$) and, in addition, are, respectively, homothetic, homogeneous of degree s, and linear homogeneous. Consider now the second case, $\sigma \neq 1$.

Case 2 If $\sigma \neq 1$, integrating both sides of equation (10-35) yields

$$\alpha \int \frac{\partial x_1}{x_1^{1/\sigma}} = -(1 - \alpha) \int \frac{\partial x_2}{x_2^{1/\sigma}} + g(y)$$

where again, the arbitrary constant of integration is some function of output y, designated $g(y)$, since y is held constant in finding the slope $\partial x_2/\partial x_1$ of an isoquant. Performing the indicated operations and rearranging yields, incorporating the factor $(-1/\sigma) + 1$ into $g(y)$,

$$g(y) = \alpha x_1^{(-1/\sigma)+1} + (1 - \alpha)x_2^{(-1/\sigma)+1} \tag{10-39}$$

It will simplify matters if we let $\rho = 1/\sigma - 1$; that is, $\sigma = 1/(1 + \rho)$; then

$$g(y) = \alpha x_1^{-\rho} + (1 - \alpha)x_2^{-\rho} \tag{10-40}$$

Assuming again that $g(y)$ is monotonic, (10-40) can be written

$$y = F(\alpha x_1^{-\rho} + (1 - \alpha)x_2^{-\rho}) \tag{10-41}$$

Equation (10-41) is the most general form of homothetic production functions exhibiting constant elasticity of substitution. As before, again using theorem 6 of Chap. 3, if we wish $y = f(x_1, x_2)$ to be homogeneous of degree 1, then, of necessity, $F = kz^{-1/\rho}$ and

$$y = k(\alpha x_1^{-\rho} + (1 - \alpha)x_2^{-\rho})^{-1/\rho} \tag{10-42}$$

Equation (10-42) is what is commonly referred to as the CES production function. It assumes linear homogeneity. The elasticity of substitution, of course, varies between 0 and ∞. When $\sigma \to 0$, $\rho = \to +\infty$; when $\sigma = 1$, $\rho = 0$, and when $\sigma \to +\infty$, $\rho \to -1$. Hence the range of values for ρ is $-1 < \rho < +\infty$. When $\sigma \to 0$ ($\rho \to \infty$), the isoquants become L-shaped; i.e., the function becomes a fixed-proportions production function. When $\sigma \to \infty$ ($\rho \to -1$), the isoquants become straight lines, as inspection of (10-42) reveals.

Although we have proved that when $\sigma = 1$ $(\rho = 0)$, the CES production function becomes Cobb-Douglas, that fact is not obvious from equation (10-42). In order to show this result directly, we need a mathematical theorem known as L'Hospital's rule.

L'Hospital's rule Suppose that $f(x)$ and $g(x)$ both tend to 0 (have a limit of 0) as $x \to 0$. Then if the ratio $f'(x)/g'(x)$ exists,

$$\lim_{x \to 0} \frac{f(x)}{g(x)} = \lim_{x \to 0} \frac{f'(x)}{g'(x)} \tag{10-43}$$

The limit of the ratio of the functions, if it exists, equals the ratio of the derivatives of $f(x)$ and $g(x)$, respectively.

The formal proof of this theorem can be found in any advanced calculus text; we shall not present it here.

Consider the CES function (10-42) again, and take the logarithms of both sides:

$$\log y = \log k - \frac{\log (\alpha x_1^{-\rho} + (1 - \alpha)x_2^{-\rho})}{\rho} \tag{10-44}$$

The right-hand side of (10-44) consists, aside from the constant, of a ratio of two functions, each of which tends to 0 as $\rho \to 0$. We find the limit as $\rho \to 0$, letting $f(\rho) =$ numerator, remembering that if $y = a^{-t}$, $dy/dt = -a^{-t} \log a$:

$$f'(\rho) = \frac{1}{\alpha x_1^{-\rho} + (1 - \alpha)x_2^{-\rho}} [x_1^{-\rho}\alpha \log x_1 + x_2^{-\rho}(1 - \alpha) \log x_2](-1)$$

$$\lim_{\rho \to 0} f'(\rho) = -\frac{1}{1} [\alpha \log x_1 + (1 - \alpha) \log x_2]$$

$$= -\log x_1^{\alpha} x_2^{1-\alpha}$$

The denominator of (10-44) is simply ρ, and thus $g'(\rho) = 1$; hence, $\lim_{\rho \to 0} g'(\rho) = 1$. Therefore, as $\rho \to 0$,

$$\log y = \log k + \log x_1^{\alpha} x_2^{1-\alpha}$$

or

$$y = kx_1^{\alpha} x_2^{1-\alpha}$$

the Cobb-Douglas function, as expected.

Generalizations to *n* Factors

Consider again the definition of elasticity of substitution given in equation (10-27) but now assuming that the two factors in question are two of *n* factors that enter the production function:

$$\sigma_{ij} = \frac{f_i/f_j \, d(x_i/x_j)}{x_i/x_j \, d(f_i/f_j)} \tag{10-45}$$

This number is a measure of how fast the ratio of two inputs changes when the marginal rate of substitution between them changes. In order for this definition to make sense, the other factors must be held constant at some parametric levels $x_k = x_k^0$, $k \neq i, j$. When more than two factors are involved, a marginal rate of substitution of one variable for another can only be defined in some two-dimensional subspace of the original space, i.e., along a plane (hyperplane) parallel to the x_i, x_j axes, in which the other variables are held constant. Thus definitions of elasticity of substitution analogous to equation (10-27), for the n-factor case, are "partial" elasticities of substitution. By holding the other factors constant, they do not represent the full degree of substitution possibilities present in the production function. These partial measures would be especially deceptive if one or more of the factors held constant were either close substitutes or highly complementary to the variable factors.

As an alternative, one could develop elasticities of substitution based on equation (10-26):

$$\sigma_{ij}^* = \frac{w_{ij}}{u_{ij}} \frac{\partial u_{ij}}{\partial w_{ij}} \tag{10-46}$$

where $w_{ij} = w_i/w_j$, $u_{ij} = x_i/x_j$. In this definition, all other *wages* are to be held constant with the other factors allowed to vary. This definition overcomes most of the objections stated above for the fixed-input definition (10-45). Clearly, σ_{ij}^* will relate to the cross-elasticities of factor demand. As such, they are less of a technological datum of the production function but most likely a more useful concept since in reality it will be unlikely that the other factors will remain fixed.

The obvious generalization of the CES functional form to many factors

$$y = A(\alpha_1 x_1^{-\rho} + \cdots + \alpha_n x_n^{-\rho})^{-1/\rho} \tag{10-47}$$

has been shown to yield constant elasticities of the type given in (10-26); that is, the other factor *prices* are held fixed.[†] They are also called the *Allen elasticities*.[‡] However, all the partial elasticities are equal to each other and to $1/(1 + \rho)$. Also, when $\rho = 0$ ($\sigma_{ij} = 1$), the form reduces, as in the two-factor case, to a Cobb-Douglas or multiplicatively separable function

$$y = A x_1^{\alpha_1} x_2^{\alpha_2} \cdots x_n^{\alpha_n}$$

where $\sum \alpha_i = 1$ to preserve linear homogeneity.

PROBLEMS

1 If a production function is homogeneous of degree $r > 1$ ($r < 1$), it exhibits increasing (decreasing) returns to scale. The converse, however, is false. Explain.

[†] See H. Uzawa: Production Functions with Constant Elasticities of Substitution, *The Review of Economic Studies*, **29**: 291–299, October 1962.

[‡] See R. G. D. Allen: "Mathematical Analysis for Economists," Macmillan & Co., Ltd., London, 1938; reprinted by St. Martin's Press, New York.

2 Suppose all firms in a competitive industry have the same production function, $y = f(x_1, x_2)$, where $f(x_1, x_2)$ is homogeneous of degree $r < 1$. Show that all firms in this industry will be receiving "rents," i.e., positive accounting profits. To which factor of production do these rents accrue? In the long run, if entry is free in this industry, what will be the industry price, output, and number of firms?

3 Find the production function associated with each of the following cost functions:

(a) $C = \sqrt{w_1 w_2}\, e^{y/2}$

(b) $C = w_2[1 + y + \log(w_1/w_2)]$

(c) $C = y(w_1^2 + w_2^2)^{1/2}$

4 It is often said that the reason for U-shaped average cost curves is indivisibility of some factors. However, indivisibility does not necessarily lead to such properties. Suppose a firm's production function is homogeneous of some degree. Suppose the production function is also homogeneous in any $n - 1$ factors when the nth factor is held fixed at some level. Show that the only function with these properties is the multiplicatively separable form, $y = kx_1^{\alpha_1} x_2^{\alpha_2} \cdots x_n^{\alpha_n}$.

5 What class of *homothetic* functions $y = f(x_1, \ldots, x_n)$ is also homothetic in any $n - 1$ factors, with the nth factor held fixed at some level?

6 Show that for homothetic production functions, at the point of minimum average cost, the AC function is a function of factor prices only.

7 Suppose a production function $y = f(x_1, x_2)$ is homothetic, that is, $f(x_1, x_2) = F(h(x_1, x_2))$, where $h(x_1, x_2)$ is linear homogeneous. Show that the elasticity of substitution is given by $\sigma = (h_1 h_2)/h_{12} h$.

BIBLIOGRAPHY

Allen, R. G. D.: "Mathematical Analysis for Economists," Macmillan & Co., Ltd., London, 1938; reprinted by St. Martin's Press, New York.

Arrow, K. J., H. Chenery, B. Minhas, and R. M. Solow: Capital-Labor Substitution and Economic Efficiency, *The Review of Economics and Statistics*, **43:** 225–250, 1961. The seminal paper on CES production functions.

Carlson, Sune: "A Study on the Theory of Production," Kelley & Millman, New York, 1956.

Diewert, W. E.: Applications of Duality Theory, Department of Manpower and Immigration, Canada, 1973.

Frisch, Ragnar: "Theory of Production," Rand McNally & Company, Chicago, 1965.

Hicks, J. R.: "Value and Capital," 2d ed., Clarendon Press, Oxford, 1946.

Jorgenson, D. W., L. R. Christensen, and L. J. Lau: Transendental Logarithmic Production Frontiers, *Review of Economics and Statistics*, **55:** 28–45, February 1973.

McFadden, Daniel: Constant Elasticity of Substitution Production Functions, *Review of Economic Studies*, **30:** 73–83, June 1963.

Samuelson, Paul A.: "Foundations of Economic Analysis," Harvard University Press, Cambridge, Mass., 1947.

Shephard, Ronald W.: "Cost and Production Functions," Princeton University Press, Princeton, N.J., 1953; also the revised version of this book, 1970, which has become a classic.

Uzawa, H.: Production Functions with Constant Elasticities of Substitution, *The Review of Economic Studies*, **29:** 291–299, October 1962.

ELEVEN

SPECIAL TOPICS IN CONSUMER THEORY

11.1 REVEALED PREFERENCE AND EXCHANGE

Any given economic system solves, in some way, the problems of production and allocation of goods and resources. Starting with various factor endowments, resources are somehow organized and combined, and a certain set of finished goods emerges. All along the way, decisions are made concerning two fundamental problems:

1. What final set of goods shall be produced?
2. How shall factors of production be combined to produce those goods?

These problems are not independent. The choice of factors and their least-cost combinations will vary depending on the level of demand for the goods. A person building a car in the back yard will use inputs different from those used by General Motors. As Adam Smith indicated some 200 years ago in the "Wealth of Nations," "the division of labor [and other resources] is limited by the extent of the market." These matters aside, how does it come to pass that producers of goods have any idea at all what to produce? What is it that guides these decision makers in selecting a certain, usually small, set of goods to produce, out of the vast array of conceivable alternative goods and services?

 The problem is by no means trivial. Imagine yourself as the chief economic planner of a society in which it has been mandated by the ruling political party that all goods are to be handed out free of charge. To make life easy for you, the government has provided you with a complete set of costs of producing all existing and potential goods. How much of each should you produce, assuming you had the best interests of the consumers in mind? To achieve your goal, you would need to know how much consumers valued the alternative goods. Without this information, a planner might decide to produce meat for a nation of vegetarians, or, on a less grandiose scale, acres of wheat for people who would rather consume rice or corn, or trains and buses for people who would rather drive their own cars. What mix of these goods and services should be produced?

The solution of this allocation problem in any economy depends upon the production of information concerning the valuation of goods by consumers and the ability of individuals to utilize that information. The latter problem has to do with the system of property rights developed in the nation in question. We shall not inquire into these matters here. Suffice it to say that a system which allows private ownership and free contracting between individuals will in all likelihood produce a different set of goods than a society where these rights are attenuated.

The former problem, how information is produced regarding consumers' valuations of goods, is the topic at hand here. Recall the definition of *value*. The value of goods (at the margin) is the amount of other goods consumers are willing to give up in order to consume an additional increment of the good in question. In most private exchange, information about these marginal values is produced automatically by the willingness or reluctance of the participants to engage in trade. When a trade takes place, the value of the goods traded is revealed to the traders and other observers. Since, under the usual behavioral postulates of Chap. 8, individuals will purchase goods until the marginal value of those goods falls to the value of the next best alternative, *prices*, in a voluntary exchange economy, provide the information of consumers' *marginal* (though not total) value of each traded good. Any producer whose marginal costs of production are less than that price can benefit by producing more of that good but in so doing will be directing resources from low-valued to higher-valued uses. In this way the gains from trade will be further exhausted.

The value of goods will also be revealed, though not as precisely, when other means of allocation are used. When goods are price-controlled, e.g., gasoline in the winter of 1973–1974, waiting lines and other nonprice discrimination appeared. These phenomena provided evidence that the good was valued higher, at the margin, than the official controlled price. But exactly how much higher (a subject of intense debate at the time) was not known. The information on the precise marginal evaluation of gasoline during that time was never allowed to be produced. And, in the extreme case, where goods are handed out " free," very little information is produced concerning consumers' valuations of those goods.

In the usual case of so-called private goods in which congestion is so extreme that only one person can consume the item, preferences are revealed automatically through the act of exchange. Intensity of preference will be revealed through the level of purchase of goods and services. An important class of goods for which this does not easily occur is made up of the so-called public goods, in which congestion is absent, so that adding an additional consumer to the consumption of that service in no way diminishes the level of service provided the other consumers.

The services national defense, lighthouses, or uncrowded freeways are classic examples of such goods. In some cases, the ability to *exclude* nonpayers from the benefits of these services would be difficult to arrange. (The right of exclusion, a fundamental part of property rights, is not peculiar to public goods, nor are all public goods incapable of having rights of exclusion cheaply enforced.) In the case of nonexclusive public goods, particularly, information concerning consumers' valuations of the good will be difficult to observe. Consumers will often have an incentive to understate the intensity of their preferences, and to "free-ride." Imagine how the production of such goods might be attempted: if the costs of production are to be assessed on the basis of the value of the service to the consumers, the consumers will tend to indicate how little they value the service (if at all), each hoping that enough others will indicate a high enough level of willingness to pay to make the project viable. The end result may be that the service is not produced at all, or that "too little" is produced. In these situations, coercive schemes such as government provision of the good through mandatory taxation or the formation of private clubs with assessment of dues are often resorted to as a means of lowering the contracting costs between consumers eager to exhaust the gains from exchange. But the preferences of individuals for these types of services will not be completely revealed, since individuals in the group will still, in all likelihood, have different marginal evaluations of the final level of public good produced.

Is it possible, given the nature of exchange explored above, to replace the utility-maximization hypothesis with one based entirely on observable quantities? That is, can a behavioral postulate be formulated in terms of exchanges which yields refutable hypotheses? This question was initiated by Samuelson, Houthakker, and others in the 1930s and 1940s, resulting in what is known as the *theory of revealed preference*. It is intimately tied in with another classical question of the theory of the consumer, viz., whether the Slutsky relations of Chap. 8 constitute the entire range of implications of the utility-maximization hypothesis. That is, is it possible, starting with a set of demand relations which obey symmetry and negative semidefiniteness of the pure substitution terms, to infer that there exists some utility function (together with all its monotonic transformations) from which those demand functions are derivable? This issue is known as the problem of *integrability*. A complete discussion of these issues is beyond the scope of this book, the integrability issue in particular being dependent upon subtle mathematical details. We shall, however, indicate the general nature of the problems.

Let us suppose that a consumer possesses a well-defined set of demand relations,

$$x_i = x_i^M(p_1, \ldots, p_n, M) \qquad i = 1, \ldots, n \tag{11-1}$$

At this point we need not even assume that these relations are single-valued; i.e., we allow, for the moment, that confronted with a set of prices $p_1, \ldots, p_n$ and a given money income M, the consumer might be willing to choose from more than one consumption bundle. Strictly speaking, then, the relations (11-1) are not functions, since single-valuedness of the dependent variable is part of the definition of a function; instead system (11-1) represents what are sometimes

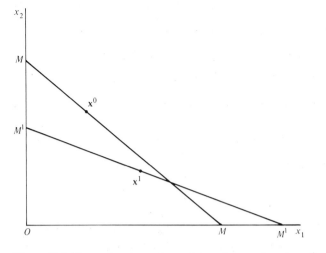

Figure 11-1 The weak axiom of revealed preference. At prices $\mathbf{p}^0$, the consumption bundle $\mathbf{x}^0$ is chosen, implying a budget line MM. The consumption bundle $\mathbf{x}^1$, since it lies interior to MM, could have been chosen but wasn't. Hence, $\mathbf{x}^0$ is said to be revealed preferred to $\mathbf{x}^1$. This does not mean that $\mathbf{x}^1$ will never be chosen. What it does mean is that when $\mathbf{x}^1$ is chosen, at some price vector $\mathbf{p}^1$, implying a budget line M^1M^1, $\mathbf{x}^0$ will be more expensive than $\mathbf{x}^1$ at those new prices. In other words, if $\mathbf{p}^0\mathbf{x}^0 \geq \mathbf{p}^0\mathbf{x}^1$, when $\mathbf{x}^1$ is chosen at $\mathbf{p}^1$, necessarily $\mathbf{p}^1\mathbf{x}^1 < \mathbf{p}^1\mathbf{x}^0$. This is illustrated in this diagram, since $\mathbf{x}^0$ lies outside the budget line M^1M^1.

called *correspondences* or just simply *relations*. What is being insisted on here is that a consumer *will choose* some consumption bundle $\mathbf{x}^0 = (x_1^0, \ldots, x_n^0)$ when confronted with a price-income vector $(\mathbf{p}^0, M^0) = (p_1^0, \ldots, p_n^0, M^0)$. Let us also assert that the consumer, in so choosing, will spend his or her entire budget; i.e., the choice $\mathbf{x}^0$ will satisfy the budget relation $\sum p_i^0 x_i^0 = M^0$.

It will be much easier going if some elementary matrix and vector notation is used in the following discussion. Recall the definitions of vectors and matrix multiplication in Chap. 5. The scalar (or inner) product of two vectors $\mathbf{x} = (x_1, \ldots, x_n)$ and $\mathbf{y} = (y_1, \ldots, y_n)$ is defined as $\mathbf{xy} = \sum_{i=1}^{n} x_i y_i$. With this notation the budget equation $\sum p_i x_i = M$ is simply written $\mathbf{px} = M$. The set of differentials $dx_1, \ldots, dx_n$ is written simply $\mathbf{dx}$. The expression $\mathbf{p}\,\mathbf{dx}$ means $\sum_{i=1}^{n} p_i\,dx_i$, etc. The entire set of demand relations (11-1) is written simply as $\mathbf{x} = \mathbf{x}^M(\mathbf{p}, M)$. Now, on with economics.

In Fig. 11-1, a consumer is faced with a price-income vector $(\mathbf{p}^0, M^0)$ and chooses the consumption bundle $\mathbf{x}^0$, where $\mathbf{p}^0\mathbf{x}^0 = M^0$; that is, the budget equation is satisfied. In so doing, we shall say that the consumer reveals a preference for bundle $\mathbf{x}^0$ over some other bundle, say $\mathbf{x}^1$, which was not chosen. We say $\mathbf{x}^0$ is *revealed preferred* to $\mathbf{x}^1$. We cannot yet speak of the consumer being indifferent between $\mathbf{x}^0$ and $\mathbf{x}^1$, since indifference is a utility-related concept, which is not yet defined. The phrase "$\mathbf{x}^0$ revealed preferred to $\mathbf{x}^1$" simply means that where the consumer was confronted with two *affordable* consumption bundles $\mathbf{x}^0$ and $\mathbf{x}^1$, $\mathbf{x}^0$ was chosen and $\mathbf{x}^1$ not, although $\mathbf{x}^1$ was no more expensive than $\mathbf{x}^0$. It is not likely that we would be able to formulate a hypothesis about choices if the chosen bundle were less expensive than the nonchosen one; people choose Chevrolets instead of Cadillacs not necessarily because they prefer Chevrolets to Cadillacs but because the latter cost more. The statement that $\mathbf{x}^1$ is no more expensive than $\mathbf{x}^0$ is written $\mathbf{p}^0\mathbf{x}^0 \geq \mathbf{p}^0\mathbf{x}^1$.

Having so *defined* revealed preference, let us now assert something about behavior in terms of it.

The weak axiom of revealed preference Assume that $\mathbf{x}^0$ is revealed preferred to $\mathbf{x}^1$, that is, at some price vector $\mathbf{p}^0$, $\mathbf{x}^0$ is chosen, and $\mathbf{p}^0\mathbf{x}^0 \geq \mathbf{p}^0\mathbf{x}^1$, so that $\mathbf{x}^1$ could have been chosen but was not. Then $\mathbf{x}^1$ *will never be revealed preferred to* $\mathbf{x}^0$.

The weak axiom (we shall presently explain the reason for the adjective *weak*) does not say that $\mathbf{x}^1$ will never be chosen under any circumstances. Quite the contrary. The bundle $\mathbf{x}^1$ may very well be chosen at some price vector $\mathbf{p}^1$. What the weak axiom indicates is that if $\mathbf{x}^1$ is chosen at some price $\mathbf{p}^1$, then $\mathbf{x}^0$ will be more expensive than $\mathbf{x}^1$ at prices $\mathbf{p}^1$. Consider Fig. 11-1 again. At prices $\mathbf{p}^0$, the consumer chooses $\mathbf{x}^0$ even though $\mathbf{x}^1$ could have been chosen, since $\mathbf{x}^1$ lies below the implied budget line MM defined as $\mathbf{p}^0\mathbf{x}^0 = \mathbf{M}^0$. At some other set of prices $\mathbf{p}^1$, $\mathbf{x}^1$ might be the chosen bundle, forming a new budget equation $\mathbf{p}^1\mathbf{x}^1 = M^1$. But note that at prices $\mathbf{p}^1$, $\mathbf{x}^0$ is more expensive than $\mathbf{x}^1$, that is, $\mathbf{p}^1\mathbf{x}^0 > \mathbf{p}^1\mathbf{x}^1$. Hence, $\mathbf{x}^1$ is *not* revealed preferred to $\mathbf{x}^0$ merely because it was chosen, for the same reason that one would not want to infer that Chevrolets are preferred to Cadillacs. The bundle $\mathbf{x}^1$ is simply cheaper than $\mathbf{x}^0$ at prices $\mathbf{p}^1$; nothing can be inferred about the desirability of $\mathbf{x}^0$ and $\mathbf{x}^1$ from $\mathbf{p}^1\mathbf{x}^0 > \mathbf{p}^1\mathbf{x}^1$ alone.

Algebraically, then, the weak axiom of revealed preference says:

if $$\mathbf{p}^0\mathbf{x}^0 \geq \mathbf{p}^0\mathbf{x}^1$$

then $$\mathbf{p}^1\mathbf{x}^0 > \mathbf{p}^1\mathbf{x}^1 \tag{11-2}$$

where the consumption bundle chosen is the one whose superscript is the same as that on the price vector. Figure 11-2 shows a price-consumption situation which would contradict the weak axiom. There, $\mathbf{x}^1$ is chosen at $\mathbf{p}^1$ when $\mathbf{x}^0$ could have been chosen; we have both $\mathbf{p}^0\mathbf{x}^0 \geq \mathbf{p}^0\mathbf{x}^1$ and $\mathbf{p}^1\mathbf{x}^1 \geq \mathbf{p}^1\mathbf{x}^0$. The weak axiom therefore does imply some restrictions in the range of observable behavior. What are they?

Proposition 1 The demand relations (11-1) are homogeneous of degree zero in all prices and money income; that is, $x_i^M(tp_1, \ldots, tp_n, tM) \equiv x_i^M(p_1, \ldots, p_n, M)$.

PROOF Let the consumption bundle $\mathbf{x}^0 = (x_1^0, \ldots, x_n^0)$ be chosen by the consumer when prices and income are $(\mathbf{p}^0, M^0) = (p_1^0, \ldots, p_n^0, M^0)$, and let $\mathbf{x}^1 = (x_1^1, \ldots, x_n^1)$ be chosen at prices and income $(\mathbf{p}^1, M^1) = (p_1^1, \ldots, p_n^1, M^1)$.

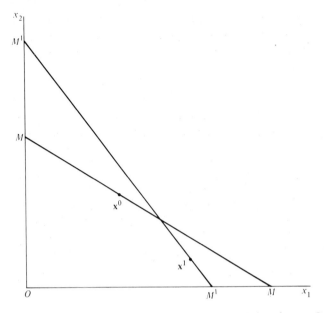

Figure 11-2 Violation of the weak axiom of revealed preference. In the initial situation at prices $\mathbf{p}^0$, $\mathbf{x}^0$ is chosen even though $\mathbf{x}^1$ could have been chosen. Hence, $\mathbf{x}^0$ is revealed preferred to $\mathbf{x}^1$. When $\mathbf{x}^1$ is chosen at prices $\mathbf{p}^1$, implying a budget line M^1M^1, $\mathbf{x}^0$ could still have been chosen, and thus $\mathbf{x}^1$ would be revealed preferred to $\mathbf{x}^0$. This contradicts the weak axiom, which says that if $\mathbf{x}^0$ is revealed preferred to $\mathbf{x}^1$, then $\mathbf{x}^1$ will never be preferred to $\mathbf{x}^0$. Note that if one were to try to draw an indifference locus tangent to MM and M^1M^1 at $\mathbf{x}^0$ and $\mathbf{x}^1$, respectively, the locus would be concave to the origin. This behavior is ruled out by the weak axiom.

By hypothesis, $\mathbf{p}^1 = t\mathbf{p}^0$, $M^1 = tM^0$. Assume now that $\mathbf{x}^1 \neq \mathbf{x}^0$, that is, that two distinct points are chosen in these situations. We shall show that a contradiction arises. Since $t\mathbf{M}^0 = \mathbf{M}^1$ and the consumer spends the entire budget,

$$t\mathbf{p}^0\mathbf{x}^0 = \mathbf{p}^1\mathbf{x}^1$$

However, $\mathbf{p}^1 = t\mathbf{p}^0$. Hence,

$$t\mathbf{p}^0\mathbf{x}^0 = t\mathbf{p}^0\mathbf{x}^1$$

or
$$\mathbf{p}^0\mathbf{x}^0 = \mathbf{p}^0\mathbf{x}^1 \tag{11-3}$$

Equation (11-3) says that $\mathbf{x}^0$ is revealed preferred to $\mathbf{x}^1$, since $\mathbf{x}^1$ could have been chosen and was not. Therefore, when $\mathbf{x}^1$ *is* chosen, $\mathbf{x}^0$ must be more expensive, i.e.,

$$\mathbf{p}^1\mathbf{x}^1 < \mathbf{p}^1\mathbf{x}^0 \tag{11-4}$$

by the weak axiom of revealed preference. However, $\mathbf{p}^1 = t\mathbf{p}^0$. Substituting this into (11-4) yields

$$t\mathbf{p}^0\mathbf{x}^1 < t\mathbf{p}^0\mathbf{x}^0$$

or
$$\mathbf{p}^0\mathbf{x}^1 < \mathbf{p}^0\mathbf{x}^0 \tag{11-5}$$

330 THE STRUCTURE OF ECONOMICS

However, (11-5) and (11-3) are contradictory; hence, the assumption that $\mathbf{x}^1 \neq \mathbf{x}^0$ must be false, and the weak axiom of revealed preference implies that the demand relations (11-1) are homogeneous of degree zero.

Proposition 2 The weak axiom implies that the demand relations (11-1) are single-valued; i.e., for any price-income vector $(\mathbf{p}, M)$ the consumer chooses a single point of consumption.

PROOF This proposition is actually a special case of proposition 1. Simply let $t = 1$ in the above proof. Proposition 1 includes the case where $t = 1$ (since it holds for all $t > 0$), so when $\mathbf{p}^1 = \mathbf{p}^0$, $M^1 = M^0$, one and only one consumption bundle is chosen. If two points were chosen, each would be revealed preferred to the other, by symmetry; an obvious contradiction.

Thus, two properties of demand functions implied by utility analysis, single-valuedness and homogeneity of degree zero, are also implied by the weak axiom of revealed preference. Most important, however, the axiom also implies the negativity of the Hicks-Slutsky type substitution terms $\partial x_i^M/\partial p_i + x_i \, \partial x_i^M/\partial M$. Let us define

$$s_{ij} = \frac{\partial x_i^M}{\partial p_j} + x_j \frac{\partial x_i^M}{\partial M} \tag{11-6}$$

We are not yet entitled to call these terms *pure-substitution effects*, or *compensated changes* because we have not yet shown (the weak axiom is insufficient for that purpose) that a utility function exists for this consumer. With utility as yet undefined, the concept of indifference or utility held constant has no meaning. However, we can show the following.

Proposition 3 The matrix of s_{ij}'s is negative semidefinite, under the assumption of the weak axiom of revealed preference.

PROOF Let us assume also that the demand functions (11-1), $\mathbf{x} = \mathbf{x}^M(\mathbf{p}, M)$, are differentiable. Let $\mathbf{p}^1 = \mathbf{p}^0 + d\mathbf{p}$, $\mathbf{x}^1 = \mathbf{x}^0 + d\mathbf{x}$, where the differentials indicate movements along the tangent planes. Then from the weak axiom,

$$\mathbf{p}^0\mathbf{x}^0 = \mathbf{p}^0\mathbf{x}^1 \qquad \text{implies} \qquad \mathbf{p}^1\mathbf{x}^1 < \mathbf{p}^1\mathbf{x}^0$$

With $\mathbf{p}^1$ and $\mathbf{x}^1$ defined as above this becomes

$$\mathbf{p}^0\mathbf{x}^0 = \mathbf{p}^0(\mathbf{x}^0 + d\mathbf{x}) \tag{11-7}$$

implies

$$(\mathbf{p}^0 + d\mathbf{p})(\mathbf{x}^0 + d\mathbf{x}) < (\mathbf{p}^0 + d\mathbf{p})\mathbf{x}^0 \tag{11-8}$$

Equation (11-7) simplifies to $\mathbf{p}^0 \, d\mathbf{x} = 0$, and (11-8) reduces to

$$(\mathbf{p}^0 + d\mathbf{p})\mathbf{x}^0 + (\mathbf{p}^0 + d\mathbf{p}) \, d\mathbf{x} < (\mathbf{p}^0 + d\mathbf{p})\mathbf{x}^0$$

or

$$(\mathbf{p}^0 + d\mathbf{p}) \, d\mathbf{x} < 0$$

Hence, for differentiable demand functions, the weak axiom can be stated as

$$\mathbf{dp}\ \mathbf{dx} \leq 0 \qquad (11\text{-}9)$$

whenever

$$\mathbf{p}\ \mathbf{dx} = 0 \qquad (11\text{-}10)$$

That is, $\sum dp_i\, dx_i \leq 0$ whenever $\sum p_i\, dx_i = 0$, where the equality holds in (11-9) only when all prices change in the same proportion; otherwise $\mathbf{dp}\ \mathbf{dx} < 0$. Now relate equations (11-9) and (11-10) to Hicks-Slutsky terms, the s_{ij}'s, defined in (11-6). For each demand function $x_i = x_i^M(p_1, \ldots, p_n, M)$,

$$dx_i = \sum_{j=1}^{n} \left(\frac{\partial x_i^M}{\partial p_j}\, dp_j \right) + \frac{\partial x_i^M}{\partial M}\, dM \qquad (11\text{-}11)$$

However, when $\sum_{j=1}^{n} p_j\, dx_j = 0$,

$$dM = \sum_{j=1}^{n} x_j\, dp_j + \sum_{j=1}^{n} p_j\, dx_j = \sum_{j=1}^{n} x_j\, dp_j \qquad (11\text{-}12)$$

Substituting (11-12) into (11-11) gives

$$dx_i = \sum_{j=1}^{n} \frac{\partial x_i^M}{\partial p_j}\, dp_j + \sum_{j=1}^{n} \frac{\partial x_i^M}{\partial M}\, x_j\, dp_j$$

or

$$dx_i = \sum_{j=1}^{n} \left(\frac{\partial x_i^M}{\partial p_j} + x_j \frac{\partial x_i^M}{\partial M} \right) dp_j = \sum_{j=1}^{n} s_{ij}\, dp_j \qquad (11\text{-}13)$$

Applying equation (11-9) to (11-13) gives

$$\sum_{i=1}^{n} dx_i\, dp_i = \sum_{i=1}^{n} \sum_{j=1}^{n} s_{ij}\, dp_i\, dp_j \leq 0 \qquad (11\text{-}14)$$

where the equality holds when all prices change in the same proportion. Equation (11-14) says, by definition, that the matrix of Slutsky terms is negative semidefinite. As such, with the methods employed in deriving the conditions for maximization, $s_{ii} \leq 0$ (usually $s_{ii} < 0$); that is, the pure-substitution own effects are negative.

What is the meaning of (11-9) and (11-10)? The condition $\sum p_i\, dx_i = 0$ is precisely what is implied when, starting from the utility framework, utility is held constant. When $U(x_1, \ldots, x_n) = U_0$, a constant,

$$dU = \sum U_i\, dx_i = \lambda \sum p_i\, dx_i = 0$$

using the first-order equations for utility-maximization subject to a budget constraint. Hence, in that case, assuming nonsatiation ($\lambda \neq 0$), $\sum p_i\, dx_i = 0$. Thus, the dx_i's would be interpretable as pure substitution movements. If only one price p_j is changed, that is, $dp_i = 0$, $i \neq j$, then equation (11-9) says that $dp_j\, dx_j < 0$, or that the own substitution effect is negative, as implied by utility analysis. But again, these are mere analogies at this point, since the existence of a utility function has not yet been shown.

The revealed-preference approach to consumer theory was originally offered as an operational alternative to the sometimes vague and mysterious utility analysis. We see that, in fact, the weak axiom of revealed preference implies almost as much as utility analysis itself and hence is practically equivalent to it. The only result not implied by the weak axiom is the symmetry of the Slutsky terms; that is, $s_{ij} = s_{ji}$. Without this, a utility function cannot exist, since $s_{ij} = s_{ji}$ is a necessary consequence of utility theory. The question thus remains: Can the weak axiom of revealed preference be strengthened so that it implies symmetry and hence the possible equivalence of revealed-preference theory and utility analysis? The answer was provided by Houthakker in 1950, with results discussed in the next section.

11.2 THE STRONG AXIOM OF REVEALED PREFERENCE AND INTEGRABILITY

The inability to deduce the symmetry of Slutsky-type substitution terms from the weak axiom of revealed preference seems at first to be mainly an annoying detail. However, if a utility function does not exist for a given consumer, we should expect occasionally to observe behavior that most of us would regard as strange and not in conformity with the usual observations on consumer behavior. Let us see what type of behavior is *not* ruled out by the weak axiom.

Consider three consumption bundles, $\mathbf{x}^0$, $\mathbf{x}^1$, and $\mathbf{x}^2$, which the consumer purchases at price vectors $\mathbf{p}^0$, $\mathbf{p}^1$, and $\mathbf{p}^2$, respectively. Each bundle represents consumption levels of three separate goods. Let $\mathbf{x}^j = (x_1^j, x_2^j, x_3^j)$, $\mathbf{p}^j = (p_1^j, p_2^j, p_3^j)$, $j = 1, 2, 3$.

$$\mathbf{x}^0 = (2, 2, 2) \qquad \mathbf{p}^0 = (2, 2, 2)$$
$$\mathbf{x}^1 = (3, 1, 2) \qquad \mathbf{p}^1 = (1, 3, 2)$$
$$\mathbf{x}^2 = (4, 1, 1\tfrac{1}{2}) \qquad \mathbf{p}^2 = (2, 1\tfrac{1}{2}, 5)$$

In the initial situation, when each good is priced at \$2, 2 units each are bought, for a total expenditure of \$12. When p_1 is lowered from \$2 to \$1 and p_2 raised to \$3 from \$2, to produce $\mathbf{p}^1 = (1, 3, 2)$, this consumer evidently increases consumption of the first good x_1 and lowers that of x_2. This is in accordance with substitution toward the lower-priced good. Similarly, when p_3 is raised from \$2 to \$5, among other changes, the consumer decreases consumption of x_3, from 2 units to $1\tfrac{1}{2}$ units. Although p_1 increases absolutely from \$1 to \$2, relative to the change in p_3, x_1 becomes relatively cheaper and consumption of x_1 increases. Hence, these consumption bundles and prices seem plausible enough.

They are even more plausible in that the weak axiom of revealed preference is satisfied for these points. In particular, we note

$$\mathbf{p}^0\mathbf{x}^0 = \mathbf{p}^0\mathbf{x}^1 = 12$$

and thus $\mathbf{x}^0$ is revealed preferred to $\mathbf{x}^1$. When $\mathbf{x}^1$ is in fact purchased, $\mathbf{x}^0$ is more expensive than $\mathbf{x}^1$:

$$\mathbf{p}^1\mathbf{x}^1 = 10 < \mathbf{p}^1\mathbf{x}^0 = 12$$

What is more, $\mathbf{x}^1$ is revealed preferred to $\mathbf{x}^2$:

$$\mathbf{p}^1\mathbf{x}^1 = \mathbf{p}^1\mathbf{x}^2 = 10$$

and when $\mathbf{x}^2$ is purchased, $\mathbf{x}^1$ is more expensive:

$$\mathbf{p}^2\mathbf{x}^2 = 17 < \mathbf{p}^2\mathbf{x}^1 = 17\tfrac{1}{2}$$

Now, however, something utterly revolting occurs: $\mathbf{x}^2$ is revealed preferred to $\mathbf{x}^0$.

$$\mathbf{p}^2\mathbf{x}^2 = \mathbf{p}^2\mathbf{x}^0 = 17$$

and, when $\mathbf{x}^0$ is purchased, $\mathbf{x}^2$ is more expensive:

$$\mathbf{p}^0\mathbf{x}^0 = 12 < \mathbf{p}^0\mathbf{x}^2 = 13$$

We see from the above example that the weak axiom of revealed preference allows intransitivity of preferences to occur. If revealed preference is to be associated with the usual notions of consumers' preferences, we cannot allow the situation where $\mathbf{x}^0$ is preferred to $\mathbf{x}^1$ and $\mathbf{x}^1$ is preferred to $\mathbf{x}^2$ and then have $\mathbf{x}^2$ preferred to the original bundle $\mathbf{x}^0$. Such intransitivity could not occur under the usual assumptions of utility analysis—in particular, the assumption that indifference curves are nonintersecting. Yet this situation is precisely what occurs in the above example, an example in complete conformity with the weak axiom of revealed preference.

It is therefore not surprising that something less than what is implied by utility-maximization is implied by the weak axiom. This took the form of allowing $s_{ij} \neq s_{ji}$. It is not obvious or easy to explain but nonetheless true that this asymmetry and the occurrence of nontransitive revealed preferences are equivalent in the sense that, together with the weak axiom, eliminating either one rules out the other also. In other words, if the weak axiom of revealed preference is strengthened to include the additional assertion that revealed preferences will not be nontransitive, i.e., that nontransitivity will not occur, then in fact it can be shown that a utility function exists for that consumer with the usual properties. These properties include the condition that $s_{ij} = s_{ji}$, $i, j = 1, \ldots, n$. Conversely, if, in addition to the weak axiom, it is also assumed that $s_{ij} = s_{ji}$, $i = 1, \ldots, n$, this too guarantees the existence of a utility function consistent with the observed behavior and hence nontransitivity of revealed preferences. This latter issue is the classic problem of integrability of the demand functions, i.e., the question of whether a given set of demand functions is capable of being generated by some utility function.

Let us formally state the strong axiom of revealed preferences, due to H. S. Houthakker.†

---

† H. S. Houthakker, Revealed Preference and the Utility Function, *Economica*, **17**: 159–174, May 1950.

The strong axiom of revealed preference Let the bundle of goods purchased at price vector $\mathbf{p}^i$ be denoted $\mathbf{x}^i$. For any finite set of bundles $(\mathbf{x}^1, \ldots, \mathbf{x}^k)$, if $\mathbf{x}^1$ is revealed preferred to $\mathbf{x}^2$, $\mathbf{x}^2$ revealed preferred to $\mathbf{x}^3$, etc., $\ldots$, $\mathbf{x}^{k-1}$ revealed preferred to $\mathbf{x}^k$, or, algebraically, if $\mathbf{p}^1\mathbf{x}^1 \geq \mathbf{p}^1\mathbf{x}^2$, $\mathbf{p}^2\mathbf{x}^2 \geq \mathbf{p}^2\mathbf{x}^3$, $\ldots$, $\mathbf{p}^{k-1}\mathbf{x}^{k-1} \geq \mathbf{p}^{k-1}\mathbf{x}^k$, then $\mathbf{p}^k\mathbf{x}^k < \mathbf{p}^k\mathbf{x}^0$; that is, $\mathbf{x}^k$ is *not* revealed preferred to $\mathbf{x}^0$.

"THEOREM" A set of individual demand functions $x_i = x_i^M(p_1, \ldots, p_n, M)$, $i = 1, \ldots, n$, which are consistent with the strong axiom of revealed preference are derivable from utility analysis. That is, there exists a class of utility functions $F(U(x_1, \ldots, x_n))$, where F is any monotonic transformation, which, when maximized subject to the budget constraint $\sum p_i x_i = M$ results in those particular demand functions.

The above "theorem" is subject to certain technical mathematical conditions concerning differentiability and other details (hence the quotation marks). In essence, however, the strong axiom is equivalent to the utility-maximization hypothesis; either one implies the other. The proof of this theorem is unfortunately beyond the scope of this book. The interested reader should consult Houthakker's original paper and the later literature.

The strong axiom is a straightforward generalization of the weak axiom. It merely extends the notion of the weak axiom to a chain of more than two consumption bundles. In general, pairwise comparison of consumption points is too weak a basis for making statements about multidimensional curvature properties of functions. Suppose, for example, a consumer possesses well-defined indifference curves, all nonconcave, etc., for two commodities x_1 and x_2. Likewise, assume a similarly well-behaved indifference map between x_2 and some other good x_3 and another well-behaved set for x_3 and x_1. Are these separate indifference maps consistent with an overall utility function $U(x_1, x_2, x_3)$? Not necessarily. No such integral function need exist. The indifference maps may all be well-behaved taken alone, but they may be inconsistent with each other algebraically or they may allow the intransitivity demonstrated in the previous example. Suppose, for example, at a given point, this consumer's MRS of apples for oranges is three apples for one orange. And suppose the consumer will trade one orange for two pears and two pears for four apples. These marginal rates of substitution could not be generated by a three-dimensional utility function, for the consumer would spiral around the original point and wind up being indifferent between the original bundle of goods and one which had more of one good and the same amount of the others. Yet it is perfectly easy to draw these indifference curves in two-dimensional space.

In addition, the usual convexity of the separate two-dimensional curves is insufficient to guarantee usual convexity of the three-dimensional indifference surfaces, assuming it exists. If each two-dimensional curve is convex to the origin, the bordered hessians of the form

$$H_2 = \begin{vmatrix} U_{ii} & U_{ij} & -p_i \\ U_{ji} & U_{jj} & -p_j \\ -p_i & -p_j & 0 \end{vmatrix}$$

are all nonnegative. However, even if they are all positive, the full bordered hessian

$$H_3 = \begin{vmatrix} U_{11} & U_{12} & U_{13} & -p_1 \\ U_{21} & U_{22} & U_{23} & -p_2 \\ U_{31} & U_{32} & U_{33} & -p_3 \\ -p_1 & -p_2 & -p_3 & 0 \end{vmatrix}$$

need not have the appropriate sign (nonpositive). The resulting indifference surface can, at least locally, be concave to the origin at some point, even though all two-dimensional projections of that surface exhibit strict quasi-concavity. These are all subtle geometric issues. It is remarkable that as simple a statement as the strong axiom of revealed preference contains the same behavioral implications as the quasi-concavity of a multidimensional utility function.

Integrability

Suppose an econometrician estimates a set of demand relations $x_i = x_i^M(p_1, \ldots, p_n, M)$, $i = 1, \ldots, n$, and asks you to check whether these estimated functions are capable of being derived by utility analysis. That is, is it possible (and if so, how) to determine that a given set of demand functions is consistent with standard utility analysis? Consider the two demand functions

$$x_1 = \frac{M}{2p_1} \qquad x_2 = \frac{M}{2p_2} \tag{11-15}$$

Let us make such a determination here (even though we know the answer, these demand functions having been derived in Chap. 8). Both functions are clearly homogeneous of degree zero in all prices and money income. Also,

$$p_1 x_1 + p_2 x_2 = \frac{M}{2} + \frac{M}{2} \equiv M$$

Thus, the budget constraint is satisfied identically. Let us calculate the matrix of Slutsky terms s_{ij} (remember, we cannot yet call these pure-substitution effects, since that notion has not yet been established). We have

$$s_{11} = \frac{\partial x_1}{\partial p_1} + x_1 \frac{\partial x_1}{\partial M} = -\frac{M}{2p_1^2} + \frac{M}{2p_1}\frac{1}{2p_1} = -\frac{M}{4p_1^2}$$

and hence $s_{11} < 0$ as needed. Similarly, $s_{22} = -M/4p_2^2 < 0$. For the cross-effects,

$$s_{12} = \frac{\partial x_1}{\partial p_2} + x_2 \frac{\partial x_1}{\partial M} = 0 + \frac{M}{2p_2}\frac{1}{2p_1} = \frac{M}{4p_1 p_2}$$

and

$$s_{21} = \frac{\partial x_2}{\partial p_1} + x_1 \frac{\partial x_2}{\partial M} = 0 + \frac{M}{2p_1}\frac{1}{2p_2} = \frac{M}{4p_1 p_2}$$

Thus, $s_{12} = s_{21}$, also as needed. The last requirement on these s_{ij}'s is that their matrix be negative semidefinite; that is, s_{11}, $s_{22} < 0$ (already shown) and $s_{11}s_{22} - s_{12}^2 = 0$. For the latter,

$$s_{11}s_{22} - s_{12}^2 = -\frac{M}{4p_1^2}\left(-\frac{M}{4p_2^2}\right) - \left(\frac{M}{4p_1p_2}\right)^2 \equiv 0$$

Thus these demand functions exhibit all the usual properties. But is that enough? How can we be sure that there are not other conditions that must be satisfied in order for a utility function to exist? Let us try to find a utility function (if it exists) which would generate these demand functions. Since the demand functions are solutions to first-order conditions (partial derivatives of a lagrangian function), this problem is known as *integrating* back to the utility function. We proceed as follows. If a utility function $U(x_1, x_2)$ exists for these demand functions, then along any indifference curve

$$dU = U_1\,dx_1 + U_2\,dx_2 = 0$$

or
$$dx_1 + \frac{U_2}{U_1}dx_2 = 0 \tag{11-16}$$

This is equivalent to

$$\frac{dx_2}{dx_1} = -\frac{U_1}{U_2} \tag{11-17}$$

This is the familiar statement that at any point, the MRS between two goods equals the ratio of the marginal utilities of the two goods. However, at the chosen point, $U_1/U_2 = p_1/p_2$. For these demand functions, $p_1 = M/2x_1$, $p_2 = M/2x_2$. Hence,

$$\frac{U_1}{U_2} = \frac{p_1}{p_2} = \frac{x_2}{x_1}$$

The differential equation (11-17) then becomes

$$\frac{dx_2}{dx_1} = -\frac{x_2}{x_1} \tag{11-18}$$

This can be integrated by separating variables:

$$\frac{dx_2}{x_2} = -\frac{dx_1}{x_1}$$

Integrating gives

$$\log x_2 = -\log x_1 + \log F(U)$$

or
$$F(U) = x_1x_2 \tag{11-19}$$

where the constant of integration $F(U)$ is the arbitrary indifference level chosen for the slope element dx_2/dx_1. This situation is depicted in Fig. 11-3.

Several things happened to go right in this puzzle. There was no problem

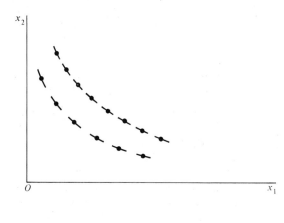

Figure 11-3 Integrability: the two-variable case. The differential equation (11-16) or (11-17) defines a direction at each point $(x_1 x_2)$ of the $x_1 x_2$ plane. These directional elements are depicted in the above graph as short line segments through each point. The problem of integrability is to find a function which links these directions up, for constant (the arbitrary constant of integration) levels of the functions. In utility analysis, these level-curve linkups of the slope element given by the differential equation (11-16) are the indifference curves. For two commodities, this integration is always possible.

expressing the slope element dx_2/dx_1 in terms of the consumption variables x_1 and x_2 only, and the differential equation itself was easy to integrate. The resulting utility function is that which was used in earlier chapters to derive the above demand functions. Let us investigate these matters more closely.

The first step was to express the slope element in terms of x_1 and x_2. This involved inverting the demand functions, which were originally functions of the prices and income, for functions of the quantities. In most cases, this can be done, with one qualification. The demand functions $x_i = x_i^M(p_1, \ldots, p_n, M)$ are homogeneous of degree zero in prices and money income. Therefore, it is clearly *not* possible to write $p_i = p_i^*(x_1, \ldots, x_n)$, since any given consumption bundle is associated with an infinity of price vectors, all multiples of each other. However, we can expect to solve for the x_i's in terms of *relative* prices, or prices relative to income. Using the homogeneity property, we have

$$x_i^M(tp_1, \ldots, tp_n, tM) \equiv x_i^M(p_1, \ldots, p_n, M)$$

If we let $t = 1/M$, the demand function can be written

$$x_i^M(p_1, \ldots, p_n, M) \equiv x_i^M\left(\frac{p_1}{M}, \ldots, \frac{p_n}{M}, 1\right) \equiv g_i(r_1, \ldots, r_n) \qquad (11\text{-}20)$$

where $r_i = p_i/M$, $i = 1, \ldots, n$. The r_i's represent that fraction of a consumer's income necessary for the purchase of 1 unit of x_i. In general, we can expect the jacobian matrix of the g_i relative-price demand functions to have a nonzero determinant and to be able to solve for these relative prices in terms of the x_i's, or

$$r_i = h_i(x_1, \ldots, x_n) \qquad (11\text{-}21)$$

Then, since $p_i/p_j = r_i/r_j$, the slope elements $dx_i/dx_j = -p_j/p_i$ are expressible in terms of the quantity variables, using the inverted demand functions (11-21). This was accomplished in the above example, in the differential equation (11-18).

Having now found $r_i = h_i(x_1, \ldots, x_n)$ or, for the two-variable case, $r_1 = h_1(x_1,$

x_2), $r_2 = h_2(x_1, x_2)$, it remains to solve the differential equation (11-16) or (11-17),

$$\frac{dx_2}{dx_1} = -\frac{p_1}{p_2} = -\frac{h_1(x_1, x_2)}{h_2(x_1, x_2)}$$

or $\qquad\qquad h_1(x_1, x_2)\, dx_1 + h_2(x_1, x_2)\, dx_2 = 0 \qquad\qquad (11\text{-}22)$

These differential equations are not, in general, easy to solve. However, for the *two-variable* case only, a solution is assured, by a well-known mathematical theorem.

How is equation (11-22) to be integrated, i.e., solved? Remember, this differential equation is supposed to represent the total differential of a utility function along an indifference curve; that is, $dU = 0$. Then for $U = U(x_1, x_2)$, from equation (11-16) we must have $U_1 = h_1$, $U_2 = h_2$. Moreover, since cross-partials are invariant to the order of differentiation, we must have $U_{12} = U_{21}$, or

$$\frac{\partial h_1}{\partial x_2} = \frac{\partial h_2}{\partial x_1} \qquad\qquad (11\text{-}23)$$

This condition happened to be satisfied for the demand functions in the above example. There, $h_1 = 1/2x_1$, $h_2 = 1/2x_2$, $\partial h_1/\partial x_2 = \partial h_2/\partial x_1 = 0$. Whereas it is clear that $\partial h_1/\partial x_2 = \partial h_2/\partial x_1$ is a *necessary* condition which must exist if an integral function $U(x_1, x_2)$ is to exist, it is also the case that this condition is *sufficient* for the existence of such an integral function, by a well-known theorem of differential equations. Hence, since $\partial h_1/\partial x_2 = \partial h_2/\partial x_1$ in the above example, some integral utility function $U = U(x_1, x_2)$ necessarily existed, with $\partial U/\partial x_1 = h_1$, $\partial U/\partial x_2 = h_2$.

The point of the above discussion is that if one starts with an arbitrary set of demand functions $x_i = x_i^M(p_1, \ldots, p_n, M)$, $i = 1, \ldots, n$, satisfying the usual budget and homogeneity conditions, it will be rather fortuitous if the resulting differential generalization of equation (11-16) has a solution:

$$h_1(x_1, \ldots, x_n)\, dx_1 + \cdots + h_n(x_1, \ldots, x_n)\, dx_n = 0 \qquad\qquad (11\text{-}24)$$

In general, a solution to this differential equation does not exist; i.e., there may be no utility function $U(x_1, \ldots, x_n)$ such that $\partial U/\partial x_i = h_i$, $i = 1, \ldots, n$. Special restrictions on the h_i's must be imposed in order to guarantee a solution.

Curiously enough, however, for the two-variable case, the differential equation (11-16) or (11-24) *always* has a solution. That is, starting with two demand functions $x_1 = x_1^M(p_1, p_2, M)$ and $x_2 = x_2^M(p_1, p_2, M)$ which satisfy the budget and homogeneity condition, the resulting $h_1(x_1, x_2)$ and $h_2(x_1, x_2)$ are always integrable. The resulting differential expression

$$h_1(x_1, x_2)\, dx_1 + h_2(x_1, x_2)\, dx_2 = 0$$

may not in fact exhibit $\partial h_1/\partial x_2 = \partial h_2/\partial x_1$. However, in this two-variable case, it happens that there will always be an *integrating factor* $G(x_1, x_2)$ such that

$$G(x_1, x_2)h_1(x_1, x_2)\, dx_1 + G(x_1, x_2)h_2(x_1, x_2)\, dx_2 = 0$$

is integrable, i.e., that $\partial(Gh_1)/\partial x_2 = \partial(Gh_2)/\partial x_1$. The proof of this nontrivial theorem is available in most calculus texts and will not be reproduced here. Notice, though, that $dx_2/dx_1 = -Gh_1/Gh_2 = -h_1/h_2$, and hence the G function corresponds to $F'(U)$, where $F(U)$ is any monotonic transformation of the utility function.

The reason the two-variable system is always integrable can be seen with the help of Fig. 11-3, and at the same time the relationship of integrability and revealed preference will be more clearly exhibited. The differential equations (11-16) or (11-17) serve to define at each point (x_1, x_2) of the $x_1 x_2$ plane a slope element, or direction, $-h_1/h_2$. Every point has such a direction defined. Some of these are exhibited by the short line segments drawn through each point. The integral function $U(x_1, x_2)$ connects up these directional elements for constant functional values. Under some technical mathematical conditions, this can always be done, guaranteeing the existence of a solution to the differential equation (11-16) for the two-dimensional case.

In the three-good case, however, the story is different. In each of the $x_1 x_2$, $x_2 x_3$, and $x_3 x_1$ planes, a slope element $dx_j/dx_i = -h_i/h_j$ will be defined. These

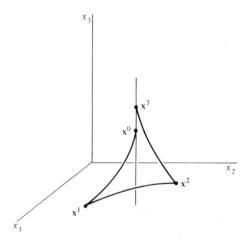

Figure 11-4 Integrability: the three-commodity case. Consider some point $\mathbf{x}^0 = (x_1^0, x_2^0, x_3^0)$. A slope element in the $x_1 x_3$ direction, $-h_1/h_3$, is defined by the differential equation (11-24). Integrating in that plane, parallel to the x_1, x_3 axes, we come to some other point $\mathbf{x}^1$. At $\mathbf{x}^1$, a directional element $-h_1/h_2$ is defined in an $x_1 x_2$ plane parallel to the x_1, x_2 axes. Integrating along some level curve there, we can get to another point $\mathbf{x}^2$ at which the original x_1 value is restored. At $\mathbf{x}^2$, a directional element $-h_3/h_2$ is defined in the $x_2 x_3$ plane. Integrating along that level curve, we may get back to a point such as $\mathbf{x}^3$ which has the same level of x_1 and x_2 as $\mathbf{x}^1$ but has more of the third commodity x_3. This spiraling process is what is ruled out by the integrability conditions. In order for a well-defined indifference *surface* to exist, relating to a utility function $U(x_1, x_2, x_3)$, a point such as $\mathbf{x}^3$ cannot occur but must coincide with $\mathbf{x}^0$. Then the path $\mathbf{x}^0 \to \mathbf{x}^1 \to \mathbf{x}^2 \to \mathbf{x}^3$ represents a movement along one indifference surface. A path like $\mathbf{x}^0 \to \mathbf{x}^1 \to \mathbf{x}^2 \to \mathbf{x}^3$ in the diagram is what can occur if only the *weak* axiom of revealed preference is asserted. The numerical example illustrated this. The strong axiom, by asserting that the last point in the chain will not be revealed preferred to the first, effectively eliminates the situation depicted in the diagram.

will be the indifference elements described in the revealed-preference section. However, there is no guarantee that these directional elements will all link up with each other; the possibility remains that a consumer can spiral around some point and reach a point that is indifferent to the original while having more of one good and not less of the others. The situation leaves open the possibility of the nontransitive behavior exhibited earlier. The force of the integrability condition $\partial h_i/\partial x_j = \partial h_j/\partial x_i$ is to guarantee that such behavior does not exist; like the strong axiom of revealed preference, integrability rules out nontransitive behavior by guaranteeing the existence of a utility function. This is illustrated in Fig. 11-4.

The consequences of this analysis with regard to revealed-preference theory are that for the two-commodity case, the *weak* axiom is in fact sufficient to guarantee the existence of a utility function. The type of intransitive behavior exhibited earlier cannot occur with only two commodities if the weak axiom is satisfied. The fundamental difference between the two- and many-commodity situations is that for two commodities there is only one relative price. With only one price, the consumer cannot circle around the original point to a new position of greater commodity levels while remaining on the same indifference curve, as is possible in three dimensions if only the weak axiom is asserted.

What conditions on the demand functions themselves lead to integrability? Although it cannot be shown here, unfortunately, as advanced techniques are required, the symmetry of the Slutsky terms $s_{ij} = \partial x_i^M/\partial p_j + x_j\partial x_i^M/\partial M$ is sufficient to guarantee the existence of a utility function from which the demand curves are derived. Given this symmetry, the terms s_{ij} are interpretable as the slopes of compensated demand curves, i.e., the partial derivatives $\partial x_i^U(p_1, \ldots, p_n, U)/\partial p_j$. Since $\partial x_i^U/\partial p_j = \partial x_j^U/\partial p_i$, the differential expression $x_1^U\, dp_1 + \cdots + x_n^U\, dp_n$ is exact; i.e., it is integrable. Since by the envelope theorem we know that the expenditure, or cost, function $M^*(p_1, \ldots, p_n, U)$ has the property $\partial M^*/\partial p_j = x_j^U$, clearly, the above differential expression is simply

$$dM^* = \frac{\partial M^*}{\partial p_1}\, dp_1 + \cdots + \frac{\partial M^*}{\partial p_n}\, dp_n = x_1^U\, dp_1 + \cdots + x_n^U\, dp_n$$

Hence, $M^*(p_1, \ldots, p_n, U)$ is the integral of this expression and is known to exist since $\partial^2 M^*/(\partial p_i\, \partial p_j) = \partial x_i^U/\partial p_j = \partial x_j^U/\partial p_i = \partial^2 M^*/(\partial p_j\, \partial p_i)$. Thus, the expenditure function is well defined if the Slutsky terms are symmetrical. From the discussion in the previous chapter, the corresponding utility function must exist also.

Let us check that the two-variable case is always integrable. Consider two demand functions $x_1 = x_1^M(p_1, p_2, M)$ and $x_2 = x_2^M(p_1, p_2, M)$. Assume that

$$p_1 x_1^M + p_2 x_2^M \equiv M \tag{11-25}$$

and $\qquad x_i^M(tp_1, tp_2, tM) \equiv x_i^M(p_1, p_2, M) \qquad i = 1, 2 \tag{11-26}$

That is, the demand functions satisfy the budget and homogeneity conditions. If these demand curves are integrable, i.e., if there exists some utility function which generates these functions, then we should find $s_{12} = s_{21}$. Let us see if this is the case. Superscripts will be omitted to save notational clutter.

From homogeneity and (11-25), using Euler's theorem, we get

$$\frac{\partial x_1}{\partial p_1} p_1 + \frac{\partial x_1}{\partial p_2} p_2 + \frac{\partial x_1}{\partial M} (p_1 x_1 + p_2 x_2) \equiv 0$$

since $M = p_1 x_1 + p_2 x_2$. Collecting terms gives

$$p_1 \left(\frac{\partial x_1}{\partial p_1} + x_1 \frac{\partial x_1}{\partial M} \right) + p_2 \left(\frac{\partial x_1}{\partial p_2} + x_2 \frac{\partial x_1}{\partial M} \right) \equiv 0$$

or

$$p_1 s_{11} + p_2 s_{12} \equiv 0 \qquad (11\text{-}27a)$$

In like fashion, applying Euler's theorem to $x_2(p_1, p_2, M)$ gives

$$p_1 s_{21} + p_2 s_{22} \equiv 0 \qquad (11\text{-}27b)$$

Equations (11-27) generalize to n commodities in a straightforward manner. In general,

$$\sum_{j=1}^{n} p_j s_{ij} = 0, \qquad i = 1, \ldots, n \qquad (11\text{-}28)$$

Now consider the budget relation (11-25). Differentiating with respect to p_1 yields

$$p_1 \frac{\partial x_1}{\partial p_1} + p_2 \frac{\partial x_2}{\partial p_1} \equiv -x_1$$

Differentiating (11-25) with respect to M yields

$$p_1 \frac{\partial x_1}{\partial M} + p_2 \frac{\partial x_2}{\partial M} \equiv 1$$

Multiplying this expression by $-x_1$ and substituting into the above leads to

$$p_1 \frac{\partial x_1}{\partial p_1} + p_2 \frac{\partial x_2}{\partial p_1} \equiv -p_1 x_1 \frac{\partial x_1}{\partial M} - p_2 x_1 \frac{\partial x_2}{\partial M}$$

Combining terms, we have

$$p_1 \left(\frac{\partial x_1}{\partial p_1} + x_1 \frac{\partial x_1}{\partial M} \right) + p_2 \left(\frac{\partial x_2}{\partial p_1} + x_1 \frac{\partial x_2}{\partial M} \right) \equiv 0$$

or

$$p_1 s_{11} + p_2 s_{21} \equiv 0 \qquad (11\text{-}29a)$$

In like fashion, by differentiating the budget relation with respect to p_2, one can derive

$$p_1 s_{12} + p_2 s_{22} \equiv 0 \qquad (11\text{-}29b)$$

In general, for n commodities,

$$\sum_{i=1}^{n} p_i s_{ij} \equiv 0 \qquad j = 1, \ldots, n \qquad (11\text{-}30)$$

Note that in equation (11-28) the sum runs over j, whereas in (11-30) it runs over i. These relations say that the weighted sum of the Slutsky terms for any good or for any price equals zero, where the weights are the prices. These relations were derived without any reference to utility theory; the only assumption was that the consumer had well-defined choice functions satisfying the budget and homogeneity conditions.

It is apparent from equations (11-27a) and (11-29a) that for the two-commodity case, $s_{12} = s_{21}$. Hence, it is indeed always possible to find a utility function $U(x_1, x_2)$ which generates the money-income demand curves $x_i = x_i(p_1, p_2, M)$, $i = 1, 2$. If the additional property of negative semidefiniteness is imposed on the Slutsky terms, that is, $s_{11} < 0$, $s_{22} < 0$, $s_{11}s_{22} - s_{12}^2 = 0$ following from either equations (11-27) or (11-29), then the utility function will have the usual convex indifference curves of consumer theory.

The importance of these results is that they demonstrate that negative semidefiniteness and symmetry of the Slutsky terms constitute all the implications of utility theory. Since it is possible to work backward from these assumptions and demonstrate the existence of quasi-concave utility functions, there can be no other independent results of utility theory. Any other results, e.g., Le Châtelier effects, can be derived from these assumptions as well as from utility theory. In addition, since the strong axiom of revealed preference also guarantees the existence of utility functions, these approaches are all equivalent aspects of consumer theory.

11.3 THE COMPOSITE-COMMODITY THEOREM

One feature of economic systems is the interplay of a large number of variables. The number of commodities produced in a modern economy runs into the millions or billions; the variety of tasks, skills, and capital is enormous. Indeed, analysis of such systems would be impossible for most minds without some simplification or abstraction from reality. In the first chapter we discussed the role of assumptions in science, in particular the necessary simplification in order to make a theory tractable. In this section we shall investigate one aspect of this procedure, the lumping together of many commodities into one composite commodity.

Most textbooks and articles in economics generally reduce the world to two commodities or two factors of production, etc. One is usually the good under analysis, and the other is usually labeled "all other goods," or all other "closely related" goods. To what extent is this procedure justifiable? Under what circumstances can all other goods be treated as one good?

It might be appropriate at the start to recognize that what is in fact called a *commodity* is not a technological datum. Most commodities have several characteristics, each of which presumably generates utility to consumers. Yet usually, only one of these characteristics is used to label the commodity. Consider the example of eggs. Eggs come in various volumes, weights, colors, and degrees of firmness of yolk and white. The fact that egg sizes are by weight rather than volume is due to the relative ease, i.e., lower cost, of measuring that dimension than, say, volume. (The last characteristic, firmness, is the one used by the U.S. Department of Agriculture in grading. It is difficult to measure in a nondestructive manner.) Diamonds, on the other hand, are extensively measured. They are classified by color (white, blue-white, yellow, etc.), various degrees of departure from flawless crystal structure, shape of cut (round, marquise, emerald, etc.). Each of these characteristics is carefully measured, and prices vary accordingly. Diamonds are so extensively measured and categorized because, given the "high" price of the basic material of diamonds, measurement is relatively cheap. Hence, a great deal of measuring is done on diamonds, and relatively less measuring is done on lower-valued commodities. As a last example, much produce is sold by the piece in season and by weight out of season. When the produce is in season, i.e., in relatively greater supply, its price is lower. The cost of measuring, e.g., weighing at the check-out counter, or bunching together uniform packages, is relatively high. Hence, less measuring is done, and consumers are left to do whatever measuring they please on their own. Thus, the units of the commodity are apt to be different at different times or even at different retail establishments, depending upon the level of retail services offered. The notion of a commodity is thus not a technological datum but dependent in large part on the economic costs of characterization of the good.

We shall ignore these matters, however, in the forthcoming discussion. Assume that there are n well-defined commodities, $x_1, \ldots, x_n$, which the consumer purchases in positive amounts, at prices $p_1, \ldots, p_n$, respectively. Suppose now that the prices of some subset of these commodities all change simultaneously in the same proportion. Mathematically, let $\mathbf{p}^0 = (p_1^0, \ldots, p_n^0)$ be the initial price vector. Suppose, by suitable relabeling of the commodities that $p_{k+1}, \ldots, p_n$ all vary in the same proportion; that is, $p_{k+1} = tp_{k+1}^0, \ldots, p_n = tp_n^0$, where initially $t = 1$. (If, for example, t became 2, then all prices would have doubled.) How would the consumer react to changes in t, that is, proportionate changes in $n - k$ of the prices?

As we have indicated in the previous sections, the behavioral implications of utility theory are summarized and exhausted in the statement that the compensated, or Slutsky, changes s_{ij} form a symmetric negative semidefinite matrix. These pure-substitution effects are derivable from the cost-minimization problem:

$$\text{minimize} \qquad \sum_{i=1}^{n} p_i x_i = M$$

$$\text{subject to} \qquad U(x_1, \ldots, x_n) = U^0$$

The expenditure function $M^*(p_1, \ldots, p_n, U^0)$ has the property that $\partial M^*/\partial p_i = M_{p_i}^* = x_i^U(p_1, \ldots, p_n, U^0)$, $M_{p_i p_j}^* = \partial x_i^U/\partial p_j$. In the present problem, a new parameter t is introduced. To derive the compensated changes in the x_i's when t changes, one must consider the model:

$$\text{minimize} \qquad M = \sum_{i=1}^{n} p_i x_i = \sum_{i=1}^{k} p_i x_i + \sum_{i=k+1}^{n} t p_i x_i \qquad (11\text{-}31)$$

subject to $$U(x_1, \ldots, x_n) = U^0 \tag{11-32}$$

The objective function (11-31) can be written:

minimize $$M = \sum_{i=1}^{k} p_i x_i + ty \tag{11-33}$$

where $y = \sum_{i=k+1}^{n} p_i x_i$, the total expenditure on commodities $k + 1$ through n, the ones whose prices are all changing proportionately. When $t = 1$, (11-33) is identical to (11-31); hence the same demand point results. We can thus analyze a change in t from 1 by use of the envelope results of Chap. 9. Since $\partial M^*/\partial t = M_t^* = y^U = \sum_{i=k+1}^{n} p_i^0 x_i^U$,

$$M_{t, p_j}^* = \frac{\partial y^U}{\partial p_j} \qquad j = 1, \ldots, k$$

The $(k + 1) \times (k + 1)$ matrix of terms,

$$\mathbf{M}_{pt}^* = \begin{pmatrix} \dfrac{\partial x_1^U}{\partial p_1} & \cdots & \dfrac{\partial x_k^U}{\partial p_1} & \dfrac{\partial y^U}{\partial p_1} \\ \cdots\cdots\cdots\cdots\cdots\cdots \\ \dfrac{\partial x_1^U}{\partial p_k} & \cdots & \dfrac{\partial x_k^U}{\partial p_k} & \dfrac{\partial y^U}{\partial p_k} \\ \dfrac{\partial x_1^U}{\partial t} & \cdots & \dfrac{\partial x_k^U}{\partial t} & \dfrac{\partial y^U}{\partial t} \end{pmatrix} \tag{11-34}$$

must be negative semidefinite. The factor of proportion t enters this matrix exactly as do the prices $p_1, \ldots, p_k$, and total expenditure y^U on $x_{k+1}, \ldots, x_n$ enters just like any other quantity variable. Thus this system of compensated changes is no different from any other well-behaved set of $n + 1$ compensated demand functions. Therefore, when prices of several commodities vary simultaneously, in the same proportion, total expenditures on those commodities behave exactly like any other commodity. This new variable y is called a *composite commodity*, and was introduced first by John R. Hicks in "Value and Capital." The composite commodity is just like any other decision variable; e.g., the response to a change in its own "price" t is negative:

$$\frac{\partial y^U}{\partial t} < 0 \tag{11-35}$$

Also, from the symmetry of the cross-partials in (11-34)

$$\frac{\partial y^U}{\partial p_i} = \frac{\partial x_i^U}{\partial t} \qquad i = 1, \ldots, k \tag{11-36}$$

in addition to the usual reciprocity conditions $\partial x_i^U/\partial p_j = \partial x_j^U/\partial p_i$.

This important theorem justifies the use of two-dimensional graphical analysis in much of economic theory. It is easy to imagine that in many empirically important cases where a single, outstanding price change takes place in the economy, variations in prices of a group of commodities will not vary significantly within the group. The group can thus be regarded as a single commodity. Since one price will have changed, say, this is equivalent, for relative price changes, to a proportionate change in all prices of goods within the group. Thus, the highly convenient simplification of economic analysis by considering the good in question vs. all other goods is at least consistent with utility theory and perhaps empirically sound in many instances.

Shipping the Good Apples Out

Consider now another type of simultaneous price change, that of adding a fixed amount to several prices. That is, consider the effects of changing a parameter t added to $p_1, \ldots, p_k$, yielding prices $p_1 + t, \ldots, p_k + t, p_{k+1}, \ldots, p_n$. Such a situation might occur if the first k goods are subject to the same tax or transportation charge. In this case, the composite good $z = \sum_{i=1}^{k} x_i$ acts as a single good.

Again, consider the relevant cost-minimization problem:

minimize
$$M = \sum_{i=1}^{k} (p_i + t)x_i + \sum_{i=k+1}^{n} p_i x_i \tag{11-37}$$

subject to
$$U(x_1, \ldots, x_n) = U^0$$

from which the compensated demands

$$x_i = x_i^U(p_1, \ldots, p_n, t, U^0) \tag{11-38}$$

are derived. However, M is linear in the parameter t, and letting M^* denote the expenditure function $M^*(p_1, \ldots, p_n, t, U^0)$, we have

$$\frac{\partial M^*}{\partial t} = \sum_{i=1}^{k} x_i^U \equiv z^U(p_1, \ldots, p_n, t, U^0) \tag{11-39}$$

Hence, z^U exhibits the properties of any other good. The matrix of second partials of M^* with respect to just $p_1, \ldots, p_n$ and t is symmetric and negative semidefinite:

$$\mathbf{M}_{pt}^* = \begin{vmatrix} \dfrac{\partial x_1^U}{\partial p_1} & \cdots & \dfrac{\partial x_1^U}{\partial p_n} & \dfrac{\partial x_1^U}{\partial t} \\ \cdots\cdots\cdots\cdots\cdots\cdots\cdots\cdots \\ \dfrac{\partial x_n^U}{\partial p_1} & \cdots & \dfrac{\partial x_n^U}{\partial p_n} & \dfrac{\partial x_n^U}{\partial t} \\ \dfrac{\partial z^U}{\partial p_1} & \cdots & \dfrac{\partial z^U}{\partial p_n} & \dfrac{\partial z^U}{\partial t} \end{vmatrix} \tag{11-40}$$

From the symmetry of this matrix,

$$\frac{\partial z^U}{\partial p_i} = \frac{\partial x_i^U}{\partial t} \tag{11-41}$$

From the definition of z^U, and the fact that $s_{ij} = s_{ji}$,

$$\frac{\partial x_i^U}{\partial t} = \sum_{j=1}^{k} \frac{\partial x_j^U}{\partial p_i} = \sum_{j=1}^{k} s_{ji} = \sum_{j=1}^{k} s_{ij} \tag{11-42}$$

The own effect of the composite commodity z^U is negative; i.e.,

$$\frac{\partial z^U}{\partial t} < 0 \tag{11-43}$$

This result is also derivable from the original substitution matrix. Letting $s_{ij} = \partial x_i^U / \partial p_j$, as before, with $s_{it} = \partial x_i^U / \partial t$, $s_{ti} = \partial z^U / \partial p_i$, by negative semidefiniteness we have

$$\sum_{i=1}^{n} \sum_{j=1}^{n} s_{ij} h_i h_j \le 0 \tag{11-44}$$

where the equality holds when the h_i's are proportional to the prices. Let h_i, $h_j = 1$, $i = 1, \ldots, k$, and h_i, $h_j = 0$, $i, j = k+1, \ldots, n$. Then (11-44) becomes

$$\sum_{i=1}^{k} \sum_{j=1}^{k} s_{ij} < 0$$

which is equation (11-43), assuming all prices are not the same number (all proportional to unity).

Let us now investigate the empirical effects of this type of price change more closely. Using the composite-commodity theorem, we can consider a three-good world, x_1, x_2, x_3, where x_3 is the composite commodity of the previous section. Suppose goods 1 and 2 are transported from another location, with x_3 produced locally, producing a set of prices $p_1 + t, p_2 + t, p_3$, where p_1 and p_2 are the point of origin prices of x_1 and x_2, respectively.† The transportation charge is apt to produce a predictable change in the mix of goods consumed in the origin vs. the destination of the goods. Consider the following complaint mailed into the "Troubleshooter" column of the *Seattle Times* by an irate consumer:‡

> Why are Washington apples in local markets so small and old-looking? The dried-up stems might seem they were taken out of cold storage from some gathered last year.
>
> Recently, some apple-picking friends brought some apples they had just picked, and they were at least four times the size of those available for sale here.
>
> Where do these big Delicious apples go? Are they shipped to Europe, to the East or can they be bought here in Seattle?
>
> M.W.P.

---

† This situation was first analyzed by A. Alchian and W. Allen in their principles texts, "University Economics," and its condensation, "Exchange and Production," Wadsworth Publishing Company, Inc., Belmont, Calif., 1969.

‡ *Seattle Times*, Sunday, October 19, 1975.

An answer from a trade representative allowed that "itinerant truckers" (price-cutters) were at fault:

> The apples [she] is seeing in her local markets may have been some left from the 1974 crop, or could be lower-grade fruit sold store-to-store by itinerant truckers.

The textbook answer was supplied by this economist several days later:†

Comparing apples to apples

> Regarding M.W.P.'s complaint (Sunday, October 19) that all the good apples were being shipped to the East, you might be interested to know that "shipping the good apples out" has been a favorite classroom and exam question in the economics department at U.W. for many years.
>
> It is a real phenomenon, easily explained:
>
> Suppose, for example, a "good" apple costs 10 cents and a "poor" apple 5 cents locally. Then, since the decision to eat one good apple costs the same as eating two poor apples, we can say that a good apple in essence "costs" two poor apples. Two good apples cost four poor apples.
>
> Suppose now that it costs 5 cents per apple (any apple) to ship apples East. Then, in the East, good apples will cost 15 cents each and poor ones 10 cents each. But now eating two good apples will cost three—not four poor apples.
>
> Though both prices are higher, good apples have become relatively cheaper, and a higher percentage of good apples will be consumed in the East than here.
>
> It is no conspiracy—just the laws of supply and demand.

This appealing line of argument, though possibly empirically correct, was challenged by J. Gould and J. Segall, who pointed out that in a three-good world, interactions with the third good might destroy the effect.‡

The problem with the above textbook answer is that when t changes in a three-good world, more than one relative price change is involved: $p_1 + t$ and $p_2 + t$ both change relative to p_3. The law of demand strictly applies only to situations in which one and only one relative price in the system changes. Yet the argument seems empirically valid in a wide range of circumstances. Cheap French wines, sold in France in cans, are never exported to the United States. Surely there are French consumers irate about the best French wines being shipped out. Restaurants buy most of the U.S. Department of Agriculture prime beef because when the various amenities of restaurants, e.g., waiters and waitresses, cooks, fancy decor, etc., are added to the food costs, the higher-priced item becomes *relatively* cheaper. Houses situated on attractive (and thus expensive) sites will in

---

† *Seattle Times*, Tuesday, October 28, 1975.

‡ John Gould and Joel Segall, The Substitution Effects of Transportation Costs, *Journal of Political Economy*, 1968, pp. 130–137. These authors made an interesting mistake: they cited the case of having to go to Maine to get a truly delectable lobster or having to drive out to the countryside to get truly fresh vegetables as counterexamples of Alchian and Allen's hypothesis. If this occurs because of spoilage en route, this is an irrelevant consideration. More important, it doesn't matter if the lobsters are shipped to you or you are shipped to the lobsters. Going to Maine involves a transportation cost to people not from Maine. We should expect to observe, if Alchian and Allen's hypothesis is correct, that tourists in Maine consume a higher quality of lobster than the natives. The act of going to Maine to eat lobsters in no way contradicts Alchian and Allen's thesis.

general be more attractive houses than average. Let us analyze the situation mathematically.

Alchian and Allen's thesis is that if x_1 is the premium-quality good (higher-priced) and x_2 the inferior quality, then

$$\frac{\partial(x_1^U/x_2^U)}{\partial t} > 0 \tag{11-45}$$

(Superscripts will now be dropped. The student must remember that these are all compensated changes. The introduction of income effects complicates the analysis in predictable ways; viz., income effects are always indeterminate.) Expanding the quotient in (11-45)† gives

$$\frac{\partial(x_1/x_2)}{\partial t} = \left(x_2 \frac{\partial x_1}{\partial t} - x_1 \frac{\partial x_2}{\partial t}\right) \frac{1}{x_2^2}$$

From equation (11-42), $\partial x_1/\partial t = s_{11} + s_{12}$, $\partial x_2/\partial t = s_{21} + s_{22}$. Thus,

$$\frac{\partial(x_1/x_2)}{\partial t} = \frac{x_1}{x_2}\left(\frac{s_{11}}{x_1} + \frac{s_{12}}{x_1} - \frac{s_{21}}{x_2} - \frac{s_{22}}{x_2}\right)$$

Let us convert these terms to elasticities. Letting $\varepsilon_{ij} = (p_j/x_i)(\partial x_i/\partial p_j)$, we have

$$\frac{\partial(x_1/x_2)}{\partial t} = \frac{x_1}{x_2}\left(\frac{\varepsilon_{11}}{p_1} + \frac{\varepsilon_{12}}{p_2} - \frac{\varepsilon_{21}}{p_1} - \frac{\varepsilon_{22}}{p_2}\right)$$

However, from the homogeneity of the compensated demand, $\sum_{j=1}^{n} p_j s_{ij} = 0$ and hence by dividing by x_i yields

$$\varepsilon_{11} + \varepsilon_{12} + \varepsilon_{13} = 0 \qquad \text{and} \qquad \varepsilon_{21} + \varepsilon_{22} + \varepsilon_{23} = 0$$

for this three-good model. Using these expressions to substitute for ε_{12} and ε_{21} in the above equation, we have

$$\frac{\partial(x_1/x_2)}{\partial t} = \frac{x_1}{x_2}\left[\frac{\varepsilon_{11}}{p_1} + \left(-\frac{\varepsilon_{11}}{p_2} - \frac{\varepsilon_{13}}{p_2}\right) - \frac{\varepsilon_{21}}{p_1} - \left(-\frac{\varepsilon_{21}}{p_2} - \frac{\varepsilon_{23}}{p_2}\right)\right]$$

or

$$\frac{\partial(x_1/x_2)}{\partial t} = \frac{x_1}{x_2}\left[(\varepsilon_{11} - \varepsilon_{21})\left(\frac{1}{p_1} - \frac{1}{p_2}\right) + (\varepsilon_{23} - \varepsilon_{13})\left(\frac{1}{p_2}\right)\right] \tag{11-46}$$

Let us examine equation (11-46). Since x_1 is the higher-quality good, $p_1 > p_2$, and thus $1/p_1 - 1/p_2 < 0$. Also, $\varepsilon_{11} < 0$ and $\varepsilon_{21} > 0$ since two qualities of the same good are presumably substitutes. Alchian and Allen's thesis is that $\partial(x_1/x_2)/\partial t > 0$; the first compound term in (11-46) confirms this. In a two-good world, this would be the entire expression, and then Alchian and Allen would be entirely correct. The last term, $\varepsilon_{23} - \varepsilon_{13}$, however, is indeterminate. If, however, we assume that the lower- and higher-quality good interact in the same manner with the composite good x_3, that is, that $\varepsilon_{13} = \varepsilon_{23}$, then the hypothesis will be valid. The hypothesis

---

† The author is indebted to Thomas Borcherding for demonstrating this algebra.

becomes invalid only in the asymmetrical case, where, say, the premium good is a much closer substitute for the third good than the inferior good ($\varepsilon_{13} > \varepsilon_{23}$). Then when p_1 and p_2 are both raised, say, to $p_1 + t$ and $p_2 + t$, respectively, the consumer substitutes x_3 for x_1 in greater proportion than x_2 for x_1, confounding the hypothesis. This asymmetry seems to be empirically insignificant to this casual observer.

A similar result can be derived for the *difference*, as opposed to the ratio of consumption of x_1 to x_2, when t changes. Letting $p_1 = p_2 + k$, $k > 0$, from homogeneity we get

$$(p_2 + k)s_{11} + p_2 s_{12} + p_3 s_{13} = 0$$

$$(p_2 + k)s_{21} + p_2 s_{22} + p_3 s_{23} = 0$$

Since $\partial x_1/\partial t = s_{1t} = s_{11} + s_{12}$ and $\partial x_2/\partial t = s_{2t} = s_{21} + s_{22}$,

$$p_2 s_{1t} + k s_{11} + p_3 s_{13} = 0$$

$$p_2 s_{2t} + k s_{21} + p_3 s_{23} = 0$$

Subtracting gives

$$p_2(s_{1t} - s_{2t}) = -k(s_{11} - s_{21}) + p_3(s_{23} - s_{13}) \tag{11-47}$$

Assuming that the lower- and higher-quality goods are substitutes for each other (otherwise the whole exercise is meaningless), $s_{21} > 0$. Thus the first term on the right side of (11-47), $-k(s_{11} - s_{21})$, is positive. This tends to confirm the idea that an increase in transport cost will raise the absolute level of consumption of the premium good relative to the lower-quality good. The validity of the inference in a three-good model boils down to the term $(s_{23} - s_{13})$, a term similar to that appearing in equation (11-46), dealing with the ratio x_1/x_2. If these interactions with the third good are similar, then the higher-quality good will be shipped to distant places in greater amounts than the lower-quality good.

It should be noted that a higher-quality good and lower quality of the *same good* should be fairly close substitutes. Therefore, as an empirical matter one should expect relatively high absolute values of s_{11}, s_{12}, and s_{22}, or the corresponding elasticities. This will make the first term in equations (11-46) and (11-47) relatively large. And if these goods are not closely related to the composite commodity, s_{13} and s_{23} should be fairly small, even if not approximately equal. Hence, as an empirical matter, the Alchian and Allen hypothesis that the higher-quality good will tend to increase relative to the lower-quality good when like transport (or other) costs are added to each item might be expected to be true for most commodities.

In general, simultaneous price changes of the form $p_i = p_i^0 + p_i(t)$, $i = 1, \ldots, k$, $k \le n$, with $p_i(0) = 0$ can be defined. These changes will in general not produce interesting comparative-statics theorems. The resulting composite commodities will be complicated expressions involving the derivatives of $p_i(t)$. The empirical usefulness of such constructions is likely to be small.

11.4 CONSUMER'S SURPLUS

One of the most vexing problems in the theory of exchange is the measurement, in units of money income, of the gains from trade. Consider Fig. 11-5, in which the consumer is initially at point $\mathbf{x}^0 = (x_1^0, x_2^0)$ on indifference curve U^0, having faced prices of p_1^0, p_2^0 and money income M^0. Suppose that p_1 is now lowered to p_1^1, the consumer moving to point $\mathbf{x}^1 = (x_1^1, x_2^1)$ on indifference curve U^1. How much better off is the consumer at $\mathbf{x}^1$ compared with being back at $\mathbf{x}^0$? One answer might be to ask how much income can be taken away from the consumer and still leave him or her no worse off than before, at point $\mathbf{x}^0$. This represents a parallel shift of the budget line from $\mathbf{x}^1$ to a point $\mathbf{x}^a$ on the original indifference curve U^0. This amount of income is the maximum amount the consumer would be willing to pay for the right to face the lower price of x_1; it is called a *compensating variation*. Call this amount M^{1a}. Now consider another answer: How much income must this consumer be given at the original prices to be as well off as with the lowered price of x_1? This amount, call it M^{0b}, is the amount of income needed to shift the budget line parallel to itself from point $\mathbf{x}^0$ to a point $\mathbf{x}^b$ on U^1, since the consumer

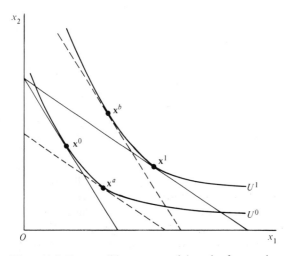

Figure 11-5 Two possible measures of the gains from exchange. Suppose the consumer is initially at point $\mathbf{x}^0$, at prices $\mathbf{p}^0 = (p_1^0, p_2^0)$. If p_1 is lowered to p_1^1, the consumer moves to point $\mathbf{x}^1$. The maximum amount this consumer would pay for the *right* to face this lower price is the amount of income M^{1a} that would shift the budget plane from $\mathbf{x}^1$ back to $\mathbf{x}^a$, which is on the original indifference surface U^0. This amount is known as the *compensating variation for a fall in price*. In that case, the consumer would be indifferent between consuming the original bundle $\mathbf{x}^0$ and facing the lower price but consuming bundle $\mathbf{x}^a$. Similarly, if the consumer already has the right, i.e., sufficient income, to consume $\mathbf{x}^1$, raising p_1 from p_1^1 to p_1^0 would move the consumer back to $\mathbf{x}^0$. The consumer will have to be paid at least the amount of income M^{1b} needed to shift the budget plane from $\mathbf{x}^0$ to $\mathbf{x}^b$ on U^1 in order to face the higher price of x_1 voluntarily. For then, the consumer will be no worse off than at $\mathbf{x}^1$. This amount of income is known as the *compensating variation to a rise in price*. These two measures of the gain in going from $\mathbf{x}^0$ to $\mathbf{x}^1$ will not in general be equal. If x_1 is a normal good, then $M^{1a} < M^{0b}$ (why?).

is indifferent between $\mathbf{x}^b$ and $\mathbf{x}^1$. This amount, M^{0b}, is the amount the consumer would have to be bribed to accept the higher price p_1^0 of x_1, voluntarily instead of the lower price. These are two plausible measures of the gains from going to $\mathbf{x}^1$ from $\mathbf{x}^0$. The problem arises because these two measures, M^{1a} and M^{0b} (and others that could be considered) are not in general equal. The consumer might be willing to pay \$10 to face a lower price of some good; having achieved that point, however, the consumer might be unwilling to relinquish it for the original situation for any payment less than \$15. Having achieved a higher indifference level (an increase in real income), if the good is not inferior, the consumer will value it more; hence, more will have to be paid to make the consumer give up the good than to get more units starting at the lower real income. (The reverse is true for inferior goods.) What to do?

Suppose the consumer faces prices $\mathbf{p}^0 = (\$1, \$1)$ initially with an income of, say, \$100. Consider the following series of questions. We could ask this consumer the maximum amount she (for verbal convenience) would be willing to pay to have p_1 lowered a penny, to \$.99. Let's say the amount offered is \$.10. (We should expect the consumer to be consuming 10 units of x_1. Why?) The \$.10 is not to be collected, however. If it were, the consumer by definition would remain on the same indifference level; i.e., she would move along a *compensated* demand curve. Since we would like to measure gains from moving to a higher indifference level, the \$.10 is not collected but merely noted. Now suppose the consumer is now asked, facing a price of \$.99 for x_1, how much she is willing to pay to face the price \$.98 for x_1. Suppose she says \$.11. Again, the amount is noted but not collected. Suppose this is continued, penny by penny, until $p_1 = .75$, $p_2 = 1.00$, $M = \$100$ (since no amounts have been collected). Some total amount, say \$2.53, will have been recorded as the maximum amounts this consumer would have been willing to pay for the lowered price of x_1. Is this the gain from this movement along the money-income-held-constant demand curve for x_1? Let us examine this situation geometrically. Consider Fig. 11-6, and suppose at price p_1^0 the consumer buys none of x_1. The price p_1^0 is her *reservation price*. How much will she pay to consume some given amount of x_1? Since the height of the demand curve represents the subjective price of x_1, that is, the trade-offs she is willing to make to acquire additional units, if the *maximum* is extracted for that first unit, she will move down her compensated (utility-held-constant) demand curve. The maximum she will pay for $x_1^U(p_1^1)$ is the trapezoidal area $Oace$, where $Oa = p_1^0$, $Oe = bc = x_1^U(p_1^1)$. However, since when Oe units are purchased at $p_1 = p_1^1$, she will pay out the rectangle $Obce$, the amount she will pay for the *right* to consume Oe at price p_1^1 is the triangular amount abc. In our construction, this amount is not to be collected, or else the consumer will continue to move down the compensated demand curve through point a, $x_1^U(p_1, p_2^0, U^0)$. If the consumer faces price p_1^1 and has kept all her original money income, she will consume a larger amount of x_1, if x_1 is a normal good, $x_1^M(p_1^1, p_2^0, M^0) = bd$. Suppose the consumer is now consuming bd units at price p_1^1 and p_1 is lowered to p_1^2. Then she would be willing to pay up to the trapezoidal area $bdgf$ for the *right* to consume x_1 at this new lower price. The curved section dg is part of a compensated demand curve starting at point d,

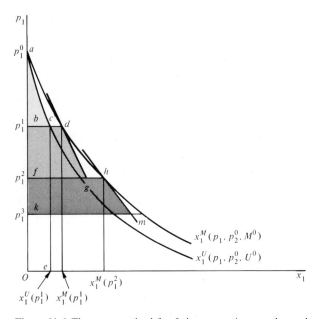

Figure 11-6 The area to the left of the money-income demand curve defined as the limit of a sum of compensating variations in income. Starting at price p_1^0, the consumer buys no x_1. If p_1 is lowered to p_1^1, the consumer will be willing to pay $Oace$ for $Oe = x_1^U(p_1^1, p_2^0, U^0)$ of x_1. At each point along a demand curve, the price (or height of the curve) is the marginal evaluation of that good in terms of all other goods, expressible in units of income. If the consumer actually pays that amount for each unit, she will move down along the compensated demand curve; for the amount paid out is that amount which leaves the consumer indifferent between the new and old points. After subtracting the rectangle $p_i q_i$ of expenditures actually paid when the goods are all offered at some price, the triangle abc represents the amount the consumer would pay to have the *right* to purchase Oe units at price Ob. If $p_1 = p_1^1 = Ob$ and the consumer keeps all her original income, Od will be purchased, given by the money-income-held-constant demand curve. The amount she will then pay for a further price decrease is the shaded trapezoidal area $bdgf$, where gf is a new compensated demand curve through point d. This process is continued until the final price is reached. If the price changes are all small, these shaded areas approach the area to the left of the money-income demand curve.

where the consumer now starts from. If this amount is not in fact collected, the consumer continues to move down her *money*-income demand curve to point h. Likewise, the maximum amount the consumer would pay for a further price decrease if no previous amounts had been collected is the trapezoidal area $fhmk$, where hm is along a compensated demand curve through h.

If these price changes are made very small, the shaded areas approach the area to the left of the money-income-held-constant demand curve. Thus, this famous triangle can be regarded as the limit of a sum of compensating variations in income for a fall in price. This area, ABC in Fig. 11-7, is $-\int x_1 \, dp_1$. (The negative sign appears because p_1 is being *lowered*.) Note that $ABC = OACD - OBCD$, or

$$-\int x_1^M \, dp_1 = \int p_1 \, dx_1 - p_1 x_1 \Big|_{p^0}^{p^1} \qquad (11\text{-}48)$$

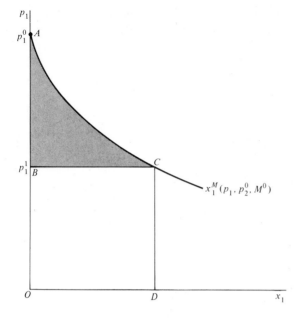

Figure 11-7 The marshallian triangle. The area to the left of the money-income-held-constant demand curve can be regarded as one particular series of compensating variations in income in response to a fall in price from OA to OB. However, other paths of price changes leading to the same fall in price will have other amounts of income gains associated with them. The above triangle ABC therefore cannot be regarded as *the* income gain from a fall in price. The triangle $ABC = -\int x_1 \, dp_1$.
Since $ABC = OACD - OBCD$,
$$-\int x_1 \, dp_1 = \int p_1 \, dx_1 - p_1 x_1$$
with appropriate endpoint limits.

where the appropriate endpoint limits are to be applied. The integral $p_1 \, dx_1$ gives the area *under* the demand curve; subtracting $p_1 x_1 \big|_{p_1^0}^{p_1^1} = p_1^1 x_1^1 - p_1^0 x_1^0$, the change in total expenditures on x_1, leaves the triangle $-\int x_1^M \, dp_1$, the area to the *left* of the demand curve above the market price.

Is this the answer to our puzzle, the money-income value of a price change? Unfortunately, the answer is no. Let's say this area ABC on Fig. 11-7 represents the $2.53 figure mentioned previously as the sum of the amounts the consumer would pay but not have collected to face successively lower prices of p_1 from the situation $(\mathbf{p}^0, M^0) = (\$1, \$1, \$100)$ to $(\mathbf{p}^1, M^0) = (\$.75, \$1, \$100)$. Consider an alternative series of questions: How much would the consumer be willing to pay to face in turn the prices $(.99, 1)$, $(.98, .99)$, $(.97, .98)$, $(.96, .99)$, $(.95, 1)$, ..., some other path of prices, *but ending with the same* terminal price vector $(.75, 1)$ with income 100? *The answer is in general different from before*, say $2.17. The answer is different even though the initial and final price vectors are identical. Thus, the area to the left of the ordinary (money-income) demand curve cannot be regarded as the money equivalent of the fall in price of x_1; other series of compensating variations yield different evaluations. What is the reason for all this strange business?

The simple truth is that there is no unique dollar or money-income equivalent of a change in utility. There is nothing to do about it. Let us investigate the mathematical structure of the problem more closely. For one price change, the integral $-\int x_i^M \, dp_i$ represents the limit of the sum of the compensating variations for a change in p_i, in units of income. If more than one price changed, the appropriate expression would be

$$W = -\sum \int x_i^M \, dp_i = -\int \sum x_i^M \, dp_i \qquad (11\text{-}49)$$

where $x_i = x_i^M(p_1, \ldots, p_n, M)$, the money-income demand curves for an n-good model. Equation (11-49) is a complicated integral, called a *line integral*. It is not enough to specify the terminal prices (income is to be held constant throughout here) in evaluating (11-49). The actual *path* of prices must also be specified.

Example Consider the utility function $U = x_2 + \log x_1$. The associated demand curves are $x_1 = p_2/p_1$, $x_2 = (M/p_2) - 1$ (for $p_2 < M$). Then the integral W is

$$W = -\int \frac{p_2}{p_1} \, dp_1 - \int \left(\frac{M}{p_2} - 1 \right) dp_2$$

In the first integral, p_2 is treated as a constant; in the second integral p_1 is treated as a constant. Let us evaluate these integrals between the points $\mathbf{p}^0 = (2, 2)$ and $\mathbf{p}^1 = (1, 1)$, as depicted in Fig. 11-8, with $M = 4$. Then at $\mathbf{p}^0$, $\mathbf{x}^0 = (1, 1)$, and at $\mathbf{p}^1$, $\mathbf{x}^1 = (1, 3)$. Let us arrive at $\mathbf{p}^1$ through two different paths.

Path 1. Lower p_1 to 1; then lower p_2 to 1. This is the path through point $\mathbf{p}^a$, denoted C_1.

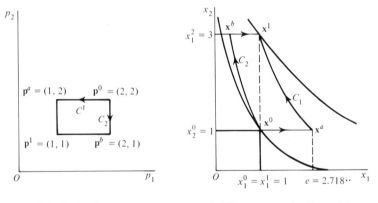

Path of price changes

Indifference curves for $U = x_2 + \log x_1$ and path of quantity changes

Figure 11-8 (*a*) Path of price changes. Two paths, C_1 and C_2, are given for changing prices from $\mathbf{p}^0 = (2, 2)$ to $\mathbf{p}^1 = (1, 1)$. For C_1, first p_1 is lowered from 2 to 1 (point $\mathbf{p}^a$), and then p_2 is lowered to 1 also. (*b*) Indifference curves for $U = x_2 + \log x_1$ and path of quantity changes. The corresponding demands are presented. When $\mathbf{p} = \mathbf{p}^0$, $M = 4$, $x_1^0 = 1$, $x_2^0 = 1$. When prices are at $\mathbf{p}^a = (1, 2)$, $x_1 = 2$, $x_2 = 1$ [point $\mathbf{x}^a$ in (*b*)]. Then quantities move from $\mathbf{x}^a$ to $\mathbf{x}^1$ as prices move from $\mathbf{p}^a$ to $\mathbf{p}^1$. Similarly, along curve C_2, through $\mathbf{p}^2 = (2, 1)$, the quantities move through point $\mathbf{x}^b = (\frac{1}{2}, 3)$ in (*b*). The total imputed gains to the price change are different along each path.

Path 2. Lower p_2 to 1; then lower p_1 to 1. This is the path through point $\mathbf{p}^b$, denoted C_2.

These two paths and the corresponding quantity levels are depicted in Fig. 11-8a and b. For path 1, when p_2 is held constant, that is, $dp_2 = 0$ (along the first leg of C_1), the second integral is 0. Along the second leg of C_1, the first integral is 0, since $dp_1 = 0$. Thus

$$W_{C_1} = -\int_{p_1=2}^{p_1=1} \frac{2}{p_1} \, dp_1 - \int_{p_2=2}^{p_2=1} \left(\frac{4}{p_2} - 1\right) dp_2$$

$$= -2(\log 1 - \log 2) - 4(\log 1 - \log 2) + (1 - 2)$$

$$= 6 \log 2 - 1 = (\log 2^6) - 1 = (\log 64) - 1$$

Along path C_2, first p_1 is held constant (hence, the first integral is 0, then p_2 is held constant at $p_2 = 1$ (hence the other integral is 0). Thus,

$$W_{C_2} = -\int_{p_2=2}^{p_2=1} \left(\frac{4}{p_2} - 1\right) dp_2 - \int_{p_1=2}^{p_1=1} \frac{1}{p_1} \, dp_1$$

$$= +[4(\log 2) - 1] + \log 2 = \log 2^5 - 1 = (\log 32) - 1$$

Thus we see that $W_{C_2} \neq W_{C_1}$. The sum of the amounts the consumer would be willing to pay to face these lower prices, in successive small increments, is not a unique number. It depends on the path of price changes. Again, there is nothing to do about it.

Let us return to the integral (11-49). Consider the utility-maximization model: maximize $U(x_1, \ldots, x_n)$ subject to $\sum p_i x_i = M$, from which the money-income demand curves are derived. The lagrangian, again, is $\mathcal{L} = U(x_1, \ldots, x_n) + \lambda^M(M - \sum p_i x_i)$. The indirect utility function is $U(x_1^M, \ldots, x_n^M) = U^*(p_1, \ldots, p_n, M)$. The total differential of the indirect utility function is

$$dU^* = \sum \left(\frac{\partial U^*}{\partial p_i}\right) dp_i + \frac{\partial U^*}{\partial M} \, dM$$

However, by the envelope theorem, $\partial U^*/\partial p_i = \partial \mathcal{L}/\partial p_i = -\lambda^M x_i^M$; $\partial U^*/\partial M = \lambda^M$. Hence,

$$dU^* = -\lambda^M \sum x_i^M \, dp_i + \lambda^M \, dM$$

Dividing by λ^M and rearranging terms gives

$$-\sum x_i^M \, dp_i = \frac{1}{\lambda^M} dU^* - dM \tag{11-50}$$

Integrating both sides of (11-50) between the price-income vectors $(\mathbf{p}^0, M^0)$ and $(\mathbf{p}^1, M^1)$ *along some specified path* C, we have

$$-\int_C \sum x_i^M \, dp_i = \int_C \frac{1}{\lambda^M} dU^* - (M^1 - M^0) \tag{11-51}$$

What is the meaning of the integral $\int_C (1/\lambda^M) \, dU^*$? The Lagrange multiplier λ^M is the marginal utility of money income. Its reciprocal is the marginal cost of utility, the Lagrange multiplier λ^U derived in the cost-minimization model. Then $1/\lambda^M$ *can be regarded as an imputed rent, or shadow price, of acquiring additional utility.* The integral (11-51) is the sum of these subjective evaluations of utility at the margin and hence represents the total value, in units of income ($x_i \, dp_i$ has the units of income, e.g., dollars) of the change in utility due to a change in prices and money income, along a specified path of price changes. If only prices change, as in Fig. 11-7,

$$W_C = -\int \sum x_i^M \, dp_i = \int \frac{1}{\lambda^M} \, dU^*$$

since $M^0 = M^1$.

The integral $\int (1/\lambda^M) \, dU^*$ is in fact the area under all the demand curves. This area is $\int \sum p_i \, dx_i$. However, from the first-order conditions for the utility-maximization problem, $p_i = U_i/\lambda^M$, $i = 1, \ldots, n$. Thus

$$\int \sum p_i \, dx_i = \int \frac{1}{\lambda^M} \sum U_i \, dx_i = \int \frac{1}{\lambda^M} \, dU^*$$

The path dependence of $W_C = -\int \sum x_i^M \, dp_i$ can be visualized by noting that if, say, p_i changes, the demand curves for the other commodities begin to shift at the rate $\partial x_j^M/\partial p_i$, $j \neq i$. If, however, some other price p_j changes, the demand for commodity i changes at the rate $\partial x_i^M/\partial p_j$. Since these rates are not in general equal, how p_i and p_j are changed, e.g., first p_i, then p_j, or vice versa, will affect the areas to the left of the demand curves, $-\int x_i^M \, dp_i$, and hence the value of the sum of these areas, $-\int \sum x_i^M \, dp_i$. It turns out, in fact, that the condition $\partial x_i^M/\partial p_j = \partial x_j^M/\partial p_i$ is precisely the condition under which this integral is independent of the path, i.e., dependent solely on the terminal price vectors.

This integrability condition appeared earlier in the section on revealed preference and integrability. If some function $W(p_1, \ldots, p_n)$ exists such that $W_{p_i} = \partial W/\partial p_i = -x_i^M(p_1, \ldots, p_n, M)$, then since $W_{p_i p_j} = W_{p_j p_i}$, it follows that $\partial x_i^M/\partial p_j = \partial x_j^M/\partial p_i$. And the reverse is true also. If $\partial x_j^M/\partial p_j = \partial x_j^M/\partial p_i$, the integral W_C is independent of the path; for then

$$W_C = -\int \sum x_i^M \, dp_i = W(p^1, M) - W(p^0, M)$$

the difference between two values of the integral function $W(p_1, \ldots, p_n, M)$. The path will not matter.

Example Consider the demand functions $x_1 = M/2p_1$, $x_2 = M/2p_2$, derived from the utility function $U = x_1 x_2$ (or any monotonic transformation thereof). Note that $\partial x_1^M/\partial p_2 = 0 = \partial x_2^M/\partial p_1$.

$$W_C = -\int_{p_1^0}^{p_1^1} \frac{M}{2p_1} \, dp_1 - \int_{p_2^0}^{p_2^1} \frac{M}{2p_2} \, dp_2$$

$$= -\frac{M}{2}(\log p_1^1 - \log p_1^0) - \frac{M}{2}(\log p_2^1 - \log p_2^0)$$

Here, W_C is dependent solely on the terminal price vectors $\mathbf{p}^0$ and $\mathbf{p}^1$, since each integral is an ordinary definite integral. The fact that $\partial x_1^M/\partial p_2 = 0$ $(= \partial x_2^M/\partial p_1)$ simplified the calculations, but the results hold because $\partial x_1^M/\partial p_2 = \partial x_2^M/\partial p_1$. And this latter condition holds only because $\partial W/\partial p_1 = M/2p_1$, $\partial W/\partial p_2 = M/2p_2$; that is, the money income demands are the first partials of some integral function.

Let us investigate the situations under which the integral W_C is independent of the path of price changes. Suppose that when the prices change, money income also changes so as to hold the utility level constant. Then the x_i's will in fact be the *compensated* demands $x_i^U(p_1, \ldots, p_n, U^0)$. Then from equation (11-51)

$$-\int \sum x_i^U \, dp_i = \int \lambda^U \, dU^* - (M^1 - M^0) \tag{11-52}$$

Since utility is being held constant, $dU^* = 0$; hence

$$-\int \sum x_i^U \, dp_i = M^0 - M^1 \tag{11-53}$$

As indicated, this integral must be path-independent since it depends only on the initial and final money-income levels. This independence of path occurs because of the symmetry of the Slutsky terms, $\partial x_i^U/\partial p_j = \partial x_j^U/\partial p_i$, which is the mathematical condition for such independence of path.

Equation (11-52) can be derived in the following manner. The compensated-demand curves $x_i^U(p_1, \ldots, p_n, U^0)$ are derived from the cost-minimization problem: minimize $M = \sum p_i x_i$ subject to $U(x_1, \ldots, x_n) = U^0$. The lagrangian is $\mathscr{L} = \sum p_i x_i + \lambda^U(U^0 - U(x_1, \ldots, x_n))$. The expenditure function is $M = \sum p_i x_i^U = M^*(p_1, \ldots, p_n, U^0)$. Taking the total differential of M^* leads to

$$dM^* = \sum \frac{\partial M^*}{\partial p_i} \, dp_i + \frac{\partial M^*}{\partial U^0} \, dU^0$$

However, using the envelope theorem gives $\partial M^*/\partial p_i = x_i^U$, $i = 1, \ldots, n$, and $\partial M^*/\partial U^0 = \lambda^U$. Thus

$$dM^* = \sum x_i^U \, dp_i + \lambda^U \, dU^0$$

Integrating both sides thus yields, after rearrangement of terms,

$$-\int_{p^0}^{p^1} \sum x_i^U \, dp_i = \int_{U^0}^{U^1} \lambda^U \, dU - (M^1 - M^0) \tag{11-54}$$

Since $\lambda^U = 1/\lambda^M$, this is equation (11-52), that is, equation (11-50) for compensated demand curves. But these integrals are all path-independent, since $\partial x_i^U/\partial p_j = \partial x_j^U/\partial p_i$ and $\partial \lambda^U/\partial p_i = \partial x_i^U/\partial U^0$, all these partials being the second partials of the integral function $M^*(p_1, \ldots, p_n, U^0)$.

If only one price changes, say p_1, then

$$-\int x_1^U \, dp_1 = M^0 - M^1 \tag{11-55}$$

This equation says that the area to the left of the compensated-demand curve between two prices (say $p_1^1 < p_1^0$; that is, p_1 has been lowered) equals the amount of money income that can be taken from the consumer leaving him or her on the same indifference level. This is the *compensating variation* for a fall in price discussed earlier. It is the maximum amount that a consumer will pay for the *right* to purchase x_1 at the lower price p_1^1 instead of p_1^0.

Thus the areas to the left of the *compensated*-demand curves have the unambiguous interpretation of amounts of money-income, e.g., dollars, that can be extracted from consumers for the right to face a lower price or the bribe necessary to get the consumer to accept a higher price voluntarily. These numbers are unambiguous because the line integral (11-53) generating them is always independent of the path of price changes. The money equivalents of a change *in utility* due to a price change, however, will not in general be well defined. For any given increase, say, in utility due to the lowering of some price or prices, different money evaluations of that gain will be forthcoming, for different arrangements of price changes, even though the terminal price-income vectors are the same in each case. Sad, but true.

There is one important case where the money equivalents of utility changes are well defined, i.e., path-independent. As indicated earlier, this occurs when $\partial x_i^M/\partial p_j = \partial x_j^M/\partial p_i$. What types of demand curves does this represent? From the Slutsky equation, by this hypothesis,

$$\frac{\partial x_i^M}{\partial p_j} = \frac{\partial x_i^U}{\partial p_j} - x_j \frac{\partial x_i^M}{\partial M} = \frac{\partial x_j^U}{\partial p_i} - x_i \frac{\partial x_j^M}{\partial M} = \frac{\partial x_j^M}{\partial p_i}$$

However, $\partial x_i^U/\partial p_j = \partial x_j^U/\partial p_i$ always. Hence,

$$x_j \frac{\partial x_i^M}{\partial M} = x_i \frac{\partial x_j^M}{\partial M} \qquad i, j = 1, \ldots, n \tag{11-56}$$

When we multiply through by $M/x_i x_j$, this says that the income elasticities must all be equal:

$$\varepsilon_{iM} = \frac{M}{x_i} \frac{\partial x_i^M}{\partial M} = \frac{M}{x_j} \frac{\partial x_j^M}{\partial M} = \varepsilon_{jM} \qquad i, j = 1, \ldots, n \tag{11-57}$$

Since the weighted sum of the income elasticities equals unity, that is, $\Sigma \kappa_i \varepsilon_{iM} = 1$, where $\kappa_i = p_i x_i/M$, if all the income elasticities are equal, they are all equal to 1, $\varepsilon_{iM} = 1$, $i = 1, \ldots, n$. Unitary income elasticities are the demand curves derived from homothetic indifference maps, i.e., indifference curves for which the income-consumption paths are straight lines out of the origin. For them, the ratio of goods consumed, x_i/x_j, is independent of the income level. Thus,

$$\frac{\partial(x_i^M/x_j^M)}{\partial M} = 0$$

Using the quotient rule, we get

$$\left(x_j^M \frac{\partial x_i^M}{\partial M} - x_i^M \frac{\partial x_j^M}{\partial M} \right) \left(\frac{1}{x_j^M} \right)^2 = 0$$

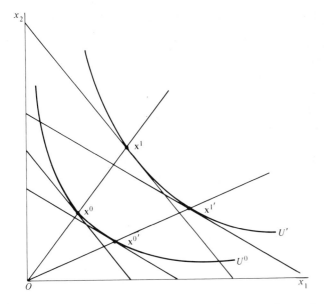

Figure 11-9 Homethic indifferences map. A given proportionate change in money income will lead to the same gain in utility no matter what point on U^0 the consumer starts at. Hence, for these indifference curves, the marginal utility of money income is independent of relative prices.

from which equation (11-56) and unitary income elasticities follow. The converse is clearly true also; i.e., income elasticities equal to 1 imply homotheticity of $U(x_1, \ldots, x_n)$, as these steps are easily reversed.

Why the money equivalents are unique in the homothetic case can be seen geometrically. Figure 11-9 shows a homothetic indifference map. Suppose the consumer is at point $\mathbf{x}^0$ on U^0. Suppose income is doubled, prices held constant, or all prices halved. Then the consumer will achieve point $\mathbf{x}^1$ on indifference level U^1, consuming twice the previous level of x_1 and x_2. Now suppose the consumer had started at point $\mathbf{x}^{0'}$ on U^0. If income is now doubled (or prices halved), the consumer will achieve a consumption point on the same new indifference level U^1 as before, at some point $\mathbf{x}^{1'}$ at twice his original consumption of x_1 and x_2. This occurs for homothetic functions, the level surfaces (indifference curves, here) are all radial blowups of each other. Wherever the consumer starts, a given utility increase is equivalent to the same proportionate gain in money income.

Since the monetary equivalent of the utility increase is independent of which point on an indifference curve the consumer starts at, this suggests that the marginal utility of money income λ^M should be independent of *relative* prices for these utility functions. Indeed, this is the case. Any homothetic utility function can be written as $U = F(y)$, where $y = h(x_1, \ldots, x_n)$ is a homogeneous function of degree 1 and $F'(y) > 0$. Since $F' > 0$, one can also write $y = F^{-1}(U) = G(U)$, with

$G'(U) = dy/dU = 1/F'(y) = 1/(dU/dy)$. From the first-order conditions for utility maximization we get

$$\lambda^M = \frac{1}{M} \sum U_i x_i = \frac{1}{M} \sum F'(y) h_i x_i$$

But $\sum h_i x_i \equiv h(x_1, \ldots, x_n) = y$. Thus

$$\lambda^M = \frac{1}{M} F'(y) y = \frac{1}{M} \frac{1}{G'(U)} F^{-1}(U) \qquad \text{or} \qquad \lambda^M = J(M, U)$$

Thus, for homothetic indifference maps, the marginal utility of money income depends only on income and the utility level, irrespective of which bundle is being consumed. Thus, the relative prices being faced don't matter.

The converse is also true; i.e., if λ^M is independent of relative prices, the utility function must be homothetic. This can all be seen in another manner. From the utility function for the utility-maximization problem, $\partial U^*/\partial p_i = -\lambda^M x_i^M$. Hence, $\partial(\lambda^M x_i^M)/\partial p_j = \partial(\lambda^M x_j^M)/\partial p_i$, or, using the product rule,

$$\lambda^M \frac{\partial x_i^M}{\partial p_j} + x_i^M \frac{\partial \lambda^M}{\partial p_j} = \lambda^M \frac{\partial x_j^M}{\partial p_i} + x_j^M \frac{\partial \lambda^M}{\partial p_i} \tag{11-58}$$

Now, $\lambda^M(p_1, \ldots, p_n, M)$ is homogeneous of degree -1. (Since $\lambda^M = U^i/p_i$, if all prices and money income are multiplied by the same scalar t, the numerator remains constant but the denominator changes to $t p_i$.) Thus, $\lambda^M(t\mathbf{p}, tM) = t^{-1} U_i/p_i$. Hence, by definition, $\lambda^M(t p_1, \ldots, t p_n, tM) \equiv (1/t)\lambda^M(p_1, \ldots, p_n, M)$. Let $t = 1/M$. Then

$$\lambda^M\left(\frac{p_1}{M}, \ldots, \frac{p_n}{M}, 1\right) \equiv M\lambda^M(p_1, \ldots, p_n, M)$$

Thus
$$\frac{\partial \lambda^M}{\partial(p_i/M)} = M \frac{\partial \lambda^M}{\partial p_i} \qquad i = 1, \ldots, n \tag{11-59}$$

If λ^M is independent of relative prices, $\partial \lambda^M/\partial(p_i/M) = 0$, and thus $\partial \lambda^M/\partial p_i = 0$. But then equation (11-58) reduces to

$$\lambda^M \frac{\partial x_i^M}{\partial p_j} = \lambda^M \frac{\partial x_j^M}{\partial p_i}$$

which, after canceling the λ^M's, implies homotheticity as before.

We can see how this relates to the integral $-\int \sum x_i^M \, dp_i$. If λ^M is a function of the utility level only (ignoring M, which is being held constant), then $\int (1/\lambda^M) \, dU$ is an ordinary integral of one variable only, U, and is hence a function of only the terminal utility levels, given by the bounds of integration. This is the relevance of the constancy of the marginal utility of money income.

A source of confusion on these matters is that the phrase "constant marginal utility of *money*" is also used to denote the situation where one good, plotted on the vertical axis and denoted as the composite good money, exhibits constant marginal utility. This is saying something entirely different from the above. In this case, for two goods, x_1, x_2, with a utility function $U(x_1, x_2)$, $U_2 = $ constant. Hence, $U_{21} = U_{12} = U_{22} = 0$. It quickly follows that the indifference curves are vertically parallel; i.e., the slope does not change as one moves vertically through the indifference map. Mathematically, $\partial(U_1/U_2)/\partial x_2 = 0$, since U_1/U_2 is the (negative) slope of the indifference curves. But

$$\frac{\partial(U_1/U_2)}{\partial x_2} = (U_2 U_{12} - U_1 U_{22})\frac{1}{U_2^2} = 0$$

by the above conditions. The converse is *not* true. A monotonic transformation of the utility function leaves the indifference map unchanged but will in general change the size and sign of the second partials. The utility function used before in an example, $U = x_2 + \log x_1$, exhibits $U_{22} = U_{21} = U_{12} = 0$. However, for $V = F(U) = e^U = x_1 e^{x_2}$, $V_{22}, V_{21}, V_{12} \neq 0$.

The importance of vertically parallel indifference curves is that the income effects on x_1 (plotted horizontally) are 0. (See Chap. 8, problem 18.) Then, from the Slutsky equation,

$$\frac{\partial x_1^M}{\partial p_j} = \frac{\partial x_1^U}{\partial p_j} - x_j \frac{\partial x_1^M}{\partial M} = \frac{\partial x_1^U}{\partial p_j}, \qquad j = 1, \ldots, n \qquad (11\text{-}60)$$

This means that for the appropriate money income and utility levels, the compensated and uncompensated demand curve for x_1 are coincident (since there is no income effect on x_1). In this case, the area to the left of the money-income (uncompensated) demand curve can be regarded the same way (since it is identical to it) as the area to the left of the compensated demand curve, or the amount the consumer is willing to pay to face a lower price of x_1. This is the basis of the discussion presented in Hicks' "Value and Capital" and elsewhere. Much of the confusion on these matters stems from the ambiguous use of the term money. Some economists use it to denote money income; others mean a numeraire commodity which enters the individual's utility function. They are two entirely separate concepts.

Summary and Conclusions

The phrase *consumer's surplus* is used in two contexts. As a tool of positive economic analysis, consumer's surplus is simply another term for the gains from trade. The fact that there is no unique evaluation of this gain in units of income does not constitute a denial that such gains exist. These gains, in fact, are the cornerstone of the theory of exchange. The law of demand implies that individuals participating in voluntary trade will always pay less for a total quantity of goods than they would if that quantity were offered on an all-or-none basis. It follows that individuals can be expected to devote some resources to enlarging this gain for themselves. The concept of consumer's surplus should therefore be the behavioral basis for theories of the formation of monopolies and cartels and the political economy of legislation aimed at altering the terms of trade, i.e., the property rights, of the participants in exchange.

The most widespread use of an explicit concept of consumer's surplus, however, has been in the area of welfare economics and social policy. In this context, a function measuring the "welfare loss" due to, for example, a set of excise taxes is formulated to measure the costs, in terms of forgone opportunities to trade (sometimes called *deadweight loss*) of a given tax policy. This loss function is construed as a function of the deviations of prices p_i from marginal costs or, symbolically,

$$\mathscr{L} = f(p_1 - MC_1, \ldots, p_n - MC_n) \tag{11-61}$$

Similarly, the areas to the left of demand curves are used to measure the potential gains from erecting various public works, e.g., dams, to lower the marginal cost of some good.

It should be clear by now that no such functions can exist. There is no way to identify a unique amount of money income as the amount gained (or lost) through different trading arrangements. The usual defense of this procedure is to observe that in fact, for "small" price changes or in situations in which the income elasticity of a given good is "not too high," the area to the left of the ordinary (money-income) demand curves approximates the compensating variations for the price change, i.e., those well-defined amounts consumers would pay or be paid to face the new price situation. This, however, is using the inappropriate to measure the undefinable. The area to the left of the ordinary demand curve does not measure the gain from trade, as there is no unique "gain from trade." Moreover, it is odd to use as a measure of the gains from moving from one indifference surface to another a measure which explicitly holds utility constant. The compensating variations are independent of all behavior which may occur at points other than on the one indifference surface in question.

Allocative efficiency is generally defined with reference to a world without transactions costs. Inefficiency implies forgone gains from trade, a denial of the postulate that more is preferred to less, unless some unspecified costs of trading are being ignored. The measurement of inefficiency must begin with the alternative cost of resources used to alter the terms of trade. This author would argue also that attempts to measure the unmeasurable will be unsuccessful. It seems that a fruitful analysis of potential gains to consumers can still be realized with the use of marginal analysis. Perhaps, however, a more interesting question than the measurement of so-called inefficiency is the political economy of why such losses should appear in a model based on maximizing behavior. We shall deal with these matters in greater detail in Chap. 15, Welfare Economics.

PROBLEMS

1 Consider the class of utility functions which are *additively separable*; i.e.,

$$U(x_1, \ldots, x_n) \equiv U_1(x_1) + \cdots + U_n(x_n)$$

For this class of utility functions, show:

(a) At most one good can exhibit increasing marginal utility and in that case (i) that good is normal whereas all remaining goods are inferior and (ii) that good is a *net* substitute $(\partial x_i^U/\partial p_j > 0)$ for the remaining goods whereas the remaining goods are all complementary to each other.

(b) If all goods exhibit diminishing marginal utility, (i) all goods are normal, and (ii) all goods are net substitutes.

2 For demand functions derived from additively separable utility functions, show that

(a) $\dfrac{\partial x_i/\partial p_k}{\partial x_j/\partial p_k} = \dfrac{\partial x_i/\partial M}{\partial x_j/\partial M}$

(b) $s_{ij} = -k \dfrac{\partial x_i^M}{\partial M} \dfrac{\partial x_j^M}{\partial M}$ where $k = \dfrac{\lambda^M}{\partial \lambda^M/\partial M}$

3 Consider the indirect utility function $U(p_1, \ldots, p_n, M) \equiv U(p_1/M, \ldots, p_n/M, 1) \equiv V(r_1, \ldots, r_n)$, where $r_i = p_i/M$. Show that if V is additively separable in $r_1, \ldots, r_n$, then

$$\frac{\partial x_i^M/\partial p_k}{\partial x_j^M/\partial p_k} = \frac{x_i}{x_j}$$

4 Using the results of the previous two problems, show that if $U(\mathbf{x})$ and $V(\mathbf{r})$ are both additively separable, then $U(\mathbf{x})$ is homothetic.

5 Consider the class of utility functions

$$U(x_1, \ldots, x_n) \equiv (x_1 - x_1^0)^{\alpha_1}(x_2 - x_2^0)^{\alpha_2} \cdots (x_n - x_n^0)^{\alpha_n}$$

where $x_1^0, \ldots, x_n^0$ can be thought of as subsistence levels of the goods; i.e., if $x_i < x_i^0$ for any i, then $U(\mathbf{x}) = 0$. This class of utility functions is known as *Stone-Geary*. Show that this utility function generates demand systems with the characteristic that the *expenditure* $p_j x_j$ on any good x_j is a linear function of all prices and money income.

6 Consider a set of demand functions $x_i = x_i^*(p_1, \ldots, p_n, M)$ whose only known properties are homogeneity and satisfying a budget constraint; i.e.,

$$\sum_{j=1}^{n} \frac{\partial x_i^*}{\partial p_j} p_j + \frac{\partial x_i^*}{\partial M} M \equiv 0 \qquad i = 1, \ldots, n \tag{1}$$

and

$$\sum_{i=1}^{n} p_i x_i^* \equiv M \tag{2}$$

Show that under (1) and (2) alone, Hicks' third law holds, i.e.,

$$\sum_{i=1}^{n} p_i s_{ij} = \sum_{j=1}^{n} p_j s_{ij} = 0 \qquad \text{where } s_{ij} = \frac{\partial x_i^*}{\partial p_j} + x_j^* \frac{\partial x_i^*}{\partial M}$$

7 Suppose a consumer's utility function is additively separable and, in addition, the marginal utility of money income is independent of prices. Show that the elasticity of each money-income demand curve is everywhere unity.

8 The development of utility theory can be regarded as the attempt to provide a theory which explains the phenomenon of downward-sloping demand curves. It was soon discovered that the hicksian pure-substitution terms were symmetric, a result, said Samuelson, "which would not have been discovered without the use of mathematics."

(a) Explain why it is something of a non sequitur to assert the symmetry of the substitution terms.

(b) What behavioral differences are there, if any, in terms of observable price-quantity combinations, between a theory of the consumer which includes such symmetry and one which does not require such symmetry?

9 Which of the following sets of observations of price-quantity data are consistent with utility maximization?

(a) $\mathbf{p}^1 = (1, 2, 3)$ $\quad \mathbf{x}^1 = (3, 2, 1)$
$\quad\mathbf{p}^2 = (2, 1, 2)$ $\quad \mathbf{x}^2 = (2, 2, 1)$
$\quad\mathbf{p}^3 = (3, 5, 1)$ $\quad \mathbf{x}^3 = (1, 2, 1)$
(b) $\mathbf{p}^1 = (3, 4, 1)$ $\quad \mathbf{x}^1 = (5, 1, 3)$
$\quad\mathbf{p}^2 = (2, 3, 2)$ $\quad \mathbf{x}^2 = (3, 3, 3)$
$\quad\mathbf{p}^3 = (5, 3, 1)$ $\quad \mathbf{x}^3 = (4, 2, 2)$
(c) $\mathbf{p}^1 = (4, 3, 2)$ $\quad \mathbf{x}^1 = (2, 2, 2)$
$\quad\mathbf{p}^2 = (5, 3, 3)$ $\quad \mathbf{x}^2 = (1, 3, 3)$
$\quad\mathbf{p}^3 = (5, 2, 3)$ $\quad \mathbf{x}^3 = (1, 3, 2)$

10 A certain consumer is observed to purchase bundles $\mathbf{x}^i$ at prices $\mathbf{p}^i$:

$$\mathbf{p}^1 = (4, 2, 3) \quad \mathbf{x}^1 = (1, 3, 3)$$
$$\mathbf{p}^2 = (3, 2, 3) \quad \mathbf{x}^2 = (2, 3, 2)$$
$$\mathbf{p}^3 = (2, 3, 3) \quad \mathbf{x}^3 = (.5, 1, 5)$$

What is the sex of this consumer?

11 Consider the two demand functions

$$x_1 = \frac{p_2}{p_1} \qquad x_2 = \frac{M}{p_2} - 1 \qquad p_2 < M$$

Integrate these demand functions to find the class of utility functions from which they are derived.

12 Answer the previous question for the demand functions

$$x_1 = \frac{p_2 M}{p_1 p_2 + p_1^2}$$

$$x_2 = \frac{p_1 M}{p_1 p_2 + p_2^2}$$

13 A consumer faced with prices $p_1 = 9$, $p_2 = 12$ consumes at some point $\mathbf{x}^0$, where $x_1 = 4$, $x_2 = 7$, $U(\mathbf{x}^0) = 10$. When p_1 is lowered to $p_1 = 8$, the consumer would move to point $\mathbf{x}^1$, where $x_1 = 6$, $x_2 = 6$, $U(\mathbf{x}^1) = 15$. From these data, estimate the following values:

(a) How much would the consumer be willing to pay to face the lower price of x_1?

(b) How much would a consumer initially at $\mathbf{x}^1$ have to be paid to accept the higher price of x_1 voluntarily?

(c) Are your answers in (a) and (b) exact calculations of these values, or are they approximations? If the latter, is the direction of bias predictable?

(d) How much better off is the consumer at $\mathbf{x}^1$ than at $\mathbf{x}^0$?

14 In his "Principles," Marshall gave the following definition of consumer's surplus:

1. The amount a consumer would pay over which he does pay for a given amount of a good rather than none at all.

Several other consumer's surplus measures have been proposed, e.g.,

2. The amount the consumer would pay for the *right* to purchase the good at its market price rather than have no good at all.

3. The amount the consumer would have to be paid to voluntarily forgo entirely consumption of the good at its present level.

4. The monetary equivalent of the gain in utility that the consumer receives by being able to purchase the good at the market price rather than purchase none at some higher price.

5. The monetary equivalent of the fall in utility a consumer would experience if the right to purchase the good at the market price were taken away.

(*a*) Discuss the relationship, if any, between these measures.

(*b*) Show that measure 2 is greater than measure 1.

(*c*) Show that if the good is normal over the whole range of consumption, then measure 3 is greater than measure 2.

(*d*) Would knowledge of measures 1 to 3 enable one to determine which of two mutually exclusive projects would result in maximizing the consumer's utility?

15 Show that if a consumer's income consists of a numeraire commodity that enters the utility function, then the line integral generating consumer's surplus measures will be path-independent only if all nonnumeraire commodities have zero income elasticities.

BIBLIOGRAPHY

Barten, A. P.: Consumer Demand Functions under Conditions of Almost Additive Preferences, *Econometrica*, **32:** 1–38, 1964.

Chipman, J. S., L. Hurwicz, M. K. Richter, and H. F. Sonnenschein (eds.): "Preferences, Utility, and Demand," Harcourt Brace Jovanovich, New York, 1971.

Debreu, Gerard: "The Theory of Value," John Wiley & Company, Inc., New York, 1959.

Georgescu-Roegen, N.: The Pure Theory of Consumer Behavior, *Quarterly Journal of Economics*, **50:** 545–593, 1936.

Hicks, J. R.: "Value and Capital," 2d ed., Oxford University Press, London, 1946.

————: "A Revision of Demand Theory," Oxford University Press, London, 1956.

Houthakker, H. S.: Revealed Preference and the Utility Function, *Economica*, **17:** 159–174, 1950. The original discussion of the strong axiom of revealed preference.

————: Additive Preferences, *Econometrica*, **28:** 244–257, 1960.

————: The Present State of Consumption Theory, *Econometrica*, **29:** 704–740, 1961.

Lau, L. J.: Duality and the Structure of Utility Functions, *Journal of Economic Theory*, **1:** 374–395, December 1969.

Morgan, J. N.: The Measurement of Gains and Losses, *Quarterly Journal of Economics*, **62:** 287–308, February 1948.

Samuelson, P. A.: "Foundations of Economic Analysis," Harvard University Press, Cambridge, Mass., 1947.

————: Consumption Theory in Terms of Revealed Preference, *Economica*, **15:** 243–253, 1948.

————: The Problem of Integrability in Utility Theory, *Economica*, **17:** 355–385, 1950.

Silberberg, E.: Duality and the Many Consumers' Surpluses, *American Economic Review*, **62:** 942–956, December 1972.

TWELVE

MAXIMIZATION WITH INEQUALITY AND NONNEGATIVITY CONSTRAINTS

12.1 NONNEGATIVITY

In the previous pages we have largely ignored the issues raised by constraining the variables in a maximization model to be nonnegative. In the model of the firm, for example, we did not consider the possibility that simultaneous solution of the first-order equations might lead to negative values of one or more inputs. Such an occurrence would nullify the condition for profit-maximization that wages be equal to marginal revenue product. In a more general sense, there are many factors of production which a firm chooses not to use at all. Similarly, consumers choose to consume only a small fraction of the myriad of consumer goods available. It is possible to characterize mathematically the conditions under which nonnegativity becomes a binding constraint. It might be remarked first, however, that since the refutable comparative-statics theorems are concerned with how choice variables change when parameters change, the comparative statics of variables *not* chosen is fairly trivial. In a local sense (the evaluation of the partial derivatives of the choice functions at a given point) these variables continue not to be chosen; that is, $\partial x_i^*/\partial \alpha_j = 0$ for these variables. In a global sense, e.g., price changes of finite magnitude, factors or goods previously not chosen may enter the relevant choice set. For these situations, more powerful assumptions must be made to yield refutable theorems than in our previous discussions, where strictly *local* phenomena were analyzed.

Consider the monopolist of the first chapter. A profit function of the type

$$\pi(x) = R(x) - C(x) \tag{12-1}$$

is asserted to be maximized, where $R(x)$ and $C(x)$ denote, respectively, the revenue and cost associated with a given level of output x. (We are ignoring the tax aspect of the model as it is not germane to this discussion.) The first-order conditions for a maximum of $\pi(x)$ are

$$\pi'(x) = R'(x) - C'(x) = 0 \tag{12-2}$$

However, this condition is meant to apply only to those situations where the solution to (12-2) is nonnegative. The firm might choose to produce zero output, however, if, for example, $R'(x) < C'(x)$ for all $x > 0$. In that case, where the marginal revenue is less than marginal cost, increasing output *reduces* profits $\pi(x)$. The existence of a *maximum* of profits (not necessarily *positive* profits, another issue entirely) at some *positive* level of output x^* presupposes that for some $0 \leq x \leq x^*$, MR > MC; that is, $R'(x) > C'(x)$ so that it "paid" for the firm to start operations in the first place. The only reason the profit *maximum* would occur at $x = 0$ is that MR(0) $\leq$ MC(0). That is, *if* maximum π occurs at $x = 0$, *then* $\pi' = R'(x) - C'(x) \leq 0$ at $x = 0$. The converse is not being asserted; it is in fact false. If $R'(x) - C'(x) < 0$ at $x = 0$, this does not imply that an interior maximum cannot occur at some x distant from the origin. Again, the only aspect of the firm's behavior under consideration here is the attainment of *maximum* profits, not whether the firm shall exist or not [presumably dependent upon $\pi(x) > 0$].

Let us summarize this condition for maximization of functions of one variable. Consider some function $y = f(x)$. Then the first-order condition for $f(x)$ to achieve a maximum *subject to the nonnegativity constraint $x \geq 0$*, is

$$f'(x) \leq 0 \qquad \text{if } f'(x) < 0 \qquad \text{then } x = 0 \tag{12-3}$$

Alternatively, one can express the same idea as

$$f'(x) \leq 0 \tag{12-4a}$$

$$xf'(x) = 0 \tag{12-4b}$$

Geometrically, the situation is as depicted in Fig. 12-1. In Fig. 12-1a the usual, *interior* maximum is illustrated. This solution is called an interior maximum because the value of x which maximizes $f(x)$ does not lie on the boundary of the set over which x is defined (here, the nonnegative real axis; its only boundary is the point $x = 0$). The set of positive real numbers is the *interior* of this domain of definition of x; hence the terminology. In Fig. 12-1b and c, corner solutions are depicted. That is, the maximum value of $f(x)$, for $x \geq 0$, occurs when $x = 0$. (The fact that the function in Fig. 12-1b achieves a regular maximum at a negative value of x is irrelevant.) When the maximum occurs at $x = 0$, it is impossible to have $f'(x) > 0$ there. If $f'(0) > 0$, increasing x would increase $f(x)$ and $f(0)$ could not be a maximum. However, it is possible that $f'(0) = 0$, as in Fig. 12-1c. There, the nonnegativity constraint is nonbinding. That is, the maximum $f(x)$ would occur at $x = 0$ anyway, even without the restriction $x \geq 0$. Thus, if a maximum occurs when $x > 0$, $f'(x) = 0$. If the maximum occurs when $x = 0$, then necessarily $f'(x) \leq 0$. This condition is expressed in relation (12-3) or, equivalently, (12-4).

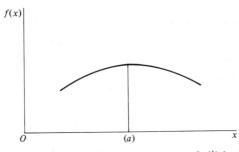

$f(x)$ has an interior maximum, that is, $x > 0, f'(x) = 0$

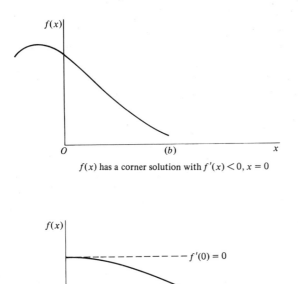

$f(x)$ has a corner solution with $f'(x) < 0, x = 0$

$f(x)$ has a corner solution, with $f'(x) = 0, x = 0$

Figure 12-1 (*a*) $f(x)$ has an interior maximum; that is, $x > 0$, $f'(x) = 0$. (*b*) $f(x)$ has a corner solution with $f'(x) < 0, x = 0$. (*c*) $f(x)$ has a corner solution, with $f'(x) = 0$, $x = 0$.

These more general first-order conditions can be derived algebraically by the device known as adding a *slack variable*. The constraint $x \geq 0$ is an elementary form of the more general inequality constraint, $g(x) \geq 0$. By converting this inequality to an *equality constraint*, ordinary lagrangian methods can be used to derive the first-order conditions.

The constraint $x \geq 0$ is equivalent to

$$x - s^2 = 0 \tag{12-5}$$

where s takes on any real value. When $s \neq 0$, an interior solution is implied, since $x = s^2 > 0$. When $s = 0$, a corner solution is present.

We can now state this as the constrained-maximum problem:

maximize $$y = f(x)$$

subject to $$x - s^2 = 0$$

The lagrangian for this problem is

$$\mathscr{L} = f(x) + \lambda(x - s^2) \tag{12-6}$$

Taking the first partials of $\mathscr{L}$ with respect to x, s, and λ gives

$$\mathscr{L}_x = f'(x) + \lambda = 0 \tag{12-7a}$$

$$\mathscr{L}_s = -2\lambda s = 0 \tag{12-7b}$$

$$\mathscr{L}_\lambda = x - s^2 = 0 \tag{12-7c}$$

From equation (12-7b) we see that if $s \neq 0$, that is, an *interior* solution is obtained, then $\lambda = 0$ and hence from (12-7a), $f'(x) = 0$. Thus, as expected, the usual condition $f'(x) = 0$ is obtained for noncorner solutions. Using the second-order conditions for constrained maximization, we can show that $\lambda \geq 0$. The second-order condition is that

$$\mathscr{L}_{xx}h_x^2 + 2\mathscr{L}_{xs}h_xh_s + \mathscr{L}_{ss}h_s^2 \leq 0 \tag{12-8}$$

for all h_x, h_s satisfying

$$g_x h_x + g_s h_s = 0 \tag{12-9}$$

where $g(x, s) = x - s^2$, the constraint. From the lagrangian (12-6), $\mathscr{L}_{xx} = f''(x)$, $\mathscr{L}_{xs} = 0$, $\mathscr{L}_{ss} = -2\lambda$. From the constraint $g(x, s) = x - s^2$, $g_x = 1$, $g_s = -2s$. Hence, (12-8) and (12-9) become

$$f''(x)h_x^2 - 2\lambda h_s^2 \leq 0 \tag{12-10}$$

for all h_x, h_s satisfying

$$h_x - 2sh_s = 0 \tag{12-11}$$

We already know from equation (12-7b) that if $s \neq 0$, then $\lambda = 0$. Suppose now that $s = 0$. Then from equation (12-11), $h_x = 0$, but no restriction is placed on h_s. When we use $h_x = 0$, $h_s =$ anything, equation (12-10) becomes

$$-2\lambda h_s^2 \leq 0$$

implying, since $h_s^2 > 0$,

$$\lambda \geq 0 \tag{12-12}$$

We now have a complete statement of the first-order conditions for maximizing $f(x)$ subject to $x \geq 0$. From (12-7a), since $\lambda \geq 0$,

$$f'(x) \leq 0 \tag{12-13}$$

If $f'(x) < 0$, then $\lambda > 0$. From (12-7b) $s = 0$ and thus $x = 0$ from (12-7c). Therefore:

if $$f'(x) < 0 \qquad x = 0 \tag{12-14}$$

Equations (12-13) and (12-14) are equivalent to

$$f'(x) \leq 0 \tag{12-15}$$

$$xf'(x) = 0 \tag{12-16}$$

commonly written

$$f'(x) \leq 0 \qquad \text{if} <, x = 0$$

Notice that if the maximum occurs at $x = 0$, no restrictions on $f''(0)$ are implied. In Fig. 12-1b, $f(x)$ could be either convex (as drawn) or concave, and the maximum would still occur at $x = 0$.

These conditions can also be derived using the determinantal conditions on the bordered hessian of second partials of $\mathscr{L}$:

$$|\mathscr{L}| = \begin{vmatrix} \mathscr{L}_{xx} & \mathscr{L}_{xs} & g_x \\ \mathscr{L}_{sx} & \mathscr{L}_{ss} & g_s \\ g_x & g_s & 0 \end{vmatrix} > 0$$

Using the values previously calculated for these partials, we have

$$|\mathscr{L}| = \begin{vmatrix} f''(x) & 0 & 1 \\ 0 & -2\lambda & -2s \\ 1 & -2s & 0 \end{vmatrix} = -4s^2 f''(x) + 2\lambda \geq 0 \tag{12-17}$$

From (12-17), if $s = 0$ (corner solution), $2\lambda \geq 0$; hence $\lambda \geq 0$. Thus, from (12-7a), $f'(x) \leq 0$.

The first-order conditions for obtaining a *minimum* value of $f(x)$ subject to $x \geq 0$ are obtained in a similar manner. One quickly shows that these conditions are

$$f'(x) \geq 0 \qquad \text{if} >, x = 0 \tag{12-18}$$

That is, if a minimum occurs at $x = 0$, it must be the case that $f(x)$ is rising (or horizontal) at $x = 0$. Otherwise, i.e., if the function were falling at $x = 0$, making x positive would lower the value of $f(x)$ and $f(x)$ could not have a minimum at $x = 0$.

Functions of Two or More Variables

The principles delineated above for maximization of functions of one variable generalize in an obvious manner to functions of two or more variables. Consider the problem:

maximize $$z = f(x_1, x_2)$$

subject to $$x_1 \geq 0 \qquad x_2 \geq 0$$

Let us now add slack variables s_1^2, s_2^2 in the manner of the first example. The problem then becomes one of maximization subject to two *equality* constraints:

maximize $$y = f(x_1, x_2)$$

subject to $$g^1(x_1, s_1) = x_1 - s_1^2 = 0$$
$$g^2(x_2, s_2) = x_2 - s_2^2 = 0$$

The lagrangian for this problem is

$$\mathcal{L} = f(x_1, x_2) + \lambda_1(x_1 - s_1^2) + \lambda_2(x_2 - s_2^2)$$

The first-order conditions for maximization are

$$\mathcal{L}_{x_1} = f_1 + \lambda_1 = 0 \tag{12-19a}$$

$$\mathcal{L}_{x_2} = f_2 + \lambda_2 = 0 \tag{12-19b}$$

$$\mathcal{L}_{s_1} = -2\lambda_1 s_1 = 0 \tag{12-19c}$$

$$\mathcal{L}_{s_2} = -2\lambda_2 s_2 = 0 \tag{12-19d}$$

$$\mathcal{L}_{\lambda_1} = x_1 - s_1^2 = 0 \tag{12-19e}$$

$$\mathcal{L}_{\lambda_2} = x_2 - s_2^2 = 0 \tag{12-19f}$$

From equations (12-19c) and (12-19d), if either constraint is nonbinding, i.e., if $s_1 \neq 0$ or $s_2 \neq 0$, then, respectively, $\lambda_1 = 0$, $\lambda_2 = 0$. In that case $(x_1 > 0, x_2 > 0)$, the ordinary first-order relations $f_1 = 0, f_2 = 0$ obtain.

We can show that $\lambda_1 \geq 0, \lambda_2 \geq 0$ by using the second-order conditions. For a constrained maximum,

$$\sum_{i=1}^{2} \sum_{j=1}^{2} \mathcal{L}_{x_i x_j} h_i h_j + 2 \sum_{i=1}^{2} \sum_{j=1}^{2} \mathcal{L}_{x_i s_j} h_i k_j + \sum_{i=1}^{2} \sum_{j=1}^{2} \mathcal{L}_{s_i s_j} k_i k_j \leq 0 \tag{12-20}$$

for all values h_1, h_2, k_1, k_2 such that

$$g_{x_1}^1 h_1 + g_{s_1}^1 k_1 = 0 \tag{12-21a}$$

$$g_{x_2}^2 h_2 + g_{s_2}^2 k_2 = 0 \tag{12-21b}$$

By inspection of the lagrangian [or equations (12-19)] we have

$$\mathcal{L}_{x_i x_j} = f_{ij} \qquad i, j = 1, 2$$

$$\mathcal{L}_{x_i s_j} = 0 \qquad i, j = 1, 2$$

$$\mathcal{L}_{s_i s_j} = \begin{cases} -2\lambda_i & \text{if } i = j \\ 0 & \text{if } i \neq j \end{cases}$$

$$g_{x_j}^i = \begin{cases} 1 & \text{if } i = j \\ 0 & \text{if } i \neq j \end{cases}$$

$$g_{s_j}^i = \begin{cases} -2s_i & \text{if } i = j \\ 0 & \text{if } i \neq j \end{cases}$$

Relations (12-20) and (12-21) therefore become

$$\sum_{i=1}^{2} \sum_{j=1}^{2} f_{ij} h_i h_j - 2\lambda_1 k_1^2 - 2\lambda_2 k_2^2 \leq 0 \qquad (12\text{-}22)$$

for all h_1, h_2, k_1, k_2 such that

$$h_1 - 2s_1 k_1 = 0 \qquad (12\text{-}23a)$$
$$h_2 - 2s_2 k_2 = 0 \qquad (12\text{-}23b)$$

We already know that if $s_i \neq 0$, then $\lambda_i = 0$. Suppose therefore that $s_i = 0$. Then from (12-23), $h_i = 0$. Then equation (12-22) becomes

$$-2\lambda_1 k_1^2 - 2\lambda_2 k_2^2 \leq 0$$

This must hold for *all* k_1, k_2. Setting $k_1 = 0$, $k_2 = 0$ in turn therefore yields

$$\lambda_1 \geq 0 \qquad (12\text{-}24a)$$
$$\lambda_2 \geq 0 \qquad (12\text{-}24b)$$

From the nonnegativity of the Lagrange multipliers, equations (12-19a) and (12-19b) become

$$f_1 \leq 0 \qquad f_2 \leq 0$$

And if $f_i < 0$ (meaning $\lambda_i > 0$), then from (12-19c) and (12-19d), $s_i = 0$, and hence $x_i = 0$. Thus the first-order conditions for a maximum subject to nonnegativity constraints are

$$f_i \leq 0 \qquad \text{if } <, x_i = 0 \qquad i = 1, 2 \qquad (12\text{-}25)$$

This reasoning generalizes to functions of n variables in a straightforward manner, yielding analogous results. The first-order conditions for:

maximize $\qquad z = f(x_1, \ldots, x_n)$

subject to $\qquad x_i \geq 0 \qquad$ some or all $i = 1, \ldots, n$

are $\qquad\qquad f_i \leq 0 \qquad$ if $<, x_i = 0 \qquad (12\text{-}26)$

for variables constrained to be nonnegative, and simply

$$f_i = 0$$

for variables not constrained to be nonnegative.

Let us see what these conditions imply for the profit-maximizing firm. We previously considered the model:

maximize $\qquad \pi = pf(x_1, x_2) - w_1 x_1 - w_2 x_2$

Let us now specify explicitly that the factors x_1 and x_2 can only be employed in positive amounts, as physical reality would dictate.† With $x_1, x_2 \geq 0$, the first-order conditions for profit-maximization become

$$\pi_1 = pf_1 - w_1 \leq 0 \qquad \text{if} <, x_1 = 0$$

$$\pi_2 = pf_2 - w_2 \leq 0 \qquad \text{if} <, x_2 = 0 \qquad (12\text{-}27)$$

Equations (12-27) say that if the profit maximum occurs at zero input of some factor, then the value of the marginal product of that factor is less than its wage. This is in accord with intuition. If the marginal value product were initially greater than the wage of some factor, the firm could increase its profits by employing that factor in positive amounts.

Notice carefully the direction of implication intended by equations (12-26) and, for the firm, (12-27). These relations do *not* say that if the marginal value product is initially, i.e., at $x_i = 0$, less than the wage of some factor, that factor will not be used. We might *initially* find $pf_i < w_i$, but, as x_i increased, f_i might increase and then decrease, yielding $pf_i = w_i$ at some finite, positive value of x_i. The "law" of diminishing returns is in fact usually stated to allow this possibility; the usual assertion is that f_i declines after some level of use of x_i (holding the other factors constant). The above first-order equations say only that *if* the maximum of profits (or anything else) is observed to occur when $pf_i < w_i$, *then* it must be the case that that input is not used; that is, $x_i = 0$. The converse of this statement is *not* implied by this analysis and will in general be false. These are strictly local conditions around the maximum position.

To illustrate this important point, consider a farmer who has to decide which of two tractors, a large model x_L or a small one x_S, to purchase. Either one alone may yield positive profits, with a marginal value product initially greater than the rental wage. This particular farmer would never find it profitable to use two tractors. It turns out, say, that using only the smaller tractor yields the highest profits. At zero (or small) input levels of the other tractor, the marginal value product of either tractor is greater than the rental wage. But at *maximum* profits, $x_S > 0$, $x_L = 0$ because at that point, $pf_{x_L} < w_L$. But the nonuse of some factor does *not* imply that the value of the marginal product of that factor is always less than its wage.

The generalized first-order conditions (7-26), while providing a conceptual generalization of the conditions for a maximum, are not useful for actually finding that maximum. As the previous paragraph indicates, these conditions describe the maximum position after the fact. They don't tell us in advance which variables will equal zero at the maximum position. Consider, for example, that firms usually

---

† Some general mathematical treatments of the firm treat inputs as negative outputs. This type of black-box approach to the theory of the firm generates a mathematical symmetry that is convenient in some analyses. Also, in more sophisticated models of the firm involving physical stocks of certain inputs, drawing down of some such stock (disinvestment) can be regarded as negative accumulation but probably still positive service flow from that stock.

employ only a few of the hundreds or thousands of potential factors of production available to them. Firms typically reject one type of machinery in favor of another, they set skill levels for employees, etc., rejecting certain factors outright. The above first-order conditions merely indicate that for the rejected factors, the marginal value product must have been less than the wage, even at zero input levels. But that is precious little to go on in predicting in advance exactly which factors will be employed and which factors won't.

More importantly, as indicated earlier, the only interesting refutable comparative-statics relations are those which predict a direction (or magnitude, if possible) of change in a choice variable as parameters change. The comparative statics of variables not chosen is rather elementary: $\partial x_i^*/\partial \alpha_j \equiv 0$ for all x_i not chosen, by definition. Hence the meaningful results that are forthcoming with mathematical model building will de facto be derived from the classical maximum conditions of first-order *equalities*. Models involving nonnegativity (or other inequality constraints) will in general require an *algorithm* for solution. That is, some iterative trial-and-error process will be required to see which, if any, constraints are in fact binding. In the chapter on linear programming, an example of such an algorithm will be presented.

12.2 INEQUALITY CONSTRAINTS

Let us now consider the imposition of an inequality constraint $g(x_1, x_2) \geq 0$ in addition to the nonnegativity constraints in a two-variable problem. That is, consider:

maximize $\qquad\qquad z = f(x_1, x_2)$

subject to $\qquad g(x_1, x_2) \geq 0 \qquad$ and $\qquad x_1 \geq 0, x_2 \geq 0$

(No loss of generality is involved by writing the constraint as ≥ 0; multiplying the constraint by -1 reverses the sign.) Again, we first convert these inequalities to equalities, yielding the constrained-maximum problem:

maximize $\qquad\qquad z = f(x_1, x_2)$

subject to $\qquad\qquad g(x_1, x_2) - x_3^2 = 0$

$$g^1(x_1, s_1) = x_1 - s_1^2 = 0 \qquad g^2(x_2, s_2) = x_2 - s_2^2 = 0$$

Here the slack variables are x_3, s_1, and s_2. The lagrangian is

$$\mathcal{L} = f(x_1, x_2) + \lambda(g(x_1, x_2) - x_3^2) + \lambda_1(x_1 - s_1^2) + \lambda_2(x_2 - s_2^2) \quad (12\text{-}28)$$

The first-order conditions for a maximum are thus

$$\mathcal{L}_{x_1} = f_1 + \lambda g_1 + \lambda_1 = 0 \qquad\qquad (12\text{-}29a)$$

$$\mathcal{L}_{x_2} = f_2 + \lambda g_2 + \lambda_2 = 0 \qquad\qquad (12\text{-}29b)$$

$$\mathcal{L}_{x_3} = -2\lambda x_3 = 0 \qquad\qquad (12\text{-}30a)$$

$$\mathcal{L}_{s_1} = -2\lambda_1 s_1 = 0 \tag{12-30b}$$

$$\mathcal{L}_{s_2} = -2\lambda_2 s_2 = 0 \tag{12-30c}$$

and the constraints

$$\mathcal{L}_\lambda = g(x_1, x_2) - x_3^2 = 0 \tag{12-31a}$$

$$\mathcal{L}_{\lambda_1} = x_1 - s_1^2 = 0 \tag{12-31b}$$

$$\mathcal{L}_{\lambda_2} = x_2 - s_2^2 = 0 \tag{12-31c}$$

Using exactly the same reasoning as before, we note from equations (12-30) that if any constraint is nonbinding (holds as a strict inequality), then the associated Lagrange multiplier is 0. Suppose, at the maximum point, x_1, $x_2 > 0$, and $g(x_1, x_2) > 0$; then all these constraints turn out to be completely irrelevant. From equations (12-30), $\lambda = \lambda_1 = \lambda_2 = 0$, and equations (12-29) become the ordinary equations for unconstrained maximum, $f_1 = f_2 = 0$. If in fact $g(x_1, x_2) = 0$, that is, the constraint is binding, and x_1, $x_2 > 0$, then equations (12-29) give the ordinary first-order conditions for a constrained maximum, $\mathcal{L}_1 = f_1 + \lambda g_1 = 0$, $\mathcal{L}_2 = f_2 + \lambda g_2 = 0$.

It must also be the case that λ, λ_1, $\lambda_2 \geq 0$. The second-order conditions for constrained maximum are

$$\sum_{j=1}^{3} \sum_{i=1}^{3} \mathcal{L}_{x_i x_j} h_i h_j + 2 \sum_{j=1}^{2} \sum_{i=1}^{3} \mathcal{L}_{x_i s_j} h_i k_j + \sum_{j=1}^{2} \sum_{i=1}^{2} \mathcal{L}_{s_i s_j} k_i k_j \leq 0 \tag{12-32}$$

for all h_1, h_2, h_3, k_1, k_2 satisfying

$$g_1 h_1 + g_2 h_2 + g_3 h_3 = 0 \tag{12-33a}$$

$$g_{x_1}^1 h_1 + g_{s_1}^1 k_1 = 0 \tag{12-33b}$$

$$g_{x_2}^2 h_2 + g_{s_2}^2 k_2 = 0 \tag{12-33c}$$

Now

$$\mathcal{L}_{x_i x_j} = f_{ij} + \lambda g_{ij} = \mathcal{L}_{ij} \qquad \mathcal{L}_{x_i s_j} = 0 \qquad \begin{array}{l} i = 1, 2, 3 \\ j = 1, 2 \end{array}$$

$$\mathcal{L}_{x_3 x_3} = -2\lambda \qquad \mathcal{L}_{x_i x_3} = 0 \qquad \text{if } i \neq 3$$

$$\mathcal{L}_{s_i s_j} = \begin{cases} -2\lambda_i & \text{if } i = j \\ 0 & \text{if } i \neq j \end{cases}$$

Then the relations (12-32) and (12-33) become

$$\sum_{j=1}^{2} \sum_{i=1}^{2} \mathcal{L}_{ij} h_i h_j - 2\lambda h_3^2 - 2\lambda_1 k_1^2 - 2\lambda_2 k_2^2 \leq 0 \tag{12-34}$$

for all h_1, h_2, h_3, k_1, k_2 such that

$$g_1 h_1 + g_2 h_2 - 2x_3 h_3 = 0 \tag{12-35a}$$

$$h_1 - 2s_1 k_1 = 0 \tag{12-35b}$$

$$h_2 - 2s_2 k_2 = 0 \tag{12-35c}$$

Again, we already know that if s_1, $s_2 \neq 0$, then λ_1, $\lambda_2 = 0$, respectively. Also, if $x_3 \neq 0$, then $\lambda = 0$, from (12-30a). Therefore, suppose $s_1 = s_2 = 0$. Then, as before, from (12-35b) and (12-35c), $h_1 = h_2 = 0$. Then (12-34) becomes

$$-2\lambda h_3^2 - 2\lambda_1 k_1^2 - 2\lambda_2 k_2^2 \leq 0$$

Letting any *two* of h_3, k_1, and $k_2 = 0$ [this is valid since (12-34) must hold for *all* h_i's and k_i's] yields

$$\lambda \geq 0 \qquad \lambda_1 \geq 0 \qquad \lambda_2 \geq 0$$

The first-order equations (12-29) to (12-31) therefore can be stated as

$$\mathscr{L}_{x_i} = f_i + \lambda g_i \leq 0 \qquad \text{if} <, x_i = 0 \tag{12-36}$$

$$\mathscr{L}_\lambda = g(x_1, x_2) \geq 0 \qquad \text{if} >, \lambda = 0 \tag{12-37}$$

and we note that $\lambda \geq 0$.

These conditions generalize in a straightforward fashion to the case of n variables and m inequality constraints. In general, consider:

maximize $\qquad\qquad z = f(x_1, \ldots, x_n)$

subject to $\qquad\qquad g^1(x_1, \ldots, x_n) \geq 0$

$\qquad\qquad\qquad \cdots\cdots\cdots\cdots\cdots$

$\qquad\qquad\qquad g^m(x_1, \ldots, x_n) \geq 0$

$\qquad\qquad\qquad x_1, \ldots, x_n \geq 0$

There is no a priori need to restrict m to be less than n (as might be the case with *equality* constraints) since some (or all) of these constraints may turn out to be nonbinding.

Define the lagrangian

$$\mathscr{L} = f(x_1, \ldots, x_n) + \sum_{j=1}^{m} \lambda_j g^j(x_1, \ldots, x_n)$$

Then the first-order conditions for a maximum are

$$\mathscr{L}_{x_i} = f_i + \sum_{j=1}^{m} \lambda_j g_i^j \leq 0 \qquad \text{if} <, x_i = 0 \tag{12-38}$$

$$\mathscr{L}_{\lambda_j} = g^j \geq 0 \qquad \text{if} >, \lambda_j = 0 \tag{12-39}$$

These relations are known as the *Kuhn-Tucker* conditions for a maximum subject to inequality constraints.[†] Again, these conditions are not very useful for determining the actual solution of such a problem. They are descriptions of the maxi-

---

† The original paper is H. W. Kuhn and A. W. Tucker, Nonlinear Programming, in J. Neyman (ed.), *Proceedings of the Second Berkeley Symposium on Mathematical Statistics and Probability*, University of California Press, Berkeley, 1951.

mum position, after the fact, so to speak. *If it turns out that at the maximum position,* $f_i + \lambda g_i < 0$, *then* $x_i = 0$. Nothing more is implied.

The conditions for a constrained *minimum* are similarly derived. Consider the problem:

minimize $\qquad\qquad\qquad z = f(x_1, \ldots, x_n)$

subject to $\qquad\qquad g^j(x_1, \ldots, x_n) \leq 0 \qquad j = 1, \ldots, m$

$$x_i \geq 0 \qquad i = 1, \ldots, n$$

The constraints are written as ≤ 0 to preserve symmetry. No loss of generality is involved; merely multiplying any constraint by -1 reverses the sign of any constraint. Again, the lagrangian, as before, is

$$\mathscr{L} = f(x_1, \ldots, x_n) + \sum_{j=1}^{m} \lambda_j g^j(x_1, \ldots, x_n)$$

The first-order conditions are then

$$\mathscr{L}_{x_i} = f_i + \sum_{j=1}^{m} \lambda_j g_i^j \geq 0 \qquad \text{if} >, x_i = 0, i = 1, \ldots, n$$

$$\mathscr{L}_{\lambda_j} = g^j \leq 0 \qquad \text{if} <, \lambda_j = 0, j = 1, \ldots, m$$

Writing the constraints as $g^j \leq 0$ ensures that $\lambda_j \geq 0$.

Let us illustrate these Kuhn-Tucker conditions using the model of a consumer who maximizes his or her utility $U(x_1, x_2)$ subject to a budget constraint. Let us now assume that the consumer need not spend all of his or her money income. The model then becomes

maximize $\qquad\qquad\qquad U(x_1, x_2)$

subject to $\qquad\qquad p_1 x_1 + p_2 x_2 \leq M \qquad x_1, x_2 \geq 0$

The lagrangian for this problem is

$$\mathscr{L} = U(x_1, x_2) + \lambda(M - p_1 x_1 - p_2 x_2)$$

The constraint has been incorporated in the lagrangian in the form $M - p_1 x_1 - p_2 x_2 \geq 0$, to conform with the previous analysis.

The first-order conditions are thus

$$\mathscr{L}_1 = U_1 - \lambda p_1 \leq 0 \qquad \text{if} <, x_1 = 0 \qquad\qquad (12\text{-}40a)$$

$$\mathscr{L}_2 = U_2 - \lambda p_2 \leq 0 \qquad \text{if} <, x_2 = 0 \qquad\qquad (12\text{-}40b)$$

$$\mathscr{L}_\lambda = M - p_1 x_1 - p_2 x_2 \geq 0 \qquad \text{if} >, \lambda = 0 \qquad\qquad (12\text{-}40c)$$

The Lagrange multiplier λ represents the consumer's marginal utility of money income. Briefly, suppose $x_1, x_2 > 0$. Then $U_1 = \lambda p_1$, $U_2 = \lambda p_2$, and

$$\lambda = \frac{U_1}{p_1} = \frac{U_2}{p_2}$$

The term U_1/p_1 represents the marginal utility, per dollar, of income spent on x_1. Likewise, U_2/p_2 represents the marginal utility of income spent on x_2. At a constrained maximum, these two ratios are equal, their common value being simply the marginal utility of money income.

Consider the last condition (12-40c). This can now be interpreted as saying that if the budget constraint is not binding, that is, $p_1 x_1 + p_2 x_2 < M$ (the consumer doesn't exhaust his or her income), then λ, the marginal utility of income, must be 0. The consumer is *satiated* in all commodities. This is confirmed by (12-40a) and (12-40b). If $\lambda = 0$, then $U_1 = U_2 = 0$; that is, the marginal utilities of both goods are 0. Hence, the consumer would not consume more of these goods even if they were given outright, i.e., free. This consumer is at a *bliss point*.

Now consider the situation where $\lambda > 0$ (the consumer would prefer to have more income) and $x_2 = x_2^* > 0$, but at the maximum point, $U_1 - \lambda p_1 < 0$, so that $x_1 = x_1^* = 0$. Assuming positive prices, we have at $x_1^* = 0$, $x_2^* > 0$,

$$\lambda = \frac{U_2}{p_2} > \frac{U_1}{p_1}$$

Rearranging terms gives

$$\frac{U_1}{U_2} < \frac{p_1}{p_2}$$

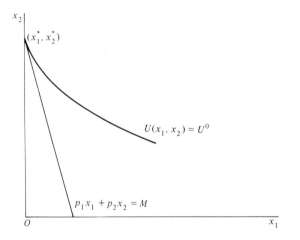

Figure 12-2 Maximization of utility at a corner. A consumer achieves maximum utility when $x_1^* = 0$, $x_2^* > 0$. The consumption of x_1 is 0 because $U_1 - \lambda p_1 < 0$. Assuming positive prices, this inequality is equivalent to $\lambda > U_1/p_1$. However, $\lambda = U_2/p_2$, since x_2 is consumed in positive amounts. That is, for x_2, the marginal utility of income is the marginal utility per dollar spent on x_2. However, the marginal utility per dollar spent on x_1 is less than that spent on x_2 at the utility maximum; hence $x_1 = 0$. Combining these two relations gives $U_2/p_2 > U_1/p_1$ or $U_1/U_2 < p_1/p_2$, as exhibited in the above diagram, where U_1/U_2 represents the slope of an indifference curve (the consumer's marginal evaluation of x_1) and p_1/p_2 represents the market's evaluation of x_1. As depicted, with convexity, $U_1/U_2 < p_1/p_2$ all along the indifference surface. This consumer, no matter how little x_1 is consumed, always values x_1 less than the market does. Hence, no x_1 is consumed.

This situation is depicted in Fig. 12-2. At any point, the consumer's subjective marginal evaluation of x_1, in terms of the x_2 the consumer would willingly forgo to consume an extra unit of x_1, is given by U_1/U_2, the ratio of marginal utilities. This is the (negative) slope of the indifference curve at any point. If the consumer chooses to consume no x_1 at all at the utility maximum, then the consumer's subjective marginal evaluation must be less than the value the market places on x_1. The market will exchange x_2 for x_1 at the ratio p_1/p_2. If, for example, $p_1 = \$6$ and $p_2 = \$2$, the market will exchange 3 units of x_2 for 1 unit of x_1. At zero x_1 consumption, a consumer valuing x_1 at only 2 units of x_2 would not be purchasing any x_1 at all at the utility maximum. In Fig. 12-2, this situation is represented by having the budget line cut the vertical x_2 axis at a steeper slope than the indifference curve $U(x_1, x_2) = U^0$, where U^0 is the maximum achievable utility. That is, $U_1/U_2 < p_1/p_2$ at $x_1^* = 0$, $x_2^* > 0$.

12.3 THE SADDLEPOINT THEOREM

Let us now return to the first-order conditions for the problem:

maximize $\qquad\qquad z = f(x_1, \ldots, x_n)$

subject to $\qquad\qquad g^1(x_1, \ldots, x_n) \geq 0$

$$\ldots\ldots\ldots\ldots\ldots\ldots$$

$$g^m(x_1, \ldots, x_n) \geq 0$$

$$x_1, \ldots, x_n \geq 0$$

For the lagrangian

$$\mathscr{L} = f(x_1, \ldots, x_n) + \sum_{j=1}^{m} \lambda_j g^j(x_1, \ldots, x_n)$$

the Kuhn-Tucker conditions are, again,

$$\mathscr{L}_{x_i} = f_i + \sum_{j=1}^{m} \lambda_j g_i^j \leq 0 \qquad \text{if } <, \ x_i = 0 \qquad\qquad (12\text{-}38)$$

and $\qquad\quad \mathscr{L}_{\lambda_j} = g^j \geq 0 \qquad \text{if } >, \ \lambda_j = 0 \qquad\qquad (12\text{-}39)$

Noting the direction of the inequalities, we see that these conditions are suggestive of the *lagrangian* function $\mathscr{L}(x_1, \ldots, x_n, \lambda_1, \ldots, \lambda_m)$ achieving a *maximum* in the x directions and a *minimum* in the λ directions. That is, consider the lagrangian above as just some function of x_i's and λ_j's. If $\mathscr{L}$ achieved a *maximum* with regard to the x_i's, the first-order necessary conditions would be equations (12-38). Likewise, if $\mathscr{L}$ achieved a *minimum* with respect to the λ_j's, the first-order necessary conditions would be precisely equations (12-39).

A point on a function which is a maximum in some directions and a minimum in the others is called a *saddlepoint* of the function. The terminology is suggested by the shape of saddles: in the direction along the horse's backbone, the center of the saddle represents a minimum point, but going from one side of the horse to the other, the center of the saddle represents a maximum.

Consider a function $f(x_1, \ldots, x_n, y_1, \ldots, y_m)$, or, more briefly, $f(\mathbf{x}, \mathbf{y})$, where $\mathbf{x} = (x_1, \ldots, x_n)$, $\mathbf{y} = (y_1, \ldots, y_m)$. The point $(\mathbf{x}^0, \mathbf{y}^0)$ is said to be a saddlepoint of $f(\mathbf{x}, \mathbf{y})$ if

$$f(\mathbf{x}, \mathbf{y}^0) \leq f(\mathbf{x}^0, \mathbf{y}^0) \leq f(\mathbf{x}^0, \mathbf{y})$$

Let us now apply this concept to the lagrangian above. *If* the lagrangian $\mathcal{L} = f(x_1, \ldots, x_n) + \sum_{j=1}^{m} \lambda_j g^j(x_1, \ldots, x_n)$ has a saddlepoint at some values $x_i = x_i^*$, $i = 1, \ldots, n$; $\lambda_j = \lambda_j^*$, $j = 1, \ldots, m$ (briefly, at $\mathbf{x} = \mathbf{x}^*$, $\lambda = \lambda^*$), then, as a necessary consequence, the relations (12-38) and (12-39) are implied. That is, *if*

$$\mathcal{L}(\mathbf{x}, \lambda^*) \leq \mathcal{L}(\mathbf{x}^*, \lambda^*) \leq \mathcal{L}(\mathbf{x}^*, \lambda) \tag{12-41}$$

then it is being asserted that $\mathcal{L}(\mathbf{x}, \lambda)$ has a maximum in the $\mathbf{x}$ directions and a minimum in the λ directions. The first-order necessary conditions for such an extremum of $\mathcal{L}(\mathbf{x}, \lambda)$ are

$$\mathcal{L}_{x_i} \leq 0 \qquad \text{if } <, x_i = 0$$

and
$$\mathcal{L}_{\lambda_j} \geq 0 \qquad \text{if } >, \lambda_j = 0$$

However, the mere fact that two assertions [constrained maximum of $f(x_1, \ldots, x_n)$ and saddlepoint of $\mathcal{L}(\mathbf{x}, \lambda)$] imply the same conditions [equations (12-38) and (12-39)] does *not* imply that those two assertions are equivalent or that a particular one implies the other. It *is* the case, however, under fairly general mathematical conditions, that the saddlepoint criterion implies that $f(\mathbf{x})$ has a constrained maximum. The converse is *not* true, however, unless stronger conditions are attached. If it assumed, in addition, that (1) $f(\mathbf{x})$ and the $g^j(\mathbf{x})$'s are all concave functions and (2) there exists an $\mathbf{x}^0 > 0$ such that $g^j(\mathbf{x}^0) > 0$, $j = 1, \ldots, m$ (this condition is known as Slater's *constraint qualification*), then if $(\mathbf{x}^*, \lambda^*)$ is a solution of the constrained-maximum problem, $(\mathbf{x}^*, \lambda^*)$ is also a saddlepoint of the lagrangian function.

This theorem is known as the *Kuhn-Tucker saddlepoint theorem* (there are actually many variants of it). Part of the proof appears in the Appendix to this chapter. Vector notation will be used throughout.

Suppose $(\mathbf{x}^*, \lambda^*)$ is in fact a saddlepoint of $\mathcal{L}(\mathbf{x}, \lambda)$. Then, by definition, for $\mathbf{x} \geq 0$, $\lambda \geq 0$,

$$f(\mathbf{x}) + \lambda^* \mathbf{g}(\mathbf{x}) \leq f(\mathbf{x}^*) + \lambda^* \mathbf{g}(\mathbf{x}^*) \tag{12-42}$$

and
$$f(\mathbf{x}^*) + \lambda^* \mathbf{g}(\mathbf{x}^*) \leq f(\mathbf{x}^*) + \lambda \mathbf{g}(\mathbf{x}^*) \tag{12-43}$$

where $\lambda \mathbf{g}(\mathbf{x})$ means $\sum_{j=1}^{m} \lambda_j g^j(\mathbf{x})$, the inner product of the vectors $\lambda = (\lambda_1, \ldots, \lambda_m)$ and $\mathbf{g}(\mathbf{x}) = (g^1(\mathbf{x}), \ldots, g^m(\mathbf{x}))$. From (12-43), after canceling $f(\mathbf{x}^*)$ from both sides and rearranging, we have

$$(\lambda - \lambda^*) \mathbf{g}(\mathbf{x}^*) \geq 0 \tag{12-44}$$

Since (12-44) must hold for *any* λ, by hypothesis, for sufficiently large λ, $\lambda - \lambda^* \geq 0$ and hence

$$\mathbf{g}(\mathbf{x}^*) \geq 0 \tag{12-45}$$

Thus we have shown that $\mathbf{x}^*$ is *feasible*; i.e., it satisfies the constraints of the maximum problem. Moreover, we can set $\lambda = 0$ in (12-44) (again, since this must hold for *all* λ), obtaining, after multiplying by -1,

$$\lambda^* \mathbf{g}(\mathbf{x}^*) \leq 0 \tag{12-46}$$

However, $\lambda^* \geq 0$, $\mathbf{g}(\mathbf{x}^*) \geq 0$. Therefore, in order to satisfy (12-46), it must be that

$$\lambda^* \mathbf{g}(\mathbf{x}^*) = 0 \tag{12-47}$$

Now consider the first inequality, (12-42), which refers to the maximum in the $\mathbf{x}$ directions. When we use equation (12-47), (12-42) becomes

$$f(\mathbf{x}^*) \geq f(\mathbf{x}) + \lambda^* \mathbf{g}(\mathbf{x}) \tag{12-48}$$

However, $\lambda^* \geq 0$, and for any *feasible* $\mathbf{x}$, that is, an $\mathbf{x}$ which satisfies the constraints, $\mathbf{g}(\mathbf{x}) \geq 0$. Therefore, $\lambda^* \mathbf{g}(\mathbf{x}) \geq 0$, and thus

$$f(\mathbf{x}^*) \geq f(\mathbf{x}) \tag{12-49}$$

for any feasible $\mathbf{x}$. Therefore, $\mathbf{x}^*$ maximizes $f(\mathbf{x})$ subject to the constraints $\mathbf{g}(\mathbf{x}) \geq 0$. We have therefore shown that the saddlepoint condition implies that a constrained maximum exists.

To repeat, the converse of the above is in general false. If conditions 1 and 2 above are added, viz., that $f(\mathbf{x})$ and $g^j(\mathbf{x})$, $j = 1, \ldots, m$, are all concave and that there exists an $\mathbf{x}^0$ such that $g^j(\mathbf{x}^0) > 0$, $j = 1, \ldots, m$, then the "converse" follows. The proof of this proposition unfortunately requires more advanced methods of linear algebra dealing with convex sets. It is presented in the Appendix to the chapter. Note, however, that the right-hand part of the saddlepoint inequality follows readily from the assumption of a constrained maximum. If $\mathbf{x}^*$, λ^* are the values which maximize $f(\mathbf{x})$ subject to $\mathbf{g}(\mathbf{x}) \geq 0$, then

$$\mathscr{L}(\mathbf{x}^*, \lambda^*) = f(\mathbf{x}^*) + \lambda^* \mathbf{g}(\mathbf{x}^*)$$

However, from the first-order conditions, $\lambda^* \mathbf{g}(\mathbf{x}^*) = 0$. Hence,

$$\mathscr{L}(\mathbf{x}^*, \lambda^*) = f(\mathbf{x}^*)$$

By definition
$$\mathscr{L}(\mathbf{x}^*, \lambda) = f(\mathbf{x}^*) + \lambda \mathbf{g}(\mathbf{x}^*)$$

But $\mathbf{g}(\mathbf{x}^*) \geq 0$, and $\lambda \geq 0$ by assumption; thus

$$\mathscr{L}(\mathbf{x}^*, \lambda^*) = f(\mathbf{x}^*) \leq f(\mathbf{x}^*) + \lambda \mathbf{g}(\mathbf{x}^*) = \mathscr{L}(\mathbf{x}^*, \lambda)$$

i.e., the right-hand part of the relation (12-41).

Example We shall show by example that achieving a constrained maximum does not imply that the lagrangian has a saddlepoint there. Consider a consumer who maximizes the utility function $U = x_1 x_2$ subject to the constraint

$p_1 x_1 + p_2 x_2 \leq M$. Since the level (indifference) curves of the utility function, $x_1 x_2 = U^0$, never cross the axes and $U_1, U_2 > 0$ for all positive x, the consumer will in fact spend his or her entire income; that is, $M - p_1 x_1 - p_2 x_2 = 0$. Thus, the problem is solved by formulating

$$\mathscr{L} = x_1 x_2 + \lambda(M - p_1 x_1 - p_2 x_2) \tag{12-50}$$

with first-order equations

$$\mathscr{L}_1 = x_2 - \lambda p_1 = 0$$
$$\mathscr{L}_2 = x_1 - \lambda p_2 = 0$$
$$\mathscr{L}_\lambda = M - p_1 x_1 - p_2 x_2 = 0 \tag{12-51}$$

The consumer's demand functions are found by first eliminating λ:

$$x_2 = \lambda p_1 \qquad x_1 = \lambda p_2$$

and thus
$$\frac{x_2}{x_1} = \frac{p_1}{p_2} \qquad \text{or} \qquad p_1 x_1 = p_2 x_2$$

Substituting this relation into the budget constraint ($\mathscr{L}_\lambda = 0$) gives

$$p_1 x_1 + p_1 x_1 = M$$

and thus
$$x_1^* = \frac{M}{2p_1} \tag{12-52a}$$

Similarly,
$$x_2^* = \frac{M}{2p_2} \tag{12-52b}$$

Also,
$$\lambda^* = \frac{x_2^*}{p_1} = \frac{x_1^*}{p_2} = \frac{M}{2p_1 p_2} \tag{12-53}$$

We therefore find

$$\mathscr{L}(\mathbf{x}^*, \lambda^*) = x_1^* x_2^* + \lambda^*(M - p_1 x_1^* - p_2 x_2^*) \tag{12-54}$$

However, the budget constraint is satisfied by x_1^*, x_2^*, and thus

$$\mathscr{L}(\mathbf{x}^*, \lambda^*) = \frac{M}{2p_1} \frac{M}{2p_2} = \frac{M^2}{4p_1 p_2} = U(x_1^*, x_2^*)$$

By definition

$$\mathscr{L}(\mathbf{x}^*, \lambda) = U(x_1^*, x_2^*) + \lambda(M - p_1 x_1^* - p_2 x_2^*)$$

Since the budget constraint is binding at x_1^*, x_2^*,

$$\mathscr{L}(\mathbf{x}^*, \lambda) = U(x_1^*, x_2^*) = \frac{M^2}{4p_1 p_2} = \mathscr{L}(\mathbf{x}^*, \lambda^*)$$

Hence, the right-hand side of the saddlepoint is satisfied as an equality,

$$\mathscr{L}(\mathbf{x}^*, \lambda^*) = \mathscr{L}(\mathbf{x}^*, \lambda) \tag{12-55}$$

The left-hand side of the saddlepoint condition is *not* satisfied, however:

$$\mathscr{L}(\mathbf{x}, \lambda^*) = U(x_1, x_2) + \lambda^*(M - p_1 x_1 - p_2 x_2)$$

$$= x_1 x_2 + \frac{M}{2p_1 p_2}(M - p_1 x_1 - p_2 x_2)$$

If we let $x_1 = x_2 = 0$,

$$\mathscr{L}(\mathbf{x}, \lambda^*) = \frac{M^2}{2p_1 p_2} > \frac{M^2}{4p_1 p_2} = \mathscr{L}(\mathbf{x}^*, \lambda^*)$$

The saddlepoint condition is violated because although $U = x_1 x_2$ is quasi-concave in x_1 and x_2, it is not *concave*. Thus the mere attainment of a constrained maximum is *not* sufficient for the lagrangian to possess a saddlepoint at the maximum position.

12.4 NONLINEAR PROGRAMMING

The general class of problems involving maximization of a function subject to inequality and nonnegativity constraints is called *nonlinear programming problems*. These problems, of the form:

maximize $\qquad\qquad y = f(x_1, \ldots, x_n)$

subject to $\qquad\qquad g^1(x_1, \ldots, x_n) \geq 0$

$$\ldots\ldots\ldots\ldots\ldots$$

$$g^m(x_1, \ldots, x_n) \geq 0$$

$$x_1, \ldots, x_n \geq 0$$

do not contain specific enough structure to permit description of the solution. The determination of exactly which constraints will be binding and which will not makes this class of problems significantly more complex than the classical problem of maximizing a function subject to equality constraints with nonnegativity not imposed. Once it is shown which constraints are binding, the above problem reduces to a classical maximization problem, solvable (*in principle*—the equations may admit of no easily expressible solution) by standard lagrangian techniques.

Solutions to nonlinear programming problems will be found only by some *iterative* procedure, i.e., an *algorithm* which leads one toward the maximum in a stepwise fashion. In general, such algorithms begin with an arbitrary *feasible* point, i.e., an $\mathbf{x} = (x_1, \ldots, x_n)$, which satisfies all the constraints, including nonnegativity. Then in the neighborhood of that point some evaluation is made of how $f(\mathbf{x})$ could be increased, e.g., by decreasing some x_i's and increasing others. When a new point is reached, the evaluation is repeated. A successful algorithm is one which leads to the maximum position in a finite (but not astronomically large) number of steps.

A number of algorithms have been developed, assuming various specific structures on the f and g^j functions. The most famous is the *simplex algorithm*, developed by George Dantzig in 1947 for solving the class of *linear* programming problems.† This type of problem results when f and the g^j's are all linear functions, or:

maximize

$$y = \sum_{i=1}^{n} p_i x_i$$

subject to

$$\sum_{j=1}^{n} a_{ij} x_j \le b_i \qquad i = 1, \ldots, m$$

$$x_j \ge 0 \qquad j = 1, \ldots, n$$

This class of problems will be investigated in the chapter on linear general equilibrium models.

No general algorithm for all nonlinear programming problems exists. The specific algorithms that exist for some nonlinear problems are not of central interest to most economists and are outside the scope of this book. We shall only briefly indicate some structures for which algorithms have been more successful.

One of the central problems encountered in nonlinear programming problems is the determination of whether a *local* solution is in fact the *global* solution of the problem. That is, suppose $f(\mathbf{x}^*) \ge f(\mathbf{x})$ for all $\mathbf{x}$ in some neighborhood of $\mathbf{x}^*$. Then $\mathbf{x}^*$ is a *local* maximum. How can we be sure that $\mathbf{x}^*$ is the *global* solution, that is, $f(\mathbf{x}^*) \ge f(\mathbf{x})$, for all feasible $\mathbf{x}$? In general, of course, one can't be sure, but under certain structures local solutions are in fact global solutions. Let us explore these circumstances.

Consider Fig. 12-3, in which a consumer attempts to maximize some utility function $U(x_1, x_2)$ whose indifference curves, U^1 and U^2, are shown. Suppose, contrary to the usual assumptions, that the budget constraint is *not* the usual linear form, $p_1 x_1 + p_2 x_2 \le M$, but the area bounded by the curved line MM'. Given this situation, *two* local constrained maxima exist: $\mathbf{x}^*$ and $\mathbf{x}^{**}$. At $\mathbf{x}^*$, $U(\mathbf{x}^*) > U(\mathbf{x})$ for all $\mathbf{x}$ in *some* neighborhoods of $\mathbf{x}^*$. An iterative procedure which led to $\mathbf{x}^*$ as the solution to this problem might be insufficiently powerful to indicate that if the neighborhood is made large enough, some $\mathbf{x}$'s will be found for which $U(\mathbf{x}) > U(\mathbf{x}^*)$. In the given example, $\mathbf{x}^{**}$ is the *global* maximum, since clearly $U(\mathbf{x}^{**}) > U(\mathbf{x})$ for all other $\mathbf{x}$ in the budget set.

The problem of nonglobal maxima occurs here because points connecting $\mathbf{x}^*$ and $\mathbf{x}^{**}$ lie outside the *feasible region*, i.e., the set of all feasible $\mathbf{x}$'s. That is, a straight line joining $\mathbf{x}^*$ and $\mathbf{x}^{**}$ contains points not admissible under the conditions of the model. A very important construct in analyses of nonlinear programming problems is therefore that of a *convex set*.

---

† G. Dantzig, Maximization of a Linear Function of Variables Subject to Linear Inequalities, in T. C. Koopmans (ed.), Activity Analysis and Allocation, *Cowles Commission Monograph* 13, John Wiley & Sons, Inc., New York, 1951.

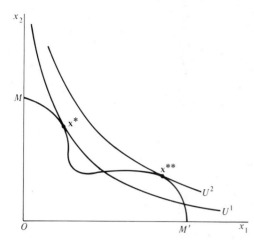

Figure 12-3 Utility maximization subject to nonlinear budget constraint. $\mathbf{x}^*$ and $\mathbf{x}^{**}$ are both *local* maxima of $U(x_1, x_2)$. However, $\mathbf{x}^{**}$ is the *global* maximum point. The nonlinear budget constraint MM' produces a feasible set which is not convex. Under these circumstances, and with nonconcave objective functions, such nonglobal local maxima can occur. If the feasible set is convex and the objective function is a concave function, then any local maximum is the global maximum. The efficiency of solution algorithms can be vastly increased under those circumstances.

Definition A set S is said to be convex if, for all $x_1 \in S$, $x_2 \in S$ (the symbol "$\in$" means "belonging to" or, "is an element of"), the points $x = kx_1 + (1 - k)x_2$ belong to S, for all $0 \le k \le 1$.

Geometrically, a convex set is one such that all points along a straight line joining any two points in the set also belong to the set. The straight line joining any two points in the set never leaves the set. All squares, triangles, circles, spheres, and parallelograms are convex sets; sets like that depicted in Fig. 12-3, the points bounded by the axes and the curve MM', are nonconvex.

The principal result on local vs. global maxima is, as indicated in the above discussion, the following theorem.

Theorem Let $f(\mathbf{x})$, $\mathbf{x} = (x_1, \ldots, x_n)$ be a concave function defined over some convex set S. Then if $f(\mathbf{x}^*)$ is a unique local maximum in S, it is in fact the *global* maximum.

PROOF Suppose there exists an $\mathbf{x}^{**}$ such that $f(\mathbf{x}^{**}) > f(\mathbf{x}^*)$. Then, by concavity,

$$
\begin{aligned}
f(k\mathbf{x}^* + (1 - k)\mathbf{x}^{**}) &\ge kf(\mathbf{x}^*) + (1 - k)f(\mathbf{x}^{**}) \\
&> kf(\mathbf{x}^*) + (1 - k)f(\mathbf{x}^*) \\
&= f(\mathbf{x}^*) \qquad 0 < k < 1
\end{aligned}
$$

However, by choosing k arbitrarily close to 1, the point $(k\mathbf{x}^* + (1 - k)\mathbf{x}^{**})$ becomes arbitrarily close to $\mathbf{x}^*$, and yet the function is greater there than at $\mathbf{x}^*$, a local maximum. This contradiction demonstrates the result.

Heuristically, if $\mathbf{x}^*$ and $\mathbf{x}^{**}$ are any two finitely separated points of local maxima, the chord joining them must lie in the convex set S. The function evaluated along that chord must be at least as large as the smaller of $f(\mathbf{x}^*)$ and $f(\mathbf{x}^{**})$. If, say, $f(\mathbf{x}^*) > f(\mathbf{x}^{**})$, points $\mathbf{x}$ arbitrarily near $\mathbf{x}^{**}$ must also yield $f(\mathbf{x}) > f(\mathbf{x}^{**})$, contradicting the assumption that $\mathbf{x}^{**}$ is a local maximum. If $f(\mathbf{x}^*) = f(\mathbf{x}^{**})$, the function must be weakly concave, with $f(\mathbf{x}) = f(k\mathbf{x}^* + (1-k)\mathbf{x}^{**}) = kf(\mathbf{x}^*) + (1-k)f(\mathbf{x}^{**})$, $0 \le k \le 1$. The function must be constant along the chord joining $\mathbf{x}^*$ and $\mathbf{x}^{**}$. It follows, therefore, that if a local maximum is unique, it is the global maximum over the convex set S.

Under what conditions will the set of variables over which a maximum problem is posed be convex? That is, under what conditions is the feasible region of a nonlinear programming problem a convex set? It is easy to show that if the constraints are all concave functions, the feasible region is in fact convex.

Consider the set S defined as the $\mathbf{x} = (x_1, \ldots, x_n)$ such that $g(\mathbf{x}) \ge a$, where a is any real number. Then S is convex; for consider any $\mathbf{x}^1, \mathbf{x}^2$ for which $g(\mathbf{x}^1) \ge a$, $g(\mathbf{x}^2) \ge a$. From concavity

$$g(k\mathbf{x}^1 + (1-k)\mathbf{x}^2) \ge kg(\mathbf{x}^1) + (1-k)g(\mathbf{x}^2) \ge ka + (1-k)a = a \qquad 0 \le k \le 1$$

Therefore the point $k\mathbf{x}^1 + (1-k)\mathbf{x}^2$ lies in the set, and S is convex. If some functions $g^1(\mathbf{x}), \ldots, g^m(\mathbf{x})$ are all concave, then the set of $\mathbf{x}$'s which satisfy

$$g^1(\mathbf{x}) \ge a_1$$
$$\cdots\cdots\cdots$$
$$g^m(\mathbf{x}) \ge a_m$$

simultaneously clearly also constitutes a convex set, as would be the case if nonnegativity constraints are added. (The intersection of convex sets is a convex set.) Hence, if the constraints of a programming problem are all concave, the feasible region will be a convex set. If the objective function is also concave, we can be assured that any local maximum is the global maximum of the model.

The principal application of the above theorem, to be discussed in the next chapter, is in the theory of linear programming in which $f(\mathbf{x})$, $g^1(\mathbf{x})$, $\ldots$, $g^m(\mathbf{x})$ are all linear functions. In that case, the feasible region is convex, and an efficient algorithm for finding the solution to the problem has been developed.

12.5 AN "ADDING-UP" THEOREM

Many economic models have the general structure:

maximize $\qquad\qquad y = f(x_1, \ldots, x_n)$

subject to $\qquad\quad g^1(x_1, \ldots, x_n) \le b_1$

$$\cdots\cdots\cdots\cdots\cdots$$

$\qquad\qquad\qquad g^m(x_1, \ldots, x_n) \le b_m \qquad x_1, \ldots, x_n \ge 0$

Let us now assume that $f, g^1, \ldots, g^m$ are all homogeneous of the same degree r.

Assume that the problem admits of a solution found by standard Lagrange-Kuhn-Tucker techniques. The lagrangian is

$$\mathscr{L} = f(x_1, \ldots, x_n) + \sum_{j=1}^{m} \lambda_j^*(b_j - g^j(x_1, \ldots, x_n)) \tag{12-56}$$

The first-order conditions are therefore

$$f_i \leq \sum_{j=1}^{m} \lambda_j^* g_i^j \qquad \text{if } <, \, x_j = 0 \tag{12-57}$$

and
$$b_j - g^j \geq 0 \qquad \text{if } >, \, \lambda_j = 0 \tag{12-58}$$

Alternatively,
$$f_i x_i^* = \sum_{j=1}^{m} \lambda_j^* g_i^j x_i^* \tag{12-59}$$

and
$$b_j \lambda_j^* = g^j \lambda_j^* \tag{12-60}$$

Let us now sum (12-59) over i and (12-60) over j. This yields

$$\sum_{i=1}^{n} f_i x_i^* = \sum_{j=1}^{m} \lambda_j^* \sum_{i=1}^{n} g_i^j x_i^* \tag{12-61}$$

and
$$\sum_{j=1}^{m} b_j \lambda_j^* = \sum_{j=1}^{m} g^j \lambda_j^* \tag{12-62}$$

Now let us use Euler's theorem. Since f and $g^1, \ldots, g^m$ are all homogeneous of degree r, $\sum f_i x_i \equiv rf$, $\sum g_i^j x_i \equiv rg^j$, and hence from (12-61), letting $y^* = f(\mathbf{x}^*)$, we have

$$ry^* = rf(\mathbf{x}^*) = \sum \lambda_j^* rg^j(\mathbf{x}^*) = r \sum_{j=1}^{m} \lambda_j^* b_j$$

or
$$y^* = \sum_{j=1}^{m} \lambda_j^* b_j \tag{12-63}$$

Now from general envelope considerations,

$$\lambda_j^* = \frac{\partial y^*}{\partial b_j}$$

If the constraint $g^j(\mathbf{x}) \leq b_j$ is thought of as a *resource constraint*, wherein b_j represents the amount of some resource used by the economy, $\lambda_j^* = \partial y^*/\partial b_j$ represents the *imputed rent*, or shadow price, of that resource, measured in terms of y. In other words, $\lambda_j^* b_j$ can be thought of as the total factor cost of some factor associated with some resource allocation. Equation (12-63) then says that under these assumptions, the output being maximized can be allocated to each resource, with nothing left over on either side. This type of adding-up, or exhaustion-of-the-product, theorem appeared in the chapters on production and cost, when linear homogeneous production functions were involved. The above is a generalization of those results.

Moreover, consider the indirect objective function

$$\phi(b_1, \ldots, b_m) = f(x_1^*, \ldots, x_n^*) = y^*$$

Since $y^* \equiv \sum_{j=1}^m \lambda_j^* b_j$ and $\lambda_j^* = \partial y^* / \partial b_j = \partial \phi / \partial b_j$,

$$\phi(b_1, \ldots, b_m) \equiv \sum_{j=1}^m \frac{\partial \phi}{\partial b_j} b_j \qquad (12\text{-}64)$$

Therefore, under these conditions, the indirect objective function is homogeneous of degree 1 in the parameters $b_1, \ldots, b_m$, from the converse of Euler's theorem.

PROBLEMS

1 Explain the error in the following statement: For a profit-maximizing firm, if the value of the marginal product of some factor is initially less than its wage, the factor will not be used. State the condition correctly.

2 Consider the constrained-*minimum* problem:

minimize $\qquad\qquad\qquad z = f(x_1, x_2)$

subject to $\qquad\qquad\qquad g(x_1, x_2) \le 0 \qquad x_1, x_2 \ge 0$

Derive the Kuhn-Tucker first-order conditions for a minimum.

3 Consider the cost-minimization problem:

minimize $\qquad\qquad\qquad C = w_1 x_1 + w_2 x_2$

subject to $\qquad\qquad\qquad f(x_1, x_2) \ge y_0 \qquad x_1, x_2 \ge 0$

Derive and interpret the first-order conditions for a minimum. Under what conditions on the production function will the lagrangian have a saddlepoint at the cost-minimizing solution?

4 Consider a consumer who maximizes the utility function $U = x_2 e^{x_1}$ subject to a budget constraint. Characterize the implied demand levels via the Kuhn-Tucker conditions, i.e., indicate when positive demand levels are present for both commodities, etc.

5 Consider the quadratic utility function, $U = ax_1^2 + 2bx_1 x_2 + cx_2^2$. Discuss the nature of the implied consumer choices for this utility function in terms of the values a, b, and c.

6 Find the solution to the following nonlinear programming problem:

maximize $\qquad\qquad\qquad y = x_1 x_2$

subject to $\qquad\quad x_1 + x_2 \le 10 \qquad x_1 + 2x_2 \le 18 \qquad x_1, x_2 \ge 0$

7 Consider the nonlinear programming problem:

maximize $\qquad\qquad\qquad y = x_1 x_2$

subject to $\qquad\quad x_1 + x_2 \le 10 \qquad x_2 \le k \qquad x_1, x_2 \ge 0$

What is the maximum value of k for which that constraint is binding?

8 Solve:

minimize $\qquad\qquad\qquad y = x_1 + 2x_2$

subject to $\qquad\quad x_1 x_2 \ge 8 \qquad x_1 \ge 5 \qquad x_1, x_2 \ge 0$

9 Solve the above problem with $x_1 \leq 5$ replacing $x_1 \geq 5$.

10 An individual has the utility function $U = x_1^{1/3}x_2^{2/3}$ for consumption in two time periods, with x_1 = present consumption, x_2 = next year's consumption. This person has an initial stock of capital of \$10, which can yield consumption along an "investment possibilities frontier," given by $2x_1^2 + x_2^2 = 200$. The person can, however, borrow and lend at some market rate of interest r to rearrange consumption.

   (*a*) Explain why maximization of utility requires a prior maximization of wealth W, where $W = x_1 + x_2/(1 + r)$. That is, explain why if W is not maximized, $U(x_1, x_2)$ cannot be maximized.

   (*b*) Suppose the consumer can borrow or lend at $r = 30$ percent. Find the utility-maximizing consumption choices. Is the consumer a borrower or a lender?

   (*c*) Suppose the consumer can lend money at only 20 percent interest and can borrow at no less than 40 percent interest. What consumption plan maximizes utility, and what is the present value of that consumption?

APPENDIX CHAPTER 12

The proof that if $f(\mathbf{x})$, $g^1(\mathbf{x})$, ..., $g^m(\mathbf{x})$ are all concave functions, then

$$\mathscr{L}(\mathbf{x}, \boldsymbol{\lambda}^*) \leq \mathscr{L}(\mathbf{x}^*, \boldsymbol{\lambda}^*) = f(\mathbf{x}^*)$$

where $\mathbf{x}^*$ solves the maximum problem, is based on a famous theorem of convex-set analysis. Consider two nonintersecting (disjoint) convex sets S_1 and S_2. It is geometrically obvious, though messy to prove, that a *hyperplane* (the generalization of a *line* in two dimensions, *plane* in three dimensions, etc.) can be passed between S_1 and S_2. This proposition is known as the *separating-hyperplane theorem*. The theorem also holds if the sets are tangent at one point.

   Consider Fig. 12-4. S_1 and S_2 are two convex sets which do not intersect. It is therefore possible to pass between them a line $p_1 x_1 + p_2 x_2 = k$ or, in vector

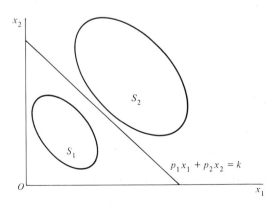

Figure 12-4 A separating hyperplane. Sets S_1 and S_2 are both convex, and they are *disjoint*; i.e., they have no point in common. Under these circumstances it is always possible to pass a hyperplane (in two dimensions, a straight line) between the two sets. The equation of this hyperplane, in two dimensions is $p_1 x_1 + p_2 x_2 = k$. Since S_2 lies above this plane, for all x_1^2, x_2^2 in S_2, $p_1 x_1^2 + p_2 x_2^2 \geq k$. Similarly, for all $x_1^1 x_2^1$ in S_1, $p_1 x_1^1 + p_2 x_2^1 \leq k$. Hence, the separating hyperplane theorem says that if S_1 and S_2 are disjoint convex sets in n space, there exists scalars $p_1, \ldots, p_n$, not all 0, such that $\sum_{i=1}^{n} p_i x_i^1 \leq \sum_{i=1}^{n} p_i x_i^2$, for all $\mathbf{x}^1$ in S_1 and $\mathbf{x}^2$ in S_2. The theorem also holds if the sets intersect at only one point, that is, S_1 and S_2 are tangent to each other.

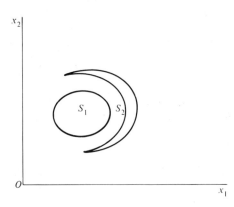

Figure 12-5 Nonconvex sets. It is not always possible to separate nonconvex sets with a hyperplane.

notation, $\mathbf{px} = k$. Figure 12-5 shows why such may not be the case if the sets are nonconvex.

Since all the points in S_2 lie "above" the hyperplane, for all $\mathbf{x}^2 \in S_2$, $\mathbf{px}^2 \geq k$. (The weak inequality is used since the hyperplane might be tangent to S_2.) Similarly, since S_1 lies "below" the hyperplane, for all $\mathbf{x}^1 \in S_1$, $\mathbf{px}^1 \leq k$. Therefore, for any two disjoint convex sets S_1 and S_2, there exists scalars p_1, p_2 not both 0 such that

$$\mathbf{px}^1 \leq \mathbf{px}^2$$

The direction of the inequality is actually arbitrary. Reversing the signs of p_1, p_2 changes the direction of the inequality. The theorem generalizes to n dimensions. If S_1 and S_2 are any two disjoint convex sets in euclidean n space, for any $\mathbf{x}^1 \in S_1$, $\mathbf{x}^2 \in S_2$, there exist scalars $p_1, \ldots, p_n$, not all zero, such that

$$\sum_{i=1}^{n} p_i x_i^1 \leq \sum_{i=1}^{n} p_i x_i^2 \tag{12A-1}$$

Let us return now to the saddlepoint problem. We are assuming that $\mathbf{x}^*$ maximizes $f(\mathbf{x})$ subject to $g^j(\mathbf{x}) \geq 0$, $j = 1, \ldots, m$, $\mathbf{x} \geq 0$. We shall also assume Slater's constraint qualification that there exists an $\mathbf{x}^0 \geq 0$ such that $g^j(\mathbf{x}^0) > 0$, $j = 1, \ldots, m$. For any given $\mathbf{x}$, there exist the $m + 1$ values $(f(\mathbf{x}), g^1(\mathbf{x}), \ldots, g^m(\mathbf{x}))$, an $(m + 1)$-dimensional vector.

1. Define the set S_1 as the vectors $\mathbf{U} = (U_0, U_1, \ldots, U_m)$ such that $U_0 \leq f(\mathbf{x})$, $U_j \leq g^j(\mathbf{x})$, $j = 1, \ldots, m$, for all feasible $\mathbf{x}$.
2. Define S_2 as the vectors $\mathbf{V} = (V_0, V_1, \ldots, V_m)$ such that $V_0 > f(\mathbf{x}^*)$, $V_j > 0, j = 1, \ldots, m$.

The sets S_1 and S_2 are convex, disjoint sets. S_1 is convex because $f, g^1, \ldots, g^m$ are all concave functions. The results at the end of Sec. 12.4 imply convexity for S_1. S_2 is convex because S_2 is essentially the positive quadrant in $m + 1$ space, except that the first coordinate, V_0, starts at $f(\mathbf{x}^*)$. Finally, since $f(\mathbf{x}^*) \geq f(\mathbf{x})$, and since $V_0 > f(\mathbf{x}^*)$, there can be no $\mathbf{V}$ vector which lies in S_1. The first coordinate, V_0, violates the definition of S_1.

Since S_1 and S_2 are disjoint convex sets, by the separating-hyperplane theorem there exist scalars $\lambda_0, \lambda_1, \ldots, \lambda_m$ such that

$$\sum_{j=0}^{m} U_j \lambda_j \leq \sum_{j=0}^{m} V_j \lambda_j \tag{12A-2}$$

for all $\mathbf{U} \in S_1$, $\mathbf{V} \in S_2$. Moreover, although the point $(f(\mathbf{x}^*), 0, \ldots, 0)$ is not in S_2, it is on the boundary of S_2 and hence the theorem applies to that point as well. The point $(f(\mathbf{x}), g^1(\mathbf{x}), \ldots, g^m(\mathbf{x}))$ is in S_1. Hence, applying equation (12A-2) gives

$$\lambda_0 f(\mathbf{x}) + \sum_{j=1}^{m} \lambda_j g^j(\mathbf{x}) \leq \lambda_0 f(\mathbf{x}^*) \tag{12A-3}$$

It can be seen from equation (12A-2) that $\lambda_0, \lambda_1, \ldots, \lambda_m$ are all nonnegative. The vectors $\mathbf{U}$ include the entire negative "quadrant," or orthant of this $m + 1$ space. Any of the U_j's can be made arbitrarily large, negatively. Note that $V_1, \ldots, V_m$ are all greater than 0. If any $\lambda_j, j = 1, \ldots, m$, were negative, making that U_j sufficiently negative would violate the inequality (12A-2). Lastly, since $f(\mathbf{x}^*) \geq f(\mathbf{x})$, and since $\mathbf{x}^*$ maximizes $f(\mathbf{x})$, $\lambda_0 \geq 0$ for essentially the same reasons.

Therefore, all the λ's in (12A-3) are nonnegative. Moreover, given the constraint qualification, $\lambda_0 > 0$; for suppose $\lambda_0 = 0$; then (12A-3) says that

$$\sum \lambda_j g^j(\mathbf{x}) \leq 0$$

However, since the separating-hyperplane theorem says that not all the λ_j's are 0 and the constraint qualification says that $g^j(\mathbf{x}^0) > 0, j = 1, \ldots, m$, it must be the case that at $\mathbf{x}^0$

$$\sum \lambda_j g^j(\mathbf{x}^0) > 0$$

contradicting the above. Hence, $\lambda_0 > 0$. We can therefore divide (12A-3) by λ_0, and if we define

$$\lambda_j^* = \frac{\lambda_j}{\lambda_0} \qquad j = 1, \ldots, m$$

equation (12A-3) becomes

$$f(\mathbf{x}) + \sum_{j=1}^{m} \lambda_j^* g^j(\mathbf{x}) \leq f(\mathbf{x}^*) \tag{12A-4}$$

When $\mathbf{x} = \mathbf{x}^*$, (12A-4) yields

$$\sum \lambda_j^* g^j(\mathbf{x}^*) \leq 0$$

but since $\lambda_j^* \geq 0$, $g^j(\mathbf{x}^*) \geq 0, j = 1, \ldots, m$,

$$\sum \lambda_j^* g^j(\mathbf{x}^*) = 0$$

Defining the lagrangian,

$$\mathscr{L}(\mathbf{x}, \lambda) = f(\mathbf{x}) + \sum_{j=1}^{m} \lambda^j g^j(\mathbf{x})$$

we find, with $\mathbf{x} \geq \mathbf{0}$, $\lambda \geq \mathbf{0}$,

$$\mathscr{L}(\mathbf{x}^*, \lambda^*) = f(\mathbf{x}^*)$$

and therefore

$$\mathscr{L}(\mathbf{x}, \lambda^*) = f(\mathbf{x}) + \sum_{j=1}^{m} \lambda_j^* g^j(\mathbf{x}) \leq f(\mathbf{x}^*) = \mathscr{L}(\mathbf{x}^*, \lambda^*) \tag{12A-5}$$

satisfying the saddlepoint criterion. We showed in the chapter proper that

$$\mathscr{L}(\mathbf{x}^*, \lambda^*) \leq \mathscr{L}(\mathbf{x}^*, \lambda)$$

Hence, if $f(\mathbf{x})$, $g^1(\mathbf{x})$, ..., $g^m(\mathbf{x})$ are all concave, and if there exists an $\mathbf{x}^0$ such that $g^j(\mathbf{x}^0) > 0$, $j = 1$, ..., m, solving the constrained-maximum problem implies that the saddlepoint condition will be satisfied.

BIBLIOGRAPHY

The following articles and books all require advanced mathematical training.

Arrow, K. J., and A. C. Enthoven: Quasi-concave Programming, *Econometrica*, **29**: 779–800, 1961.
———, L. Hurwicz, and H. Uzawa (eds.): "Studies in Linear and Nonlinear Programming," Stanford University Press, Stanford, 1958.
Dantzig, G. B.: Maximization of a Linear Function of Variables Subject to Linear Inequalities, in T. C. Koopmans (ed.), Activity Analysis of Production and Allocation, *Cowles Commission Monograph* 13, John Wiley & Sons, Inc., New York, 1951.
El Hodiri, M.: Constrained Extrema: Introduction to the Differentiable Case, with Economic Application, *Lecture Notes in Operations Research and Mathematical Systems*, vol. 56, Springer, 1970.
———: The Math-Econ Trick, *Manifold*, **17**, 8–15, Autumn 1975.
John, F.: Extremum Problems with Inequalities as Subsidiary Conditions, in "Studies and Essays, Courant Anniversary Volume," Interscience, Publishers, New York, 1948.
Kuhn, H. W., and A. W. Tucker: Nonlinear Programming, in J. Neyman (ed.), *Proceedings of the Second Berkeley Symposium on Mathematical Statistics and Probability*, University of California Press, Berkeley, 1951. The seminal work.
Rockafellar, R. T.: "Convex Analysis," Princeton University Press, Princeton, N.J., 1970.
Valentine, F.: The Problem of Lagrange with Differential Inequalities as Side Conditions, in "Contributions to the Calculus of Variations, 1933–1937," University of Chicago Press, Chicago, 1937.

THIRTEEN

GENERAL EQUILIBRIUM I: LINEAR MODELS

13.1 INTRODUCTION: FIXED-COEFFICIENT TECHNOLOGY

In the previous chapters, the models analyzed were derived from the marshallian framework of partial equilibrium. That is, the models related to *one* firm or *one* individual, with the rest of the market taken as given. No attempt was made to consider the aggregate effects of the simultaneous actions of consumers or firms in response to some parameter change. The actions of each consumer or each firm by itself may in general have no significant impact on market prices or aggregate quantities. However, if all firms or consumers react to a given parameter change in the same direction, one would expect to observe changes in the aggregate levels of other variables formerly held constant in the analysis.

Consider, for example, the effects of an increase in the price of some final good, produced by a rightward shift of the demand curve for that good. Each firm in the industry will simultaneously attempt to increase its output of that good. If a competitive factor market is assumed, each firm takes factor prices as given. That is, individual adjustments of factor levels by a given firm are not expected to affect factor prices. However, if *all* firms simultaneously wish to employ more labor and capital, the prices of labor and capital can be expected to change. If this industry is a significant part of the economy, then whether or not factor prices rise or fall might not be determinable by considering this one industry alone. In a *closed economy*, an increase in the demand for this industry's output means a *decrease* in demand for some alternative commodity. If the labor and capital markets for the two industries are interrelated, i.e., resources can move from one industry to the other, the change in factor prices depends upon the relative intensity of factor use in each industry.

The above phenomena are usually labeled *general-equilibrium problems*. The terms *partial equilibrium* and *general equilibrium* should not connote the superiority of one model over another. One model is not uniformly more general than the other. The differences between the models are best described as differences in test conditions. That is, different parameters are held fixed in the two classes of models. In the partial-equilibrium framework, in which one very small part of an economy is analyzed, prices of factors and goods in unrelated industries are assumed constant. Total quantities of goods and factors are generally considered variable. In the general-equilibrium models, as we shall see, total quantities of resources are usually assumed fixed, and the emphasis of the analysis is on interindustry reactions. The appropriateness of the model depends on the problem to be studied. Generality, while desirable *ceterus paribus*, is not necessarily to be preferred in all cases. Greater generality is usually accompanied by greater complexity. The proper trade-offs to be made for an efficient analysis of some problem cannot be assigned a priori.

This point was made earlier in Chap. 1, in the discussion of the realism of assumptions. To take a particular example, the analysis of price controls and rationing on one industry in the United States, even a large industry like the oil industry, is probably most easily handled by most economists within the standard marshallian framework of partial equilibrium. Although large in absolute size, in relation to the rest of the economy, even the oil industry is comparatively small. On the other hand, the analysis of the introduction of, say, a national value-added tax to replace other economy-wide taxes would most likely require the general-equilibrium approach for empirically valid predictions. The selection of test conditions, i.e., the parameters to be held constant, is again a function of the problem at hand and not an a priori determinable procedure.

Let us now consider an economy in which n final goods, $y_1, \ldots, y_n$, are produced. These goods are produced using m factors of production, $x_1, \ldots, x_m$. The prices of the n final goods, $p_1, \ldots, p_n$, respectively, are assumed fixed by the world market. This is known as the *small-country assumption*. This economy is sufficiently small in terms of the *world* economy for changes in its output levels not to affect world prices. (Shades of partial-equilibrium analysis!) Let

$x_{ij} =$ amount of factor i used in the production of good j

$$i = 1, \ldots, m; j = 1, \ldots, n$$

The production function for good j is then written as

$$y_j = f^j(x_{1j}, \ldots, x_{mj})$$

The total resource levels of this economy are fixed at the levels $x_1, \ldots, x_m$. That is, the quantities $x_1, \ldots, x_m$ are not choice variables but parameters in this model. With competitive markets (or, more precisely, in the absence of transactions costs), the exhaustion of gains from trade implies that the value of total (final) output, or GNP (there are no depreciable assets here, hence no distinction between GNP and NNP) is maximized. Otherwise, some individual could gain by transferring a resource from a lower-valued use to a higher-valued use. In the words of Adam Smith,

> As every individual . . . endeavors as much as he can both to employ his capital in the support of domestic industry, and so to direct that industry that its produce may be of greatest value, every individual necessarily labors to render the annual revenue of the society as great as he can . . . . [He] is in this, as in many other cases, led by an invisible hand to promote an end which was no part of his intention.†

The assertion of exhaustion of gains from exchange subject to fixed resource constraints is stated mathematically as

maximize
$$z = \sum_{j=1}^{n} p_j y_j = \sum_{j=1}^{n} p_j f^j(x_{1j}, \ldots, x_{mj})$$

subject to
$$\sum_{j=1}^{n} x_{ij} \le x_i \qquad i = 1, \ldots, m \tag{13-1}$$

We shall investigate this very general model in several stages of simplification. Consider first the model reduced to only *two* goods and *two* factors. Let us denote the factors labor L and capital K. Let the labor and capital allocated to industry j be denoted L_j and K_j, respectively. Then we can write this reduced model as follows:

maximize
$$p_1 f^1(L_1, K_1) + p_2 f^2(L_2, K_2)$$

subject to $\quad L_1 + L_2 \le L \quad\quad K_1 + K_2 \le K \quad\quad L_1, L_2, K_1, K_2 \ge 0$ $\tag{13-2}$

Here, L and K are, respectively, the parametrically "fixed" total resource endowments of labor and capital.

Of perhaps greater significance is another simplification commonly introduced into the analysis, viz., the assumption that $f^1(L_1, K_1)$ and $f^2(L_2, K_2)$ exhibit *constant returns to scale*. That is,

$$f^j(tL_j, tK_j) \equiv tf^j(L_j, K_j) = ty_j \qquad j = 1, 2$$

Since this relation holds for *all* t, let $t = 1/y_j$. Then the production relation becomes

$$1 \equiv f^j\left(\frac{L_j}{y_j}, \frac{K_j}{y_j}\right)$$

If we let $a_{Lj} = L_j/y_j$ and $a_{Kj} = K_j/y_j$, the production functions become

$$f^j(a_{Lj}, a_{Kj}) \equiv 1$$

This construction indicates that constant-returns-to-scale production functions are completely described by the knowledge of *one* isoquant, here, the unit isoquant, i.e., the isoquant representing 1 unit of output. This is as should be expected

---

† Adam Smith, "Wealth of Nations," bk. IV, chap. II.

since the level curves of linear homogeneous functions are all radial blowups of each other.

The quantities a_{ij} represent the amount of resource i used to produce 1 unit of output j. They are often known as *input-output coefficients*. They are in general considered to be *variable*, changing continuously over a wide range (0 to $+\infty$ in the case of isoquants which are asymptotic to each axis).

When this formulation of the production functions is used, the model expressed in equations (13-2) can be transformed into:

maximize
$$z = p_1 y_1 + p_2 y_2$$

subject to
$$a_{L1} y_1 + a_{L2} y_2 \leq L \qquad (13\text{-}3)$$

$$a_{K1} y_1 + a_{K2} y_2 \leq K$$

$$f^1(a_{L1}, a_{K1}) \equiv 1$$

$$f^2(a_{L2}, a_{K2}) \equiv 1$$

$$y_1, y_2 \geq 0$$

In this form, the theorems of international trade theory (the factor-price equalization, Stolper-Samuelson, and Rybczynski theorems) are derivable. We shall derive these theorems at this level of generality in the next chapter. In this chapter, however, we shall consider this model in a still simpler framework, that of fixed-coefficient technology. In so doing, we shall develop the body of analysis known as *linear programming* and illustrate its empirical usefulness. By fixed coefficients we mean the very special case where the a_{ij}'s are constants—fixed, as it were, by nature at preassigned values. In this case, the model described by equations (13-3) becomes a *linear programming* problem:

maximize
$$z = p_1 y_1 + p_2 y_2$$

subject to
$$a_{L1} y_1 + a_{L2} y_2 \leq L$$

$$a_{K1} y_1 + a_{K2} y_2 \leq K \qquad y_1, y_2 \geq 0$$

Here, p_1, p_2, L, K and all the a_{ij}'s are constants. The problem becomes one of maximizing a linear function subject to linear inequality constraints, hence, a *linear* programming problem. (In general, one could deal with several goods and factors.) Even in this highly restrictive form, the model is capable of yielding insights into the general equilibrium economy. This will be the object of this chapter. Let us first examine more closely the nature of fixed-coefficient technology.

Production functions of this type were discussed briefly in Chap. 10. They can be represented as

$$y_j = \min \left(\frac{L_j}{a_{Lj}}, \frac{K_j}{a_{Kj}} \right) \qquad (13\text{-}4)$$

The isoquants of this production function (the term is applied loosely) are L-shaped, as depicted in Fig. 13-1. For example, consider the function $y = \min (L/1,$

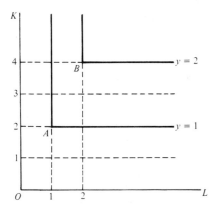

Figure 13-1 Fixed coefficient production functions. The assumption that input-output coefficients of production are fixed leads to L-shaped isoquants. Production of 1 unit of output *requires* a certain amount of each factor. In the figure production of 1 unit of output requires 1 unit of labor and 2 units of capital. This input combination is labeled as point A. With 2 units of K available, no additional output occurs if more than 1 unit of labor is added. Thus, the isoquant is horizontal to the right of A, and $\mathrm{MP}_L = 0$. Similarly, the isoquant is vertical above A, since $\mathrm{MP}_K = 0$ for $L = 1$, $K > 2$. If both labor *and* capital are increased in the same proportion, then (since the input-output coefficients are constants) output will rise by the same proportion. Hence, this function is a special case of constant-returns-to-scale production functions. For example, in the figure when $L = 2$, $K = 4$, output is $y = 2$.

$K/2$); 1 unit of output can be produced using 1 unit of labor and 2 units of capital. Thus, $a_{L1} = 1$, $a_{K1} = 2$. If either factor is increased, holding the other factor constant, output remains the same. For example, if L is increased to 2 units, holding K at 2, then

$$\min\left(\tfrac{2}{1}, \tfrac{2}{2}\right) = \min\left(\tfrac{1}{1}, \tfrac{2}{2}\right) = 1 \text{ unit of } y$$

The marginal products of labor and capital are never simultaneously nonzero. For example, to the right of point A, $\mathrm{MP}_L = 0$, since additional amounts of labor yield no increases in output. However, increases in capital will yield increases in output there, and hence $\mathrm{MP}_K > 0$. At point A, the marginal products of labor and capital are undefined. Any movement at all to the right of A, no matter how small, will yield $\mathrm{MP}_K > 0$. To the left of A, $\mathrm{MP}_K = 0$; however, $\mathrm{MP}_L > 0$. Thus, this production function yields discontinuous marginal product functions. The points of discontinuity are the corners of the isoquants, where the marginal technical rate of substitution, $\mathrm{MP}_L/\mathrm{MP}_K$ is undefined, since no unique slope of the isoquant exists there.

Constancy of the a_{ij}'s is clearly a highly restrictive assumption about productive processes. It can be generalized somewhat by assuming that the firm is faced with not one but several (though finite) distinct production coefficient possibilities, called *activities*. That is, suppose, in addition to the input-output coefficients $(a_{L1}, a_{K1}) = (1, 2)$ as in the example in Fig. 13-1, the firm could produce 1 unit of output with the coefficients $(b_{L1}, b_{K1}) = (3, 1)$, or $(c_{L1}, c_{K1}) = (2, 3)$. This situation is depicted in Fig. 13-2. The three activities are denoted A, B, and C, respectively.

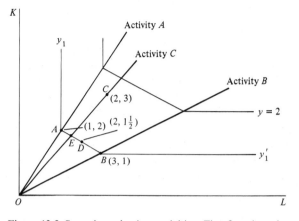

Figure 13-2 Several production activities. The firm has three distinct production activities, or technologies, available to it. The first, represented by point A, is the technology discussed in Fig. 13-1, wherein 1 unit of output requires 1 unit of labor L and 2 units of capital K. However, the firm can also produce 1 unit of output using 3 units of L and 1 unit of K (point B), or 2 units of L and 3 units of K (point C). In addition, the firm can use any *convex combination* of these processes. That is, any input combination whose coordinates lie along the straight line joining any two processes is also feasible. Thus, 1 unit of output can be produced by using 2 units of L and $1\frac{1}{2}$ units of K (point D). This is accomplished by using processes A and B simultaneously, at half the unit output rate each. If process A is used k percent and B is used $1 - k$ percent, the process $kA + (1 - k)B$ is generated, represented geometrically by the line segment AB.

It is clear that process C will never be used at positive factor prices. There is a process E utilizing activities A and B in some proportion (what proportions?) which yields 1 unit of output using less of *both* labor and capital than activity C. The unit isoquant for this firm is therefore a vertical line above A, the segment AB, and a horizontal line to the right of B. These points represent minimum combinations of L and K needed to produce 1 unit of output. Constant returns to scale imply that all other isoquants will have corners along the rays OA, OB.

Let us now assume, in addition, that *the firm can choose to use one or more processes, or activities, simultaneously*. That is, assume that these activities are not mutually exclusive but can be used simultaneously side by side.

Suppose, for example, 1 unit of output was to be produced by producing $\frac{1}{2}$ unit using activity A and $\frac{1}{2}$ unit by activity B. To produce $\frac{1}{2}$ unit of output by A will require $\frac{1}{2}$ unit of labor and 1 unit of capital (halfway along the ray from the origin to point A). Similarly, using the B activity coefficients, producing $\frac{1}{2}$ unit of output will require $1\frac{1}{2}$ units of labor and $\frac{1}{2}$ unit of capital. Together, then, production of 1 unit of output using activities A and B together at equal (half) intensities will require 2 $(= \frac{1}{2} + 1\frac{1}{2})$ units of labor and $1\frac{1}{2}$ $(= 1 + \frac{1}{2})$ units of capital. Geometrically, this new composite activity $D = (d_{L1}, d_{K1}) = (2, 1\frac{1}{2})$ lies midway on the straight line joining points A and B. In fact, if each original activity can be used in any proportion with another, then 1 unit of output can be produced by the activities defined by the coordinates of all points lying on the straight line joining the original activity levels. Producing 1 unit by using A to produce $\frac{1}{4}$ unit and B $\frac{3}{4}$ unit will be represented by the point three-fourths of the way toward B on the line segment AB.

Algebraically, this is represented as follows. Suppose $A = (L^A, K^A)$ and $B = (L^B, K^B)$ are any two processes which yield 1 unit of output. Points A and B are two points on the unit isoquant. Under the assumptions of constant returns to scale and complete divisibility of these processes, 1 unit of output can be produced using any *weighted average* of processes A and B as long as the weights sum to unity. Thus, 1 unit of output can be produced using $\mathbf{x} = kA + (1 - k)B$, where $0 \leq k \leq 1$. That is, $L^x = kL^A + (1 - k)L^B$, $K^x = kK^A + (1 - k)K^B$. As k varies from 0 to 1, $\mathbf{x}$ traces out the points on the straight line joining A and B.

More generally, suppose that $\mathbf{x}^1, \ldots, \mathbf{x}^m$ represent m points in n space. The set of points $\mathbf{x} = \sum_{i=1}^{m} k_i \mathbf{x}^i$ such that $k_i \geq 0$, $\sum k_i = 1$, is called a *convex combination* of $\mathbf{x}^1, \ldots, \mathbf{x}^m$. The convex combination of points A, B, and C in Fig. 13-2 would be represented by all points within and on the boundary of a triangle formed by joining points A, B, and C. In linear models of this type the assumption is generally made that the convex combinations of unit processes are all alternative processes for the firm to consider.

It is clear from the geometry in Fig. 13-2, however, that activity C will never be used by a cost-minimizing firm. Point E on the line AB, representing some mix of the activities A and B, leads to production of 1 unit of output using less of both labor and capital than point C. Activities A and B dominate activity C. Activity C becomes irrelevant because it will never be observed.

The unit isoquant for a firm endowed with activities A, B, and C is therefore the kinked line consisting of: (1) the vertical segment emanating from point A (designated Ay_1, though this line proceeds to infinity); (2) the line AB, and (3) a line horizontal from B, denoted By_1'. Since these production activities are linear homogeneous, isoquants for other levels of production will be radial blowups of this unit isoquant, with the kinks or corners along extensions of the rays OA, OB. Most important, an isoquant map which is convex to the origin has been obtained.

Consider now the nature of a cost-minimizing solution, say for $y_1 = 1$ (perfectly representative, due to homotheticity), as depicted in Fig. 13-3. The slope of line segment AB is $-\frac{1}{2}$. Thus, along this segment the ratio of the marginal product of labor to that of capital is constant at $MP_L/MP_K = \frac{1}{2}$. Let

> w be the wage rate of labor and r be the "rental" rate on capital

then the ordinary tangency condition for cost-minimization is that $MP_L/MP_K = w/r$. Here, however, if the wage rate is ever so slightly more than half the rental rate, so that $w/r > \frac{1}{2}$, the cost-minimizing solution will occur at point A. This will be where an isocost line, wr in Fig. 13-3, just touches the isoquant $y_1 ABy_1'$. Only the relatively capital-intensive activity will be used. If the wage rate falls so that $w/r < \frac{1}{2}$, as depicted by the isocost segment $w'r'$, the cost-minimizing solution jumps to point B. With this shift in factor prices, only the labor-intensive activity, or process, will be used. We see that small changes in factor prices, from $\frac{1}{2} + \varepsilon$ to $\frac{1}{2} - \varepsilon$, where $\varepsilon > 0$ can be as small as one likes, can produce a substantial change in the factor mix. When $w/r = \frac{1}{2}$, the isocost line will be tangent to the isoquant along the whole segment AB, producing an infinite number of solutions.

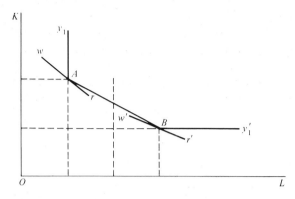

Figure 13-3 Cost minimization with linear-segment isoquants. When isoquants consist of straight-line segments with corners, as generated by constant-coefficient production functions with more than one technology, the cost-minimizing solution will not in general be the tangency condition $MP_L/MP_K = w/r$. This occurs simply because the isoquant will have only a finite number of slopes (above, only three: $-\infty$, $-\frac{1}{2}$, 0), whereas w/r can vary continuously from $+\infty$ to 0. For finite factor prices, only if $w/r = \frac{1}{2}$ will an actual tangency occur. If $w/r > \frac{1}{2}$, the cost-minimizing solution will be at point A. If $w/r < \frac{1}{2}$, the solution will be at point B. If $w/r = \frac{1}{2}$, all points along the line segment AB will be cost-minimizing solutions. Notice that changes in the factor-price ratio will often produce no change at all in the input combination. Only if in changing, w/r passes through the value of $\frac{1}{2}$ (even ever so slightly), will the input combination change. And any such small change around the value $\frac{1}{2}$ will produce a *discontinuous* change in the factor mix.

Let us formulate algebraically the problem of minimizing the cost of achieving some parametric level of output y^0, given the three possible activities above. The objective function is to minimize $z = wL + rK$, where w and r are parametric factor prices and L and K are the total amounts of labor and capital used. Labor and capital can be used in any of the three processes. Denote the amounts of labor allocated to processes A, B, and C as L_A, L_B, and L_C, respectively, and likewise K_A, K_B, and K_C for capital. Thus, $L = L_A + L_B + L_C$, and $K = K_A + K_B + K_C$.

If process A is used, with coefficients (1, 2), then $L_A = K_A/2$, and $y_A = L_A$. Likewise, for process B, $L_B = 3K_B$ and $y_B = L_B/3$. For process C, $L_C/2 = K_C/3$, and $y_C = L_C/2$. The problem can thus be posed as,

minimize
$$w(L_A + L_B + L_C) + r\left(2L_A + \frac{L_B}{3} + \frac{3}{2}L_C\right)$$

subject to
$$L_A + \frac{L_B}{3} + \frac{L_C}{2} \geq y^0$$

and
$$L_A, L_B, L_C \geq 0 \qquad\qquad (13\text{-}5)$$

Although the problem posed in (13-5) involves only simple linear equations, it is not at all trivial to solve. The lagrangian is,

$$\mathscr{L} = w(L_A + L_B + L_C) + r\left(2L_A + \frac{L_B}{3} + \frac{3}{2}L_C\right) + \lambda\left(y^0 - L_A - \frac{L_B}{3} - \frac{L_C}{2}\right)$$

producing the first-order relations,

$$w + 2r - \lambda \geq 0 \qquad \text{if} >, L_A = 0$$

$$w + \frac{r}{3} - \frac{\lambda}{3} \geq 0 \qquad \text{if} >, L_B = 0$$

$$w + \frac{3}{2}r - \frac{\lambda}{2} \geq 0 \qquad \text{if} >, L_C = 0 \qquad (13\text{-}6)$$

$$y^0 - L_A - \frac{L_B}{3} - \frac{L_C}{2} \leq 0 \qquad \text{if} <, \lambda = 0 \qquad (13\text{-}7)$$

The Lagrange multiplier λ is interpretable as marginal cost as in the neoclassical case. Since $MC = w + 2r$ if process A is used, $MC = 3w + r$ if process B is used, and $MC = 2w + 3r$ if process C is used; relations (13-6) say that at the cost-minimum point the only process that will be used is the process for which MC is minimized (unless several are equally minimal). Of course, for linear homogeneous production functions, of which this is a special case, $MC = AC$, and thus this procedure minimizes total cost. But this does not help us much in actually *finding* the solution, i.e., finding which process or processes to use. Problems of this type require solution by *algorithm*. That is, some iterative procedure is required to approach the solution in a finite number of steps. This algorithm must be able to reveal which first-order conditions are in fact binding and which are to be ignored. This is not usually possible without some search procedure, in which changes in the variables which move the program closer to solution are revealed as the algorithm, or routine, is carried out.

The assumption of constant coefficients in any model of economic behavior can generally be counted on to be in violation of the facts over some finite time period. The assumption may nonetheless be useful, however, if it enlarges the tractability of the model. As pointed out in Chap. 1, assumptions are always simplifications of reality by definition and are incorporated into the analysis to improve the manageability of the model or theory. In the case of linear models, the benefit of this assumption is that a well-established, easy-to-use algorithm exists for finding the solution to the model. Reality of assumptions is traded off for tractability—in this case, actually obtaining solutions. We shall now investigate this class of models and their solution.

13.2 THE LINEAR ACTIVITY-ANALYSIS MODEL: A SPECIFIC EXAMPLE

In this section we shall investigate a particular linear programming problem and use it to illustrate the general nature of such models. In the next section, the general theorems and methodology will be presented.

Consider a firm (or an economy made up of many such identical firms) which can produce two goods, food y_1 and clothing y_2. Let us now suppose that *three* inputs are used to produce these outputs: H, land; L, labor; and K, capital (to use an historically important but misleading taxonomy). These inputs must be combined in fixed proportions to produce 1 unit of either food or clothing. In particular, assume that to produce 1 unit of food requires 3 acres, 2 worker-hours, and 1 "machine" (unit of capital). To produce 1 unit of clothing requires 2 acres, 2 worker-hours, and 2 machines (the same machines as for food). This technology, or state of the art, is representable by the following input-output matrix $\mathbf{A}$:

$$\mathbf{A} = \begin{pmatrix} 3 & 2 \\ 2 & 2 \\ 1 & 2 \end{pmatrix} \tag{13-8}$$

where a_{ij} = amount of factor i used to produce 1 unit of output j
$\quad i = H, L, K; j = 1, 2$

Since three factors and two outputs are involved, the resulting input-output matrix contains three rows and two columns. These coefficients are *fixed*, i.e., constant at their given values. No other processes or activities are available to this firm or economy.†

Let us assume now that this firm is endowed with 54 acres of land, 40 worker-hours, and 35 machines, representing the resource constraints. Further, assume that food sells for $40 per unit and clothing for $30 per unit; that is, $p_1 = \$40$, $p_2 = \$30$.

We now assert that this firm or an economy made up of many such firms maximizes the total value of output of food and clothing, subject to the constraints imposed by the scarcity of resources (factors) and the nonnegativity of factors. The mathematical statement of this model is:

maximize $\quad z = 40y_1 + 30y_2$

subject to $\quad 3y_1 + 2y_2 \leq 54 \quad$ land constraint

$\qquad\qquad 2y_1 + 2y_2 \leq 40 \quad$ labor constraint

$\qquad\qquad y_1 + 2y_2 \leq 35 \quad$ capital constraint $\quad y_1, y_2 \geq 0$ $\qquad$ (13-9)

Mathematically, the problem is to maximize a linear function subject to linear inequality constraints and nonnegativity of the decision variables. The constraints

---

† More general models, called *Leontief input-output models*, after their inventor, Wassily Leontief, allow variables to be *both* the objects of final consumption (outputs) *and* inputs. For example, some food will likely be used in the production of clothing, and vice versa. The matrix of coefficients would have to be suitably expanded. If $\mathbf{B} = (b_{ij})$ represents the amount of outputs i used to produce 1 unit of output j, if $\mathbf{C} = (c_1, \ldots, c_n)$ represents a vector of final consumption of these outputs, and if $\mathbf{X} = (x_1, \ldots, x_n)$ represents total production of these goods, then, by arithmetic, $\sum_{j=1}^{n} b_{ij} x_j + c_i = x_i, i = 1, \ldots, n$. In matrix form, $\mathbf{BX} + \mathbf{C} = \mathbf{X}$, or $\mathbf{C} = (\mathbf{I} - \mathbf{B})\mathbf{X}$, where $\mathbf{I}$ represents the $n \times n$ identity matrix. The production $\mathbf{X}$ needed to sustain consumption $\mathbf{C}$ is $\mathbf{X} = (\mathbf{I} - \mathbf{B})^{-1}\mathbf{C}$. It can be shown that the inverse $(\mathbf{I} - \mathbf{B})^{-1}$ exists only if $(\mathbf{I} - \mathbf{B})^{-1} = \mathbf{I} + \mathbf{B} + \mathbf{B}^2 + \cdots$ is a convergent series, analogous to the sum of an infinite geometric series in ordinary algebra.

in (13-9) say that no more than 54 acres, 40 worker-hours, and 35 machines may be used by this firm. However, it is possible to use *less* than these amounts. That is, the firm is not bound to use all its resources. And we can quickly see that it cannot be the case that all three factors will be fully utilized; in that case, the constraints in (13-9) would represent three independent equations in two unknowns, yielding no solution. How shall we discover which resources to utilize fully?

A graphical solution The solution to this linear programming problem can be obtained graphically, since only two decision variables, y_1 and y_2, are present. In Fig. 13-4, coordinate axes have been drawn, with y_1 the abcissa and y_2 the ordinate. Since outputs are constrained to be nonnegative, only the first (nonnegative) quadrant of euclidean space is relevant. If all land were to be used, the combinations of food and clothing that could be produced would satisfy $3y_1 + 2y_2 = 54$, a strict equality. This is the line denoted "land" in Fig. 13-4, having horizontal

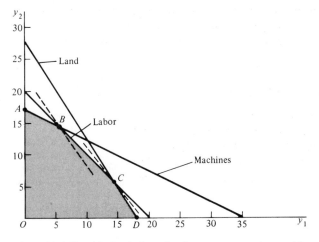

Figure 13-4 Graphical solution of a linear programming problem. The feasible region of a linear programming problem is the set of points which satisfy all the constraints (including nonnegativity) simultaneously. In the above model, this is represented by the region $OABCD$. Along AB, the capital, or machine, constraint $y_1 + 2y_2 = 35$ is binding, but the land and labor constraints are nonbinding. Those two constraints lie above and to the right (except at point B) of the capital constraint there. At point B, both the capital and labor constraints are binding, while along BC (excluding point C), only the labor constraint is binding, i.e., holds as an *equality*. Similarly, along CD (excluding C) only the land constraint holds as an equality. The feasible region is a *convex set*. If *any* two points in $OABCD$ are selected, all points on the straight line joining those two points also lie in $OABCD$.

The (maximum) solution of the linear programming problem occurs where the isorevenue line $z = 40y_1 + 30y_2$ is shifted as far from the origin as is consistent with its remaining in contact with the feasible region $OABCD$. This occurs, for this problem, at point C, where the labor and land constraints are binding and the capital constraint is nonbinding. The slope of the isorevenue line is $p_1/p_2 = 40/30 = \frac{4}{3}$. This is *greater* than the slope of the production possibilities frontier along BC (1) and less than the slope along CD ($\frac{3}{2}$). No tangency (in the sense of equal slopes) occurs. Instead the inequality conditions that for each good, MR < MC for increases in output, MR > MC for decreases in output, hold at point C. The maximum is global because $OABCD$ is a convex set. There are no corners jutting out at points removed from C.

intercept 18, vertical intercept 27. However, the constraint says merely that *not more than 54* units of land may be used, and possibly less. Hence, the set of all output combinations possible under the land constraint is the triangular area bound by this line and the positive axes. It is not possible to obtain output combinations outside this triangle.

However, the above is only one of three constraints (aside from nonnegativity). In addition, no more than 40 worker-hours are available. This implies that no output combinations are attainable which lie outside the line $2y_1 + 2y_2 = 40$ (denoted "labor" in Fig. 13-4). Output is further constrained to lie within (boundaries included) the triangle defined by this line and the nonnegative axes. Lastly, since only 35 machines are available, all output combinations must lie within the triangle whose boundaries are the nonnegative axes and the line $y_1 + 2y_2 = 35$.

The set of all output combinations which satisfy all the constraints (including nonnegativity) is called the *feasible region* for the problem. The feasible region for this problem is the shaded polygonal area $OABCD$ in Fig. 13-4. It is called the feasible region simply because this set of points represents all possible outputs, given the constraints imposed by scarcity of resources.

The feasible regions of all linear programming problems have the important property of being *convex sets*. Recall from the previous chapter that a convex set is one in which the straight line joining any two points in the set lies entirely in the set. The feasible region is convex here because the constraints, being linear, are therefore *concave* functions (though weakly so). As we saw in Chap. 12, if $g^j(x_1, \ldots, x_n)$ is a concave function, the area defined by $g^j \geq 0, j = 1, \ldots, m$ is a convex set. We shall show this again, in more detail, for linear functions in the next section. The objective function, also linear, is therefore also concave. Therefore, we know that if a *local* maximum of this function is achieved over the (convex) feasible region, it is also a *global* maximum. And if the maximum is not unique, there are an infinite number of local maxima, all equal, along the straight line joining any two maxima.

Let us now move on to the solution of the problem. The objective is to maximize the linear function $z = 40y_1 + 30y_2$ such that the point (y_1, y_2) lies in the feasible region $OABCD$. This isorevenue line (hyperplane, in more than three dimensions) achieves higher values the farther it is from the origin. This isorevenue line has a slope $= -\frac{4}{3}$. One such line is the dotted line through point B. It clearly is not the maximum z, which is in fact obtained when $z = 40y_1 + 30y_2$ passes through point C. At point C, only the land and labor constraints are binding. Point C lies wholly within the machine constraint, that is, $y_1 + 2y_2 < 35$. The solution values of y_1 and y_2 are thus obtained by solving simultaneously the land and labor constraints, *as equalities*, ignoring the machine constraint entirely. That is, point C is the intersection of

$$3y_1 + 2y_2 = 54 \quad \text{and} \quad 2y_1 + 2y_2 = 40 \tag{13-10}$$

Solving simultaneously quickly yields the solution values $y_1^* = 14$, $y_2^* = 6$, with $z^* = 40(14) + 30(6) = \$740$.

We can also determine the allocation of factor resources to each industry or final good. Since $y_1 = 14$, the amounts of land, labor, and capital used to produce food, y_1, are $a_{11} y_1$, $a_{21} y_1$ and $a_{31} y_1$, respectively, or 42 acres, 28 worker-hours, and 14 machines. For clothing, y_2, the resource requirements are $a_{12} y_2$, $a_{22} y_2$, and $a_{32} y_2$, respectively, or, since $y_2 = 6$, 12 acres, 12 worker-hours, and 12 machines. All together, $42 + 12 = 54$ acres, $28 + 12 = 40$ worker-hours, and $14 + 12 = 26$ machines are used. Land and labor are fully employed and machines are only partially employed, as indicated by the observation that the machine constraint is the only constraint which is nonbinding.

Geometrically, it is clear that point C provides the maximum value of z. It is also visually obvious for this problem that C is the *global* maximum of z. This latter statement is a consequence of $OABCD$ being a convex set, and $z = 40y_1 + 30y_2$ being a (weakly) concave function. The impact of the theorem on maximization of concave functions over convex sets is geometrically clear in this example. (Remember, of course, that one example proves little!)

That point C is the solution is clear from economic reasoning as well. The boundary of the feasible region, the broken line $ABCD$, is the production possibilities frontier for this firm or economy. The slope of this frontier represents the marginal cost of obtaining more y_1. Along line segment AB, this marginal cost is $\frac{1}{2}$ unit of y_2. The 5 units of y_1 produced at B are achieved at the expense of $2\frac{1}{2}$ units of y_2 ($17\frac{1}{2}$ at A minus 15 at B). However, the marginal *benefit* of producing y_1 is given by the slope of the isorevenue line, or $\frac{4}{3}$ unit of y_2. Since MR > MC for y_1, it pays to increase production of y_1. When point B is reached, the marginal cost changes discontinuously. Along the segment BC, marginal cost $= 1$. This is still less than marginal revenue, hence it pays to move all the way along BC to point C. However, it does not pay to move beyond point C. Along CD, MC of y_1 is $\frac{3}{2}$, which is greater than MR $= \frac{4}{3}$. There is no point on this frontier where MC $=$ MR. However, there is a point C for which, in terms of y_1, MC < MR to the left of C and MC > MR to the right of C. That is, at point C, $y_1 = 14$. For $y_1 < 14$, MC < MR, whereas for $y_1 > 14$, MC > MR. (Marginal cost is undefined at $y_1 = 14$ since the frontier has a corner there, i.e., the frontier is nondifferentiable there.) We can thus expect no marginal *equalities* as defining the extreme values of the objective functions, but we can expect a series of marginal *inequalities*, indicating that a move in any direction will leave the firm or economy in a lower-valued option.

There is one instance in which marginal equalities do occur. Suppose p_1 had been \$30 instead of \$40. Then the MR of y_1 would be unity. This is precisely MC all along segment BC. In this case there would not be one solution to the linear programming problem but an infinite number of solutions. The isorevenue line would be tangent to the feasible region at all points along BC; all those points would therefore be the solution of the problem. This is the situation where if two local maxima exist for a concave function defined over a convex set, all points along the straight line joining those maxima are also maxima.

To economists, the interest in this problem goes beyond the mere attainment of a solution. We have seen that in constrained-maximization models, new variables, the Lagrange multipliers, imputed some sort of value to the constraint, e.g., the marginal utility of money income, or marginal cost of production with resources. These imputed values are present here also, though we have not yet expressly introduced them as Lagrange multipliers in the analysis.

Consider that since land is scarce, output is not as large as it otherwise would be. In particular, suppose this firm or economy possessed 55 acres of land instead of just 54. How would this affect the value of output? The maximum value of output would now occur at a new point C', the intersection of the constraint boundaries

$$3y_1 + 2y_2 = 55 \quad \text{land}$$

$$2y_1 + 2y_2 = 40 \quad \text{labor}$$

Solving, we get $y_1^* = 15$, $y_2^* = 5$. The value of total income, z^*, is now $z^* = 40(15) + 30(5) = \$750$, a gain of \$10.

The fact that income would grow by \$10 if one additional acre of land were available imputes a value, a *shadow price*, or *imputed rent* as it is called, to land. Clearly, the marginal value product of land is \$10. In a competitive economy, this land would rent for \$10 per acre. Moreover, the marginal value of land will remain constant as long as the maximum value of income is determined by the intersection of the land and labor constraints only.

Suppose land is increased to $54 + \Delta H$. Then the value of total income is determined using the solution of

$$3y_1 + 2y_2 = 54 + \Delta H \qquad 2y_1 + 2y_2 = 40 \qquad (13\text{-}11)$$

Thus $$y_1^* = 14 + \Delta H \qquad y_2^* = 6 - \Delta H$$

Formerly, $z^* = 740$. The new value of z^* is

$$z^* + \Delta z^* = 40(14 + \Delta H) + 30(6 - \Delta H) = 740 + 10\,\Delta H$$

Thus, $\Delta z^* = 10\,\Delta H$, or, taking limits,

$$\frac{\partial z^*}{\partial H} = 10 \qquad (13\text{-}12)$$

This is precisely the envelope theorem, which says that the rate of change of the objective function (here z^*) with respect to a parameter representing a resource constraint is the imputed value of that resource.

We shall denote this imputed value, or shadow price, of the first factor, land, as

$$u_1 = \frac{\partial z^*}{\partial H} \qquad (13\text{-}13a)$$

Note that u_1 is *constant* at \$10. It does not depend on the parametric values of either the land or labor resource constraints, 54 acres and 40 worker-hours, respectively. This result is the basis of what is known as the Stolper-Samuelson and factor-price equalization theorems. In the next chapter we shall show that for the general case of linear homogeneous production functions (of which fixed coefficients are a special case), factor prices are functions of output prices only. Hence, the above result, that the factor price of land is constant (subject to the qualification below), independent of the resource endowments in some neighborhood of the initial solution.

We shall see more explicitly how the factor prices become Lagrange multipliers (called *dual variables* there) in the next section. Note, however, in the solution to equations (13-11) above, that ΔH must be less than 6; otherwise y_2 would become negative. The algebraic algorithm for solving these problems is vitally dependent on these changes. When ΔH becomes greater than 6, the solution will move to a new corner of the feasible region and the marginal valuation of resources will change. (In fact, the marginal value of land will fall to zero. Why?)

In a similar manner, we can determine the imputed wage rate in this "economy." If the amount of labor is increased by an amount ΔL, the new value of output is determined by

$$3y_1 + 2y_2 = 54 \qquad 2y_1 + 2y_2 = 40 + \Delta L$$

Thus
$$y_1^* = 14 - \Delta L \qquad y_2^* = 6 + \tfrac{3}{2}\,\Delta L$$

Therefore,

$$z^* + \Delta z^* = 40(14 - \Delta L) + 30(6 + \tfrac{3}{2}\,\Delta L) = 740 + 5\,\Delta L$$

Subtracting $z^* = 740$, we have $\Delta z^*/\Delta L = 5$, or, taking limits,

$$u_2 = \frac{\partial z^*}{\partial L} = 5 \tag{13-13b}$$

The marginal value of labor is \$5. A competitive economy would result in labor's receiving this wage. Here, since $y_1^* = 14 - \Delta L$, $\Delta L \leq 14$. If labor increased by more than 14 worker-hours, the marginal values of the factors would change since a new corner of the feasible region would be reached. (In fact, the marginal value of labor would fall to 0 if $\Delta L \geq 4.5$. Why?)

Lastly, consider what the effects on z^* would be if more machines ΔK were available. The machine constraint is already nonbinding. Only 26 machines are used, in spite of 35 being available. An additional machine would add nothing to income; its marginal value is 0. Machines, though limited, are not scarce. They are a free good, being available in greater supply than the quantity demanded at zero price. Thus,

$$u_3 = \frac{\partial z^*}{\partial K} = 0 \tag{13-13c}$$

Do not assume that since the *marginal* evaluation of capital (machines) is 0 capital is redundant in this economy. In fact, 26 machines are used. Moreover, with fixed coefficients, production, by definition, is impossible without certain amounts of each factor. The *marginal* product of capital is 0 because the nine *extra* machines are incapable of being combined productively with the available land and labor. This is a feature of fixed-coefficient technology. The *total* product of capital is certainly not zero. Capital is merely redundant at the particular margin in question, where $y_1 = 14$, $y_2 = 6$.

The above phenomena are special cases of the factor-price equalization theorem. With unchanging output prices, factor prices remain the same when endowments are changed. This holds until endowments change sufficiently to cause new factors to be brought in and one or more formerly positively used factors to fall from use.

13.3 THE RYBCZYNSKI THEOREM

Let us now consider the effects on output of changes in the land H and labor L endowments. We found $y_1^* = 14 + \Delta H$, $y_2^* = 6 - \Delta H$, and $y_1^* = 14 - \Delta L$, $y_2^* = 6 + \frac{3}{2} \Delta L$. Combining these into one total differential expression gives

$$dy_1^* = dH - dL \qquad dy_2^* = -dH + \tfrac{3}{2} dL$$

These results are examples of the *Rybczynski theorem*. This important theorem says that if the endowment of some resource increases, the industry that uses that resource most intensively will increase its output while the other industry will decrease its output. The relative factor intensity is measured by the ratio of factor use in each industry. For example, L_1/K_1, L_2/K_2, the labor-capital ratios in industry 1 and industry 2, are compared. The industry for which this ratio is higher is relatively labor-intensive; the other is relatively capital-intensive. However, note that

$$\frac{L_j}{K_j} = \frac{L_j/y_j}{K_j/y_j} = \frac{a_{Lj}}{a_{Kj}}$$

Hence, the factor intensities can also be determined by the ratios of the a_{ij}'s, in the appropriate manner.

In the present example, the only two factors which are relevant at the solution point are land and labor. The food industry y_1 is relatively *land*-intensive, since $a_{11}/a_{21} > a_{12}/a_{22}$, that is, $\frac{3}{2} > \frac{2}{3}$. Clothing y_2 is relatively *labor*-intensive. When the endowment of land *increases* by dH, food production is *increased* by dH while clothing production actually *decreases*, also by dH. On the other hand, if the endowment of labor were to *increase* by dL, the labor-intensive industry y_2 would *increase* by $\frac{3}{2} dL$, whereas food output would *decline* by dL. These results are shown graphically in Fig. 13-5.

Algebraically, the Rybczynski theorem results from the simple solution of simultaneous equations. In our example, the solution values of the model are determined by the land and labor constraints,

$$a_{11}y_1 + a_{12}y_2 = H \qquad \text{land} \tag{13-14a}$$

$$a_{21}y_1 + a_{22}y_2 = L \qquad \text{labor} \tag{13-14b}$$

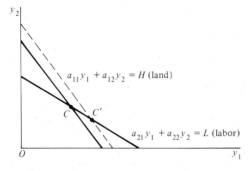

Figure 13-5 The Rybczynski theorem in a linear model, showing the land and labor constraints. The capital constraint, being nonbinding, is omitted. Maximum income occurs at point C. The slope of the land constraint is $-a_{11}/a_{12} = -\frac{3}{2}$ in our model. The slope of the labor constraint is $-a_{21}/a_{22} = -1$. Since $a_{11}/a_{12} > a_{21}/a_{22}$, $a_{11}/a_{21} > a_{12}/a_{22}$, or industry 1, food, is *land*-intensive. Industry 2, clothing, is labor-intensive. Notice how the solution to the problem changes when the amount of land H is increased. The land constraint shifts to the right, producing a new output mix designated by point C'. At C', output of y_1, the land-intensive good, is increased, while the output of the labor-intensive good decreases.

Solving by Cramer's rule yields

$$y_1 = \frac{a_{22}H - a_{12}L}{a_{11}a_{22} - a_{12}a_{21}} \qquad y_2 = \frac{-a_{21}H + a_{11}L}{a_{11}a_{22} - a_{12}a_{21}} \qquad (13\text{-}15)$$

The factor intensities determine the sign of the denominator. If, say, the food (y_1) industry is relatively *land*-intensive, then $H_1/L_1 > H_2/L_2$. This is equivalent to $a_{11}/a_{21} > a_{12}/a_{22}$ or $a_{11}a_{22} - a_{12}a_{21} > 0$. (It is clearly critical that $a_{11}a_{22} - a_{12}a_{21} \neq 0$. Otherwise, with equal factor intensities, the constraints determining the solution would be parallel to each other, i.e., linearly dependent. In that case, no solution to the model in its present form could exist; one constraint would have to be discarded as nonbinding.) If the denominator is positive, then by simple differentiation,

$$\frac{\partial y_1}{\partial H} = \frac{a_{22}}{(+)} > 0 \qquad \frac{\partial y_1}{\partial L} = -\frac{a_{12}}{(+)} < 0$$

$$\frac{\partial y_2}{\partial H} = -\frac{a_{21}}{(+)} < 0 \qquad \frac{\partial y_2}{\partial L} = \frac{a_{11}}{(+)} > 0 \qquad (13\text{-}16)$$

the Rybczynski results. Moreover, it is easy to show that these output changes will occur in *greater* absolute proportion than the parameter changes. For example,

$$y_1 = k_1 H + k_2 L$$

where

$$k_1 = a_{22}/(a_{11}a_{22} - a_{12}a_{21}), \quad k_2 = -a_{12}/(a_{11}a_{22} - a_{12}a_{21})$$

Thus

$$\frac{\Delta y_1/y_1}{\Delta H/H} = \frac{H}{y_1}\frac{\partial y_1}{\partial H} = \frac{H}{y_1}k_1 = \frac{k_1 H}{k_1 H + k_2 L}$$

Since

$$k_2 < 0, \quad k_1 H > k_1 H + k_2 L,$$

hence

$$\frac{H}{y_1}\frac{\partial y_1}{\partial H} > 1$$

The same result obtains for the other variables. Outputs respond *elastically* (absolute elasticity greater than unity) to changes in resource endowments.

13.4 THE STOLPER-SAMUELSON THEOREM

The solution to this linear model will remain at point C in Fig. 13-4 as long as p_1/p_2, the ratio of output prices, is less than $\frac{3}{2}$ and greater than 1. In our present example, $p_1/p_2 = \frac{40}{30} = \frac{4}{3}$. Let us calculate the effect on factor prices produced by an increase in the price of clothing, say, to $p_2 = 33$, i.e., by 10 percent.

The new shadow-factor prices can be calculated as before. However, consider the unit factor cost of y_1 and y_2. The first column of the (a_{ij}) matrix gives the amounts of land, labor, and capital needed to produce 1 unit of y_1. The unit factor cost of y_1 is therefore

$$a_{11}u_1 + a_{21}u_2 + a_{31}u_3 = 3(10) + 2(5) + 1(0) = \$40 = p_1 \qquad (13\text{-}17a)$$

Similarly, the second column of a_{ij}'s gives the amounts of land, labor, and capital needed to produce 1 unit of y_2. The unit factor cost of y_2 is therefore

$$a_{12}u_1 + a_{22}u_2 + a_{32}u_3 = 2(10) + 2(5) + 2(0) = \$30 = p_2 \qquad (13\text{-}17b)$$

Unit factor cost equals output price. Equations (13-17) represent zero-profit conditions. Since the production function here exhibits constant returns to scale, zero profits are to be expected. Since in this example $u_3 = 0$ (the marginal product of capital is 0) at point C, the zero-profit conditions are

$$\begin{aligned} a_{11}u_1 + a_{21}u_2 &= p_1 \\ a_{12}u_1 + a_{22}u_2 &= p_2 \end{aligned} \qquad (13\text{-}18)$$

These are two equations in two unknowns, from which we can solve for u_1 and u_2 in terms of p_1 and p_2, using our data about the a_{ij}'s. [Remember, though, that these equations apply only when the solution is at point C. If the solution were at point B, u_1 would be 0 and equations (13-18) would involve the coefficients a_{31} and a_{32}.] Most importantly, note that the coefficients of these equations are the transpose of the coefficients in equations (13-14). The only difference is that a_{12} and a_{21} are interchanged. The algebra of the relations between factor and output prices is therefore virtually identical to the relations between physical outputs and resource endowments.

Solving equations (13-18) by Cramer's rule gives

$$u_1 = \frac{a_{22}p_1 - a_{21}p_2}{a_{11}a_{22} - a_{12}a_{21}} = \frac{2p_1 - 2p_2}{2} = p_1 - p_2 \qquad (13\text{-}19a)$$

$$u_2 = \frac{a_{11}p_2 - a_{12}p_1}{a_{11}a_{22} - a_{12}a_{21}} = \frac{3p_2 - 2p_1}{2} = \frac{3}{2}p_2 - p_1 \qquad (13\text{-}19b)$$

Notice the direction of change: if p_1 increases (the price of the land-intensive good increases), then the price of land u_1 increases while the price of labor decreases. Likewise, if the price of the labor-intensive good y_2 increases, land decreases in price while labor increases in price. With $p_1 = 40$, $p_2 = 30$, we derived $u_1 = 10$, $u_2 = 5$, in accordance with equations (13-13). With, say, $p_1 = 40$, $p_2 = 33$, we find $u_1 = 7$, $u_2 = 9.5$. With the price of the labor-intensive good rising by 10 percent, the price of land falls by 30 percent, whereas the price of labor nearly doubles. These results are known as the *Stolper-Samuelson theorem*.

The Stolper-Samuelson theorem states that if, say, the price of the labor-intensive good *rises*, the price of labor will not only *rise* but will rise in greater proportion to the output-price increase. Likewise, the price of the other factor will

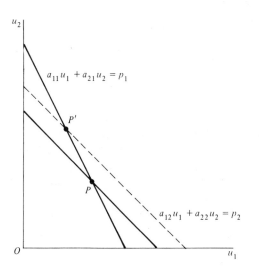

Figure 13-6 The Stolper-Samuelson theorem in a linear model, showing plot of the two zero-profit conditions (13-17). Capital is nonscarce, with $u_3 = 0$, and is thus omitted from the diagram. The slopes of the two lines depend on the factor intensities. For y_1, the slope of the zero-profit equation is $-a_{11}/a_{21}$. For y_2, the slope is $-a_{12}/a_{22}$. Given the numbers in our example, $a_{11}/a_{21} = \frac{3}{2}$, $a_{12}/a_{22} = 1$, and hence y_1, food, is *land*-intensive, whereas y_2, clothing, is labor-intensive. Under these conditions, an increase in p_2, which causes a parallel shift in (13-17b), produces a new solution at P'. This lowers u_1 and raises u_2. In words, if the price of, say, the labor-intensive good rises, the price of labor will rise while the price of the other factor (here, land) will fall.

fall in greater proportion to the rise in output-price. The same elastic response that was observed for the physical quantities occurs for prices. This duality is apparent from the similar structures of equations (13-14) and (13-19). Since the algebra is identical (save for interchanging a_{12} and a_{21}), we shall not repeat it.

The direction of change of factor prices can be seen geometrically in Fig. 13-6. There, the zero-profit equations (13-17) are plotted in the $u_1 u_2$ plane. The steeper line is equation (13-17a). The slope of this line is $-a_{11}/a_{21} = -\frac{3}{2}$. The less steep line is equation (13-17b), which has slope $-a_{12}/a_{22} = -1$. The intersection, point P, represents the solution values of u_2 and u_1. Suppose now that p_2 increases. This is represented geometrically by a parallel shift in (13-17b), as shown by the dotted line. The new intersection is at P'. At P', u_2 has increased and u_1 has decreased. Again, an increase in the price of the labor-intensive good will raise the price of labor and lower the price of the other factor, in this instance land.

13.5 THE DUAL PROBLEM

Let us summarize the analysis of the problem just solved. The problem, again, was to:

maximize $\qquad z = 40y_1 + 30y_2$

subject to $\qquad 3y_1 + 2y_2 \le 54 \qquad$ land constraint

$\qquad\qquad\qquad 2y_1 + 2y_2 \le 40 \qquad$ labor constraint

$\qquad\qquad\qquad\quad y_1 + 2y_2 \le 35 \qquad$ capital constraint

$\qquad\qquad\qquad\qquad y_1, y_2 \ge 0 \qquad\qquad\qquad\qquad\qquad$ (13-9)

The coefficients in the constraints, the a_{ij}'s, represent the (constant) amounts of factor i used in the production of 1 unit of output j. The solution to this particular linear programming problem is $y_1^* = 14$, $y_2^* = 6$. At that point, the land and labor constraints are binding, but the capital constraint is nonbinding. That is,

$$3y_1^* + 2y_2^* = 54 \qquad 2y_1^* + 2y_2^* = 40 \qquad y_1^* + 2y_2^* < 35$$

By considering how much income would change if factor endowments were altered incrementally, marginal evaluations, or shadow prices, were imputed to the three factors. Letting u_1, u_2, and u_3 represent the shadow-factor prices of land, labor, and capital, respectively, we found, at point C, where total income was maximized,

$$u_1 = \$10 \qquad u_2 = \$5 \qquad u_3 = 0$$

We also found again that the unit factor costs of y_1 and y_2 equaled the output prices, \$40 and \$30, respectively. For food, y_1, the first column of the (a_{ij}) matrix gives the amounts of land, labor, and capital needed to produce a unit of y_1. Thus, the unit cost of y_1 given the above shadow-factor prices is

$$u_1 a_{11} + u_2 a_{21} + u_3 a_{31} = 10(3) + 5(2) + 0(1) = \$40 = p_1$$

Likewise, for y_2, total unit factor cost is

$$u_1 a_{12} + u_2 a_{22} + u_3 a_{32} = 10(2) + 5(2) + 0(3) = \$30 = p_2$$

The linear model implies the zero-profit conditions:

$$a_{11} u_1 + a_{21} u_2 + a_{31} u_3 = p_1$$

$$a_{12} u_1 + a_{22} u_2 + a_{32} u_3 = p_2 \qquad (13\text{-}17)$$

In general, we would expect the unit factor cost to be *greater than or equal to the price* of that good. If unit cost were *less* than the price, no finite solution to the linear programming problem could exist; increasing the output of such a good would lead to ever-increasing total revenues. It might be the case, however, that unit factor cost *exceeded* price in a finite solution. Then we should expect the output of that good to be zero (negative outputs are not admissable).

There is a symmetry, or duality, in the above analysis. In the original model, in which income (revenue) was maximized, the constraints were statements of limited resource endowments. When these constraints held as equalities, a non-negative, generally positive new variable, a shadow-factor price, appeared. This "price" was 0 when the constraint was nonbinding, i.e., when a strict inequality appeared, as in the capital constraint above.

However, achieving an actual maximum of revenue also implies that unit costs will be at least as great as output-prices,

$$a_{1j} u_1 + a_{2j} u_2 + a_{3j} u_3 \geq p_j \qquad \text{for all } j \qquad (13\text{-}20)$$

Moreover, revenue maximization implies that if this relation holds as a strict *inequality*, output y_j will be zero. Otherwise, $y_j \geq 0$ (with $y_j > 0$ expected). This is the same "algebra" as when the constraints were the original resource constraints involving y_1 and y_2 and the new, dual variables were the shadow prices u_1, u_2, and u_3. The above symmetry, or duality, occurs because the u_i's are the Lagrange multipliers for the original, primal problem, whereas the outputs y_1 and y_2 are Lagrange multipliers for an associated constrained minimization problem. It is an example of the Kuhn-Tucker saddlepoint theorem. Let us see how this occurs.

Denote the original revenue-maximization problem (13-9) as the primal problem. When we let u_1, u_2, and u_3 represent the Lagrange multipliers associated with the three resource constraints, the lagrangian for this problem is

$$\mathscr{L} = p_1 y_1 + p_2 y_2 + u_1(H - a_{11} y_1 - a_{12} y_2)$$

$$+ u_2(L - a_{21} y_1 - a_{22} y_2) + u_3(K - a_{31} y_1 - a_{32} y_2) \qquad (13\text{-}21)$$

Among the Kuhn-Tucker first-order conditions for a maximum are that the first partials of $\mathscr{L}$ with respect to y_1 and y_2 be nonpositive, and if $\partial \mathscr{L}/\partial y_j < 0$, $y_j = 0$. At an interior solution, $\partial \mathscr{L}/\partial y_j = 0$. If a maximum should occur at $y_j = 0$, some j, this must happen because the lagrangian would become larger if *smaller*, i.e., negative, values of y_j were allowed. Hence, it must be that if a maximum occurs at

$y_j = 0$, $\partial \mathscr{L}/\partial y_j \le 0$ there. Applying these conditions to the lagrangian (13-21), we have

$$\frac{\partial \mathscr{L}}{\partial y_1} = p_1 - a_{11}u_1 - a_{21}u_2 - a_{31}u_3 \le 0 \qquad \text{if} <, \; y_1 = 0 \qquad (13\text{-}22a)$$

$$\frac{\partial \mathscr{L}}{\partial y_2} = p_2 - a_{12}u_1 - a_{22}u_2 - a_{32}u_3 \le 0 \qquad \text{if} <, \; y_2 = 0 \qquad (13\text{-}22b)$$

These first-order conditions are precisely the nonpositive profit conditions (13-20) discussed above. The remaining first-order conditions are, of course, the inequality constraints, obtained by differentiation with respect to the Lagrange multipliers, here u_1, u_2, and u_3:

$$\frac{\partial \mathscr{L}}{\partial u_1} = H - a_{11}y_1 - a_{12}y_2 \ge 0 \qquad \text{if} >, \; u_1 = 0$$

$$\frac{\partial \mathscr{L}}{\partial u_2} = L - a_{21}y_1 - a_{22}y_2 \ge 0 \qquad \text{if} >, \; u_2 = 0$$

$$\frac{\partial \mathscr{L}}{\partial u_3} = K - a_{31}y_1 - a_{32}y_2 \ge 0 \qquad \text{if} >, \; u_3 = 0$$

These are precisely the resource constraints with the added stipulation that if the resource constraint is nonbinding, the imputed shadow price of that factor is 0, in accordance with our previous reasoning and results.

There is more to the lagrangian (13-21) than first meets the eye. Let us rearrange the terms of (13-21) as follows:

$$\mathscr{L} = Hu_1 + Lu_2 + Ku_3 + y_1(p_1 - a_{11}u_1 - a_{21}u_2 - a_{31}u_3)$$
$$+ y_2(p_2 - a_{12}u_1 - a_{22}u_2 - a_{32}u_3) \qquad (13\text{-}23)$$

This functional form can be interpreted as a lagrangian for an extremum problem with choice variables u_1, u_2, and u_3 whose objective function is $w = Hu_1 + Lu_2 + Ku_3$, the total value of the resource endowment. The outputs y_1 and y_2 appear in the position of Lagrange multipliers for profit constraints.

A competitive economy can be expected to utilize its resources efficiently. We should expect in this model that revenue maximization implies, and is implied by, *minimization of the total value of resources*, subject to the constraints that profits are nonpositive. The lagrangian (13-23), if *minimized* with respect to u_1, u_2, and u_3, yields the following first-order inequality conditions:

$$\frac{\partial \mathscr{L}}{\partial u_1} = H - a_{11}y_1 - a_{12}y_2 \ge 0 \qquad \text{if} >, \; u_1 = 0 \qquad (13\text{-}24a)$$

$$\frac{\partial \mathscr{L}}{\partial u_2} = L - a_{21}y_1 - a_{22}y_2 \ge 0 \qquad \text{if} >, \; u_2 = 0 \qquad (13\text{-}24b)$$

$$\frac{\partial \mathscr{L}}{\partial u_3} = K - a_{31}y_1 - a_{32}y_2 \ge 0 \qquad \text{if} >, \; u_3 = 0 \qquad (13\text{-}24c)$$

and

$$\frac{\partial \mathscr{L}}{\partial y_1} = p_1 - a_{11}u_1 - a_{21}u_2 - a_{31}u_3 \leq 0 \qquad \text{if } <, \ y_1 = 0 \qquad (13\text{-}25a)$$

$$\frac{\partial \mathscr{L}}{\partial y_2} = p_2 - a_{12}u_1 - a_{22}u_2 - a_{32}u_3 \leq 0 \qquad \text{if } <, \ y_2 = 0 \qquad (13\text{-}25b)$$

exactly the same resource and nonpositive profit conditions derived from the primal problem.

Thus, the following two problems yield the same first-order conditions:

1. The primal problem:

   maximize $\qquad z = p_1 y_1 + p_2 y_2$

   subject to $\qquad a_{11} y_1 + a_{12} y_2 \leq H$

   $\qquad\qquad\quad a_{21} y_1 + a_{22} y_2 \leq L$

   $\qquad\qquad\quad a_{31} y_1 + a_{32} y_2 \leq K \qquad y_1, y_2 \geq 0$

2. The dual problem:

   minimize $\qquad w = Hu_1 + Lu_2 + Ku_3$

   subject to $\qquad a_{11}u_1 + a_{21}u_2 + a_{31}u_3 \geq p_1$

   $\qquad\qquad\quad a_{12}u_1 + a_{22}u_2 + a_{32}u_3 \geq p_2 \qquad u_1, u_2, u_3 \geq 0$

Moreover, the values of the objective functions of these two problems are identical when the solutions are obtained. In this model, this is a statement that the total value of output equals the total value of resource endowment when resources are used efficiently. In the above example, the maximum value of output was

$$z^* = p_1 y_1^* + p_2 y_2^* = 40(14) + 30(6) = \$740$$

as computed earlier. The total value of the resource endowment at that point is

$$w^* = Hu_1^* + Lu_2^* + Ku_3^* = 54(10) + 40(5) + 35(0) = \$740$$

the same as for the primal problem.

This adding-up or exhaustion-of-product theorem is a consequence of the homogeneity of the objective and constraint functions. As we showed in Chap. 12, when the objective and constraint functions in a maximum problem are all homogeneous of the same degree [the constraints appearing as $g^j(x_1, \ldots, x_n) \leq k^j$], then the indirect objective function $\phi(k^1, \ldots, k^m)$ is homogeneous of degree 1 in the k^j's. Hence, by Euler's theorem,

$$z^* \equiv \frac{\partial z^*}{\partial H} H + \frac{\partial z^*}{\partial L} L + \frac{\partial z^*}{\partial K} K = u_1^* H + u_2^* L + u_3^* K = w^*$$

where w^* is the minimum value of the objective function of the dual objective function (total factor cost) and the u_i^*'s are the u_i's that achieve that minimum.

This remarkable duality was first noted and explored by Koopmans and others.† They converted a purely mathematical puzzle into an interesting (albeit highly restrictive) economic model.

In general, consider the linear programming problem:

maximize
$$z = \sum_{i=1}^{n} p_i x_i$$

subject to
$$\sum_{j=1}^{n} a_{ij} x_j \le b_j \qquad i = 1, \ldots, m \qquad (13\text{-}26)$$

$$x_j \ge 0, j = 1, \ldots, n$$

There is no need for m, the number of constraints, to be less than the number of decision variables, since these are *inequality* constraints. Some of these constraints will in general be nonbinding, though it is not easy to discover which ones will be binding. In fact, finding the solution to this problem consists precisely of discovering which constraints are binding and which are not. (The algorithm for doing so will be presented in the next section.)

The above problem can be written using matrix notation. Denote the column vector of x_i's as

$$\mathbf{x} = \begin{pmatrix} x_1 \\ \vdots \\ x_n \end{pmatrix}$$

the objective coefficient matrix of p_i's as

$$\mathbf{p} = \begin{pmatrix} p_1 \\ \vdots \\ p_n \end{pmatrix}$$

and the right-hand-side coefficients, the b_i's, as

$$\mathbf{b} = \begin{pmatrix} b_1 \\ \vdots \\ b_m \end{pmatrix}$$

Denote the matrix of technical coefficients, the a_{ij}'s, as $\mathbf{A}$:

$$\mathbf{A} = \begin{pmatrix} a_{11} & \cdots & a_{1n} \\ \cdots\cdots\cdots\cdots\cdots \\ a_{m1} & \cdots & a_{mn} \end{pmatrix}$$

Let $\mathbf{x} \ge \mathbf{0}$ mean $x_i \ge 0$, $i = 1, \ldots, n$. The prime denotes the transpose of a matrix.

---

† Activity Analysis of Production and Allocation, *Cowles Commission Monograph* 13, John Wiley & Sons, Inc., New York, 1951.

The general linear programming problem can then be written:

maximize $\qquad\qquad\qquad\qquad z = \mathbf{p}'\mathbf{x}$

subject to $\qquad\qquad\qquad\quad \mathbf{Ax} \le \mathbf{b} \qquad \mathbf{x} \ge \mathbf{0}$ $\qquad\qquad$ (13-27)

Associated with this linear programming problem is a dual problem:

minimize $\qquad\qquad\qquad\qquad w = \mathbf{b}'\mathbf{u}$

subject to $\qquad\qquad\qquad\quad \mathbf{A}'\mathbf{u} \ge \mathbf{p} \qquad \mathbf{u} \ge \mathbf{0}$ $\qquad\qquad$ (13-28)

where

$$\mathbf{u} = \begin{pmatrix} u_1 \\ \vdots \\ u_m \end{pmatrix}$$

is a new vector of decision variables, the *dual variables*.

Note that the primal problem involves n decision variables and m linear inequality constraints. The dual problem involves m decision variables and n linear inequality constraints. The coefficient matrix of the constraints of the dual problem is simply the transpose of the coefficient matrix of the primal problem. The right-hand-side coefficients of one problem appear as the objective function coefficients of the other. *These problems are self-dual;* i.e., the dual problem of the dual problem is the original primal problem. In fact, either problem can be considered the primal problem.

We shall now state and briefly discuss the fundamental theorem of linear programming.

Theorem Suppose there exists an $\mathbf{x}^0 \ge \mathbf{0}$ which satisfies the constraints of the primal problem, that is, $\mathbf{Ax}^0 \le \mathbf{b}$ ($\mathbf{x}^0$ is a *feasible* solution) and a $\mathbf{u}^0 \ge \mathbf{0}$ which satisfies the constraints of the dual problem; that is, $\mathbf{A}'\mathbf{u}^0 \ge \mathbf{p}$ ($\mathbf{u}^0$ is a solution of the dual problem). *Then both problems possess an optimal solution,* i.e., a finite solution to the problem posed, *and these two solution values are in fact identical.* That is, suppose $\mathbf{x}^* \ge \mathbf{0}$ is that $\mathbf{x}$ vector which maximizes $z = \mathbf{p}'\mathbf{x}$ subject to $\mathbf{Ax} \le \mathbf{b}$. The maximum value of $\mathbf{p}'\mathbf{x}$ is $z^* = \mathbf{p}'\mathbf{x}^*$. Similarly, let $\mathbf{u}^* \ge \mathbf{0}$ be the $\mathbf{u}$ vector for which $w = \mathbf{b}'\mathbf{u}$ is a minimum, and let $w^* = \mathbf{b}'\mathbf{u}^*$. Then $z^* = w^*$.

Discussion It is easy to show that $z^* \le w^*$. The constraints of the primal problem are

$$\sum_{j=1}^{n} a_{ij}x_j \le b_i \qquad i = 1, \ldots, m$$

Multiply each constraint by $u_i \ge 0$ and add:

$$\sum_{i=1}^{m} \sum_{j=1}^{n} u_i a_{ij} x_j \le \sum_{i=1}^{m} b_i u_i = w$$

In matrix notation, this is simply premultiplying $\mathbf{Ax} \leq \mathbf{b}$ by the vector $\mathbf{u}'$, yielding

$$\mathbf{u}'\mathbf{Ax} \leq \mathbf{u}'\mathbf{b} = w \tag{13-29}$$

(Note that the term $\mathbf{u}'\mathbf{Ax}$ is the product of matrices of respective size $1 \times m$, $m \times n$, and $n \times 1$. Hence, $\mathbf{u}'\mathbf{Ax}$ has size (1×1); that is, it is a simple number, or scalar.)
   Now consider the constraints of the dual problem,

$$\sum_{i=1}^{m} a_{ij}u_i \geq p_j \qquad j = 1, \ldots, n$$

Multiply each constraint by $x_j \geq 0$ and add:

$$\sum_{j=1}^{n} \sum_{i=1}^{m} x_j a_{ij} u_i \geq \sum_{j=1}^{n} p_j x_j = z$$

Again, in matrix terms, this is simply multiplying, on the right, $\mathbf{u}'\mathbf{A} \geq \mathbf{p}'$ by the vector $\mathbf{x}$, yielding

$$\mathbf{u}'\mathbf{Ax} \geq \mathbf{p}'\mathbf{x} = z \tag{13-30}$$

From (13-29) and (13-30)

$$z \leq \mathbf{u}'\mathbf{Ax} \leq w \tag{13-31}$$

Since this holds for *all* feasible $\mathbf{u}$ and $\mathbf{x}$ vectors (including $\mathbf{u}^*$ and $\mathbf{x}^*$),

$$z^* \leq w^* \tag{13-32}$$

   Consider now the statement of the fundamental theorem above. Suppose $\mathbf{x}^0$ and $\mathbf{u}^0$ are (finite) feasible solutions to the primal and dual problems, respectively. Then from (13-31),

$$\mathbf{p}'\mathbf{x}^0 \leq \mathbf{u}^{0'}\mathbf{b}$$

This relation implies that a finite maximum exists for the primal problem and a finite minimum exists for the dual problem. For consider that

$$\mathbf{p}'\mathbf{x}^0 \leq \mathbf{p}'\mathbf{x}^* \leq \mathbf{u}^{*'}\mathbf{b} \leq \mathbf{u}^{0'}\mathbf{b} \tag{13-33}$$

by the definition of the optimality of $\mathbf{x}^*$ and $\mathbf{u}^*$ and equation (13-31). But since $\mathbf{u}^{0'}\mathbf{b}$ and $\mathbf{p}'\mathbf{x}^0$ are finite numbers, $\mathbf{p}'\mathbf{x}^*$, the maximum, or optimal, value of $z = \mathbf{p}'\mathbf{x}$, is bounded from above by $\mathbf{u}^{0'}\mathbf{b}$. Likewise, $\mathbf{u}^{*'}\mathbf{b}$ is bounded from below by $\mathbf{p}'\mathbf{x}^0$. Therefore, if *feasible* solutions exist to both the primal and dual problems, finite *optimal* solutions must exist for each problem.
   That $z^* = \mathbf{p}'\mathbf{x}^* = \mathbf{u}^*\mathbf{b} = w^*$ at this optimum is a consequence of the Kuhn-Tucker saddlepoint theorem. Since the objective and constraint functions are all linear, they are all concave. Therefore, the existence of a solution $\mathbf{x}^*$ to the maximum (primal) problem implies and is implied by the lagrangian of the primal problem having a saddlepoint.
   Write the constraints of the primal problem as

$$b_i - \sum_{j=1}^{n} a_{ij}x_j \geq 0 \qquad i = 1, \ldots, m$$

Multiply each constraint by a Lagrange multiplier u_i and add. This yields the lagrangian

$$\mathscr{L} = \sum_{j=1}^{n} p_j x_j + \sum_{i=1}^{m} u_i \left(b_i - \sum_{j=1}^{n} a_{ij} x_j \right)$$

In matrix notation this lagrangian is

$$\mathscr{L}(\mathbf{x}, \mathbf{u}) = \mathbf{p}'\mathbf{x} + \mathbf{u}'(\mathbf{b} - \mathbf{A}\mathbf{x}) \tag{13-34}$$

The saddlepoint theorem says that if $\mathbf{x}^*$ is the solution to the primal problem, there exists a $\mathbf{u}^* \geq 0$ such that

$$\mathscr{L}(\mathbf{x}, \mathbf{u}^*) \leq \mathscr{L}(\mathbf{x}^*, \mathbf{u}^*) \leq \mathscr{L}(\mathbf{x}^*, \mathbf{u}) \tag{13-35}$$

However, $\mathscr{L}(\mathbf{x},\mathbf{u})$ can be rewritten

$$\mathscr{L}(\mathbf{x}, \mathbf{u}) = \mathbf{u}'\mathbf{b} + (\mathbf{p}' - \mathbf{u}'\mathbf{A})\mathbf{x} \tag{13-36}$$

Define $M(\mathbf{u}, \mathbf{x}) \equiv -\mathscr{L}(\mathbf{x}, \mathbf{u}) = -\mathbf{u}'\mathbf{b} + (\mathbf{u}'\mathbf{A} - \mathbf{p}')\mathbf{x}$. Then, from (13-35),

$$M(\mathbf{u}, \mathbf{x}^*) \leq M(\mathbf{u}^*, \mathbf{x}^*) \leq M(\mathbf{u}^*, \mathbf{x}) \tag{13-37}$$

Since $M(\mathbf{u}, \mathbf{x})$ has a saddlepoint at $(\mathbf{u}^*, \mathbf{x}^*)$, $\mathbf{u}^*$ maximizes

$$-w = -\mathbf{u}'\mathbf{b} = -\sum_{i=1}^{m} b_i u_i$$

subject to $\qquad\qquad \mathbf{u}'\mathbf{A} - \mathbf{p}' \geq 0$

or $\qquad\qquad\qquad \sum_{i=1}^{m} a_{ij} u_i \geq p_j \qquad j = 1, \ldots, n$

This is precisely the dual problem (13-28). (Of course, minimizing $\sum b_i u_i$ is equivalent to maximizing $- \sum b_i u_i$.)

From the first-order conditions for maximizing $\mathscr{L}$ with respect to x,

$$\mathscr{L}_{\mathbf{x}} = \mathbf{p}' - \mathbf{u}'\mathbf{A} \leq 0 \qquad \text{if } <, \mathbf{x} = 0 \tag{13-38a}$$

$$\mathscr{L}_{\mathbf{u}} = \mathbf{b} - \mathbf{A}\mathbf{x} \geq 0 \qquad \text{if } >, \mathbf{u} = 0 \tag{13-38b}$$

where $\mathscr{L}_{\mathbf{x}}$ simply means the whole vector of $\mathscr{L}_{x_j}$'s, $j = 1, \ldots, n$, etc. Equivalently, from (13-38a),

$$(\mathbf{p}' - \mathbf{u}'^*\mathbf{A})\mathbf{x}^* = 0 \tag{13-39a}$$

and from (13-38b),

$$\mathbf{u}^{*'}(\mathbf{b} - \mathbf{A}\mathbf{x}^*) = 0 \tag{13-39b}$$

Hence, at $\mathbf{x}^*, \mathbf{u}^*$, the lagrangian has the common value

$$\mathscr{L}(\mathbf{x}^*, \mathbf{u}^*) = \mathbf{p}'\mathbf{x}^* + \mathbf{u}^{*'}(\mathbf{b} - \mathbf{A}\mathbf{x}^*) = \mathbf{p}'\mathbf{x}^* = z^*$$

and $\qquad\quad \mathscr{L}(\mathbf{x}^*, \mathbf{u}^*) = \mathbf{u}^{*'}\mathbf{b} + (\mathbf{p}' - \mathbf{u}^{*'}\mathbf{A})\mathbf{x}^* = \mathbf{u}^{*'}\mathbf{b} = w^*$

Therefore, $z^* = w^*$ at the saddlepoint, which represents the *maximum* in the **x** directions (the solution to the primal problem) and a *minimum* in the **u** directions (representing the solution to the dual problem).

As a final note, from the envelope theorem,

$$u_i^* = \frac{\partial z^*}{\partial b_i}$$

We showed in Chap. 12 that when the objective and constraint functions $f(\mathbf{x})$ and $g(\mathbf{x})$ [the constraints being $g(\mathbf{x}) \le \mathbf{b}$] are all homogeneous of the same degree, then $z^* = \phi(b_1, \ldots, b_m)$ is homogeneous of degree 1 in the b_i's. Therefore, by the converse of Euler's theorem,

$$w^* = \sum_{i=1}^m b_i u_i^* = \sum_{i=1}^m \frac{\partial z^*}{\partial b_i} b_i \equiv z^*$$

Equivalently,
$$x_j^* = \frac{\partial w^*}{\partial p_j}$$

and therefore
$$z^* = \sum p_j x_j^* = \sum \frac{\partial w^*}{\partial p_j} p_j \equiv w^*$$

13.6 THE SIMPLEX ALGORITHM†

In the previous sections we discussed some of the economic aspects of the solutions to linear programming problems. In particular, we have shown that there is often an interesting dual problem associated with any linear maximization model. The primary reason for considering as restrictive a model as that of constant coefficients, however, is the trade-off in terms of ease of empirical solution. In fact, a relatively simple, easily programmable (in the computer sense) algorithm, or routine, exists for finding the solution to linear programming problems. Let us explore this aspect of these models now, and then apply it to the earlier example of maximization of total revenue, or income.

Mathematical Prerequisites

Consider the general linear programming problem:

maximize
$$z = \sum_{j=1}^r p_j x_j \tag{13-40}$$

† This section uses concepts developed in the Appendix to Chap. 5.

subject to
$$a_{11}x_1 + \cdots + a_{1r}x_r \le b_1$$
$$\cdots\cdots\cdots\cdots\cdots\cdots\cdots\cdots$$
$$a_{m1}x_1 + \cdots + a_{mr}x_r \le b_m$$
$$x_1, \ldots, x_r \ge 0 \qquad\qquad (13\text{-}41)$$

Here, we have r decision variables and m linear inequality constraints.

The first step in solving such a problem is to convert the *inequality* constraints to *equalities* (which are easier to deal with) through the introduction of *slack variables*. The constraints (13-41) are replaced by the set

$$a_{11}x_1 + \cdots + a_{1r}x_r + x_{r+1} = b_1$$
$$a_{21}x_1 + \cdots + a_{2r}x_r + x_{r+2} = b_2$$
$$\cdots\cdots\cdots\cdots\cdots\cdots\cdots\cdots\cdots\cdots$$
$$a_{m1}x_1 + \cdots + a_{mr}x_r + x_{r+m} = b_m \qquad (13\text{-}42)$$
$$x_1, \ldots, x_{r+m} \ge 0$$

Since the slack variables $x_{r+1}, \ldots, x_{r+m}$ are constrained to be nonnegative, the equalities (13-42) define the same feasible region as the inequalities (13-41). We see, therefore, that no generality is lost by considering a linear programming problem in which a linear function is maximized subject to linear *equality* constraints, plus nonnegativity. If the constraints are of the form $\sum_j a_{ij}x_j \ge b_i$, however, the slack variable must enter with a *negative* sign, to preserve the meaning of the inequality. Thus, if the constraint were $x_1 + x_2 \ge 10$, the relevant equality constraint would be $x_1 + x_2 - x_3 = 10$, $x_1, x_2, x_3 \ge 0$.

Thus, the problem we shall attempt to solve is:

maximize
$$z = \sum_{i=1}^{n} p_i x_i$$

subject to
$$\sum_{j=1}^{n} a_{ij}x_j = b_i \qquad i = 1, \ldots, m$$
$$x_j \ge 0 \qquad j = 1, \ldots, n$$

In matrix notation, this problem can be written:

maximize
$$\mathbf{p'x}$$

subject to
$$\mathbf{Ax = b} \qquad \mathbf{x \ge 0}$$

where $\mathbf{p}, \mathbf{x} = n \times 1$ matrices, or *column vectors*
$\mathbf{A} = m \times n$ matrix of coefficients
$\mathbf{b} = m \times 1$ column vector

No generality is lost if we assume that these m constraints are all *independent*, i.e., that it is not possible to derive any constraint by combining the remaining $m - 1$. Mathematically, we say that the matrix $\mathbf{A}$ has *rank* m.

Example Consider the constraints

$$x_1 + 2x_2 + x_4 = 2$$
$$2x_1 - 2x_2 + x_3 = 3$$
$$4x_1 + 2x_2 + x_3 + 2x_4 = 6$$

If the first equation is multiplied by 2 and added to the second equation, the resulting equation is

$$4x_1 + 2x_2 + x_3 + 2x_4 = 7$$

The left-hand side is identical to the third constraint above. The three constraints are obviously inconsistent with each other, since $6 \neq 7$. If the 6 had been a 7 in the original third constraint, that constraint could have been ignored, since it would be redundant. We could then simply consider this a two-constraint system.

Denote the rows of the matrix $\mathbf{A}$ by $\mathbf{A}_1, \ldots, \mathbf{A}_m$, respectively. The matrix $\mathbf{A}$ has rank m if there do not exist scalars $k_1, \ldots, k_m$ such that

$$\mathbf{A}_j = \sum_{\substack{i=1 \\ i \neq j}}^{m} k_i \mathbf{A}_i$$

That is, $\mathbf{A}$ has rank m if no row is a linear combination of the remaining rows. This assures that any $m \times m$ determinant formed from $\mathbf{A}$ will be nonzero. The number of decision variables n must be greater than the number of constraints m to have any meaningful problem. If $m = n$, a unique solution of the constraints exists; the feasible region consists of that one point, and hence, the maximization part of the problem is trivial. If $m > n$, the feasible region is void.

With m independent equations, it is possible to solve for any m x_j's, uniquely, in terms of the remaining $n - m$. If these remaining $n - m$ x_j's are set equal to 0, a *basic feasible* solution results (assuming that nonnegativity, as always, holds as well). That is, a *basic feasible* solution is a feasible solution in which $n - m$ of the x_j's equal 0, or the number of positive x_j's is no greater than the number of constraints. The m x_j's in the basic feasible solution are called the *basis*.

Geometrically, the set of basic feasible solutions corresponds to the *corners* of the feasible region, e.g., the origin and points A, B, C, and D in Fig. 13-4. We can see this as follows. A corner is a point which does *not* lie between two other points in the feasible region. Suppose $\mathbf{y} = (y_1, \ldots, y_m, 0, \ldots, 0)$ is a basic feasible solution, that is, $\mathbf{Ay} = \mathbf{b}$, $\mathbf{y} \geq \mathbf{0}$, where the coordinates have been numbered so that the last $n - m$ y_j's are zero. If $\mathbf{y}$ is not on a corner of the feasible region, then there exist two other feasible solutions, $\mathbf{u}$ and $\mathbf{v}$, such that $\mathbf{y}$ lies on the straight line joining $\mathbf{u}$ and $\mathbf{v}$, that is,

$$\mathbf{y} = k\mathbf{u} + (1 - k)\mathbf{v} \qquad 0 < k < 1$$

For the last $n - m$ components of $\mathbf{u}$ and $\mathbf{v}$,

$$0 = ku_j + (1 - k)v_j \qquad j = m + 1, \ldots, n$$

Since $u_j \geq 0$ and $v_j \geq 0$, this can happen only if $u_j = v_j = 0, j = m + 1, \ldots, n$. Thus, $\mathbf{u}$ and $\mathbf{v}$ are also basic feasible solutions. However, $\mathbf{y}$, $\mathbf{u}$, and $\mathbf{v}$ must all be the same point. With the last $n - m$ components of each vector equal to zero, the matrix equation of constraints, $\mathbf{Ax} = \mathbf{b}$, reduces to

$$\sum_{j=1}^{m} a_{ij} y_j = b_i \qquad i = 1, \ldots, m$$

$$\sum_{j=1}^{m} a_{ij} u_j = b_i \qquad i = 1, \ldots, m$$

$$\sum_{j=1}^{m} a_{ij} v_j = b_i \qquad i = 1, \ldots, m$$

These are the same m equations in m unknowns. The equations are all linearly independent by assumption. Hence, there is a unique solution; that is, $\mathbf{y} = \mathbf{u} = \mathbf{v}$. This contradicts the assumption that $\mathbf{y}$ lies *between* two other feasible solutions. Hence, the set of *basic feasible* solutions is the corners of the feasible region.

As indicated earlier, the feasible region is always a *convex set* for linear programming problems. This was illustrated earlier. The proof is quite simple and follows from more general considerations since the constraints are all concave functions. Suppose $\mathbf{u}$ and $\mathbf{v}$ are any two feasible solutions, that is, $\mathbf{Au} = \mathbf{b}$, $\mathbf{Av} = \mathbf{b}$, $\mathbf{u}, \mathbf{v} \geq \mathbf{0}$. Then any point $\mathbf{y} = k\mathbf{u} + (1 - k)\mathbf{v}$, $0 \leq k \leq 1$ is also a feasible solution:

$$\mathbf{Ay} = \mathbf{A}(k\mathbf{u} + (1 - k)\mathbf{v}) = k\mathbf{Au} + (1 - k)\mathbf{Av} = k\mathbf{b} + (1 - k)\mathbf{b} = \mathbf{b}$$

Hence, $\mathbf{Ay} = \mathbf{b}$. Clearly, $\mathbf{y} \geq \mathbf{0}$, since $\mathbf{u}, \mathbf{v} \geq \mathbf{0}$, and the scalar $k \geq 0$. Hence, $\mathbf{y}$, which represents all points on the straight line joining $\mathbf{u}$ and $\mathbf{v}$, is feasible whenever $\mathbf{u}$ and $\mathbf{v}$ are, and thus by definition the feasible region is convex.

The importance of these results is that they tell us that any local maximum must be the global maximum (though not necessarily unique) of the problem. There can be no "hills further on" with higher maxima than the given one.

It is geometrically obvious from Fig. 13-4 that in general the maximum, or *optimal solution* as it is usually called, *will be at a corner of the feasible region.* We shall not prove this important theorem, as it depends upon more advanced techniques of linear algebra. It may be the case that there are an infinite number of solutions. This occurs when the objective hyperplane is parallel to a flat portion of the feasible region at the maximum position. In the example in Sec. 13.2, if $p_1 = p_2$, so that $p_1/p_2 = 1$, for example, the maximum will occur at all points along the line segment BC in Fig. 13-4. However, the *basic* feasible solutions B and C will still be optimal. *In any linear programming problem in which a finite optimum exists, there exists an optimal solution which is a basic feasible solution. If the optimal solution is unique, it is a basic feasible solution.*

These results drastically reduce the number of points over which we have to search for the optimal solution. One approach to the problem would be simply to program a computer to search all the corners, evaluate $z = \mathbf{p}'\mathbf{x}$ at each one, and pick the largest. However, vastly more efficient routines are available. The number of corners can be quite large; e.g., a model with 10 equations and 20 variables may contain

$$\binom{20}{10} = \frac{20!}{10!\,10!} = 184{,}756$$

basic feasible solutions.

The Simplex Algorithm: Example

We shall now illustrate the simplex algorithm for solving linear programming models by using the algorithm on the three-factor, two-good model analyzed in Sec. 13.2. The problem, again, is:

maximize $\qquad\qquad z = 40y_1 + 30y_2$

subject to $\qquad\qquad 3y_1 + 2y_2 \le 54$

$\qquad\qquad\qquad\quad 2y_1 + 2y_2 \le 40$

$\qquad\qquad\qquad\quad\ y_1 + 2y_2 \le 35 \qquad y_1, y_2 \ge 0$

The first step is to convert the constraints to equalities, by adding slack variables:

maximize $\qquad\qquad\qquad z = 40y_1 + 30y_2$ $\qquad\qquad$ (13-43)

subject to $\qquad\qquad\qquad 3y_1 + 2y_2 + y_3 = 54$ $\qquad\qquad$ (13-44a)

$\qquad\qquad\qquad\qquad 2y_1 + 2y_2 + y_4 = 40$ $\qquad\qquad$ (13-44b)

$\qquad\qquad\qquad\qquad\ y_1 + 2y_2 + y_5 = 35$ $\qquad\qquad$ (13-44c)

$\qquad\qquad\qquad\qquad y_1, y_2, y_3, y_4, y_5 \ge 0$

We now have three independent constraints in five variables. A basic feasible solution is a vector $\mathbf{y} = (y_1, \ldots, y_5)$ such that any *two* $(= 5 - 3)$ y_j's are set equal to 0, and the remaining y_j's are nonnegative and satisfy the above constraints. Let us arbitrarily set $y_4 = y_5 = 0$ and see if this yields a basic feasible solution. However, let us keep y_4 and y_5 in the equations and *solve for y_1, y_2, and y_3 in terms of y_4 and y_5*.

Subtracting (13-44c) from (13-44b) and rearranging terms gives

$$y_1 = 5 - y_4 + y_5 \qquad\qquad (13\text{-}45a)$$

Substituting this into (13-44c) and solving for y_2, we have

$$2y_2 = 35 - y_5 - (5 - y_4 + y_5)$$

or $\qquad\qquad\qquad y_2 = 15 + 0.5y_4 - y_5 \qquad\qquad (13\text{-}45b)$

Lastly, we substitute (13-45a) and (13-45b) into (13-44a) to solve for y_3 :

$$y_3 = 54 - 3(5 - y_4 + y_5) - 2(15 + 0.5y_4 - y_5)$$

or $\qquad y_3 = 9 + 2y_4 - y_5 \qquad\qquad\qquad\qquad (13\text{-}45c)$

Consider this solution, equations (13-45). Setting $y_4 = y_5 = 0$, we get $y_1 = 5$, $y_2 = 15$, $y_3 = 9$. This is a basic *feasible* solution since $y_1, y_2, y_3 \geq 0$. It corresponds to point B in Fig. 13-4. Notice that the slack variable y_3 is positive. Hence, the first (land) constraint is nonbinding, but with $y_4 = y_5 = 0$, the labor and capital constraints are binding.

However, is this solution optimal; i.e., does it maximize the objective function? Let us substitute these values of y_1 and y_2 into the objective function [y_3 does not appear in (13-43)], carrying y_4 and y_5 along:

$$z = 40(5 - y_4 + y_5) + 30(15 + 0.5y_4 - y_5)$$

$$z = 650 - 25y_4 + 10y_5 \qquad\qquad\qquad\qquad (13\text{-}46)$$

Equation (13-46) is the indirect objective function for this solution vector. It quickly reveals that the solution $y_1 = 5$, $y_2 = 15$, $y_3 = 9$ just obtained is *not* optimal. Using the envelope theorem, we get

$$\frac{\partial z}{\partial y_5} = 10 > 0 \qquad\qquad\qquad\qquad (13\text{-}47)$$

This relation says that the value of the objective function z can be increased by increasing the variable y_5. In fact, z will increase by a factor of 10 for each unit increase in y_5.

Thus, we should seek to make y_5 as large as possible. How large is "possible"? We have to make sure that the remaining variables remain nonnegative. Consider equations (13-45) again. We know we have to bring y_5 into the basis, but which variable, y_1, y_2, or y_3, shall we take out to leave only three basic variables? There is no reason, from equation (13-45a), why y_5 cannot be increased indefinitely (along with y_1). However, (13-45b) tells us, for example, that y_5 cannot be made larger than 15. Ignoring y_4 (which remains at 0), nonnegativity and equations (13-45) mean that we must satisfy, simultaneously,

$$y_1 = 5 + y_5 \geq 0$$

$$y_2 = 15 - y_5 \geq 0$$

$$y_3 = 9 - y_5 \geq 0$$

In fact, the last inequality indicates that $y_5 \leq 9$ is required for nonnegativity. This relation tells us both that "as large as possible" for y_5 is in fact $y_5 = 9$ and that y_3 is the variable that comes out of the basis.

The new basis is therefore y_1, y_2, and y_5. We must now solve for these variables and in the same manner check whether this solution is optimal. We know it will be an improvement, since $\partial z/\partial y_5 > 0$. In fact, we know (since $\partial z/\partial y_5 = 10$ and $y_5 = 9$) that z will increase by $10(9) = 90$, yielding $z = 650 + 90 = 740$. Let us proceed.

From (13-45c),

$$y_5 = 9 + 2y_4 - y_3 \tag{13-48a}$$

Substituting this into (13-45a) yields

$$y_1 = 5 - y_4 + (9 + 2y_4 - y_3)$$

or

$$y_1 = 14 - y_3 + y_4 \tag{13-48b}$$

Substituting (13-48a) into (13-45b) gives

$$y_2 = 15 + 0.5y_4 - (9 + 2y_4 - y_3)$$

or

$$y_2 = 6 + y_3 - 1.5y_4 \tag{13-48c}$$

Equations (13-48) are the new basic feasible solution. Setting $y_3 = y_4 = 0$, we get $y_1 = 14$, $y_2 = 6$, $y_5 = 9$, and $z = 40(14) + 30(6) = 740$, as expected. This is point C in Fig. 13-4.

Is this solution optimal? Using (13-48b) and (13-48c), we get

$$z = 40(14 - y_3 + y_4) + 30(6 + y_3 - 1.5y_4)$$

or

$$z = 740 - 10y_3 - 5y_4 \tag{13-49}$$

Equation (13-49), the indirect objective function for this solution, tells us that this is indeed the optimal solution. This relation implies that $\partial z/\partial y_3 < 0$, $\partial z/\partial y_4 < 0$. Bringing in either of the nonbasic variables will only *reduce* the value of the objective function. Moreover, this solution is *globally* optimal. Convexity of the feasible region and concavity of the objective function (weak concavity here; the objective function is linear) tells us that any local maximum must be a global maximum. We have thus found the maximum solution in one easy iteration, a combination of luck and the efficiency of the simplex algorithm.

To summarize, the simplex algorithm consists of first finding some basic feasible solution by rote, if necessary. The basic variables are solved in terms of the nonbasic variables. These values are then substituted into the objective function, a procedure by which the objective function becomes expressed in terms of the nonbasic variables only. If $\partial z/\partial y_j > 0$ for any nonbasic variable, the original solution is not optimal. Suppose one or more y_j is such that $\partial z/\partial y_j > 0$. Pick one of them (perhaps the one for which $\partial z/\partial y_j$ is largest, though this will not ensure that the optimal solution will be reached the fastest). Use the previously obtained solutions to determine how large that nonbasic variable can be made and which previously basic variable must be set equal to zero, i.e., taken out of the basis. Solve for the new basic feasible solution. Repeat this process until $\partial z/\partial y_j \leq 0$ for all nonbasic variables. When this condition holds, the solution is optimal, since bringing new variables into the basis will not increase z.

Remark 1 If $\partial z / \partial y_j = 0$ for some nonbasic variable, bringing that y_j into the basis will neither increase nor decrease z. If this occurs at an optimal solution, multiple optima are indicated.

Remark 2 For a *minimization* problem, the criterion that must be satisfied is $\partial z / \partial y_j \geq 0$ for all nonbasic y_j. For minimization problems, the optimal solution is characterized by having the nonbasic variables *increase* the objective function if they are introduced.

Example Let us consider the following minimization problem, stripped of any economic content, for the purposes of exhibiting the simplex algorithm once more:

minimize $\qquad z = 2x_1 + x_2 + 2x_3$

subject to $\qquad x_1 - 2x_2 + x_3 \geq 16$

$\qquad\qquad\qquad 2x_2 + x_3 \leq 10$

$\qquad\qquad\qquad\qquad x_3 \leq 6 \qquad x_1, x_2, x_3 \geq 0$

The first step is to add slack variables to convert the constraints into equalities. Note the direction of the inequalities:

minimize $\quad z = 2x_1 + x_2 + 2x_3$

subject to $\quad x_1 - 2x_2 + x_3 - x_4 = 16$

$\qquad\qquad\quad 2x_2 + x_3 + x_5 = 10 \qquad x_1, x_2, x_3, x_4, x_5, x_6 \geq 0$

$\qquad\qquad\quad x_3 + x_6 = 6$

Let us choose x_1, x_2, and x_3 as a basis. Solving for these variables in terms of the remaining ones yields (the student should work through this algebra):

$$x_3 = 6 - x_6$$

$$x_2 = 2 - 0.5x_5 + 0.5x_6$$

$$x_1 = 14 + x_4 - x_5 + 2x_6$$

Computing z, we get

$$z = 2(14 + x_4 - x_5 + 2x_6) + (2 - 0.5x_5 + 0.5x_6) + 2(6 - x_6)$$

or $\qquad z = 42 + 2x_4 - 2.5x_5 + 2.5x_6$

We see that $\partial z / \partial x_5 < 0$; bringing x_5 into the basis will decrease z. Hence, this solution is not optimal. How large can we make x_5? From the above solution, to ensure nonnegativity of x_1, x_2, and x_3, we must have (ignoring x_4 and x_6, which remain at 0)

$$x_2 = 2 - 0.5x_5 \geq 0 \qquad x_1 = 14 - x_5 \geq 0$$

Since these must both be satisfied, we cannot increase x_5 beyond 4. Hence, x_2 comes out of the basis. The new basis is x_1, x_3, and x_5. Solving for these variables yields

$$x_3 = 6 - x_6$$

$$x_5 = 4 - 2x_2 + x_6$$

$$x_1 = 10 + 2x_2 + x_4 + x_6$$

Computing the new z [we expect this z to be less than the old z by $2.5(4) = 10$] gives

$$z = 2(10 + 2x_2 + x_4 + x_6) + x_2 + 2(6 - x_6)$$

or $\qquad z = 32 + 5x_2 + 2x_4$

Notice that $\partial z/\partial x_2 > 0$, $\partial z/\partial x_4 > 0$ but that $\partial z/\partial x_6 = 0$. This solution is optimal, since there is no variable to be brought in which would *lower* z. However, this is not the only solution. Bringing x_6 into the basis will keep z the same. There are an infinite number of solutions along the line segment between this solution ($x_1 = 10$, $x_2 = 0$, $x_3 = 6$) and the one which results from bringing x_6 in. The remainder of this problem is left as an exercise for the student.

PROBLEMS

1 Consider an economy made up of many identical fixed-coefficient firms, each of which produces food y_1 and clothing y_2. There are three inputs, land, labor, and capital, inputs 1, 2, and 3, respectively. The matrix of technological coefficients is

$$\mathbf{A} = \begin{pmatrix} 1 & 1 \\ 1 & 2 \\ 1 & 4 \end{pmatrix}$$

Each firm has available to it 30 units of land, 40 units of labor, and 72 units of capital. Prices are $20 per unit for food and $30 per unit for clothing.

(a) Find the production plan that maximizes the value of output.

(b) Find the shadow prices of land, labor, and capital.

(c) Write down the dual problem and interpret it.

(d) Solve the dual problem and verify that the optimal value of its objective function equals the maximum value of output.

(e) From the factor intensities of the goods at the optimum, predict the changes in output levels that would occur if an additional unit of labor were available. Check by actual solution.

(f) From the factor intensities, predict the change in factor prices if p_1 rises to 21. Check by actual solution.

(g) What effect does a small increase in factor endowments have on factor prices?

2 Answer the same questions as in problem 1 for an economy made up of firms with coefficient matrix

$$\mathbf{A} = \begin{pmatrix} 2 & 1 \\ 1 & 1 \\ 1 & 0 \end{pmatrix}$$

endowments of

$$\mathbf{b} = \begin{pmatrix} 40 \\ 30 \\ 15 \end{pmatrix}$$

and prices $p_1 = 15$, $p_2 = 10$. For part (f), suppose here that p_2 rises to 11.

3 Solve the following linear programming problem:

minimize $\qquad\qquad z = 4x_1 + 5x_2 + x_3$

subject to $\qquad\qquad x_1 + x_2 \geq 9$

$$x_1 + x_3 \leq 8 \qquad x_1, x_2, x_3 \geq 0$$

$$2x_2 - x_3 \geq 5$$

Start with x_1, x_2, x_3 as a basis.

4 A firm makes banjos (x_1), guitars (x_2), and mandolins (x_3). It uses three inputs: wood, labor, and brass, inputs 1, 2, and 3, respectively. Let

$$a_{ij} = \text{amount of } i\text{th input used in production}$$
$$\text{of 1 unit of product } j$$

The matrix of these technological coefficients is

$$\begin{pmatrix} 1 & 1 & 1 \\ 2 & 2 & 1 \\ 1 & 2 & 1 \end{pmatrix}$$

The firm has available to it 50 units of wood, 60 units of labor, and 55 units of brass. The firm sells banjos for $200, guitars for $175, and mandolins for $125.

(a) Find the production plan that maximizes the total value of output. Start with x_1, x_2, x_3 as your first basis.

(b) Formulate the dual for this problem and explain its economic interpretation. Solve the dual problem, using, if you wish, whatever information about its solution you can glean from the solution of the primal problem. How much would the firm be willing to pay for an additional unit of wood, labor, and brass?

5 *The Diet Problem.* Suppose a consumer has available n foods, $x_1, \ldots, x_n$. Each food contains a certain amount of nutrients (vitamins, minerals, etc.). Let $a_{ij} =$ amount of nutrient i in food j. If the foods x_i cost p_i per unit, and the consumer wishes to obtain a minimum daily requirement (MDR) b_j of nutrient j, what diet should be consumed?

(a) Formulate this problem as a linear programming problem. What assumptions about how nutrients are combined is needed?

(b) Formulate and interpret the dual problem.

(c) Suppose there are only three nutrients to consider, A, B, and C, with MDRs of 34, 32 and 50, respectively. There are three foods, x_1, x_2, and x_3 with prices $p_1 = 1$, $p_2 = 3$, $p_3 = 2$. The matrix of nutrient contents of the foods is

$$\mathbf{A} = \begin{pmatrix} 1 & 2 & 1 \\ 2 & 1 & 3 \\ 2 & 3 & 1 \end{pmatrix}$$

Find the diet that minimizes the cost of satisfying the MDRs of each nutrient. Check by solving the dual problem also.

6 Complete the discussion of the linear programming problem presented in the text preceding the problems. Bring x_6 into the basis and show that the maximum value of z is unchanged. Formulate and solve the dual problem and verify that its objective function has at its solution the same value as z^*.

BIBLIOGRAPHY

Dantzig, G. B.: Maximization of a Linear Function of Variables Subject to Linear Inequalities, in T. C. Koopmans (ed.), Activity Analysis of Production and Allocation, *Cowles Commission Monograph* 13, John Wiley & Sons, Inc., New York, 1951.

Dorfman, R., P. A. Samuelson, and R. M. Solow: "Linear Programming and Economic Analysis," McGraw-Hill Book Company, New York, 1958.

Gale, D.: "The Theory of Linear Economic Models," McGraw-Hill Book Company, New York, 1960.

Hadley, G.: "Linear Programming," Addison-Wesley Publishing Company, Inc., Reading, Mass., 1962.

Jones, R. W.: Duality in International Trade: A Geometrical Note, *Canadian Journal of Economics and Political Science*, **31**: 390–393, 1965.

————: The Structure of Simple General Equilibrium Models, *Journal of Political Economy*, **73**: 557–572, 1965.

Koopmans, T. C. (ed.): Activity Analysis of Production and Allocation, *Cowles Commission Monograph* 13, John Wiley & Sons, Inc., New York, 1951.

————: "Three Essays on the State of Economic Science," McGraw-Hill Book Company, New York, 1957.

Leontief, W. W., et al.: "Studies in the Structure of the American Economy," Oxford University Press, New York, 1953.

Rybczynski, T. M.: Factor Endowment and Relative Commodity Prices, *Econometrica*, **22**: 336–341, 1955.

Samuelson, P. A.: Frank Knight's Theorem in Linear Programming, RAND Corp., Santa Monica, Calif., 1950; reprinted in J. Stiglitz (ed.), "The Collected Scientific Papers of Paul A. Samuelson," M.I.T. Press, Cambridge, Mass., 1966.

Stigler, G. J.: The Cost of Subsistence, *Journal of Farm Economics*, **27**: 303–314, 1945.

Stolper, W. F., and P. A. Samuelson: Protection and Real Wages, *Review of Economic Studies*, **9**: 58–73, 1941.

Von Neumann, J.: A Model of General Equilibrium, *Review of Economic Studies*, **13**: 1–9, 1945.

Walras, L.: "Elements of Pure Economics," trans. W. Jaffe, Richard D. Irwin, Inc., Homewood, Ill., 1954.

FOURTEEN

GENERAL EQUILIBRIUM II: NONLINEAR MODELS

14.1 TANGENCY CONDITIONS

In this chapter, the more plausible model of general equilibrium based on *variable* coefficients of production will be investigated. The bulk of the chapter will be concerned with the derivation of the Stolper-Samuelson and Rybczynski theorems in this more general context. It is a rather remarkable feature of these models that when the production functions are assumed merely to be *linear homogeneous*, the comparative statics of the model yield the same implications as in the case of fixed-coefficient technology (indeed, the algebra is identical).

The most general model to be considered here is the one in which n final goods, $y_1, \ldots, y_n$, are produced using m factors of production, $x_1, \ldots, x_m$. The economy faces world output-prices, $p_1, \ldots, p_n$. If we let

$$x_{ij} = \text{amount of factor } i \text{ used in produc-}$$
$$\text{tion of good } j$$

the production function for y_j is

$$y_j = f^j(x_{1j}, \ldots, x_{mj}) \qquad j = 1, \ldots, n \tag{14-1}$$

We assert that an invisible hand leads the economy to:

$$\text{maximize} \qquad z = \sum_{j=1}^{n} p_j y_j = \sum_{j=1}^{n} p_j f^j(x_{1j}, \ldots, x_{mj}) \tag{14-2}$$

subject to $$\sum_{j=1}^{n} x_{ij} \leq x_i \qquad i = 1, \ldots, m \tag{14-3}$$

$$x_{ij} \geq 0 \qquad \text{all} \quad i, j$$

The model, at this point, is a general nonlinear programming problem. Without the knowledge of the specific functional forms for the production functions (14-1), no solution algorithm is available (as opposed to the linear model of the previous chapter). We shall therefore concentrate on the *comparative statics* of the model, assuming that the x_{ij}'s above are the ones which the economy uses in positive amounts. In that case, the Kuhn-Tucker first-order conditions become the classical lagrangian techniques.

All the comparative-statics results that are forthcoming in this general model can be adequately indicated by reducing the model to two goods and two factors, since we shall not be concerned with which factors are present in the first place. Let us therefore change notation to conform with the previous analysis and consider *two* factors, L, labor, and K, capital. Let L_j and K_j represent the amounts of labor and capital, respectively, which are used in the production of good j. The production functions for each of the two goods are

$$y_j = f^j(L_j, K_j) \qquad j = 1, 2$$

The model thus becomes:

maximize $$z = p_1 f^1(L_1, K_1) + p_2 f^2(L_2, K_2) \tag{14-4}$$

subject to $$L_1 + L_2 = L \tag{14-5a}$$

$$K_1 + K_2 = K \tag{14-5b}$$

We are assuming that we shall find L_1, L_2, K_1, and K_2 all positive and fully employed at the parametrically fixed levels L and K, respectively. The lagrangian for this model is

$$\mathcal{L} = p_1 f^1(L_1, K_1) + p_2 f^2(L_2, K_2) + \lambda_L(L - L_1 - L_2) + \lambda_K(K - K_1 - K_2) \tag{14-6}$$

The first-order equations for constrained maximum are obtained by differentiating $\mathcal{L}$ with respect to the four choice variables, L_1, L_2, K_1, K_2, and the two Lagrange multipliers. When we let

$$f_L^j = \frac{\partial f^j}{\partial L_j} = \frac{\partial y_j}{\partial L_j} \qquad f_K^j = \frac{\partial f^j}{\partial K_j} = \frac{\partial y_j}{\partial K_j}$$

these first-order conditions are

$$p_1 f_L^1 - \lambda_L = 0 \tag{14-7a}$$

$$p_1 f_K^1 - \lambda_K = 0 \tag{14-7b}$$

$$p_2 f_L^2 - \lambda_L = 0 \tag{14-7c}$$

$$p_2 f_K^2 - \lambda_K = 0 \tag{14-7d}$$

$$L - L_1 - L_2 = 0 \qquad (14\text{-}8a)$$

$$K - K_1 - K_2 = 0 \qquad (14\text{-}8b)$$

The second-order conditions consist of restrictions on the border-preserving principal minors of the border hessian determinant formed by differentiating equations (14-7) and (14-8) again with respect to the L_i's, K_i's and λ's. Letting $f^j_{LL} = \partial^2 f^j/(\partial L_j\, \partial L_j)$, etc., we have

$$H = \begin{vmatrix} p_1 f^1_{LL} & p_1 f^1_{LK} & 0 & 0 & -1 & 0 \\ p_1 f^1_{KL} & p_1 f^1_{KK} & 0 & 0 & 0 & -1 \\ 0 & 0 & p_2 f^2_{LL} & p_2 f^2_{LK} & -1 & 0 \\ 0 & 0 & p_2 f^2_{KL} & p_2 f^2_{KK} & 0 & -1 \\ -1 & 0 & -1 & 0 & 0 & 0 \\ 0 & -1 & 0 & -1 & 0 & 0 \end{vmatrix} \qquad (14\text{-}9)$$

Specifically, the border-preserving principal minors of order k alternate in sign, the whole determinant H having sign $+1$.

Assuming the sufficient second-order conditions hold, equations (14-7) and (14-8) can be solved for the explicit choice functions

$$L_i = L_i^*(p_1, p_2, L, K) \qquad i = 1, 2 \qquad (14\text{-}10a)$$

$$K_i = K_i^*(p_1, p_2, L, K) \qquad i = 1, 2 \qquad (14\text{-}10b)$$

and

$$\lambda_L = \lambda_L^*(p_1, p_2, L, K) \qquad (14\text{-}11a)$$

$$\lambda_K = \lambda_K^*(p_1, p_2, L, K) \qquad (14\text{-}11b)$$

Equations (14-10) show the quantities of each factor that will be used by each industry at given output prices and total resource constraints. They are in fact neither factor-supply nor factor-demand equations, since they are not functions of factor prices. The factor-supply curves to the whole economy are vertical lines at L and K, respectively. Equations (14-10) represent the solutions to the allocation problem wherein each factor is demanded by two industries.

As in the linear model of the previous chapter, the role of factor prices is filled by the Lagrange multipliers λ_L and λ_K. Substituting the L_i^*'s and K_i^*'s into the objective function z yields

$$z^* = \phi(p_1, p_2, L, K) = p_1 f^1(L_1^*, K_1^*) + p_2 f^2(L_2^*, K_2^*) \qquad (14\text{-}12)$$

Using the envelope theorem, we get

$$\frac{\partial z^*}{\partial L} = \frac{\partial \phi}{\partial L} = \frac{\partial \mathscr{L}}{\partial L} = \lambda_L^*(p_1, p_2, L, K) \qquad (14\text{-}13a)$$

$$\frac{\partial z^*}{\partial K} = \frac{\partial \phi}{\partial K} = \frac{\partial \mathscr{L}}{\partial K} = \lambda_K^*(p_1, p_2, L, K) \qquad (14\text{-}13b)$$

That is, λ_L^* is the rate of change of maximum NNP with respect to a change in the resource endowment of labor, with a similar interpretation for λ_K^*. These multipliers are the incremental increases in income that would result if an additional increment of labor or capital were available. In a competitive economy, these are the marginal revenue products of labor and capital, respectively. They indicate what labor and capital would be paid in a competitive economy. Hence, the Lagrange multipliers represent the imputed values, or shadow prices, of resources in this model. They are not exogenous, as in the previous partial-equilibrium treatments of the firm, but endogenous, appearing as part of the solution to the model.

Let us in fact designate the wage rate w as $w \equiv \lambda_L$ and the flow price of capital as $r \equiv \lambda_K$. The symbol r does *not* represent an interest rate. It is the rate at which capital is *rented*, analogous to the rate w at which labor is rented. Capital is treated as a service flow, as is labor, and not as a stock which is purchased outright, with r the wage of capital.

Industry supply curves can be defined in this model by substituting the L_i^*'s and K_i^*'s into the production function, yielding

$$y_1 = f^1(L_1^*, K_1^*) = y_1^*(p_1, p_2, L, K) \tag{14-14a}$$

$$y_2 = f^2(L_2^*, K_2^*) = y_2^*(p_1, p_2, L, K) \tag{14-14b}$$

These are the industry supply curves because they indicate how much output will be produced for a given price of output, price of the other good, and resource constraints. The demand curves for each industry are the horizontal price lines at the levels p_1 and p_2, respectively, reflecting competitive output markets.

The supply curves (14-14) are homogeneous of degree zero in output prices. Increasing both prices by the same proportion leaves output unchanged, or

$$y_j^*(tp_1, tp_2, L, K) \equiv y_j^*(p_1, p_2, L, K) \qquad j = 1, 2 \tag{14-15}$$

This is easily seen from the objective function (14-4), $z = p_1 y_1 + p_2 y_2$. If both prices are increased by the factor t, $z = t(p_1 y_1 + p_2 y_2)$, a simple monotonic (linear, in fact) transformation of the original function. The values of the factors which maximize $p_1 y_1 + p_2 y_2$ also maximize $tp_1 y_1 + tp_2 y_2$. The solutions (14-10), $L_i = L_i^*(p_1, p_2, L, K)$, etc., are thus homogeneous of degree zero in p_1 and p_2, and thus so must be $y_1^* = f^1(L_1^*, K_1^*)$ and $y_2^* = f^2(L_2^*, K_2^*)$.

The production possibility frontier for this economy is defined as the locus of points (y_1, y_2) such that for any given y_2, the maximum y_1 is obtained, or vice versa. It can be obtained by eliminating the prices from equations (14-14a) and (14-14b). In equation (14-15), let $t = 1/p_2, p = p_1/p_2$. The variable p represents the *relative* price of output y_1 (in terms of units of y_2). Then we obtain

$$y_1^*(p_1, p_2, L, K) = y_1^*\left(\frac{p_1}{p_2}, 1, L, K\right) = Y_1^*(p, L, K) \tag{14-16a}$$

and

$$y_2^*(p_1, p_2, L, K) = y_2^*\left(\frac{p_1}{p_2}, 1, L, K\right) = Y_2^*(p, L, K) \tag{14-16b}$$

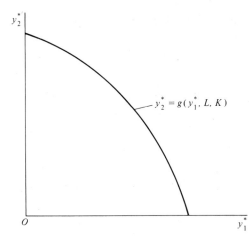

Figure 14-1 The production possibilities frontier indicates the maximum amount of one
output that is attainable for given amounts of
the other. In order for the economy to achieve
maximum NNP for given resource constraints,
a point on this frontier must be reached.
Otherwise, increasing both y_1 and y_2 will
increase NNP $= p_1 y_1 + p_2 y_2$. The second-
order conditions for the maximization of NNP
model imply that $\partial y_2^*/\partial y_1^* < 0, \partial^2 y_1^*/\partial y_1^{*2} < 0$,
as drawn above. However, this is not implied
by simply maximizing y_2 for given y_1, L, and
K unless additional restrictions are placed on
the production functions. (See problem 5.)

Assuming $\partial Y_j^*/\partial p \neq 0, j = 1, 2$, the variable p, relative output-price, can be eliminated from these two equations, leaving

$$G(y_1^*, y_2^*, L, K) = 0 \qquad (14\text{-}17)$$

or, in explicit form,

$$y_2^* = g(y_1^*; L, K) \qquad (14\text{-}18)$$

The typical assumed shape of this function is concave to the origin, as depicted in
Fig. 14-1. We shall see presently how this shape is implied by the sufficient second-
order equations for this model. As drawn, $\partial y_2^*/\partial y_1^* < 0$, and $\partial^2 y_2^*/\partial y_1^{*2} < 0$.

Before analyzing the comparative statics of this model, let us investigate the
first-order marginal relations (14-7). As we have indicated, $w (= \lambda_L)$ and $r (= \lambda_K)$
are the imputed marginal revenue products of labor and capital, respectively.
From equations (14-7a) and (14-7c), we see that the marginal revenue product of
labor must be the same in both industries. Likewise, from (14-7b) and (14-7d), the
marginal revenue product of capital must be the same in both industries. One
would expect this on the basis of intuitive reasoning. If labor, say, were more
productive, i.e., yielded more output at the margin, in industry 1 than in industry
2, the owners of labor would find competitive bids for their services more attractive in the first industry. Labor will leave industry 2 and enter industry 1. In so
doing, the marginal product of labor will rise in industry 2 and fall in industry 1.
This process will continue until the bids for labor (or capital) are the same in both
industries. It is this process of competitive bidding, with owners of labor and
capital seeking their highest valued employment, that is the essence of Adam
Smith's invisible hand mechanism, in which the value of total output is
maximized.

Combining equations (14-7a) and (14-7b) gives

$$\frac{f_L^1}{f_K^1} = \frac{w}{r} \qquad (14\text{-}19a)$$

Likewise, from (14-7c) and (14-7d) we have

$$\frac{f_L^2}{f_K^2} = \frac{w}{r} \tag{14-19b}$$

These last two equations say that the ratio of the marginal products of labor and capital, for each industry, is equal to the ratio of the (imputed) factor prices. This is analogous to the partial-equilibrium tangency condition for profit-maximization or cost-minimization, in which the isoquants are tangent to the isocost line, with common slope equal to the ratio of wage rates.

In the present model, however, this imputed ratio of wage rates or relative factor costs is common to both industries. From equation (14-19),

$$\frac{f_L^1}{f_K^1} = \frac{w}{r} = \frac{f_L^2}{f_K^2} \tag{14-20}$$

At the wealth-maximizing input combination, the slopes of the isoquants in each industry are the same. Again, if they were different, one factor would be more productive (at the margin) in one industry than the other (the reverse holding for the other factor). In that case, factors would move from the relatively low-valued use to the high-valued use, increasing both the return to that factor and the NNP of the economy.

This situation is commonly depicted in an Edgeworth-Bowley box diagram. In Fig. 14-2, industry 1 is depicted in the usual manner, with origin O_1 at the lower left, or southwest, corner of the box. The isoquants of industry 1 are the curves convex to that origin. The axes are finite, however, and extended only to the limits of resource endowments. In the horizontal direction, labor is plotted up to the parametric value L. Likewise, in the vertical direction, units of capital are plotted until the parametric value K is reached. At these limits, a rectangle is formed, yielding another origin O_2. The production function $f^2(L_2, K_2)$ is plotted upside down, starting at O_2, with increased labor plotted in a westerly direction, increased capital in the southerly direction. Various isoquants of $f^2(L_2, K_2)$ are plotted in Fig. 14-2. These curves are concave to O_1 but convex to O_2, the origin from which they are plotted.

Any point in the box represents an allocation of factors to each industry. For example, at point A, L_1 units of labor are allocated to industry 1 and L_2 to industry 2. As at all interior points, $L_1 + L_2 = L$, the horizontal dimension of the box. Likewise at A, K_1 units of capital are allocated to industry 1 and K_2 to industry 2. Since $K_1 + K_2 = K$, the vertical height of the box at all values of L_1, the entire amount of capital available to the economy is allocated between the two industries.

Point A, however, cannot be an efficient allocation, i.e., one in which NNP is maximized. At point A, the slope of industry 1's isoquant is flatter than that of industry 2. Industry 1 will be bidding relatively low for labor and high for capital. Likewise, industry 2, which at A employs relatively large amounts of capital (though this is not necessary), will bid higher amounts for labor and lower

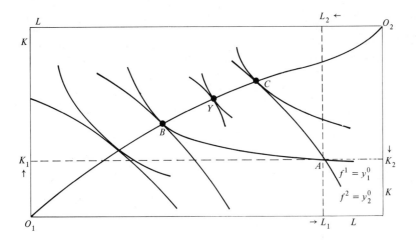

Figure 14-2 Edgeworth-Bowley box diagram for factor utilization. This famous diagram, attributed to F. Y. Edgeworth and A. L. Bowley, depicts the set of factor allocations in an economy in which all gains from trade are exhausted. The dimensions of the box are the total endowments of labor (plotted horizontally) and capital (plotted vertically). The labor L_1, used by industry 1, at some point, say A, is the horizontal distance from A to the vertical axis emanating from origin O_1. Likewise, the vertical distance from the labor axis to A is the capital K_1 used by industry 1. Continuing to the right from A to the right-hand extremity of the box is the remaining labor L_2 in the economy, which is used by industry 2. Likewise, the vertical distance above A to the top horizontal axis is the amount of capital K_2 used by industry 2. Since $L_1 + L_2 = L$ and $K_1 + K_2 = K$, where L and K are constants, a rectangle is depicted such that any point inside it defines an allocation of factors to each industry.

With this in mind, the production function $f^1(L_1, K_1)$ can be plotted with respect to the origin defined by the southwest corner of the box, and $f^2(L_2, K_2)$ can be plotted with respect to the origin defined by the northeast corner of the box. Industry 2's production function $f^2(L_2, K_2)$, however, is plotted negatively. *Increasing L_2* is a leftward movement since it represents *decreasing L_1*. Likewise, *increasing K_2* is a downward movement since it represents *decreasing K_1*. Hence, while the isoquants of f^1 appear normally, the isoquants of f^2 appear concave to O_1. Actually, though, they are to be interpreted as convex to O_2, the appropriate origin from which $f^2(L_2, K_2)$ is plotted.

The efficient factor allocations, i.e., those which result in output levels on the production frontier, are those input combinations at which the slopes of the isoquants are equal, in accordance with equation (14-20). At such points, each industry values the inputs identically. If industry 1 were willing to give up 3 units of capital for 1 unit of labor and industry 2 were willing to give up 1 unit of labor for 1 unit of capital, both industries could experience an increase in output by, say, industry 1 exchanging only 2 units of capital and getting 1 unit of labor from industry 1 in return. Such mutually advantageous reallocations are possible as long as the slopes of the isoquants for the two industries are different. The locus of points at which those slopes are identical, indicating exhaustion of gains from exchange of factors, is the curve line between O_1 and O_2, known as the *contract curve*. In the absence of transactions costs, some point on the contract curve must be achieved. If the initial point is A, say, in this diagram, then *voluntary* exchange will lead to an allocation of factors on the contract curve.

amounts for capital than industry 1. The slopes of each industry's isoquants at A indicate that labor is valued more to industry 2 than to industry 1 while capital is relatively high-valued to industry 1. The competitive mechanism will induce labor to move to industry 2 and capital to industry 1. In terms of the Edgeworth diagram, the allocation point will move to the contract curve. Eventually, some point will be reached, such as point Y, at which the slopes of industry 1's and industry 2's isoquants are identical, in accordance with equation (14-20). At such a point, the isoquants for the two industries will be tangent to each other. The locus of all such points of tangency within the Edgeworth box is called the *contract curve*. In the absence of transactions costs, a competitive economy must always be at some point on the contract curve. To be otherwise would deny the postulate that more is preferred to less. Individual self-seeking will force the economy to some point along the contract curve at which all gains from trade are exhausted.

One more tangency which is not depicted but nonetheless is implied is the response of consumers to this situation. All consumers in this economy face the prices p_1 and p_2 for the output of these industries. Utility-maximizing consumers will consume these goods where their subjective marginal valuation of the goods equals the price ratio, i.e., the relative costs to the consumers. The slope of the consumers' indifference curves, their marginal rate of substitution, will equal the price ratio, or the slope of the production possibility frontier at the final output point.

Any point on the production possibility frontier depicted in Fig. 14-1 corresponds to some point on the contract curve of Fig. 14-2, since only at efficient factor utilization can the maximum output of one good be obtained for a given amount of the other. Any factor allocation not on the contract curve of Fig. 14-2 will result in an output point inside the production frontier depicted in Fig. 14-1. In the literature, two kinds of efficiency are usually defined. If the production point achieved is perceived to be on the production possibilities frontier, then the economy is said to be *efficient in production*. However, due to, for example, monopolies in the economy, the marginal rates of substitution of consumers may not equal the relative cost of production. In that case, gains from exchange could occur, using the reasoning just described, that would allow all consumers to gain. When the MRS of all consumers equals the relative marginal costs of production, the economy is said to be *efficient in consumption*. These welfare-type considerations were first enunciated by V. Pareto. An economy in which all the gains from exchange are exhausted is called *Pareto-optimal* or *Pareto-efficient*. We shall delve into this in more detail in the next chapter.

The student should be warned that efficiency is an essentially unobservable condition. In the absence of transactions costs, all gains from exchange must at all times be exhausted, and hence efficiency follows tautologically. If an economy is asserted to be at an inefficient, or non-Pareto, point, the implied losses to consumers must be reconciled with the consumers' preferences for more rather than less. That is, some observable cost of trading, perhaps embodied in some institutional restriction on open markets, must be identified to make the theory internally consistent. (A deeper analysis would in fact have to explain why consumers sometimes get together and enact laws resulting in lost gains from trade.)

14.2 GENERAL COMPARATIVE-STATICS RESULTS

As we have repeatedly emphasized, the potentially observable, refutable hypotheses generated by a model are the goals of theory. The first-order conditions (14-7) and (14-8) are nonobservable in the absence of knowledge of the specific functional forms. The refutable hypotheses of this model are the restrictions in sign of the various partial derivatives of the explicit choice functions, equations (14-10a) and (14-10b), that are implied by the maximization hypothesis. Additional refutable hypotheses, derived from the above, are the possible restrictions in sign of the output-supply functions (14-14). Let us investigate these comparative-statics relations using the envelope analysis of Chap. 9.

The indirect national income function, defined in equation (14-12), is the maximum value of NNP for given output prices and resource endowments. It is found by substituting the explicit choice functions (14-10) into the objective function defining NNP, or

$$z^* = \text{NNP}^* = \phi(p_1, p_2, L, K) = p_1 f^1(L_1^*, K_1^*) + p_2 f^2(L_2^*, K_2^*)$$

Since this is the maximum value of NNP for given parameter values, $\text{NNP} - \text{NNP}^* \le 0$, with $\text{NNP} - \text{NNP}^* = 0$ when $L_i = L_i^*$, $K_i = K_i^*$, $i = 1, 2$. Thus, the function

$$F(L_1, L_2, K_1, K_2, p_1, p_2, L, K) = \text{NNP}(L_1, L_2, K_1, K_2, p_1, p_2, L, K)$$
$$- \text{NNP}^*(p_1, p_2, L, K)$$

has a constrained maximum (of 0) at $L_i = L_i^*$, $K_i = K_i^*$, $i = 1, 2$. The lagrangian for this primal-dual problem is

$$\mathscr{L} = \text{NNP} - \text{NNP}^* + w(L - L_1 - L_2) + r(K - K_1 - K_2)$$

The comparative-statics sign restrictions are derived from the bordered hessian of second partials of $\mathscr{L}$ with respect to the parameters p_1, p_2, L, and K. The first partials of $\mathscr{L}$ with respect to these parameters are the envelope relations

$$\frac{\partial \mathscr{L}}{\partial p_1} = y_1 - y_1^* = 0 \tag{14-21a}$$

$$\frac{\partial \mathscr{L}}{\partial p_2} = y_2 - y_2^* = 0 \tag{14-21b}$$

$$\frac{\partial \mathscr{L}}{\partial L} = -w^* + w = 0 \tag{14-21c}$$

$$\frac{\partial \mathscr{L}}{\partial K} = -r^* + r = 0 \tag{14-21d}$$

The constraints are the first partials of $\mathscr{L}$ with respect to w and r, set equal to 0:

$$\frac{\partial \mathscr{L}}{\partial w} = L - L_1 - L_2 = 0 \qquad (14\text{-}22a)$$

$$\frac{\partial \mathscr{L}}{\partial r} = K - K_1 - K_2 = 0 \qquad (14\text{-}22b)$$

The relevant bordered hessian is formed from the second partials of $\mathscr{L}$ with respect to p_1, p_2, L, K, w, and r. These second partials are the first partials of equations (14-21) and (14-22) with respect to those variables, since those equations are the first partials of $\mathscr{L}$ with respect to those variables. The bordered hessian is thus

$$|\mathscr{L}_{\alpha\alpha}| = \begin{vmatrix} -\dfrac{\partial y_1^*}{\partial p_1} & -\dfrac{\partial y_1^*}{\partial p_2} & -\dfrac{\partial y_1^*}{\partial L} & -\dfrac{\partial y_1^*}{\partial K} & 0 & 0 \\[2mm] -\dfrac{\partial y_2^*}{\partial p_1} & -\dfrac{\partial y_2^*}{\partial p_2} & -\dfrac{\partial y_2^*}{\partial L} & -\dfrac{\partial y_2^*}{\partial K} & 0 & 0 \\[2mm] -\dfrac{\partial w^*}{\partial p_1} & -\dfrac{\partial w^*}{\partial p_2} & -\dfrac{\partial w^*}{\partial L} & -\dfrac{\partial w^*}{\partial K} & 1 & 0 \\[2mm] -\dfrac{\partial r^*}{\partial p_1} & -\dfrac{\partial r^*}{\partial p_2} & -\dfrac{\partial r^*}{\partial L} & -\dfrac{\partial r^*}{\partial K} & 0 & 1 \\[2mm] 0 & 0 & 1 & 0 & 0 & 0 \\[2mm] 0 & 0 & 0 & 1 & 0 & 0 \end{vmatrix} \qquad (14\text{-}23)$$

The first comparative-statics relations that appear are the reciprocity conditions, derived from the symmetry of $\mathscr{L}_{\alpha\alpha}$. We note

$$\frac{\partial y_1^*}{\partial p_2} = \frac{\partial y_2^*}{\partial p_1} \qquad (14\text{-}24)$$

$$\frac{\partial y_i^*}{\partial L} = \frac{\partial w^*}{\partial p_i} \qquad i = 1, 2 \qquad (14\text{-}25a)$$

$$\frac{\partial y_i^*}{\partial K} = \frac{\partial r^*}{\partial p_i} \qquad i = 1, 2 \qquad (14\text{-}25b)$$

Also

$$\frac{\partial w^*}{\partial K} = \frac{\partial r^*}{\partial L} \qquad (14\text{-}26)$$

Equation (14-24) says that if the output price of y_1 is raised, say, the effect on industry 2's output is exactly the same as the effect on industry 1's output of an increase in p_2. Equations (14-25) indicate, for example, that if the resource endowment of labor is increased, the effect on the ith industry's output will be the same as the effect of an increase in the price of the ith industry's output on the imputed wage or shadow price of labor. Equations (14-24) to (14-26) demonstrate a duality of prices and quantities in this model. All the relations that are valid for quantities are also valid for prices. The reciprocity relations (14-26) are exact analogs of (14-24) with the prices of the goods or factors replacing the respective physical quantities and vice versa.

Equations (14-24) to (14-26) generalize in a straightforward manner to the case of n goods and m factors. When we let $\lambda_1, \ldots, \lambda_m$ represent the shadow-factor prices of factors $x_1, \ldots, x_m$, these equations become, respectively,

$$\frac{\partial y_i^*}{\partial p_j} = \frac{\partial y_j^*}{\partial p_i} \qquad i, j = 1, \ldots, n$$

$$\frac{\partial y_j^*}{\partial x_i} = \frac{\partial \lambda_i^*}{\partial p_j} \qquad i = 1, \ldots, m; j = 1, \ldots, n$$

$$\frac{\partial \lambda_i}{\partial x_j} = \frac{\partial \lambda_j}{\partial x_i} \qquad i, j = 1, \ldots, m$$

Thus far, however, we have not placed any sign restrictions on these partial derivatives. At this level of generality, it is not possible to say whether an increase in the endowment of labor will increase or decrease the output of either industry. (It can be shown, as one would expect with positive marginal products, that an increase in labor or capital cannot lead to a decrease in output of *both* industries.) The effect on the imputed wages of changes in output prices is likewise indeterminate. The only comparative-statics sign restrictions that are derivable at this level of generality relate to the supply of output functions $y_i = y_i^*(p_1, p_2, L, K)$. These curves must be upward-sloping in their own prices, assuming the sufficient second-order conditions. The parameters in this model are partitionable into two distinct sets, p_1 and p_2, which appear only in the objective function, and L and K, which appear only in the constraints. No signed comparative-statics relations can appear for these latter parameters, as the analysis of Chap. 9 makes clear. In the case of p_1 and p_2, the associated decision variables y_1^* and y_2^* behave the same as in an unconstrained model. Since this is a maximum problem, the diagonal elements $-\partial y_1^*/\partial p_1$ and $-\partial y_2^*/\partial p_2$ must be negative. Thus,

$$\frac{\partial y_i^*}{\partial p_i} > 0 \qquad i = 1, 2 \tag{14-27}$$

The output-supply curves are thus upward-sloping. Again, the analogous assertions for $-\partial w^*/\partial L$, $-\partial r^*/\partial K$ are *not* valid, since L and K are parameters which appear in the constraints. It is *not* possible to say at this level of generality that, for example, an increase in the amount of labor in the economy will depress the wage rate of labor. Plausible as that result sounds, it is not implied by the above model. Moreover, with the addition of other assumptions, in particular constant-returns-to-scale production functions, the wage rates are shown to be *independent* of the endowments of resources. We shall explore these issues in the next section.

Let us now consider the implied properties of the production transformation frontier, defined in equation (14-17) and depicted in Fig. 14-1. The factor-choice equations are, again,

$$L_i = L_i^*(p_1, p_2, L, K) \qquad K_i = K_i^*(p_1, p_2, L, K)$$

Since these equations are homogeneous of degree zero in p_1, p_2, they can be expressed in terms of the price ratio $p = p_1/p_2$. We shall suppress the parameters L and K in the following discussion for notational ease; these parameters are not relevant to this discussion. Writing $L_i = L_i^*(p)$, $K_i = K_i^*(p)$, we define equations (14-14) again as

$$y_1^*(p) = f^1(L_1^*(p), K_1^*(p)) \qquad (14\text{-}28a)$$

and
$$y_2^*(p) = f^2(L_2^*(p), K_2^*(p)) \qquad (14\text{-}28b)$$

Assuming these functions are invertible, the functional dependence

$$y_2^* = y_2^*(p(y_1^*)) = y_2^*(y_1^*) \qquad (14\text{-}29)$$

is valid. From the chain rule,

$$\frac{\partial y_2^*}{\partial y_1^*} = \frac{\partial y_2^*/\partial p}{\partial y_1^*/\partial p} \qquad (14\text{-}30)$$

When equations (14-28) are used, equation (14-30) becomes

$$\frac{\partial y_2^*}{\partial y_1^*} = \frac{f_L^2(\partial L_2^*/\partial p) + f_K^2(\partial K_2^*/\partial p)}{f_L^1(\partial L_1^*/\partial p) + f_K^1(\partial K_1^*/\partial p)}$$

Using the first-order conditions that $p_1 f_L^1 = p_2 f_L^2 = w$, $p_1 f_K^1 = p_2 f_K^2 = r$, we have

$$\frac{\partial y_2^*}{\partial y_1^*} = \frac{(1/p_2)[w(\partial L_2^*/\partial p) + r(\partial K_2^*/\partial p)]}{(1/p_1)[w(\partial L_1^*/\partial p) + r(\partial K_1^*/\partial p)]}$$

However, since $L_1^*(p) + L_2^*(p) \equiv L$, $K_1^*(p) + K_2^*(p) \equiv K$,

$$\frac{\partial L_1^*}{\partial p} \equiv -\frac{\partial L_2^*}{\partial p} \qquad \frac{\partial K_1^*}{\partial p} \equiv -\frac{\partial K_2^*}{\partial p}$$

The numerator (excluding the price term) is thus exactly the negative of the denominator, or

$$\frac{\partial y_2^*}{\partial y_1^*} = \frac{p_1}{p_2}(-1) = -p = -p(y_1^*) \qquad (14\text{-}31)$$

Equation (14-31) asserts that when NNP is maximized, the production possibilities frontier will be tangent to an *isorevenue* (same-revenue) line. NNP is given as a linear function of output levels,

$$\text{NNP} = p_1 y_1 + p_2 y_2$$

The values of y_1 and y_2 which maximize NNP, that is, those values which allow this line to move farthest from the origin in the output space, are those values where the production frontier has the same slope as the isorevenue line, $-p = -p_1/p_2$. This situation is depicted in Fig. 14-3. As drawn there, the production possibilities frontier is concave to the origin. This is verified mathematically by differentiating both sides of the identity (14-31) with respect to y_1^*:

$$\frac{\partial^2 y_2^*}{\partial y_1^{*2}} = -\frac{\partial p}{\partial y_1^*} = \frac{-1}{\partial y_1^*/\partial p} = \frac{-p_2}{\partial y_1^*/\partial p_1} < 0 \qquad (14\text{-}32)$$

Equations (14-31) and (14-32) assert that this economy is characterized by positive and increasing marginal costs of production in the neighborhood of the wealth-maximizing output choices. The fact that $\partial y_2^*/\partial y_1^*$ is negative means that if more y_1 is desired, some y_2 will have to be forgone. The partial derivative $\partial y_2^*/\partial y_1^*$

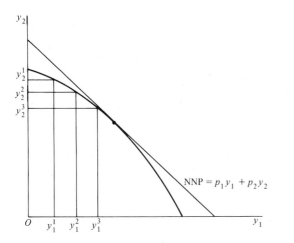

Figure 14-3 Maximization of NNP $= p_1 y_1 + p_2 y_2$. An interior maximization of NNP subject to resource constraints implies a production possibilities frontier which is concave to the origin. This feature is visually obvious in the above diagram. If the frontier were convex to the origin, maximum NNP, where the line NNP $= p_1 y_1 + p_2 y_2$ was as far from the origin as possible, would occur at a corner, implying production of one good only. The interior maximum above occurs at a point where the consumers' marginal evaluations of the two goods (measured by the slope $-p_1/p_2$ of the isorevenue line NNP $= p_1 y_1 + p_2 y_2$) equals the marginal production trade-off of y_2 for y_1. This latter trade-off is the marginal cost of y_1 measured by the ordinary slope of the production frontier. The concavity of this frontier is indicative of increasing marginal costs of production. As output of y_1 increases from y_1^1 to y_1^2, the *cost* of this increased output is measured by the *decrease* in y_2 available, $y_2^1 - y_2^2$. Increasing y_1 by the same increment, to y_1^3, leads to the *larger* sacrifice of y_2, measured by the vertical distance $y_2^2 - y_2^3$. In the limit, for small changes in y_1, the marginal cost of y_1 in terms of the rate at which y_2 must be forgone is the slope of the production possibilities frontier. The increasing (in absolute value) slope as y_1 increases indicates increasing marginal cost of y_1. The same situation obtains for y_2: the reciprocal slope measures the marginal cost of y_2 and increases with increasing y_2.

measures the rate at which y_2^* must be sacrificed in order to get more y_1. Therefore, $\partial y_2^*/\partial y_1^*$ is the (negative) marginal opportunity cost of obtaining more y_1^*. Since $\partial(\partial y_2^*/\partial y_1^*)/\partial y_1^* = \partial^2 y_2^*/\partial y_1^{*2} < 0$, the marginal cost of y_1 must be increasing. As y_1 increases, the slope, or marginal cost $\partial y_2^*/\partial y_1^*$ of y_1 becomes more negative. Hence, the more y_1 the economy produces the more y_2 must be forgone to obtain additional units of y_1. This situation is depicted in Fig. 14-3. As y_1 increases from y_1^1 to y_1^2 to y_1^3, the marginal cost of these increments, measured by the vertical declines in y_2 produced $(y_2^1 - y_2^2$ and $y_2^2 - y_2^3)$, increases.

Given the interpretation of $\partial y_2^*/\partial y_1^*$ as the marginal cost of y_1, equation (14-31) becomes the familiar condition for maximizing behavior so that marginal costs equal marginal benefits, i.e., here, marginal revenue. The world market is willing to exchange y_2 for additional units of y_1 at the rate $p = p_1/p_2$. NNP will be maximized when, at the margin, the cost of y_1 in terms of y_2 forgone is just equal to the additional revenue produced by the increased y_1 and decreased y_2 production, measured by the price ratio $p = p_1/p_2$. Equation (14-32) is the statement that at a *maximum* position, marginal costs must be rising. Of course, all this analysis can be done with the axes interchanged, i.e., in terms of marginal costs and benefits for y_2 rather than y_1. The model is perfectly symmetric in y_1 and y_2; valid results are obtainable by interchanging y_1 and y_2, and likewise labor and capital.

We note in passing that in the two-good case, since $\partial y_1^*/\partial p_1, \partial y_2^*/\partial p_2 > 0$, it must be that $\partial y_2^*/\partial p_1 = \partial y_1^*/\partial p_2 < 0$. This follows from the homogeneity of the output-supply functions and is left as a problem for the student. In the n-good case, however, no sign is implied for the off-diagonal terms $\partial y_i^*/\partial p_j$, $i \neq j$.

14.3 THE FACTOR-PRICE EQUALIZATION AND RELATED THEOREMS

Let us now move on to the analysis of the classic theorems of international trade: the factor-price equalization, Stolper-Samuelson, and Rybczynski theorems. These results were presented for the special case of fixed-coefficient technology in the previous chapter. To derive these results for the case of variable proportions, the assumption of linear homogeneous industry production functions must be added.

We have not been specific about the nature of the firms in this model, as it was not germane to the results. Let us now assume, however, that each industry is composed of many "identical" firms. They may differ in scale, but the underlying production function for each firm in a given industry must be the same. Under these conditions, an industry production function can be well defined. That is, if all firms are identical in the above sense, the aggregate output of the industry is expressible as a well-defined (single-valued) function of the total labor and capital inputs. Moreover, this aggregate production function will be linear homogeneous. Consider a 10 percent increase in the demand for the industry's output. With constant factor prices, the long-run effects will be merely to increase the number of firms in the industry by 10 percent (if the scale of each firm is the same). These new firms, being identical to the preexisting firms in the industry, will hire like proportions of labor and capital. Hence, 10 percent more labor and 10 percent more capital will be used to produce the 10 percent increase in output. Since this will occur for any initial input combination, the industry, or aggregate production, function can be characterized as having constant returns to scale.

Example Consider two firms *in the same industry*, with production functions

$$y_1 = f^1(L_1, K_1) = L_1^{1/3} K_1^{2/3}$$
$$y_2 = f^2(L_2, K_2) = L_2^{2/3} K_2^{1/3}$$

The industry output y by definition is $y \equiv y_1 + y_2$. (Remember, this is for *one good*, not the previous model for two goods.) Total factor usage for these two firms is $L \equiv L_1 + L_2$, $K \equiv K_1 + K_2$. Is it possible to define a function $y = f(L, K)$, that is, aggregate output, as a function of aggregate factor inputs? The answer is readily seen to be in the negative. Students can convince themselves of this by trying to do so. For example,

$$y = L_1^{1/3} K_1^{2/3} + L_2^{2/3} K_2^{1/3} = L_1^{1/3} K_1^{2/3} + (L - L_1)^{2/3} (K - K_1)^{1/3}$$

There is no way to eliminate L_1 and K_1 from this equation. Output y will always depend on the allocation of labor and capital between the two firms. That is, if a unit of labor and/or capital is moved from firm 1 to firm 2, then even though aggregate labor and capital remain the same, total output will change, since the firms' production functions are different. Hence, *industry* output, under these circumstances, is *not* a (single-valued) function of *total* resource utilization.

We shall therefore make the assumption that there are two industries, each consisting of many identical "small" firms. Then, although factor prices are endogenously determined in the model, each firm can be perceived as taking factor prices as given. That is, the actions of any one firm cannot affect in any substantial way either factor or output prices. The simultaneous (and identical, since all firms are identical) actions of all firms together do affect prices, but these effects are beyond the control of any given firm. Most importantly, the *industry* production functions can be assumed to be linear homogeneous, i.e., exhibiting constant returns to scale. Let us characterize this linear homogeneity as follows. By definition,

$$f^j(tL_j, tK_j) \equiv tf^j(L_j, K_j) \equiv ty_j \qquad j = 1, 2$$

Since this holds for all t, let $t = 1/y_j$. Then

$$f^j\left(\frac{L_j}{y_j}, \frac{K_j}{y_j}\right) \equiv f^j(a_{Lj}, a_{Kj}) \equiv 1 \qquad j = 1, 2 \qquad (14\text{-}33)$$

Equation (14-33) defines the production function in terms of the input-output coefficients. These a_{ij}'s were utilized in the linear model of the previous chapter.

There, they were considered to be constants. Here, they are variable, changing continuously along the firm's *unit isoquant*. Equation (14-33) says that for constant-returns-to-scale production functions, the function is completely described by the unit isoquant. This occurs since all other isoquants are linear radial blowups or contractions of the unit (or any other) isoquant.

We shall use equations (14-33) explicitly as constraints in the problem. In inequality form, we shall presume that inputs are combined such that

$$f^j(a_{Lj}, a_{Kj}) \geq 1$$

The resource constraints can also be expressed in terms of the a_{ij}'s. By simple arithmetic,

$$L_1 + L_2 = \frac{L_1}{y_1} y_1 + \frac{L_2}{y_2} y_2 = L$$

or

$$a_{L1} y_1 + a_{L2} y_2 = L \qquad (14\text{-}34a)$$

Similarly, the capital constraint is

$$a_{K1} y_1 + a_{K2} y_2 = K \qquad (14\text{-}34b)$$

The model of revenue (income) maximization subject to resource constraints can therefore be written

maximize $\qquad z = p_1 y_1 + p_2 y_2$

subject to $\qquad a_{L1} y_1 + a_{L2} y_2 \leq L \qquad a_{K1} y_1 + a_{K2} y_2 \leq K$

$$\qquad\qquad f^1(a_{L1}, a_{K1}) \geq 1 \qquad f^2(a_{L2}, a_{K2}) \geq 1 \qquad (14\text{-}35)$$

The decision variables are the *six* variables $y_1, y_2, a_{L1}, a_{K1}, a_{L2}, a_{K2}$. Remember, the a_{ij}'s are not constants, as in the linear programming model. They represent input combinations which are jointly determined with outputs.

The lagrangian for the problem posed in (14-35) is

$$\mathcal{L} = p_1 y_1 + p_2 y_2 + w(L - a_{L1} y_1 - a_{L2} y_2)$$
$$+ r(K - a_{K1} y_1 - a_{K2} y_2)$$
$$+ \lambda_1(f^1(a_{L1}, a_{K1}) - 1) + \lambda_2(f^2(a_{L2}, a_{K2}) - 1) \qquad (14\text{-}36)$$

The Lagrange multipliers w and r represent the imputed wages, or rental values, of labor and capital, as before. The Kuhn-Tucker first-order conditions are thus

$$\frac{\partial \mathcal{L}}{\partial y_1} = p_1 - a_{L1} w - a_{K1} r \leq 0 \qquad \text{if} <, y_1 = 0 \qquad (14\text{-}37a)$$

$$\frac{\partial \mathcal{L}}{\partial y_2} = p_2 - a_{L2} w - a_{K2} r \leq 0 \qquad \text{if} <, y_2 = 0 \qquad (14\text{-}37b)$$

$$\frac{\partial \mathcal{L}}{\partial a_{L1}} = -w y_1 + \lambda_1 \frac{\partial f^1}{\partial a_{L1}} \leq 0 \qquad \text{if} <, a_{L1} = 0 \qquad (14\text{-}38a)$$

$$\frac{\partial \mathscr{L}}{\partial a_{K1}} = -ry_1 + \lambda_1 \frac{\partial f^1}{\partial a_{K1}} \leq 0 \qquad \text{if} <, a_{K1} = 0 \qquad (14\text{-}38b)$$

$$\frac{\partial \mathscr{L}}{\partial a_{L2}} = -wy_2 + \lambda_2 \frac{\partial f^2}{\partial a_{L2}} \leq 0 \qquad \text{if} <, a_{L2} = 0 \qquad (14\text{-}38c)$$

$$\frac{\partial \mathscr{L}}{\partial a_{K2}} = -ry_2 + \lambda_2 \frac{\partial f^2}{\partial a_{K2}} \leq 0 \qquad \text{if} <, a_{K2} = 0 \qquad (14\text{-}38d)$$

and the constraints

$$\frac{\partial \mathscr{L}}{\partial w} = L - a_{L1}y_1 - a_{L2}y_2 \geq 0 \qquad \text{if} >, w = 0 \qquad (14\text{-}39a)$$

$$\frac{\partial \mathscr{L}}{\partial r} = K - a_{K1}y_1 - a_{K2}y_2 \geq 0 \qquad \text{if} >, r = 0 \qquad (14\text{-}39b)$$

$$\frac{\partial \mathscr{L}}{\partial \lambda_1} = f^1(a_{L1}, a_{K1}) - 1 \geq 0 \qquad \text{if} >, \lambda_1 = 0 \qquad (14\text{-}40a)$$

$$\frac{\partial \mathscr{L}}{\partial \lambda_2} = f^2(a_{L2}, a_{K2}) - 1 \geq 0 \qquad \text{if} >, \lambda_2 = 0 \qquad (14\text{-}40b)$$

Notice the relations (14-37). These are precisely the nonpositive profit conditions which formed the constraints of the dual linear programming problem of the previous chapter. They say that if the maximum position occurs such that "profits" are negative for either good, then the output of that good will be 0.

The relations (14-38) are the marginal conditions for factor utilization, with the units adjusted to reflect the constraint of being on the unit isoquant. Since $f^i(L_j, K_j)$ is homogeneous of degree 1, f^j_L is homogeneous of degree zero. Thus

$$f^j_L(L_j, K_j) \equiv f^j_L \left(\frac{L_j}{K_j} \right) \equiv f^j_{a_{Lj}} \left(\frac{a_{Lj}}{a_{Kj}} \right)$$

Dividing equations (14-38) by y_j gives

$$\frac{\lambda_j}{y_j} \frac{\partial f^j}{\partial a_{Lj}} - w \leq 0$$

etc., or

$$\frac{\lambda_j}{y_j} \frac{\partial f^j}{\partial L_j} - w \leq 0 \qquad \text{if} <, L_j = 0 \qquad (14\text{-}41a)$$

with a similar relation with respect to capital:

$$\frac{\lambda_j}{y_j} \frac{\partial f^j}{\partial K_j} - r \leq 0 \qquad \text{if} <, K_j = 0 \qquad (14\text{-}41b)$$

Equations (14-41) are equivalent to equations (14-38). They are the usual marginal conditions for factor utilization if one interprets (λ_j/y_j) as marginal cost of y_j. Equations (14-38) or (14-41) say that if the maximum position occurs where the value of the marginal product of any factor is less than its wage (or rental price), it will not be used. Otherwise, the value of the marginal product equals the wage.

Consider again the maximum problem posed in (14-35) and the associated lagrangian (14-36). This maximization takes place at six margins, i.e., for six choice variables, y_1, y_2, a_{L1}, a_{K1}, a_{L2}, and a_{K2}. It is possible to conceive of this maximization as taking place in two stages. Recall that the assertion that profits are maximized carries with it the implication that the total cost of that level of output must be minimized. The maximization can be achieved by first minimizing cost for *any* output level; then, with costs minimized, that output level which maximizes profits can be determined as the second part of a two-stage maximization procedure.

In the present model, the hypothesis that total revenue is maximized (subject to resource constraints) can be regarded as occurring in two stages also. First, the "correct" input combinations *along the unit isoquant* can be found. That is, holding $y_j = 1$, $j = 1, 2$, we select the a_{ij}'s so as to minimize total factor cost for each industry. This results in having the marginal technical rate of substitution between the factors equal the factor-price ratio. Then, given this tangency condition, outputs are varied along the expansion path [in this case, along a ray through the point (a_{Lj}^*, a_{Kj}^*) on the unit isoquant] until the y_j^*'s are found.

This process can be seen algebraically by rearranging the terms in the lagrangian (14-36) as follows:

$$\mathcal{L} = p_1 y_1 + p_2 y_2 + wL + rK$$
$$- [y_1(a_{L1}w + a_{K1}r) + \lambda_1(1 - f^1(a_{L1}, a_{K1}))]$$
$$- [y_2(a_{L2}w + a_{K2}r) + \lambda_2(1 - f^2(a_{L2}, a_{K2}))] \tag{14-42}$$

The maximum value of $\mathcal{L}$ is NNP* $= p_1 y_1^* + p_2 y_2^*$. Let us maximize $\mathcal{L}$ by first *minimizing* the two square-bracketed terms (which enter negatively) with respect to the a_{ij}'s, treating y_1 and y_2 as parametric. This is equivalent to two separate *minimizations*:

minimize $\qquad\qquad y_1(a_{L1}w + a_{K1}r)$

subject to $\qquad\qquad f^1(a_{L1}, a_{K1}) = 1 \tag{14-43a}$

and minimize $\qquad\qquad y_2(a_{L2}w + a_{K2}r)$

subject to $\qquad\qquad f^2(a_{L2}, a_{K2}) = 1 \tag{14-43b}$

The lagrangians for these two problems are exactly the square-bracketed terms in the lagrangian (14-42). Moreover, these minimization problems are equivalent to the standard cost-minimization formats: multiply the objective functions through by y_1 or y_2 as indicated in (14-43). Since $y_1 a_{L1} = L_1$, etc., and $y_j f^j(a_{Lj}, a_{Kj}) \equiv f^j(y_j a_{Lj}, y_j a_{Kj}) \equiv f^j(L_j, K_j)$ by linear homogeneity, these square-bracketed terms are respectively equivalent to

$$(wL_1 + rK_1) + \lambda_1(y_1 - f^1(L_1, K_1)) \tag{14-44a}$$

and $\qquad\qquad (wL_2 + rK_2) + \lambda_2(y_2 - f^2(L_2, K_2)) \tag{14-44b}$

[Again, from homogeneity, $f^1(a_{L1}, a_{K1}) = 1$ is equivalent to $f^1(L_1, K_1) = y_1$, etc.] The lagrangian expressions (14-44) are exactly those which result from the problems:

minimize $\qquad\qquad wL_1 + rK_1 = C_1$

subject to $\qquad\qquad f^1(L_1, K_1) = y_1$ $\qquad\qquad$ (14-45a)

and minimize $\qquad\qquad wL_2 + rK_2 = C_2$

subject to $\qquad\qquad f^2(L_2, K_2) = y_2$ $\qquad\qquad$ (14-45b)

where y_1 and y_2 are at this point parametric. Problems (14-43) and (14-45) are thus equivalent. The setup (14-45) is the classical problem of minimizing the cost of achieving some output y_j. The objective function C_j is the total cost of achieving that output level, *and λ_j is the marginal cost of that* output. The λ_j's are *not* the same, however, in (14-45) and (14-43), because the units of the constraints are different.

The lagrangian associated with the submodel (14-43a) is

$$\mathscr{L} = y_1(wa_{L1} + ra_{K1}) + \lambda_1(1 - f^1(a_{L1}, a_{K1})) \qquad (14\text{-}46a)$$

Note that since y_1 is treated as a constant here, minimizing $y_1(wa_{L1} + ra_{K1})$ yields the same solution and comparative-statics results as minimizing $wa_{L1} + ra_{K1}$. The first-order conditions obtained from (14-46a) are

$$\frac{\partial \mathscr{L}}{\partial a_{L1}} = y_1 w - \lambda_1 \frac{\partial f^1}{\partial a_{L1}} = 0 \qquad (14\text{-}47a)$$

$$\frac{\partial \mathscr{L}}{\partial a_{K1}} = y_1 r - \lambda_1 \frac{\partial f^1}{\partial a_{K1}} = 0 \qquad (14\text{-}47b)$$

$$\frac{\partial \mathscr{L}}{\partial \lambda_1} = 1 - f^1(a_{L1}, a_{K1}) = 0 \qquad (14\text{-}47c)$$

Equations (14-47) are precisely the relations (14-38a), (14-38b), and (14-40a), respectively (ignoring the possibility of corner solutions).

A similar set of results follows from the submodel (14-43b). The lagrangian for industry 2 is

$$\mathscr{L} = y_2(a_{L2}w + a_{K2}r) + \lambda_2(1 - f^2(a_{L2}, a_{K2})) \qquad (14\text{-}46b)$$

producing the first-order conditions

$$y_2 w - \lambda_2 \frac{\partial f^2}{\partial a_{L2}} = 0 \qquad (14\text{-}48a)$$

$$y_2 r - \lambda_2 \frac{\partial f^2}{\partial a_{K2}} = 0 \qquad (14\text{-}48b)$$

$$1 - f^2(a_{L2}, a_{K2}) = 0 \qquad (14\text{-}48c)$$

These equations are, respectively, the same as relations (14-38c), (14-38d), and

(14-40b). *Hence, the two suboptimizations account for six out of the ten first-order equations of the whole model.* These six equations determine the cost-minimizing input combinations (a_{L1}^*, a_{K1}^*), (a_{L2}^*, a_{K2}^*) along the unit isoquants of each industry and the two industry marginal cost functions (λ_1^*/y_1^*) and (λ_2^*/y_2^*). The remaining four variables to be determined are y_1^*, y_2^*, w, and r.

The Four-Equation Model

Let us "solve" the systems (14-47), (14-48) for the a_{ij}^*'s. Dividing (14-47a) by (14-47b) and (14-48a) by (14-48b) yields

$$\frac{\partial f^1/\partial a_{L1}}{\partial f^1/\partial a_{K1}} = \frac{w}{r} \tag{14-49a}$$

and

$$\frac{\partial f^2/\partial a_{L2}}{\partial f^2/\partial a_{K2}} = \frac{w}{r} \tag{14-49b}$$

Equations (14-49a) and (14-47c) represent two equations in the two unknowns, a_{L1} a_{K1}, and the variable w/r. Likewise, (14-49b) and (14-48c) represent two equations in the two unknowns a_{L2}, a_{K2}, and the same variable w/r. Thus, we can write the solution of the equations systems (14-47) and (14-48) as

$$a_{ij} = a_{ij}^*\left(\frac{w}{r}\right) \quad i = L, K; j = 1, 2 \tag{14-50}$$

and

$$\lambda_j/y_j = (\lambda_j^*/y_j^*)(w, r) \quad j = 1, 2 \tag{14-51}$$

These equations are a very important feature of this model. They say that the input-output coefficients are functions of the *factor-price ratio only*. In particular, the a_{ij}^*'s are *not* functions of the endowments of either factor. Second, the marginal cost functions (14-51) are not functions of output levels but only of factor prices. This all occurs because of the linear homogeneity of the production functions. The independence of marginal cost from output level was shown in Chap. 10 on cost functions. There, we showed that if $y = f(x_1, x_2)$ was linear homogeneous, the cost function could be written $C^* = yA(w_1, w_2)$. Consequently, $\partial C^*/\partial y = A(w_1, w_2)$, which is equations (14-51). Equations (14-50) occur because for linear homogeneous functions, any level curve describes the whole function. Whatever occurs at any output level y_j^0 is simply a magnification or contraction of what occurs at $y_j = 1$.

It is apparent from general comparative-statics theory that

$$\frac{\partial a_{Lj}^*}{\partial w} < 0 \tag{14-52a}$$

and

$$\frac{\partial a_{Kj}^*}{\partial r} < 0 \tag{14-52b}$$

The unit input-output factor levels are downward-sloping in their own price. Also, it is apparent that $a_{ij}^*(w/r)$ is homogeneous of degree zero in w and r, since a_{ij}^* is a function of the ratio w/r. From Euler's theorem,

$$\frac{\partial a_{Lj}^*}{\partial w} w + \frac{\partial a_{Lj}^*}{\partial r} r \equiv 0$$

Since $\partial a_{Lj}^* / \partial w < 0$,

$$\frac{\partial a_{Lj}^*}{\partial r} > 0 \qquad (14\text{-}52c)$$

Similarly, it can be shown that

$$\frac{\partial a_{Kj}^*}{\partial w} > 0 \qquad (14\text{-}52d)$$

We shall use these results later.

If we use these solutions to the *six* equations (14-47) and (14-48), the entire ten-equation model (the ten first-order conditions) can be reduced to four equations in the four unknowns y_1, y_2, w, and r. The remaining equations of the original ten are (14-37a), (14-37b), (14-39a), and (14-39b). Substituting the solution values (14-50) back into these equations (again, we ignore the possibility of corner solutions) yields

$$a_{L1}^* w + a_{K1}^* r = p_1 \qquad (14\text{-}53a)$$

$$a_{L2}^* w + a_{K2}^* r = p_2 \qquad (14\text{-}53b)$$

and

$$a_{L1}^* y_1 + a_{L2}^* y_2 = L \qquad (14\text{-}54a)$$

$$a_{K1}^* y_1 + a_{K2}^* y_2 = K \qquad (14\text{-}54b)$$

The entire model has been compressed to four equations. *Moreover, these are precisely the same four relations as were derived for the linear programming model, two zero-profit conditions equations* (14-53) *and two resource constraints* (14-54). Here, however, the a_{ij}^*'s are not constants. They are functions of the factor-price ratio w/r, as indicated by equations (14-50).

Although the above are four equations in four unknowns, these equations have a very special structure. The variables w and r and the parameters p_1 and p_2 appear only in the first two equations (14-53). And the variables y_1 and y_2 and the parameters L and K appear only in the second set of equations (14-54). Thus, these equations are actually decomposable, or separable, into two sets of two equations in two unknowns. Just as in the linear model, the coefficient matrix of a_{ij}^*'s for the first set [equations (14-53a) and (14-53b)] is the transpose of the coefficient matrix of the second set [equations (14-54)].

As a consequence of this separability, equations (14-53) can be "solved" independently of (14-54), since the a_{ij}^*'s are functions of w/r only:

$$w = w^*(p_1, p_2) \qquad (14\text{-}55a)$$

$$r = r^*(p_1, p_2) \qquad (14\text{-}55b)$$

On the other hand, although equations (14-54) can be solved for y_1 and y_2 in terms of L and K, these solutions will involve the a_{ij}^*'s, which are functions of w/r and hence p_1 and p_2 through (14-55). Thus, solving equations (14-54) and using (14-55) leads to the output-supply functions

$$y_1 = y_1^*(p_1, p_2, L, K) \tag{14-56a}$$

$$y_2 = y_2^*(p_1, p_2, L, K) \tag{14-56b}$$

just as in the original model without the homogeneity conditions. As before, the results $\partial y_1^*/\partial p_1, \partial y_2^*/\partial p_2 > 0$ are still valid; the supply curves of each industry are upward-sloping.

The Factor-Price Equalization Theorem

Equations (14-55) are the basis of what is known as the *factor-price equalization theorem*, a fundamental result in the theory of international trade. Consider the case of two countries, each producing the same two commodities and engaging in trade with one another. In the pretrade, or *autarky*, situation, output-prices in the two countries will in general differ, given different marginal costs of production, i.e., different production possibility frontiers, for the two countries. (Of course, consumers' tastes might differ systematically in the two countries, producing different output-prices even if the marginal cost functions for the two countries were identical.) However, with the opening up of trade, which will occur precisely because output-prices (and hence consumers' marginal evaluations of the goods) are different, the output-prices will tend toward equality. With no transportation or other transactions costs of trading, the gains from trade will be exhausted only when output-prices are identical in the two countries, i.e., when each country's consumers face the same set of output-prices. Given the postulate of "more preferred to less," this outcome is implied.

A less obvious question is the effect on *factor* prices of this tending to equality of output-prices. If factors were freely mobile between the two countries at zero cost, clearly, factor prices in the two countries would also have to be identical. Factors would simply move to the higher-paying country, depressing wages or rentals there and raising them in the former location. But what if factors *cannot* move from one country to another? That is, suppose goods can move costlessly from one country to the other but factors can never emigrate. What will happen to factor prices then, when output-prices converge?

Equations (14-55) say that under certain conditions, factor prices will also be equal, in the two countries, when output-prices are the same for both countries, in spite of factor immobility. This surprising result, known as the *factor-price equalization theorem*, depends upon the form of equations (14-55). Those equations indicate that factor prices are functions of *output-prices only*. Factor endowments do not enter the right-hand side of these equations and hence are irrelevant in determining factor prices. However, the specific functional form of $w^*(p_1, p_2)$ and $r^*(p_1, p_2)$ will depend upon the underlying production functions in the economy.

If the production technology, i.e., the underlying production functions, *is the same in both countries*, i.e., trade is taking place because of different endowments of factors or differences in consumers' tastes (or both) between the two countries, then the functional form of equations (14-55) will be the same for the two countries. In that case, the factor prices will be the same in both countries, since they will depend in identical fashion upon the output prices, which are the same for both countries. An additional qualification, relating to differing relative factor intensities in the two countries, will be explored presently. Notice, too, that the result depends critically on the assumption of linear homogeneous industry production functions. It is that assumption which permits the formulation of the first-order conditions in terms of the factor intensity variables, the a_{ij}'s, which, in turn, allows solution of these a_{ij}'s in terms of the relative price ratio w/r alone. It is the dependence of relative factor intensities on factor prices alone which makes equations (14-53), the zero-profit conditions, soluble for factor prices solely in terms of output-prices. Without constant returns to scale in each industry, the above procedure cannot be carried out.

The Stolper-Samuelson Theorems

Let us now investigate the effects of changes in output-prices on factor prices. Since equations (14-53) are the sole determinants of factor prices, the comparative statics of this part of the model is accomplished by differentiating equations (14-53) with respect to output-prices. Let us differentiate these equations with respect to p_1, remembering that the "solutions" $w = w^*(p_1, p_2)$, $r = r^*(p_1, p_2)$ have been substituted into these equations for w and r, respectively, and that the a_{ij}^*'s, being functions of factor prices, are thereby also functions of the output-prices. Hence, upon differentiation of (14-53a),

$$a_{L1}^* \frac{\partial w^*}{\partial p_1} + w^* \frac{\partial a_{L1}^*}{\partial p_1} + a_{K1}^* \frac{\partial r^*}{\partial p_1} + r^* \frac{\partial a_{K1}^*}{\partial p_1} \equiv 1$$

or

$$a_{L1}^* \frac{\partial w^*}{\partial p_1} + a_{K1}^* \frac{\partial r^*}{\partial p_1} \equiv 1 - w \frac{\partial a_{L1}^*}{\partial p_1} - r \frac{\partial a_{K1}^*}{\partial p_1} \qquad (14\text{-}57a)$$

Similarly differentiating (14-53b) gives

$$a_{L2}^* \frac{\partial w}{\partial p_1} + a_{K2}^* \frac{\partial r^*}{\partial p_1} \equiv - w \frac{\partial a_{L2}^*}{\partial p_1} - r \frac{\partial a_{K2}^*}{\partial p_1} \qquad (14\text{-}57b)$$

However, the last two terms on the right-hand side of (14-57a) and (14-57b) sum to zero: consider the production function $f^1(a_{L1}^*, a_{K1}^*) \equiv 1$. Differentiating this identity with respect to p_1 gives

$$\frac{\partial f^1}{\partial a_{L1}} \frac{\partial a_{L1}^*}{\partial p_1} + \frac{\partial f^1}{\partial a_{K1}} \frac{\partial a_{K1}^*}{\partial p_1} \equiv 0 \qquad (14\text{-}58)$$

Using the first-order conditions $\partial f^1/\partial a_{L1} = y_1 w/\lambda_1$, $\partial f^1/\partial a_{K1} = y_1 r/\lambda_1$, and eliminating the factor y_1/λ_1 in each term, we get

$$w\frac{\partial a_{L1}^*}{\partial p_1} + r\frac{\partial a_{K1}^*}{\partial p_1} \equiv 0 \tag{14-59a}$$

A similar procedure shows that

$$w\frac{\partial a_{L2}^*}{\partial p_1} + r\frac{\partial a_{K2}^*}{\partial p_1} \equiv 0 \tag{14-59b}$$

Therefore, the comparative-statics equations (14-57) reduce to the simple form

$$a_{L1}^*\frac{\partial w^*}{\partial p_1} + a_{K1}^*\frac{\partial r^*}{\partial p_1} \equiv 1 \tag{14-60a}$$

$$a_{L2}^*\frac{\partial w^*}{\partial p_1} + a_{K2}^*\frac{\partial r^*}{\partial p_1} \equiv 0 \tag{14-60b}$$

Equations (14-60), which give the changes in factor prices caused by changes in output-prices, *have exactly the same structure as the equations which determined these variables in the linear models.* [In the case of constant a_{ij}'s, the differential form (14-60) is directly equivalent to the undifferentiated form (14-53).] Therefore, the analysis of this model is identical, in regard to these variables, to the linear model. Proceeding as before, let

$$A = \begin{vmatrix} a_{L1}^* & a_{L2}^* \\ a_{K1}^* & a_{K2}^* \end{vmatrix}$$

Solving for $\partial w^*/\partial p_1$, $\partial r^*/\partial p_1$ by Cramer's rule, we have

$$\frac{\partial w^*}{\partial p_1} = \frac{a_{K2}^*}{A} \tag{14-61a}$$

and

$$\frac{\partial r^*}{\partial p_1} = -\frac{a_{L2}^*}{A} \tag{14-61b}$$

In like fashion, if equations (14-53) are differentiated with respect to p_2, one gets

$$\frac{\partial w^*}{\partial p_2} = -\frac{a_{K1}^*}{A} \tag{14-61c}$$

$$\frac{\partial r^*}{\partial p_2} = \frac{a_{L1}^*}{A} \tag{14-61d}$$

Let us investigate these relationships. In the first place, these solutions are valid only if $A \neq 0$. This is in fact the sufficient condition of the implicit-function theorem that the equations $w = w^*(p_1, p_2)$, $r = r^*(p_1, p_2)$ are locally well defined. Hence, this condition is also required for the factor-price equalization theorem.

The determinant A will be nonzero, in this two-factor, two-good case, if either

$$\frac{a_{L1}^*}{a_{K1}^*} > \frac{a_{L2}^*}{a_{K2}^*} \tag{14-62a}$$

or

$$\frac{a_{L1}^*}{a_{K1}^*} < \frac{a_{L2}^*}{a_{K2}^*} \tag{14-62b}$$

These equations are equivalent to

$$\frac{L_1^*}{K_1^*} > \frac{L_2^*}{K_2^*} \tag{14-63a}$$

or

$$\frac{L_1^*}{K_1^*} < \frac{L_2^*}{K_2^*} \tag{14-63b}$$

In other words, if one industry is more labor-intensive than the other, i.e., its capital-labor ratio is lower than that ratio in the other industry, then the equations defining factor prices as functions of output-prices only will be well defined. Also, the comparative-statics relations (14-61) indicating the response of factor prices to changes in output-prices will be well defined.

With regard to the comparative-statics relations (14-61), the condition that one industry be more labor-intensive is a strictly *local* condition. All comparative-statics equations, despite the name which connotes comparing separate equilibria, are in fact simply partial derivatives evaluated at a certain point. The functions defining the choice relations need only be well-behaved around that one point; i.e., they must have the various properties of differentiability, nonzero jacobian deter-minant, etc., to allow a solution for a choice function at a given point.

For purposes of asserting factor-price equalization, however, the *local* condition that $L_1/K_1 \neq L_2/K_2$ is insufficiently strong. The factor-price equalization theorem is an essentially *global* assertion. That is, it asserts that, starting at finitely different output-prices in two countries, as output-prices converge, factor prices will converge also. But this is supposed to take place over a whole path of prices. Therefore, a strictly local condition on factor intensities cannot be enough to guarantee the convergence of factor prices. If factor prices are to converge *for any initial output-prices* and for any endowments, then one industry will *always* have to be more labor- (or capital-) intensive than the other. That is, we must have $L_i/K_i > L_j/K_j$ for *all* output-prices. If industry 1 is initially the more labor-intensive industry, as output-prices change, that industry must remain the more labor-intensive. Should one industry switch from being relatively labor- to relatively capital-intensive, the direction of movement of factor prices with regard to output-price changes will reverse. In equations (14-61), the denominators will all change sign. This means that if, say, industry 1 is labor-intensive at some output-prices, wages and rents will move in one direction as output-prices converge. However, for different endowments or if output-prices are such that industry 1 is *capital*-intensive, factor prices will move in the opposite direction as output-prices converge in the two countries. What is therefore needed, in order to assert factor-price equalization (aside from the other assumptions such as linear homogeneity, etc.) is the *global* condition that $L_i/K_i > L_j/K_j$ for *all* possible output or output-price combinations along the production frontier. Strictly local conditions are insufficiently strong.

Suppose now that industry 1 is the more labor-intensive industry, i.e., that $a_{L1}/a_{K1} > a_{L2}/a_{K2}$. (To save notational clutter, the asterisks will now be dropped.) Then $A > 0$ and, from equations (14-61a) and (14-61b),

$$\frac{\partial w}{\partial p_1} > 0 \qquad (14\text{-}64a)$$

and

$$\frac{\partial r}{\partial p_1} < 0 \qquad (14\text{-}64b)$$

These results are the general Stolper-Samuelson theorem. They say, again, that if the price of the labor-intensive industry is increased, nominal wage rates will rise, whereas capital rental rates will fall. If p_1 rises, then we know that y_1 increases and y_2 decreases, that is, $\partial y_1/\partial p_1 > 0$, $\partial y_2/\partial p_1 < 0$, as the economy moves along the production possibilities frontier. Hence, in this case, the labor-intensive industry is expanding whereas the capital-intensive industry is contracting. This results in a net increase in the aggregate demand for labor and a decrease in aggregate demand for capital. Hence, the factor price of labor rises while that of capital falls. In general, the price of a factor of production will rise if the price of the industry in which that factor is most intensively used rises; it will fall if the industry which is less intensive in that factor experiences an output-price increase.

The above analysis, however, pertains to *nominal* price changes only. If p_1 and w_1 *both* rise, as in the above example, will "real" wages in fact have risen? That is, will the owners of labor be able to purchase more goods at the higher wages after these two price changes? Clearly, the owners of capital, whose money price has fallen, are worse off in real as well as money terms.

The *real* income of the owners of labor will also rise if the wage rate increases. Wages will increase at a higher percentage rate than the output-price, i.e.,

$$\lim \frac{\Delta w/w}{\Delta p_1/p_1} = \frac{\partial w}{\partial p_1} \frac{p_1}{w} > 1 \qquad (14\text{-}65)$$

If the owners of labor consume the output of industry 1 only, then equation (14-65) guarantees greater purchasing power. If the owners of labor consume some y_2 also, then since the price of y_2 hasn't changed, (14-65) represents an even greater increase in real income. (In the limit, if *only* y_2 were consumed, then *any* increase in w would be an increase in real income, since p_2 is constant here.)

From equation (14-61a), again,

$$\frac{\partial w}{\partial p_1} = \frac{a_{K2}}{A} > 0$$

From the zero-profit first-order relation (14-53a),

$$p_1 = a_{L1}w + a_{K1}r$$

or

$$\frac{p_1}{w} = a_{L1} + a_{K1}\frac{r}{w}$$

Thus

$$\frac{p_1}{w}\frac{\partial w}{\partial p_1} = \frac{a_{K2}a_{L1} + (r/w)a_{K1}a_{K2}}{a_{K2}a_{L1} - a_{K1}a_{L2}} > 1 \qquad (14\text{-}65a)$$

just as in the case of fixed coefficients. The same procedure shows that

$$\frac{p_2}{r}\frac{\partial r}{\partial p_2} > 1 \qquad (14\text{-}65b)$$

That is, since industry 2 is capital-intensive, an increase in p_2 will not only increase nominal rental rates on capital but real rates also. In addition,

$$\frac{p_1}{r}\frac{\partial r}{\partial p_1} < -1 \qquad (14\text{-}65c)$$

and

$$\frac{p_2}{w}\frac{\partial w}{\partial p_2} < -1 \qquad (14\text{-}65d)$$

That is, if the price of the labor-intensive industry rises, rental rates will not only fall, they will fall in greater absolute proportion than the rise in output-price, with a similar result for the response of wages to an increase in the price of output of the capital-intensive industry. Relations (14-65b), (14-65c), and (14-65d) are derived in the same manner as (14-65a); their proofs are left as exercises.

Another set of results coming under the heading of the Stolper-Samuelson theorem are the effects on factor intensities of changes in output-prices. That is, consider how the labor-capital ratio varies in each industry when, say, p_1 is increased. Assume as before that industry 1 is labor-intensive. The labor-capital ratio in industry j is $L_j/K_j = a_{Lj}/a_{Kj}$. Specifically, the a_{ij}'s are functions of the factor prices w and r, which are in turn functions of output-prices, or

$$\frac{a_{Lj}}{a_{Kj}} = g(w^*(p_1, p_2), r^*(p_1, p_2))$$

Using the quotient rule with the chain rule gives

$$(a_{Kj})^2 \frac{\partial(a_{Lj}/a_{Kj})}{\partial p_1} = a_{Kj}\left(\frac{\partial a_{Lj}}{\partial w}\frac{\partial w}{\partial p_1} + \frac{\partial a_{Lj}}{\partial r}\frac{\partial r}{\partial p_1}\right)$$

$$- a_{Lj}\left(\frac{\partial a_{Kj}}{\partial w}\frac{\partial w}{\partial p_1} + \frac{\partial a_{Kj}}{\partial r}\frac{\partial r}{\partial p_1}\right)$$

Rearranging terms gives

$$(a_{Kj})^2 \frac{\partial(a_{Lj}/a_{Kj})}{\partial p_1} = \left(a_{Kj} \frac{\partial a_{Lj}}{\partial w} - a_{Lj} \frac{\partial a_{Kj}}{\partial w}\right) \frac{\partial w}{\partial p_1}$$

$$+ \left(a_{Kj} \frac{\partial a_{Lj}}{\partial r} - a_{Lj} \frac{\partial a_{Kj}}{\partial r}\right) \frac{\partial r}{\partial p_1} < 0 \qquad (14\text{-}66a)$$

This result follows from the comparative-statics relations derived for the cost-minimization submodels (14-43). The comparative statics of those models yielded the results, *for both industries,*

$$\frac{\partial a_{Lj}}{\partial w} < 0 \qquad j = 1, 2 \qquad (14\text{-}52a)$$

$$\frac{\partial a_{Kj}}{\partial r} < 0 \qquad j = 1, 2 \qquad (14\text{-}52b)$$

$$\frac{\partial a_{Lj}}{\partial r} > 0 \qquad j = 1, 2 \qquad (14\text{-}52c)$$

$$\frac{\partial a_{Kj}}{\partial w} > 0 \qquad j = 1, 2 \qquad (14\text{-}52d)$$

Inserting these sign values and also equations (14-64), that is, $\partial w/\partial p_1 > 0$, $\partial r/\partial p_1 < 0$, into (14-66a) immediately shows that

$$\frac{\partial(a_{Lj}/a_{Kj})}{\partial p_1} < 0 \qquad j = 1, 2$$

when y_1 is labor-intensive.

Similarly, with regard to changes in p_2, we have

$$(a_{Kj})^2 \frac{\partial(a_{Lj}/a_{Kj})}{\partial p_2} = \left(a_{Kj} \frac{\partial a_{Lj}}{\partial w} - a_{Lj} \frac{\partial a_{Kj}}{\partial w}\right) \frac{\partial w}{\partial p_2}$$

$$+ \left(a_{Kj} \frac{\partial a_{Lj}}{\partial r} - a_{Lj} \frac{\partial a_{Kj}}{\partial r}\right) \frac{\partial r}{\partial p_2} > 0 \qquad (14\text{-}66b)$$

The only differences between (14-66b) and (14-66a) are the terms $\partial w/\partial p_2$, $\partial r/\partial p_2$ instead of $\partial w/\partial p_1$ and $\partial r/\partial p_1$. Since these latter two terms have the opposite sign of the first two, respectively,

$$\frac{\partial(a_{Lj}/a_{Kj})}{\partial p_2} > 0 \qquad j = 1, 2$$

Note that equations (14-66) say that if the price of the labor-intensive good (y_1 here) rises, then the labor-capital ratio will fall *in both industries.* With the rise in p_1, more of the labor-intensive good will be produced and less of the capital-intensive good. This results in a net increase in the demand for labor. However, total labor to the economy is fixed. The economy responds to this increase in demand in two ways: the price of labor w rises, and the rental price of capital falls, in accordance with equations (14-64). To economize on the now higher-priced labor, *both* industries reduce the ratio of labor to capital utilized in production. (It may be a surprising piece of arithmetic that this is possible.) This situation is

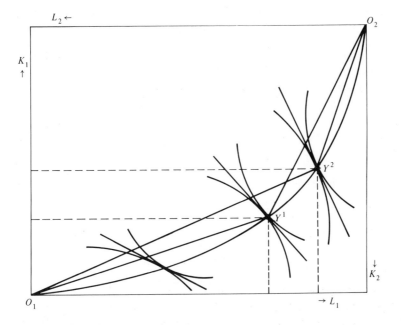

Figure 14-4 Diagrammatic exposition of the Stolper-Samuelson theorem: variable proportions. Consider an Edgeworth-type diagram as in Fig. 14-2, with labor plotted along the horizontal axes and capital plotted vertically. A contract curve O_1O_2 connecting the two origins has been drawn. It has a special shape: it is convex to the labor axis from O_1; that is, the contract curve rises toward O_2 at an increasing rate. It is this shape that guarantees that industry 1 will always be more labor-intensive than industry 2. Consider point Y^1 along O_1O_2. The slope of the chord O_1Y^1 is K_1/L_1. The slope of the chord connecting Y^1 and O_2, Y^1O_2, is K_2/L_2. As drawn, $K_1/L_1 < K_2/L_2$, or $L_1/K_1 > L_2/K_2$. Moreover, this is true along any point of the contract curve. Industry 1 is always more labor-intensive than industry 2.

Consider now the slopes of the isoquants as they cross the contract curve. Near O_1, where the contract curve is close to the labor axis, the isoquants are quite flat; i.e., they have a low absolute slope. As one moves along O_1O_2 toward O_2, the isoquants cut the curve at increasing slopes, as depicted at points Y^1 and Y^2. The slope of the isoquants is w/r, the ratio of wages to rental rates. Thus, with industry 1 always the more relatively intensive, as output y_1 expands, in response to increases in p_1, wage rates rise relative to rental rates. This is in accordance with equations (14-61) and the subsequent analysis. The increase in *real* wages is not easily depicted geometrically, however. Notice, too, that as p_1 and thus y_1 increase, *both* industries become less labor-intensive (though industry 1 remains more so than industry 2). As output moves from Y^1 to Y^2, for example, the capital-labor ratio, measured for industry 1 by the slope of the chord O_1Y^2 and for industry 2 by the slope of Y^2O_2, increases. That is, the labor-capital ratio decreases, or both industries become less labor-intensive. This can be viewed as a response to the increase in real wage rates and the fall of real capital rental rates.

illustrated in Fig. 14-4. These results cannot be observed in the model with fixed-coefficient technology. There, the a_{ij}'s are constant and hence unchanged by output prices.

The Rybczynski Theorem

Let us now turn to the comparative statics of this two-factor, two-good variable-proportions model with respect to changes in endowments. Under the hypotheses of the factor-price equalization theorem, which includes the assumption that one industry is always more labor-intensive than the other, a change in the resource endowment of either labor or capital (or both) will have *no effect* on factor prices. Again [equations (14-50)] $a_{ij} = a_{ij}^*(w/r)$, and equations (14-53) imply that factor prices are functions of *output-prices only* [equations (14-55)]. Thus, the first result is

$$\frac{\partial w}{\partial L} = \frac{\partial w}{\partial K} = \frac{\partial r}{\partial L} = \frac{\partial r}{\partial K} = 0 \tag{14-67}$$

Do not forget that in these relations, output-*prices* are being held fixed. Only resource endowments are changing. As endowments shift, the NNP plane $p_1 y_1 + p_2 y_2$ depicted in Fig. 14-3 shifts *parallel* to itself and becomes tangent to a new production frontier (not depicted) at the same output-prices. Since output-prices remain the same, factor prices are unchanged, given our assumptions.

Let us now consider the effects of changing the endowment of labor, say, on output levels. Since equations (14-53) involve prices only, the comparative-statics relations are derivable from equations (14-54) alone, repeated here:

$$a_{L1}^* y_1 + a_{L2}^* y_2 = L \tag{14-54a}$$

$$a_{K1}^* y_1 + a_{K2}^* y_2 = K \tag{14-54b}$$

These two identities are the original resource constraints of the model, with the important added condition that the linear-homogeneity assumption for the production function has been used to express the a_{ij}'s as functions of factor prices w and r (in particular w/r) only. If now either L or K changes, the a_{ij}'s remain constant, since $\partial a_{ij}^*/\partial L = [\partial a_{ij}^*/\partial(w/r)][\partial(w/r)/\partial L] = 0$, since the latter term is 0, from the above discussion. Hence, for the comparative statics of this model *with regard to changes in endowments, the a_{ij}^*'s can be treated as constants, even in this variable-proportions model!*

Let us then differentiate equations (14-54), partially of course, with respect to L. (Again, the asterisks will be dropped to save clutter. But do not forget the assumptions needed to perform these operations.) Differentiating gives

$$a_{L1} \frac{\partial y_1}{\partial L} + a_{L2} \frac{\partial y_2}{\partial L} \equiv 1$$

$$a_{K1} \frac{\partial y_1}{\partial L} + a_{K2} \frac{\partial y_2}{\partial L} \equiv 0$$

Thus, using Cramer's rule, we find, as in the linear programming model,

$$\frac{\partial y_1}{\partial L} \equiv \frac{a_{K2}}{A} = \frac{a_{K2}}{a_{L1}a_{K2} - a_{L2}a_{K1}} \tag{14-68a}$$

$$\frac{\partial y_2}{\partial L} \equiv -\frac{a_{K1}}{A} = -\frac{a_{K1}}{a_{L1}a_{K2} - a_{L2}a_{K1}} \tag{14-68b}$$

Under the assumption that industry 1 is labor-intensive, $A > 0$, and thus $\partial y_1/\partial L > 0$, $\partial y_2/\partial L < 0$. Differentiation of (14-54) with respect to K yields

$$\frac{\partial y_1}{\partial K} \equiv -\frac{a_{L2}}{A} = \frac{-a_{L2}}{a_{L1}a_{K2} - a_{L2}a_{K1}} \tag{14-68c}$$

$$\frac{\partial y_2}{\partial K} \equiv \frac{a_{L1}}{A} = \frac{a_{L1}}{a_{L1}a_{K2} - a_{L2}a_{K1}} \tag{14-68d}$$

Again, assuming industry 1 is labor-intensive, (14-68c) says that $\partial y_1/\partial K < 0$, and (14-68d) shows that $\partial y_2/\partial K > 0$.

These results, known as the *Rybczynski theorem*, state that under the hypotheses of the factor-price equalization theorem, an increase, say, in the endowment of labor (holding output-prices constant) will increase the output of the labor-intensive industry and decrease the output of the capital-intensive industry. Likewise, an increase in the endowment of capital, *ceteris paribus*, will increase the output of the capital-intensive industry and decrease the output of the labor-intensive industry. Again, under our strong assumptions, all these repercussions will leave factor *prices* unchanged. These results were illustrated for the linear models in Fig. 13-5.

Equations (14-68) are in fact derivable from earlier results. Recall the reciprocity conditions (14-25a) and (14-25b), which were derived from the general model, without the homogeneity restrictions:

$$\frac{\partial y_1}{\partial L} = \frac{\partial w}{\partial p_1} \qquad \frac{\partial y_2}{\partial L} = \frac{\partial w}{\partial p_2} \tag{14-25a}$$

and

$$\frac{\partial y_1}{\partial K} = \frac{\partial r}{\partial p_1} \qquad \frac{\partial y_2}{\partial K} = \frac{\partial r}{\partial p_2} \tag{14-25b}$$

Inspection of equations (14-61) and (14-68) confirms these reciprocity conditions. For example, from (14-61a) and (14-68a),

$$\frac{\partial w}{\partial p_1} = \frac{a_{K2}}{A} = \frac{\partial y_1}{\partial L}$$

The Rybczynski theorems are in fact merely the dual relationships of the Stolper-Samuelson theorems. The relations between factor and output-*prices* are identical to the relations between *physical* factors and outputs. All the results for factor prices have exact analogs for the factors themselves and vice versa.

In particular, the elasticity relationships (14-65) for real factor-price changes have corresponding results for the factors themselves. The algebra is identical, since the comparative-statics formulas (14-61) and (14-68) are identical. For example, suppose the endowment of labor increases, again assuming that industry 1 is labor-intensive. Then the output of industry 1 will not only increase but will increase at a faster rate than the increase in labor, i.e.,

$$\frac{L}{y_1}\frac{\partial y_1}{\partial L} > 1$$

As before, since $L = a_{L1} y_1 + a_{L2} y_2$, $L/y_1 = a_{L1} + a_{L2}(y_2/y_1)$. Thus

$$\frac{L}{y_1}\frac{\partial y_1}{\partial L} = \frac{a_{K2}a_{L1} + a_{K2}a_{L2}(y_2/y_1)}{a_{K2}a_{L1} - a_{K1}a_{L2}} > 1 \tag{14-69a}$$

A similar procedure shows

$$\frac{K}{y_2}\frac{\partial y_2}{\partial K} > 1 \tag{14-69b}$$

$$\frac{K}{y_1}\frac{\partial y_1}{\partial K} < -1 \tag{14-69c}$$

$$\frac{L}{y_2}\frac{\partial y_2}{\partial L} < -1 \tag{14-69d}$$

in perfect analogy with equations (14-65).

14.4 SUMMARY AND CONCLUSIONS

Let us now briefly summarize the results and the underlying assumptions of the two-good, two-factor model. The fundamental hypothesis is that in a competitive economy, the owners of factors will contract with each other in such a way as to maximize the value of national income. This invisible hand process is not the intention of any person in the economy. Self-seeking owners of resources, in trying to maximize the return of such ownership, can be expected if transactions costs are 0, to combine in a way that all gains from trade are exhausted. This must place the economy on the production frontier and at that point on that frontier where the marginal evaluations by consumers of each good, in terms of forgone consumption of the other good, equals the marginal cost of production of each good, measured in terms of forgone production of the other good. This occurs at a point of tangency of the line, or plane, defining NNP, $z = p_1 y_1 + p_2 y_2$, and the production possibilities frontier.

Since factors are completely mobile between the two industries, factor prices must be the same in both industries. Factor prices emerge as the Lagrange multipliers associated with the resource constraints. Although the wage and capital rental rates are determined endogenously by the model, these factor prices are taken exogenously by the relatively "small," identical firms that make up each industry. It is the simultaneous actions of each firm that change factor prices and aggregate output levels.

Under these general conditions, it is possible to show that the supply of output curves, $y_j = y_j^*(p_1, p_2)$, are upward-sloping in their own price. This is a direct consequence of the concavity of the production possibilities frontier with respect to the origin. This shape of the production frontier is indicative of increasing marginal costs (hence, upward-sloping supply curves) for each industry. These matters are discussed in Sec. 14.2.

Lastly, for the general model, certain reciprocity conditions appear, equations (14-24) to (14-26). These relations indicate a duality between physical quantities and their respective prices. The relation of outputs to resource endowments is the same as the relation of resource *prices* to output *prices*. These results are independent of any homogeneity assumptions concerning the production functions.

In Sec. 14.3, the assumption that each industry is characterized by constant returns to scale is added to the model. This permits representation of the production function in terms of the unit isoquant only (since all isoquants are radial blowups or contractions of that or any other isoquant). Mathematically, letting $a_{ij} = $ the amount of input i used to produce 1 unit of output j, where $i = L, K$, $j = 1, 2$, the production relations become $f^1(a_{L1}, a_{K1}) = 1$ and $f^2(a_{L2}, a_{K2}) = 1$. These a_{ij}'s are the fundamental quantities in this more restricted model. When we use the production relations above and the first-order marginal relations (14-38), the a_{ij}'s are shown to depend only on the factor prices, the Lagrange multipliers, w, and r; in particular, $a_{ij} = a_{ij}^*(w/r)$. This critical step allows the model to be defined by two independent sets of two equations each, equations (14-53) and (14-54). The former indicate that profits are zero in each industry, i.e., that the amount of labor used to produce 1 unit of y_1 times the price of labor plus the amount of capital used to produce 1 unit of y_1 times the unit price of capital exactly equals the price of 1 unit of y_1. Similarly, the total unit factor cost of y_2 equals the unit price of y_2. The second set of equations constitutes the original resource constraints, with the added feature that the a_{ij}'s are functions of w/r only. Because of the dependence of the a_{ij}'s on w/r only, the comparative statics of this model is the same as in the case where the a_{ij}'s are technologically fixed. The variable-proportions model (including the assumption of linear homogeneous production functions) yields the same comparative-statics results as the fixed-proportions linear programming model.

Equations (14-53), dealing with prices, yield as solutions equations (14-55), factor prices expressed as functions of *output-prices only*. This result yields the factor-price equalization theorem, under the global assumption that in each country, one industry is always more labor-intensive than the other. This theorem then indicates that if two countries trade with each other, then as output-prices converge in the two countries, the factor prices in each country will be functions of output-prices only and not dependent in any way on resource endowments. If the production functions are the same in the two countries, the functional relationship $w = w^*(p_1, p_2)$, $r = r^*(p_1, p_2)$ will be the same for both countries. Then, since with free trade both countries will face the same output-prices, factor prices will also equalize in both countries even though factors are immobile between countries.

Differentiation of equations (14-53), dealing with prices only, yields the set of results known as the Stolper-Samuelson theorem. It is shown in equations (14-61) and (14-65) that if the price of the, say, labor-intensive industry rises (inducing an expansion of that industry), nominal *and* real wages will rise and capital rental rates will fall. Likewise, if the price of the capital-intensive industry rises, the capital-goods industry expands, the labor-intensive industry contracts, and thus rental rates rise, in real as well as nominal terms, and the wage rate falls. Also, if the price of the labor-intensive industry rises, *both* industries become less labor-intensive, with similar results holding if the price of the capital-intensive good rises.

Analogous results for the physical quantities are known as the Rybczynski theorem. By using the reciprocity conditions (14-24) to (14-26), the algebra of the Rybczynski theorem is shown to be the same as that used in the Stolper-Samuelson theorem. Alternatively, these results are derivable from the second set of two equations defining the model [equations (14-59)], the resource constraints. In equations (14-68) and (14-69), it is shown that if, say, the amount of labor available to the whole economy increases, the output of the labor-intensive industry will not only expand but will expand in greater proportion to the increase in labor. The capital-intensive industry will contract in greater proportion than the increase in labor. Analogous results hold for an autonomous increase in capital.

This completes our discussion of the two-good, two-factor model. Let us briefly comment on the many-good, many-factor generalization of this model. This generalization is in fact exceedingly complex and beyond the scope of this book. The general model of maximization of NNP subject to resource constraints proceeds in an obvious way, with no difficulty. One derives the upward slope of the supply functions and the reciprocity conditions analogous to (14-24) to (14-26) in the same manner. The difficulty begins with trying to generalize the factor-price equalization, Stolper-Samuelson, and Rybczynski-type theorems. In general, if the number of goods exceeds the number of factors, certain goods, not determinable without an algorithmic process, will not be produced. Similarly, if the number of factors exceeds the number of goods in these models, certain factors will not be used and their associated Lagrange multiplier shadow prices will equal 0. The relation of factor-price to output-price changes is much more complex than a simple dependence upon factor intensities, since higher-order determinants are involved. Under restricted conditions, however, the factor-price equalization theorem is valid. However, no easy or intuitive factor intensity rules can be stated to give the results analogous to those derived in Sec. 14.3.

PROBLEMS

1 In the n-good, m-factor model, with y_i^* the output of the ith industry, show that $\sum_{j=1}^{n} \varepsilon_{ij} = 0$, where $\varepsilon_{ij} = (p_j/y_i^*)(\partial y_i^*/\partial p_j)$. Show therefore in the two-good model that $\partial y_1^*/\partial p_2 > 0$.

2 Show that with linear homogeneous production functions, the model with n goods and m factors has the property that the (maximum) total value of output equals total factor cost.

3 Explain why it is critical, from the standpoint of deriving the Stolper-Samuelson and Rybczynski theorems, for the technological coefficients a_{ij} to be dependent on factor prices only and not the factor endowments. Explain what assumptions in the model produce this result.

4 Explain the assumptions needed to yield the result that factor prices are dependent on output-prices only. Does it follow from this alone that if two countries engage in costless trade, factor prices will be the same in both countries? Why or why not?

5 The production possibilities frontier is derivable by treating one output level, say y_1, as fixed (parametric) and then using the resources to maximize the output level of y_2. As y_1 is varied parametrically, the production possibilities locus will be traced out.

(*a*) Set up this problem for two goods and two factors and interpret the (three) Lagrange multipliers.

(*b*) Show that the production frontier is not necessarily concave in this formulation. What distinguishes these assumptions from the ones used in the text, in which concavity of the production frontier is implied?

(*c*) Show that if both production functions are concave, the production possibilities frontier is concave.

6 Consider the maximization of NNP model with $y_1 = L_1^{1/3} K_1^{2/3}$, $y_2 = L_2^{2/3} K_2^{1/3}$.

(*a*) Show that the capital-labor ratio in industry 1 will always be 4 times the capital-labor ratio in industry 2.

(*b*) Derive equations (14-50) for this specification; i.e., verify for this model that each a_{ij}^* is a function of the factor-price ratio only.

(*c*) Show that $\partial a_{Lj}^*/\partial w_j < 0$, $\partial a_{Kj}^*/\partial r < 0$ directly from the equations for a_{ij}^*.

(*d*) On the basis of the factor intensities in each industry, which factor price would you expect to increase and which to decrease when p_1 increases?

(*e*) Find the explicit functions $w = w^*(p_1, p_2)$ and $r = r^*(p_1, p_2)$ and verify the predictions in part (*d*).

(*f*) On the basis of factor intensities, which industry will increase output and which will decrease output when the endowment of labor increases?

(*g*) Verify this result by applying equations (14-54) for this model.

7 Derive the Rybczynski theorem from the Stolper-Samuelson theorem using the reciprocity relations present in the two-good, two-factor model.

BIBLIOGRAPHY

Arrow, K. J.: Economic Equilibrium, "International Encyclopedia of the Social Sciences," vol. 4, pp. 376–388, The Macmillan Company and the Free Press, New York, 1968.

Debreu, G.: Theory of Value, *Cowles Foundation Monograph* 17, John Wiley & Sons, Inc., New York, 1959.

Dorfman, R., P. A. Samuelson, and R. M. Solow: "Linear Programming and Economic Analysis," McGraw-Hill Book Company, New York, 1958.

Edgeworth, F. Y.: "Mathematical Psychics," Routledge & Kegan Paul, Ltd., London, 1881.

Hicks, J. R.: "Value and Capital," 2d ed., Oxford University Press, New York, 1946.

Jones, R. W.: Duality in International Trade: A Geometrical Note, *Canadian Journal of Economics and Political Science*, **31**: 390–393, 1965.

———: The Structure of Simple General Equilibrium Models, *Journal of Political Economy*, **73**: 557–572, 1965.

Koopmans, T. C., ed.: Activity Analysis of Production and Allocation, *Cowles Commission Monograph* 13, John Wiley & Sons, Inc., New York, 1951.

———: "Three Essays on the State of Economic Science," McGraw-Hill Book Company, New York, 1957.

Patinkin, D.: "Money, Interest, and Prices," 2d ed., Harper & Row, Publishers, New York, 1965.

Quirk, J., and R. Saposnik: "Introduction to General Equilibrium Theory and Welfare Economics," McGraw-Hill Book Company, New York, 1968.

Rybczynski, T. M.: Factor Endowment and Relative Commodity Prices, *Econometrica*, **22**: 336–341, 1955.

Samuelson, P. A.: Prices of Factors and Goods in General Equilibrium, *Review of Economic Studies*, **21**: 1–20, 1953–1954.

Walras, L.: "Elements of Pure Economics," trans. W. Jaffe, Richard D. Irwin, Inc., Homewood, Ill., 1954.

FIFTEEN

WELFARE ECONOMICS

15.1 SOCIAL WELFARE FUNCTIONS

Throughout this book it has been stressed repeatedly that the goal of any empirical science is the development of refutable propositions about some set of observable phenomena. Refutable propositions which survive repeated testing form the important principles on which the science is based. (It is easy, of course, to conceive of refutable hypotheses which are in fact refuted.)

Parallel to the development of economics along the above lines has arisen a discipline called *welfare economics*, which seeks not to explain observable events but to *evaluate* the desirability of alternative institutions and the supposed resulting economic choices. For example, it is commonly alleged that "too many" fish are being caught in the oceans, that tariffs and other specific excise taxes cause an "inefficient" allocation of resources ("too little" production of the taxed item), that "too much" pollution and congestion occur in metropolitan areas, and the like. In this chapter we shall investigate the basis of these assertions and comment on the empirical content of such pronouncements.

It was common for classical economists to speak of "the benefits to society," the interest of the "working class" and other such phrases that implied a sufficient harmony of interests between members of the relevant class to permit speaking of them as a group. Even today, we often hear of individuals representing "the interests of consumers" or of someone taking the position of "big business."

A difficulty in the concept of group preferences, or interests, was pointed out by Kenneth Arrow in his classic paper, A Difficulty in the Concept of Social Welfare.† The use of such phrases implies that there is a well-defined function of individual preferences, or utility functions, representing the utility, or "welfare," of the group. Such a function was first posed explicitly by A. Bergson in 1938.‡ The social welfare function posited by Bergson had the form

$$W = f(U^1, \ldots, U^m) \tag{15-1}$$

where $U^1, \ldots, U^m$ were the utility functions of the m individuals in the group being considered, perhaps the whole economy. Bergson considered various first-order marginal conditions for the maximization of W subject to the resource constraints of the economy.

Arrow's discussion of these matters began with a 200-year-old example of the problem of construction of a group preference function. The example was based upon majority voting. Voting is a very common way for groups to reach decisions. Suppose one were to attempt to define collective preferences on the basis of what a majority of the community would vote for. Suppose there are three alternatives, **a**, **b**, and **c**, and three individuals in the group. Let P represent "is preferred to," so that **a**P**b** means that **a** is preferred to **b**.

Suppose now that the three individuals have the following preferences:

Individual 1: **a**P**b**, **b**P**c**
Individual 2: **b**P**c**, **c**P**a**
Individual 3: **c**P**a**, **a**P**b**

Assume, in accordance with ordinary utility theory, that these consumers' preferences are *transitive*. That is, for individual 1, **a**P**b** and **b**P**c** means that **a**P**c**, etc. Then it can be quickly seen that a majority-rule social welfare function will have the unsatisfactory property of being *intransitive*. Consider, for example, alternative **a**. A majority of voters, namely voters 2 and 3, prefer **c** to **a**. Likewise, a majority of voters (1 and 3) prefer **a** to **b**, and another, different majority (1 and 2) prefer **b** to **c**. Whichever alternative is selected, a majority of voters will prefer some other alternative. Thus, the social welfare function based on what the majority wishes will exhibit the properties **a**P**b**, **b**P**c** *and* **c**P**a**.§

---

† *The Journal of Political Economy*, **58**, 328–46, 1950. This paper was part of a larger study, Social Choice and Individual Values, 2d ed., *Cowles Commission Monograph* 12, John Wiley & Sons, Inc., New York, 1963.

‡ Abram Bergson, A Reformulation of Certain Aspects of Welfare Economics, *Quarterly Journal of Economics*, **52**, 310–334, 1938.

§ This voting paradox illustrates one of the outstanding differences between *market* choices and *political* choices. In the former, the consumer has the option of expressing the *intensity* of a preference by the simple act of choosing to purchase differing amounts of goods. In political choice, however, ordinary voters get one and only one vote. The consumer under these circumstances is unable to express intensity of preference. In the above example, the three alternatives were merely *ranked*. The

Let us now summarize Arrow's theorem about social welfare functions. Arrow uses a weaker form of the preference relation: let aR_ib represent the statement, " **a** is *preferred or indifferent* to **b**, according to individual i." Suppose there are n individuals in this society. Then, by a *social welfare function*, in this terminology, we mean a relation R which corresponds to the individual orderings, $R_1, \ldots, R_n$, of all social states by the n individuals in the society. That is, given the preference orderings of all people in the polity, there exists some social ordering R which denotes "society's" values and rankings of the alternatives being considered.

Arrow proceeded to list five conditions which he felt almost any reasonable social welfare function ought to contain. The first of these is that the social welfare function is in fact defined for all sets of individual orderings which obey some set of individualistic hypotheses about behavior, e.g., the usual economic postulates of convex indifference curves and the like.

Condition 1 The social welfare function is defined for every admissible pair of individual orderings R_1, R_2.

Second, the social ordering should describe welfare and not, in Arrow's word, "illfare." The social welfare function should react in the same direction, or at least not oppositely to, alterations in individual values.

Condition 2 If a social state **a** rises or does not fall in the ordering of each individual without any other change in those orderings, and if **a**R**b** before the change, for any other alternative **b**, then **a**R**b** after the change in individual orderings.

The most controversial of Arrow's *conditions* is the third, the independence of irrelevant alternatives. Consider an election in which three candidates, **a**, **b**, and **c**, are running. Suppose an individual's preferences are aR_ibR_ic. Suppose, before the election, candidate **b** dies. Then we would expect to observe aR_ic. In like manner, we expect the social welfare function's ranking of any two alternatives to be unaffected by the addition or removal of some other alternative.

---

voters were not able to say, for example, that they preferred **a** a great deal more than **b** and **b** only slightly more than **c**. In legislative bodies, in which there are only relatively few voters, the individuals can *trade* votes on successive issues. Suppose, for example, individual 1 has the above-stated intensities of preferences and individual 2 was almost indifferent between **a**, **b**, and **c**. Then voter 1 could make a contract or a deal to vote for some other issue which voter 2 felt strongly about (and which voter 1 had no strong preferences about) in exchange for an agreement from voter 2 to vote for alternative **a** in the text example. The paradox would be resolved through trade. However, more trade is not necessarily preferred to less trade for individuals, and voter 3 might end up worse off for such political trading. It is for these reasons that many people believe that special-interest legislation is more apt to be enacted by legislative bodies than by referendum vote. But such vote trading also protects minorities who feel intensely about some issue from the "tyranny of the majority." The gains-from-trade aspect of political trading is emphasized in James Buchanan and Gordon Tullock, "The Calculus of Consent," University of Michigan Press, Ann Arbor, 1963.

Condition 3 Let R_1, R_2 and R'_1, R'_2 be two sets of individual orderings. Let S be the entire set of alternatives. Suppose, for both individuals and all alternatives **a**, **b** in S, that $\mathbf{a}R_i\mathbf{b}$ if and only if $\mathbf{a}R'_i\mathbf{b}$. Then the social choice made from S is the same whether the individual orderings are R_1 and R_2 or R'_1 and R'_2.

Conditions 4 and 5 imposed by Arrow amount to assertions that individual preferences *matter*. That is, individual values are to "count," in determining the social welfare function. Conditions 4 and 5 say that the social welfare function is not to be either *imposed* or *dictatorial*. A social welfare function is said to be *imposed* if, for some pair of alternatives **a** and **b**, $\mathbf{a}R\mathbf{b}$ for any set of individual orderings R_1, R_2, that is, irrespective of the individual orderings R_1, R_2, where R is the social ordering corresponding to R_1, R_2. Likewise, a social welfare function is said to be *dictatorial* if there exists an individual i such that for all **a** and **b**, $\mathbf{a}R_i\mathbf{b}$ implies $\mathbf{a}R\mathbf{b}$ regardless of the orderings of all individuals other than i, where R is the social preference ordering corresponding to the R_i's.

Condition 4 The social welfare function is not to be imposed.

Condition 5 The social welfare function is to be nondictatorial.

Arrow succeeded in showing that these five conditions could not all hold simultaneously. In particular, he showed that any social welfare function that satisfied the first three conditions was either imposed or dictatorial. This very strong result is called the *possibility theorem*.† It says that no matter how complicated a scheme might be constructed for determining a set of social preferences, social ordering R cannot meet all conditions 1 to 5. It will be impossible to construct *any* welfare function of the type described in equation (15-1), $W = f(U_1, \ldots, U_n)$, that is, some function of individual utility levels, obeying the above conditions.

Another interpretation of the possibility theorem is that interpersonal comparisons of social utility are ruled out. It is impossible to say that taking a dollar away from a rich person and giving it to a poor person will make society better off, in some nondictatorial or imposed sense. The problem of interpersonal comparisons of utility was a vehicle by which ordinal utility replaced the older cardinal utility idea.

On a less rigorous but more intuitive basis, the reason sensible social welfare functions cannot exist is that they conflict in a fundamental way with the notion that more is preferred to less. At any given moment, there is a frontier of possibilities for the consumers in any society. Any movement *along* this frontier involves gains for some individuals and losses for others. Without a measure for comparing these gains and losses between individuals, there is no sense to the phrase social welfare. (We shall explore these matters in more detail in Sec. 15.3.)

---

† The author would have called it the impossibility theorem.

A rigorous proof of the possibility theorem is beyond the scope of this book. It can be found in the reference cited. We conclude this section by noting that in spite of this theorem, hundreds, perhaps thousands of articles have been written in economics journals using social welfare functions. Indeed, a whole new area of mathematical theology has arisen. However, to quote Samuelson,† "the theorems enunciated under the heading of welfare economics are not meaningful propositions of hypotheses in the technical sense. For they represent the deductive implications of assumptions which are not themselves meaningful refutable hypotheses about reality."

15.2 THE PARETO CONDITIONS

Faced with the impossibility of constructing a meaningful social welfare function, economists have opted for a weaker criterion by which to evaluate alternative situations. This criterion, known as the *Pareto condition*, after the Italian economist Vilfredo Pareto, states that a social state **a** is to be preferred to **b** if there is at least one person better off in **a** than in **b**, and no one is worse off in **a** than in **b**. This is a weaker value judgment only in the sense that more people would probably accept this judgment over more specific types of social orderings wherein some individuals lose and others gain. A state **a** which is preferred to **b** in the paretian senses is said to be *Pareto-superior* to **b**. One can imagine some sort of frontier of possible states of the economy such that there are no Pareto-superior points. That is, along this frontier, any movement entails a loss for at least one individual. The points for which no Pareto-superior states exist are called *Pareto-optimal.*

In general, we shall find that the set of Pareto-optimal points is quite large. Whether or not these points are a useful guide to policy is debatable. Even so, to say that the economy *ought* to be at a Pareto-optimal state is a value judgment and therefore a part of moral philosophy and not part of the empirical science of economics. We can, however, as economists, investigate the conditions under which various ideal Pareto-optimal states will be obtained. In this section we shall investigate certain famous conditions which achieve Pareto optimality. It is useful, in these discussions, to maintain the perspective indicated in the above quotation from Samuelson.

Pure Exchange

Consider an economy containing two individuals who consume two commodities, x and y. Let x_i, y_i denote the amounts of x and y consumed by the ith person, whose utility function is $U^i(x_i, y_i)$. Suppose that the total amounts of x and y are fixed, that is, $x_1 + x_2 = x$, $y_1 + y_2 = y$, where x and y are constants. Under what

---

† "Foundations of Economic Analysis," pp. 220–221, Harvard University Press, Cambridge, Mass, 1947.

circumstances will the allocation of x and y between the two individuals be Pareto-optimal?

This problem can be formulated mathematically as follows:

maximize $\qquad\qquad\qquad U^2(x_2, y_2)$

subject to $\qquad\qquad\qquad U^1(x_1, y_1) = U_0^1$

$$x_1 + x_2 = x \qquad y_1 + y_2 = y \qquad (15\text{-}2)$$

It is meaningless to attempt to maximize both individual's utilities simultaneously.† Instead, we first fix either individual's utility at some arbitrary level; then, the other person's utility is maximized. In this way, a position is attained in which neither party can be made better off without lowering the other person's utility.

The lagrangian for the above problem is

$$\mathcal{L} = U^2(x_2, y_2) + \lambda(U_0^1 - U^1(x_1, y_1)) + \lambda_x(x - x_1 - x_2) + \lambda_y(y - y_1 - y_2)$$
$$(15\text{-}3)$$

Differentiating with respect to x_1, y_1, x_2, y_2 and the Lagrange multipliers yields

$$\mathcal{L}_{x_2} = U_x^2 - \lambda_x = 0 \qquad (15\text{-}4a)$$

$$\mathcal{L}_{y_2} = U_y^2 - \lambda_y = 0 \qquad (15\text{-}4b)$$

$$\mathcal{L}_{x_1} = -\lambda U_x^1 - \lambda_x = 0 \qquad (15\text{-}4c)$$

$$\mathcal{L}_{y_1} = -\lambda U_y^1 - \lambda_y = 0 \qquad (15\text{-}4d)$$

and $\qquad\qquad \mathcal{L}_\lambda = U_0^1 - U^1(x_1, y_1) = 0 \qquad (15\text{-}5a)$

$$\mathcal{L}_{\lambda_x} = x - x_1 - x_2 = 0 \qquad (15\text{-}5b)$$

$$\mathcal{L}_{\lambda_y} = y - y_1 - y_2 = 0 \qquad (15\text{-}5c)$$

where $U_x^i = \partial U^i / \partial x_i$, etc. Combining equations (15-4) gives

$$\frac{U_x^1}{U_y^1} = \frac{\lambda_x}{\lambda_y} = \frac{U_x^2}{U_y^2} \qquad (15\text{-}6)$$

Equation (15-6) is the tangency condition that the consumer's indifference curves have the same slope. The marginal rate of substitution of x for y must be the same for both consumers. This is the familiar condition which must hold if the gains from trade are to be exhausted. The set of all points which satisfy (15-6) (and the constraints) is called the *contract curve* as depicted in Fig. 15-1. This diagram is the Edgeworth box diagram first shown in the chapter on general-equilibrium theory. (There, though, the axes were quantities of factors of production, not final goods as is the case here. The mathematics is, of course, formally identical.)

---

† We leave such constructions to those who aspire to find that economic system which seeks "the greatest good for the greatest number of people."

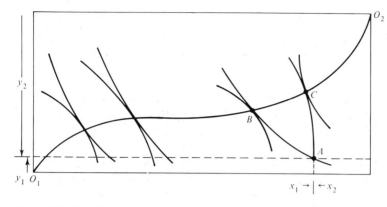

Figure 15-1 The Edgeworth box diagram is useful for depicting the set of Pareto-optimal points in a pure-trade, zero-transaction-cost world. The dimensions of the box are the total amounts of each good available, x and y. Any point, such as A in the interior of the box, represents an allocation of x and y to the two individuals. Individual 1's utility function is plotted in the usual direction from the origin marked O_1. Individual 2's utility function is plotted opposite (right to left and down) from origin O_2. The set of points for which the slopes of U^1 and U^2 are identical at the same point, i.e., a level curve of U^1 is tangent to a level curve of U^2, is called the *contract curve*, designated O_1O_2. This curve represents the set of points for which the gains from trade are exhausted. It is occasionally referred to as the conflict curve because movements *along* O_1O_2 represent conflicts of interest: one individual gains and the other loses. For that reason, it is the set of Pareto-optimal points in this economy.

The set of Pareto-optimal points is the set of allocations for which the gains from exchange are exhausted. If the consumers were presented a different allocation, e.g., point A in Fig. 15-1, then with no cost of trading we should expect them to move to some point on the contract curve $O_1 O_2$. If the trade is voluntary, the final allocation must lie between (or on) the two original indifference curves, i.e., some point on the segment BC of the contract curve. Without a further specification of the constraints of the bargaining process, the theory is inadequate to determine the actual final point. But in the absence of transactions costs and coercion self-seeking maximizers must wind up at *some* point along BC.

The problem as posed in (15-2) does not actually start at some particular point such as A and then move to the contract curve. As formulated in (15-2), the indifference level of individual 1 is fixed, say at the level which goes through point A. The resulting solution of the problem, i.e., solution to equations (15-4) and (15-5), would place the economy at point B, where person 2 achieves maximum utility, leaving person 1 on the original indifference curve. Hence, the problem posed in (15-2) admits of a unique answer, even if a bargaining process which starts *both* individuals at A is unspecified.

The indirect utility function for individual 2 is obtained first by solving equations (15-4) and (15-5) and substituting the chosen values of x_2 and y_2 into $U^2(x_2, y_2)$. Let the solutions to (15-4) and (15-5) be designated

$$x_i = x_i^*(U_0^1, x, y) \qquad y_i = y_i^*(U_0^1, x, y) \tag{15-7}$$

and likewise for the Lagrange multipliers:

$$\lambda = \lambda^*(U_0^1, x, y)$$

$$\lambda_x = \lambda_x^*(U_0^1, x, y) \qquad \lambda_y = \lambda_y^*(U_0^1, x, y) \tag{15-8}$$

Then $\qquad U^{2*} = U^2(x_2^*, y_2^*) = f(U_0^1, x, y) \tag{15-9}$

Holding constant x and y, the total amounts of the goods, one can imagine a utility frontier, defined by equation (15-9). Starting with $U_0^1 = 0$, the maximum level of utility for person 2 is that which is achieved when person 2 consumes all of both goods, i.e.,

$$f(0, x, y) \equiv U^{2*}(x, y)$$

Likewise some maximum level of U^1 exists, represented by the indifference curve for person 1 which passes through O_2, for which $U^2 = 0$.

This utility frontier is plotted as the curve UU in Fig. 15-2, where the subscript 0 on U^1 has been suppressed. Using the envelope theorem and equations (15-4) leads to

$$\frac{\partial U^{2*}}{\partial U^1} = \lambda = -\frac{U_x^2}{U_x^1} = -\frac{U_y^2}{U_y^1} < 0 \tag{15-10}$$

Assuming the tangencies defining the contract curve take place at positive marginal utilities (downward-sloping indifference curves), $\partial U^{2*}/\partial U^1 < 0$, as indicated. The Pareto frontier could not very well exhibit $\partial U^{2*}/\partial U^1 > 0$, since then movements along it in the northeast direction would imply gains for *both* individuals, contradicting the notion of Pareto optimality. It is *not* possible to infer that the Pareto frontier UU is concave to the origin; this follows from the ordinal nature of utility. A monotonic transformation of $U^1(x_1, y_1)$, say, could bend the frontier as desired, though keeping it downward-sloping.

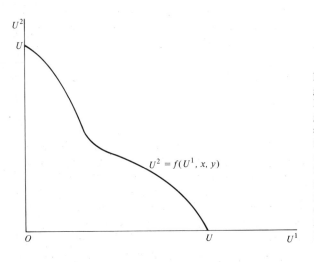

Figure 15-2 The utility frontier for given total quantities of goods. For any given amount of the goods x and y there exist a whole set of points for which neither individual can gain without the other person's losing. This Pareto frontier consists of reading off the (ordinal) utility levels for each person at every point along the contract curve O_1O_2. The frontier is necessarily downward-sloping, by definition of Pareto optimality.

Production

Suppose now we generalize the preceding discussion to the case where x and y are produced using two (or more) factors of production. In the preceding chapter on general equilibrium, an Edgeworth box diagram was constructed for the two-factor case. In order for consumers to be on the Pareto frontier in consumption, the goods must be produced efficiently. That is, a production point interior to the production possibilities frontier cannot result in a Pareto-optimal state for consumers. The consumers could both (or all, in the n-person case) have more of all goods and hence higher utility if production were moved to the production possibilities frontier in the appropriate manner. Hence, the problem of defining the Pareto frontier for consumers in the case in which x and y are *produced*, and not fixed constants, begins with the problem of defining the production possibilities frontier. Points on the production frontier are called *efficient in production*.

The mathematics for the production case is formally identical to the above analysis of final goods. Let there be two factors of production, L and K, and let L_x denote the amount of labor used in producing x, etc. Then the problem of efficient production can be stated:

maximize $$y = f(L_y, K_y)$$

subject to $$g(L_x, K_x) = x$$

$$L_x + L_y = L \qquad K_x + K_y = K \tag{15-11}$$

where $f(L_y, K_y)$ and $g(L_x, K_x)$ are the production functions of y and x, respectively. The value x is taken as a parameter above; it is *not* a decision variable. The lagrangian for the problem (15-11) is

$$\mathscr{L} = f(L_y, K_y) + \lambda(x - g(L_x, K_x)) + \lambda_L(L - L_x - L_y) + \lambda_K(K - K_x - K_y) \tag{15-12}$$

The resulting first-order relations are

$$f_L - \lambda_L = 0 \tag{15-13a}$$

$$f_K - \lambda_K = 0 \tag{15-13b}$$

$$-\lambda g_L - \lambda_L = 0 \tag{15-13c}$$

$$-\lambda g_K - \lambda_K = 0 \tag{15-13d}$$

and the constraints

$$x - g(L_x, K_x) = 0 \tag{15-14a}$$

$$L - L_x - L_y = 0 \tag{15-14b}$$

$$K - K_x - K_y = 0 \tag{15-14c}$$

From equations (15-13),

$$\frac{f_L}{f_K} = \frac{\lambda_L}{\lambda_K} = \frac{g_L}{g_K} \tag{15-15}$$

The ratio of marginal products must be equal for both goods along the production contract curve. This is the tangency condition illustrated in Fig. 14-2. Solving equations (15-13) and (15-14) simultaneously gives

$$L_y = L_y^*(x, L, K) \tag{15-16a}$$

$$K_y = K_y^*(x, L, K) \tag{15-16b}$$

$$L_x = L_x^*(x, L, K) \tag{15-16c}$$

$$K_x = K_x^*(x, L, K) \tag{15-16d}$$

and

$$\lambda = \lambda^*(x, L, K) \tag{15-17a}$$

$$\lambda_L = \lambda_L^*(x, L, K) \tag{15-17b}$$

$$\lambda_K = \lambda_K^*(x, L, K) \tag{15-17c}$$

Equations (15-16) give the chosen values of labor and capital in both industries. Substituting these values into the objective function gives the maximum y, y^* for any value of x:

$$y^* = f(L_y^*, K_y^*) = y^*(x, L, K) \tag{15-18}$$

Using the envelope theorem, we have

$$\frac{\partial y^*}{\partial x} = \frac{\partial \mathscr{L}}{\partial x} = \lambda^* \tag{15-19}$$

Hence, λ^* has the interpretation of the *marginal cost of x*, since it shows how much y^* must be given up in order to get an additional unit of x. The multiplier λ^* is the slope of the production possibility frontier by definition, since $\lambda^* = \partial y^*/\partial x$. Assuming the marginal products of the factors are positive, $\lambda^* < 0$, i.e., the production frontier is negatively sloped. As before, from equations (15-13)

$$\lambda^* = -\frac{\lambda_L^*}{g_L} = -\frac{f_L}{g_L} = -\frac{f_K}{g_K} < 0 \tag{15-20}$$

This equation has the interesting interpretation that the marginal cost of x is the same if only labor is varied (the ratio f_L/g_L) or if only capital is varied (f_K/g_K) or both are varied. In the partial-equilibrium framework this phenomenon was encountered in the formula

$$MC = \frac{w_L}{f_L} = \frac{w_K}{f_K} \tag{15-21}$$

where the w's were the respective factor prices. Here, of course, λ_L and λ_K are the factor prices, *measured in terms of the physical output y*, i.e.,

$$\lambda_L^* = \frac{\partial y^*}{\partial L} \tag{15-22a}$$

$$\lambda_K^* = \frac{\partial y^*}{\partial K} \tag{15-22b}$$

This interpretation of λ_L and λ_K makes (15-21) and (15-20) equivalent except for units.

The production possibilities curve yields the set of "efficient" production plans. A necessary condition for overall Pareto optimality is to be on this frontier. However, that in itself is not sufficient. To exhaust all the gains from trade, the goods produced must be allocated to the consumers in an efficient manner. This requires at least that the previous analysis of the *consumer's* Edgeworth box diagram apply, i.e., the consumers must be on their contract curve, for any production levels (x, y). However, one more tangency condition must also apply: for each consumer, the marginal rates of substitution of x for y, that is, the marginal evaluation of x in terms of y forgone, must equal the marginal cost of producing x (in terms of y forgone). This condition implies that the consumers are on their contract curve, since *each* consumer's marginal evaluation of x must equal the marginal cost of x. Let us see how this last condition is derived.

The only difference between this last, and most general problem and the first one posed in (15-2) is that instead of x and y being fixed, they are determined by the production possibilities frontier derived in the production model as equation (15-18). Thus, the locus of overall efficient (Pareto-optimal) points is defined by:

maximize $\qquad\qquad\qquad U^2(x_2, y_2)$

subject to $\qquad\quad U^1(x_1, y_1) = U_0^1 \qquad x_1 + x_2 = x$

$$y_1 + y_2 = y \qquad y = y^*(x, L, K) \qquad\qquad (15\text{-}23)$$

It will simplify the algebra to combine the last three constraints into one. These three equations define the production possibility curve, written in implicit form, as

$$h(x, y) = h(x_1 + x_2, y_1 + y_2) = 0$$

where the parameters L and K have been suppressed because they will not be used. The problem above is then simply:

maximize $\qquad\qquad\qquad U^2(x_2, y_2)$

subject to $\qquad\qquad\qquad U^1(x_1, y_1) = U_0^1$

$$h(x_1 + x_2, y_1 + y_2) = 0 \qquad\qquad (15\text{-}24)$$

The lagrangian for (15-24) is

$$\mathcal{L} = U^2(x_2, y_2) + \lambda_1(U_0^1 - U^1(x_1, y_1)) + \lambda h(x, y) \qquad (15\text{-}25)$$

Noting that $\partial h/\partial x_i = (\partial h/\partial x)(\partial x/\partial x_i) = \partial h/\partial x$, etc., we see that the first-order conditions are

$$U_x^2 + \lambda h_x = 0 \qquad\qquad (15\text{-}26a)$$

$$U_y^2 + \lambda h_y = 0 \qquad\qquad (15\text{-}26b)$$

$$-\lambda_1 U_x^1 + \lambda h_x = 0 \qquad\qquad (15\text{-}26c)$$

$$-\lambda_1 U_y^1 + \lambda h_y = 0 \qquad\qquad (15\text{-}26d)$$

and the two constraints

$$U_0^1 - U^1(x_1, y_1) = 0 \qquad (15\text{-}27a)$$

$$h(x, y) = 0 \qquad (15\text{-}27b)$$

Eliminating the Lagrange multipliers from equations (15-26), we find

$$\frac{U_x^1}{U_y^1} = \frac{U_x^2}{U_y^2} = \frac{h_x}{h_y} \qquad (15\text{-}28)$$

The quantity h_x/h_y is the absolute slope of the production possibilities frontier; i.e., in explicit form, by the chain rule,

$$\frac{\partial y}{\partial x} = -\frac{h_x}{h_y}$$

Hence, equation (15-28) gives the marginal condition stated above: *for overall (production and consumption) Pareto optimality, the marginal evaluation of each commodity must be the same for all individuals, and that common marginal evaluation must equal the marginal cost of producing that good.* (The words *all* and *each* have been used instead of *both*. The generalization of these results to n goods and m consumers is straightforward.)

The overall utility frontier is found by solving equations (15-26) and (15-27) for $x_i = x_i^*(U_0^1)$, $y_i = y_i^*(U_0^1)$. Substituting these values into the objective function, we derive

$$U^2 = U^2(x_2^*, y_2^*) = U^{2*}(U_0^1) \qquad (15\text{-}29)$$

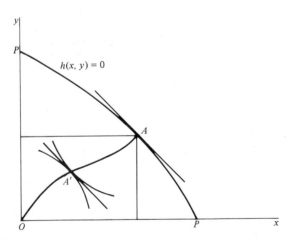

Figure 15-3 Overall Pareto optimality. The curve PP represents the *production* possibilities frontier of the economy for given resource endowments. The slope of this frontier is the marginal cost of producing x, in terms of y forgone. At any point, say A, along the frontier, an Edgeworth box can be constructed as shown. The points in the box represent allocations of x and y to the two consumers. These consumers will presumably trade to the contract curve OA. At some point or points on OA, the slopes of the indifference curves will equal the slope of the transformation curve at A. This is an overall Pareto-efficient point, since the MRSs of each consumer are equal and equal to marginal cost.

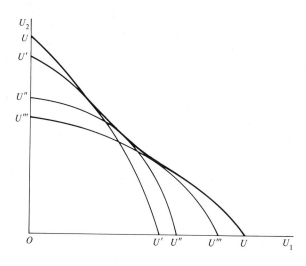

Figure 15-4 Partial and overall utility frontiers. For any given x and y, that is, for some particular point on the production possibilities curve, some *utility* frontier is implied. Several of these are drawn: $U'U'$, $U''U''$, and $U'''U'''$. The *envelope* curve for all these partial frontiers is the overall, or *grand*, utility frontier UU. The frontier UU represents the maximum utility any one consumer can achieve for given level of the other person's utility. Each point on UU represents, in general, a different production point, though there is no reason why some partial frontier could not be tangent to UU at more than one point.

This situation is shown geometrically in Fig. 15-3. The curve PP represents the production possibilities frontier for given resource endowments. At any point, say A, the slope of this frontier is the marginal cost of x. From this point, which represents a certain total amount of x and y, an Edgeworth box diagram is constructed. The points in the interior of the box represent the allocations of x and y to the two consumers. The curve OA represents the implied contract curve for the consumers. At some point (or points) along OA, say, A', the marginal evaluations of x (the marginal rates of substitution) will equal the slope of the tangent line at A, the marginal cost of x. This is an overall Pareto-optimal allocation, i.e., efficient in production and consumption. The point A' represents one particular point on the implied *utility* frontier, as depicted in Fig. 15-2. It is a special point, however, in that marginal cost equals marginal benefits there.

At each point along the *production* possibilities frontier, an Edgeworth box can be drawn and the overall efficient allocation(s) can be determined. In Fig. 15-4 the utility frontiers for several production points are drawn. The *envelope* curve for all these partial frontiers is equation (15-29), $U^2 = U^{2*}(U_0^1, x, y)$. The partial frontiers are those for specific values of x and y, that is, holding x and y constant. From general envelope considerations

$$\frac{\partial U^{2*}}{\partial U_1^0} = \left(\frac{\partial U^{2*}}{\partial U_1^0}\right)_{x, y} \tag{15-30}$$

That is, along the overall frontier, the slope of the frontier at any point is the same if x and y are held constant or allowed to vary.

The grand utility frontier UU represents the complete set of Pareto-optimal, or efficient, productions and distributions of the goods x and y. The choice of *which* Pareto-optimal point is somehow "best for society" is a value judgment and outside the scope of positive economics. If some social welfare function is posited (social welfare functions can exist, but not with all the properties outlined by Arrow), its indifference curves can be plotted in Fig. 15-4, and some optimal point along the frontier UU will be selected. There are some who believe that governments consciously seek some overall optimum as just described. It is difficult to explain political behavior with such a model.

15.3 THE CLASSICAL "THEOREMS" OF WELFARE ECONOMICS

In this section we shall present the classical "theorems" of welfare economics. The quotation marks are used because the propositions derived below are not in fact refutable theorems. At best, they represent unobservable first-order conditions for maximization, i.e., general statements that at an optimum, marginal benefits equal marginal costs. As was indicated in the quotation above from Samuelson's "Foundations of Economic Analysis," these propositions represent the logical implications of propositions which are not themselves refutable.

The first theorem is that *perfect competition leads to a Pareto-optimal allocation of goods and services.* This proposition holds only under certain restrictive conditions. Specifically, the formulation of the problems posed in the previous section ruled out two major classes of phenomena: interdependence of the consumer's utility functions, and interdependence of the production functions. In the above presentation, there were no *externalities*, or side effects, present between any of the maximizing agents. Such interdependence would be indicated by writing, say,

$$y = f(L_y, K_y, x) \tag{15-31a}$$

or
$$U^2 = U^2(x_2, y_2, U^1) \tag{15-31b}$$

In the case of (15-31a), the output of y depends not only on the labor and capital inputs in the production function for y but also the level of x produced. In the next section we shall consider a particular example of this, where the output of a farm depends in part on a neighboring rancher's output of cattle, who trample some of the farmer's output. Similarly, (15-31b) indicates that another person's happiness is an influence on one's own utility.

In the absence of occurrences (15-31a) and (15-31b) and in the absence of monopoly, the prices of goods and services offered in the economy will equal their respective marginal costs of production. The condition for profit maximization under competitive factor and output markets yields, for each industry h,

$$p_h f_i^k - w_i = 0 \qquad i = 1, \ldots, n \tag{15-32}$$

where $f^k(x_1, \ldots, x_n) = k$th firm's production function
$\qquad w_i$ = wage of x_i
$\qquad p_h$ = output-price

Suppose there are m firms. The supply function of the firms is the solution of

$$p_h - \frac{\partial C_k^*}{\partial y_k} = 0 \tag{15-33}$$

where $C_k^*(y_k, w_1, \ldots, w_n)$ is the firm's total cost function. From (15-32),

$$\frac{w_i}{w_j} = \frac{f_i^k}{f_j^k} \qquad k = 1, \ldots, m \tag{15-34}$$

This is precisely the condition that the economy be on the production possibilities frontier: the ratio of marginal products for all pairs of factors is the same for all firms, equal to the ratio of factor prices.

Moreover, utility-maximizing consumers with utility functions $U^k(y_1, \ldots, y_n)$ in the n output goods will set the ratios of marginal utilities equal to the price ratios; i.e.,

$$\frac{U_i^k}{U_j^k} = \frac{p_i}{p_j} \qquad \text{for all } i, j, k \tag{15-35}$$

Since all consumers will face the same prices, equation (15-35) says that all consumers' marginal evaluations of the good will be identical, the condition for efficient consumption for given outputs. Lastly, using equation (15-33),

$$\frac{U_i^k}{U_j^k} = \frac{p_i}{p_j} = \frac{MC_i}{MC_j} \qquad \text{for all } i, j, k \tag{15-36}$$

Hence, not only are all consumers' marginal evaluations equal, they are equal to the ratio of marginal costs of those goods, expressed in money terms. This ratio of money marginal costs is precisely the marginal cost of good i, in terms of good j forgone. That is, converting to units of good j makes $MC_j \equiv 1$. [Note that the units of MC_i/MC_j are $(\$/y_i) \div (\$/y_j) = y_j/y_i$, the amount of y_j forgone to produce another increment of y_i, or the *real* marginal cost of y_i.]

Thus, under perfect competition with no side effects (externalities), the Pareto conditions for overall efficiency hold. Therefore, in such a perfectly competitive economy, no individual will be able to improve himself or herself without making someone else worse off.

It does *not* follow from the above that it is desirable for the economy to be perfectly competitive. Consider Fig. 15-5, where the grand utility frontier UU has been plotted. Suppose, somehow, the economy has situated the two individuals at point A, a nonparetian allocation. Any movement to the right or upward from A, resulting in a point on the utility frontier along the segment BC, is clearly Pareto-superior to A. However, a movement to D, a Pareto-optimal point, leaves consumer 2 worse off; it is not an improvement from consumer 2's standpoint. Hence, aside from being a value judgment, a move to the Pareto frontier may involve losses.

The second "theorem" of classical welfare economics is the statement that there is an allocation under perfect competition for any overall Pareto optimum.

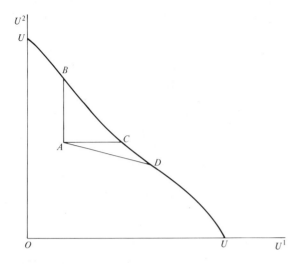

Figure 15-5 A non-Pareto move. Suppose the economy is at point A. Then any move northeast will be to a Pareto-superior position: each consumer will gain. Any point along the segment BC of the Pareto frontier UU is Pareto-superior to A. However, not every point along UU is Pareto-superior to A. Point D, for example, leaves consumer 1 better off and consumer 2 worse off than at A. Consumer 2 will not advocate economic efficiency if it results in the economy's moving to point D. It is not possible to argue, even with the weak paretian value judgment, that the economy "ought" to be at a Pareto-optimal point.

That is, starting now with a point on the Pareto frontier, there exists a competitive solution which achieves that optimum. The proof of this proposition, for general functional forms of utility and production functions, is a formidable mathematical problem, which has been analyzed by K. Arrow,[†] G. Debreu,[‡] L. Hurwicz,[§] and others. A rigorous discussion is considerably beyond the scope of this book.

Note what this second "theorem" does *not* say: it does not say that in order to achieve a Pareto position the economy must be competitive. An omniscient dictator could mandate the correct prices and quantities so that the economy would reach the same position as a competitive economy would.

Two of the outstanding reasons why an economy might not be on the overall Pareto frontier are (1) excise taxes and (2) monopolistic raising of price over marginal cost. With regard to the latter, a *perfectly discriminating monopolist*, who extracts all the gains from trade via some sort of all-or-nothing pricing, does *not* disturb the Pareto conditions. The reason, fundamentally, is that all the gains from trade are exhausted. The only difference is that only the perfectly discriminating monopolist gains whereas with open markets the buyers and sellers both gain. But as long as all the gains from trade are exhausted, there can be no Pareto-*superior* moves.

[†] The principal investigation of both the above theorems is in K. Arrow, An Extension of the Basic Theorems of Classical Welfare Economics, in J. Neyman (ed.), *Proceedings of the Second Berkeley Symposium on Mathematical Statistics and Probability*, University of California Press, Berkeley, 1951.

[‡] Gerard Debreu, "Theory of Value," John Wiley & Sons, Inc., New York, 1959.

[§] Leonid Hurwicz, Optimality and Informational Efficiency in Resource Allocation Processes, in "Mathematical Methods in the Social Sciences 1959," Stanford University Press, Stanford, California, 1960.

15.4 A "NONTHEOREM" ABOUT TAXATION

It was at one point believed that to raise any given amount of tax revenue it is best, from the standpoint of consumers' achieving the highest possible indifference curve, to collect those taxes via proportional excise taxes or income taxes. (With no savings in the economy, these taxes are equivalent.) The argument was loosely based on the observation that the Pareto conditions $p_j/p_i = \text{MRS}^k = \text{MC}_j/\text{MC}_i$ would not be disturbed if $p_j = (1 + t)\text{MC}_j$, where the tax rate t is constant across all commodities. This, however, is a logical error, since these first-order marginal conditions for Pareto optimality, while necessary, are not sufficient. Other criteria may lead to the same conditions.

The "theorem" was criticized on the empirical grounds that not all goods are easily taxed. A person's labor-leisure choice is affected by any tax on income. The price of leisure is the forgone wage; a tax on that wage income is a *subsidy* on leisure. In addition, many commodities, for more or less technological reasons, may be difficult to tax, e.g., services one provides for oneself or family. Under these conditions, a proportional tax on all taxable items is not a proportional tax on all items.

These empirical matters aside, however, the theorem itself is false. Even if one could tax all goods and services proportionately, this would not in general lead to a Pareto allocation, as we shall presently see. The most famous "proof" of this nontheorem was presented by Harold Hotelling in 1938.† Hotelling's proof went essentially as follows. Suppose a consumer currently consumes n goods, q_i, $i = 1$, ..., n, at prices $p_i = \text{MC}_i$. The consumer's *income* is taxed, however, and money income after taxes is $m = \sum p_i q_i$. Since the commodity bundle $\mathbf{q} = (q_1, \ldots, q_n)$ was chosen at prices $\mathbf{p} = (p_1, \ldots, p_n)$ and income m, any other bundle of goods $\mathbf{q}' = \mathbf{q} + \Delta\mathbf{q}$ which the consumer *could* have chosen must be inferior. Hotelling was asserting (without using the phraseology, which was not yet invented) that $\mathbf{q}$ was *revealed preferred* to $\mathbf{q}'$ if

$$\sum p_i q_i \geq \sum p_i q_i'$$

or
$$\sum p_i \Delta q_i \leq 0 \tag{15-37}$$

Now suppose prices are changed by amounts Δp_i, representing excise taxes but money income (tax) is also changed so that the consumer can have the same opportunities to purchase goods as before. By definition,

$$m + \Delta m = \sum (p_i + \Delta p_i)(q_i + \Delta q_i)$$

Subtracting $m = \sum p_i q_i$ gives

$$\Delta m = \sum p_i \Delta q_i + \sum \Delta p_i(q_i + \Delta q_i)$$

---

† H. Hotelling, The General Welfare in Relation to Problems of Taxation and of Railway and Utility Rates, *Econometrica*, **6**, 242–269, 1938; reprinted in "A.E.A. Readings in Welfare Economics," Richard D. Irwin, Homewood, Ill., 1969.

Rearranging terms, we have

$$\sum p_i \, \Delta q_i = \Delta m - \sum \Delta p_i (q_i + \Delta q_i) \tag{15-38}$$

Consider this last equation. The term $q_i + \Delta q_i$ represents the q_i's sold if taxed; hence, the last term represents the total tax revenue from the excise taxes, Δp_i, $i = 1, \ldots, n$. The term Δm represents the change in income taxes. Therefore, this expression says that if the change in excise taxes results in revenue absolutely greater than or equal to the income tax change, $\sum p_i \, \Delta q_i \leq 0$. In this case, it is argued, that since prices were set at marginal costs, replacing income taxes by excise taxes leads the consumer to purchase some bundle q' which was shown to be revealed inferior to q. Hence, to quote Hotelling,

> *If government revenue is produced by any system of excise taxes there exists a possible distribution of personal levies among the individuals of the community such that the abolition of the excise taxes and their replacement by these levies will yield the same revenue while leaving each person in a state more satisfactory to himself than before.*[†]

This "proof" is not a proof of this proposition at all. It is merely a theorem about revealed *preferences*. Starting at *any* set of prices whatsoever, making the above-stated changes in prices and income will leave the consumer worse off. Nowhere is the condition $p_i = MC_i$ used in this "proof." That marginal condition is irrelevant to the argument. No assumptions about *production* are contained in the argument; only assumptions concerning *preferences* are used. The same "proof" follows if initially $p_i \neq MC_i$ and the Δp_i's and m are changed so as to make $p_i = MC_i$ in the final position.

The fact that Hotelling's proof was invalid, however, does not in itself render the theorem invalid. The proposition *is* false, however, for considerations known as the *theory of the second best*.

15.5 THE THEORY OF THE SECOND BEST[‡]

The problem of optimal excise taxation cannot be handled without considering the ends of this taxation. Suppose there are *three* goods—two private goods, x and y, and government services, z. If these government services are services for which normal pricing is possible, e.g., postal services, the optimal taxes are zero. The government merely sells its services at marginal cost, which, together with selling x and y at their respective marginal costs, will yield a Pareto optimum. The question of optimal taxation makes sense only in the context that some good, say the services of the government, is not, for some reason, to be sold at marginal cost.

[†] Italics in the original. There is no apparent distinction in Hotelling's paper between income tax, proportional excise tax, and lump-sum or personal-levy tax.

[‡] R. G. Lipsey and K. Lancaster, The General Theory of the Second Best, *Review of Economic Studies*, **24**, 11–32, 1956.

In some cases, e.g., national defense, it would be difficult to do so. Also, an important class of goods exists, e.g., the so-called *public goods* discussed in the next section, for which marginal costs are less than average costs—the declining-AC industries. It is impossible to sell these goods at marginal cost without subsidies raised via taxation. The question thus becomes: Suppose some good z is not sold at marginal cost. Is it possible to infer that consumers will be on the highest indifference curves if the remaining goods are sold at prices proportional to their marginal costs, e.g., by proportional excise or income taxes? The answer is no, as the following argument shows.

Consider the simplest case of one consumer. The consumer maximizes utility subject to the production possibilities frontier, or:

maximize $\qquad\qquad\qquad\qquad U(x,\ y,\ z)$

subject to $\qquad\qquad\qquad\qquad g(x,\ y,\ z) = 0$

The lagrangian is

$$\mathcal{L} = U(x,\ y,\ z) + \lambda g(x,\ y,\ z)$$

producing the first-order conditions

$$U_x + \lambda g_x = 0 \qquad U_y + \lambda g_y = 0 \qquad U_z + \lambda g_z = 0$$

or $\qquad\qquad\qquad\qquad \dfrac{U_x}{U_y} = \dfrac{g_x}{g_y} \qquad \dfrac{U_z}{U_y} = \dfrac{g_z}{g_y} \qquad\qquad$ (15-39)

The marginal rates of substitution equal the respective marginal costs. Suppose now that z is not sold at MC. A simple constraint which expresses this is $U_z = kg_z$, where $k \neq U_y/g_y$. Let us now maximize $U(x,\ y,\ z)$ subject to this new constraint also, in addition to the resource constraint $g(x,\ y,\ z) = 0$. The lagrangian for this problem is

$$\mathcal{L} = U(x,\ y,\ z) + \lambda g(x,\ y,\ z) + \mu(U_z - kg_z)$$

The first-order conditions for this maximization are (excluding the constraints)

$$\mathcal{L}_x = U_x + \lambda g_x + \mu(U_{zx} - kg_{zx}) = 0$$
$$\mathcal{L}_y = U_y + \lambda g_y + \mu(U_{zy} - kg_{zy}) = 0$$
$$\mathcal{L}_z = U_z + \lambda g_z + \mu(U_{zz} - kg_{zz}) = 0$$

Since the constraint $U_z - kg_z$ is assumed to be binding, $\mu \neq 0$. Solving for the marginal rates of substitution,

$$\frac{U_x}{U_y} = \frac{-\lambda g_x - \mu(U_{zx} - kg_{zx})}{-\lambda g_y - \mu(U_{zy} - kg_{zy})} \qquad\qquad (15\text{-}40)$$

with a similar expression for U_x/U_z or U_y/U_z.

The left-hand side of equation (15-40) is the MRS between x and y. It cannot be inferred that this MRS should be equal to $\text{MC}_x/\text{MC}_y = g_x/g_y$. For arbitrary values of the cross-partials U_{zx}, g_{zx}, U_{zy}, and g_{zy}, *nonproportional* excise taxes on x and y will in general satisfy (15-40). It might be noted that if these cross-partials are all 0, Hotelling's "theorem" holds, but this is a special case.

In general, therefore, it cannot be argued that if some distortion, that is, $p_j \neq \mathrm{MC}_j$, is removed in the economy, consumers will move closer to the Pareto frontier if other distortions are present. If the industries involved are unrelated, a case might be made that the above cross-partials are 0. In that case, a more efficient allocation is implied by removal of the distortion.

Hotelling correctly argued for a nondistorting, or lump-sum, tax. As previously mentioned, an income tax is a subsidy on leisure and hence distorts the labor-leisure choice. A poll tax is cited as an example of a lump-sum tax. More precisely, an existence tax is advocated. Even with this type of tax, however, we shall find, in the long run, less existence, i.e., fewer children, less spent on lifesaving devices, etc. For all practical purposes, it is probably safe to conclude that there is no such thing as a lump-sum tax.

15.6 PUBLIC GOODS

There is an important class of goods which have the characteristic of being *jointly consumed* by more than one individual. These goods, known as *public goods*, are goods for which there is *no congestion*. Ordinary private goods are goods for which congestion is so severe that only one person can consume the good.

The most famous example of a public good is perhaps the service national defense. The protection afforded any individual by the nation's foreign policy and military prowess is substantially unaffected if additional recipients are added to that service flow. Similarly, driving on an uncrowded freeway, watching a movie or play in an uncrowded theater, or watching a television program are services for which the marginal cost, in terms of resources used up, of accommodating an additional consumer is essentially 0. These goods are the polar case of goods for which average costs are forever declining.

The problem such goods raise for welfare economic considerations is that the Pareto frontier is reached only if all goods and services are sold at their marginal cost of production. If public goods are sold at marginal cost, no revenues will be generated to finance the production of those goods. If production of the public good is financed by revenues derived from taxation of other goods, these other goods will be sold to consumers at prices other than marginal cost, thereby moving the economy off the Pareto frontier. The problems of second best, just discussed, apply to these goods.

Matters of financing aside, assuming that the public good is to be sold at marginal cost, that is, 0, what level of the good is to be produced in the first place, i.e., how many uncrowded highways, open-air concerts, etc., are to be produced? The *production* of public goods is not free; these goods are "free" only in the sense that the marginal cost of having an additional individual consume the good, once produced, is 0. In the case of private goods, this problem does not arise (except in the case of declining average costs). The goods are produced by profit-maximizing firms and sold at marginal cost. No private firm, however, could produce a public good and satisfy the Pareto condition $p = MC = 0$.

Suppose there are two consumers with utility functions $U^1(x_1, y_1)$ and $U^2(x_2, y_2)$, where x is the public good and y is the ordinary private good. By definition of a public good, both consumers consume the total amount x of the good produced. Hence,

$$x_1 = x_2 = x \tag{15-41}$$

For the private good, as before, $y_1 + y_2 = y$. Suppose there is a transformation surface $g(x, y)$ defining the production possibilities frontier for the economy. The Pareto optimum is achieved by solving:

maximize $\qquad\qquad\qquad U^2(x, y_2)$

subject to $\qquad\qquad U^1(x, y_1) = U_0^1 \qquad g(x, y) = 0 \tag{15-42}$

with $y = y_1 + y_2$. The lagrangian is

$$\mathscr{L} = U^2(x, y_2) + \lambda_1(U_0^1 - U^1(x, y_1)) + \lambda g(x, y) \tag{15-43}$$

Differentiating $\mathscr{L}$ with respect to x, y_1, y_2 and the multipliers, noting that $g_{y_i} = g_y(\partial y/\partial y_i) = g_y$, $i = 1, 2$, we have, denoting $U_{x_j}^j = U_x^j$, etc.

$$\mathscr{L}_x = U_x^2 - \lambda_1 U_x^1 + \lambda g_x = 0 \tag{15-44a}$$

$$\mathscr{L}_{y_1} = -\lambda_1 U_y^1 + \lambda g_y = 0 \tag{15-44b}$$

$$\mathscr{L}_{y_2} = U_y^2 + \lambda g_y = 0 \tag{15-44c}$$

with the constraints

$$\mathscr{L}_{\lambda_1} = U_0^1 - U^1(x, y_1) = 0 \tag{15-45a}$$

$$\mathscr{L}_{\lambda} = g(x, y) = 0 \tag{15-45b}$$

From (15-44c), $\lambda = -U_y^2/g_y$. Substituting this in (15-44b) gives $\lambda_1 = -U_y^2/U_y^1$. Using these two expressions in (15-44a) leads to

$$U_x^2 + \frac{U_y^2}{U_y^1} U_x^1 - \frac{U_y^2}{g_y} g_x = 0 \tag{15-46}$$

Dividing through by U_y^2 yields

$$\frac{U_x^2}{U_y^2} + \frac{U_x^1}{U_y^1} = \frac{g_x}{g_y} \tag{15-47}$$

Equation (15-47) admits of an interesting interpretation. U_x^1/U_y^1 and U_x^2/U_y^2 are, respectively, the marginal rates of substitutions, or the marginal evaluations, of the public good x. The expression g_x/g_y is the marginal rate of transformation of y into x or the marginal cost of the public good in terms of private good forgone.

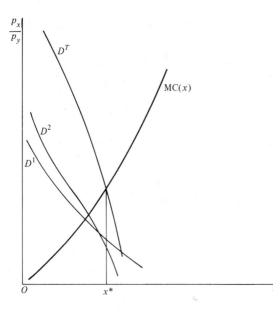

Figure 15-6 Market demand for public good. If D^1 and D^2 are the two individual demand curves for the public good, the total demand D^T is the *vertical* sum of D^1 and D^2. That is, D^T represents the sum of each consumer's marginal evaluation of the public good. This vertical summation occurs because both consumers consume the total quantity of public good produced. The output x^* at which D^T intersects the marginal cost curve for producing x yields consumption on the Pareto frontier.

Since both consumers consume the *total* amount of x produced, the marginal benefits to society of the public good are the *sum* of each consumer's marginal benefits. Equation (15-47) therefore says that when the Pareto frontier is achieved, the total consumers' marginal benefits equal marginal cost. The usual reasoning of equating benefits and costs at the margin is preserved. The rule is adapted for goods with the characteristic of joint consumption.

Equation (15-47) says that to find the market demand curve for a public good, the individual demand curves are to be added *vertically*, as shown in Fig. 15-6. The market demand for ordinary goods is, of course, the *horizontal* sum of individual demands, because each consumer consumes a part of the total. For public goods, each consumer jointly consumes the total. The height of the individual demand curves, D^1 and D^2 in Fig. 15-6, are the marginal evaluations of the public good x.† The curve D^T is the vertical sum of D^1 and D^2, representing the benefits of x at the margin to both consumers jointly. The quantity x^* where D^T intersects the marginal-cost curve of producing x is the point which satisfies the Pareto conditions for production of a public good.

The above analysis generalizes in a straightforward manner to the case of K consumers. In that case, the Pareto conditions for public-good production become

$$\sum_{i=1}^{K} \text{MRS}^i = \text{MC} \tag{15-48}$$

---

† The income being held constant in these demand curves is the total value of x and y given by the transformation surface $g(x, y) = 0$.

The problem of private production of public goods is that the ordinary market transactions are not likely to yield the Pareto allocation. In order to arrive at production of x at the level x^* where $\sum \text{MRS} = \text{MC}$, each consumer's differing marginal evaluations would have to be known. However, consumers will have no occasion to reveal these preferences. With private goods, consumers reveal their preferences by their choices in the market, purchasing additional units of a good until the marginal evaluation falls to the market price. There is no comparable mechanism for public goods. Each consumer consumes the total amount produced, and each has in general a different marginal evaluation of that good. Moreover, since the good is to be dispersed in total, it will pay consumers to understate their evaluation of the benefits of the good, lest the government attempt to allocate the good on the basis of fees based on each consumer's personal evaluations of benefits. Lastly, a fee charged for per unit use of the public good will result in "too little" consumption of the good. Consider the case of an uncrowded bridge. When a toll is charged, consumers will not cross the bridge if their marginal evaluation of the benefits is greater than 0 but less than the toll. But since the resource cost to society for the consumer's use of the bridge is 0, the ideal Pareto optimum cannot be achieved. Thus, the ordinary contracting in the marketplace for public-goods production is not likely to lead to an efficient allocation of resources in terms of the Pareto ideal.

15.7 CONSUMER'S SURPLUS AS A MEASURE OF WELFARE GAINS AND LOSSES

We have previously investigated the problems associated with defining, in units of money income, the gains from trade. One of the most prominent uses of these measures is the evaluation of costs and benefits of alternative tax schemes or the benefits of public-good production. Let us briefly recapitulate these issues and apply the analysis to the problem of public-good production.

Since the publication of Marshall's "Principles," economists have attempted to measure the benefits of consumption by some sort of calculation based on the area beneath a consumer's demand curve. In Fig. 15-7, the height of the consumer's demand curve at each point represents the consumer's marginal evaluation of the good in terms of other goods forgone, measured in terms of money. It is therefore tempting to integrate, or add up, these marginal gains to arrive at the total gain received from consuming some positive level of the good rather than none at all. However, we have seen in Chap. 11 that this is not possible. If the demand curve in Fig. 15-7 is a *utility- or real-income-held-constant* demand curve, the area $OACD$ represents the maximum dollar amount a consumer would pay to have OD units of x rather than none at all. It likewise follows that for these demand curves, ABC represents the maximum amount a consumer would pay for the *right* to consume x at unit price OB. If the license fee is actually paid, OD will be purchased and the consumer will remain on the same indifference level before and after the purchase, by definition of ABC as the *maximum* license fee the

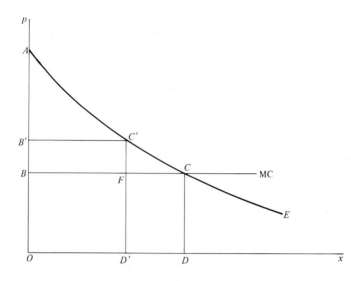

Figure 15-7 The attempt to measure welfare losses by consumer's surplus. The analysis of welfare losses is an attempt to have a money measure of the loss in utility incurred from selling commodities at prices other than marginal cost. Let $OB = \text{MC}$ of x, and suppose $OD' = B'C'$ of x is sold at OB'. The traditional analysis asserts that the benefits from consuming OD is the trapezoidal area $OACD$. At price OB', total benefits are supposed to be $OAC'D'$. The difference, $D'C'CD$, is partitioned into $FC'C$ and $D'FCD$. The latter area is an amount of income spent on other commodities, presumed to be sold at marginal cost. The remaining area $FC'C$ is called *deadweight loss*, a money measure of the loss due to the price distortion BB'. This distortion is commonly attributed to excise taxation or monopolistic sale of x. The problem with such a measure is that it is not related to any observable measure in the real world. If the demand curve AE is a *money*-income-held-constant demand curve, then $FC'C$ is only one of an infinite number of imputed shadow prices of the monetary loss associated with a fall in utility, as explained in Chap. 11. If AD is a *real-income*, or *utility-held-constant*, demand curve, then although these areas represent well-defined measures of willingness to pay to face different prices, since these measures hold utility *constant*, they cannot very well measure utility *changes*.

consumer would pay. This measure has the desirable property of being well defined and at least in principle observable.

If, on the other hand, the demand curve in Fig. 15-7 is a *money-income*-held-constant demand curve, the area ABC does *not* represent an observable quantity. This area measures *one particular* imputed rent to the gain in utility a consumer receives from being able to consume x at price OB rather than have no x at all. The gain in utility associated with the terminal prices OA and OB is generated by a line integral which is in general path-dependent; different adjustments of prices leading to the same initial and final price-income vectors will in general lead to different monetary evaluations of the consumer's gain in utility. This is an inescapable index-number problem for nonhomothetic utility functions. Only in the case of homothetic utility functions are changes in utility proportional to changes in income for any set of initial prices.

The above considerations, discussed in greater detail in Chap. 11, foreclose the use of consumer's surplus as a measure of welfare losses (or gains) due to excise taxation or the sale of public goods at other than marginal cost. Consider Fig. 15-7, where the marginal cost of some good x is drawn horizontally for convenience. The curve AE is a demand curve; it is presently unspecified whether money or real income is held constant along it.

The quantity OD is special in the sense that the marginal benefits to consumers from x exactly equal the consumer's evaluation of the resources used to produce x in producing something else—the marginal opportunity cost of x. If there are no "distortions" of prices from marginal costs elsewhere in the economy, this occurrence is part of the Pareto conditions. However, if there are other goods whose prices differ from MC so that such efficient consumption levels do not occur, then, again, it is not possible to conclude that selling this good x at MC will lead the economy closer to the Pareto frontier. In general, if one good is sold at some price other than MC, say due to an excise tax on that good, then the set of excise taxes $(t_1, \ldots, t_n)$ on the n commodities in the economy which will lead to the Pareto frontier will not consist of zero tax rates on the other commodities, nor will they all necessarily be proportional to their respective marginal costs.

The specification of such an optimal set of taxes $(t_1^*, \ldots, t_n^*)$, which leads the economy to the Pareto frontier for given deviations from MC of certain goods or for the purpose of financing government services, is too protracted a discussion to consider here. We wish instead to demonstrate that consumer's surplus measures are not reliable indicators of the losses due to nonoptimal taxes.

Following the early French economist Dupuit, and stimulated greatly by Marshall's discussion of consumer's surplus, the monetary evaluation of the welfare loss associated with consuming OD' instead of OD units of x is usually given as the triangular area $FC'C$, in Fig. 15-7. The total benefits of consuming x are reduced by the trapezoidal area $D'C'CD$. However, the rectangular area $D'FCD$ represents income spent on other goods, *presumably at the marginal cost of those other goods*, eliminating this area as a part of welfare loss. The only remaining deadweight loss of the sale of x at price $OB' > $ MC is the area $FC'C$. Summing these areas over all commodities is supposed to yield the welfare loss associated with a set of departures of price from marginal cost. That is, suppose $t_i = p_i - \text{MC}_i$, where t_i can be thought of as an excise tax on x_i, the revenues from which are to produce and efficiently allocate some government project or subsidize the production of some good with declining average costs. Then a function of the type

$$w = f(p_1, \ldots, p_n, t_1, \ldots, t_n) \tag{15-49}$$

is postulated, where w stands for welfare loss. Now one is perfectly entitled to construct some such function of excise taxes or price changes and calculate a bunch of areas, say, thereby. The relevant question is whether a calculation corresponds to something operational and useful in the real world. Let us investigate two famous cases.

One such welfare loss function is constructed off of money-income demand curves as a monetary measure of loss of utility. This measure is

$$w^M = - \int_c \sum x_i(\mathbf{p}, M) \, dp_i \tag{15-50}$$

In this particular case, except for the case of equal income elasticities in all goods considered (unitary elasticity if all goods consumed are included), a function like (15-49) is a priori undefinable. The value of the integral (15-50) is not dependent solely on the initial and final prices or the initial prices and the price changes. There simply is no unique money measure of a gain or loss in utility, for the reasons explored in Chap. 11. The consumer will impute a different dollar gain for a utility change, perhaps ranging from 0 to the entire budget, depending on how the order or path of price changes takes place. Therefore, a construction (15-49) based on areas calculated from money-income demand curves corresponds, *in principle*, to nothing in the real world. There is no observable or measurable quantity which corresponds to the construction (15-49) derived from money-income-held-constant demand curves.

Recognizing the difficulties posed by path dependence, various writers have turned to the hicksian compensating variations in income derived from utility- or real-income-held-constant demand curves. The measure

$$w^U = - \int_{p_i + t_i}^{p_i} \sum x_i(\mathbf{p}, U) \, dp_i \tag{15-51}$$

represents a well-defined quantity. Here, w^U represents the amount of money income *the consumer would be willing to pay* to face the prices p_i instead of $p_i + t_i$, $i = 1, \ldots, n$. (If some $t_i < 0$ and $w^U < 0$, w^U represents the amount a consumer *would have to be paid* to accept $p_i + t_i$ voluntarily instead of p_i, $i = 1, \ldots, n$.) The problem of using w^U as a measure of the benefits from increased utility is that w^U *depends only on one indifference level.* Utility is held constant in the above integral. That it is peculiar at best and unreliable at worst to use as a measure of the gains from trade a measure which specifically holds utility *constant* is perhaps best seen by example.

In Fig. 15-8, we set $p_y = 1$ arbitrarily. Since the vertical intercepts are $M/p_y = M$ in this case, changes in income can be read directly off the vertical axis. The consumer initially faces price p_x for x, producing the budget line emanating from A, with income OA. From the graph, the consumer is willing to pay an amount AB to have the price of x reduced to p'_x and willing to pay AC to have the price of x reduced to p''_x. Suppose $AB = \$10$ and $AC = \$20$. Suppose the consumer is actually going to have to pay \$5 (AB') to have p_x reduced to p'_x or is actually going to pay \$14 (AC') to have p_x reduced to p''_x. Suppose AB' and AC' represent the cost of two alternative, mutually exclusive public works projects. Are these data sufficient to evaluate these projects in terms of answering which will place this consumer on a higher indifference level? Although the gain measured by the compensating variation minus the cost is greater for the second project, one

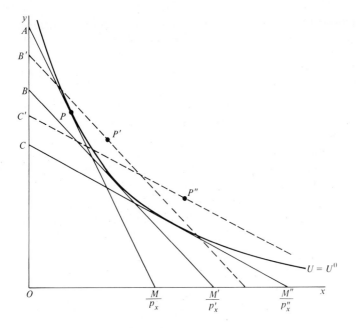

Figure 15-8 Measuring gains from trade by compensating variations in income. The consumer has income M and faces prices p_x, $p_y = 1$. Money income is therefore measurable as distances along the vertical axis since the budget line intercepts that axis at $M/p_y = M$. At price p_x, the consumer consumes at point P on utility level U^0. The consumer is willing, according to this diagram, to pay amounts AB, AC to face the lower prices p'_x, p''_x, respectively. Suppose the consumer only *has* to pay AB', AC' to face those lower prices. Suppose the differences between what the consumer is *willing* to pay and what is actually paid, that is, BB' and CC', are not equal; e.g., suppose $BB' < CC'$. Can one infer that the second situation leaves the consumer on a higher indifference curve? Alas, no. For the first case, the consumer faces price p'_x with income OB', winding up at some point P'. In the second situation, the consumer faces price p''_x and income OC', winding up at some point P''. There is no way in general to tell which if either of P' and P'' is on a higher indifference level. The only indifference curve specified is $U = U^0$; no information is provided (except convexity) about where preferred indifference levels lie. Hence, the differences between compensating variations. and actual costs of, say, two mutually exclusive projects will be unreliable measures of their ultimate benefits for consumers.

cannot conclude that the consumer would be best off with it. With the first project, lowering p_x to p'_x, the consumer will wind up at some point P' on the budget line emanating from B' with slope p'_x. For the second project, the consumer will be at some point P'' on the budget line emanating from C' with slope p''_x. Now within a broad range of price changes, there is no way to determine whether P' is more preferred or less preferred than P''. The reason is that nothing has been said of the properties of this consumer's utility function other than the one indifference curve $U = U^0$ from which all the compensating variations are derived. One must therefore conclude that integrals of the form (15-51) are not reliable measures of gains from trade; they cannot be because they hold utility constant throughout.

We conclude therefore that attempts to use consumer's surplus to measure welfare losses are largely the application of the inappropriate to measure the undefinable.

15.8 THE COASE THEOREM WITH AN APPLICATION TO THE THEORY OF SHARECROPPING

The analysis to this point has been concerned with the enunciation of conditions under which a hypothetical economy achieves a point on the Pareto frontier. That is, we have asked: What conditions must hold at points where all the gains from trade are exhausted so that the only way to make one person better off is to make someone else worse off? This analysis, sometimes referred to as the *new* welfare economics (the *old* welfare economics was concerned with finding the best output plan for society) is deficient in at least two respects. First, as we have repeatedly emphasized in this book, the goal of empirical science is to develop refutable propositions which upon testing are consistent with the data. The marginal conditions of welfare economics are unobservable and hence not refutable by data. There is no way ever to know whether marginal costs equal marginal benefits by direct inspection. These functions are beyond the realm of practical empirical economics. The statements of marginal conditions for optimization are uninteresting; they always say that marginal benefits are to equal marginal costs. It is only the refutable propositions—the positive analysis which is sometimes deducible from these marginal conditions—that are a part of (empirical) science.

On a second front, the new welfare economics as outlined above is deficient in terms of incomplete specification and logical consistency. The fundamental postulates of economics are maintained throughout. Consumers are presumed to possess utility functions with the usual properties; i.e., they prefer more to less, convexity, etc. Most importantly, there are no costs of transacting or contracting between consumers in this analysis. Yet somehow consumers are supposed to get together and *not* exhaust the gains from trade in certain circumstances. But how can this be? If all consumers prefer more to less and there are no contracting costs, *Pareto optimality is necessarily implied.* To say otherwise is to deny the fundamental postulates of economics, most probably a premature stand to take. The only way the gains from exchange will not be fully exhausted is if consumers are somehow prevented from exhausting them by the existence of positive transaction costs. These costs may involve direct negotiations between the parties involved, the hiring of attorneys and drawing up of lengthy contracts, or the existence of government rules which inhibit exchange. The latter conditions may be regarded as infinite costs for certain actions, though in many cases the expenditure of resources on different margins can sometimes evade, if only partially, governmental restrictions on trade. These expenditures may be an empirically important cost of transacting, especially under systems of price controls, quotas, etc.

It is often claimed that "tariffs misallocate resources," urban areas are "overcrowded," the atmosphere and water supplies are "overpolluted," etc. It is less

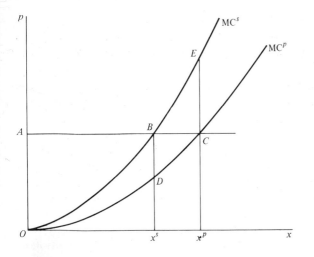

Figure 15-9 Private and social marginal costs. Diagrams of this type are often used to indicate the difference between social and private costs. The curve MC^p misspecifies the marginal cost of producing cattle in the present example by excluding the cost of destroyed crops. The marginal destruction of crops, the side effect, or externality, is represented by the vertical difference between MC^s, social, i.e., actual, marginal cost, and MC^p. It was formerly alleged that if the rancher was not legally liable for damaged crops, x^p would be produced. This analysis never came to grips with why individual maximizers would not reach the contract curve. In order to analyze where production will take place, the cost of contracting, i.e., the test conditions between the rancher and farmer, must be specified. If these transactions costs are 0, the rancher and farmer are essentially one person. They will never allow x^p to be produced instead of x^s since the additional net profits gained BCD are less than the crop damage $BECD$. If the rancher is not liable for damage done to crops, the farmer will contract to pay the rancher more than BCD (but less than $BECD$) for the rancher to produce x^s instead of x^p. Since both parties will gain, such a contract is implied.

from trade or transacting are being lost. *If* the cost of transacting is 0 (and no specific mention of transactions costs was presented in the new welfare economics), it cannot be that individual maximizers would arrive at some point *off* the contract curve. It would be a denial that more is preferred to less for two people to agree to a non-Pareto allocation or misallocation, of resources.

The assignment of legal liability for the wandering cattle constitutes a specification of *endowments* only. Any rancher who does not have to pay damages for trampled crops will be wealthier. It is an expansion of the rancher's property rights and an attenuation of the farmer's property rights. Likewise, a court ruling that the rancher *is* liable for crop damage is a transfer of assets only, from the rancher to the farmer, not a change in production possibilities or preferences. There is no reason why a change in endowments should foreclose a movement to the contract curve, i.e., the Pareto frontier. The classical theorems of welfare economics indicate that individuals will move to the contract curve irrespective of where the endowment point is placed in the Edgeworth box.

The error of assuming a non-Pareto solution hinged upon a failure to consider the range of contracting possibilities available to individuals, e.g., the ran-

frequently asked why individual maximizers would ever do these things to (
other. Indeed, in a world without transaction costs, they would not. All of w
says that the enunciation of conditions under which the gains from trade wi
exhausted under the assumption of zero transaction costs is apt to be a ra
sterile endeavor. Comparing the actual to the ideal will yield the nonstart
conclusion that the actual is deficient in certain regards and if only certain c
could be reduced, we could all be better off.

The first systematic discussion of the role of transaction costs in relatior
the allocation of resources was Ronald Coase's pathbreaking article, The Prob
of Social Cost.† The context of the alleged misallocations were various "techn(
gical externalities"—the situation where production of one good was, in this c;
a negative input in the production of some other good. The example first cited $
the historically important case of straying cattle: a rancher-producer raises ca
who invariably trample some of a neighboring farmer's crop.

The classical welfare economic treatment of this problem, in the tradition
A. C. Pigou, took place as follows. Consider Fig. 15-9. The marginal private c(
of cattle, disregarding the trampled crops, is labeled MC^p. This curve descrit
all the usual forgone opportunities of production, expressed in terms of costs
feed, land, shelter, fences, etc. However, an additional cost of production is al
incurred by society. Each additional steer raised tramples some crops, loweri
output of the adjacent farmer. With this damage treated as a cost of producii
cattle, a marginal social cost curve MC^s is drawn, the difference $MC^s(x) - MC^p($
being the marginal damage to the farmer's crops.

Suppose the price of cattle is OA. Traditional (pigovian) welfare analysis he
that unless the rancher were somehow made liable for the crop damage, th
rancher would have no occasion to consider marginal *social* costs; cattle would k
produced in the amount x^p, where $p = MC^p$. There would be a misallocation (
resources in that too many cattle (and too little food) would be produced. Th
marginal conditions for Pareto optimality require that output x^s, where $p = MC$
be produced, since MC^s represents the actual marginal-cost function for produc
ing cattle. The curve MC^p leaves out part of the cost of cattle production, the cos
of the lost food production.

If x^p is produced, the total private cost is the area OCx^p, the total damage t(
crops is the area between the two marginal cost curves OEC, and thus the tota
cost of production is the area OEx^p. At this level of output, resources are misallocated: at output greater than x^s, the marginal opportunity cost of producing
cattle is greater than the marginal benefits to consumers, measured by the price
OA. By producing x^p instead of x^s, additional benefits x^sBCx^p are generated,
resulting in a deadweight loss in the amount of BEC.

Coase's contribution was to point out that the above argument could be valid
only if the rancher and the farmer were somehow prevented from further contracting with each other. A misallocation of resources means that some mutual gains

† Ronald Coase, The Problem of Social Cost, *Journal of Law and Economics*, October 1960,
pp. 1–44.

cher and farmer in the above case. If the rancher is liable for crop damage, no further contracting is necessary; the state enforces the contract that the rancher pay the farmer for damage. If the rancher is *not* liable, however, there are still options to consider. In particular, the farmer has the option of contracting with the rancher to reduce cattle production for some fee. Consider Fig. 15-9. The damage to the farmer's crops caused by producing x^p instead of x^s is the area *DBEC*. However, the net profit to the rancher derived from this extra production is only part of that area, *DBC*, representing $x^s BCx^p - x^s DCx^p$, revenues minus cost. Since the damage to the farmer is greater by the amount *BEC* than the gain to the rancher from producing x^p instead of x^s, the farmer will be able to offer the rancher more than *DBC*, the rancher's gain, but less than *DBEC* to induce the rancher to reduce production to x^s. With no transactions cost, this contract is implied, since both the farmer and the rancher are better off. At any level of production beyond x^s, the damages to the farmer exceed the incremental gains to the rancher; both parties will gain by a contract wherein the farmer pays the rancher something in between these two amounts to reduce cattle production to x^p.

If transactions costs are not 0, forgone gains from trade may exist. To point this out, however, is to only begin the problem. The parties involved still have an incentive to consider various contracts to extract some of the mutual benefits. Different contracts have different negotiation and enforcement costs associated with them. Merger or outright purchase of one firm by another can be used to internalize side effects such as trampled crops. With merger or outright purchase, the rancher will produce x^s cattle, since it will now be the rancher's crops that are being trampled. We should expect to see individuals devising contracts that lead to the greatest extraction of mutual gains from exchange. In fact, this hypothesis is the basis for an emerging theory of contracts, based on maximizing behavior.†

The Theory of Share Tenancy: An Application of the Coase Theorem

Perhaps the first empirical application of Coase's analysis was the analysis of sharecropping by Steven N. S. Cheung.‡ Sharecropping is a form of rent payment in agriculture in which the landlord takes some share of the output, specified in advance, instead of a fixed amount, as payment for the use of the land (rent). This

---

† Coase also showed that when transactions costs were not 0, it is not possible to deduce a priori which assignment of liability would reduce misallocation more. Consider the famous case of a railroad which occasionally sets fire to fields adjacent to the tracks because of sparks from the locomotive. If the railroad is made liable for all damage, the farmers lose an incentive to reduce the damage by not planting flammable crops too close to the tracks. The land close to the tracks may have as its highest value use a repository for sparks. On the other hand, if the railroad is not liable, it may run too many trains, i.e., produce beyond where $MC^s = p$. One form of contract which may emerge is for the railroad to purchase land near the tracks, eliminating most, if not all, of the problems.

‡ Stevens N. S. Cheung, "The Theory of Share Tenancy," University of Chicago Press, Chicago, 1969.

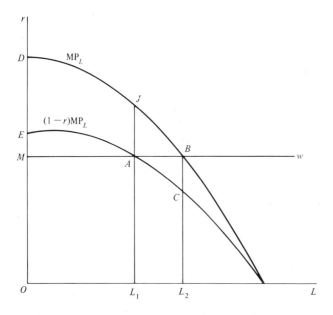

Figure 15-10 The tax-equivalent approach to sharecropping. This diagram has been used to show that sharecropping is an inefficient contract. Using a tax analogy, if MP_L is the marginal product of labor, and if r percent of the tenant's output is collected as rent, the net marginal product to the tenant is $(1 - r)MP_L$. With such a tax, the tenant would produce at L_1, where the actual marginal benefits MP_L exceed the opportunity cost of labor measured by its wage OM. This argument, while correct with regard to an excise tax on labor, cannot easily be extended to the case of sharecropping. In a share *contract*, many more variables are specified than the share itself. Farm size, nonlabor inputs in general, and labor inputs are negotiable. Under the postulate that the landlord maximizes the rent on the land subject to the constraint of competing for labor at labor's alternative cost, the Pareto condition $MP_L = w$ is implied. (*From S.N.S. Cheung, "The Theory of Share Tenancy, p. 43, University of Chicago Press, Chicago, 1969.*)

form of contract is somehow less enthusiastically regarded by many social reformers than the fixed-rent contract.

Sharecropping as a contractual form of rent payment came under attack by various economists on the grounds that it misallocated resources relative to the fixed-rent contract. In its neoclassical formulation, the rental share paid to the landlord was regarded as equivalent to an excise tax on the sharecropper's efforts, inducing sharecroppers to reduce output below the level where the marginal value product of the sharecropper equaled their alternative wage.

Consider Fig. 15-10. The top curve is the marginal product of labor. Under a fixed-rent or fixed-wage contract, labor input L_2 would be hired, where the marginal product of labor equals its alternative wage OM. Suppose, however, the tenant has contracted to pay r percent of the output to the landlord as payment for rent. Then the lower curve $(1 - r)MP_L$ represents the tenant's marginal product curve net of rental payments. It is concluded that the tenant, under these conditions, will produce at input level L_1, an inefficient point since there the true marginal product of labor is higher than its next best use, measured by the wage line w.†

The argument is correct up to this point. A *tax* on labor of r percent of the tenant's output would indeed lead the tenant to produce at L_1. The mistake is to apply this tax analysis to sharecropping, a situation in which a landlord and tenant voluntarily *contract* with each other. Again, the fundamental issue raised by Coase is invoked: Why would utility maximizers get together and *not* exhaust the gains from trade? If L_1 instead of L_2 is used, the total output lost is $L_1 JBL_2$, whereas the alternative cost to society of this labor differential, $L_2 - L_1$, is $L_1 ABL_2$. Hence, mutual gains JAB are lost. Why should the landlord be willing to forgo this additional rental value on the land?

Applying the tax analysis to sharecropping amounts to assuming that the only variable that can be specified is the rental share or the wage rate. A contract, however, need not contain only one clause. It is possible to specify more than one variable in a contract. (Indeed, why else would contracts exist?) Even in the normal wage contract, often an informal agreement between employer and employee, the hourly wage is not the only thing specified. The employer expects the employee to show up on time, work a certain number of hours at some minimum level of intensity, etc. If only the wage were specified, maximizing behavior indicates that the worker would show up and proceed to do no work at all. Contracts in general specify more than one variable.

So it is with sharecropping. Real-world share contracts specify such things as amount of land to be cultivated, nonlabor inputs to be supplied by the tenant, "the droppings [of water buffalo] go to the [landowner's] soil," etc.‡ Under these conditions, the tax analysis is simply inapplicable. The test conditions of the experiment are entirely different.

That sharecropping as a contractual form is consistent with the Pareto conditions is shown by the following argument. Suppose the landlord owns an amount of land (capital) K. Labor is available at wage rate w, representing the alternative value of labor. The landlord can subdivide his land into m tenant farms, *where m is a choice variable.* Similarly, *the rental share r going to the landlord is not fixed but is also a choice variable.* Let the amount of labor supplied to each tenant farm be L. The amount of land supplied to each farm is $k = K/m$. The tenant's production function can therefore be written

$$y = f(L, k) = f\left(L, \frac{K}{m}\right)$$

The landlord will seek to maximize the rent on the land, $R = mry$. However, this is not an unconstrained maximization. Landlords must compete for tenants. Under

---

† Curiously enough, much social criticism of sharecropping appears to be based upon the landlord's working his tenants to an undue degree, perhaps, as we shall see, a more astute observation than the above economic argument.

‡ Cheung, op. cit.

this constraint of competition, the rental share to the tenant cannot be lower than the tenant's alternative earnings in wage labor. The model thus becomes

$$\max_{(m, r, L)} R = mrf(L, k) \quad \text{subject to} \quad wL = (1 - r)f(L, k) \quad (15\text{-}52)$$

From the constraint,

$$rf(L, k) = f(L, k) - wL$$

Hence, the problem can be posed in the unconstrained form when the variable r has been eliminated:

$$\max_{m, L} R = m[f(L, k) - wL] \quad (15\text{-}53)$$

Differentiating and remembering that $k = K/m$, we have

$$\frac{\partial R}{\partial m} = m \frac{\partial f}{\partial k}\left(-\frac{K}{m^2}\right) + [f(L, k) - wL] = 0 \quad (15\text{-}54a)$$

$$\frac{\partial R}{\partial L} = m \frac{\partial f}{\partial L} - mw = 0 \quad (15\text{-}54b)$$

From equation (15-54b), we immediately see that the landlord will contract with the tenant so as to set the (value of the) marginal product of labor equal to the alternative cost of labor. Thus, the labor input in Fig. 15-9 will be L_2, not L_1. The Pareto conditions will be satisfied. Substituting $w = \partial f/\partial L$ into equation (15-54a) and rearranging leads to

$$\frac{\partial f}{\partial k}(-k) + f(L, k) - \frac{\partial f}{\partial L}L = 0$$

or

$$\frac{\partial f}{\partial k}k + \frac{\partial f}{\partial L}L = f(L, k) \quad (15\text{-}55)$$

Equation (15-55) is a statement of product exhaustion (*not* the Euler expression, which is an *identity*). The imputed value of land (capital) measured by its marginal product times the land input plus the same expression for labor equals the total output of the farm.

The share of output going to the landlord, $rf(L, k)$, from the original constraint in (15-52) is

$$rf(L, k) = f(L, k) - \frac{\partial f}{\partial L}L$$

or, from (15-55),

$$rf(L, k) = \frac{\partial f}{\partial k}k \quad (15\text{-}56)$$

The landlord's share is precisely the imputed land value of the farm. In Fig. 15-10 this is the area *MDB*. When *r is chosen so as to maximize the rent of the land*, the landlord's share is also represented by the area $EDBC = MDB$. However, $EDBC$ is not the landlord's share for *any* arbitrary r, only for the rent-maximizing r. This rent-maximizing share, from (15-56), is

$$r^* = \frac{f_k k}{y}$$

This share is not determined by custom or tradition; it is a *contracted* amount. It varies with the fertility of the land, the cost of labor, and other variables specified in the share contract.

Showing that sharecropping is consistent with the Pareto conditions, however, is to merely state a normative condition. The interesting question of *positive* economic analysis is why the form of contract varies, i.e., why is it sometimes a fixed rent and other times a share contract? The reader is referred to Cheung for detailed answers to this question. We shall merely indicate here that some answers lie in the area of contracting cost and risk aversion. Share contracting is likely to be a more costly contract to enforce. However, to cite one example from agriculture, if the variance in output, due, say, to weather, is high, the landlord and tenant may *share the risk* of uncertain output by using a share contract. Indeed, empirical evidence from Taiwan indicates that share contracting is more prevalent in wheat than rice farming, wheat having a much higher coefficient of variation of output than rice. Other tests of these hypotheses are available.

The important methodological point being made here is that it is generally sterile merely to pronounce some economic activity inefficient. Since efficiency is unobservable, statements about efficiency are in themselves useless. The normative statements of welfare analysis may be useful, however, if they are used to investigate why it is that certain ideal marginal conditions are being violated. The analysis then becomes positive rather than normative. Instead of labeling certain actions as irrational or inefficient, one asserts that the participants will seek to contract with each other to further exhaust the mutual gains from trade and one derives refutable propositions therefrom.

PROBLEMS

1 Explain why it is nonsense to seek the greatest good for the greatest number of people.

2 Suppose two consumers have the utility functions $U^1 = x_1^{1/3} y_1^{2/3}$, $U^2 = x_2^{2/3} y_2^{1/3}$. Suppose $x = x_1 + x_2$, $y = y_1 + y_2$ represent the total amount of goods available. Find the equation representing the contract curve for these consumers.

3 Suppose there are two goods, x and y, which are *both* public goods. There are two individuals whose entire consumption is made up of these two goods. There is a production possibilities frontier given by $g(x, y) = 0$. Find the marginal conditions for production levels of x and y which satisfy the Pareto conditions.

4 Suppose all firms except one in an economy are perfect competitors, the remaining firm being a perfectly discriminating monopolist. Explain why the Pareto conditions will still be satisfied. What differences in allocation and distribution of income result from that firm's not being a perfect competitor also?

5 Two farmers, A and B, live 8 and 12 miles, respectively, from a river and are separated by 15 miles along the river, as shown in Fig. 15-11. The river is their only source of water. Pumphouses cost P dollars each and must be located on the river. Laying pipe costs $100 per mile. Once the pipe is laid and pumphouses installed, the water is available at no extra cost.

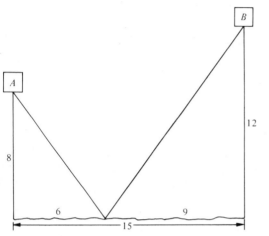

Figure 15-11

(a) Do farmers have an incentive to minimize the total (to both farmers) cost of obtaining water?

(b) If one pumphouse is used to supply both farmers, show that it will be located 6 miles from the point on the river closest to farm A. (Use either calculus or similar triangles). What will the cost of water be for each farmer and totally in terms of P?

(c) Suppose the farmers build their own pumps. What will the cost to each be and the total cost?

(d) Show that in a certain range of pumphouse costs, one farmer will induce the other to share a pumphouse if transactions costs are low enough. (Assume for simplicity that pumphouse cost is shared equally. Then relax that assumption.)

6 Explain why the utility frontier must be downward-sloping and why it is not necessarily concave to the origin on the basis of the elementary properties of utility functions.

7 "Interdependencies in individuals' utility functions or in production functions will lead to non-Pareto allocations of resources." Evaluate.

8 The cases where markets allocate resources less efficiently than the Pareto ideal is often called *market failure.*

(a) Why isn't the case where governments allocate resources less than the Pareto ideal called *government failure?*

(b) Under what conditions will there be market failure?

(c) Suppose, to cite a famous example, that in a certain region there is apple growing and beekeeping and that bees feed on apple blossoms. If the apple farmers increase their production of apples, they will allegedly increase honey production. The apple farmers acting alone will not, it is said, perceive the true marginal product of apple trees and hence will misallocate resources. Devise a model for this problem. Would the existence of actual contracts between beekeepers and apple farmers affect your conclusions as to whether market failure is a necessary consequence of production externalities, or interdependencies?

BIBLIOGRAPHY

Arrow, K. J.: An Extension of the Basic Theorems of Classical Welfare Economics, in J. Neyman (ed.), *Proceedings of the Second Berkeley Symposium on Mathematical Statistics and Probability*, University of California Press, Berkeley, 1951.

————: Social Choice and Individual Values, 2d ed., *Cowles Foundation Monograph* 12, John Wiley & Sons, Inc., New York, 1963.

Bator, F.: The Simple Analytics of Welfare Maximization, *American Economic Review*, **47**: 22–59, 1957.

————: The Anatomy of Market Failure, *Quarterly Journal of Economics*, **72**: 351–379, 1958.

Bergson, A.: A Reformulation of Certain Aspects of Welfare Economics, *Quarterly Journal of Economics*, **52**: 310–334, February 1938; reprinted in K. Arrow and T. Scitovsky (eds.), "Readings in Welfare Economics," Richard D. Irwin, Homewood, Ill., 1969.

Buchanan, J., and G. Tullock: "The Calculus of Consent," University of Michigan Press, Ann Arbor, 1963.

Cheung, S. N. S.: "The Theory of Share Tenancy," University of Chicago Press, Chicago, 1969.

————: The Fables of the Bees: An Economic Investigation, *Journal of Law and Economics*, **16**: 11–33, April 1973.

Coase, R. H.: The Problem of Social Cost, *Journal of Law and Economics*, **3**: 1–44, October 1960.

Davis, Otto A., and Andrew B. Whinston: Welfare Economics and the Theory of Second Best, *Review of Economic Studies*, **32**: 1–14, 1965.

Demestz, H.: Information and Efficiency, Another Viewpoint, *Journal of Law and Economics*, **12**: 1–22, April 1969.

Harberger, A. C.: Monopoly and Resource Allocation, *American Economic Review Proceedings*, **44**: 77–87, May 1954.

————: Taxation, Resource Allocation and Welfare, in "The Role of Direct and Indirect Taxes in the Federal Revenue System," Princeton University Press, Princeton, N.J., 1964.

————: Three Basic Postulates for Applied Welfare Economics: An Interpretive Essay, *Journal of Economic Literature*, **9**: 785–797, September 1971.

Hotelling, H.: The General Welfare in Relation to Problems of Taxation and Railway and Utility Rates, *Econometrica*, **6**: 242–269, 1938.

Lerner, A. P.: "The Economics of Control," The Macmillan Company, New York, 1944.

Lipsey, R. G., and K. Lancaster: The General Theory of the Second Best, *Review of Economic Studies*, **24**: 11–32, 1956.

Little, L. M. D.: "A Critique of Welfare Economics," 2d ed., The Clarendon Press, Oxford, 1957.

Mishan, E. J.: "Welfare Economics," Random House, Inc., New York, 1964.

Quirk, J., and R. Saposnik: "Introduction to General Equilibrium Theory and Welfare Economics," McGraw-Hill Book Company, New York, 1968.

Samuelson, P. A.: "Foundations of Economic Analysis," Harvard University Press, Cambridge, Mass., 1947.

————: The Pure Theory of Public Expenditure, *Review of Economics and Statistics*, **36**: 387–390, 1954.

————: Diagrammatic Exposition of a Theory of Public Expenditure, *Review of Economics and Statistics*, **37**: 350–356, 1955.

Silberberg, E.: Duality and the Many Consumers' Surpluses, *American Economic Review*, **62**: 942–956, December 1972.

SIXTEEN

EQUILIBRIUM, DISEQUILIBRIUM, AND THE STABILITY OF MARKETS

16.1 THREE SOURCES OF REFUTABLE HYPOTHESES

In the past chapters, the choice functions of comparative statics were derived from a specific behavioral assertion of maximizing behavior. The first-order necessary conditions for a maximum or a minimum served to define what is commonly called the *equilibrium position* of the model. Specifically, these equations indicate the choices made by economic agents for various parameter values. They are the logical deductions of the behavioral hypothesis and assumed functional forms of the model. The comparative statics of such models are derived via the implicit-function theorem or envelope relations described in Chap. 9.

Mathematically, the general model derived from a specific maximization hypothesis can be represented by:

maximize $\qquad\qquad\qquad f(\mathbf{x}, \boldsymbol{\alpha})$

subject to $\qquad\qquad\quad g^1(\mathbf{x}, \boldsymbol{\alpha}) = 0$

$$\cdots\cdots\cdots\cdots\cdots$$

$$g^r(\mathbf{x}, \boldsymbol{\alpha}) = 0 \qquad\qquad (16\text{-}1)$$

where $\mathbf{x} = (x_1, \ldots, x_n)$ is the vector of choice variables and $\boldsymbol{\alpha} = (\alpha_1, \ldots, \alpha_m)$ is a vector of parameters, or test conditions, under which the experiment is performed.

The choice functions implied by these hypotheses are the first-order conditions of the lagrangian

$$\mathscr{L} = f(\mathbf{x}, \boldsymbol{\alpha}) + \boldsymbol{\lambda} \mathbf{g}(\mathbf{x}, \boldsymbol{\alpha}) \tag{16-2}$$

where $\boldsymbol{\lambda} = (\lambda_1, \ldots, \lambda_r)$ and $\boldsymbol{\lambda} \mathbf{g}(\mathbf{x}, \boldsymbol{\alpha})$ is the scalar product $\sum_{j=1}^{m} \lambda_j g^j(\mathbf{x}, \boldsymbol{\alpha})$. Specifically,

$$\mathscr{L}_\mathbf{x} = \mathbf{f}_\mathbf{x} + \boldsymbol{\lambda} \mathbf{g}_\mathbf{x} = \mathbf{0} \qquad \mathscr{L}_\lambda = \mathbf{g}(\mathbf{x}, \boldsymbol{\alpha}) = \mathbf{0} \tag{16-3}$$

represent the $n + r$ equations defining the choices of the economic agents. The maximization hypothesis need not represent any one individual's choices; it may be the result of many individuals' choices. For example, the assertion in the general-equilibrium models of Chaps. 13 and 14 that the value of output is maximized subject to resource constraints is not specified to be the conscious aim of any one person.

The explicit choice functions implied by this model are the simultaneous solution values of the x_i's, in terms of the α_j's, found by solving equations (16-3) explicitly,

$$\mathbf{x} = \mathbf{x}^*(\boldsymbol{\alpha}) \tag{16-4}$$

The refutable theorems generated by models like these will in general consist of restrictions of the signs of the various partial derivatives of (16-4). That is, consider the $n \times m$ matrix of terms $\partial x_i / \partial \alpha_j$. If certain restrictions in sign are deducible from the maximization hypothesis and the specific functional forms, e.g., for three choice variables and four parameters,

$$\begin{pmatrix} - & ? & ? & + \\ ? & + & ? & ? \\ + & ? & ? & ? \end{pmatrix} \tag{16-5}$$

then meaningful theorems or refutable hypotheses are implied. We showed earlier that if parameters entered one and only one first-order relation (but not the constraints), certain sign patterns were deducible; in particular, for $\mathscr{L}_{x_i \alpha_i} > 0$,

$$\frac{\partial x_i^*}{\partial \alpha_i} > 0 \tag{16-6}$$

The signs of these diagonal terms are in fact the only qualitative comparative-statics implications of the general maximizing models formulated above in which the only functional restriction is that a given parameter enter one and only one first-order equation. These sign restrictions are deducible from the sufficient second-order conditions for a maximum.

The assertion of maximization of some objective function is a fundamental part of many economic models. In past chapters we have been concerned principally with the implications of such models. In general, however, there are two other categories of hypotheses used to specify economic models. Thus, in addition to the hypothesis:

1. Some objective function $f(\mathbf{x}, \boldsymbol{\alpha})$ is maximized, possibly subject to other, constraint functions.

one may consider the alternative, or additional hypotheses:

2. The parameters and functions in the model take on certain values or specific forms, e.g., assumptions of linearity in the parameters, linear overall, Cobb-Douglas production functions, etc.
3. The equations defining the choice variables in terms of the parameters (the equilibrium equations) exhibit some sort of dynamic stability which restricts the values of certain $\partial x_i^*/\partial \alpha_j$'s.

This taxonomy was first presented by Samuelson in "Foundations of Economic Analysis."

The general-equilibrium models of Chaps. 13 and 14 showed how the explicit use of assumptions of type 2, together with assertions of maximizing behavior, were used to derive refutable implications. The assertion that the value of output was maximized yielded the refutable hypotheses of upward-sloping output-supply functions and some reciprocity relations. To derive additional implications, assumptions concerning factor intensities were added. Assuming that one factor was always used more intensively in one industry than the other, the Stolper-Samuelson and Rybczynski theorems were deduced. These theorems placed additional restrictions on the movement of the choice variables when the parameters, factor endowments, and output-prices changed.

In certain models, however, no explicit maximization hypothesis is used. Instead, a system of n equations is postulated to represent the equilibrium position or the choice equations. That is, one may simply consider the system

$$f^1(\mathbf{x}, \boldsymbol{\alpha}) = 0$$
$$\cdots\cdots\cdots\cdots$$
$$f^n(\mathbf{x}, \boldsymbol{\alpha}) = 0 \tag{16-7}$$

where $\mathbf{x} = (x_1, \ldots, x_n)$ are choice variables and $\boldsymbol{\alpha} = (\alpha_1, \ldots, \alpha_m)$ are parameters. Here, f^i is *not* postulated to be the partial derivative of some objective function. Assuming the jacobian determinant of terms $\partial f^i/\partial x_j$ is not 0, the implicit-function theorem allows solution of (16-7) for the explicit choice function, as before:

$$\mathbf{x} = \mathbf{x}^*(\boldsymbol{\alpha}) \tag{16-8}$$

It is still possible to inquire about the partial derivatives of these functions, i.e., the terms in the $n \times m$ matrix $(\partial x_i/\partial \alpha_j)$. However, the information about the sign of the determinant of the jacobian matrix and its principal minors is no longer present. There are no curvature properties of an objective function to be assumed here, and hence there is less information. In this case, some other type of information about the $f^i(\mathbf{x}, \boldsymbol{\alpha})$'s must be incorporated into the model to make it possible to derive refutable implications.

For example, recall the two-factor, two-good general-equilibrium model of Chap. 14. This model was reduced to following four equations

$$a_{L1}^* w + a_{K1}^* r = p_1 \qquad a_{L2}^* w + a_{K2}^* r = p_2$$
$$a_{L1}^* y_1 + a_{L2}^* y_2 = L \qquad a_{K1}^* y_1 + a_{K2}^* y_2 = K$$

where, in general, $a_{ij}^* = a_{ij}^*(w/r)$. These equations are *not* (except for linear models) the first-order conditions for any objective function (though a maximization hypothesis is used earlier). The determination of comparative-statics results was dependent upon specific *assumptions* about the a_{ij}'s, for example, $a_{L1}^*/a_{K1}^* > a_{L2}^*/a_{K2}^*$ or the reverse. Invoking linear homogeneity and restricting the values of certain variables led to refutable propositions.

A class of models for which no explicit objective function is generally postulated is the various models of macroeconomics. To cite a famous example, consider the three-sector macromodel commonly found in intermediate textbooks. Let C, I, Y, P denote, respectively, *nominal* consumption, investment, income, and the price level. Let lowercase letters represent the corresponding *real* quantities, i.e., nominal, or money, values divided by the price level. Let i denote the nominal (market) interest rate, and assume the following functional dependence between the above variables:

$$c = \frac{C}{P} = a + b\frac{Y}{P} = a + by \tag{16-9}$$

$$z = \frac{I}{P} = \alpha + \beta i \tag{16-10}$$

$$y = c + z \tag{16-11}$$

These three equations can be combined into one expression by eliminating the terms z and c. The resulting equation gives the values of i and y which are consistent with the above equations. This new relation is called the *IS* curve:

$$y = \frac{1}{(1-b)}(a + \alpha + \beta i) \tag{16-12}$$

In addition to this output-sector relation, the monetary sector is governed by the intersection of the monetary supply and demand equations. Let $L(i, Y/P)$ denote the demand for *real* cash balances (nominal demand divided by the price level P), and let $(1/P)h(i)$ denote the supply curve of money, as determined by the monetary authorities. The monetary sector is then

$$L(i, y) - \frac{1}{P}h(i) = 0 \tag{16-13}$$

Lastly, a factor market must be described. The simplest assumption is that resources are fully employed, and thus

$$y = y_f = \text{constant} \tag{16-14}$$

(The fact that this assumption negates the one reason why macroeconomics is studied at all will be ignored here.)

Equations (16-12) to (16-14) represent three equations in the "unknowns" y, i, and P. [Consumption c is determined from (16-9) once y is known. Likewise, z is determined from (16-10).] One can use these equations to derive the implications of autonomous increases in the marginal propensity to consume, b, or a shift in the consumption function itself, a, or like parameters in the system. Suppose the parameter a increased. Substitute (16-14) into (16-12) and (16-13) to reduce the system to two equations. Differentiating with respect to a, noting that $\partial y / \partial a = 0$, we have, since $y = y_f$,

$$\frac{1}{1-b} + \frac{1}{1-b} \beta \frac{\partial i}{\partial a} = 0 \tag{16-15}$$

$$L_i \frac{\partial i}{\partial a} - \frac{1}{P} h'(i) \frac{\partial i}{\partial a} + \frac{1}{P^2} h(i) \frac{\partial P}{\partial a} = 0 \tag{16-16}$$

From (16-15), if $b \neq 1$,

$$\frac{\partial i}{\partial a} = -\frac{1}{\beta} \tag{16-17}$$

Substituting this value into (16-16) yields, after some manipulation,

$$\frac{\partial P}{\partial a} = \frac{1}{\beta L(i, y)} [PL_i - h'(i)] \tag{16-18}$$

The determination of the sign of these partial derivatives depends upon assumptions about the signs of the parameter β and the slopes of the liquidity-preference function L_i and the supply-of-money function $h'(i)$. If the investment function is downward-sloping, that is, $\beta < 0$, if the demand for cash balances is negatively sloping ($L_i < 0$), and if $h'(i) \geq 0$, then an autonomous increase in the consumption function will raise the interest rate (thereby lowering real investment z) thus increasing real consumption c. The price level will also increase, there being no automatic offsetting downward shift in the propensity to invest in this simple model.

The point of the above examples is simply that there are in fact important economic models whose choice functions, or equilibrium equations, are not the first-order equations of some objective function. This being the case, criterion 1 above for deriving refutable hypotheses is irrelevant. Refutable hypotheses will be forthcoming only via explicit assumptions about the functional forms or parameter values or an assertion about the stability of the model. It is to this last postulate that we now turn.

16.2 EQUILIBRIUM AND STABILITY

The reader will probably have noticed by now that we have largely eschewed the term equilibrium in the preceding chapters. The reason for this is twofold. First, by so doing, the choice-theoretic foundations of economic theory are emphasized.

Instead of labeling the functional relations between decision variables and parameters equilibrium conditions, the name choice functions has been used. The reason is that these equations in fact state what values of the x_i's, the choice variables, *will be chosen* for given parameter values. The term choice function is simply more descriptive.

A second and more fundamental reason for not using the term equilibrium is that in the context of models with a specific behavioral assertion it is at best redundant and at worst misleading. Consider one of the first models studied, that of a firm with the profit function $\pi = pf(x_1, x_2) - w_1 x_1 - w_2 x_2$. If we *assert* that the firm maximizes π with respect to x_1 and x_2, then the conditions $pf_1 = w_1$, $pf_2 = w_2$ are *implied*. These are not equilibrium conditions. To call these marginal relations equilibrium conditions is to imply that some sort of disequilibrium can exist; otherwise the term equilibrium is redundant. But such disequilibrium, i.e., the situation where $pf_i \neq w_i$ for some i, constitutes a denial of the original hypothesis. If $pf_i \neq w_i$ is observed, it is not disequilibrium *but a refutation of the asserted theory*.

In general, if some behavioral postulate is asserted, the logical deductions of that assertion, e.g., the first-order conditions for maximization, define the choices that will be made in the system either explicitly by individuals or as a result of the simultaneous interaction of individual choices. These deductions, which we have called choice functions, are commonly referred to as equilibrium conditions. However, since they are the logical implications of the behavioral postulate, no disequilibrium can exist without denying the theory. To imply that the reason events predicted by the theory do not occur is due to disequilibrium is to assert two sets of conflicting hypotheses.

In an explicitly dynamic system, the terms equilibrium and disequilibrium can be well defined. Let the choice variables be explicit functions of time; that is, $x_i(t)$, $i = 1, \ldots, n$. Let the choice functions defining the system be the equations

$$f^1(\mathbf{x}(t), t, \boldsymbol{\alpha}) \equiv 0$$

$$\cdots \cdots \cdots \cdots \cdots$$

$$f^n(\mathbf{x}(t), t, \boldsymbol{\alpha}) \equiv 0 \tag{16-19}$$

where $\boldsymbol{\alpha} = (\alpha_1, \ldots, \alpha_m)$ is a vector of parameters and $\mathbf{x}(t) = (x_1(t), \ldots, x_n(t))$. The functions $f^i(\mathbf{x}(t), t, \boldsymbol{\alpha})$ may be differential or integral equations of the decision variables in terms of time t. In general, as t changes, the $x_i(t)$'s will change. There may be some value of the x_i's, $x_i^0 = x_i(t_0)$, such that for all $t > t_0$,

$$f^j(\mathbf{x}^0, t, \boldsymbol{\alpha}) \equiv 0 \qquad j = 1, \ldots, n \tag{16-20}$$

Equations (16-20) indicate that there are some values, not necessarily unique, of the decision variables such that if the system generates those values, the decision variables will not change over time. Such values of the decision variables can be called equilibrium values (and, in fact, commonly are). In this context, disequilibrium is well defined: $\mathbf{x}(t) \neq \mathbf{x}^0$, but still, $f^j(\mathbf{x}(t), t, \boldsymbol{\alpha}) \equiv 0$, $j = 1, \ldots, n$, in accordance with the theory which defines the system. Even here, however, the term equilibrium can be troublesome. The system may never reach equilibrium. Indeed, for most of the dynamic-adjustment mechanisms used in economics (discussed below), the variables only approach the equilibrium values asymptotically. If a dynamic theory predicts some path of variables $x(t)$, to call this the equilibrium path involves the same problems cited above in the static context. Again there is no disequilibrium consistent with the theory if the whole path $x(t)$ representing the logical implications of the theory is called equilibrium.

Dynamic-adjustment paths $x(t)$ of the type described above are inconsistent with the static or timeless assertions like those made throughout this book. Dynamic considerations cannot be added to those models. Consider the profit-maximization model again. The implied factor-demand curves, if time is explicitly denoted, are

$$x_i(t) = x_i^*(w_1, w_2, p)$$

The adjustment of this firm to a change in a factor price is often conceptually split into stages. For example, the firm facing an increase in w_1 is presumed to move along a short-run factor-demand curve to a lower input of x_1. However, the higher w_1 induces (if x_1 and x_2 are substitutes) a rightward shift in the demand for x_2, increasing x_2. This increase in x_2, however, shifts the demand for x_1 leftward, inducing another shift in the demand for x_2, etc. These adjustments are in fact inconsistent with the original specification of the profit function and the assertion of profit-maximization. If w_1 changes, the theory as it has been asserted implies that the firm will *instantly* move to the new input levels. That is, $\partial x_i/\partial t \to +\infty$. In this model, there are no costs of adjustment. Since profit-maximization is asserted, $pf_i - w_i = 0$ must hold for each factor at all times, i.e., adjustments are instantaneous. If some sort of gradual adjustment is to be considered, a different behavioral assertion or specification of the model, e.g., one in which transition or adjustment costs are explicitly considered, must be used.

Let us now briefly indicate the nature of dynamic-stability analysis. Consider a single, isolated market for one good x. Let the demand and supply curves for x be denoted, respectively, by

$$x_D = D(p, M) \quad \text{and} \quad x_S = S(p) \tag{16-21}$$

where M is money income. Let us begin by assuming that there exists some price p^e for which $x_S = x_D$; that is,

$$D(p^e, M) - S(p^e) = 0 \tag{16-22}$$

Here, we are *not* asserting that this relation holds all the time. It is merely being asserted that *there exists some price p^e for which it holds*. This price p^e is called the *equilibrium price*.

Walrasian Stability

Instead of making specific assertions about the slopes of these functions, let us instead postulate a mechanism by which prices change. Specifically, suppose that the rate of change of price moves directly with excess demand, $E(p) = D(p, M) - S(p)$, or

$$\dot{p} = \frac{dp}{dt} = g(D(p, M) - S(p)) = g(E(p)) \tag{16-23}$$

where $g' > 0$. This relation attempts to capture the notion that if the quantity demanded exceeds the quantity supplied at some price, the sellers of the good will find it to their advantage to raise the price. This price-adjustment hypothesis was first explored by Walras and formulated mathematically by Samuelson. Walras considered the process one of *tâtonnement*, or groping, for an equilibrium. An auctioneer was imagined who called out successive prices and received bids to buy and sell. The price called would be adjusted upward or downward in accordance with the sign of excess demand. No trade would be allowed until the equilibrium-price vector was found [otherwise some sort of nonprice rationing would have to be used, generating in the process income effects which would shift the demand functions $D(p, M)$]. When p^e was located, trade would take place.

Let us make the basic behavioral postulate that this *tâtonnement* process will be successful; i.e., at least for prices "near" p^e, mechanism (16-23) will generate a path of prices which will approach p^e as t increases. That is, we *assert*

$$\lim_{t \to \infty} p(t) = p^e \tag{16-24}$$

Relation (16-24) is called *stability*. While there is an extensive taxonomy of stability concepts, only two will be considered here. If (16-24) holds for *any* initial price p, then the system is called *globally stable*, assuming p^e is unique. (If there is more than one equilibrium-price vector, then if $p(t)$ approaches any of the p^e's, the model is called *system stable*.) Global stability requires very strong mathematical properties on the functions and is a difficult problem to analyze for general functions. For that reason, the more limited, but vastly more tractable, concept of *local* stability is considered. A model is *locally stable* if (16-24) holds for all prices p *in some neighborhood of* p^e.

Let us now refine the assertion made above to mean local stability. What refutable hypotheses emerge from this assertion? At prices "close" to p^e, the function $g(E(p))$ can be represented by a Taylor series expansion. Neglecting terms of order 2 and above (the critical feature of *local* stability), relation (16-23) becomes

$$\frac{dp}{dt} = g(E(p^e)) + g'E'(p^e)(p - p^e) + \cdots \tag{16-25}$$

As long as only *local* stability is considered, the higher-order terms are negligible in comparison with the first-order term above and hence can be ignored. Since $E(p^e) = 0$ by definition of $E(p)$, the adjustment mechanism becomes the differential equation

$$\frac{dp}{dt} = (g'E')(p - p^e) \tag{16-26}$$

The solution of this differential equation, as can be verified by direct substitution, is†

$$p(t) = p^e + (p^0 - p^e)e^{(g'E')t} \tag{16-27}$$

where the initial price p^0 is the arbitrary constant of integration (presumably the old equilibrium).

The assertion of stability requires that the exponential term approach zero as $t \to \infty$. This will occur if the exponent $g'E' < 0$. Since $g' > 0$, the consequence of asserting walrasian local stability is the assertion that in some neighborhood of p^e

$$E' = D_p(p, M) - S_p(p) < 0 \tag{16-28}$$

Equation (16-28) is *not*, however, a refutable proposition about observable behavior. These supply and demand functions are themselves unobservable. Prices and quantities are observable, not these functions. The meaningful theorems are the answers to the question: Suppose some parameter (money income, here) changes; in what direction will price and quantity change?

Consider the behavior of the *equilibrium* price, as defined by (16-22), when M changes. Assuming a functional dependence $p^e = p^e(M)$, defined by solution of (16-22), differentiation of (16-22) with respect to p^e yields

$$D_p \frac{\partial p^e}{\partial M} + D_M - S_p \frac{\partial p^e}{\partial M} = 0$$

$$\frac{\partial p^e}{\partial M} = -\frac{D_M}{D_p - S_p} \tag{16-29}$$

If the good x is asserted to be normal, i.e., not inferior, so that $D_M > 0$, equation (16-29) indicates that $\partial p^e/\partial M > 0$, at least locally, using the assertion of local stability (16-28). More precisely, suppose initially that $p = p^e$. If M, say, increases, the demand curve shifts to the right. The new equilibrium price, according to (16-29), will be higher than before. It is the stability hypothesis (16-24) that $\lim p(t) = p^e$ which guarantees that in the transitional period (which is actually infinitely long in this specification) price will actually tend toward the new equilibrium. This connection between the dynamic hypothesis and the methodology of comparative statics was called the *correspondence principle* by Samuelson. This principle states that comparative statics is an essentially meaningless operation unless an underlying dynamic-adjustment mechanism is postulated and, in addition, the system is dynamically stable enough for the variables actually to tend *toward* the new equilibrium rather than away from it. We shall return to this point later in this chapter.

The implication of stability in one market, as given by (16-28), is that the demand curve has a lower slope than the supply curve. This is satisfied in the usual case, where $D_p < 0, S_p > 0$. However, it is also satisfied, for example, where $D_p < 0$

---

† When we let $p^* = p - p^e$, the deviation of price from its equilibrium value, equation (16-26) becomes $dp^*/dt = kp^*$, with $k = g'E'$; note that $dp^e/dt = 0$ since p^e is constant.

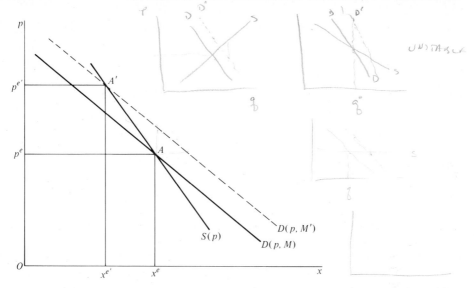

Figure 16-1 Walrasian stability. The supply and demand curves are *both* downward-sloping, though the supply curve is more so. This system is walrasian-stable. Suppose the demand curve shifts to $D(p, M')$, the dotted curve. At old equilibrium price p^e there is now positive excess demand; that is, $E(p^e, M') > 0$. The walrasian adjustment mechanism says that p must rise. In so doing, the price will move towards point A', the new equilibrium, defined by $E(pe', M') = 0$. Here however, the new equilibrium quantity is *less* than the previous one.

and $S_p < 0$, with $|S_p| < |D_p|$, as depicted in Fig. 16-1. (Remember that the dependent variable is on the *horizontal* axis.) If the demand curve shifts to $D(p, M')$, the new equilibrium price $p^{e'}$ will indeed be higher, in accordance with equation (16-29). However, the new equilibrium *quantity* $x^{e'} = D(p^{e'}, M) = S(p^{e'})$ will be *lower* than previously, unlike the case where the supply curve is positively sloped. Hence, we should expect this walrasian-stability mechanism to be insufficiently strong to assert a sign for $\partial x^e / \partial M$. Using the supply identity $x^e = S(p^e)$ leads to $\partial x^e / \partial M = S_p \, \partial p^e / \partial M$, or

$$\frac{\partial x^e}{\partial M} = \frac{-D_M S_p}{D_p - S_p} \tag{16-30}$$

From the stability hypothesis, the denominator $D_p - S_p < 0$. Hence (with $D_M > 0$), $\partial x^e / \partial M \gtrless 0$, as $S_p \gtrless 0$. Since the sign of S_p is not implied by the walrasian dynamic-stability hypothesis, no refutable hypothesis about quantity changes is forthcoming in this elementary model.

Marshallian Stability

An alternative stability mechanism is the one proposed by Alfred Marshall, who treated prices as functions of quantities. At any given quantity, the *height* of the demand curve was called the *demand price* and the height of the supply curve the *supply price.* (In more modern terminology, these values are, of course, the marginal rate of substitution and marginal cost, respectively.) Marshall postulated that whenever demand price exceeded supply price, the *quantity* offered for sale would increase. Likewise, if supply price exceeded demand price, quantity would decrease. This mechanism can be formulated mathematically as

$$\dot{x} = \frac{dx}{dt} = g(D^*(x, M) - S^*(x)) = g(E^*(x)) \tag{16-31}$$

where $g(0) = 0$, $g' > 0$ and $p = D^*(x, M)$ and $p = S^*(x)$ are the inverted demand and supply functions, respectively. As before, let us postulate that there exists an equilibrium price and quantity (p^e, x^e) such that

$$p^e = D^*(x^e, M) = S^*(x^e) \tag{16-32}$$

As in the walrasian analysis, this equation is *not* postulated to hold for all prices and quantities. Only the *existence* of such an equilibrium price and quantity is asserted here. The equation describing the paths of variables is (16-31), the quantity-adjustment equation. Equation (16-32) merely guarantees that it is *possible* to observe $dp/dt = 0$, that is, equilibrium.

The mathematical analysis is formally identical to the walrasian case above. When we expand $E^*(x)$ by a Taylor series around the point x^e, for a sufficiently small neighborhood around the equilibrium quantity, equation (16-31) becomes

$$\frac{dx}{dt} = g'E^{*\prime}(x^e)(x - x^e) \tag{16-33}$$

The solution to this differential equation is

$$x(t) = x^e + (x^0 - x^e)e^{(g'E^{*\prime})t} \tag{16-34}$$

where x^0, the arbitrary constant of integration, is the initial quantity value. The stability condition

$$\lim_{t \to \infty} x(t) = x^e$$

requires that $g'E^{*\prime} < 0$. Since $g' > 0$ by assumption, stability implies

$$E^{*\prime} = D_x^* - S_x^* < 0 \tag{16-35}$$

Again, the signs of the slopes of these (inverse) demand and supply curves are not implied; only the difference has a requisite sign.

Suppose now that the demand curve shifts upward due to a change in income, that is, $D_M^* > 0$, disturbing a preexisting equilibrium. From equation (16-32) defining equilibrium

$$D_x^* \frac{\partial x^e}{\partial M} + D_M^* = S_x^* \frac{\partial x^e}{\partial M}$$

and thus

$$\frac{\partial x^e}{\partial M} = -\frac{D_M^*}{D_x^* - S_x^*} \tag{16-36}$$

Using the assertion of marshallian stability, (16-35), we get $\partial x^e/\partial M > 0$. The new equilibrium quantity sold must be larger than previously. However, in addition to determining a sign for $\partial x^e/\partial M$, the stability condition $\lim x(t) = x^e$ is the guarantee that the new equilibrium will actually be approached. Thus, the derivation of refutable comparative-statics propositions in this model are, as in the walrasian case, dependent upon the assertion of some *dynamic*-stability hypothesis.

Although the marshallian dynamic mechanism implies a sign for *quantity* changes, no refutable proposition emerges for *price* changes. From $p^e = S^*(x^e)$, $\partial p^e/\partial M = S_x^* \, \partial x^e/\partial M$, or

$$\frac{\partial p^e}{\partial M} = -\frac{D_M^* S_x^*}{D_x^* - S_x^*} \tag{16-37}$$

Since $S_x^* \gtreqless 0$, $\partial p^e/\partial M \gtreqless 0$ as $S_x^* \gtreqless 0$. Whereas the walrasian dynamic-adjustment mechanism implies a definitive direction for *price* changes (but not quantity changes), the marshallian mechanism implies a definitive sign for *quantity* changes (but not price changes). In the usual case of downward-sloping demand curves and upward-sloping supply curves, *both* adjustment mechanisms imply the expected changes: an increase in money income (for a normal good) implies an increase in both price and quantity. But this result is dependent upon the additional assertion of the slopes of each of these curves. In Fig. 16-2, an example of a system which is marshallian-stable but not walrasian-stable is shown.

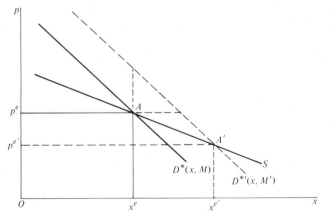

Figure 16-2 Marshallian stability. In this model, while the supply and demand curves are both downward-sloping, the demand curve is more so. Equilibrium is defined as $E^*(x, M) = 0$, where E^* is the excess of demand *price* (marginal value) over supply *price* (marginal cost). The *marshallian* adjustment mechanism postulates that *quantity* will change in the same direction as E^*. Suppose the demand curve shifts *up* to $D^{*'}(x, M')$. (Remember that price is the dependent variable here.) Then at x^e, there is now an excess of demand price over supply price. According to the dynamic postulate, quantity will increase, thereby moving the system toward the new equilibrium A'.

Notice that this model is *not* walrasian-stable. At the old equilibrium price p^e there is now positive excess demand. The walrasian mechanism says that price will increase. But this leads the system *away* from the new equilibrium. Check your understanding of these mechanisms by showing that in Fig. 16-1 the model is not *marshallian*-stable. In the usual case of downward-sloping demand and upward-sloping supply curves, the system is both walrasian-stable and marshallian-stable.

There is a formal *mathematical* similarity between the marshallian and walrasian adjustment mechanisms. It would be unwise to conclude from this, however, that the analyses of price adjustments and quantity adjustments are identical. In the real world, changing quantities is a rather different order of business from changing prices. The latter can be changed with no great resource cost: one simply posts a different price. Changing *quantities*, on the other hand, means employing different amounts of resources—hardly a costless mechanism. The problem stems from the assertion of ad hoc adjustment mechanisms not clearly related to utility- or wealth-maximization.

16.3 MULTIMARKET EQUILIBRIUM AND STABILITY

The previous discussions of stability related to one isolated market. The analysis of interrelated markets proceeds along similar lines but is mathematically more complex. We shall only briefly indicate the results of extending the discussion of stability to multiple markets.

Open Systems: Stability

Suppose first that there are only two interrelated goods, x_1 and x_2, which are transacted at prices p_1 and p_2, respectively. Assume that the demand functions for x_1 and x_2 are functions of both prices. We shall assume income constant in this discussion and thus suppress that argument in the demand functions. These two goods are *not* the entire set of goods produced; hence, this market is called an *open economy*.

The demand functions are thus

$$x_1 = x_1^D(p_1, p_2) \qquad x_2 = x_2^D(p_1, p_2) \tag{16-38}$$

Let us suppose that the supply functions are functions of the good's own price only (though this assumption is nowhere critical):

$$x_1 = x_1^S(p_1) \qquad x_2 = x_2^S(p_1) \tag{16-39}$$

Assume as before that an equilibrium-price vector exists, i.e., there is some p_1^e, p_2^e (not necessarily unique) such that

$$E_1(p_1^e, p_2^e) = x_1^D(p_1^e, p_2^e) - x_1^S(p_1^e) = 0$$

$$E_2(p_1^e, p_2^e) = x_2^D(p_1^e, p_2^e) - x_2^S(p_2^e) = 0 \tag{16-40}$$

The excess demand functions E_1 and E_2 are functions of both prices, a feature of some mathematical consequence. Equations (16-40) merely define the *equilibrium* position; however, prices and quantities are allowed to take on other values. For nonequilibrium prices, the behavioral relations defining the system are

$$\frac{dp_1}{dt} = g_1(E_1(p_1, p_2)) \qquad \frac{dp_2}{dt} = g_2(E_2(p_1, p_2)) \tag{16-41}$$

with $g_i(0) = 0$, $g_i'(E_i) > 0$. That is, in each market, positive excess demand will tend to raise the price in that market, with the rate of price change positively related to the excess demand in that market. The dynamic relations (16-41) include the equilibrium relations (16-40) as long as an equilibrium point exists.

Proceeding as before, each relation in (16-41) is approximated by the first-order terms in a Taylor series expansion. Since the E_i are functions of two variables, this yields

$$\frac{dp_1}{dt} = g_1'(E_{11}(p_1 - p_1^e) + E_{12}(p_2 - p_2^e))$$

$$\frac{dp_2}{dt} = g_2'(E_{21}(p_1 - p_1^e) + E_{22}(p_2 - p_2^e)) \tag{16-42}$$

where $E_{ij} = \partial E_i / \partial p_j$. No conceptual generality is lost by letting g_1' and g_2' be constant; for ease of exposition let $g_1' = k_1$, $g_2' = k_2$. These k_1 and k_2 values are regarded as *speeds of adjustment*. The solution to the simultaneous system of differential equations (16-42) proceeds first by defining new variables $p_1^* = p_1 - p_1^e$, $p_2^* = p_2 - p_2^e$, that is, the deviations of each price from the equilibrium price. Since p_1^e, p_2^e are constant, $dp_i^e/dt = 0$ and hence $dp_i^*/dt = dp_i/dt$. Therefore (16-42) becomes

$$\frac{dp_1^*}{dt} = k_1 E_{11} p_1^* + k_1 E_{12} p_2^*$$

$$\frac{dp_2^*}{dt} = k_2 E_{21} p_1^* + k_2 E_{22} p_2^* \tag{16-43}$$

To find the general solution to these simultaneous linear differential equations, let

$$p_i^* = A_i e^{\lambda t} \tag{16-44}$$

Substituting (16-44) into (16-43), noting that $dp_i^*/dt = \lambda A_i e^{\lambda t} = \lambda p_i^*$, yields

$$\lambda p_1^* = k_1 E_{11} p_1^* + k_1 E_{12} p_2^*$$

$$\lambda p_2^* = k_2 E_{21} p_1^* + k_2 E_{22} p_2^*$$

These equations can be written in matrix form as

$$\begin{pmatrix} k_1 E_{11} - \lambda & k_1 E_{12} \\ k_2 E_{21} & k_2 E_{22} - \lambda \end{pmatrix} \begin{pmatrix} p_1^* \\ p_2^* \end{pmatrix} = \begin{pmatrix} 0 \\ 0 \end{pmatrix} \tag{16-45}$$

Equations (16-45) are two linear equations in two "unknowns," p_1^* and p_2^*. Since the right-hand side of these equations is 0, the solution of these two equations can exist only if the determinant of the left-hand matrix equals 0:

$$\begin{vmatrix} k_1 E_{11} - \lambda & k_1 E_{12} \\ k_2 E_{21} & k_2 E_{22} - \lambda \end{vmatrix} = 0 \tag{16-46}$$

Equations of the form (16-46) are called the *characteristic equation* or *eigenvalue equation* of a matrix. The values of λ which satisfy this equation are called *eigenvalues* or *characteristic values*. There is an extensive literature on the eigenvalue problem as it relates to many important problems of maxima and minima and stability analysis, as in this application. Equation (16-46) is the quadratic equation

$$(k_1 E_{11} - \lambda)(k_2 E_{22} - \lambda) - k_1 k_2 E_{12} E_{21} = 0$$

or $\qquad \lambda^2 - (k_1 E_{11} + k_2 E_{22})\lambda + k_1 k_2 (E_{11} E_{22} - E_{12} E_{21}) = 0 \qquad$ (16-47)

The two values of λ which satisfy this equation can be obtained by use of the quadratic formula. If the solution consists of two complex numbers, these numbers are *complex conjugates*, i.e.,

$$\lambda_1 = a + bi \qquad \lambda_2 = a - bi \qquad (16\text{-}48)$$

If the roots λ_1 and λ_2 of (16-47) are not equal, the general solution of the differential equations (16-43) is

$$p_i^*(t) = A_{i1} e^{\lambda_1 t} + B_{i2} e^{\lambda_2 t} \qquad i = 1, 2$$

Under what conditions will stability result, that is, $\lim p(t) = p^e$ or, equivalently, $\lim p^*(t) = 0$? If λ_1 and λ_2 are real numbers, stability requires $\lambda_1 < 0, \lambda_2 < 0$; that is, both roots of the quadratic equation (16-47) must be negative. If λ_1 and λ_2 are complex and have the form given by (16-48), oscillatory paths of prices will be generated. However, these paths will converge to the equilibrium price *if the real part a of* λ_1 *and* λ_2 is negative; that is, $a < 0$ in (16-48).

The generalization of this analysis to n goods proceeds along similar lines. Let $E_i(\mathbf{p})$ represent the excess demand function of good i, with $\mathbf{p} = (p_1, \ldots, p_n)$. Assume there exists a $\mathbf{p}^e$ such that $E_i(\mathbf{p}^e) = 0, i = 1, \ldots, n$. The equations defining the paths of prices are

$$\frac{dp_i}{dt} = k_i E_i(\mathbf{p}) \qquad i = 1, \ldots, n \qquad (16\text{-}49)$$

By using a Taylor series expansion of $E_i(\mathbf{p})$ and letting $p_i^* = p_i - p_i^e$, equations (16-49) can be approximated by the n equations

$$\frac{dp_i^*}{dt} = k_i \sum_{j=1}^{n} E_{ij} p_j^* \qquad (16\text{-}50)$$

Upon letting $p_i^* = A_i e^{\lambda t}$, the simultaneous equations (16-50) reduce to the matrix equation

$$\begin{pmatrix} k_1 E_{11} - \lambda & k_1 E_{12} & \cdots & k_1 E_{1n} \\ k_2 E_{21} & k_2 E_{22} - \lambda & \cdots & k_2 E_{2n} \\ \cdots\cdots\cdots\cdots\cdots\cdots\cdots\cdots\cdots\cdots\cdots\cdots\cdots \\ k_n E_{n1} & k_n E_{n2} & \cdots & k_n E_{nn} - \lambda \end{pmatrix} \begin{pmatrix} p_1^* \\ p_2^* \\ \cdot \\ p_n^* \end{pmatrix} = \begin{pmatrix} 0 \\ 0 \\ \cdot \\ 0 \end{pmatrix} \qquad (16\text{-}51)$$

These equations have a solution only if the characteristic equation of the E_{ij} matrix is satisfied, i.e., for values of λ which satisfy

$$\begin{vmatrix} k_1 E_{11} - \lambda & k_1 E_{12} & \cdots & k_1 E_{1n} \\ k_2 E_{21} & k_2 E_{22} - \lambda & \cdots & k_2 E_{2n} \\ \cdots\cdots\cdots\cdots\cdots\cdots\cdots\cdots\cdots\cdots \\ k_n E_{n1} & k_n E_{n2} & \cdots & k_n E_{nn} - \lambda \end{vmatrix} = 0 \qquad (16\text{-}52)$$

This is the characteristic equation of the matrix **KE**, where **K** is a diagonal matrix of speeds of adjustment and **E** is the matrix of terms $E_{ij} = \partial E_i / \partial p_j$.

Equation (16-52) is an nth-order polynomial; it can be represented as

$$\lambda^n + b_1 \lambda^{n-1} + b_2 \lambda^{n-2} + \cdots + b_n = 0 \qquad (16\text{-}53)$$

By a famous theorem in algebra, $b_i = (-1)^i$ times the sum of the ith order principal minors of the matrix **KE**. If all the characteristic roots λ are unequal, the solution to the set of simultaneous differential equations (16-50) is given by

$$p_i^*(t) = \sum_{j=1}^{n} A_{ij} e^{\lambda_j t} \qquad (16\text{-}54)$$

where $\lambda_1, \ldots, \lambda_n$ are the n distinct characteristic roots. If a root is repeated r times, the solution to (16-50) is given by

$$p_i^*(t) = \sum_{j=1}^{n-r} (B_{i1} + B_{i2} t + \cdots + B_{i,r-1} t^{r-1}) e^{\lambda_j t} \qquad (16\text{-}55)$$

In either case, the condition that $\lim p_i^*(t) = 0$ implies that the real parts of the characteristic roots $\lambda_1, \ldots, \lambda_n$ (even if some are repeated) are all negative. A matrix whose characteristic roots are all negative is therefore called a *stable matrix*.

The above theorems are not much help in determining the quantitative properties of the E_{ij} matrix which leads to stability of the system. Further help is provided by the following well-known theorems.

Theorem 1[†] If a matrix **A** is symmetric, that is, $a_{ij} = a_{ji}$, then the eigenvalues are all real.

Theorem 2[‡] If a matrix **A** is symmetric and stable, **A** is necessarily negative definite.

[†] See, for example, G. Hadley, "Linear Algebra," Addison-Wesley Publishing Company, Inc., Reading, Mass., 1961.

[‡] Ibid.

Theorem 3 (Routh-Hurwitz)[†] Let $b_i = (-1)^i$ times the sum of all ith-order principal minors of a real $n \times n$ matrix $\mathbf{A}$. Then $\mathbf{A}$ is stable if and only if

1. $b_i > 0$, $i = 1, \ldots, n$

2. $\begin{vmatrix} b_1 & b_3 \\ 1 & b_2 \end{vmatrix} > 0 \qquad \begin{vmatrix} b_1 & b_3 & b_5 \\ 1 & b_2 & b_4 \\ 0 & b_1 & b_3 \end{vmatrix} > 0$

and so forth where $b_i = 0$ if $i > n$.

Theorem 4 (Lyapunov)[‡] A real matrix $\mathbf{A}$ is stable if and only if there exists a symmetric positive definite matrix $\mathbf{B}$ such that $\mathbf{BA} + \mathbf{A'B}$ is negative definite (where $\mathbf{A'}$ is the transpose of $\mathbf{A}$). (Of course, $\mathbf{B}$ may be a positive diagonal matrix such as the speed-of-adjustment matrix $\mathbf{K}$ above.)

A complete discussion of the known implications of these and other theorems related to matrix stability is beyond the scope of this book.[§] Let us briefly note the following, however. For 2×2 matrices, the Routh-Hurwitz theorem implies that the *sum* of the diagonal elements is negative and the whole determinant is positive if the matrix is stable. Consider then the two-equation system (16-40) and (16-41). Suppose an equilibrium position is disturbed a slight amount (within the region of local stability) by, say, a shift in the excess demand curve of the first good. We have

$$E_1(p_1^e, p_2^e, \alpha_1) = 0 \qquad E_2(p_1^e, p_2^e, \alpha_2) = 0$$

Differentiating with respect to α_1 and solving gives

$$\frac{\partial p_1^e}{\partial \alpha_1} = \frac{-E_{1\alpha}E_{22}}{E_{11}E_{22} - E_{12}E_{21}} \tag{16-56}$$

$$\frac{\partial p_2^e}{\partial \alpha_1} = \frac{E_{1\alpha}E_{21}}{E_{11}E_{22} - E_{12}E_{21}} \tag{16-57}$$

Unfortunately, local stability alone is not sufficiently powerful to sign these expressions. [Of course, (16-57) would be unsignable even under a maximization hypothesis.] By the Routh-Hurwitz theorem, the denominators are positive. But that theorem merely implies that $E_{11} + E_{22} < 0$ *not* that both $E_{11} < 0$ and

---

[†] See F. R. Gantmacher, "The Theory of Matrices," vol. II, Chelsea Publishing Company, New York, 1960.

[‡] Ibid.

[§] See, for example, J. Quirk and R. Saposnik, "Introduction to General Equilibrium Theory and Welfare Economics," McGraw-Hill, New York, 1968.

$E_{22} < 0$, as in the case of maximization models. We *can* infer that at least one of $\partial p_i^e / \partial \alpha_i > 0$ (assuming $E_{i\alpha_i} > 0$) but not *necessarily* both. Thus, local dynamic stability is a rather weak behavioral postulate when taken alone; it is, for example, insufficiently powerful to derive the law of demand in multimarket equilibrium.

Closed Economies

When combined with other hypotheses, local dynamic stability can imply some refutable hypotheses. Consider a pure-trade model with $n + 1$ commodities. That is, suppose there are fixed stocks of the $n + 1$ goods, $x_0^0, x_1^0, \ldots, x_n^0$ available. Consumers own these stocks in varying amounts and trade them in the marketplace at prices $p_0, p_1, \ldots, p_n$, respectively. In the aggregate, if the total amount purchased equals the amount sold, then

$$\sum_{i=0}^{n} p_i x_i^D(p) = \sum_{i=0}^{n} p_i x_i^0 \tag{16-58}$$

When we let the aggregate demand $E_i(p) = x_i^D - x_i^0$, equation (16-58) becomes

$$\sum_{i=0}^{n} p_i E_i = 0 \tag{16-59}$$

known as *Walras' law*. The total value of excess demand in a closed economy equals 0, *even at nonequilibrium prices*. Suppose now that n of these $n + 1$ markets, say goods 1 to n, are in equilibrium. Then, by definition, $E_i(p_i^e) = 0$, $i = 1, \ldots, n$. Then, assuming $p_0 \neq 0$, necessarily, $E_0(p_0) = 0$; that is, $p_0 = p_0^e$. The $(n+1)$st market must also be in equilibrium. This system therefore reduces to an n-equation system. If the demand curves (and hence the excess demands) are assumed homogeneous of degree zero, then one price, say p_0, can arbitrarily be set equal to unity. Good x_0 becomes the numeraire commodity, and the system reduces to

$$E_i(p_1^e, \ldots, p_n^e) = 0 \qquad i = 1, \ldots, n \tag{16-60}$$

as before, in the open economy.

With fixed initial endowments, $\partial E_i / \partial p_j = \partial x_i^D / \partial p_j$. If these are the demand curves of utility-maximizing consumers, $\partial x_i^D / \partial p_j = (\partial x_i^D / \partial p_j)_U + (x_j^D - x_j^0) \times (\partial x_i / \partial M)$, the Slutsky equation for trading models. If the income effects are all symmetric, so that $\partial x_i^D / \partial p_j = \partial x_j^D / \partial p_i$, then the matrix $\mathbf{E} = (E_{ij})$ is symmetric. If it is also stable, then by theorem 2 above, the principal minors of E alternate in sign; in particular, the $(n - 1)$st- and nth-order principal minors are of opposite sign. In this case, the comparative statics of this model follows exactly that of the corresponding maximization models. An outward shift in any demand function will cause an increase in the price of that good.

16.4 STABILITY WITH LAGGED ADJUSTMENT

In certain economic models, the assumption of a discrete time lag in the adjustment mechanism is incorporated. Two of the most famous cases of this adjustment process are the so-called *cobweb phenomenon* (usually applied to agriculture) and the Cournot duopoly solution. Let us investigate these separate (though methodologically similar) processes.

Suppose the demand for a given good is dependent upon the *current* price of that good, $q_t = f(p_t)$. Let us specify this demand function as the linear function

$$q_t^D = a - bp_t \tag{16-61}$$

Suppose now the supply is a function not of *current* price but of the price prevailing at a previous time:

$$q_t^S = c + dp_{t-1} \tag{16-62}$$

Assuming that what is brought to the market is sold at some price p_t, prices must obey the relation implied by $q_t^D = q_t^S$, or

$$a - bp_t = c + dp_{t-1} \tag{16-63}$$

This type of equation is called a *difference* equation. Its solution proceeds along lines similar to differential equations. (In fact, the algebra of difference equations is identical to that of differential equations. Knowledge of one type of equation can be applied directly to the other type by making suitable changes.)

The first question is whether there exists an equilibrium price p^e such that

$$\lim_{t \to \infty} p_t = p^e \tag{16-64}$$

If so, p^e must satisfy

$$a - bp^e = c + dp^e$$

or

$$p^e = \frac{a - c}{b + d} \tag{16-65}$$

The parameters a and b must both be positive to make the demand curve slope downward in the positive quadrant. If $d > 0$, the supply function is upward-sloping. Hence, $p^e > 0$ if $a > c$, that is, if the demand function does not intersect the quantity axis before supply becomes positive. Let us assume that this condition holds so that a $p^e > 0$ exists. Define $p_t^* = p_t - p^e$ as before; i.e., let p_t^* represent the *deviation* of price from the equilibrium price p^e. Then $p_t = p_t^* + (a - c)/(b + d)$. Making this substitution in equation (16-63) yields

$$a - bp_t^* - \frac{b(a - c)}{b + d} = c + dp_{t-1}^* + \frac{d(a - c)}{b + d}$$

This equation simplifies to

$$bp_t^* + dp_{t-1}^* = (a - c) - \frac{(b + d)(a - c)}{b + d} = 0$$

or
$$p_t^* = -\frac{d}{b}p_{t-1}^* \tag{16-66}$$

This difference equation can be solved by sight. Clearly,

$$p_t^* = A\left(-\frac{d}{b}\right)^t \tag{16-67}$$

where A is an arbitrary constant. That (16-67) is a solution to (16-66) can be verified by direct substitution. The stability condition (16-64) clearly requires that

$$\left|\frac{d}{b}\right| < 1 \tag{16-68}$$

since any number less than 1 raised to larger and larger powers approaches 0. Then, $\lim p_t^* = 0$, and thus $\lim p_t = 0 + p^e = p^e$. Figure 16-3 shows this stability condition graphically.

The relevant question for the derivation of meaningful theorems, however, is: Does the implication of stability, $|d/b| < 1$, imply refutable comparative-statics theorems? Suppose this market is initially at some equilibrium position. Let the demand curve shift by increasing the value of a. If $|d/b| > 1$, we shall expect to observe ever-larger absolute deviations in price from one time period to the next; that is, $\lim |p_t - p_{t-1}| = \infty$. If $|d/b| < 1$, the deviations must become less and less. Though not comparative-statics results, strictly speaking, these are observable events and thus subject to refutation. Note that $p_t^* = p_t - p^e$ for the *new* equilibrium price p^e is *not* observable, since p^e is not observable.

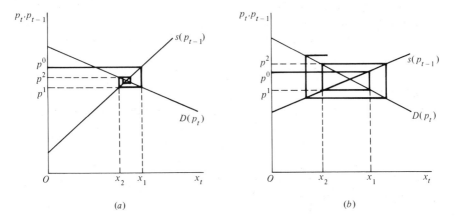

(a) (b)

Figure 16-3 (*a*) Lagged stability. Suppose price is at p^0 due to a shift in one or more of the curves. At $p = p^0$, there is excess supply. Price will fall in the next time period to p^1. At $p = p^1$, there is excess demand, and price will rise to $p = p^2$ in the next period. More specifically, when $p = p^0$, $x = x^1$ is produced. With supply vertical at this level, the current demand curve D produces a price of p^1. At $p = p^1$, suppliers produce $x = x_2$, generating price $p = p^2$, etc. Since the demand curve has a flatter slope than the supply curve ($1/b < 1/d$, or $d/b < 1$), this process *converges* to a new equilibrium. (*b*) Lagged instability. $d/b > 1$, and the adjustment process *diverges* away from equilibrium. The reason for the descriptive term cobweb theorem is obvious.

The comparative-statics results are obtained as before. Using (16-65), which defines the equilibrium price, then assuming stability, we get

$$\frac{\partial p^e}{\partial a} = \frac{1}{b + d} \tag{16-69}$$

We see from equation (16-69) that stability alone does *not* imply a sign for $\partial p^e/\partial a$. Hence, this type of lagged response stability is a very weak hypothesis in regard to the derivation of refutable comparative-statics hypotheses. If it is asserted, however, *either* that the demand curve is downward-sloping *or* that the supply curve is upward-sloping (or both), then since $|b/d| < 1$ for stability, $b + d > 0$ and $\partial p^e/\partial a > 0$ as expected. But this comparative-statics result depends on the incorporation of empirical knowledge in addition to the stability hypothesis. Similar results follow with regard to changes in the other parameters in the model.

Cournot Duopoly

Consider the situation where exactly two firms produce the same item and face the same aggregate downward-sloping demand curve. What levels of output will each firm produce? If the firms can agree to a mutually satisfactory division of the spoils, one solution to this problem is for the two firms to merge and to maximize monopolistic profits. Antitrust considerations aside, these contracts are not easy to achieve and enforce, especially if the cost functions of the two firms differ. One of the earliest nonmerger solutions was posed by the French economist A. Cournot.† Cournot assumed two interdependent demand functions, with price expressed as a function of the total amount sold, i.e.,

$$p = p(x_1 + x_2) \tag{16-70}$$

where x_i is the amount sold by the ith firm, $i = 1, 2$. Let $C_i(x_i)$ denote the cost function of firm i. The objective function of each firm is postulated as

$$\max_{x_i} p(x_1 + x_2)x_i - C_i(x_j) \tag{16-71}$$

However, the other firm's output impinges on the decision of each firm, yet neither firm can control the other firm's output. For each firm the profit-maximizing conditions are

$$x_i p'(x_1 + x_2) + p - C_i'(x_i) = 0 \qquad i = 1, 2 \tag{16-72}$$

Cournot defined a *reaction* function for each firm as the explicit solution for x_i in terms of x_j of the first-order conditions (16-72)

$$x_1 = x_1^*(x_2) \qquad x_2 = x_2^*(x_1) \tag{16-73}$$

---

† A. Cournot, "Researches into the Mathematical Principles of the Theory of Wealth," trans. Nathaniel T. Bacon, The Macmillan Company, New York, 1897.

That is, suppose, initially, $x_2 = x_2^0$. Then some level of $x_1^* = x_1^*(x_2^0) = x_1^1$ would be chosen by firm 1. Then firm 2 would react to this by choosing $x_2 = x_2^*(x_1^1) = x_2^1$; then firm 1 would react again; then firm 2, etc. Under what conditions will this process converge to the simultaneous solution of (16-72) or, equivalently, (16-73)? Let us introduce a simple specification of the model. Let the demand function $p(x_1 + x_2) = a - b(x_1 + x_2)$, and let $C_1(x_1) = k_1 x_1^2$, $C_2(x_2) = k_2 x_2^2$. Then firm 1 maximizes

$$\pi^1 = [a - b(x_1 + x_2)]x_1 - k_1 x_1^2$$

Differentiating this with respect to x_1 yields

$$a - 2bx_1 - bx_2 - 2k_1 x_1 = 0$$

or, the reaction function for firm 1,

$$x_1 = \frac{a - bx_2}{2b + 2k_1} \tag{16-74}$$

Similarly, the reaction function for x_2 is found to be

$$x_2 = \frac{a - bx_1}{2b + 2k_2} \tag{16-75}$$

Let us now explicitly introduce a *lagged* adjustment mechanism, $x_2^t = x_2^*(x_1^{t-1})$ and $x_1^t = x_1^*(x_2^{t-1})$. Then, say, (16-75) becomes

$$x_2^t = \frac{a - bx_1^{t-1}}{2b + 2k_2}$$

Substituting this expression into (16-74) (with appropriate time superscripts), noting that $x_2^{t-1} = x_2^*(x_1^{t-2})$, yields

$$x_1^t = \frac{a}{2b + 2k_1} - \frac{b}{2b + 2k_1} \frac{a - bx_1^{t-2}}{2b + 2k_2}$$

This is a *second-order* difference equation, of the form

$$x_1^t = K_1 + K_2 x_1^{t-2} \tag{16-76}$$

where, in particular, $K_2 = b^2/(2b + 2k_1)(2b + 2k_2)$. If an equilibrium x_1^e exists, it must be given by

$$x_1^e = K_1 + K_2 x_1^e$$

or

$$x_1^e = \frac{K_1}{1 - K_2}$$

Let $y_1^t = x_1^t - x_1^e = x_1^t - K_1/(1 - K_2)$. Then (16-76) reduces to

$$y_1^t = K_2 y_1^{t-2} \tag{16-77}$$

The solution to this equation is found by letting $y_1^t = \lambda^t$ as before. Then (16-77) becomes

$$\lambda^2 - K_2 = 0$$

or $\lambda = \pm K_2^{1/2}$. The general solution to (16-76) is

$$x_1^t = x_1^e + A K_2^{t/2} + B(-K_2)^{t/2} \qquad (16\text{-}78)$$

where A and B are arbitrary constants.

In this case, stability requires that $|K_2| < 1$, or

$$\left| \frac{b^2}{(2b + 2k_1)(2b + 2k_2)} \right| < 1$$

If $b, k_i > 0$, this restriction is automatically satisfied. However, this stability restriction is not as easily satisfied for all Cournot specifications. In this case, however, if $b, k_i > 0$, then a shift in the demand curve, say, will produce a new set of reactions which will ultimately converge to the new equilibrium.

Although the above is an interesting model of interindividual actions, it leaves several important questions open. Probably the most critical is the problem of policing the final prices. Each firm will find it to its own advantage to cheat and undersell the other firm. Second, this reaction process is a no-learning model. In spite of repeated failures to achieve overall profit-maximization, the firms still behave in the same fashion.

16.5 OVERVIEW AND CONCLUSIONS

The purpose of this chapter has been to evaluate in a meaningful way the notions of equilibrium, disequilibrium, and stability. One problem not analyzed was the existence of an equilibrium-price vector in the first place. It is very easy to draw supply and demand curves which never intersect or indifference curves in an Edgeworth box diagram which have no tangency. Students can practice this artwork for themselves. A vast, highly mathematical literature has arisen specifying the conditions under which equilibrium exists.

It is important, of course, to check the logical consistency of one's model. A model which purports to explain how equilibrium prices or quantities vary would be empty unless it is possible for equilibrium to exist. However, asserting that some consistent solution (equilibrium) to a system of equations exists is a weaker, perhaps much weaker, assertion than finding some set of sufficient properties so that *any* functions with those properties will generate an equilibrium. Second, and perhaps more important, the literature on existence of equilibrium has focused on achieving some solution to a system of equations in terms of *prices* only. In general, real-world contracts allow for much more complicated transactions, e.g., contracts specifying quantity, quality, and date of delivery, in addition to price. (Indeed, as mentioned earlier, why else would contracts exist?) As we saw in the section on sharecropping in the previous chapter, individuals will specify many variables in a contract in order to extract the gains from trade. Lastly, if one perceives as the function of science the explanation of events, questions of nonexistent equilibria are virtually irrelevant. Clearly something *is* happening in the world. The object of science is to explain these events. Dwelling on the possible nonexistence of those events is of questionable empirical value.

We began this book with a discussion of the structure of theories. Recall that a theory consists of three conceptually different parts. A set of behavioral postulates A (assertions, axioms) is *asserted*. These generally universal-type statements define the basic paradigm of the science. These assertions A imply that under certain observable test conditions C various observable events E will occur. In symbols, $A \cdot C \rightarrow E$. In economics, the assertions A include statements such as "individuals prefer more goods to less," "marginal rates of substitution diminish," etc. These assertions form the first class of postulates that Samuelson outlined under which meaningful theorems were derived: maximizing behavior. The second such category of empirical input in economic theories, as mentioned in Sec. 16.1, is the direct *assumption* of functional firms, parameter values, etc. These are assumptions about test conditions, i.e., about the particular nature of the problem at hand. Economists will frequently *assume* that regression equations are linear, that production functions are Cobb-Douglas, etc., in an attempt to simplify the economic paradigm and thus render it tractable. Hence, some input under category 2 is necessary in empirical science.

Samuelson's third hypothesis, that equilibrium is stable, is an attempt to replace the explicit assertions of maximizing behavior with a weaker statement of how markets operate. This methodology is a departure from the explicitly choice-theoretic microeconomic paradigm. Although it is frequently asserted that individual maximizers will behave "as if" to stabilize markets, this casts quite a different tone on the analysis. Without the unifying hypothesis of maximizing behavior, models which merely assert some mystical stability properties tend to be ad hoc, i.e., contrived to meet a specific problem. Indeed, this is the fundamental criticism of the cobweb and duopoly lagged-adjustment models presented in the last section. They are not easily made consistent with wealth-maximization.

Samuelson went on to assert a stronger proposition, however. The dynamic-adjustment mechanism is not to be merely one more behavioral assertion. It is conceived of as playing the most fundamental role in the model. Comparative-statics results are to be dependent upon the existence of a dynamic-adjustment mechanism. For, it is argued, to assert that some equilibrium price will, say, increase when income increases, one must postulate an actual mechanism by which the price gets raised. It is conceivable that the dynamic-adjustment mechanism will move the price, in this case, *away* from the new equilibrium price, rendering the system unstable.

The validity of this view is based upon one's notion of equilibrium. Consider again the logical structure of theories, $A \cdot C \rightarrow E$. In the static models, i.e., ones for which an explicit time path of variable changes is not predicted, the events E *are* the comparative-statics theorems concerning instantaneous rates of change of variables with respect to parameter changes, i.e., changes in some test conditions C. These events E are often termed equilibrium positions. However, as discussed above, there can be no disequilibrium in these models. The disequilibrium events "not E" are in fact refutations of either the asserted axioms A or the empirical validity of the test conditions, or assumptions, C (or both). Dynamic stability in these models is a *deus ex machina*, an additional assertion which may very well be in conflict with the postulates of maximixing behavior, e.g., if noninstantaneous adjustment is postulated in a world of utility or wealth maximizers with no costs of transacting. Thus, the law of demand for factors of production for static profit-maximizing firms or for income-compensated consumer demand curves is in no way dependent upon a dynamic-adjustment mechanism. The assertions of profit- or utility-maximization are sufficient to imply these results.

In the explicitly dynamic models, equilibrium is most commonly defined as that subset of the events for which the variables take on stationary values, that is, $\mathbf{dx}/dt = 0$, where $\mathbf{x}$ is the vector of choice variables. However, equilibrium is also used, for example, in some growth models, to refer to the whole time path of predicted values. Again, the events "not E" are time paths which refute the theory. In the market equilibrium models discussed above, equilibrium is defined as when $E_i = D_i - S_i = 0$. Not surprisingly, if some parameter changes, this theory as it stands is too weak (in fact, nothing at all has been asserted about behavior) to derive refutable hypotheses. The postulate of dynamic stability is merely one way of making the set of assertions A sufficiently powerful to derive a refutable hypothesis. It is not more fundamental than the assertions of maximizing behavior contained in Samuelson's category 1. It is simply that arbitrarily defining the solution to some equations as representing equilibrium is merely definitional. İt is impossible to derive refutable theorems from definitions, i.e., without adding *some* behavior, whether it is utility-maximization or some more vague hypothesis leading to stability. But it is the adequate vs. inadequate specification of models, not statics vs. dynamics, which is at issue.

The confusion of these issues has produced what this author considers to be methodologically strange theorems. One of the most famous theorems of multi-market equilibrium is the statement that if all goods in a general-equilibrium pure-trade model are gross substitutes, that is, $\partial E_i/\partial p_j = \partial x_i^D/\partial p_j > 0$, $i \neq j$, then the equilibrium defined by $E_i = 0$, $i = 1, \ldots, n$, is stable. ($E_{ii} < 0$ is also assumed.)†
The purpose of asserting *nonobservable* hypotheses such as *utility-maximization* or *stability* of markets is to derive refutable propositions such as, "if some price p_j *increases*, the consumption of some good x_i will *increase*." This latter statement represents (potentially) observable events. The above theorem uses the observable events, the goals of theory, to assert something nonobservable, stability! Of what use is such a theorem? If behavior is sufficiently well specified to imply the choice functions known as demand functions in a pure-trade situation, and if it is already known that an increase in some price will reduce the demand for that good and increase it for all other goods, what else is there left to specify? Some price changes are implied. A dynamic specification of the variables is merely a prediction in *greater detail* than the comparative-statics predictions of the response of variables to parameter changes. If the dynamic time path is inconsistent with the

---

† See Quirk and Saposnik, op. cit.

7 (a) Follows from $V_i = F'(U)U_i$. (b) Use product rule on above; $V_{ij} = F'U_{ij} + F''U_i U_j$. Although $F' > 0$ is stipulated, F'' can have either sign.

8 $\partial U/\partial p_1 = -\frac{1}{9}(x_2/x_1)^{2/3}(M/p_1^2) < 0$; yes

$\partial U/\partial p_2 = -\frac{4}{9}(x_1/x_2)^{1/3}(M/p_2^2) < 0$; yes

$\partial U/\partial M = \frac{1}{9}(x_2/x_1)^{2/3}(1/p_1) + \frac{4}{9}(x_1/x_2)^{1/3}(1/p_2) > 0$; yes

Section 3.7

2 (a) $y = \log(x_1 x_2)$; $x_1 x_2$ is homogeneous. (c) $y = F(z) = z^2 - z$, where $z = x_1 x_2$, a homogeneous function.

4 Note that $f_i = F'h_i$; slopes of level curves are f_i/f_j; result follows.

5 Apply Euler's theorem to f_1

6 Follow proof in text

CHAPTER 4

Section 4.2

1 (a) The origin; saddlepoint; (b) $(\frac{22}{7}, \frac{16}{7})$; minimum; (c) $(4, 2)$; maximum.

3 When $\alpha + \beta = 1$, $L^2 K^\beta$ is (weakly) concave.

5 $g_i = F'f_i$; since at a stationary value $f_i = g_i = 0$, $g_{ij} = F'f_{ij}$, result follows by applying second-order conditions.

Section 4.5

1 Since the term f_{12} enters the expressions for $\partial x_1^*/\partial p$ and $\partial x_2^*/\partial p$, these partials are indeterminate in sign. If one assumes, however, that both are negative, then after eliminating the positive term in the denominators, a contradiction of the second-order conditions occurs after a little manipulation.

2 Since $y^* = f(x_1^*, x_2^*)$, $\partial y^*/\partial w_1 = f_1(\partial x_1^*/\partial w_1) + f_2(\partial x_2^*/\partial w_1)$. Applying equations (4-20) gives the negative of the expression for $\partial x_1^*/\partial p$. The same analysis follows for $\partial y^*/\partial w_2$.

3 Assuming $\alpha_1 + \alpha_2 < 1$ (otherwise the second-order conditions for profit-maximization are violated), the factor demand for x_1, letting $\beta = \alpha_1 + \alpha_2 - 1$ (note $\beta < 0$) is

$$x_1^* = \alpha_1^{(\alpha_2 - 1)/\beta} \alpha_2^{-\alpha_2/\beta} p^{-\beta} w_1^{(1 - \alpha_2)/\beta} w_2^{\alpha_2/\beta}$$

Since the exponent of w_1 is negative, $\partial x_1^*/\partial w_1 < 0$. To find the factor demand for x_2, interchange all the 1s and 2s.

4 (a) Follows from $f_{12} = f_{21}$, $\partial x_1^*/\partial w_2 = \partial x_2^*/\partial w_1$. (b) Follows from equations (4-20b) and (4-20c). (c) They aren't; $\partial x_i^*/\partial w_j$ involves more than simply f_{ij}. Other second partials will be present.

5 (a) $\partial y_1^*/\partial t = \pi_{22}/(\pi_{11}\pi_{22} - \pi_{12}^2) < 0$; (b) nothing; $\pi_{12} = C''(y)$ has either sign.

7 (a) $\partial y^*/\partial t < 0$; $\partial y_i^*/\partial t \gtrless 0$, $i = 1, 2$. (b) $(dy_1/dt)_{y_2} < 0$.

CHAPTER 5

Text

1 (a) -1, (b) 2, (c) -2 (short cut: add row 3 to row 1), (d) 2.

3 Apply Cramer's rule.

5 (a) By an increase in k_1. (b) yes; find $\partial x_1^*/\partial k_1$. (c) can go either way. (d) Wages are not parameters here; one cannot write $x_i = x_i^*(w_1, w_2, p)$, as in the competitive case. (e) Essentially the same analysis as the competitive case.

APPENDIX

1 rank $\mathbf{A} = 1$, rank $\mathbf{B} = 2$, rank $\mathbf{C} = 3$; $|\mathbf{C}| \neq 0$.

3 $\mathbf{A}^{-1}(\mathbf{A}^{-1})^{-1} = \mathbf{I}$ by definition. However, $\mathbf{A}^{-1}\mathbf{A} = \mathbf{I}$. Since inverses are unique, $\mathbf{A} = (\mathbf{A}^{-1})^{-1}$.

6 Let h_i, $h_j = 0$, $i, j = 2, \ldots, n$. Then $\mathbf{h}'\mathbf{A}\mathbf{h} = a_{11}h_1^2 < 0$, hence $a_{11} < 0$. A similar procedure shows $a_{ii} < 0$, $i = 1, \ldots, n$.

7 Apply the definition of orthogonal matrices.

CHAPTER 6

3 Convexity of indifference curves means $-U_{11}p_2^2 + 2U_{12}p_1p_2 - U_{22}p_1^2 > 0$. This neither implies nor is implied by $U_{11} < 0$, $U_{22} < 0$ because of the U_{12} term.

4 (a) $x_1^* = 1$, $x_2^* = 1$; max. (b) $x_1^* = 1$, $x_2^* = 1$; min. (c) $x_1^* = M/2p_1$, $x_2^* = M/2p_2$; max. (d) $x_1^* = (p_2 U^0/p_1)^{1/2}$, $x_2^* = (p_1 U^0/p_2)^{1/2}$; min.

CHAPTER 7

3 The factor demands derived in this chapter are functions of factor prices and output level. Previously, they were functions of factor prices and output-*price*. They are different functions. They are both, however, downward-sloping in their own price, perhaps the only property useful for deriving refutable hypotheses.

4 For two factors, (i) and (ii) are equivalent (see problem 4, Sec. 4.5) whereas by (iii), the factors are always substitutes. For more than two factors, knowledge that two factors are substitutes (or complements) by any one or two definitions provides no information about the sign of the third type of expression.

7 (a) Apply Euler's theorem to f_L, f_K. (d) Follows from $dK/dL = -f_L/f_K$. (f) Apply the formulas in (a) by multiplying row 1 by L, row 2 by K and adding one row to the other. Repeat for columns. What effects do these manipulations have on Δ?

CHAPTER 8

1 Diminishing MRS is a two-dimensional concept; quasi-concavity is a much stronger restriction of the curvature of the utility function.

3 None.

7 No. If $U(x_1, \ldots, x_n)$ is a utility function and $V = F(U)$, $F'(U) > 0$, V_{ij} and U_{ij} need not have the same sign.

8 (a) (i). (b) Yes. (c) For (ii) yes, for (i), no, because of the possibility of asymmetrical income effects.

10 (a) Can change its size and sign. (b) No such law. (c) No effect. (d) No effect. (e) No effect. (f) Size can change; not the sign, however.

12 (a) Not necessarily. (b) Intuitively, if a person is a net saver this year, an increase in the interest rate will provide a larger income next year, and vice versa.

16 (a) Differentiate the identity with respect to M, noting that $\lambda^M = \partial U^*/\partial M$. (b) Differentiate the identity with respect to p_2, using the above and part (a) of problem 15.

18 (a) Vertically parallel means $\partial(U_1/U_2)/\partial x_2 = 0$. Use the quotient rule on this expression; the numerator is proportional to D_{31}, the relevant cofactor in the expression for $\partial x_1^M/\partial M$. (b) Follows from part (a) and the Slutsky equation. (c) Note that $U_1/U_2 = 1/x_1$, a function of x_1 only. Hence, U_1/U_2 is independent of x_2. (d) Show that $\partial x_2^M/\partial p_1 = 0$.

CHAPTER 9

2 In a neighborhood around some p, $\pi^* > \pi^S > \pi$. Thus, $\partial^2\pi^*/\partial p^2 = \partial y^*/\partial p \geq \partial y^S/\partial p = \partial^2\pi^S/\partial p^2$.

3 The term $\partial\lambda^*/\partial y_0$ is a diagonal element of $\mathscr{L}_{\alpha\alpha}^*$; the matrix $\mathscr{L}_{\alpha\alpha}^* - \mathscr{L}_{\alpha\alpha}^S$ is negative (semi)definite. Its diagonal terms are therefore nonpositive.

4 Same analysis as in problem 3.

5 (a) Note that AC is linear in w_1 and w_2. Hence, $AC^*(w_1, w_2)$ is concave in w_1 and w_2, and $\partial^2 AC^*/\partial w_i^2 = \partial(x_i^*/y^*)/\partial w_i \leq 0$. (b) Use quotient rule on part (a). (c) $AC_{ij}^* = AC_{ji}^*$. (d) Note that $x_1/x_2 = (x_1/y)/(x_2/y)$. Use part (a) and homogeneity of x_i^*/y^* in w_1 and w_2.

6 Set this problem up as a *constrained* maximum, with $f(x_1, x_2) = v$ as the constraint. The envelope results follow easily then.

7 (a) No. (b) These short-run factor-demand functions are not the first partials (slopes) of the profit function; hence, the curvature properties of π^* do not relate directly to these demand functions. (c) Letting $\lambda^* = \partial \pi^*/\partial M$, where M is total expenditure, note that $\lambda^* = 0$, but $\partial\lambda^*/\partial M < 0$ (why?). Note that $\pi_{w_i}^* = -x_i^*(1 + \lambda^*)$, from which useful reciprocity relations can be derived, in conjunction with $\pi_M^* = \lambda^*$. Combine with $\pi_{w_i w_i}^* > 0$.

CHAPTER 10

1 Returns to scale is a broader concept than homogeneity.

2 $C = w_1 x_1 + w_2 x_2 = pf_1 x_1 + pf_2 x_2 = rpy = rTR$. This model does not specify the recipient of these rents. (Indeed, there is no explanation of who it is that is maximizing profits.) Entry will always exist, driving firm size, output-price, and profits to 0.

3 (a) $y = \log 4x_1 x_2$

4 Suppose x_1 is held fixed. Then from Euler's theorem, $\sum_{i=1}^{n} f_i x_i = ry$ and $\sum_{i=2}^{n} f_i x_i = sy$. Combine and integrate, remembering that the arbitrary constant of integration is a function of the variables held fixed in partial differentiation. Apply to each x_i in turn.

6 Since for homothetic functions, $C = J(y)A(w_1, w_2)$, $MC = J'(y)A(w_1, w_2)$ and $AC = [J(y)/y]A(w_1, w_2)$. At min AC, $AC = MC$, or $J' = J/y$. Integration yields, for min AC outputs only, $J(y) = ky$. Hence, for such points, $AC = kA(w_1, w_2)$, a function of factor prices only.

CHAPTER 11

1 The border-preserving principal minors of order 2 are all positive; in the case of separable utility functions, this condition implies $-U_i'' p_j^2 - U_j'' p_i^2 > 0$, all $i, j, i \neq j$. Hence, there cannot be *two* U_i'''s which are both positive, otherwise one of the above conditions would be violated.

   We have $U_i'(x_i^M) = \lambda^M p_i$. Differentiating with respect to M gives $U_i''(\partial x_i^M/\partial M) = p_i \, \partial\lambda^M/\partial M$, from which parts (i) of (a) and (b) follow. For the compensated demands, $\lambda^U U_i'(x_i) = p_i$. Differentiate with respect to p_j, noting that $\partial\lambda^U/\partial p_j = \partial x_i^U/\partial U_0$. Can inferiority or superiority be defined in terms of the sign of $\partial x_i^U/\partial U_0$?

2 Use the same hints.

3 From envelope considerations, one gets *Roy's equality*, $U_{p_i}^* = -\lambda x_i^M$. Differentiate with respect to p_k, noting that $U_{p_i p_k}^* = 0$. Do the same for $U_{p_j}^*$. Note that $U_{p_i}^* = V_{r_i}^*(1/M)$.

4 Use problem 3 and part (a) of problem 2.

7 $U_i'(x_i) = \lambda^M p_i$. Therefore, $U_i''(\partial x_i^M/\partial p_j) = p_i(\partial\lambda^M/\partial p_j) = 0$. Therefore, $\partial x_i^M/\partial p_j = 0$, $i, j = 1, \ldots, n$, $j \neq i$. Result follows from budget equation.

8 (a) A theory, utility-maximization, was invented because it implied (under certain restrictions) downward-sloping demand curves. The theory also implied other things, e.g., symmetry of the substitution terms, but those properties do not follow from the assertion of downward-sloping demand functions. See the reference by El Hodiri in Chap. 12, for an amusing exposition of this point.

9 (a) consistent, (b) inconsistent, (c) consistent.

10 I wouldn't touch this one with a 10-foot pole. Strange behavior, though.

11 $U = F(x_2 + \log x_1)$

13 (a) At least \$4. (b) Less than \$6. (c) Approximations; bias indicated. (d) Not answerable.

CHAPTER 12

1 The Kuhn-Tucker conditions specify *necessary* conditions for a corner solution, not *sufficient* conditions. At some point, MP_i may be greater than w_i even if at $x_i = 0$, $MP_i < w_i$.

3 $f(x_1, x_2)$ has to be concave to achieve a saddlepoint solution.

6 $x_1 = 5$, $x_2 = 5$

7 $k = 5$

8 $x_1 = 5$, $x_2 = \frac{8}{5}$

10 (*a*) This is known as the *fisherian separation theorem* (see Irving Fisher, "The Theory of Interest," The Macmillan Company, New York, 1930, reprinted by A. Kelley, New York, 1969). If the consumer can borrow and lend, maximizing wealth leads to the largest opportunity set. Consumers can then rearrange consumption in accordance with their preferences by borrowing or lending. But don't take my word for it; read Fisher. (*b*) $x_1 = 4.93$, $x_2 = 12.82$; consumer is lender in period 1, PV = 14.78. (*c*) $x_1 = 5.15$, $x_2 = 12.36$, PV = 15.45.

CHAPTER 13

1 (*a*) $z^* = 700$. (*b*) $u_1 = 10$, $u_2 = 10$, $u_3 = 0$. (*e*) Industry 1 is relatively land-intensive; industry 2 labor-intensive. Therefore, if an additional unit of labor were available, industry 1 would expand and industry 2 would contract. (*f*) If the price of the land-intensive industry rises, the shadow price of land u_1 must rise in greater proportion than the rise in p_1 (5 percent). The shadow price of labor must fall by more than 5 percent. (*g*) None.

3 $z^* = 37$

4 $z^* = \$7000$

CHAPTER 14

1 The output-supply functions are homogeneous of degree zero in output-prices. The result follows from the application of Euler's theorem to these functions.

2 This is a direct application of the adding-up theorem of Sec. 12.5.

3 This allows analysis of the four-equation model [equations (14-53) and (14-54)] consisting of two zero-profit conditions and two resource constraints as two separate parts, with endowments appearing in only the latter two. With respect to endowment changes, the a_{ij}'s are constant, and hence this part of the model behaves like the linear models of Chap. 13 for that reason. From cost-minimization considerations, the a_{ij}'s behave as though they were constants in the first two equations dealing with output-price changes.

5 (*b*) This production frontier is not necessarily concave because no matter what the production functions themselves are, e.g., there may be extreme increasing returns to scale, as long as marginal products are finite and resources are limited, there must be some finite maximum production of either good for fixed amounts of the other good. Thus, the only curvature properties needed for this problem are convex (to the origin) isoquants, i.e., quasi-concavity. The production frontier may therefore be convex to the origin, e.g., if both production functions exhibit rapidly increasing returns to scale, and the maximum value of output may very well occur along either axis, i.e., for positive output of only one good.

CHAPTER 15

1 With finite resources and unlimited wants, a Pareto frontier of allocations exists along which any greater good for one person means lesser good for some other person.

2 $4y/y_1 - x/x_1 = 3$

4 A perfectly discriminating monopolist will produce output as long as some consumer will pay at least MC. Hence, the Pareto condition $p = MC$ will be satisfied, except that the monopolist will be the sole gainer from trade. If the monopolist's income elasticities differ from other consumers, overall production will change due to the redistribution of income only.

5 (*a*) Yes, if transactions costs are low. (*b*) $1000 + \frac{1}{2}P$ to A, $1500 + \frac{1}{2}P$ to B, $2500 + P$ total. (*c*) $800 + P$ to A, $1200 + P$ to B, $2000 + 2P$ total. (*d*) If $500 < P < 600$, A's gain from sharing a pump will be greater than B's loss from so doing. With zero contracting costs, A and B will contract to share the overall gain and will thus share.

6 The curvature of the utility frontier is sensitive to the (ordinal) units of utility. Its negative slope is a consequence of scarcity.

7 Depends on transactions costs.

8 (*a*) Curious. (*b*) Generally, when property rights are costly to define or enforce. (*c*) See several articles on this subject in the April 1973 issue of the *Journal of Law and Economics*.

CHAPTER 16

2 We do not *know* that markets are stable. Like profit-maximization, stability is a behavioral postulate which is *asserted*, with the ultimate aim of deriving refutable hypotheses from it.

3 This result follows from the elementary properties of the substitution matrix.

INDEX

Activity, production, 397–399
Adding up theorem, 386–388
Annuity, 57
Arrow, Kenneth J., 468, 482
Assertions, 7–10
  versus assumptions, 7
Assumptions, 7–8
  realism of, 8
Average cost, 178, 208
  relation to marginal cost, 178–179
Average curve, relation to marginal curve, 40

Bergson, Abram, 468
Borcherding, Thomas E., 348n.
Bowley, A. L., 436–438
Bronfenbrenner, Martin, 11
Buchanan, James M., 469n.

Chain rule:
  functions of one variable, 31–33
  functions of two variables, 72–79
  second derivatives, 77–79
Cheung, Steven N. S., 497, 498
Choice function, 12
Choice variables, 11–12
Coase, Ronald H., 494, 495
Coase "theorem," 495–497
Cobb-Douglas production function, 86
  elasticity of substitution of, 313–315, 319–321
Cobweb theorem, 523
Comparative statics:
  definition, 12
  envelope analysis of maximization systems, 284–299
Compensation, Hicks versus Slutsky, 257–259
Composite commodity theorem, 342–349
  "shipping the good apples out," 345–349
Concave function, 52–53

and convex sets, 386
and saddlepoint theorem, 380, 389–392
Confirm, 10
Constant elasticity of substitution (CES) production functions, 313–323
  (*See also* Elasticity of substitution)
Constrained maximization or minimization (*see* Maximization, constrained)
Constraints as constituting opportunities, 4
Consumer's surplus:
  compensating variation, 350, 352
  constancy of marginal utility of money income, 359–361
  as line integral, 354–358
  Marshallian, 364
  as measure of welfare loss, 362, 489–494
Continuity, 23
Contract curve, 437, 438, 473
Convex function, 52–53
Convex set:
  definition, 385
  feasible region: of linear programming problem, 403–404, 423
    of nonlinear programming problem, 384–386
Convexity of level curves, 82–83
Cost function:
  definition, 173–176
  duality with production functions, 309–313
  functional forms for: homogeneous production functions, 303–307
    homothetic production functions, 307–309
Cost minimization:
  comparative statics relations, 190–200
  envelope analysis of, 275–284
  factor demand functions: defined, 185–186
    elasticities of, 202–207
    homogeneity of, 203, 303
  first-order relations, 180
  interpretation of Lagrange multiplier as marginal cost, 186–189

reciprocity relations, 194, 197, 200, 284
second-order conditions, 180
Cournot, Augustin, 524
Cramer's rule, 130

Debreu, Gerard, 482
Decision variable, 11–12
Demand functions:
consumer's: compensated, 234
general equilibrium, 254–257
income effects, 240
money-income-held-constant, 224
pure substitution effect, 238, 243–246
real income, or utility-held-constant, 234
relation between real and money-income-
held-constant, 239–246, 248–250
Slutsky versus Hicks compensations, 257–
259
uncompensated, 224
firm's: homogeneity, 203, 207
output-held-constant, 186, 190–198
profit-maximizing, 110, 151
short-run versus long-run (see LeChatelier
principle)
Derivative:
ordinary, 26–29
chain rule, 31–33
product rule, 33
quotient rule, 34
partial, 64–65
chain rule, 73–79
Determinants:
application to comparative statics, 131–134,
164–167
Cramer's rule, 130
expansion of alien cofactors, 129–130
expansion by cofactors, 125–128
hessian, 149–150
principal minor, 149
border preserving, 162
Diet problem, 429
Differential, total: functions of one variable,
29–30
functions of two variables, 70–72
Differential equation, 60–61
Disequilibrium, 14, 215, 509–510
(See also Equilibrium)
Dual problem in linear programming, 412–417
Duality:
between cost and production functions, 309–
313
between Rybczynski and Stolper-Samuelson
theorems, 461–462
Duopoly, 524–526

Dupuit, Jules, 491
Dynamic adjustment (see Stability)

e^x, 41–45
Edgeworth, F. Y., 436–438
Edgeworth-Bowley box diagram, 436–438, 473
Eigenvalues, 518–519
Elasticity:
consumer's demand functions, 233, 250–253
definition, 35–36
output, 207, 303
Slutsky equation in terms of, 246
unitary income elasticities and homotheticity,
254
Elasticity of substitution, 315
Cobb-Douglas production function, 313–315,
319–321
constant: equal to unity, 319–321
not equal to unity, 320
derivation of CES production functions, 315–
321
Envelope theorem:
derivation (traditional method), 168–171
from primal-dual problem, 287
reciprocity relations derived from: cost minimization, 200, 284
general relations, 290–291
profit maximization, 270
Equilibrium, 14, 504, 508
Euler's theorem, 90–91
converse, 93–95

Factor demands (see Demand functions)
Factor-price equalization theorem:
linear models, 408
nonlinear models, 444, 452–453
Facts, role of, 6–7
Firms in long-run competitive equilibrium, 209–
211
First-order conditions for maximization, minim-
ization (see Maximization)
Fisher, Irving, 44n.
Fisherian investment, 44–45, 389, 536
"Faustmann" solution, 45
Function:
one variable, 21
several variables, 62

Gould, John, 347

Hessian matrix or determinant, 148–150
bordered, 162

Hicks, John R., 253
Homogeneity:
  of consumer's demand functions, 228–229,
    250–252
  of cost function, 303
  of production functions, 300
    effects on cost function, 303–307
Homogeneous functions, 84–99
  Euler's theorem, 90–91
    converse, 93–95
Homothetic functions:
  production functions, 89, 301
    effects on cost function, 307–309
  utility functions, 254
    and consumer's surplus, 358–359
Hotelling, Harold, 483–484
Houthakker, Hendrik S., 326, 333
Hurwicz, Leonid, 482
Hyperplane, 389
  separating hyperplane theorem, 389–390

Implicit function theorem, 134–139
Implicit functions, 34–35
Imputed rents to factors of production (*see* Lin-
  ear programming, shadow prices of factors)
Inferior goods, 240–241
Input-output coefficients, 396
Input-output models, 402*n*.
Integrability:
  of demand functions, 335–342
  relation to strong axiom of revealed prefer-
    ences, 340–342
Integrals, 53–59
  as area under curve, 55–57
  total cost, as integral of marginal cost, 55–56
Interest, relation of exponential function to
  continuous compounding, 41–45

Jacobian, 138

Koopmans, Tjalling C., 416
Kuhn, H. W., 376*n*.
Kuhn-Tucker conditions, 376–377

Lagged adjustment, 522–526
Lagrangian (*see* Maximization, constrained)
Lancaster, Kelvin, 484*n*.
LeChatelier principle:
  cost minimizing firms or compensated de-
    mand functions, 278–279
  general maximization problems, 293–298

profit-maximizing firms, 114–116, 272–275
Leontief, Wassily, 402*n*.
Level curves, 63, 79–83
L'Hospital's rule, 321
Limits, 23
Line integral, 354
  (*See also* Consumer's surplus)
Linear programming, 393–430
  basic feasible solution, 422–423
  basis, 422
  diet problem, 429
  dual problem, 412–416
  fundamental theorem, 417–420
  graphical solution, 403–405
  shadow prices of factors, 406–408
    (*See also* Dual problem in linear program-
      ming)
  simplex algorithm, 420–428
Lipsey, Richard G., 484*n*.
Log *x*, 45–47
Lump sum tax, 486
Lyapunov theorem, 520

Macroeconomic model, 507–508
Marginal cost:
  in first-order conditions for profit maximiza-
    tion, 13, 38
  interpretation of Lagrange multiplier as, 186–
    189
  relation to average cost, 178–179
  relation to degree of homogeneity of produc-
    tion function, 305–307
    (*See also* Cost minimization)
Marginal curve, relation to average curve, 40
Marginal product:
  definition, 64–66
  and Euler's theorem, 85, 91
  and law of diminishing returns, 108–109
  and Young's theorem, 69–71
Marginal revenue, 13, 38
Marginal utility of money income:
  constancy of, 359–361
  interpretation of Lagrange multiplier as, 229–
    230
    (*See also* Utility, maximization of)
Marshall, Alfred, 353, 364, 489, 491
Marshallian stability, 513–516
Matrix, matrices:
  associative law of multiplication, 141
  distributive law of multiplication, 141
  hessian, 148
  inverse, 148
  multiplication, 123, 140–141
  orthogonal, 145

rank, 142
symmetric, 141
Maximization:
  constrained:first-order conditions, 154–158
    more than one constraint, 157–159
    second-order conditions, 159–164
    of utility (*see* Utility)
  unconstrained: one variable, 36–40, 51–53
    first-order conditions, 37
    second-order conditions, 37
    Taylor series analysis of, 51–53
    n-variables, 102, 147–150
      first-order conditions, 102, 147
      second-order conditions, 148–150
    two variables, 100–107, 118–121
      first-order conditions, 102
      second-order conditions, 102–104
      Taylor series analysis of, 118–121
Mean value theorem, 48
Minimization (*see* Maximization)
Models versus theories, 11
Monotonic transformations:
  definition and chain rule, 76–77
  and homothetic functions, 89
  of utility functions, 84, 217, 225–228
Mosak, Jacob, 258

Nonlinear programming, 383–386
  (*See also* Kuhn-Tucker conditions; Saddle-point theorem)
Nonnegativity constraints:
  general analyis, 366–372
  and profit maximization, 373–374
  and utility maximization, 377–379

Opportunities, 3–6

Papendreou, Andreas, 11
Paradigm, 1–2
Parameter, 11–12
Parameterization of curve, 74–75, 101–102
Pareto, Vilfredo, 438, 471
Pareto conditions:
  optimality, 438, 471, 478
  and perfect competition, 480
Partial derivatives:
  definition, 65
  invariance to order of differentiation
    (Young's theorem), 68–70
Peano, 106
Product rule, 33

Production functions:
  CES (*see* Constant elasticity of substitution)
  Cobb-Douglas, 86
  definition, 63
  duality with cost functions, 309–313
  fixed or constant coefficients, 313–314, 396–399
  homogeneous, 86–88, 300
  homothetic, 89, 300
Production possibilities frontier:
  linear models, 403–405
  nonlinear models, 435, 442–444
Profit maximization:
  envelope analysis of, 263–275
  n factors, 150–153
  one factor, 13–16
  two factors, 107–118
    analysis of finite changes, 117–118
    definition of factor demand functions, 110
    long-run versus short-run demands, 114–116
      (*See also* LeChatelier principle)
    reciprocity relations, 112, 270
    relation to law of diminshing returns, 109
    slopes of factor demand curves, 112
    supply function, 113–114
Property rights, 4, 496
Public goods, 486–489

Quadratic form, 146, 148
Quasiconcave:
  definition, 164
  and LeChatelier principle, 296
  production function, 181, 195
  utility function, 221–222
Quotient rule, 34

Reciprocity conditions:
  in cost minimization, 194, 197, 200, 284
  general relations, 290–291
  in profit maximization, 112, 270
Refutable proposition, 9
Revealed preference, 324–342
  strong axiom, 332–335
    and integrability, 340–342
  weak axiom, 328
Routh-Hurwitz theorem, 520
Rybczynski theorem:
  linear models, 408–410
  nonlinear models, 460–462

Saddlepoint, 107, 380
Saddlepoint theorem, 379–383, 389–392

Sales maximization, 17–18
Samuelson, Paul A., xiv, 326, 506, 511, 527–528
Samuelson-Shephard duality theorem, 304
Scarcity, 3
  as distinct from limited, 3, 407
Second-best, 484–486
Second-order conditions (*see* Maximization)
Segall, Joel, 347
Separating hyperplane theorem, 389–390
Shadow prices, 406–408
  (*See also* Linear programming)
Share tenacy, 497–501
Shephard's lemma,, 199–200
Simplex algorithm, 420–428
Slater's constraint qualification, 380
Slutsky equation:
  derivation by envelope analysis, 248–250
  derivation by traditional methods, 239–245
  in terms of elasticities, 246
    (*See also* Utility)
Smith, Adam, 395
Social welfare functions, 467–471
  possibility theorem, 469–471
  voting paradox, 468
Stability:
  with lagged adjustment, 522–526
  local versus global, 511
  Marshallian, 513–516
  one market, 510–516
  two, or multi-markets, 516–521
  Walrasian, 510–513
Stolper, Wolfgang F. (*see* Stopler-Samuelson theorem)
Stolper-Samuelson theorem:
  linear models, 410–412
  nonlinear models, 453–460
Supply function, 18–19, 113–114

Tastes, 3–4
Tax, effect on output, 13–19

Taxation:
  income versus excise, 483–484
  lump sum, 484
Taylor's series:
  one variable, 48–51
  two variables, 118–121
Theories:
  versus models, 11
  structure of, 7
Tucker, A. W., 376n.
Tullock, Gordon, 469n.

Utility:
  cardinal versus ordinal, 216
  derivation of demand functions from, 223–224
  homothetic, 254
  maximization of: first-order conditions, 223
    with nonnegativity constraints, 377–379
    relation to cost minimization, 233–239
    second-order conditions, 223, 226–227
  monotonic transformations of, 225–228
  properties of utility functions, 216–222
    (*See also* Demand functions: Slutsky equation)
Utility frontier, 474, 479

Vectors, inner product of vectors, 124
Voting, paradox, 468

Wald, Abraham, 258
Walras, Leon, 511
Walras' law, 521
Walrasian stability, 510–513

Young's theorem, 68